ARCHITECTURAL DIAGRAMS

ARCHITECTURAL DIAGRAMS 2
346 PROJECTS OF 83 DESIGN TEAMS

The *Deutsche Nationalbibliothek* lists this publication in the *Deutsche Nationalbibliografie*; detailed bibliographic data are available in the Internet at http://dnb.d-nb.de.

ISBN 978-3-86922-148-9 (2 vol.)

© 2010 by DAMDI Publishing Co., Seoul/Korea
© 2011 by DOM publishers, Berlin/Germany
www.dom-publishers.com

This work is subject to copyright. All rights reserved. No part of this publication may be reproduced, stored in a retrieval system, or transferred, in any form or by any means, electronic, mechanical, photocopying, recording, or otherwise, without the prior written permission of the publishers. Sources and owners of rights are stated to the best of our knowledge; please signal any we might have omitted.

Editor	Miyoung Pyo
Design	Minjung Bang
Assistant	Sueun Bae, Kyungyoung Roh, Jieun Lee

ARCHITECTURAL DIAGRAMS

ARCHITECTURE
·
INTERIOR DESIGN
·
INSTALLATION
·
PROFILE & INDEX

CONTENTS

ARCHITECTURAL DIAGRAMS vol.1

010 ESSAY

016 PUBLIC SPACE

172 LANDSCAPE

262 URBAN DESIGN

ARCHITECTURAL DIAGRAMS vol.2

ARCHITECTURE

396 **AACHENMUNCHENER HEADQUARTERS** kadawittfeldarchitektur
398 **A BIG HOUSE** ECDM
400 **ADIDAS LACES** kadawittfeldarchitektur
402 **APARTMENT HOUSE GRADASKA** SADAR VUGA ARHITEKTI
404 **AQUATIC CENTER** mxg architects
406 **AZIËWEG** VMX Architects
408 **BATTERSEA WEAVE OFFICE BUILDING** UNStudio
410 **BEND UP/ BEND OVER** NL Architects
412 **BIONIC TOWER** LAVA
414 **BUREAUX BESANÇON** mxg architects
416 **BUSINESS CENTRE** MANUELLE GAUTRAND ARCHITECTURE
418 **CARBON TOWER** Axi:Ome
420 **CENTER FOR EUROPEAN CULTURE** kadawittfeldarchitektur
422 **CHO RESIDENCE** NL Architects
424 **CITROËN EXHIBITION CENTER** MANUELLE GAUTRAND ARCHITECTURE
426 **CLAUDE BERNARD** ECDM
428 **CONDOMINIUM TRNOVSKI PRISTAN** SADAR VUGA ARHITEKTI
430 **CORNICHE TOWER** LAVA
432 **DASYPUS** nodo17 Architects
434 **ECOCOON FOR RECYCLING** Vincent Callebaut Architectrue
436 **ESO HEADQUARTERS** IaN+
438 **FIVE FRANKLIN PLACE** UNStudio

440	**FRACTURED MONOLITH**	Vincent Callebaut Architectrue
442	**G55**	Bernd Kniess Architects Urban Planners
444	**HEADLANDS HOTEL**	LAVA
446	**HOTEL PRO FORMA**	nARCHITECTS
448	**HOUSING**	MANUELLE GAUTRAND ARCHITECTURE
450	**HOUSING ALMERE**	IaN+
452	**ILE DE NANTES**	PERIQHERIQUES architects
454	**IMEC TOWER**	JDS Architects
456	**LANDSCRIPT**	Vincent Callebaut Architectrue
458	**LERVIG BRYGGE**	SPACEGROUP
460	**LIFE IN TOWN**	MANUELLE GAUTRAND ARCHITECTURE
462	**LILYPADS**	Vincent Callebaut Architectrue
464	**LINZ LANDESFRAUEN KLINIK**	ONE ARCHITECTURE
466	**LIVING STEEL**	nARCHITECTS
468	**MERCEDES-BENZ MUSEUM**	UNStudio
470	**MERMAID ISLAND**	JDS Architects
472	**NL-KB**	Bernd Kniess Architects Urban Planners
474	**NL-WI**	Bernd Kniess Architects Urban Planners
476	**NUMEN**	studio asylum
478	**O-14**	Reiser + Umemoto RUR Architecture PC
480	**O.I.C HEADQUARTERS BUILDING**	Willy Müller Architects
482	**OKERN CENTER**	SPACEGROUP
484	**OMOTESANDO**	UNStudio
486	**ORDOS 100**	NL Architects
488	**PRISMA**	NL Architects
490	**PRUGIO VALLEY - UNIT & FACADE DESIGN**	jay is working.
492	**PUBLIC RECORDS OFFICE**	EM2N
494	**RESEARCH LABORATORY**	UNStudio
496	**S-HOUSE**	VMX Architects
498	**SILO**	JDS Architects
500	**SLIM TWIN**	SPACEGROUP
502	**S_MAHAL**	Moonbalsso +DN
504	**STAR HOTEL**	SPACEGROUP
506	**SUSTAINABLE OFFICE BUILDING**	VMX Architects
508	**SWITCH BUILDING**	nARCHITECTS
510	**THE MOUNTAIN**	JDS Architects

512	**THERMAL BRIDGE**	nARCHITECTS
514	**TOWER COMPLEX AT THE SULEJMAN PASHA MONUMENT AREA**	SADAR VUGA ARHITEKTI
516	**TOWER COSTA RICA**	Moho Architects
518	**TRP**	AMID [cero9]
520	**UIB**	AMID [cero9]
522	**URBAN RESORT ST. PETERSBURG**	Willy Müller Architects
524	**VERTICAL TERRACED VILLAS**	nodo17 Architects
526	**VESTBANEN**	SPACEGROUP
528	**VILLA NM**	UNStudio
530	**VILLA - VILLA**	nARCHITECTS
532	**VILLA FAMILIE MAX MAIER**	J. MAYER H. ARCHITECTS
534	**VM HOUSES**	JDS Architects
536	**WBW:WILLE URBANIE**	Bernd Kniess Architects Urban Planners
538	**ZAMBONINI HEADQUARTER**	IaN+
540	**3 Academies Ljubljana**	SADAR VUGA ARHITEKTI
542	**3 EXTENDED HOUSES**	nodo17 Architects
544	**360° HOTEL**	SPACEGROUP
546	**7-FINGERS**	Moonbalsso +DN

INTERIOR DESIGN

550	**ALMIRA SADAR BOUTIQUE**	SADAR VUGA ARHITEKTI
552	**AUTOMOTIVE SHOWROOM & LEISURE CENTRE**	MANUELLE GAUTRAND ARCHITECTURE
554	**BIG TEN BURRITO**	PLY Architecture
556	**BLUE FROG ACOUSTIC LOUNGE & STUDIOS**	Serie Architects
558	**BTB BURRITO**	PLY Architecture
560	**CLINIC THE H**	jay is working.
562	**CLOUD BOX**	servo
564	**CREATIVE HUB OF EURO RSCG**	Atelier Phileas (member of PLAN01)
566	**DANBO FUN**	MoHen Design International
568	**DIGITAL ORIGAMI**	LAVA
570	**DOUBLE JEOPARDY**	PEG office of landscape + architecture
572	**EXHIBITION DESIGN OF FISH STILL LIVES**	Studio Ramin Visch
574	**EYE OF SQUARE**	Kim Kai-chun
576	**HOTEL CASINO PARK**	SADAR VUGA ARHITEKTI
578	**HOUSEWARMING MYHOME**	J. MAYER H. ARCHITECTS

580	**INTERPOLIS**	NL Architects
582	**INTRA STUDIO**	SADAR VUGA ARHITEKTI
584	**KANTOOR DUPON**	Studio Ramin Visch
586	**KUNSTHAUS GRAZ**	the next ENTERprise
588	**LA BELLE PAUSE**	jay is working.
590	**LA GUARDIA SALON**	Z-A studio and Cheng+Snyder
592	**MAISON DU DANEMARQUE**	JDS Architects
594	**MASTERPLAN HALL 11 UNStudio**	UNStudio
596	**MTV DESIGN STAGE**	LAVA
598	**MUSIC THEATRE**	UNStudio
600	**ORIENTAL CLINIC BOM_FLOW SPACE**	jay is working.
602	**PLY LOFT**	nARCHITECTS
604	**ROBBINS ELEMENTARY SCHOOL**	PLY Architecture
606	**ROSSO RESTAURANT**	SO Architecture
608	**SCHOOL 03**	i29 interior architects
610	**SECRET STAGE**	Axi:Ome
612	**SKY OFFICE OFFSPRING**	PSA
614	**STAND AND DELIVER**	NL Architects
616	**STASH**	Maurice Mentjens Design
618	**TELEKOM STREAMS CEBIT**	kadawittfeldarchitektur
620	**THEODORE - CAFÉ BISTRO**	SO Architecture
622	**V&A WOMENS' AMENITIES**	GLOWACKA RENNIE ARCHITECTS
624	**VINEXPO 2009 ITALIAN STAND BORDEAUX**	2TR ARCHITETTURA & Laura Federici
626	**WOMEN'S SHELTER**	Axi:Ome

INSTALLATION

630	**ALISHAN TOURIST ROUTES**	Reiser+Umemoto RUR Architecture PC
632	**ALTAMIRANO WALKWAY**	EMILIO MARIN architect
634	**'AKTIPIS' FLOWERSHOP**	Point Supreme Architects
636	**BENCHES, BECOME A PART OF LANDSCAPE**	Jungwoo Ji
638	**BENCH DESIGN**	JDS Architects
640	**BIOZONE**	servo
642	**BOOKS ON EARTHQUAKE**	Smånsk Design Studio
644	**CANOPY: MoMA / P.S.1**	nARCHITECTS
646	**CIRCLE**	UNStudio

648	**CROSS-WIND BRIDGE**	Jorge Pereira
650	**CULTURAL GATE TO ALBORZ**	Guallart Architects
652	**DAS NETS**	NL Architects
654	**DISPLAY ENVIRONMENT 1**	servo
656	**DISPLAY ENVIRONMENT 2**	servo
658	**DUNE**	Moho Architects
660	**DURCHBLICK**	the next ENTERprise
662	**EARPHONE STAND**	PSA
664	**ECO-BULEVARD, NEW SUBURBAN DEVELOPMENT OF VALLECAS**	Ecosistema Urbano + TECTUM
666	**FLIP**	marco hemmerling architecture design
668	**HIGH-SPEED CAR RAMP**	Tiago Barros + Jorge Pereira
670	**HOME (FOR A HOMELESS KID) KOMATEIKA**	Zizi&Yoyo
672	**IN THE LATTICE**	servo
674	**KERYKES**	J. MAYER H. ARCHITECTS
676	**LA BALLENA PEDESTRIAN BRIDGE**	UNStudio
678	**LOBBI-PORTS**	servo
680	**LOOP-THE-LOOP**	NL Architects
682	**MACHINE IN THE GARDEN**	Responsive Systems Group
684	**OLZWEG**	R&Sie architects
686	**OPEN SPACE AWARDS TOKYO**	PSA
687	**WOOD LIGHTS**	PLY Architecture
688	**PAPER LIGHTS**	PLY Architecture
690	**PARK BENCH HOUSE**	sga : sean godsell architects
691	**STEINER GARDEN**	Zizi&Yoyo
692	**PARTY WALL**	nARCHITECTS
694	**PLAY GROUND**	Andreas Angelidakis
696	**PROXIMITY CLOUD**	servo
698	**RED+HOUSING MANIFESTO**	OBRA ARCHITECTS
700	**SCREEN WALL PROTOTYPE**	PLY Architecture
702	**SPLAT**	Andreas Angelidakis
704	**STACKED**	JDS Architects
706	**SUM**	UNStudio
708	**SUN/S.E.T**	GEOTECTURA
710	**THE EXCHANGE**	Z-A Studio
712	**TOKYO DAY-TRIPPER**	Studio Makkink & Bey bv
714	**TOUCH SCREEN**	ma0

716   **TSUMARI ART TRIENNALE 2003**   PERIQHERIQUES architects

718   **VAGABOND TRAVEL BOOKSTORE**   Smånsk Design Studio

720   **WINDSHAPE**   nARCHITECTS

722   **60CH**   EMILIO MARIN architect

724   **...!!?**   BUREAU DES MESARCHITECTURES

726   PROFILE & INDEX

ARCHITECTURE

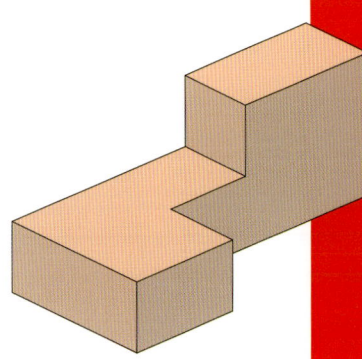 +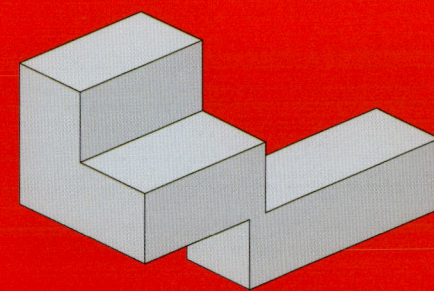

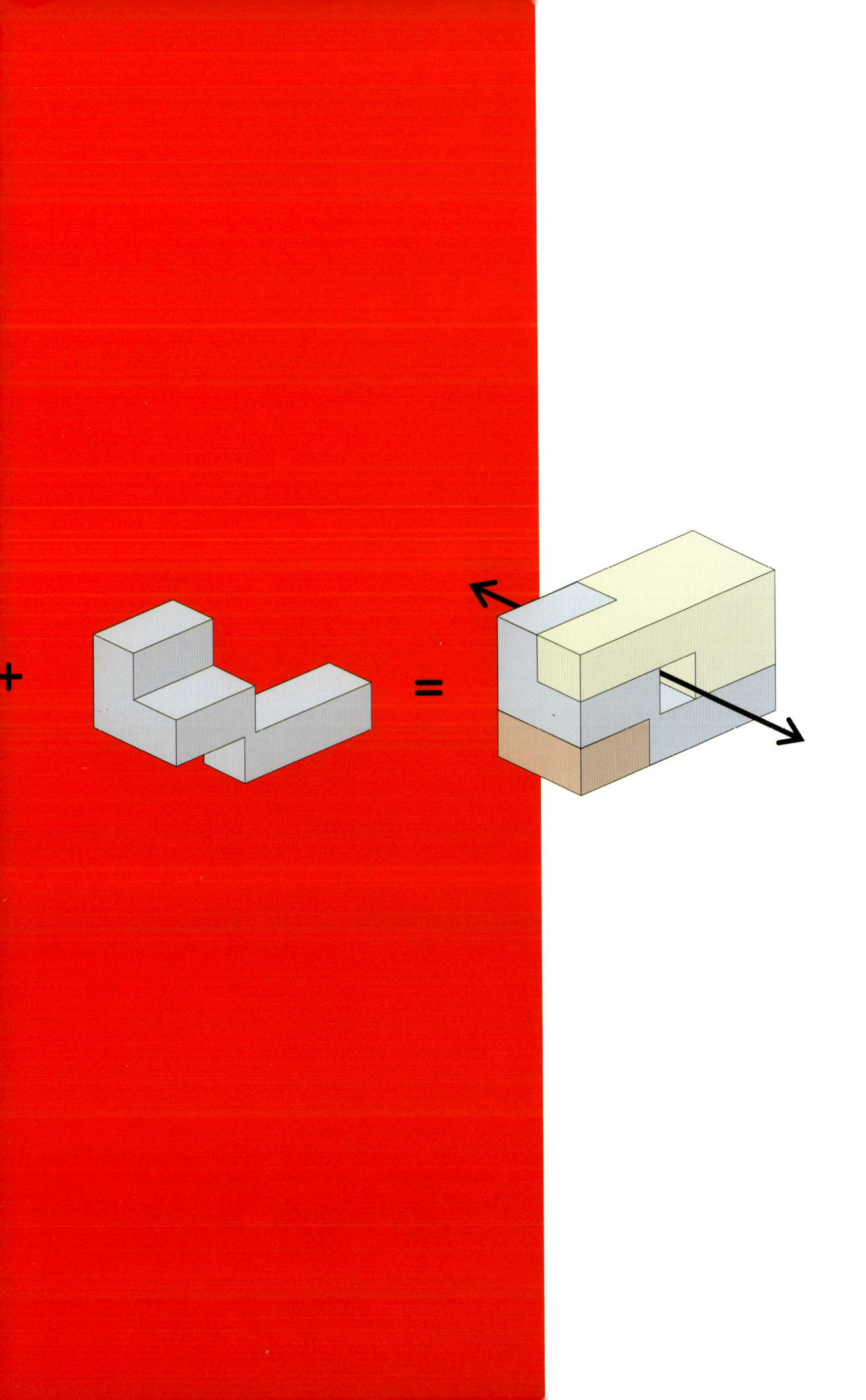

AACHENMÜNCHENER HEADQUARTERS
kadawittfeldarchitektur

"IT PROVIDES A NEW INTER- PRETATION OF THE TYPICAL PERIMETER DEVELOPMENT WITH ITS SEMI-PUBLIC AND LEAFY COURTYARDS."

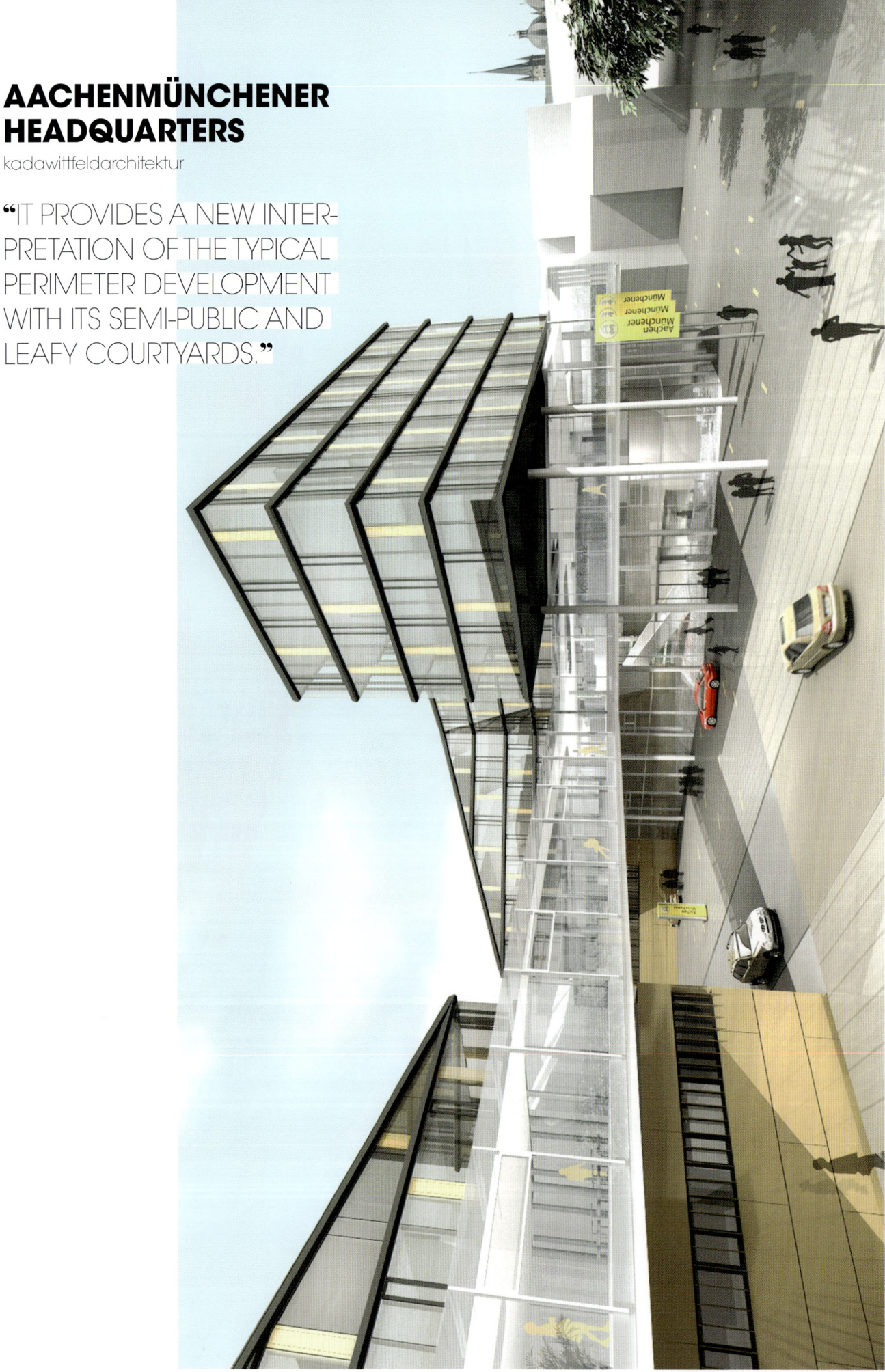

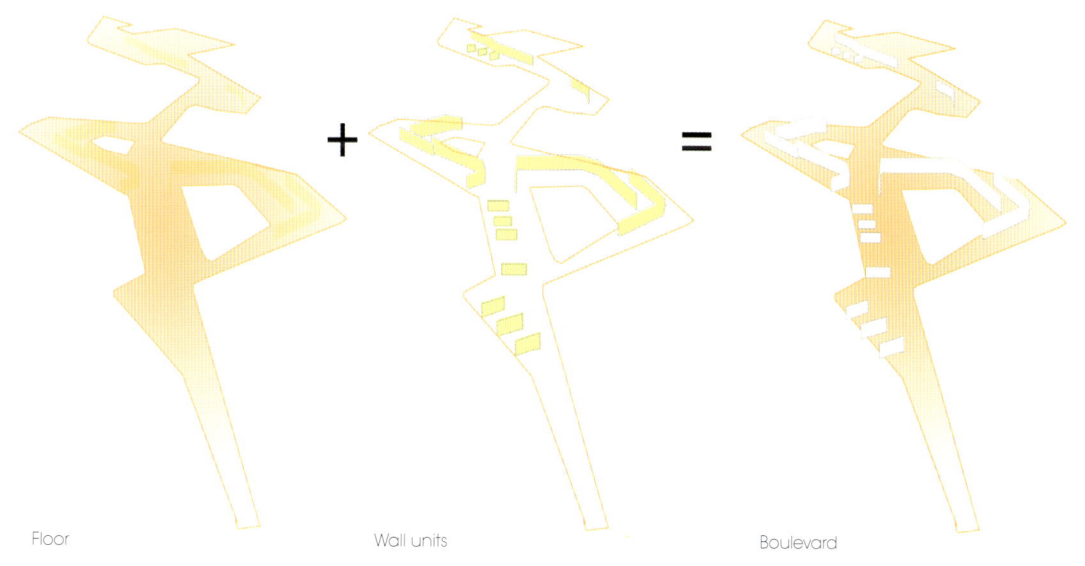

Floor + Wall units = Boulevard

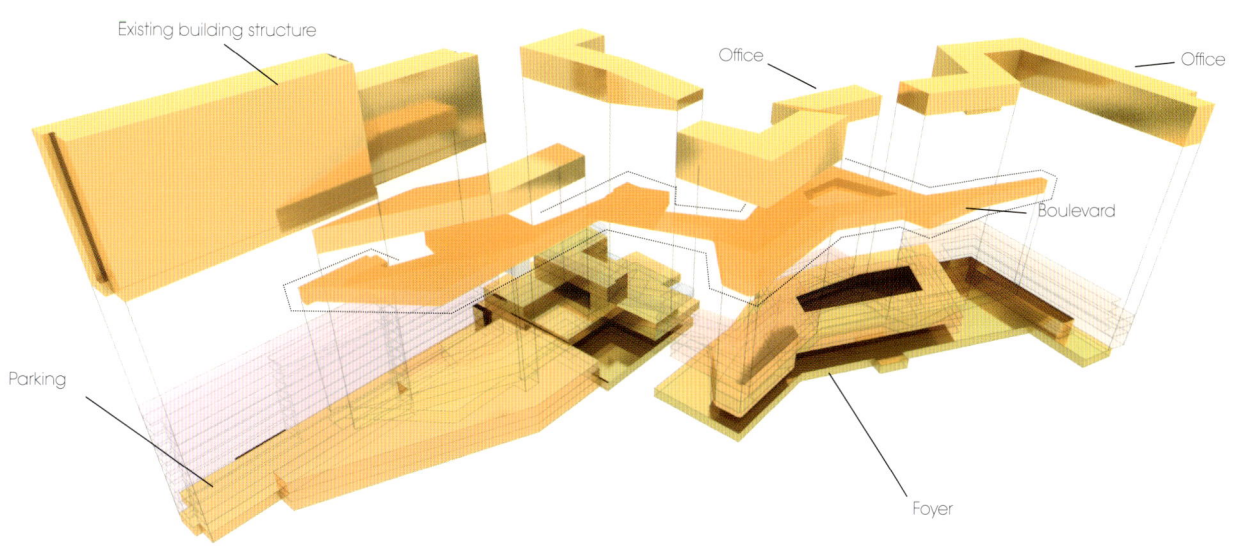

ARCHITECTURAL DIAGRAMS 397

A BIG HOUSE
ECDM

"GENEROUS WITH THE LARGE BALCONIES IT OFFERS TO EACH AND EVERY APARTMENT, ALLOWING RESIDENTS TO ENGAGE WITH THE SURROUNDING LANDSCAPE."

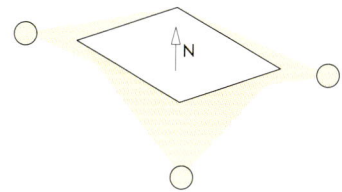
Optimum orientation

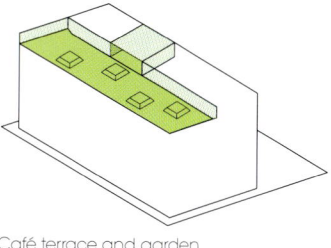
Café terrace and garden

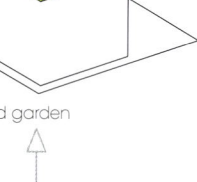
Space and outdoor use at home, feel the wind

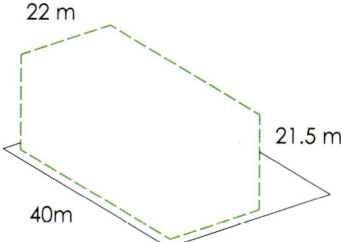
Maximum exploitation of the plot
Index compactness student

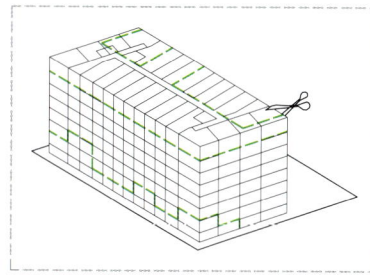
A sum of individuality
The communal areas are discovered hollow and set up with their environment, the ratio increases to heaven, the district Borderouge

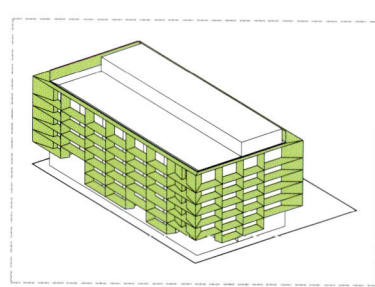
A thickness of loggias, agrement comfort and use

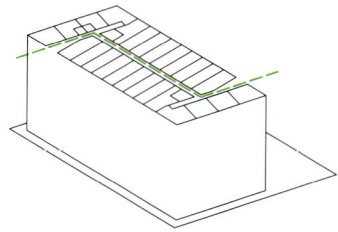
A rational plan
Circulations of natural lighting

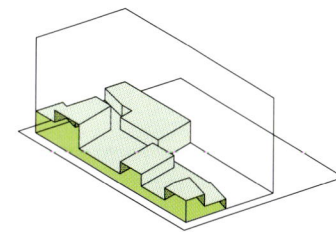
Hall, local cycling, fitness, laundry,

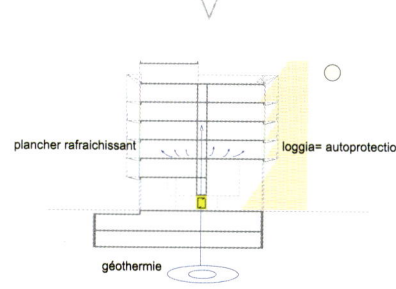
Summer comfort

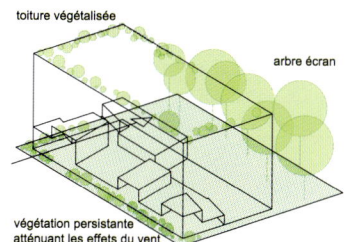
A residence in a garden

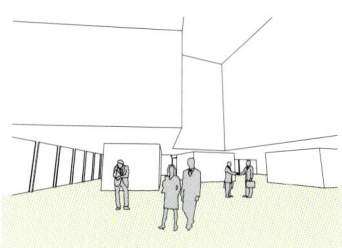
The hall, hollow expression of the density of the residence

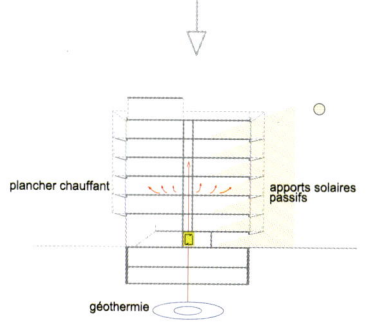
Winter comfort

ARCHITECTURAL DIAGRAMS 399

ADIDAS LACES
kadawittfeldarchitektur

"LIKE LACES, THEY TIE THE BUILDING TOGETHER, FORMING A MULTILAYER WORKSPACE AND CONVEYING AN ATMOSPHERE OF CREATIVITY."

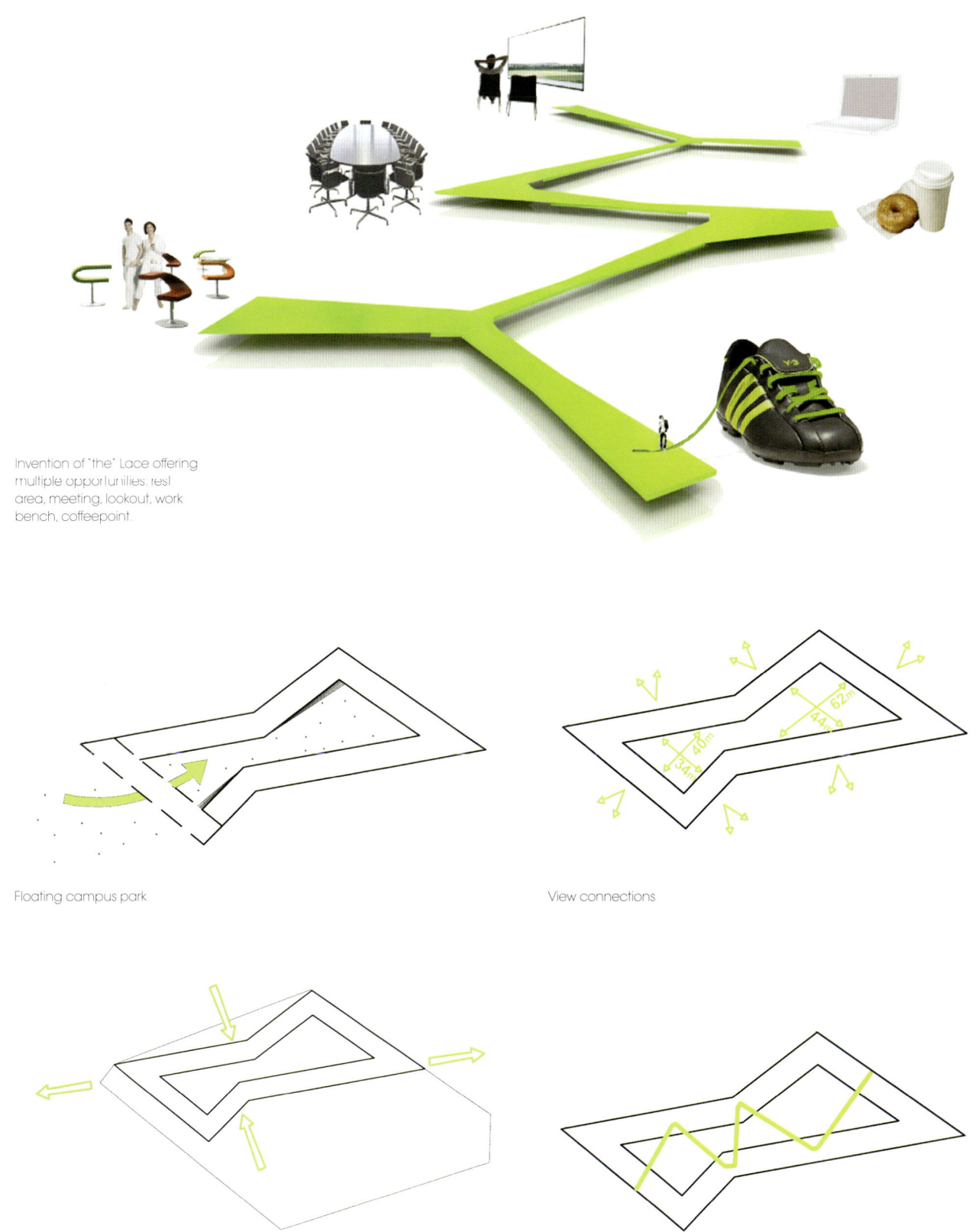

Invention of "the" Lace offering multiple opportunities: rest area, meeting, lookout, work bench, coffeepoint.

Floating campus park

View connections

Push and pull

laces

ARCHITECTURAL DIAGRAMS

APARTMENT HOUSE GRADASKA

SADAR VUGA ARHITEKTI

"THIS FACADE FUNCTIONS AS A KIND OF A SWITCHING SURFACE BETWEEN THE STRUCTURE AND THE LIVING CHARACTER."

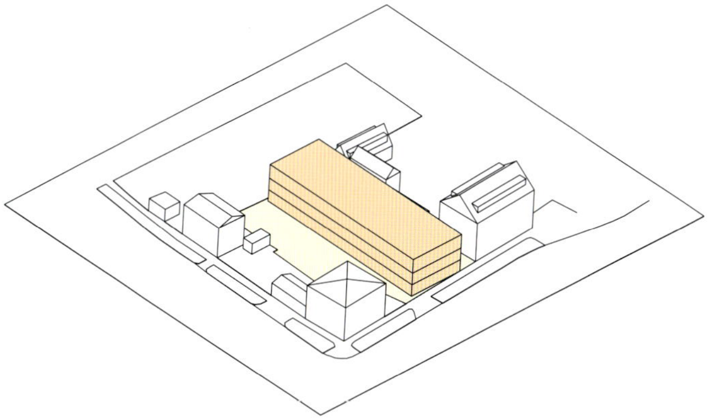

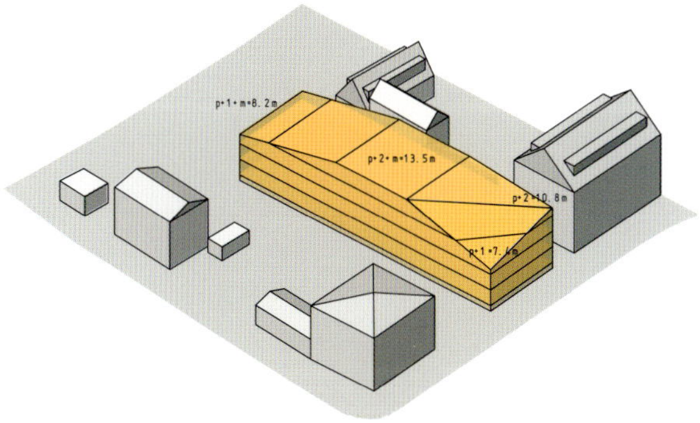

ARCHITECTURAL DIAGRAMS 403

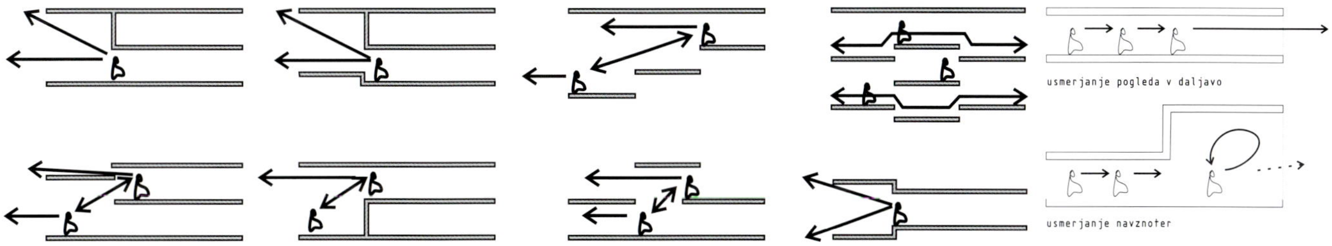

AQUATIC CENTER
mxg architectes

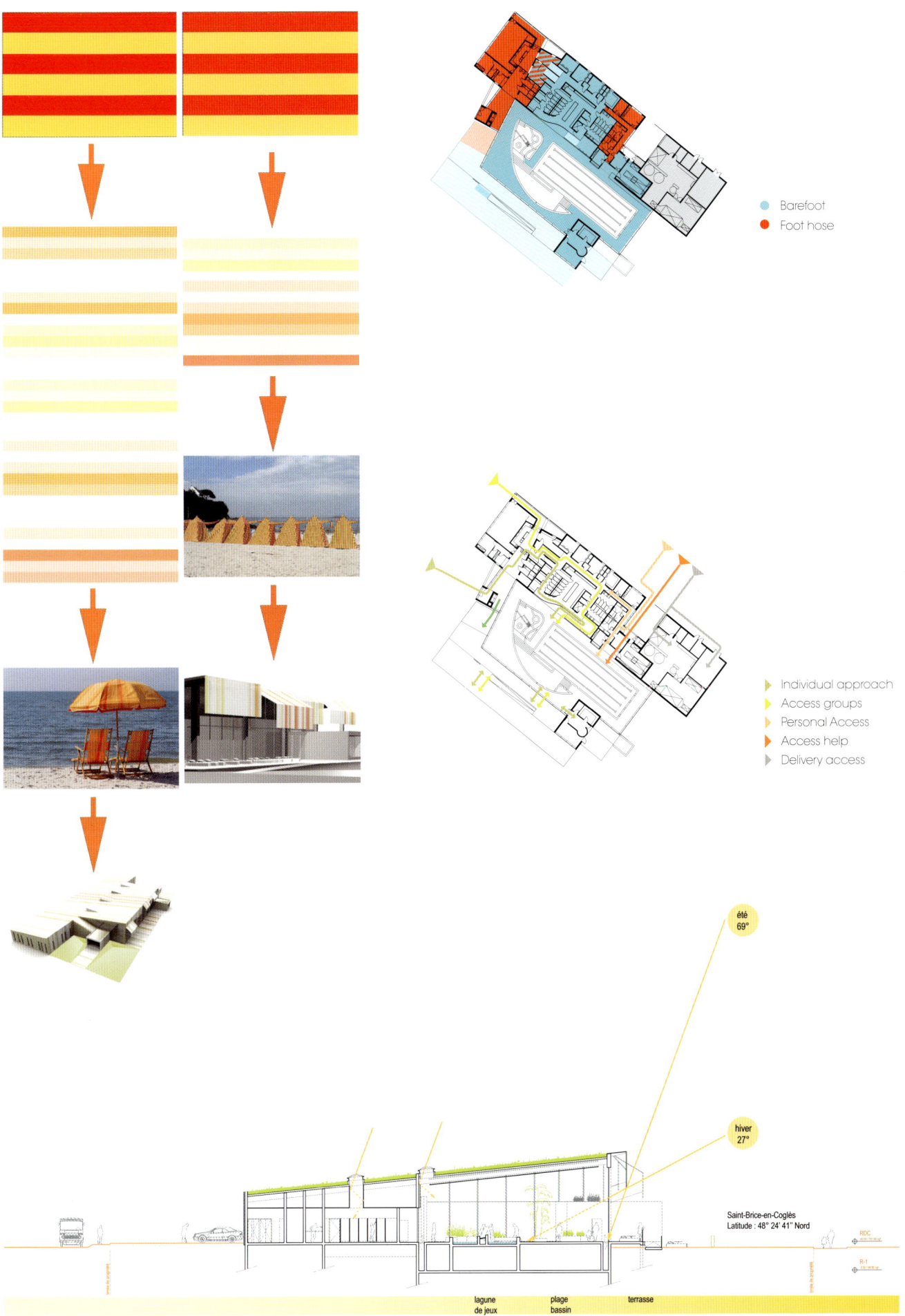

AZIËWEG VMX Architects

"THIS TYPE OF ORGANISATION SOLVES A LARGE VARIATION OF HOUSING TYPES WITHIN A COHERENT SHAPE."

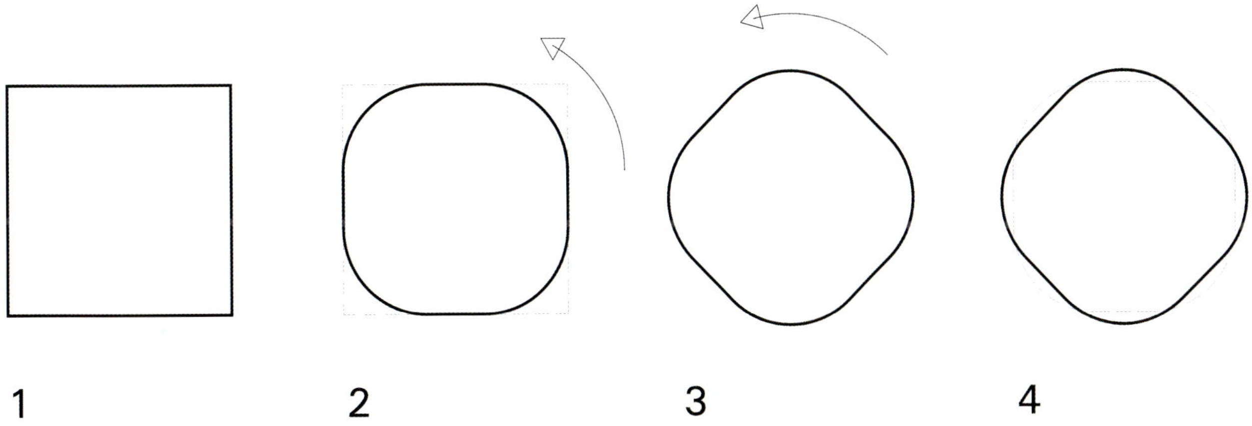

1 2 3 4

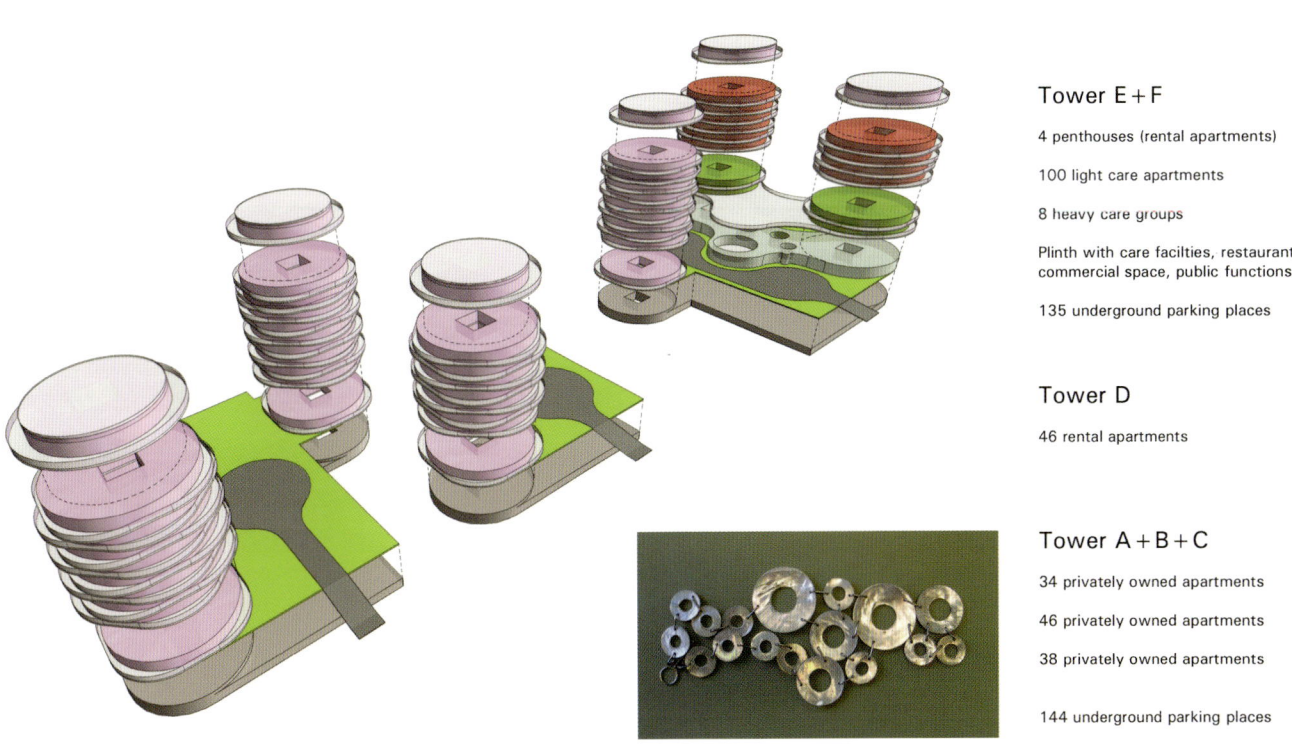

Tower E + F

4 penthouses (rental apartments)

100 light care apartments

8 heavy care groups

Plinth with care facilties, restaurant, commercial space, public functions

135 underground parking places

Tower D

46 rental apartments

Tower A + B + C

34 privately owned apartments

46 privately owned apartments

38 privately owned apartments

144 underground parking places

ARCHITECTURAL DIAGRAMS

BATTERSEA WEAVE OFFICE BUILDING UNStudio

"IDENTITY ARE TO PLAYING A IMPORTANT ROLE IN ATTRACTING BOTH FUTURE OCCUPANTS AND VISITORS."

DENSITY

**EXISTING PROPOSAL.
4 BEAMS**

18M WIDE
51000 M2

FLOORPLANS NOT IDEAL TO USE

**TEST
5 BEAMS,**

15M WIDE
51000 M2

IDEAL LIGHT CONDITION,
TOO DENSE

**ALTERNATIVE
ROTATED BEAMS
5 BEAMS,**

15M WIDE
51000 M2

INTERACTING / INTERWOVEN

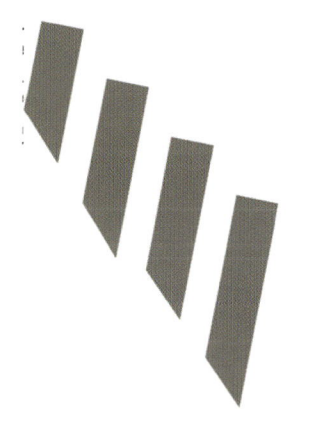

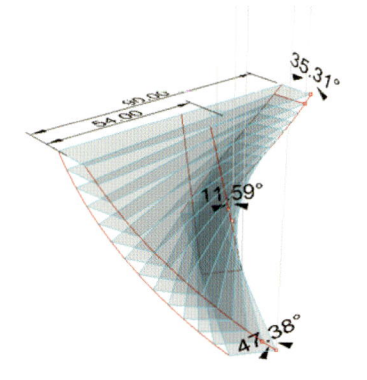

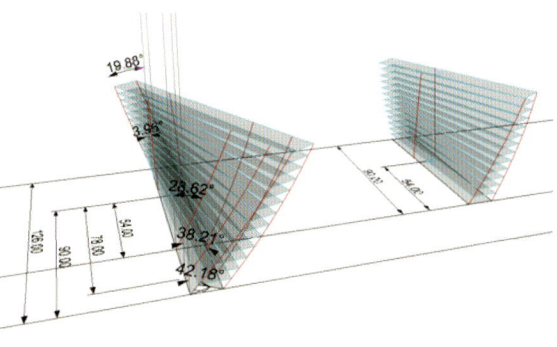

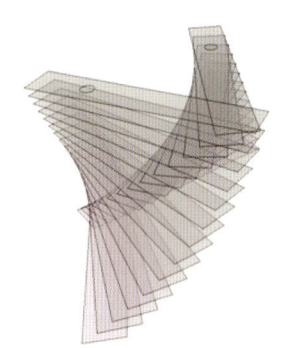

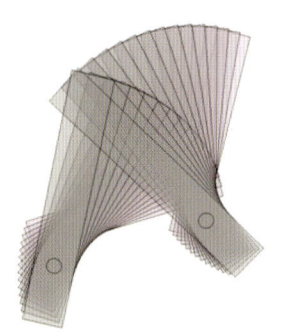

BEND UP/ BEND OVER
NL Architects

"THE GARDENS OF BOTH TYPES APPEAR ON THE ROOF: THE PARK REMAINS 100% PUBLIC."

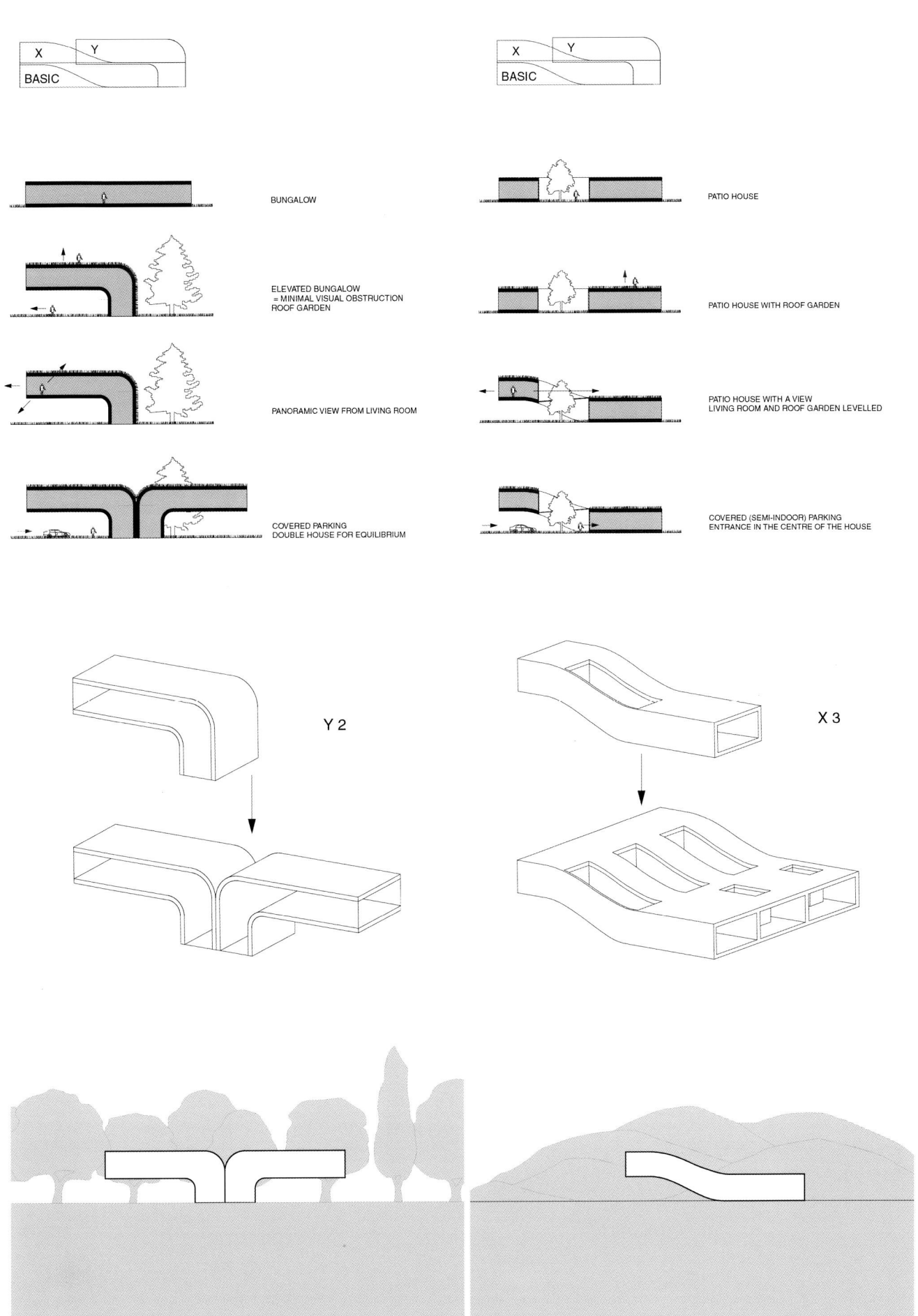

ARCHITECTURAL DIAGRAMS 411

BIONIC TOWER LAVA

"A NATURALLY OCCURING SYSTEM OF STRUCTURAL ORGANIZATION THAT GENERATES A BUILDING EMBODYING EFFICIENCIES."

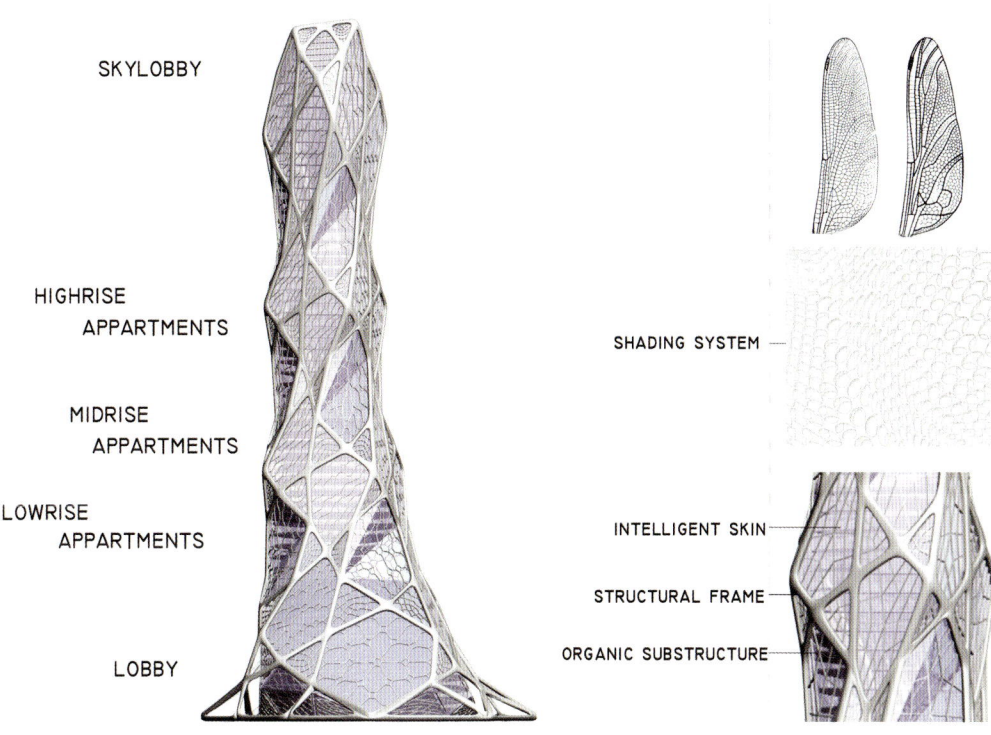

SKYLOBBY

HIGHRISE
APPARTMENTS

MIDRISE
APPARTMENTS

LOWRISE
APPARTMENTS

LOBBY

SHADING SYSTEM

INTELLIGENT SKIN
STRUCTURAL FRAME
ORGANIC SUBSTRUCTURE

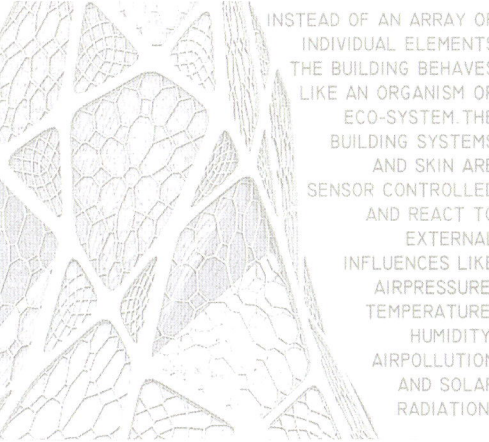

INSTEAD OF AN ARRAY OF INDIVIDUAL ELEMENTS THE BUILDING BEHAVES LIKE AN ORGANISM OR ECO-SYSTEM. THE BUILDING SYSTEMS AND SKIN ARE SENSOR CONTROLLED AND REACT TO EXTERNAL INFLUENCES LIKE AIRPRESSURE, TEMPERATURE, HUMIDITY, AIRPOLLUTION AND SOLAR RADIATION.

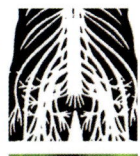

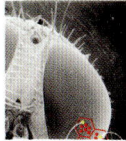

No BUILDING SKIN TODAY APPROACHES THE PERFORMANCE OF THE BIOLOGICAL WORLD. THE CURTAIN WALL IS PASSIVE, LACKING THE POWER TO ADJUST TO THE FLUCTUATING EXTERNAL ENVIRONMENT. IT SHOULD BE ABLE TO INTERVENE ACTIVELY IN THE BUILDING'S STRUGGLE TO MAINTAIN ITS INTERNAL STABILITY.

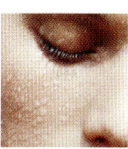

ARCHITECTURAL DIAGRAMS 413

BUREAUX BESANÇON
mxg architects + ALDO architectes

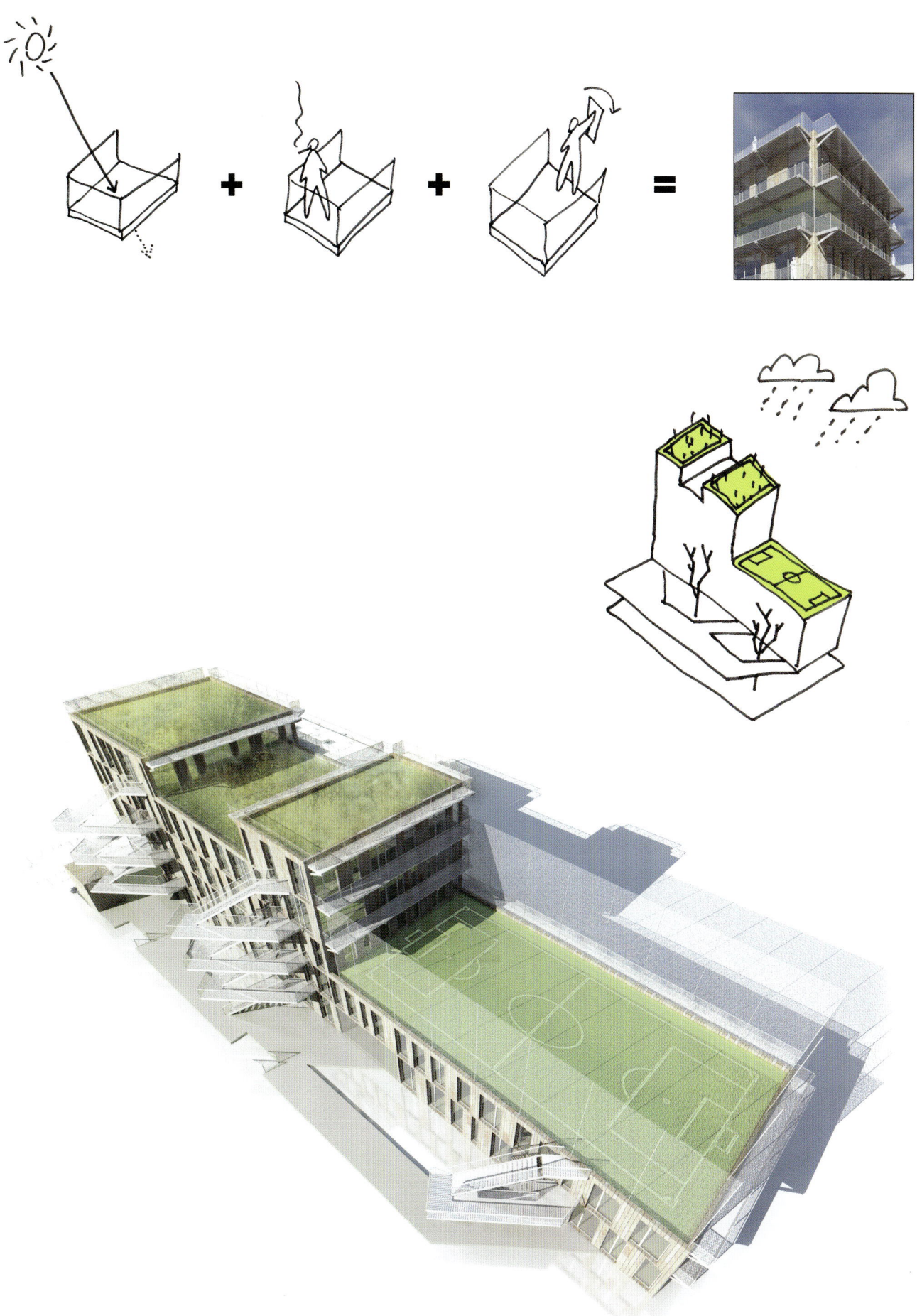

BUSINESS CENTRE
MANUELLE GAUTRAND ARCHITECTURE

"THE AZTEC SERPENT LOOK OF THE SET EXPRESSES VERTICAL AND HORIZONTAL MOVEMENT."

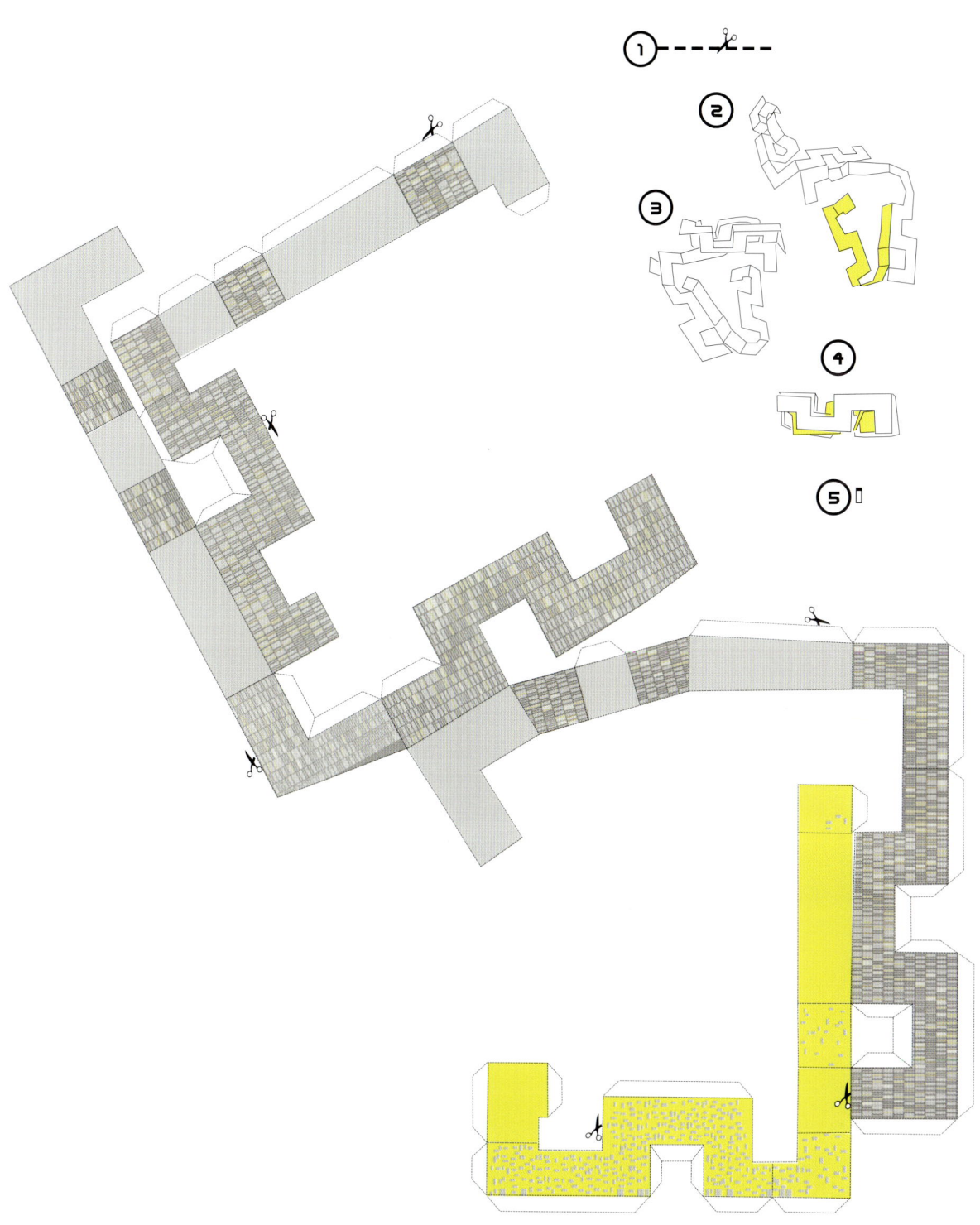

ARCHITECTURAL DIAGRAMS

CARBON TOWER Axi:Ome

"SAILS ARE AIRFOILS THAT WORK BY USING AN AIR-FLOW SET UP BY THE WIND AND GENERATE LIFT USING THE AIR."

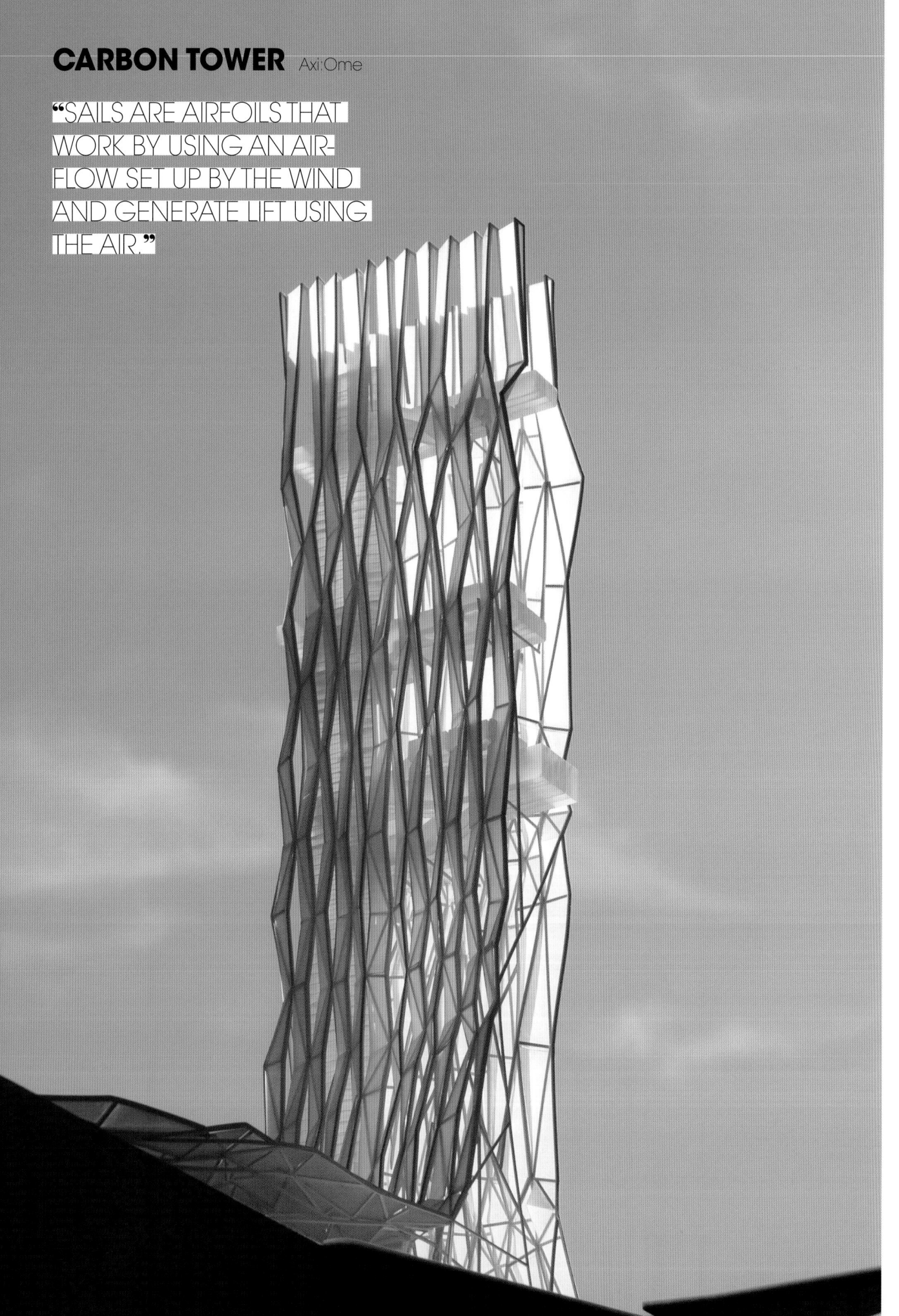

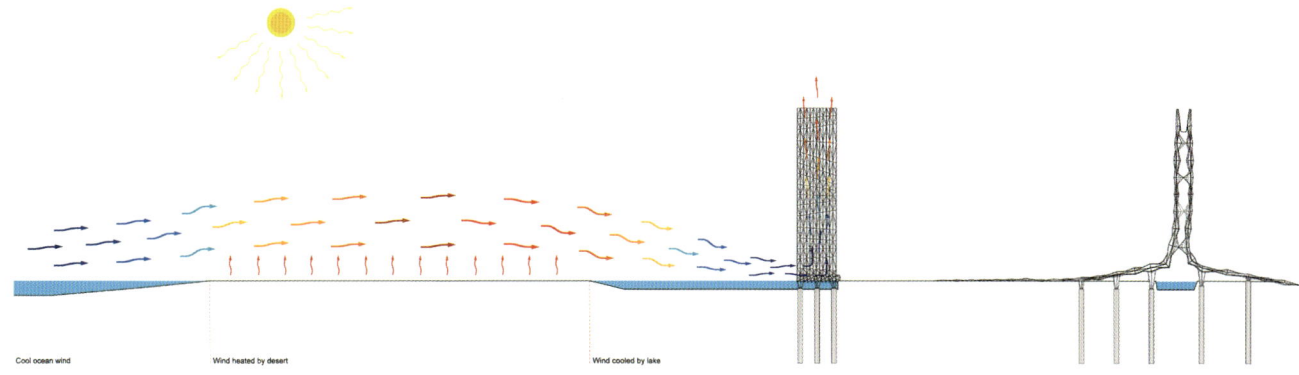

Wind and temperature diagram

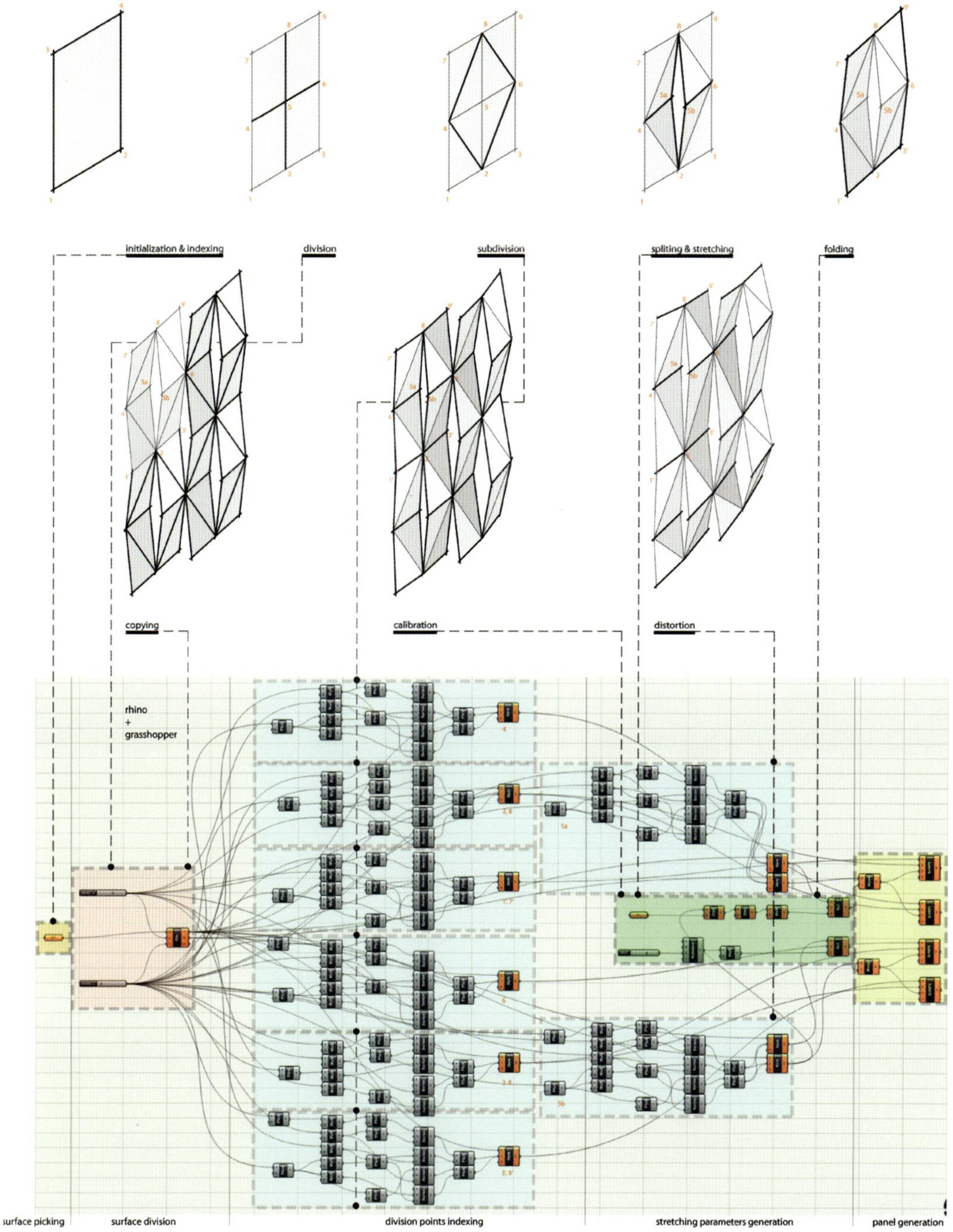

Structural generative modeling process

ARCHITECTURAL DIAGRAMS 419

CENTER FOR EUROPEAN CULTURE
kadawittfeldarchitektur

"THE BASIC SHAPE OF THE CUBIC MAIN VOLUME IS DISTORTED AS A REACTION TO THE ENVIRONMENT."

Covering

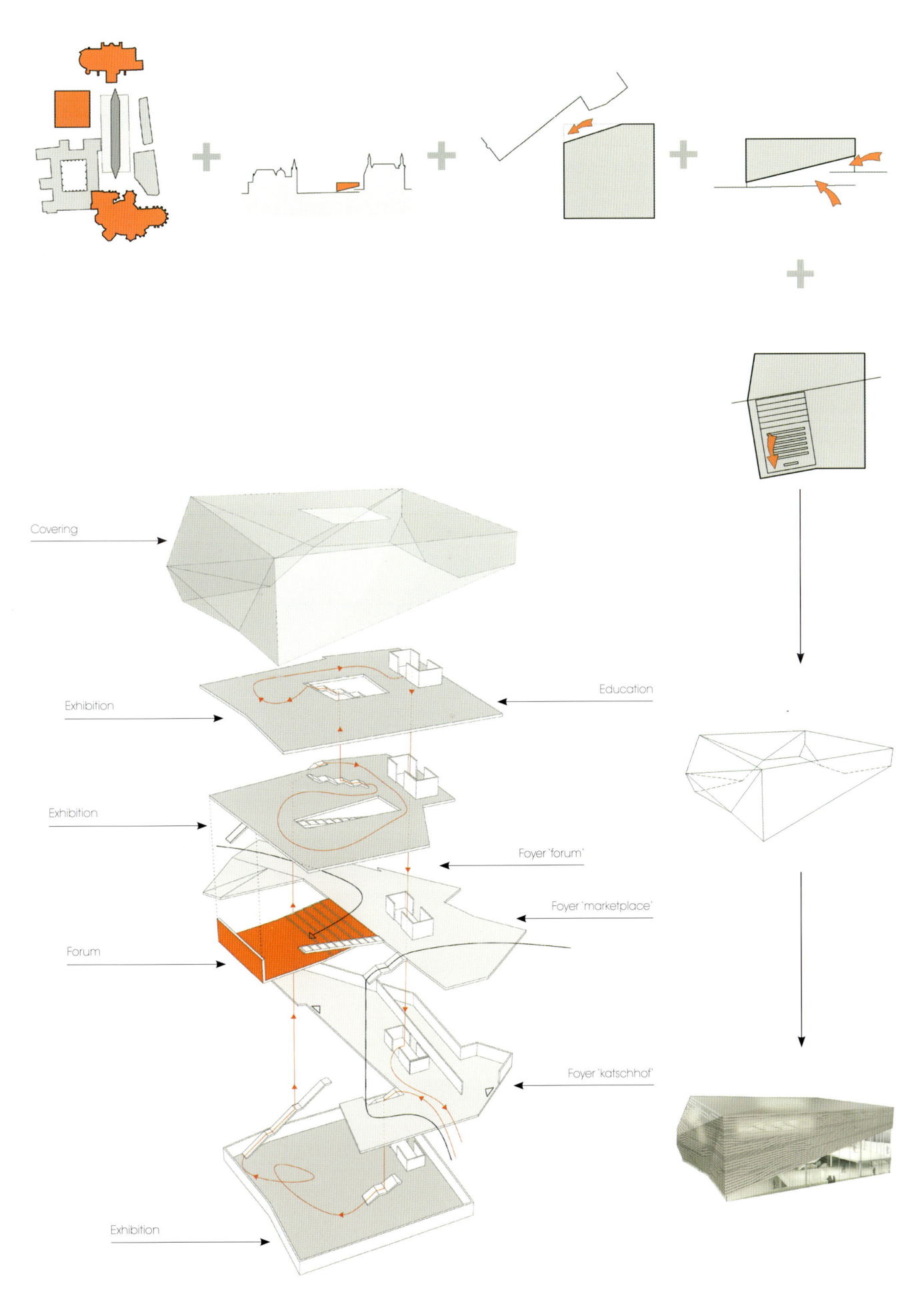

Exhibition

Exhibition

Forum

Exhibition

Education

Foyer 'forum'

Foyer 'marketplace'

Foyer 'katschhof'

ARCHITECTURAL DIAGRAMS 421

CHO RESIDENCE
NL Architects

"WE IMAGINE THAT THE GARDEN CAN BECOME THE CENTER OF THE HOUSE."

Design Concept Diagram: "The Lily"

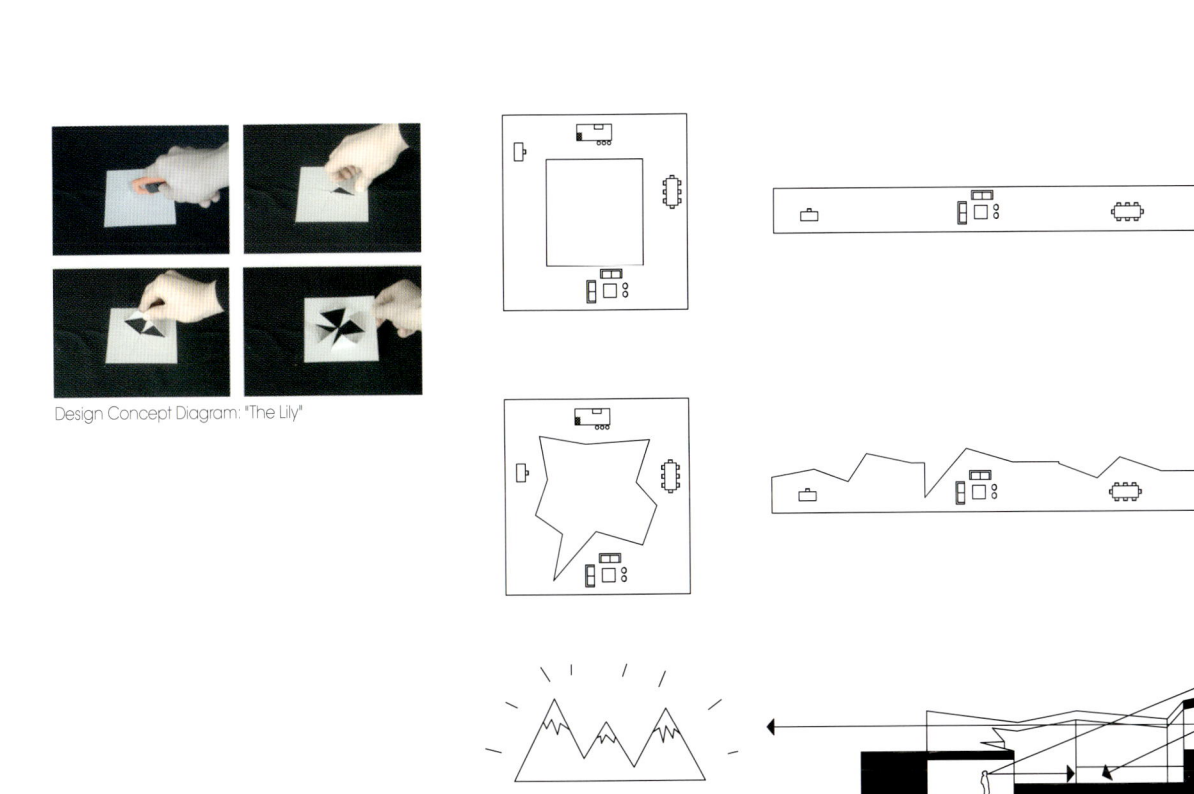

View Diagram

330m²

330m²

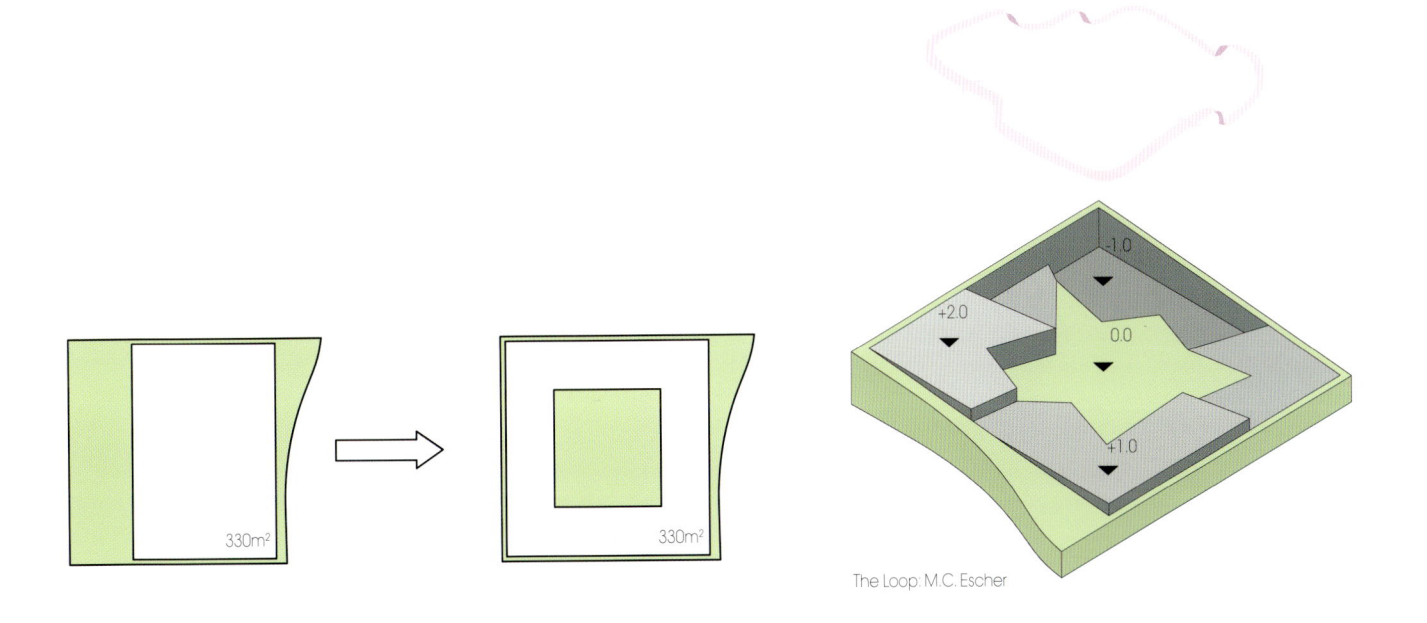

The Loop: M.C. Escher

outside patch:
10% of 534m²=55m²

inside patch:
40% of 435m²=213m²

135m2

330m²

ARCHITECTURAL DIAGRAMS 423

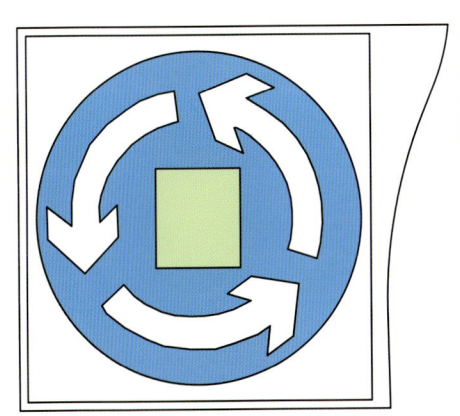

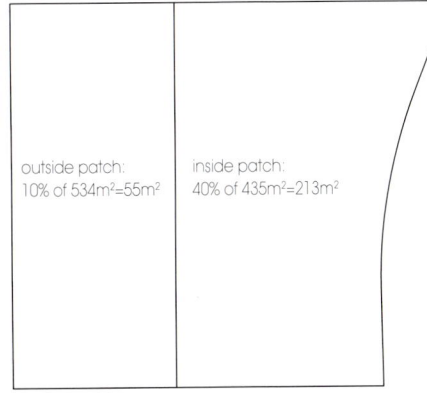

CITROËN EXHIBITION CENTER
MANUELLE GAUTRAND ARCHITECTURE

"THE CHEVRON WILL SIGNAL THE START OF SOME MUCH MORE ORIGINAL DESIGN, WITH LOZENGE SHAPES, TRIANGLES AND CHEVRONS."

Development of glass skin

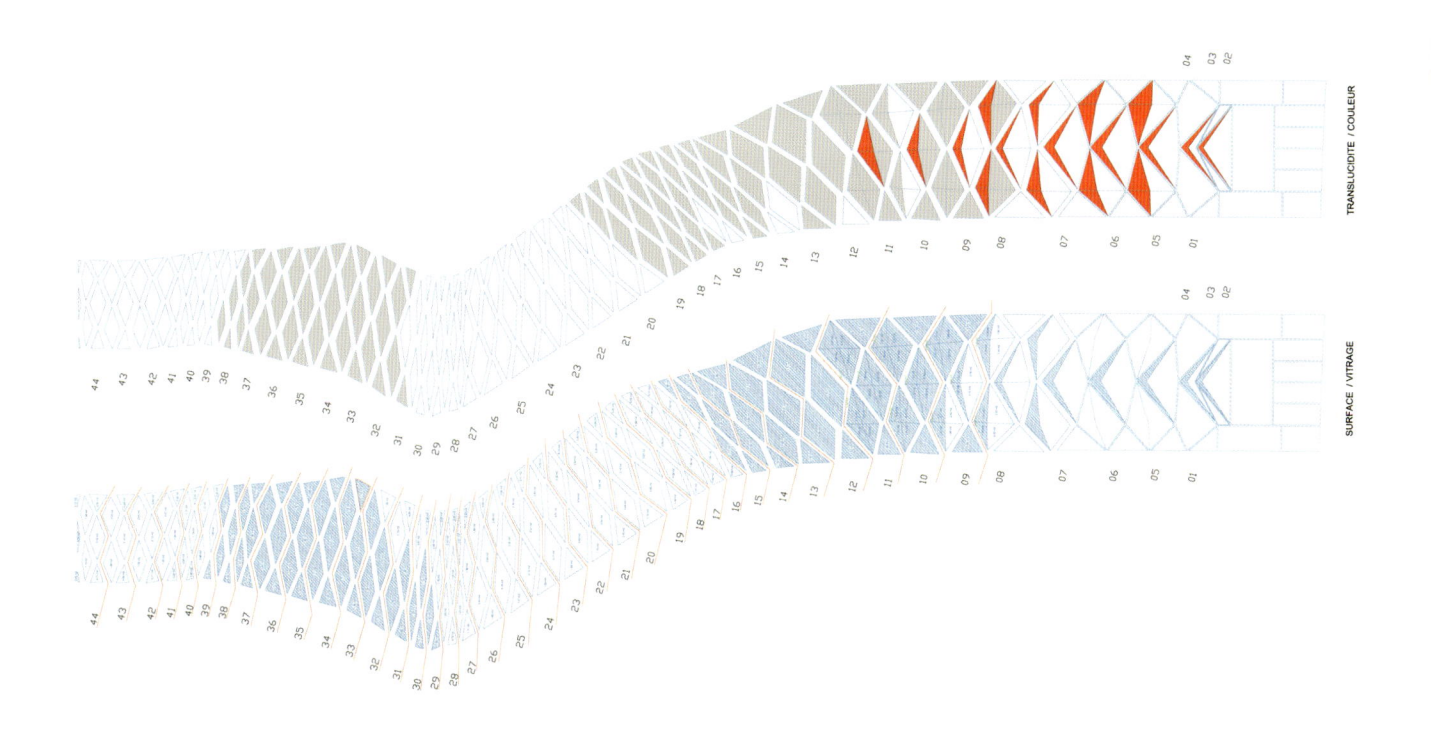

ARCHITECTURAL DIAGRAMS 425

CLAUDE BERNARD
ECDM

cm   jf   sh

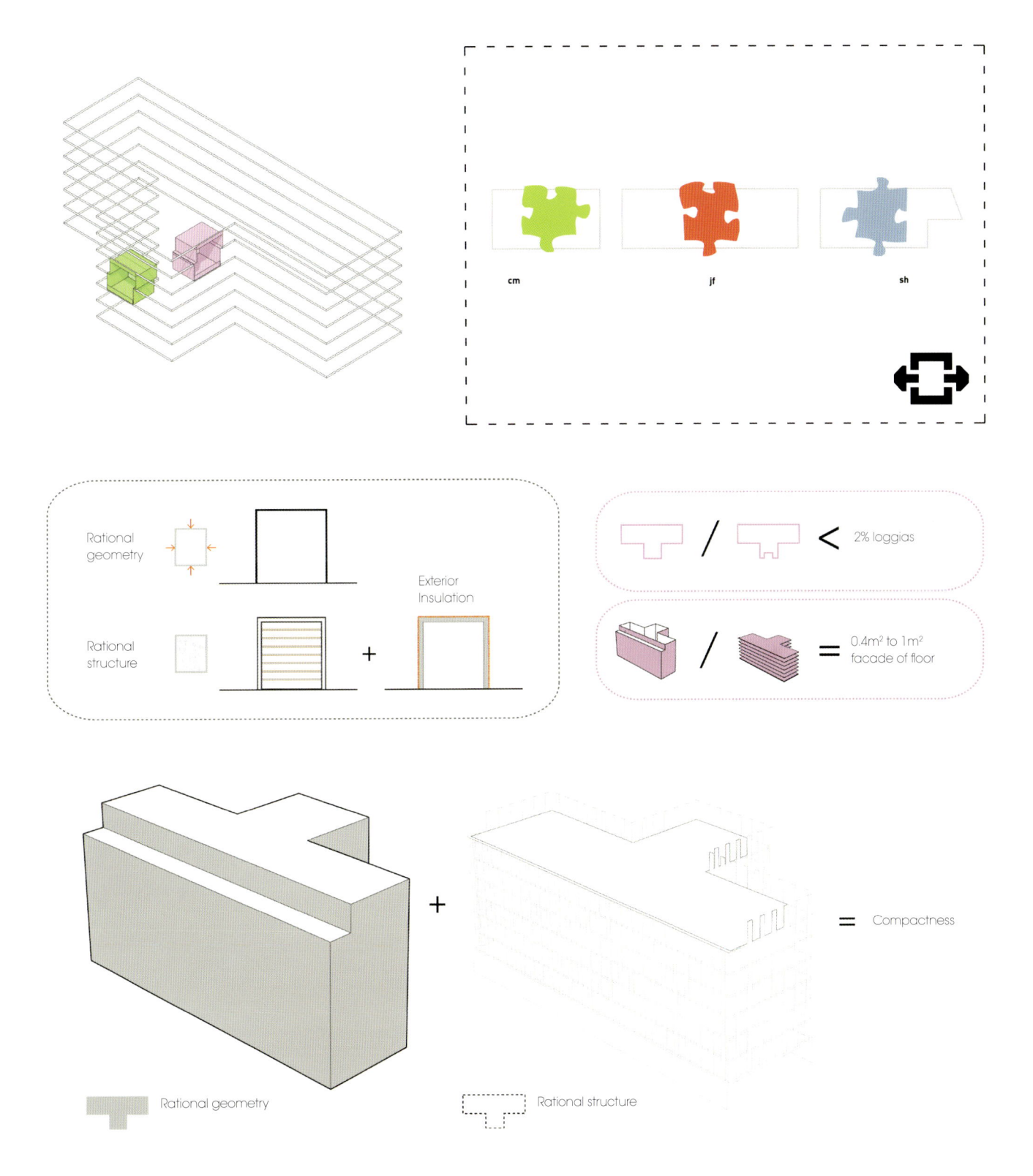

Rational geometry

Rational structure

Exterior Insulation

< 2% loggias

$0.4m^2$ to $1m^2$ facade of floor

Rational geometry + Rational structure = Compactness

ARCHITECTURAL DIAGRAMS 427

CONDOMINIUM TRNOVSKI PRISTAN
SADAR VUGA ARHITEKTI

"SALAMANDER HOUSE ADAPTS AND GENERATES A NEW CONTEXT IN ITS SURROUNDINGS."

Green terrace   Green between housing

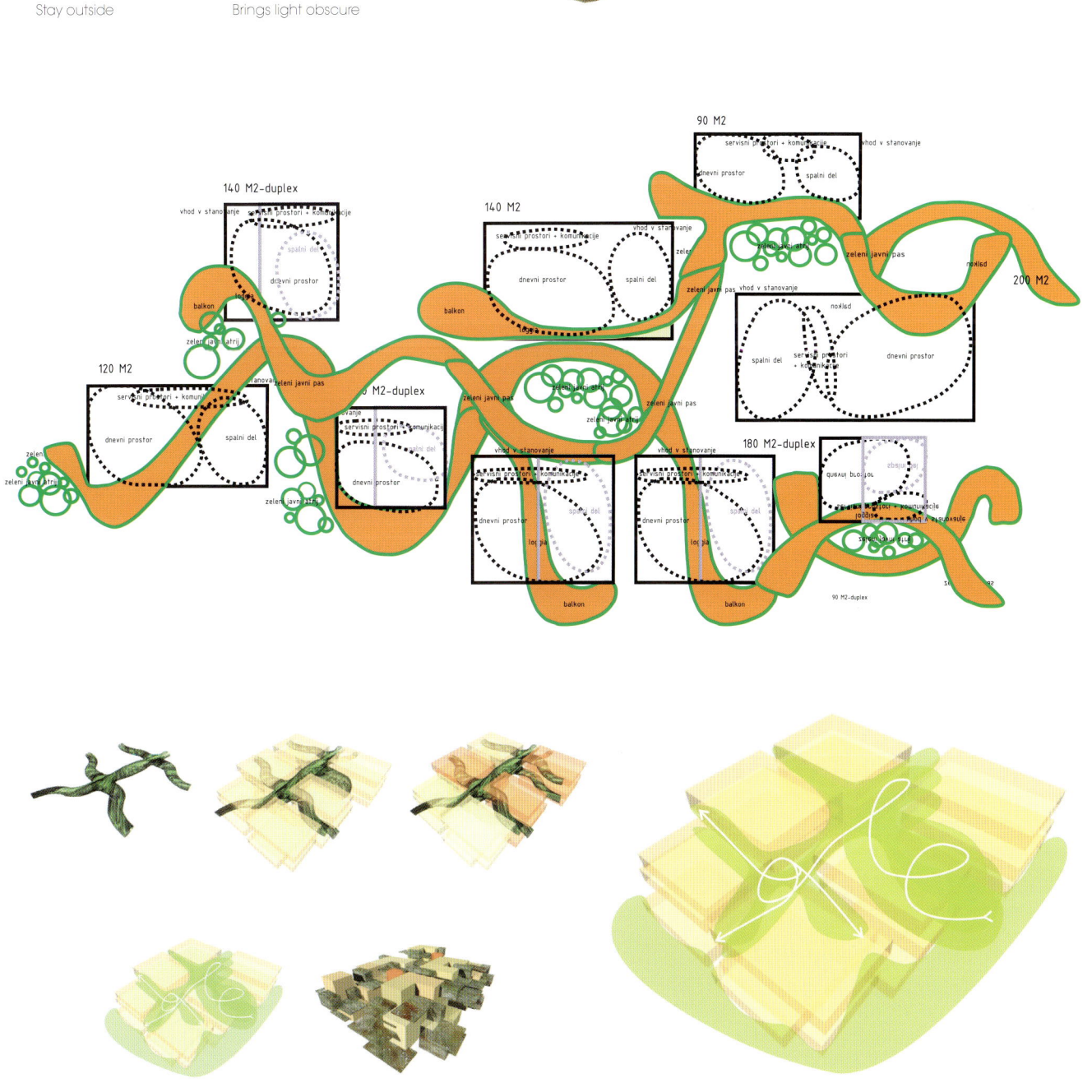

Stay outside   Brings light obscure

ARCHITECTURAL DIAGRAMS 429

CORNICHE TOWER LAVA

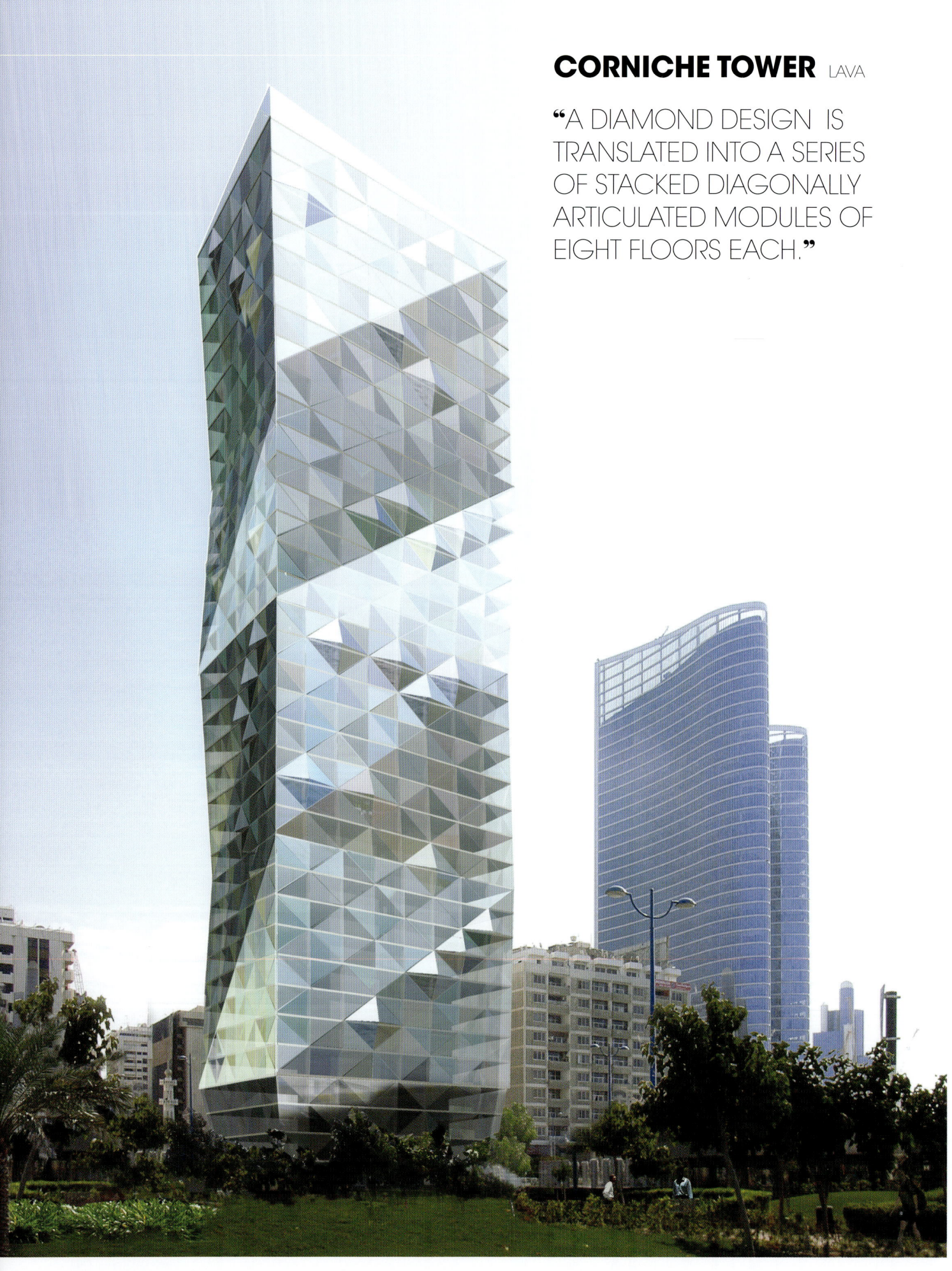

"A DIAMOND DESIGN IS TRANSLATED INTO A SERIES OF STACKED DIAGONALLY ARTICULATED MODULES OF EIGHT FLOORS EACH."

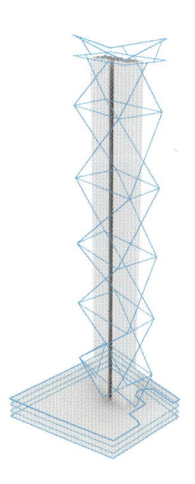

movement vertical
parking - elevator - staircase

structure vertical
columns - core - floorplates

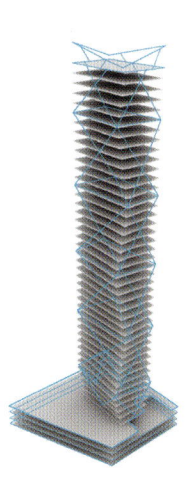

program office slabs
41 level - 2 level lobby/ mezzanine

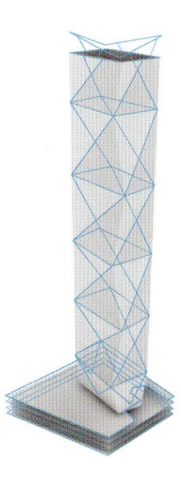

macro diamond structure
large diagonals

micro structure
small triangulated areas continued into landscape

Conceptual build-up of tower / overall organisation
The building is composed of three distinct components:

1. Infrastructural/serving elements
   Car park, main entrance lobby, the core including all elevators,
   office floor lobby areas,
2. Office slabs
3. Outer skin of building, diamond facade
   Large diagonals, small-triangulated areas; triangulation continued
   into landscape surface.

building scale

total facade area
~16965 sqm

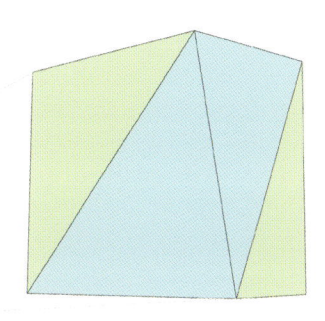

modul scale1

8 storeys, 2 main spirals

modul facade area
~3240 sqm = 100%

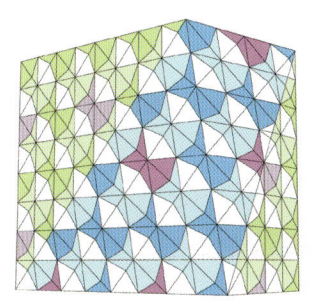

modul scale 2

- 8 storeys, 2 main spirals
- 6 different colored panels, highly
  reflective, low degree of transparency
- 1 non-colored glass panel, transparent

glas panels (area)
green light ~564 sqm
green ~420sqm
blue light ~567 sqm   = 66.3%
blue ~480sqm
red light ~133sqm
red ~ 130sqm

transparent glas ~1091sqm = 33.7% clear transparency

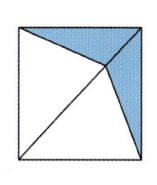

facade element scale

4 glas elements, in this case
2 blue and two transparent
elements

ARCHITECTURAL DIAGRAMS 431

DASYPUS nodo17 Architects

"ONE OF THE MAIN PREMISES OF THE PROPOSAL IS TO PRESERVE THE URBAN EMPTINESS PRESENTLY OCCUPYING THE PLOT."

Setback_8m
Bay_14m
h_14 m
L =140 m

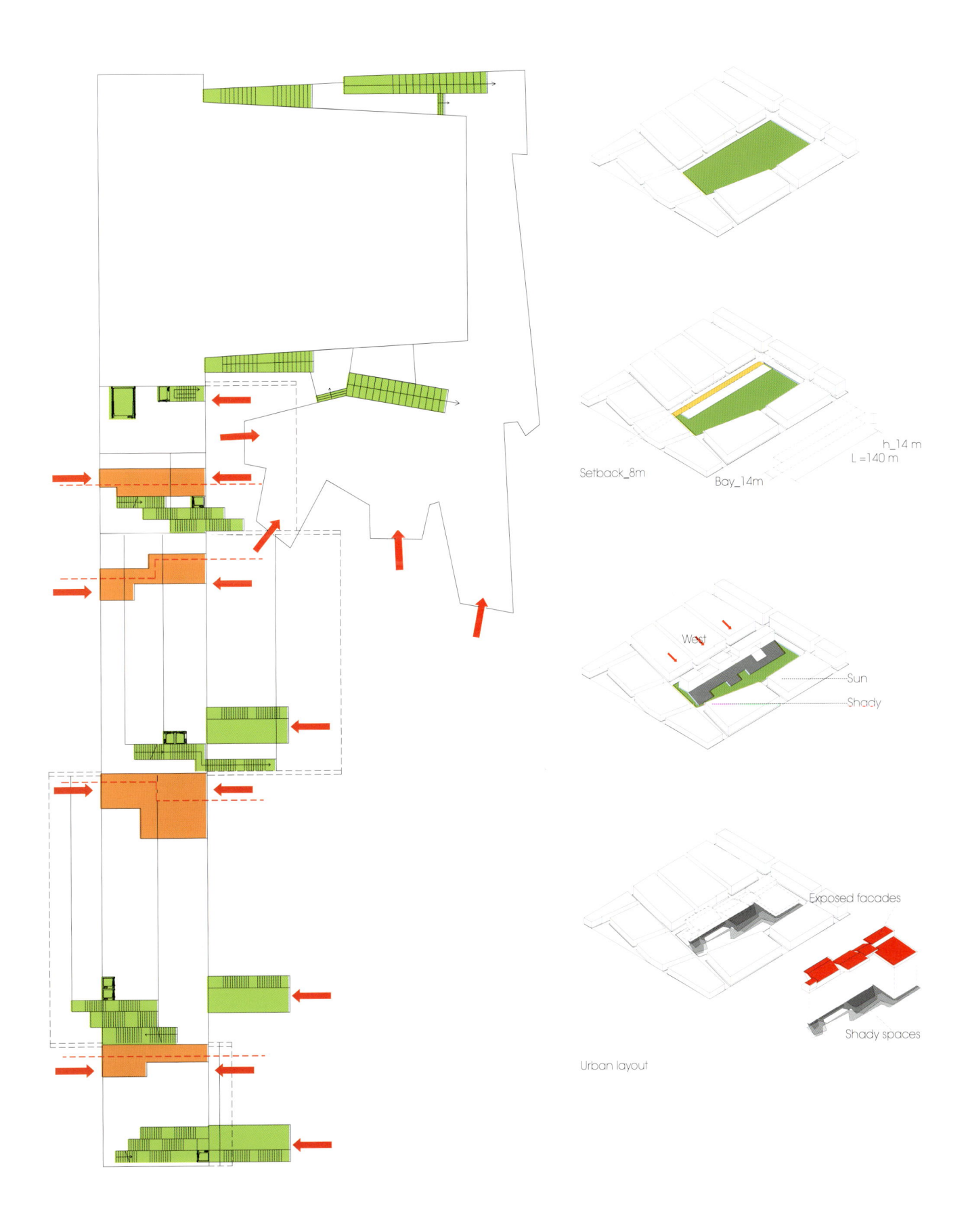

West
Sun
Shady

Exposed facades
Shady spaces

Urban layout

ARCHITECTURAL DIAGRAMS 433

ECOCOON FOR RECYCLING
Vincent Callebaut Architectures

"ECOCOON IS A MIXING BETWEEN WIND POWER SUPPLY AND URBAN HOUSING."

Silkworm concept

Electrostatic pilosity

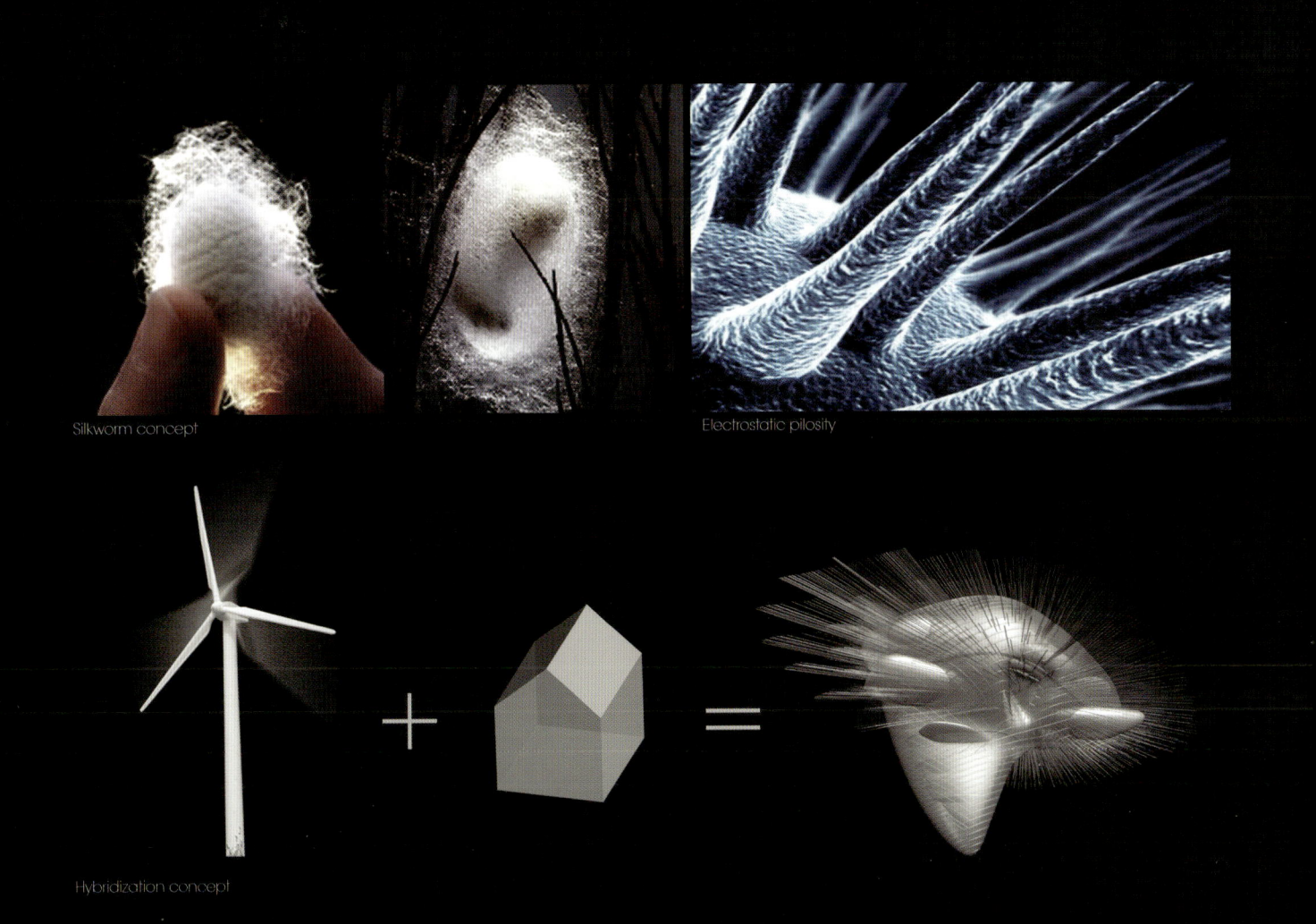

Hybridization concept

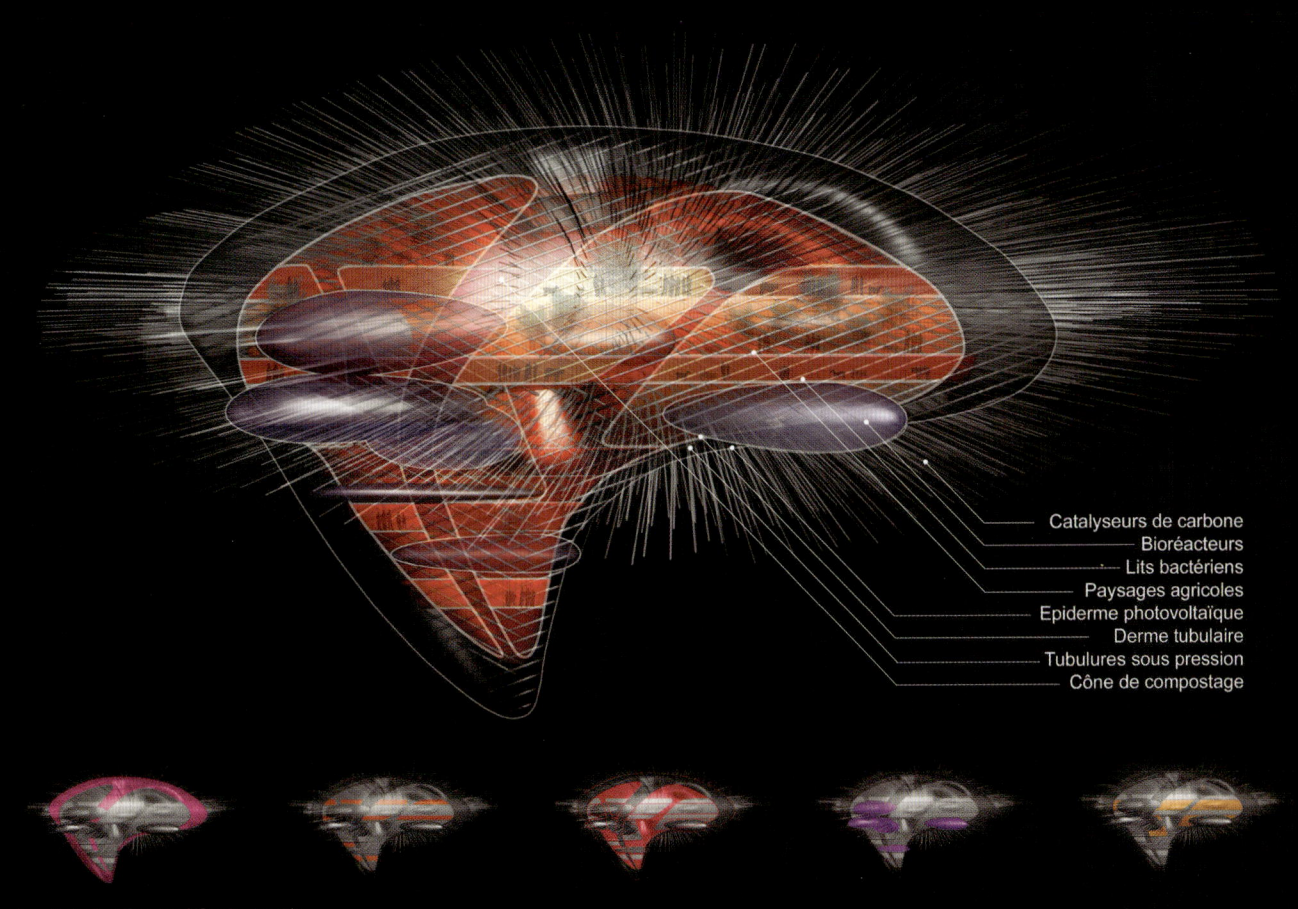

Catalyseurs de carbone
Bioréacteurs
Lits bactériens
Paysages agricoles
Epiderme photovoltaïque
Derme tubulaire
Tubulures sous pression
Cône de compostage

Typologic Section and Components

ESO HEADQUATERS
IaN+

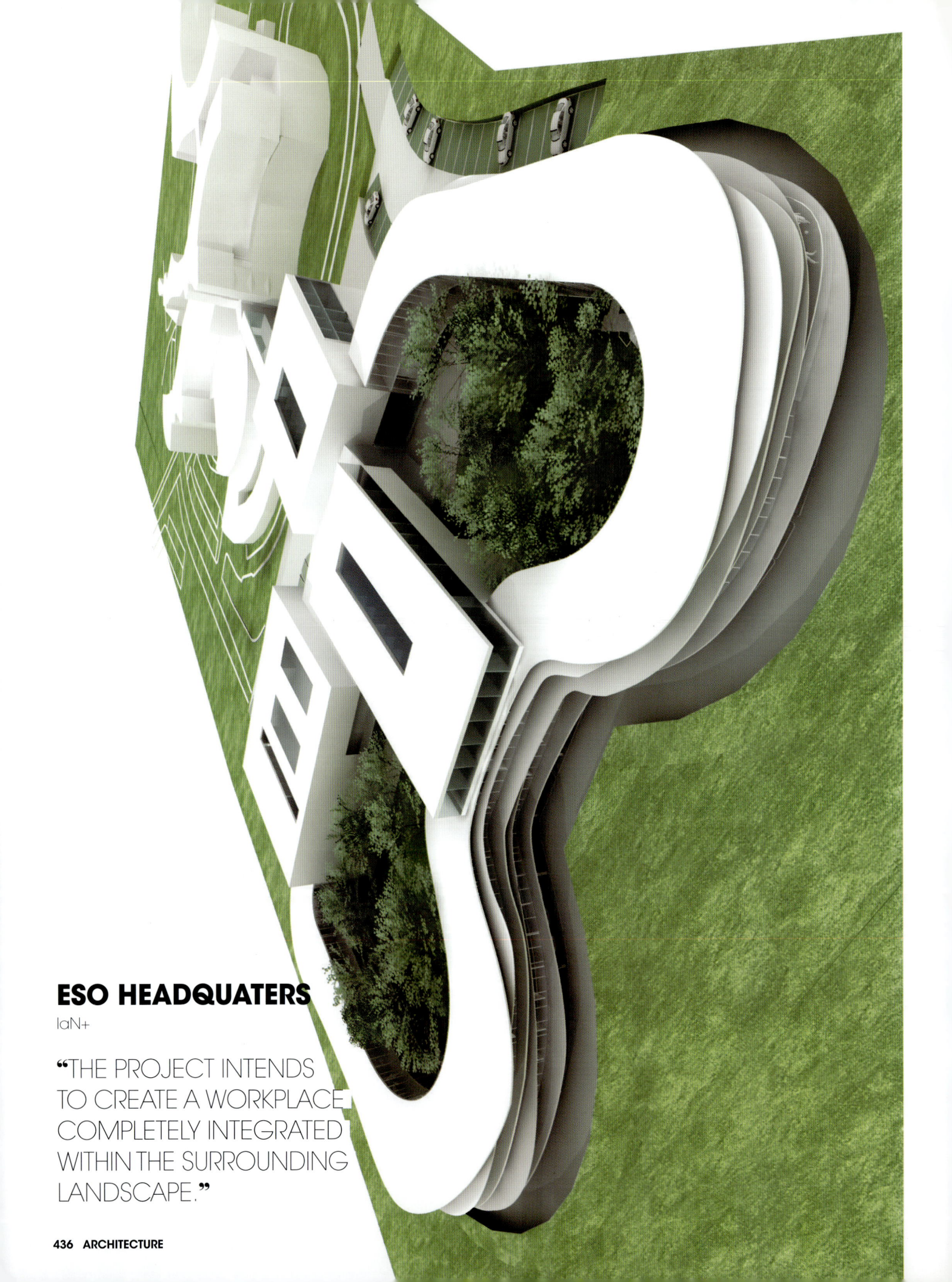

"THE PROJECT INTENDS TO CREATE A WORKPLACE COMPLETELY INTEGRATED WITHIN THE SURROUNDING LANDSCAPE."

offices orientation

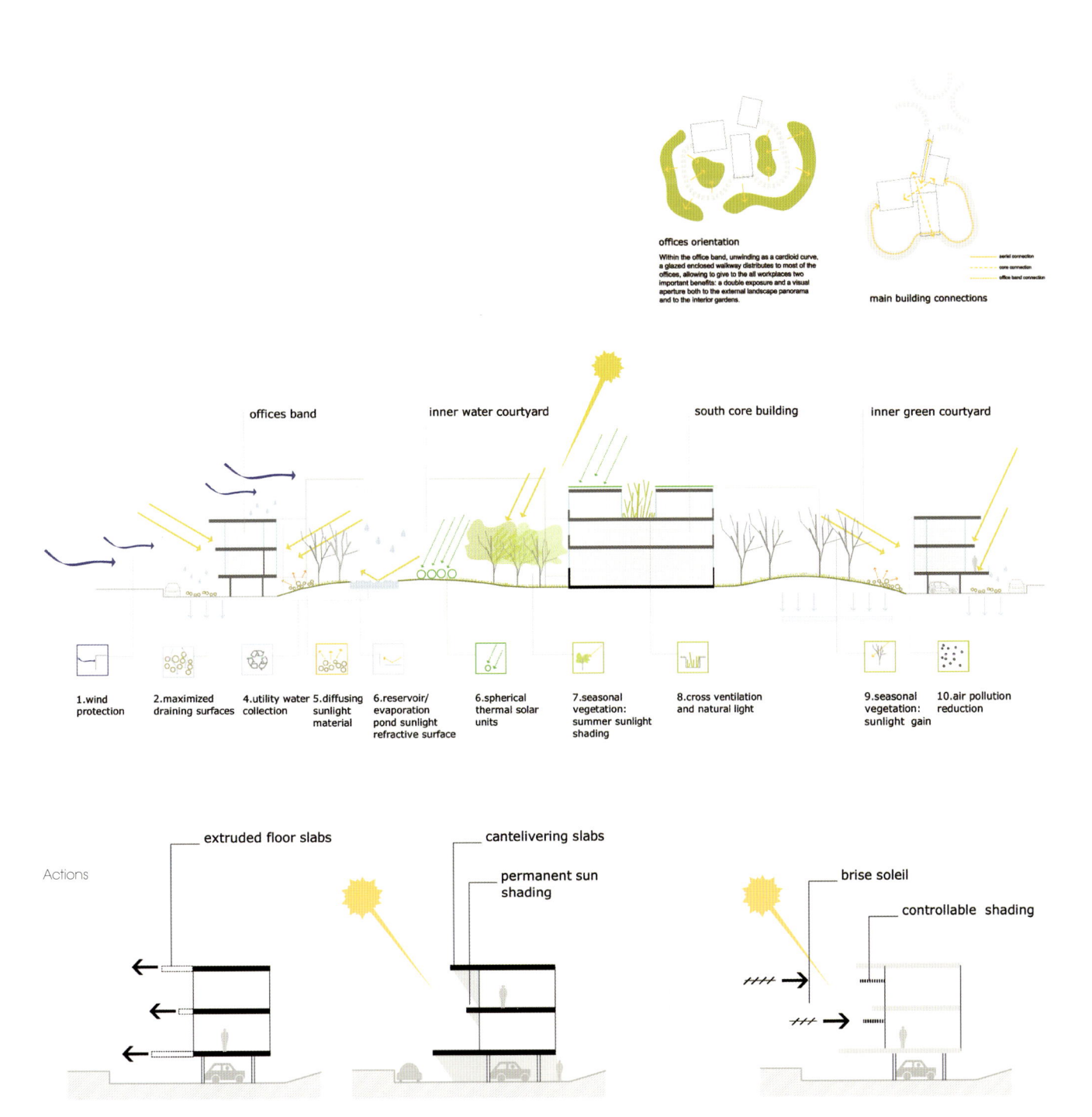

Within the office band, unwinding as a cardioid curve, a glazed enclosed walkway distributes to most of the offices, allowing to give to the all workplaces two important benefits: a double exposure and a visual aperture both to the external landscape panorama and to the interior gardens.

main building connections

aerial connection
core connection
offices band connection

offices band | inner water courtyard | south core building | inner green courtyard

1. wind protection
2. maximized draining surfaces
4. utility water collection
5. diffusing sunlight material
6. reservoir/evaporation pond sunlight refractive surface
6. spherical thermal solar units
7. seasonal vegetation: summer sunlight shading
8. cross ventilation and natural light
9. seasonal vegetation: sunlight gain
10. air pollution reduction

Actions

extruded floor slabs | cantelivering slabs | brise soleil
permanent sun shading | controllable shading

Natural lighting design strategy

ARCHITECTURAL DIAGRAMS 437

FIVE FRANKLIN PLACE
UNStudio

"THE APPLIED METAL FACADES OF TRIBECA'S 19TH CENTURY CAST IRON ARCHITECTURE AND SUCH CONTEMPORARY SOURCES AS COUTURE FASHION."

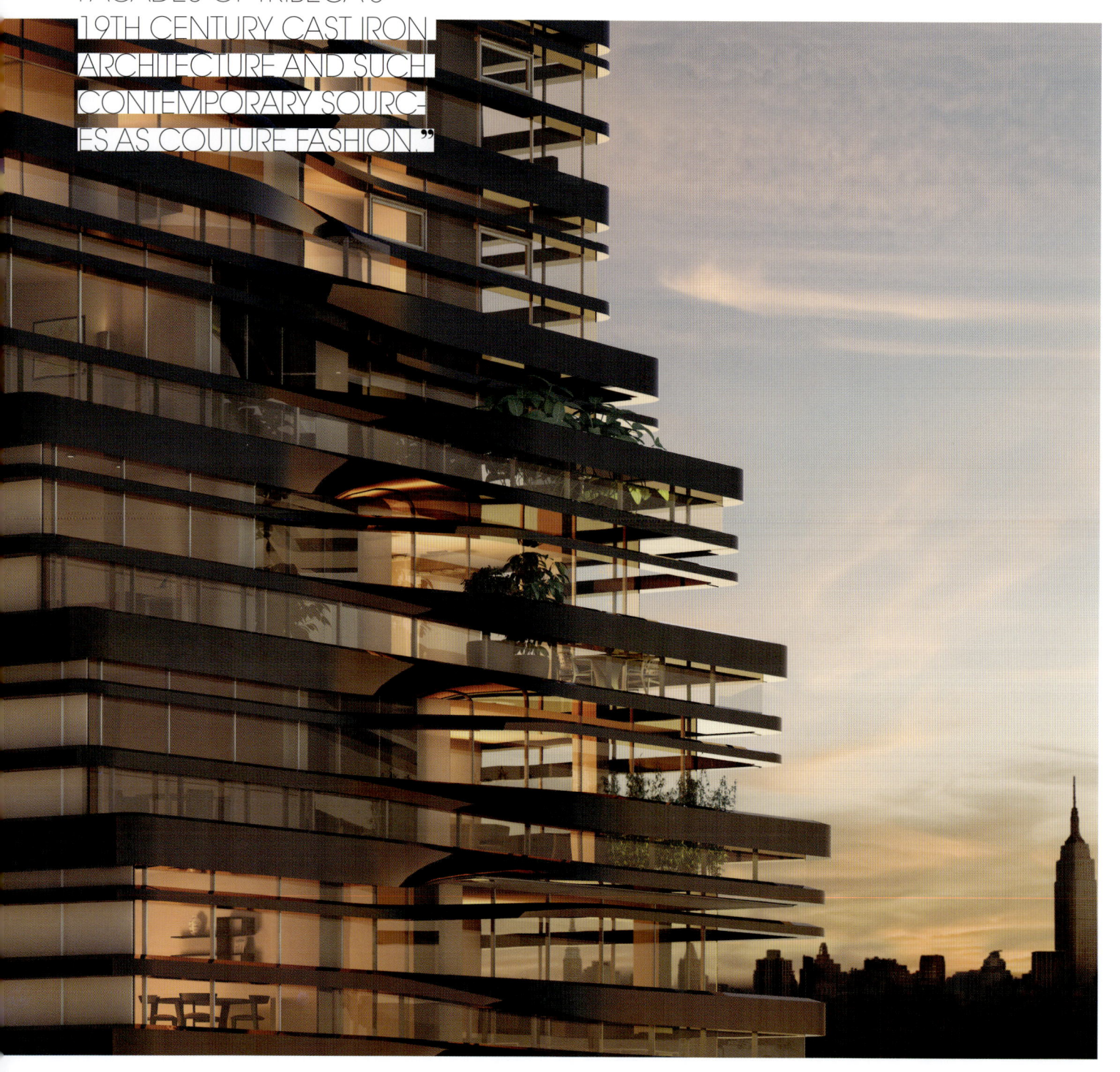

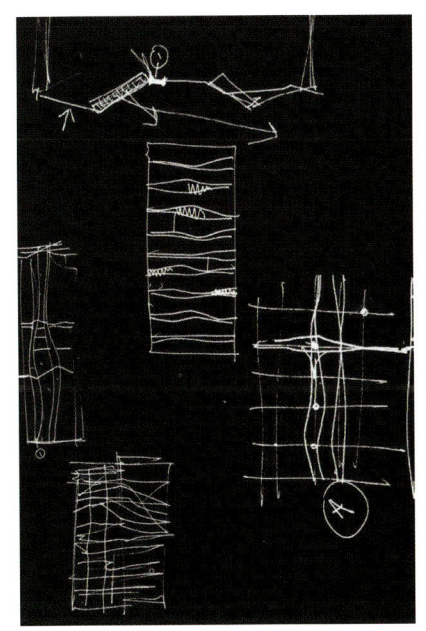

Facade pattern sketch

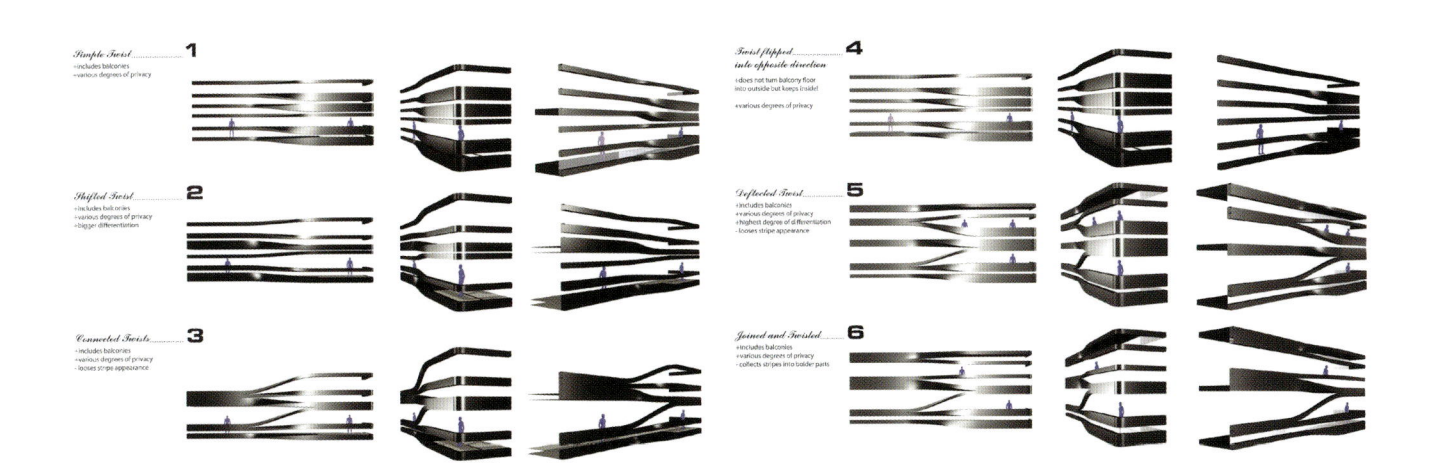

1. Simple Twist
- includes balconies
- various degrees of privacy

2. Shifted Twist
- includes balconies
- various degrees of privacy
- bigger differentiation

3. Connected Twists
- includes balconies
- various degrees of privacy
- looses stripe appearance

4. Twist flipped into opposite direction
- does not turn balcony floor into outside but keeps it inside!
- various degrees of privacy

5. Deflected Twist
- includes balconies
- various degrees of privacy
- highest degree of differentiation
- looses stripe appearance

6. Joined and Twisted
- includes balconies
- various degrees of privacy
- collects stripes into bolder parts

ARCHITECTURAL DIAGRAMS 439

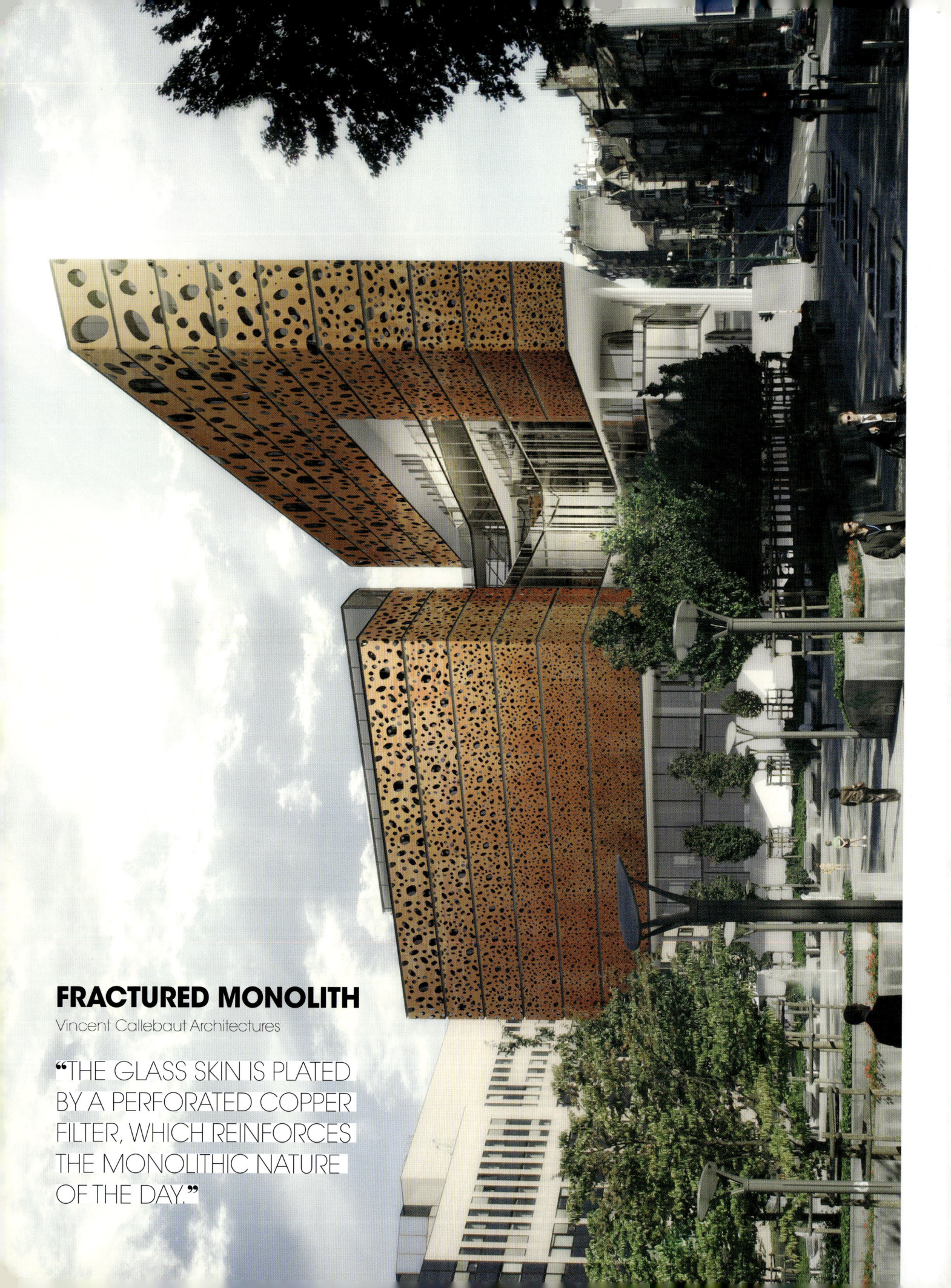

FRACTURED MONOLITH
Vincent Callebaut Architectures

"THE GLASS SKIN IS PLATED BY A PERFORATED COPPER FILTER, WHICH REINFORCES THE MONOLITHIC NATURE OF THE DAY."

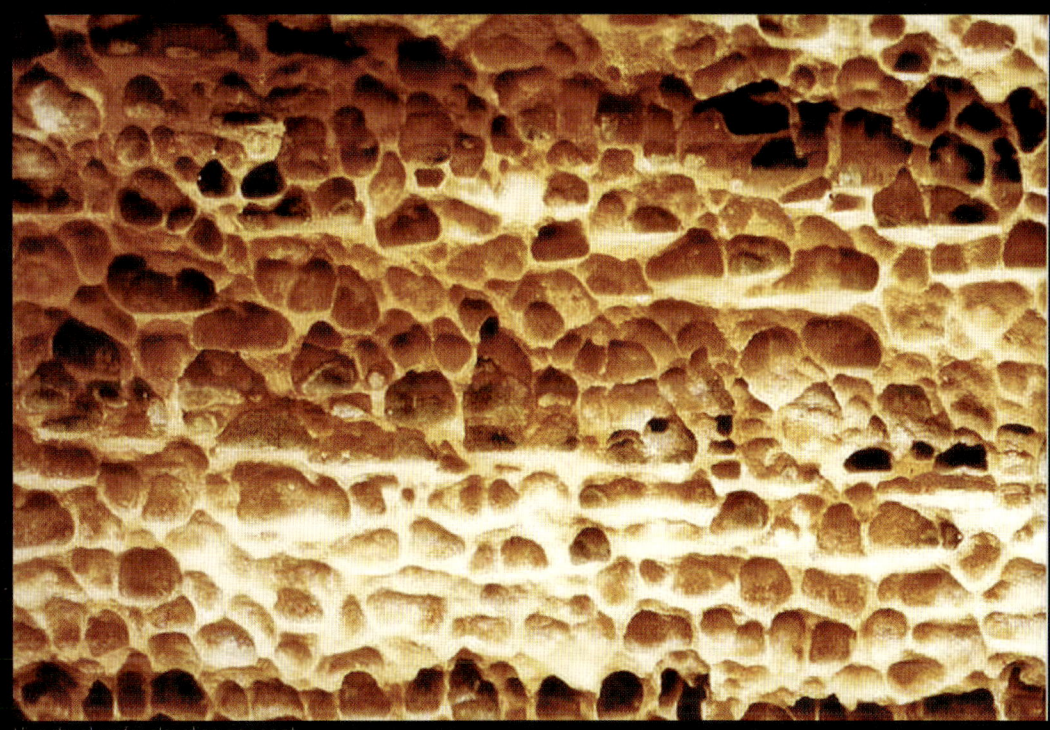

Hive structure for elevation concept

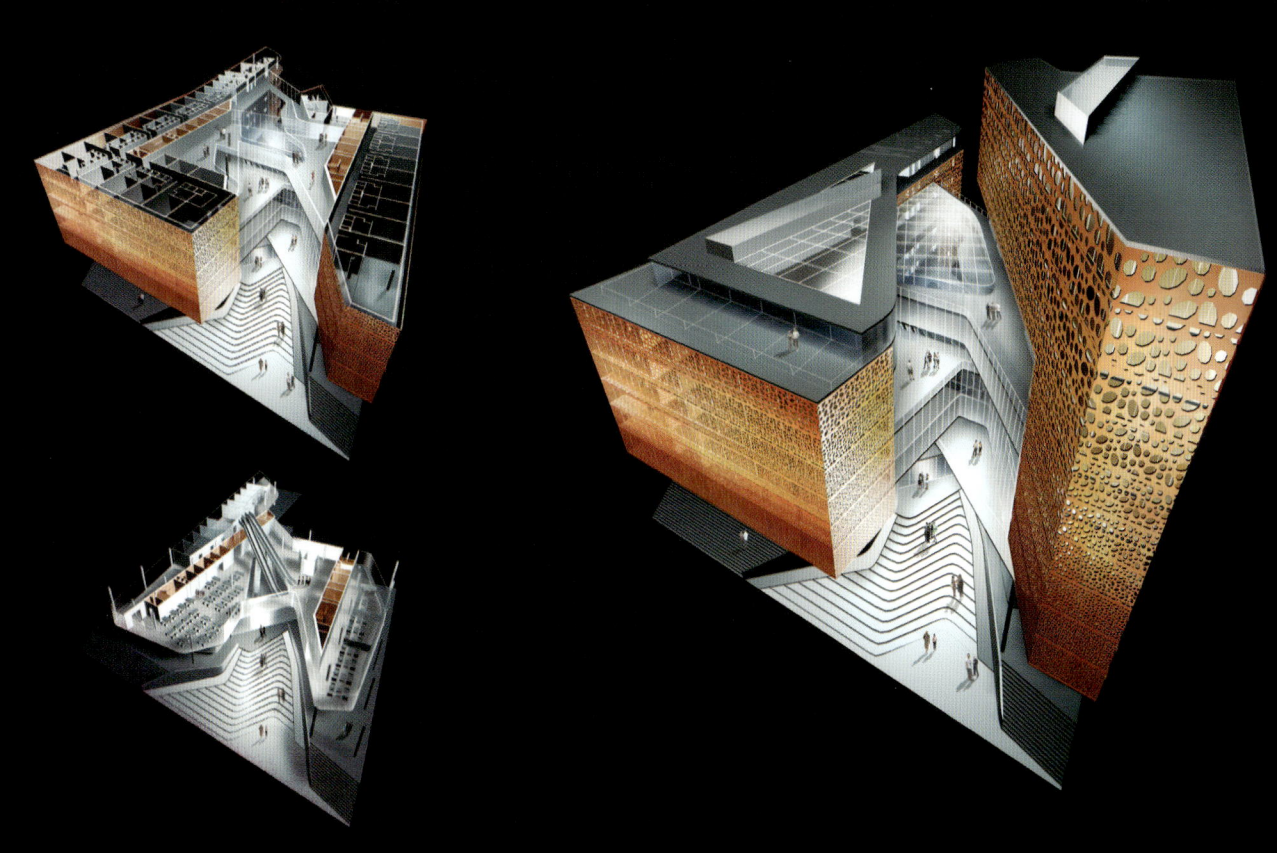

Axonometric views

ARCHITECTURAL DIAGRAMS 441

G55
Bernd Kniess Architects Urban Planners

"THE ENTIRE REMAINING OUTSIDE AREA IS CONSIDERED THE GARDEN AND BOASTS DIFFERENT AREAS OF GREENERY."

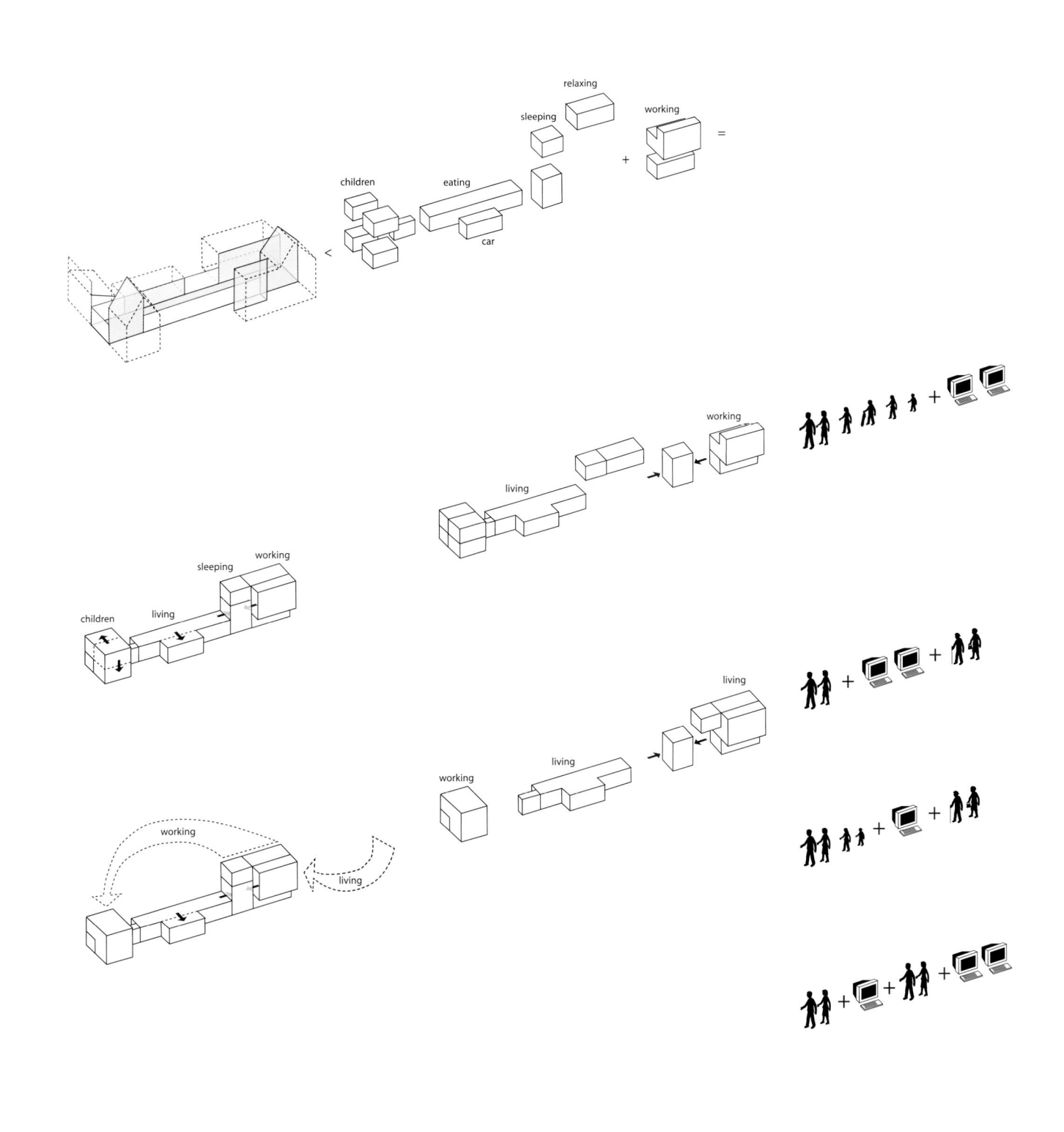

ARCHITECTURAL DIAGRAMS 443

HEADLANDS HOTEL
LAVA

"THE CURRENTLY PROPOSED DEVELOPMENT SIZE HAS BEEN CALCULATED AND BALANCED TO FULFILL BRAND AND OPERATIONAL REQUIREMENTS OF RECOGNIZED HOTEL GROUPS."

option 1

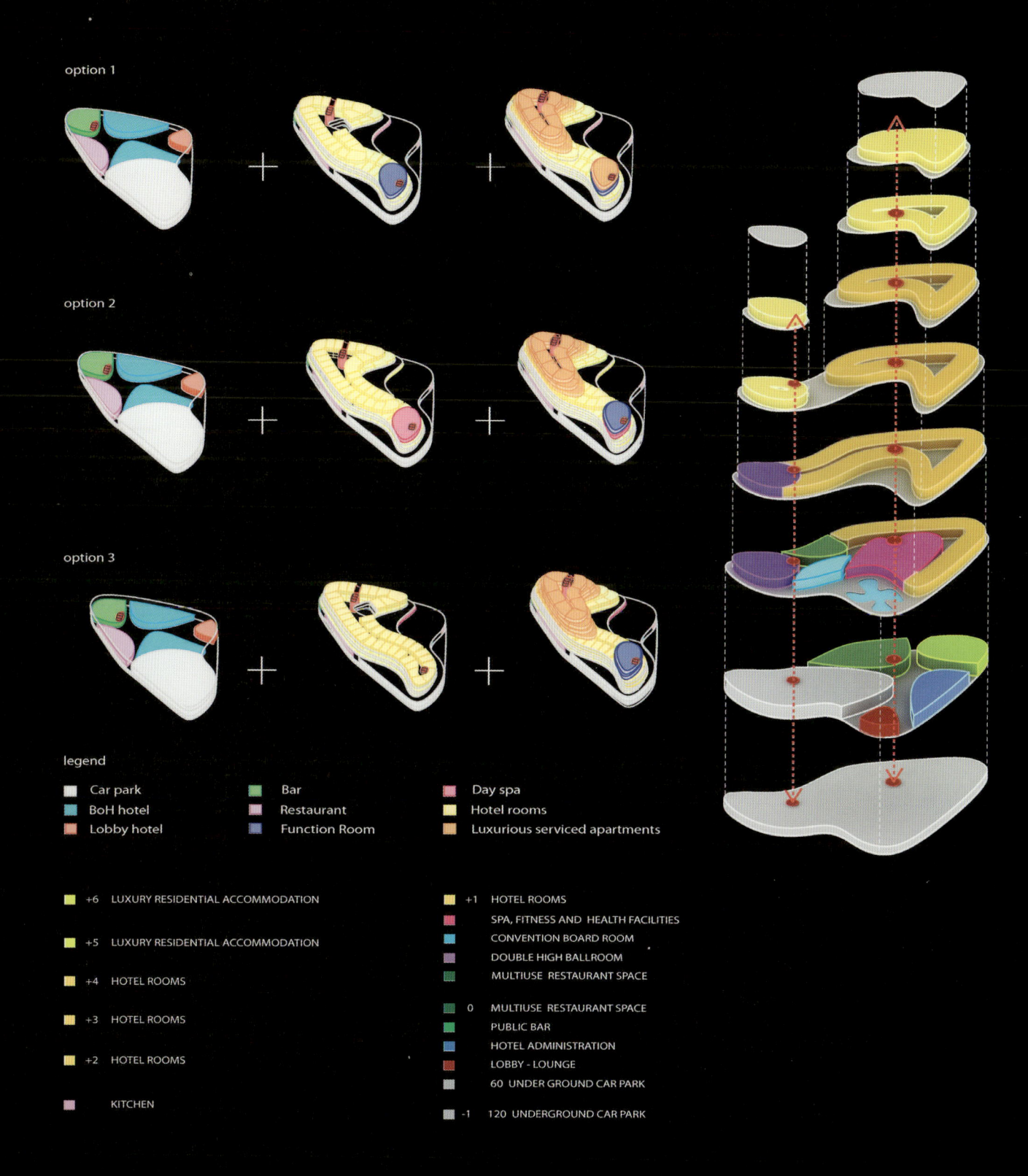

option 2

option 3

legend
- Car park
- BoH hotel
- Lobby hotel
- Bar
- Restaurant
- Function Room
- Day spa
- Hotel rooms
- Luxurious serviced apartments

+6 LUXURY RESIDENTIAL ACCOMMODATION

+5 LUXURY RESIDENTIAL ACCOMMODATION

+4 HOTEL ROOMS

+3 HOTEL ROOMS

+2 HOTEL ROOMS

    KITCHEN

+1 HOTEL ROOMS
    SPA, FITNESS AND HEALTH FACILITIES
    CONVENTION BOARD ROOM
    DOUBLE HIGH BALLROOM
    MULTIUSE RESTAURANT SPACE

0   MULTIUSE RESTAURANT SPACE
    PUBLIC BAR
    HOTEL ADMINISTRATION
    LOBBY - LOUNGE
    60 UNDER GROUND CAR PARK

-1 120 UNDERGROUND CAR PARK

ARCHITECTURAL DIAGRAMS 445

HOTEL PRO FORMA
nARCHITECTS

"IN A STANDARD HOTEL, LOBBY AND CORRIDOR ARE THE PRIMARY LOCI OF BOTH SCRIPTED AND SPONTANEOUS PERFORMANCES."

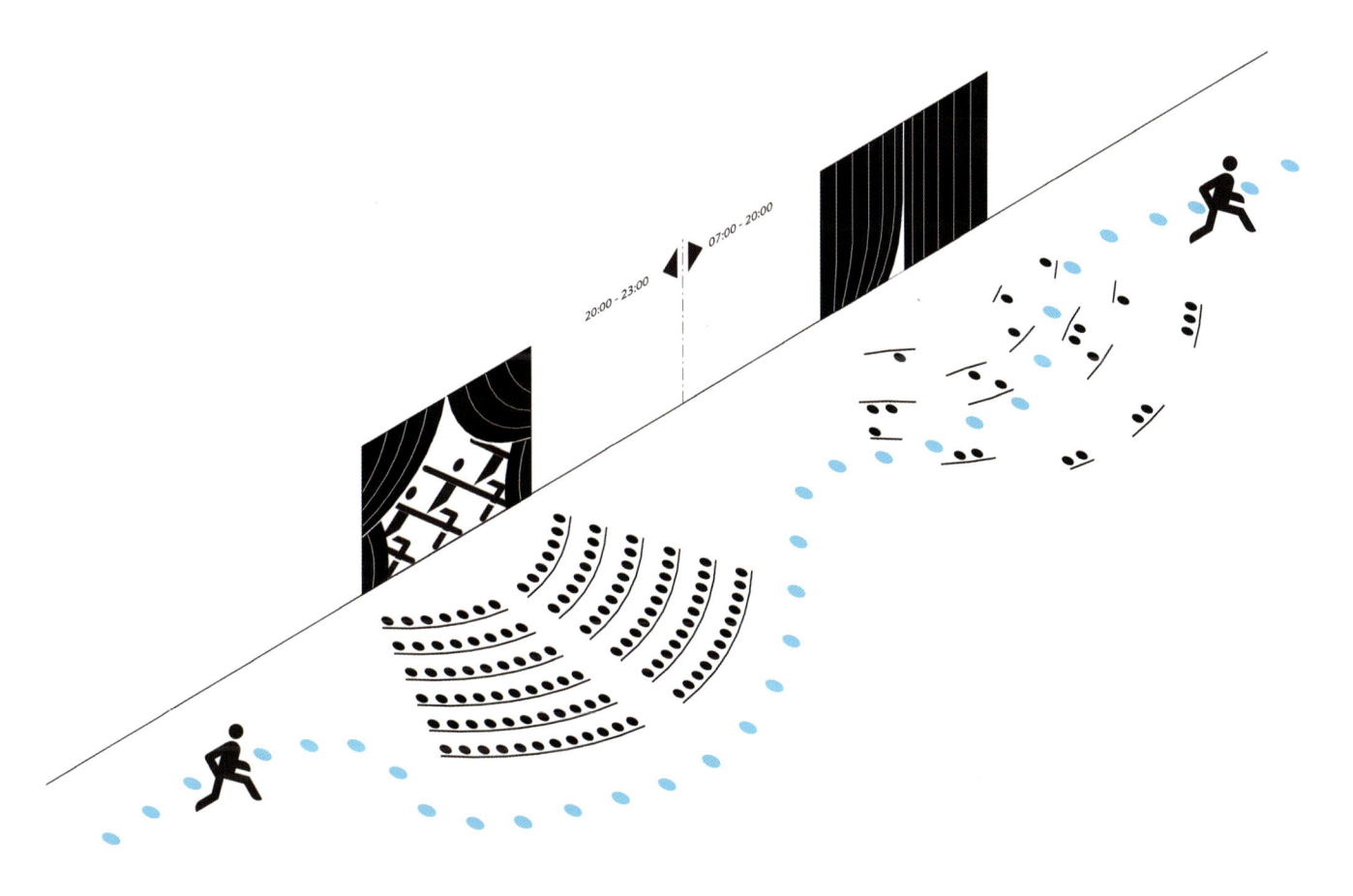

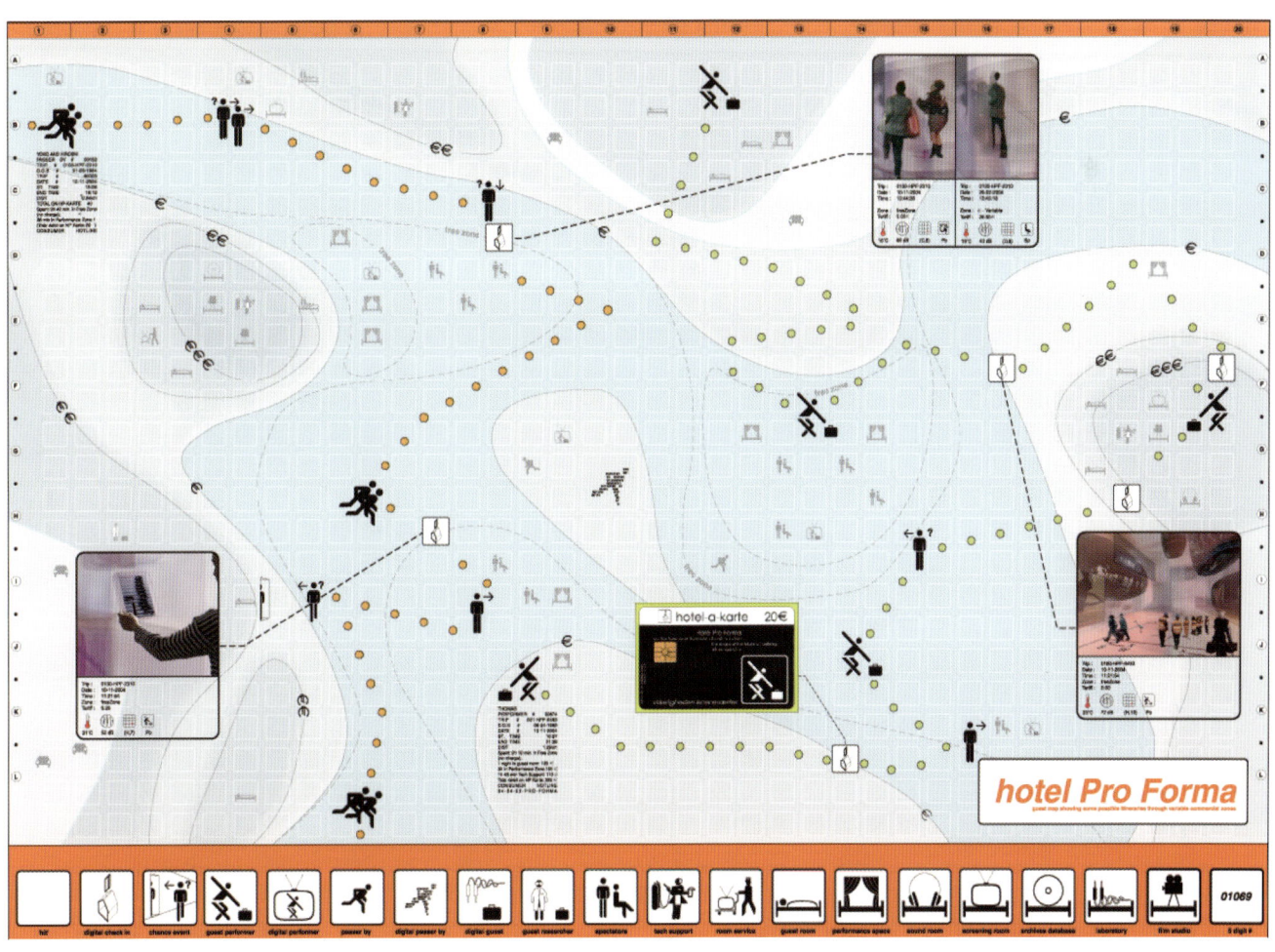

ARCHITECTURAL DIAGRAMS 447

HOUSING

MANUELLE GAUTRAND ARCHITECTURE

"I HAD TO INTEGRATE ECOLOGICAL CRITERIA FOR GREEN COLLECTIVE HOUSING LIKE INCORPORATION OF THE LANDSCAPE."

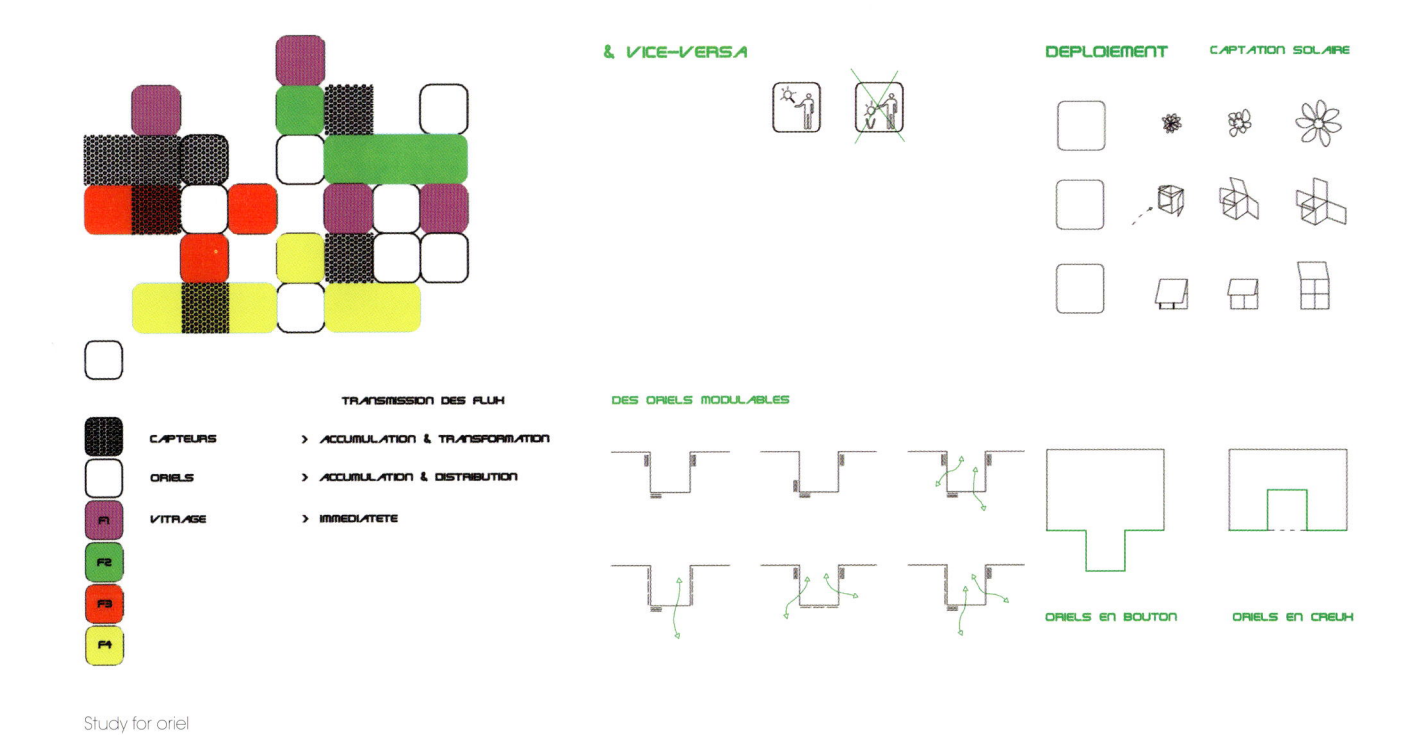

& VICE-VERSA   DEPLOIEMENT   CAPTATION SOLAIRE

TRANSMISSION DES FLUX   DES ORIELS MODULABLES

CAPTEURS   > ACCUMULATION & TRANSFORMATION
ORIELS   > ACCUMULATION & DISTRIBUTION
VITRAGE   > IMMEDIATETE

F1
F2
F3
F4

ORIELS EN BOUTON   ORIELS EN CREUX

Study for oriel

Bâtiment Nord   Bâtiment du centre   Bâtiment Sud

Typology of housing unit

6 logements de type T2
48 logements de type T3
42 logements de type T4
8 logements de type T5

ARCHITECTURAL DIAGRAMS 449

HOUSING ALMERE IaN+

"THE SOLID AND VOID ARE MERGED ONE INTO ANOTHER AND ARE EQUALLY IMPORTANT."

EXPANDED CITY   COMPACT CITY   GREEN

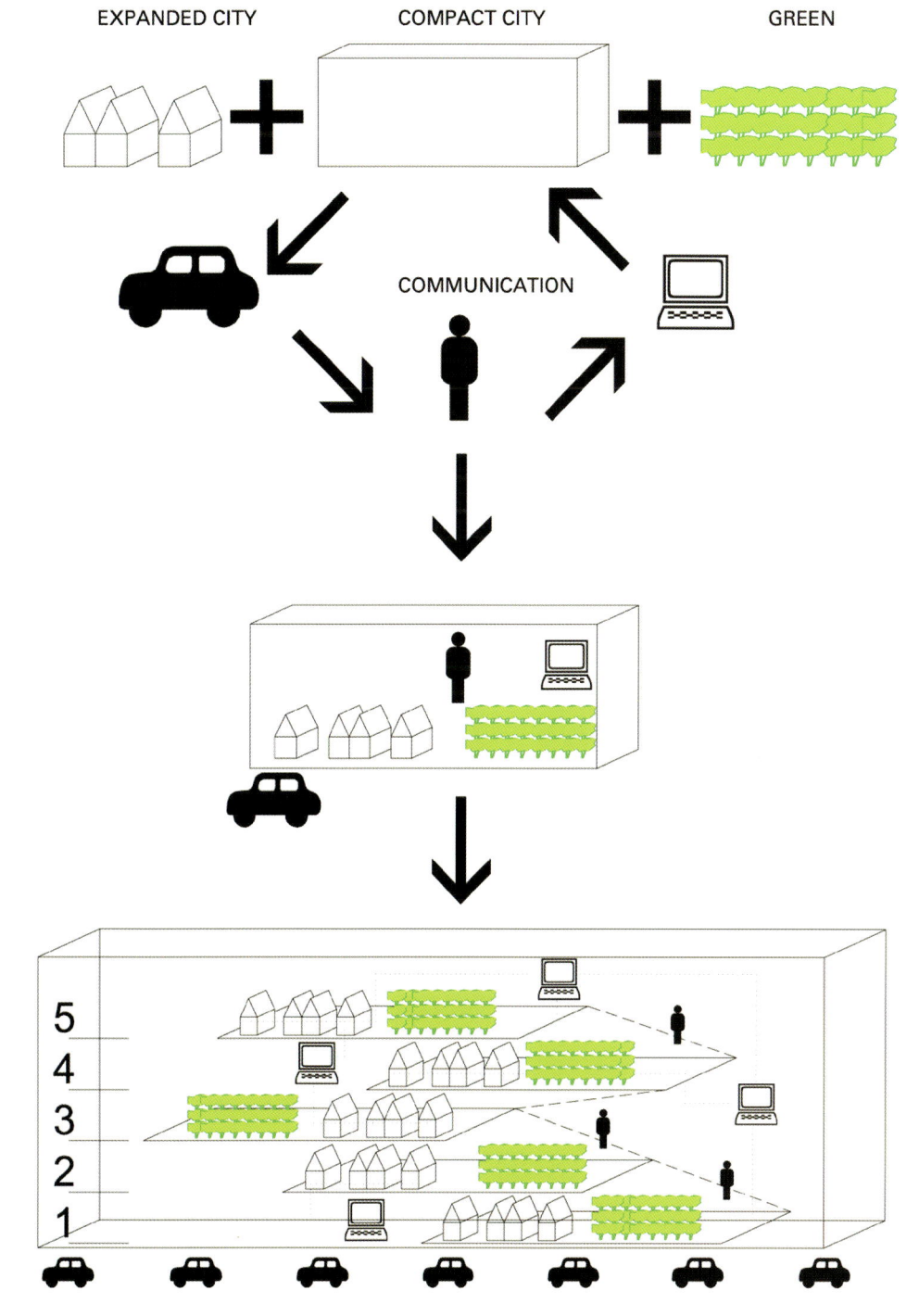

COMMUNICATION

Diagram

ARCHITECTURAL DIAGRAMS 451

ILE DE NANTES
PERIPHERIQUES architects

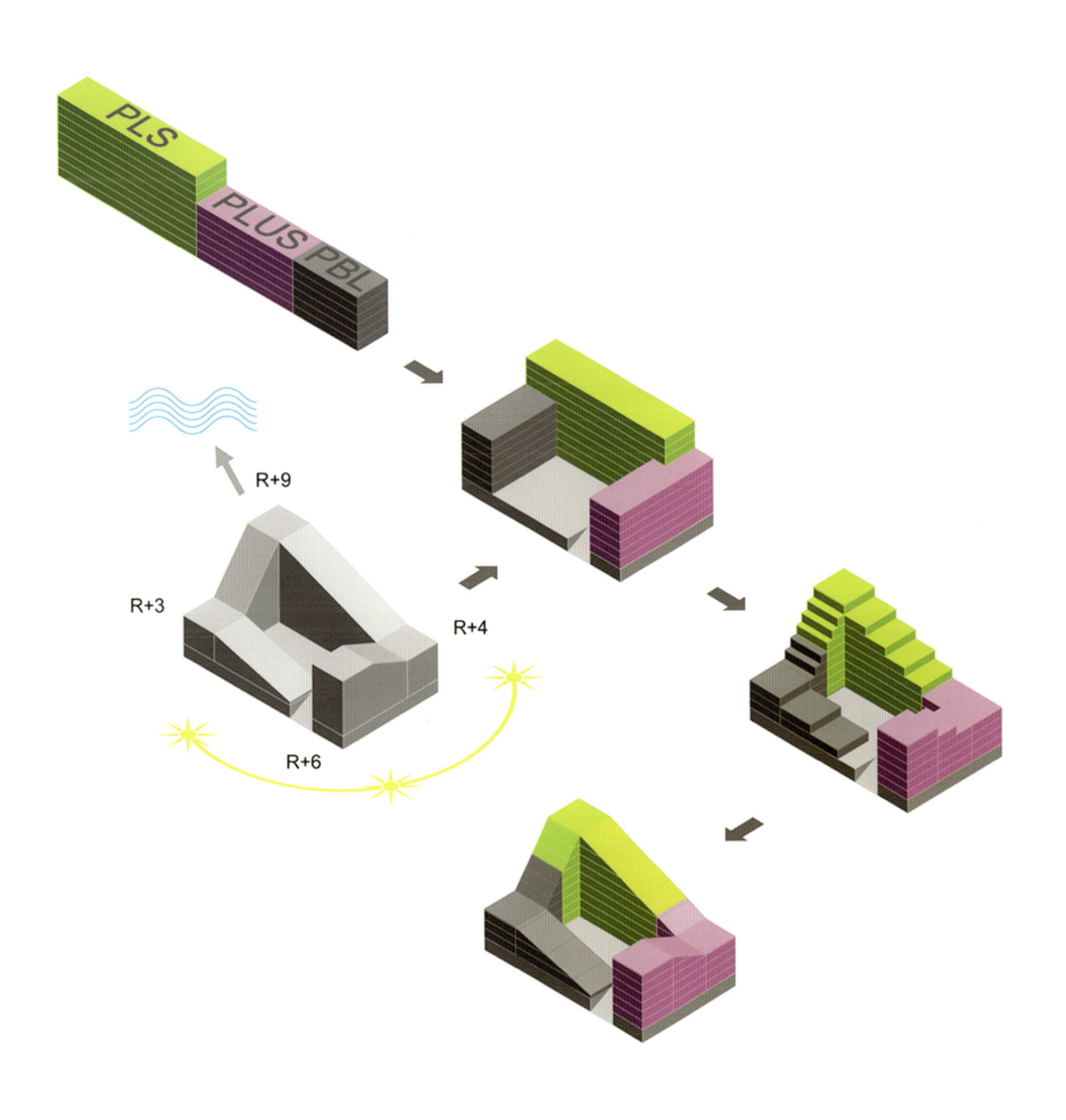

ARCHITECTURAL DIAGRAMS 453

IMEC TOWER JDS Architects

"WE FELT THE BUILDINGS'S ROLE AS AND BEACON AND A GATEWAY WERE OF VITAL IMPORTANCE, AND THE NEED TO IMPACT BOTH IMEC USERS AND THE PASSING PUBLIC WERE OF EQUAL IMPORTANCE."

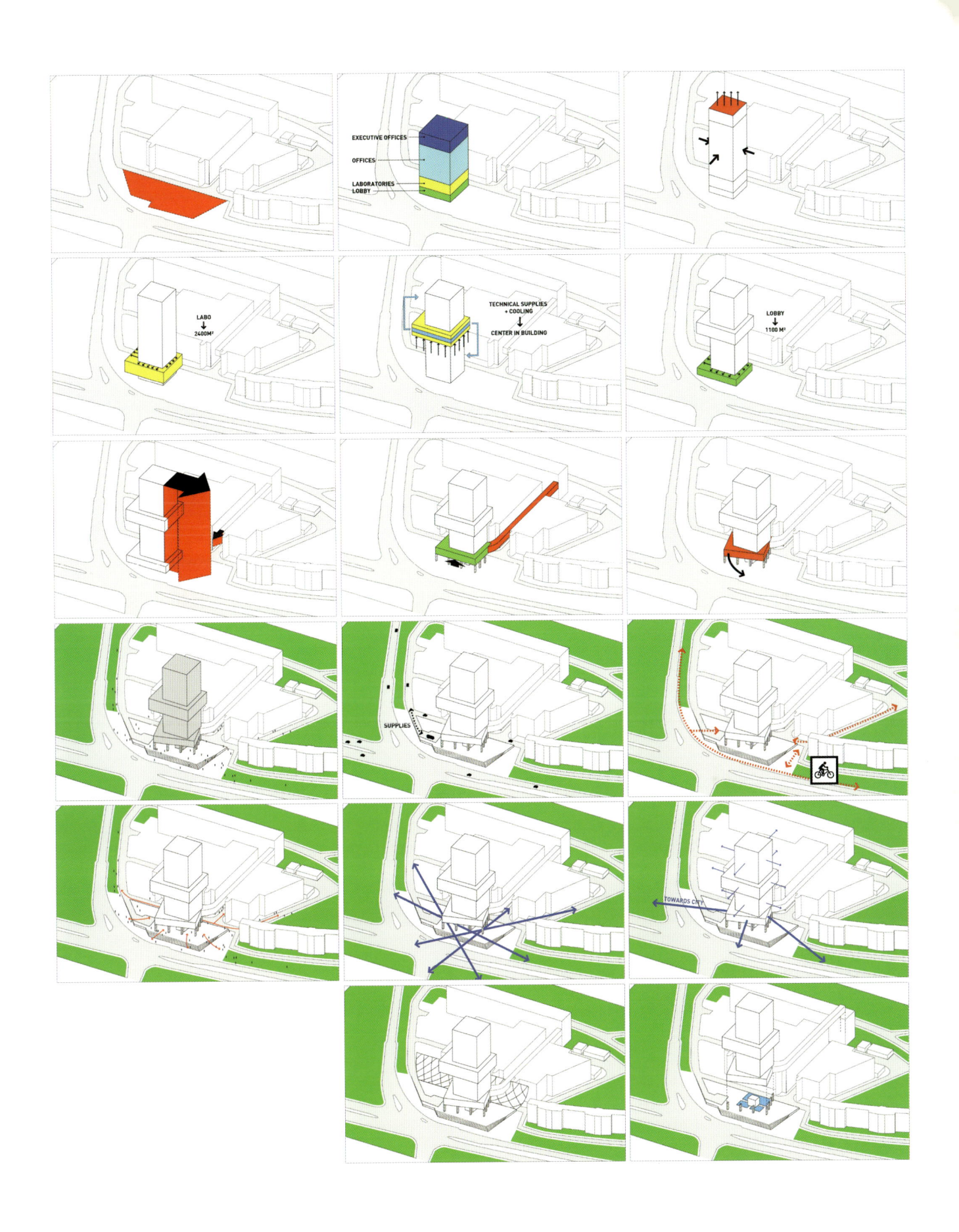

ARCHITECTURAL DIAGRAMS 455

LANDSCRIPT
Vincent Callebaut Architectures

"A MINIMUM OF FREE SPACES FOR A MAXIMUM OF DUAL SPACES, THIS IS THE OBJECTIVE."

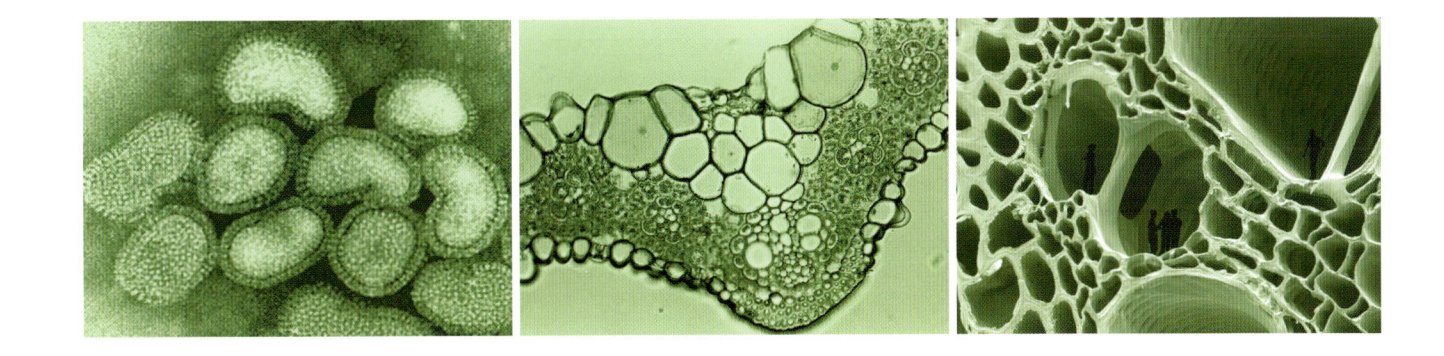

ARCHITECTURAL DIAGRAMS 457

LERVIG BRYGGE
SPACEGROUP

"REPETITION AND VARIATION IS COMBINED A REPETITIVE PRINCIPLE OF CONSTRUCTION GIVING AN EFFICIENT CONSTRUCTION."

Terrace

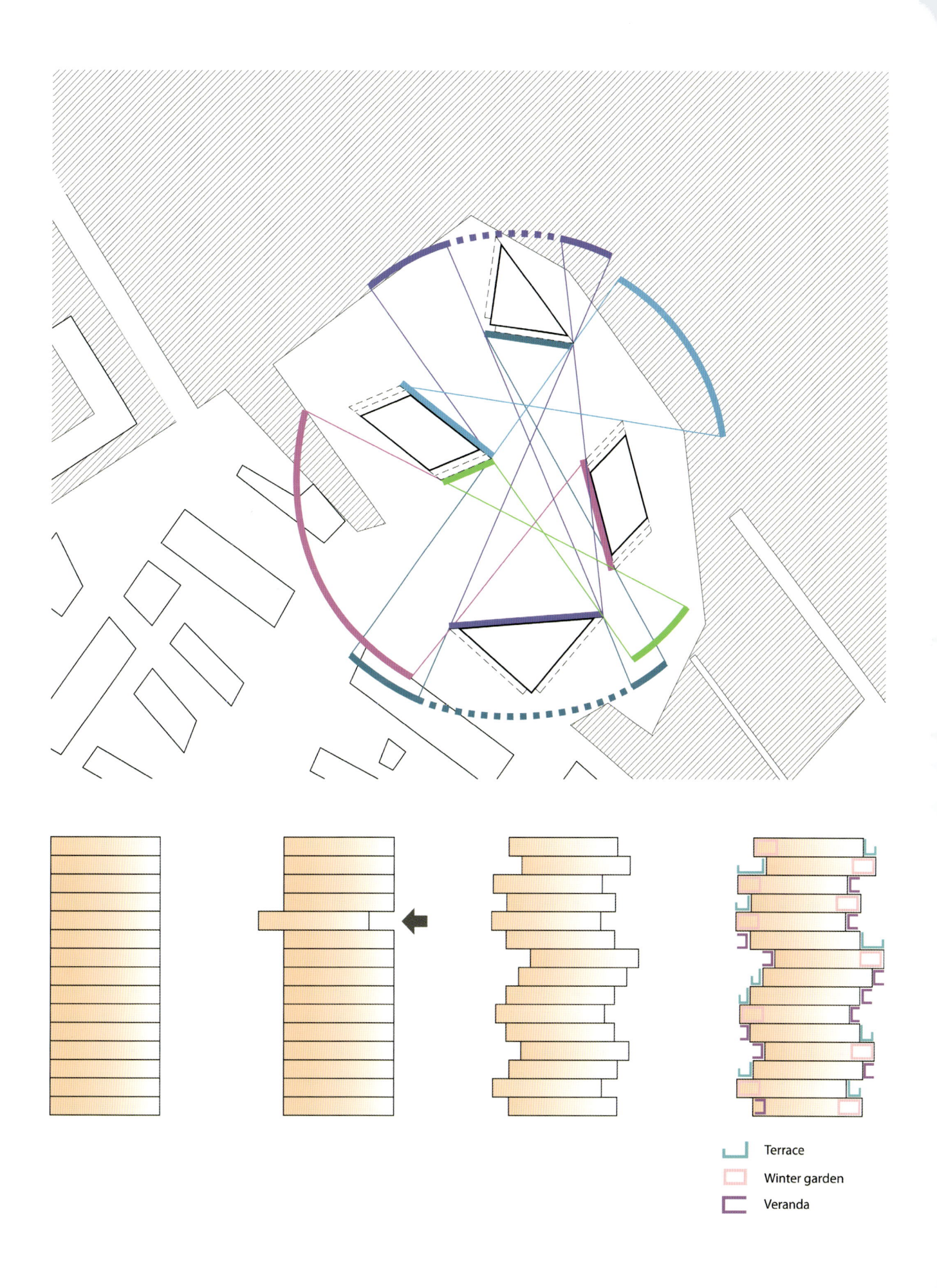

Winter garden

Veranda

ARCHITECTURAL DIAGRAMS

LIFE IN TOWN
MANUELLE GAUTRAND ARCHITECTURE

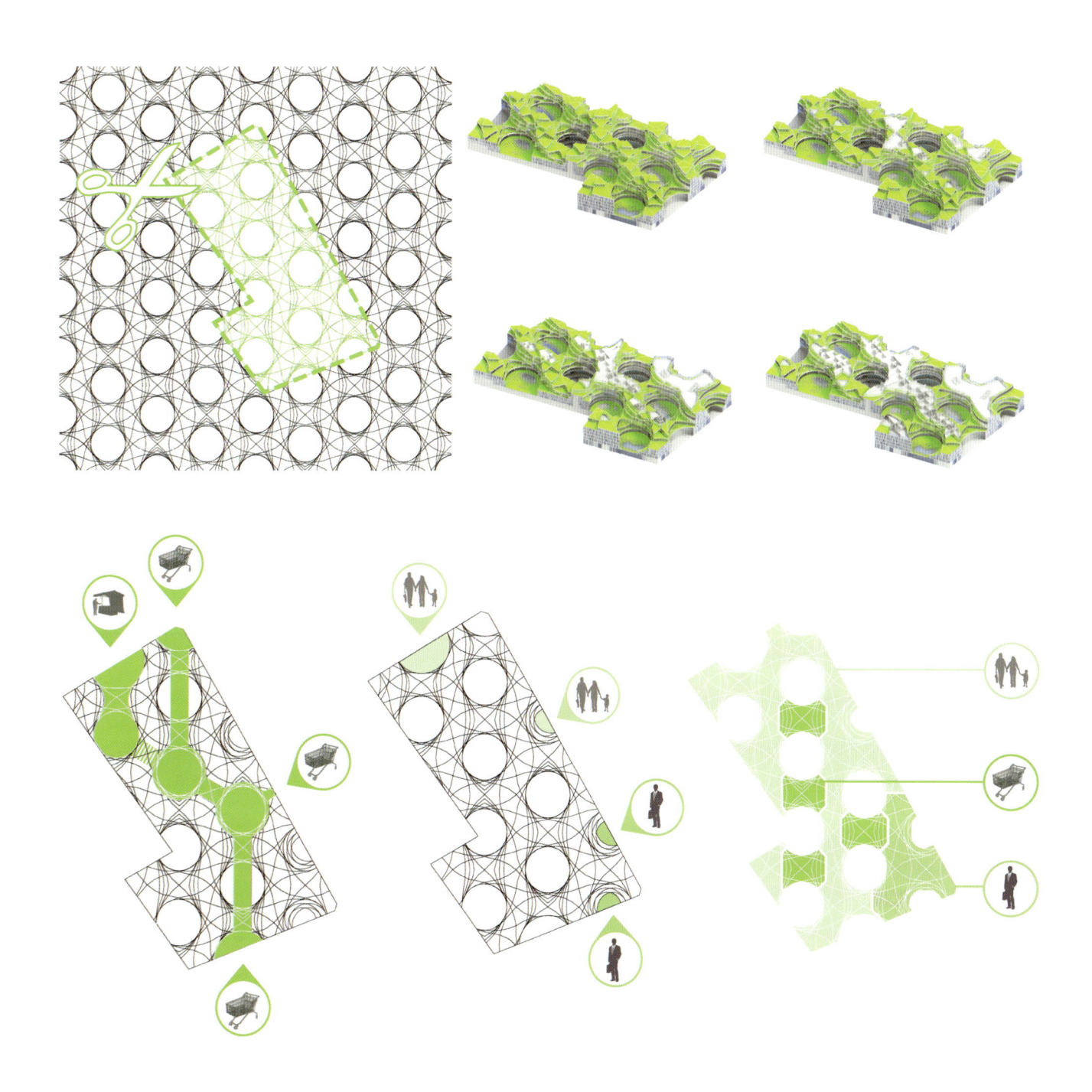

ARCHITECTURAL DIAGRAMS 461

LILYPADS

Vincent Callebaut Architectures

"TRUE BIOTOPE ENTIRELY RECYCLABLE, THIS FLOATING ECOPOLIS TENDS THUS TOWARDS THE POSITIVE ECO-ACCOUNTANCY."

ARCHITECTURAL DIAGRAMS 463

LINZ LANDESFRAUEN
KLINIK ONE ARCHITECTURE

"PRINCIPAL REASONS FROM BOTH ECONOMICAL PERSPECTIVE AND EQUIVALENCE, INDIVIDUALITY AND TOGETHERNESS FROM A SOCIOLOGICAL POINT OF VIEW."

Diagram 1 : an ideal building

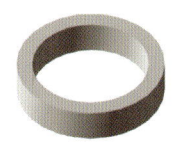

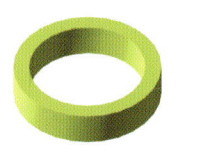

Diagram 2 : two ideal buildings

Diagram 3 : the buildings projected on the site, and the problem of left and right

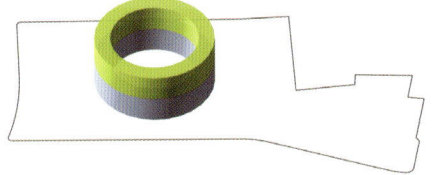

Diagram 5 : a dance

Diagram 6 : keeping distance

Diagram 7 : stretching

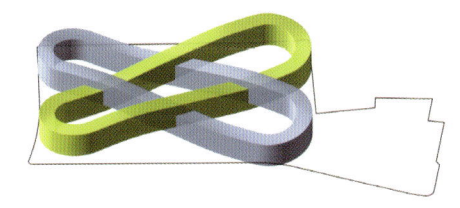

Diagram 7 : stretching

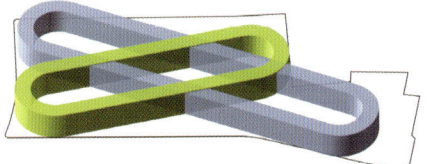

Diagram 8 : occupying the site

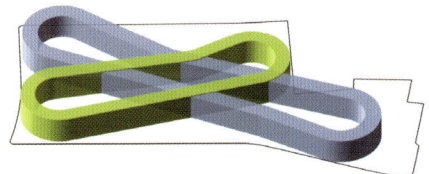

Diagram 9 : keeping the trees

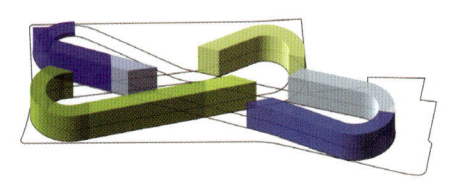

Diagram 10 : equal views

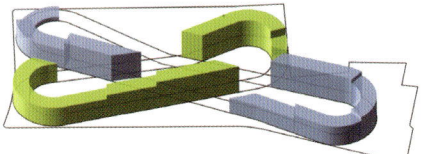

Diagram 11 : daylight

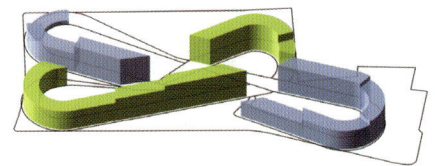

Diagram 12 : typologies

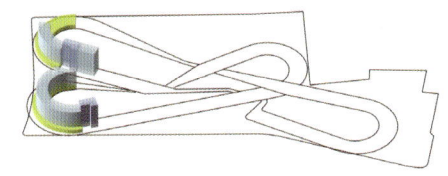

Diagram 13

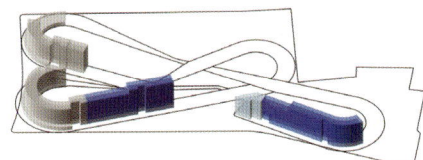

Diagram 14

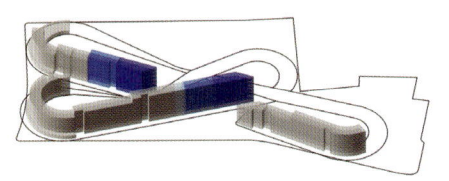

Diagram 15

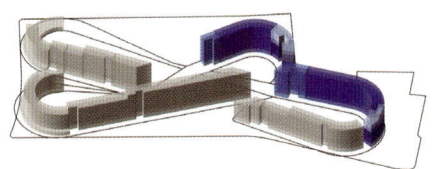

Diagram 16

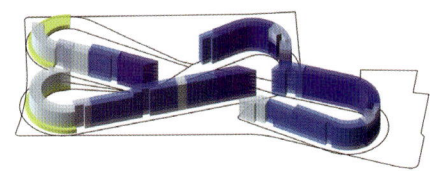

Diagram 17

ARCHITECTURAL DIAGRAMS 465

LIVING STEEL

nARCHITECTS

"A PROGRESSION OF THREE TYPOLOGIES EMERGES LIKE A TREE FROM THE GROUND..."

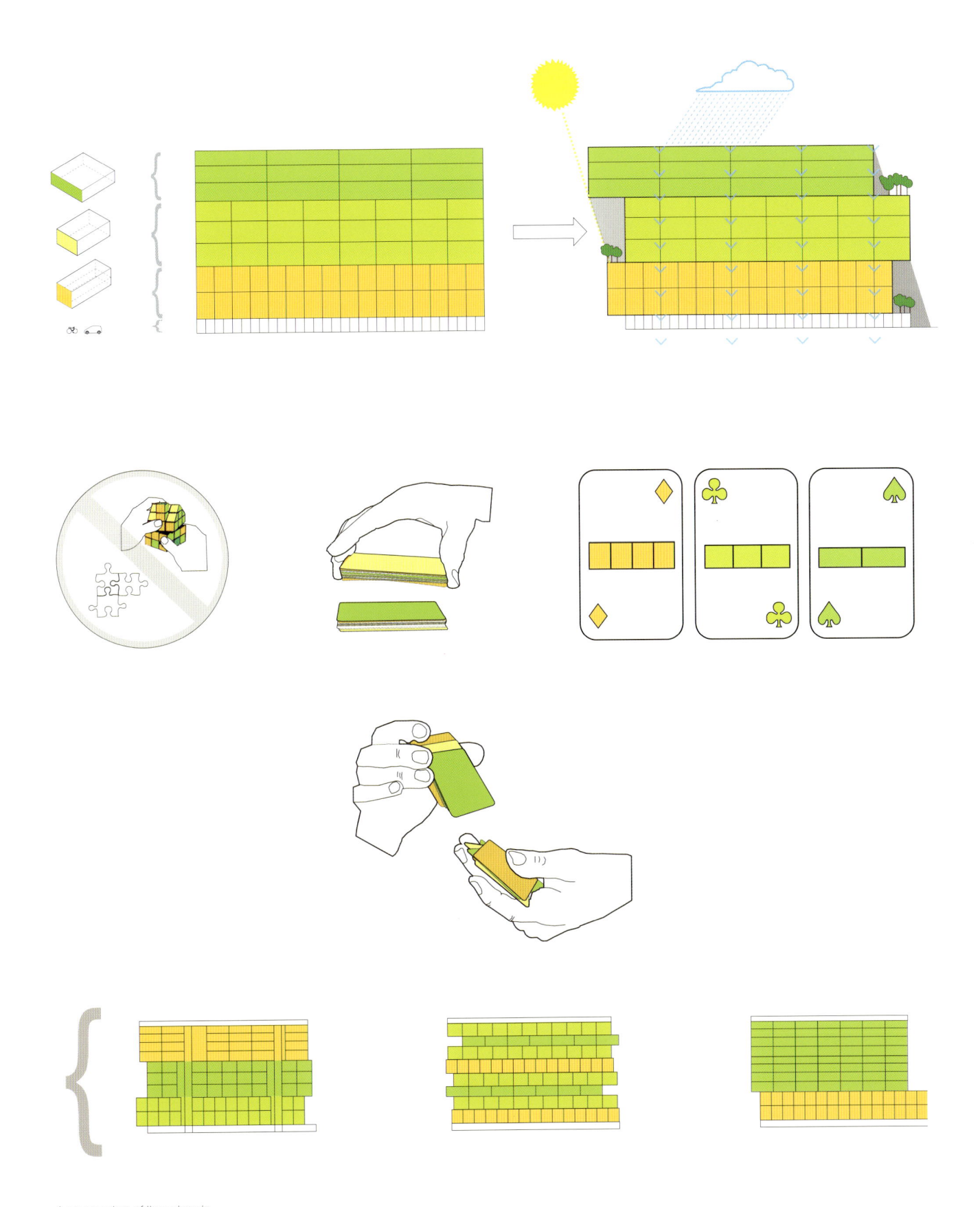

A progression of three typologies emerges like a tree from the ground...

ARCHITECTURAL DIAGRAMS 467

MERCEDES-BENZ MUSEUM UNStudio

"ITS INTERNAL ORGANIZATION AND IN ITS OUTWARD EXPRESSION THIS GEOMETRY RESPONDS TO THE CAR-DRIVEN CONTEXT OF THE MUSEUM."

ARCHITECTURAL DIAGRAMS 469

MERMAID ISLAND
JDS Architects

"FOR THE ISLAND'S FOOTPRINT WE CHOSE THE CIRCLE, SINCE ITS RADIATING SHAPE HAS NO SINGULAR DIRECTION."

SECTION SEQUENCE Ⓐ

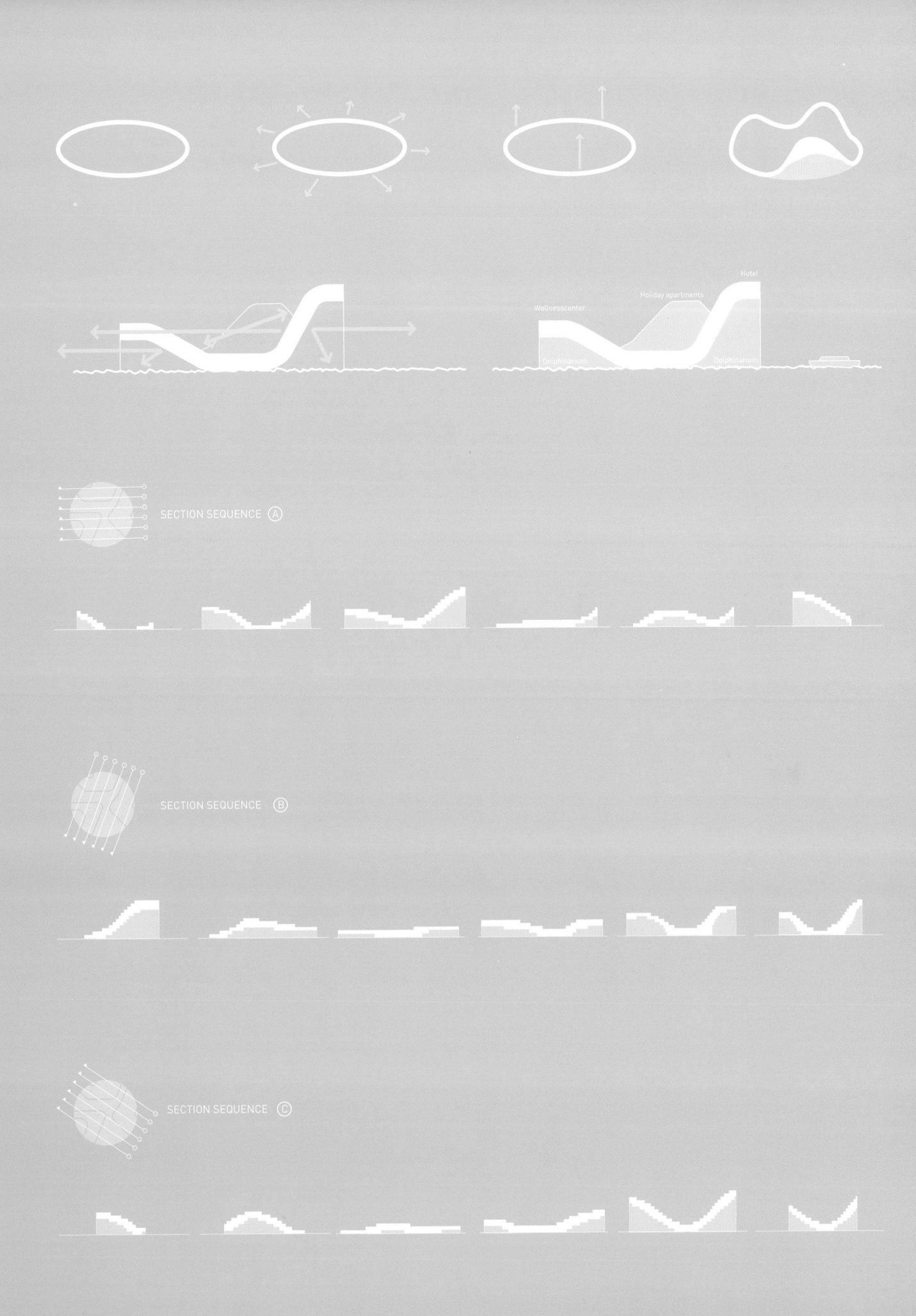

SECTION SEQUENCE Ⓑ

SECTION SEQUENCE Ⓒ

NL-KB
Bernd Kniess Architects Urban Planners

"THE 'NEW LOFT' BUILDING WAS PROMPTED IN RESPONSE TO THE LACK OF SPACE NORMALLY PROVIDED BY CLASSIC LOFTS."

ARCHITECTURAL DIAGRAMS 473

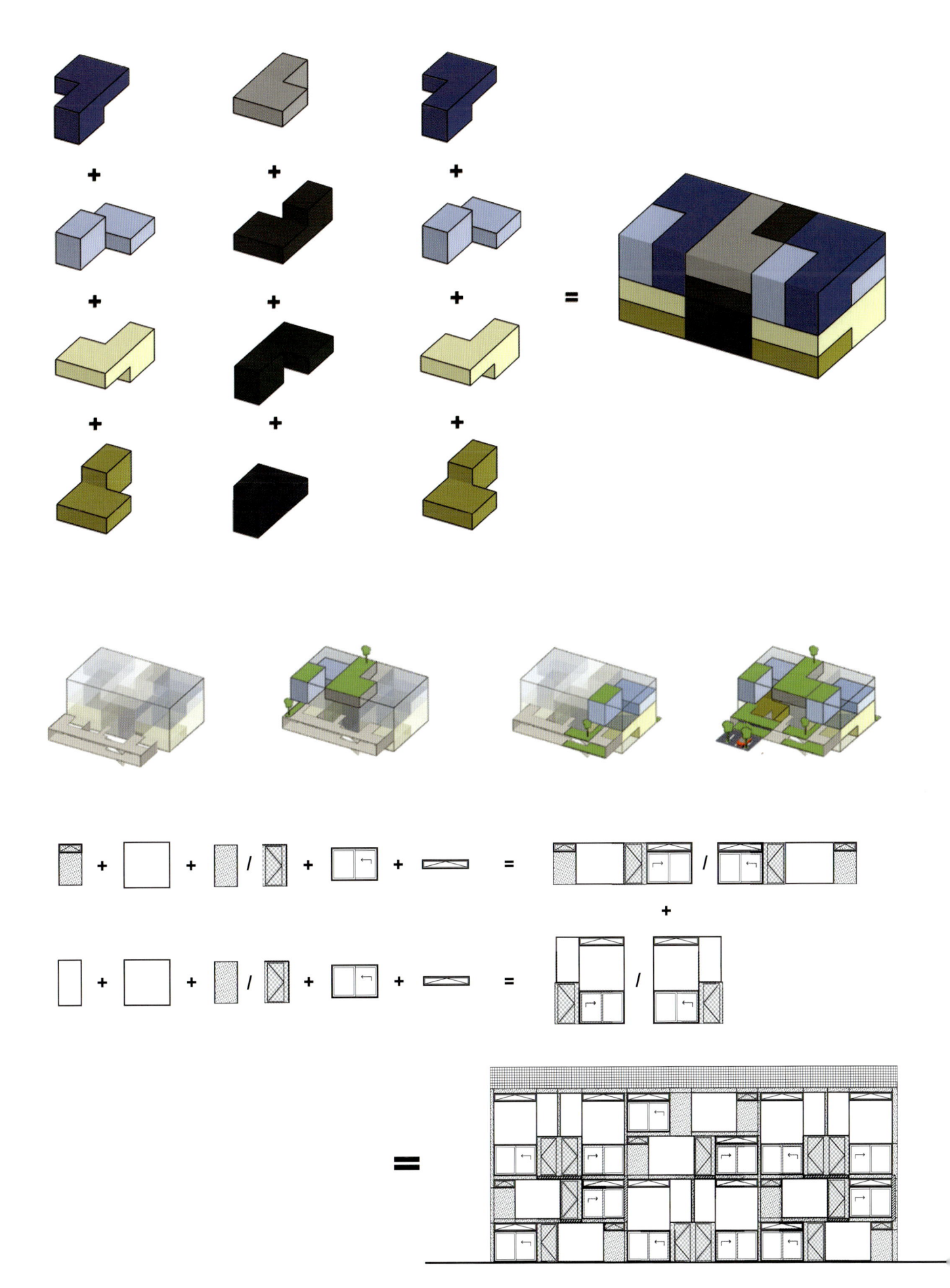

NL-WI
Bernd Kniess Architects Urban Planners

"VARIATIONS ON THIS THEME BROADEN THE INNER STRUCTURE INTO A VARIED BASIC MODEL."

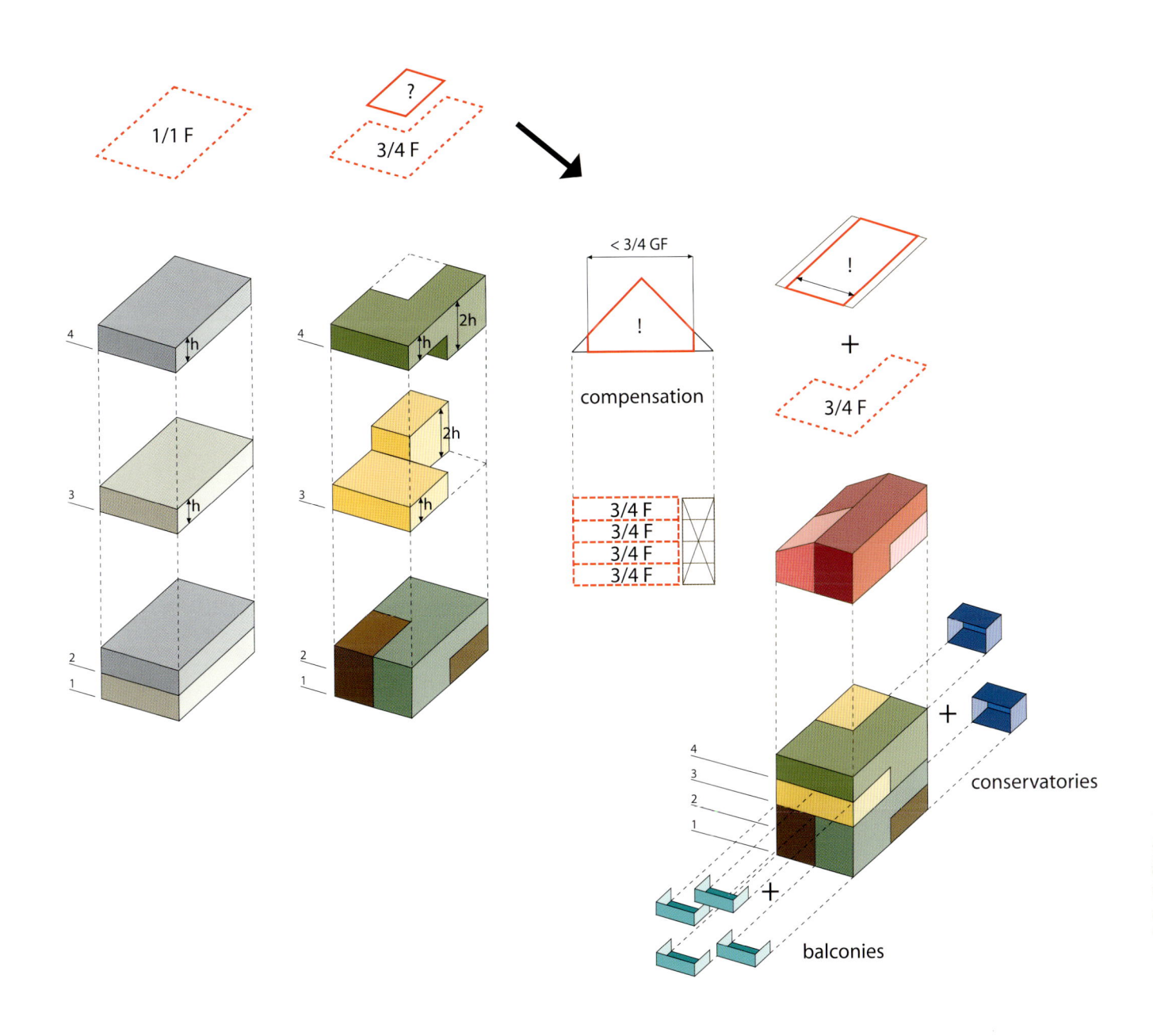

1/1 F

3/4 F ?

< 3/4 GF

compensation

3/4 F
3/4 F
3/4 F
3/4 F

!

+

3/4 F

conservatories

+

balconies

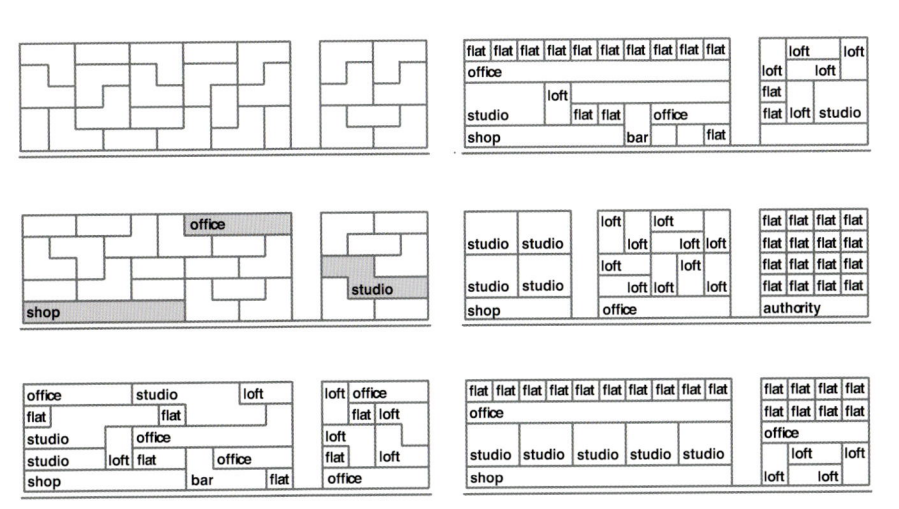

+

Structural options for different use

ARCHITECTURAL DIAGRAMS 475

NUMEN studio asylum

"THERE WAS NO EXCEPTION IN TERMS OF RETAINING MY REDUNDANT, THEMATIC SPACE, 'META-HOLLOW', BEING CARVED OUT WITHIN THE ENVELOPE OF THE STRUCTURE."

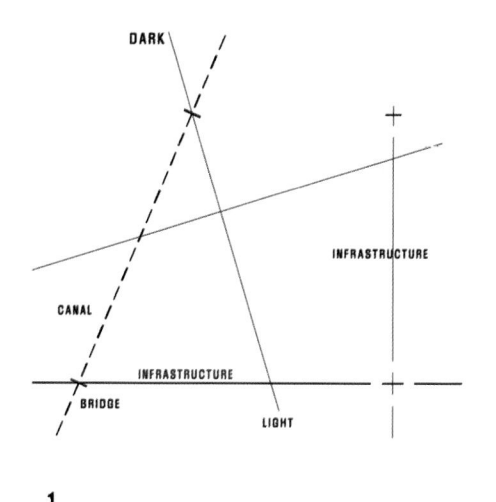

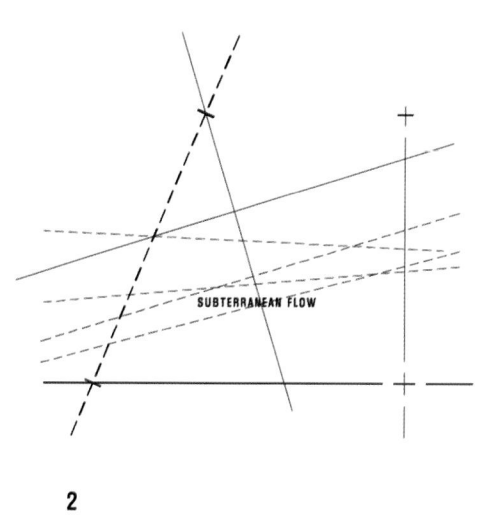

Fabrication Sequence

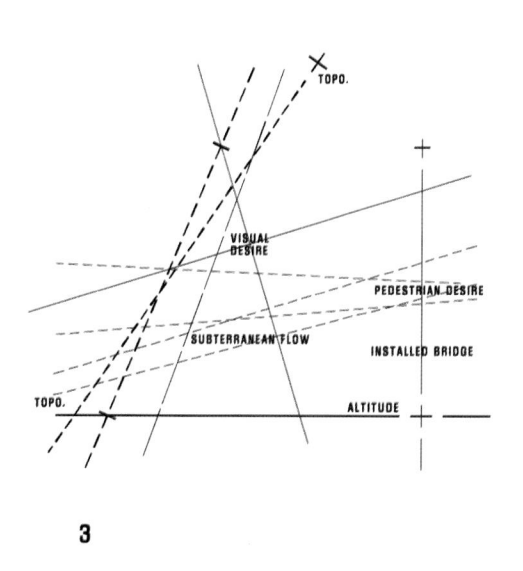

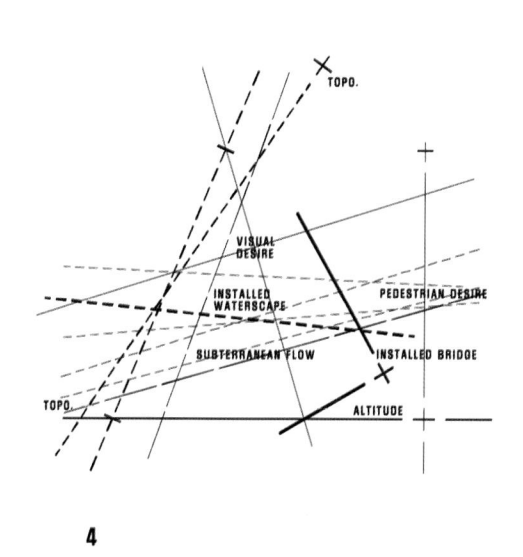

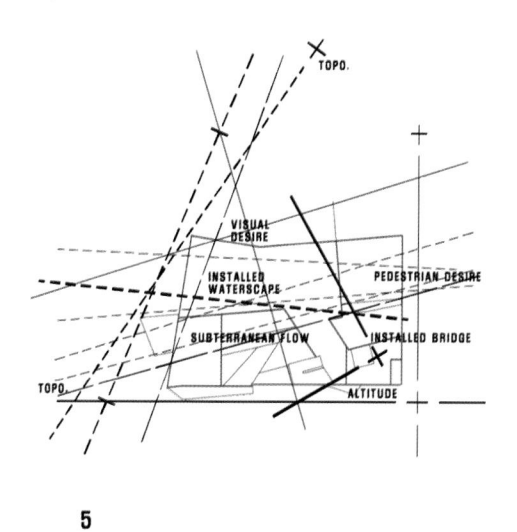

1

2

3

4

5

ARCHITECTURAL DIAGRAMS 477

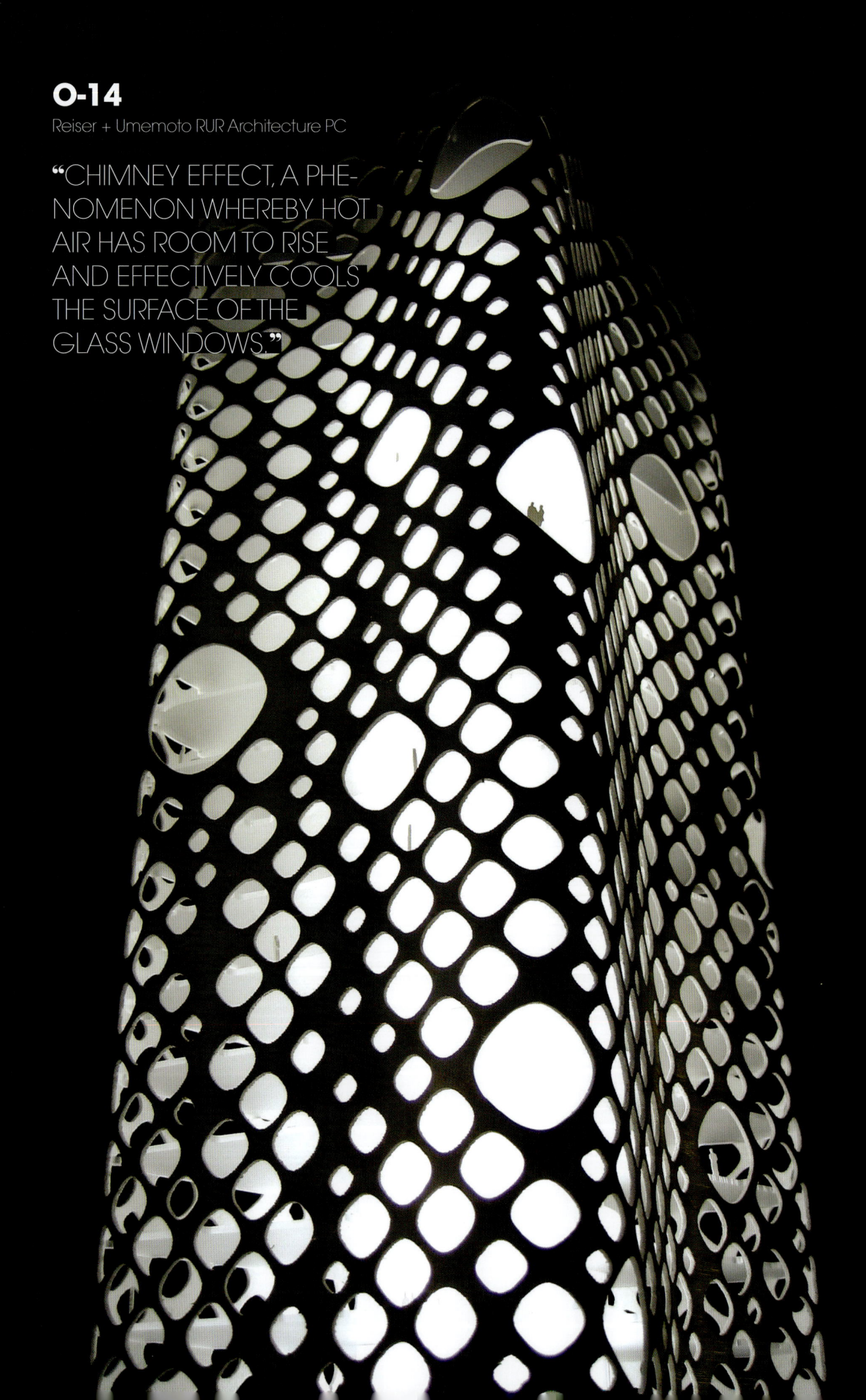

O-14
Reiser + Umemoto RUR Architecture PC

"CHIMNEY EFFECT, A PHENOMENON WHEREBY HOT AIR HAS ROOM TO RISE AND EFFECTIVELY COOLS THE SURFACE OF THE GLASS WINDOWS."

Shell Openings

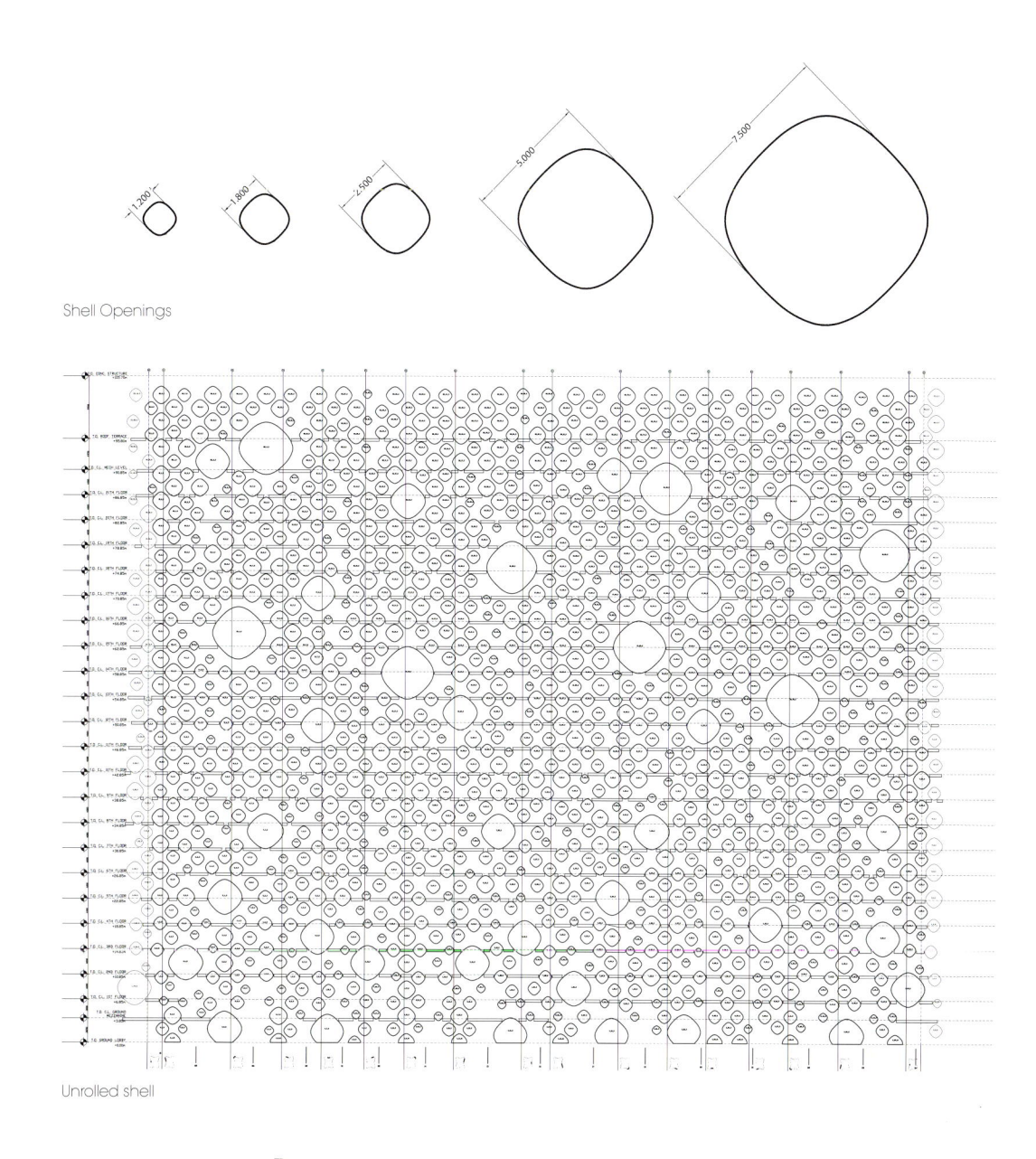

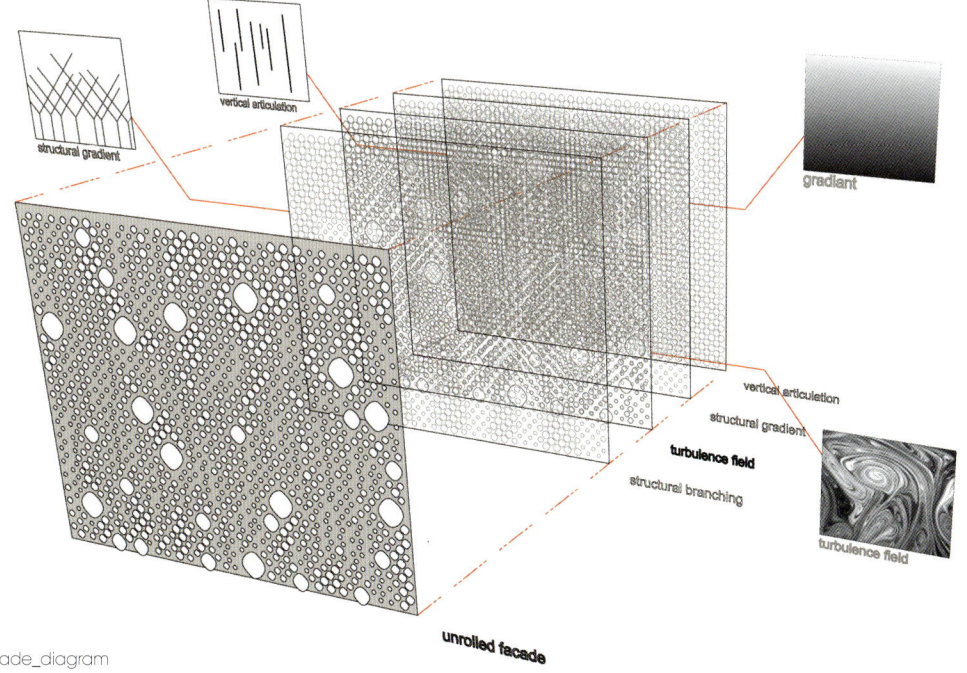

Unrolled shell

Facade_diagram

ARCHITECTURAL DIAGRAMS 479

O.I.C HEADQUARTERS BUILDING
Willy Müller Architects

"THE CUPOLA THEN IS TAKEN AS VISIBLE AND POWERFUL ICON FROM THE VAST AND RICH CULTURE AND HISTORY OF ISLAMIC ARCHITECTURE."

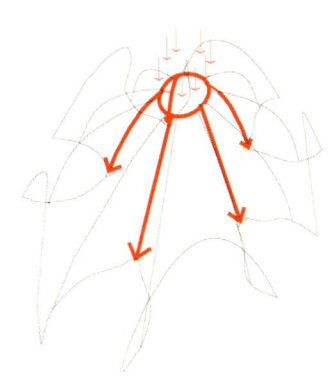

Basic structural solution [isometrical view]

Geometric principle for translational surfaces in inner structural shell [isometrical view]

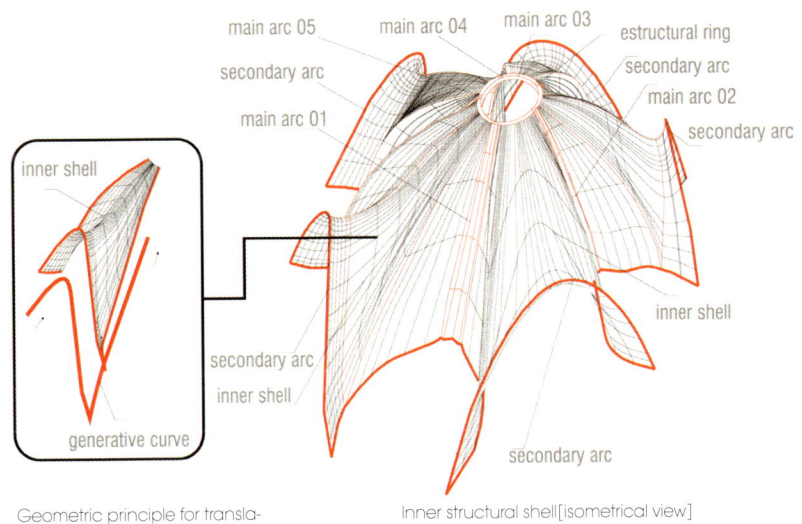

Inner structural shell [isometrical view]

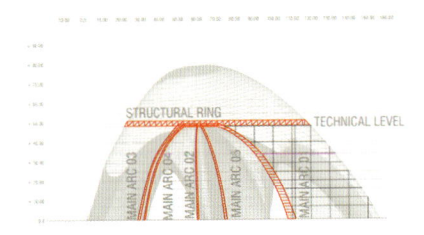

Basic structural scheme [section view]

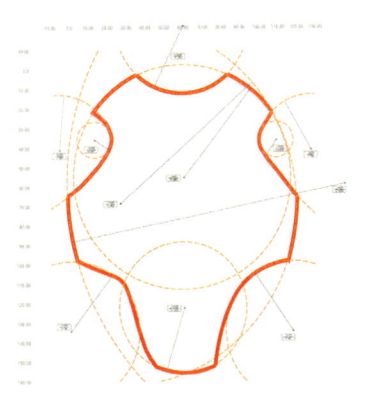

Geometrical analysis of outer shell generative curves [pain view]

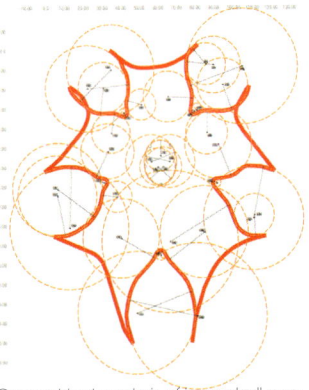

Geometrical analysis of inner shell generative curves [pain view]

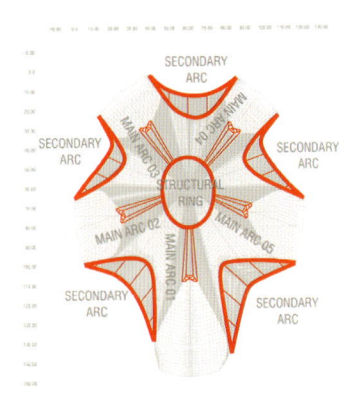

Basic structural scheme [pain view]

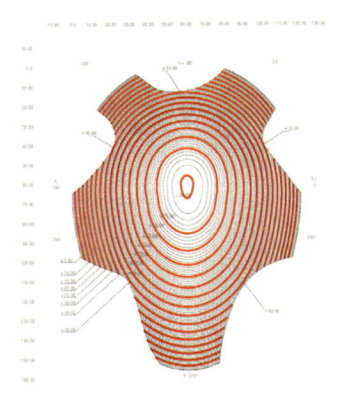

Outer shell topographical analysis / basic structural analysis of tension and compression areas [pain view]

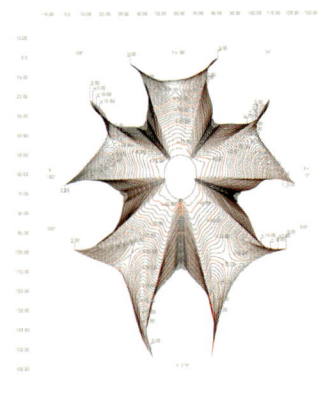

Inner shell topographical analysis / basic structural analysis of tension and compression areas [pain view]

ARCHITECTURAL DIAGRAMS 481

ØKERN CENTER
SPACEGROUP

"WE BEGAN BY STRIPPING OUR OWN ILLUSIONS AND SPECULATE FREELY ON URBAN ECOLOGIES."

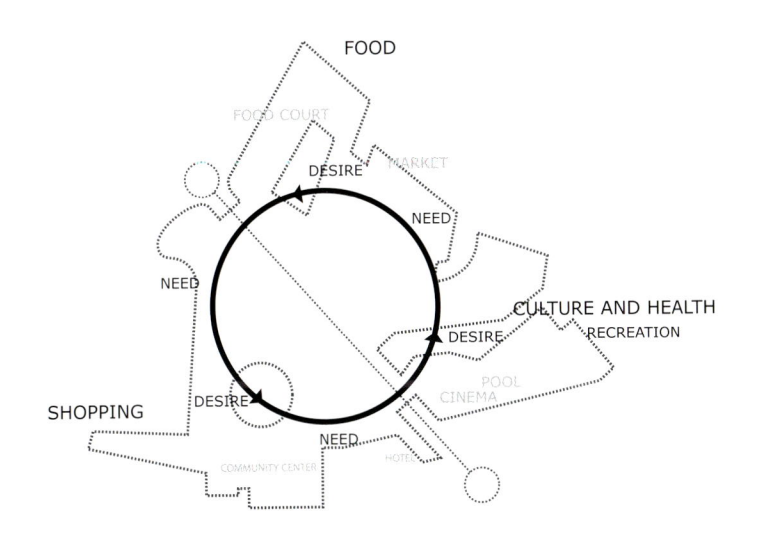

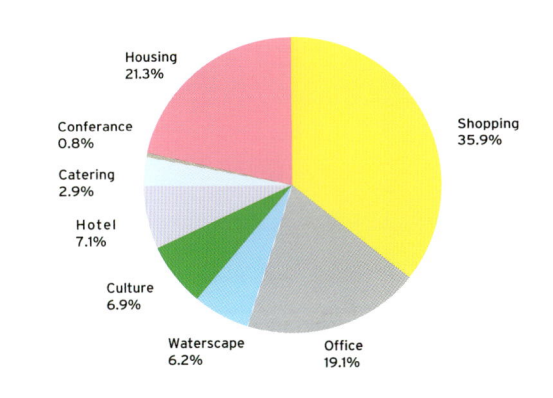

Programatic distribution

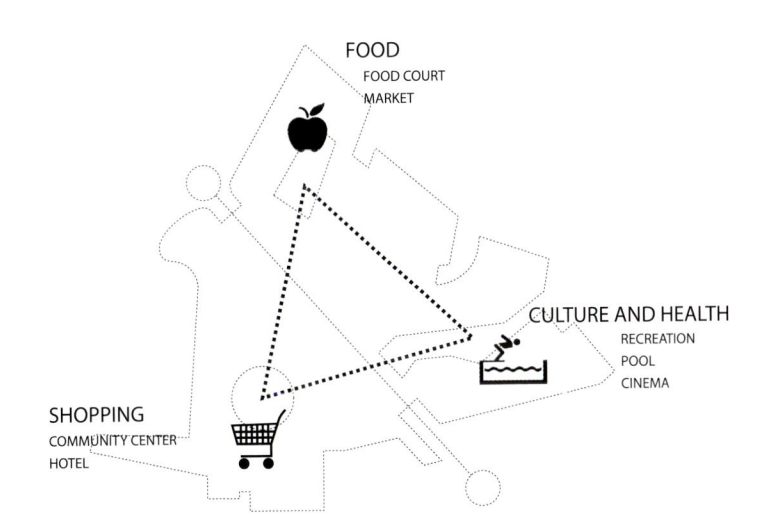

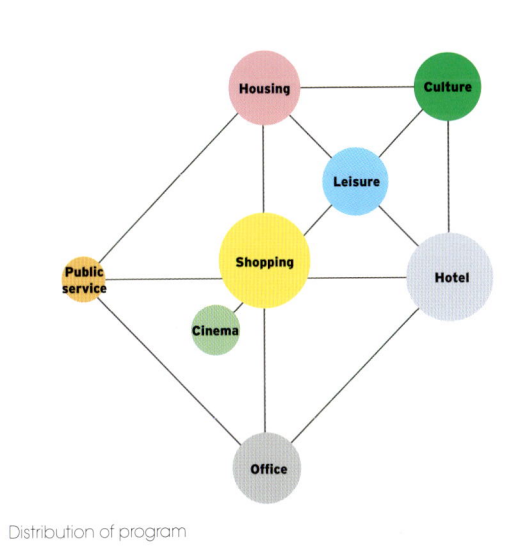

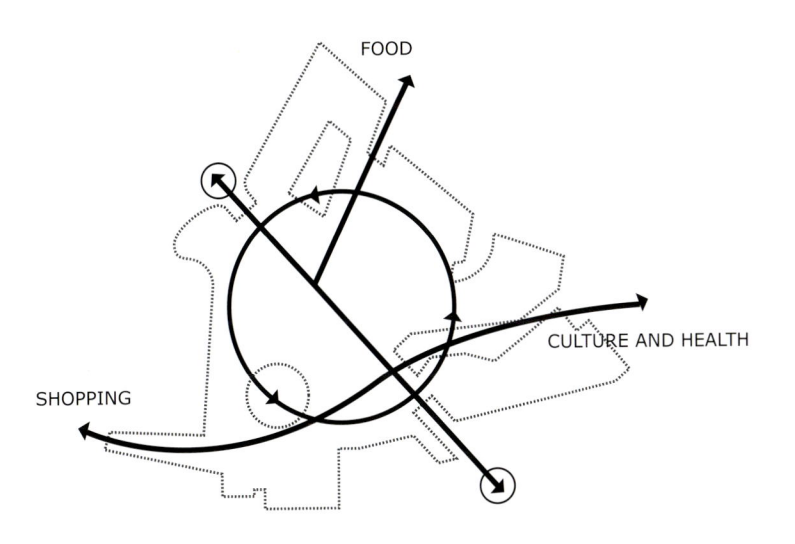

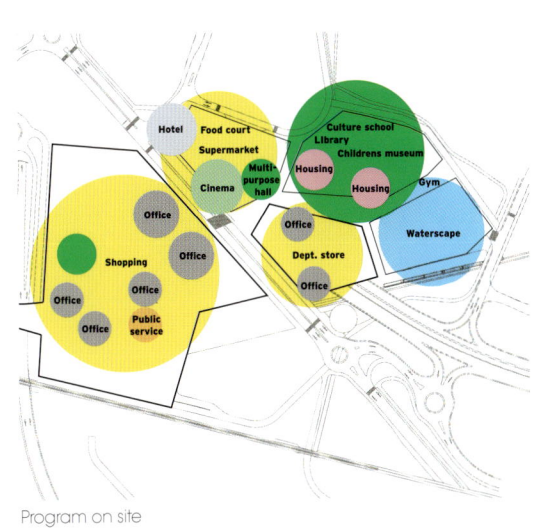

Distribution of program

Program on site

ARCHITECTURAL DIAGRAMS 483

OMOTESANDO UNStudio

"THE DESIGN ARE TO MAXI-MIZE THE POTENTIAL OF THE SITE, WHILST WORKING WITHIN THE SPATIAL AND REGULATORY CONSTRAINTS OF THE LOCATION."

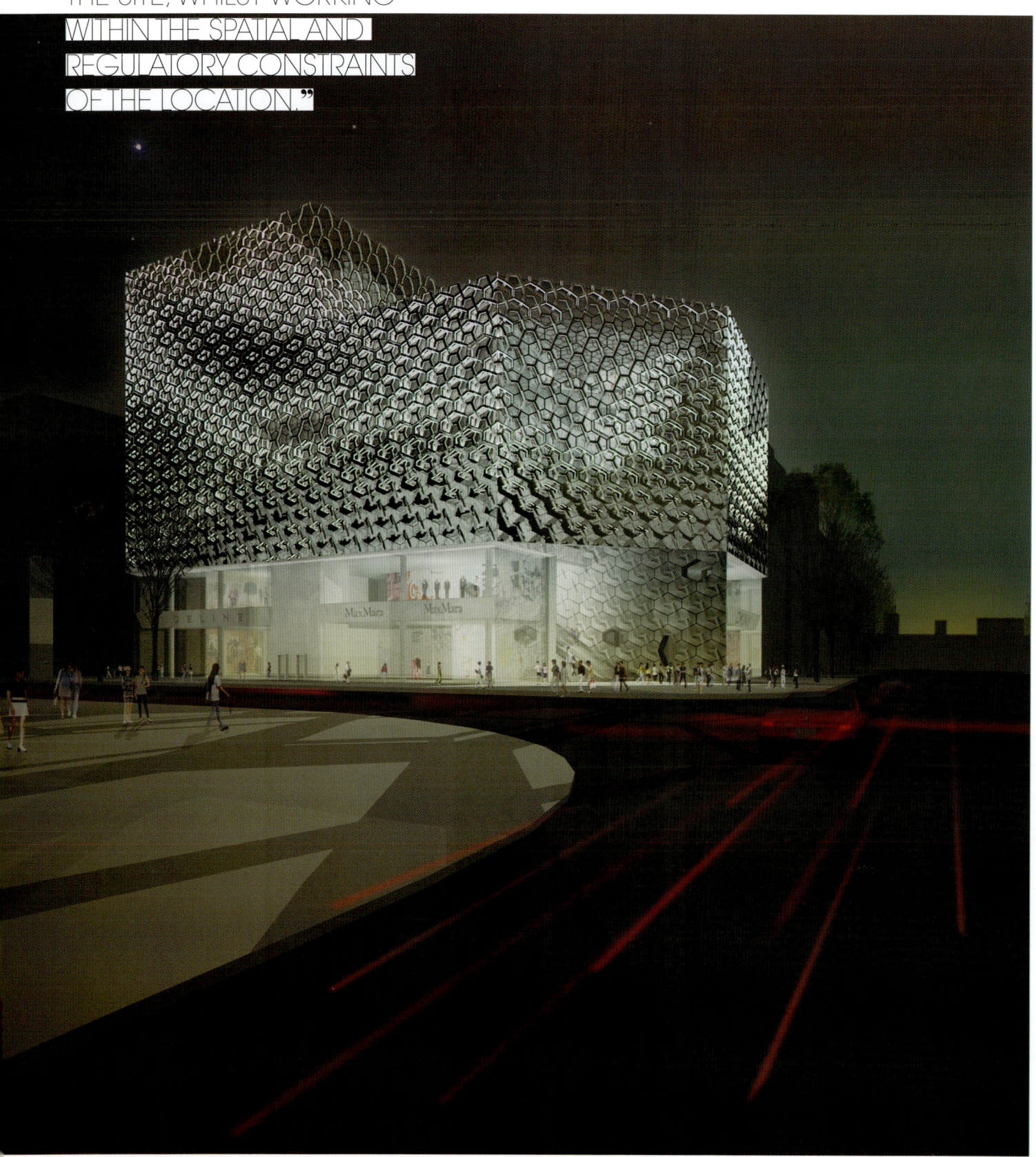

OPEN

CLOSED

Pentagon   x 4 =   Hexagon   x 4 =   Hexagon / In hexagon

ARCHITECTURAL DIAGRAMS 485

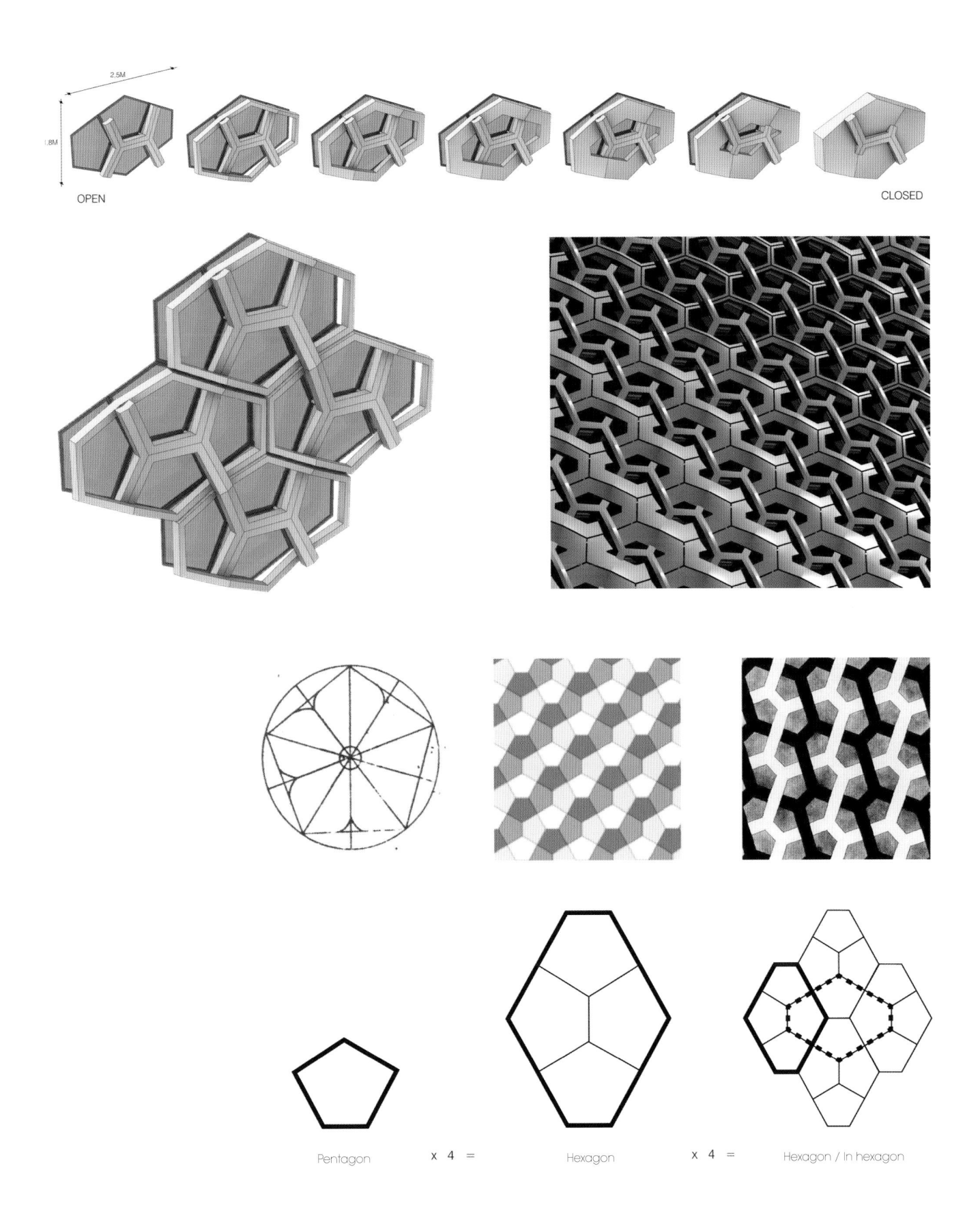

ORDOS 100 NL Architects

"NOT KNOWING THE FUTURE INHABITANTS CREATES SOME SORT OF VACUUM."

HOUSE − **GREEN HOUSE** = **GARDEN HOUSE**

Block

Subtraction

Bring in Light

Bring in Garden
= Green Heart

Interior Garden + Glass facade
= Greenhouse Inside

Position on Plot
= Drive Way

Sink for View

Parking = Sculpture

ARCHITECTURAL DIAGRAMS 487

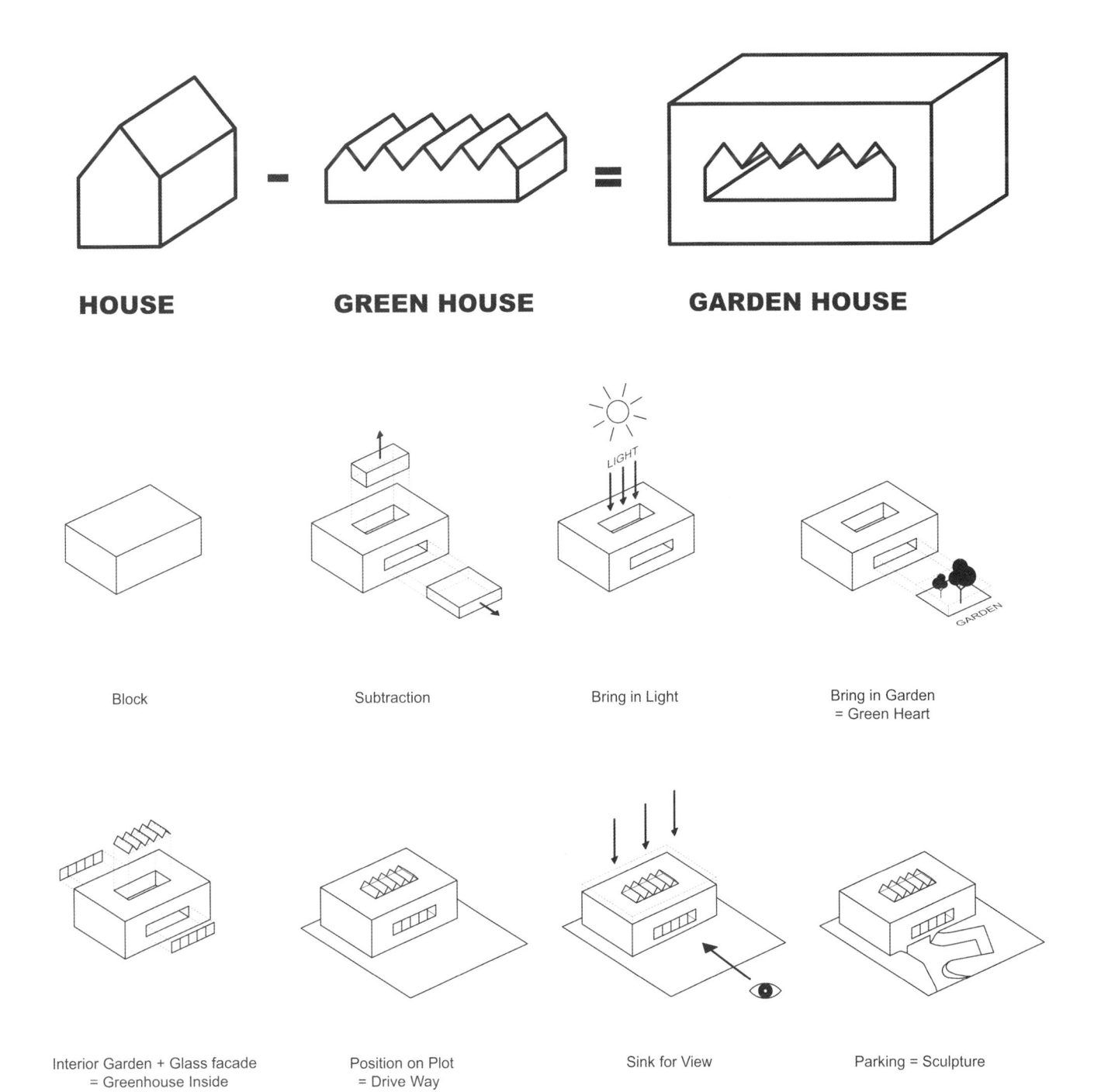

PRISMA NL Architects

"THE BUILDING CONSISTS OF A SIMPLE STACKING OF THE DESIRED APARTMENT TYPES."

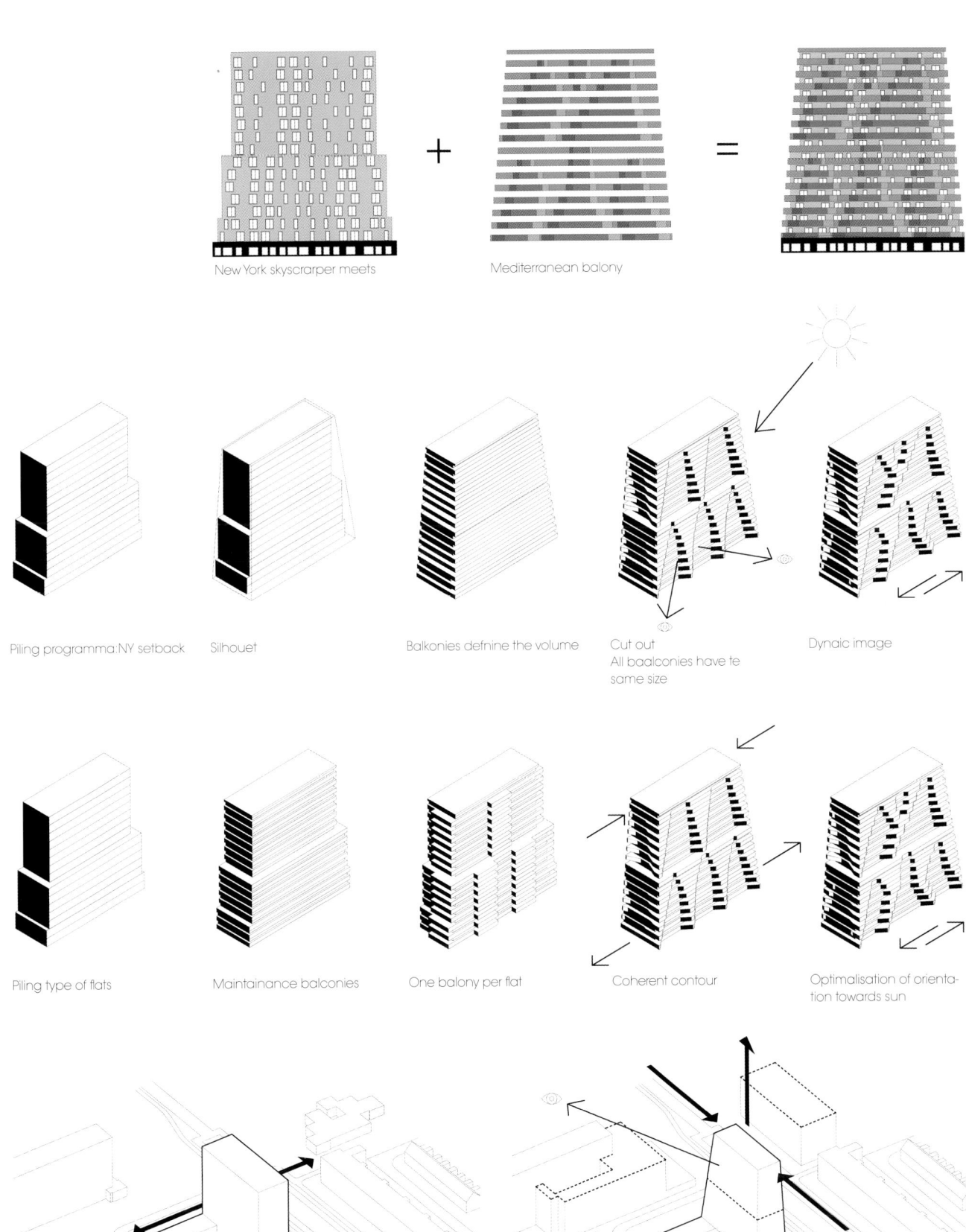

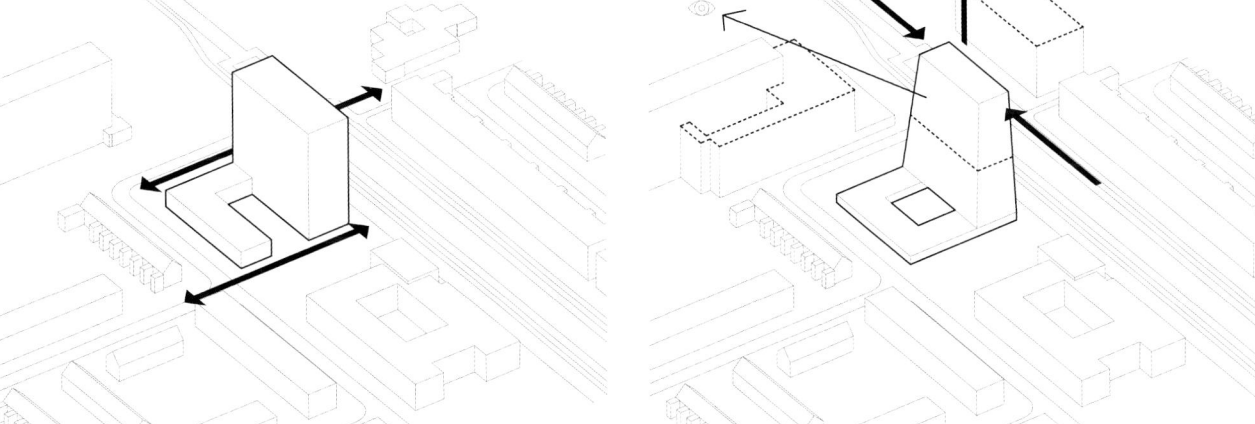

New York skyscrarper meets + Mediterranean balony =

Piling programma:NY setback | Silhouet | Balkonies defnine the volume | Cut out All baalconies have te same size | Dynaic image

Piling type of flats | Maintainance balconies | One balony per flat | Coherent contour | Optimalisation of orientation towards sun

View lines

reactons on future developments

ARCHITECTURAL DIAGRAMS 489

PRUGIO VALLEY - UNIT & FACADE DESIGN
jay is working.

"VALLEY IS TO GIVE AN INNER FOREST THAT ALLOWS THE IMAGE OF GREEN TO EVERYWHERE."

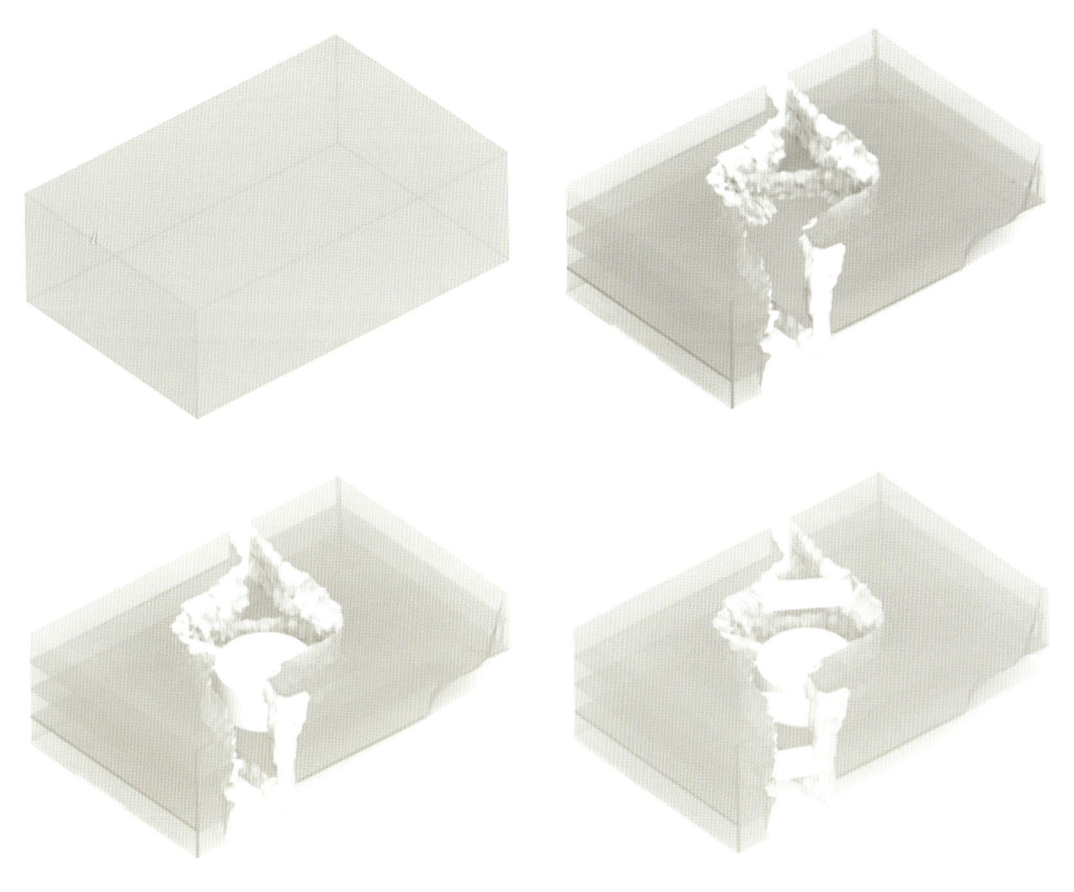

Mass process

ARCHITECTURAL DIAGRAMS 491

PUBLIC RECORDS OFFICE EM2N

"AS A CHANCE TO TRANSLATE THE EXISTING BUILDING INTO A POWERFUL, SELF-CONFIDENT FORM."

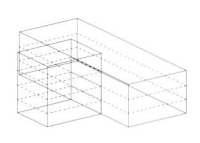

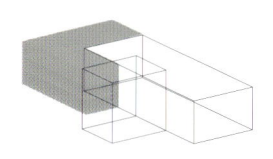

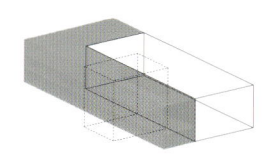

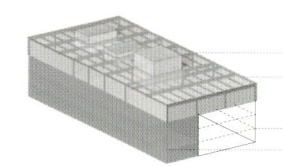

The office wing is demolished in a series of steps and new layers of space are placed around the existing records office. The new public storey is placed over both the existing and the new spaces. It profits from its urban presence and signalizes that the records office is a public building. The new archive block is surrounded by a layer of vegetation that connects the individual parts of the building to make a new entity, the softness of this layer links the building to the surrounding gardens and the embankment.

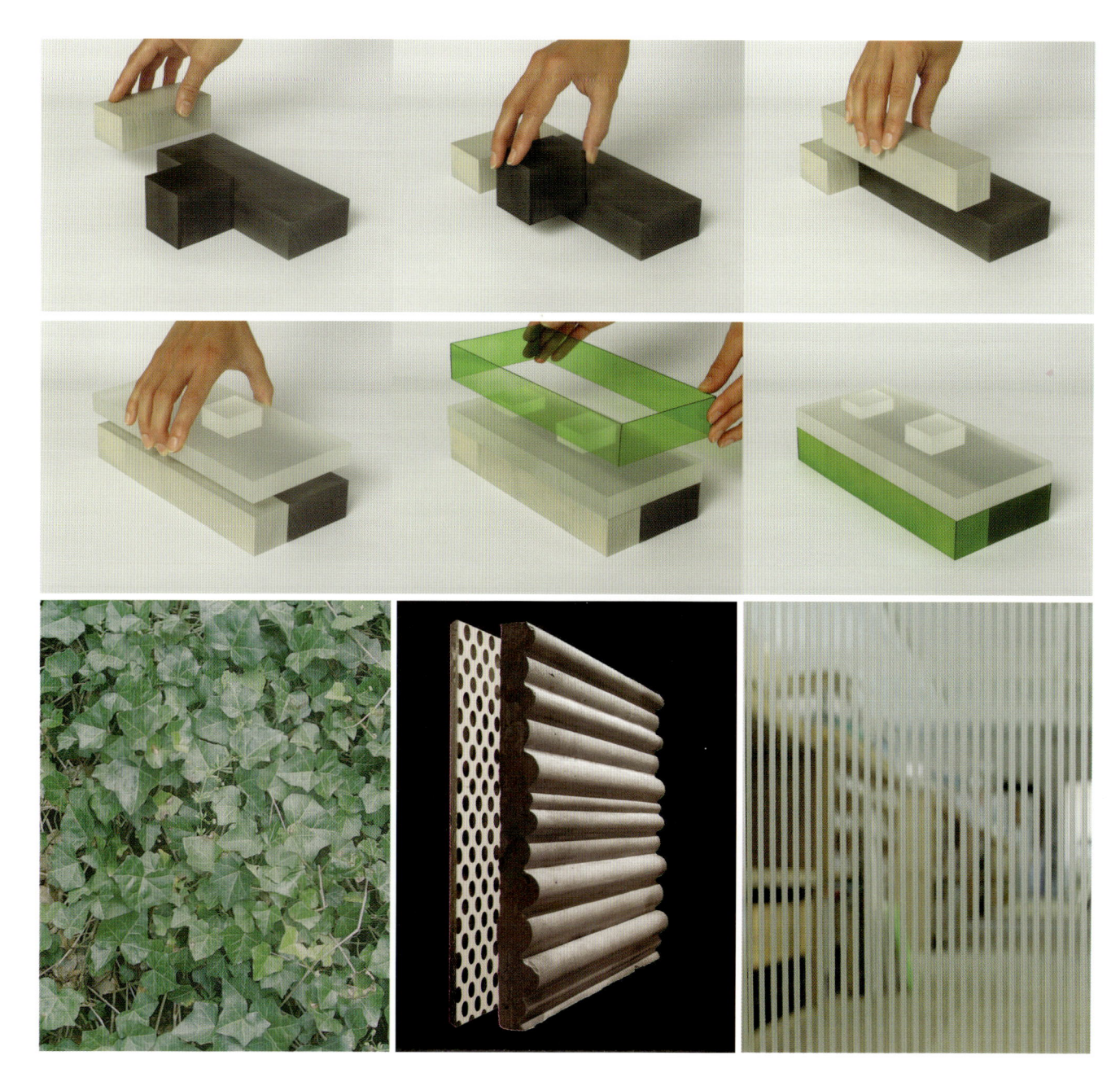

ARCHITECTURAL DIAGRAMS 493

RESEARCH LABORATORY UNStudio

"VERTICAL ALUMINUM SLATS, WHICH, IN PLACES, ARE TWISTED OUTWARDS IN BOWED FORMS."

Routing

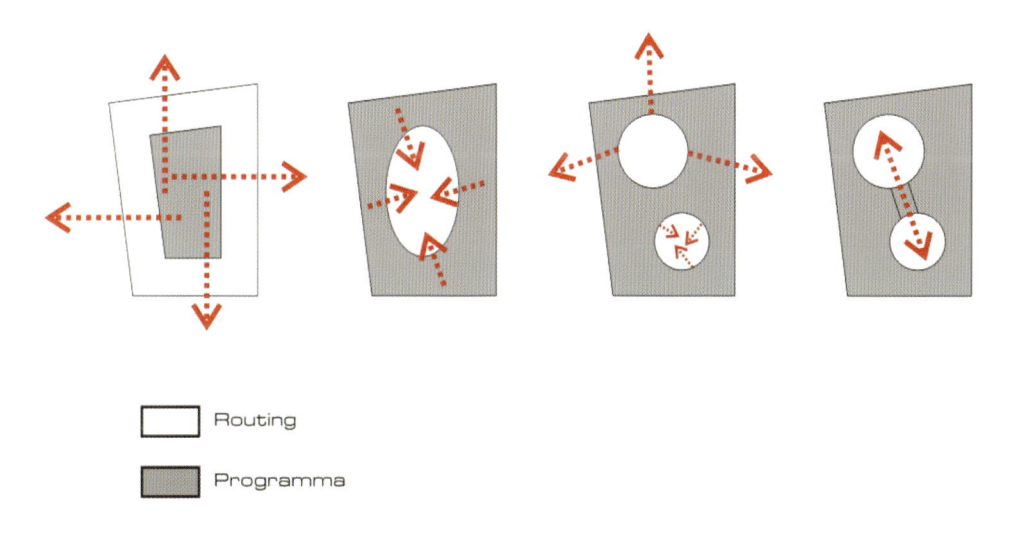

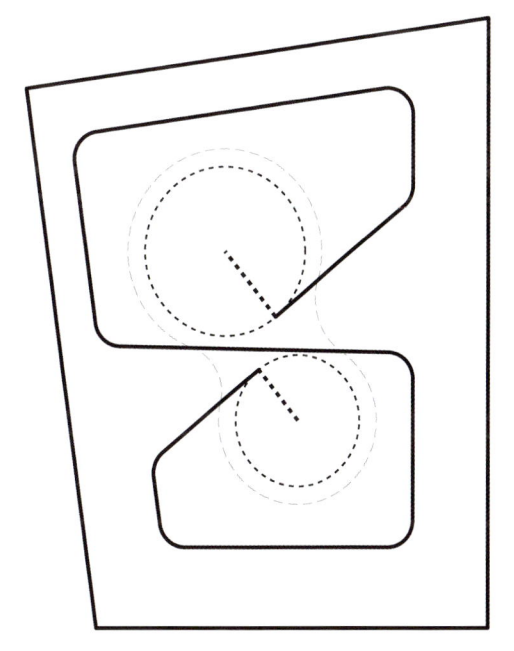

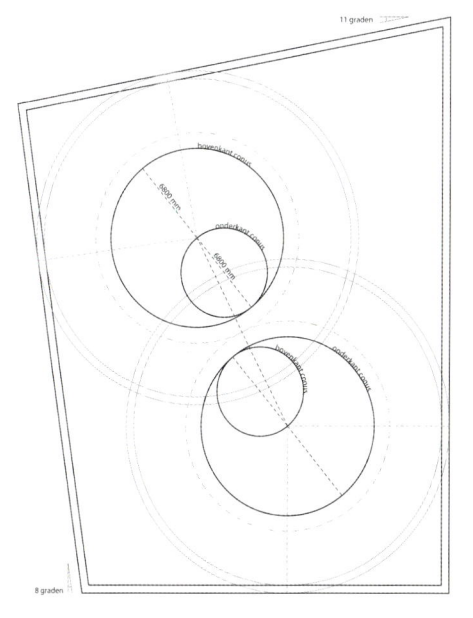

Programma

ARCHITECTURAL DIAGRAMS 495

S-HOUSE VMX Architects

"IN THE DESIGN TWO CLASSICAL TYPOLOGIES ARE COMBINED: THE PATIO VILLA AND THE MANOR HOUSE, OR DOMUS."

Street elevation

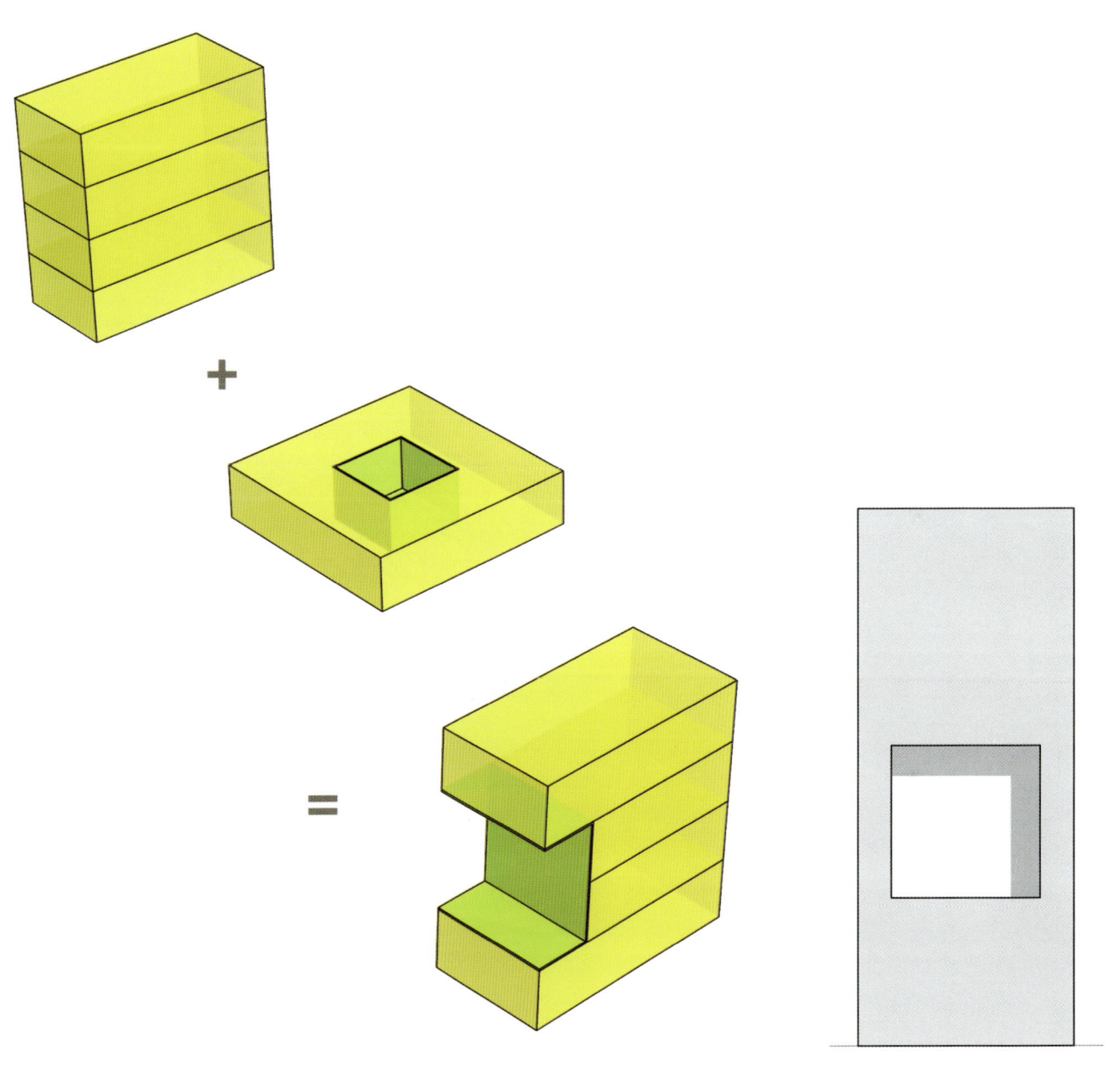

ARCHITECTURAL DIAGRAMS 497

SILO JDS Architects

"IT IS REPLETE WITH GREAT POTENTIAL BUT MUST BE RE-CONNECTED TO THE CITY."

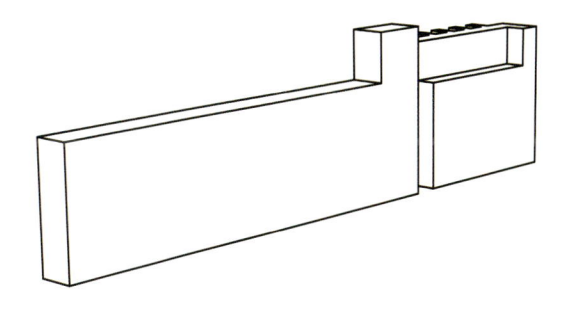

Context

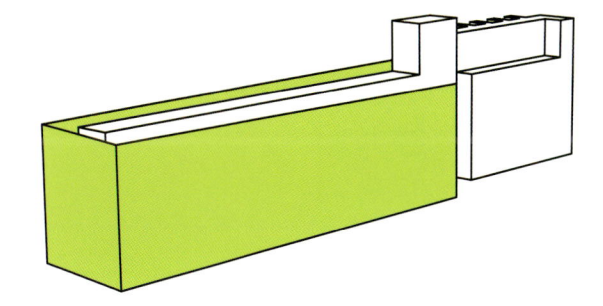

Envelope scheme

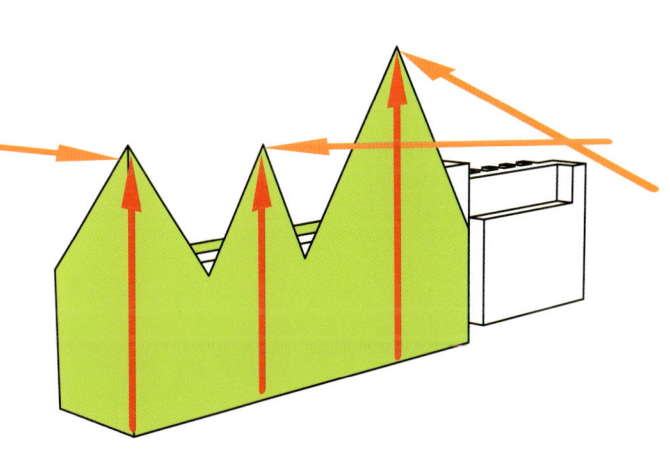

Peeks on direct views to and from streets

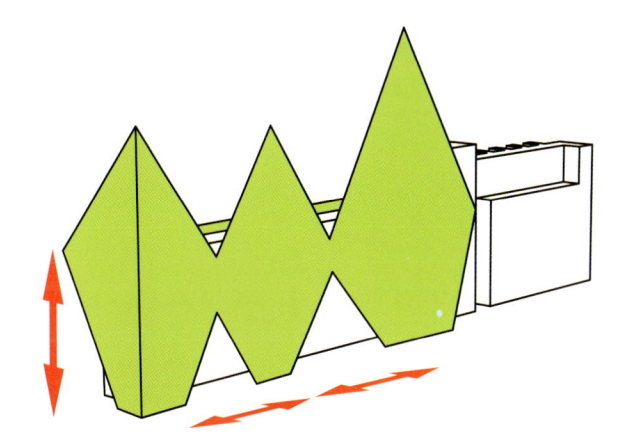

Opening to the silo and accesses

ARCHITECTURAL DIAGRAMS 499

SLIM TWIN SPACEGROUP

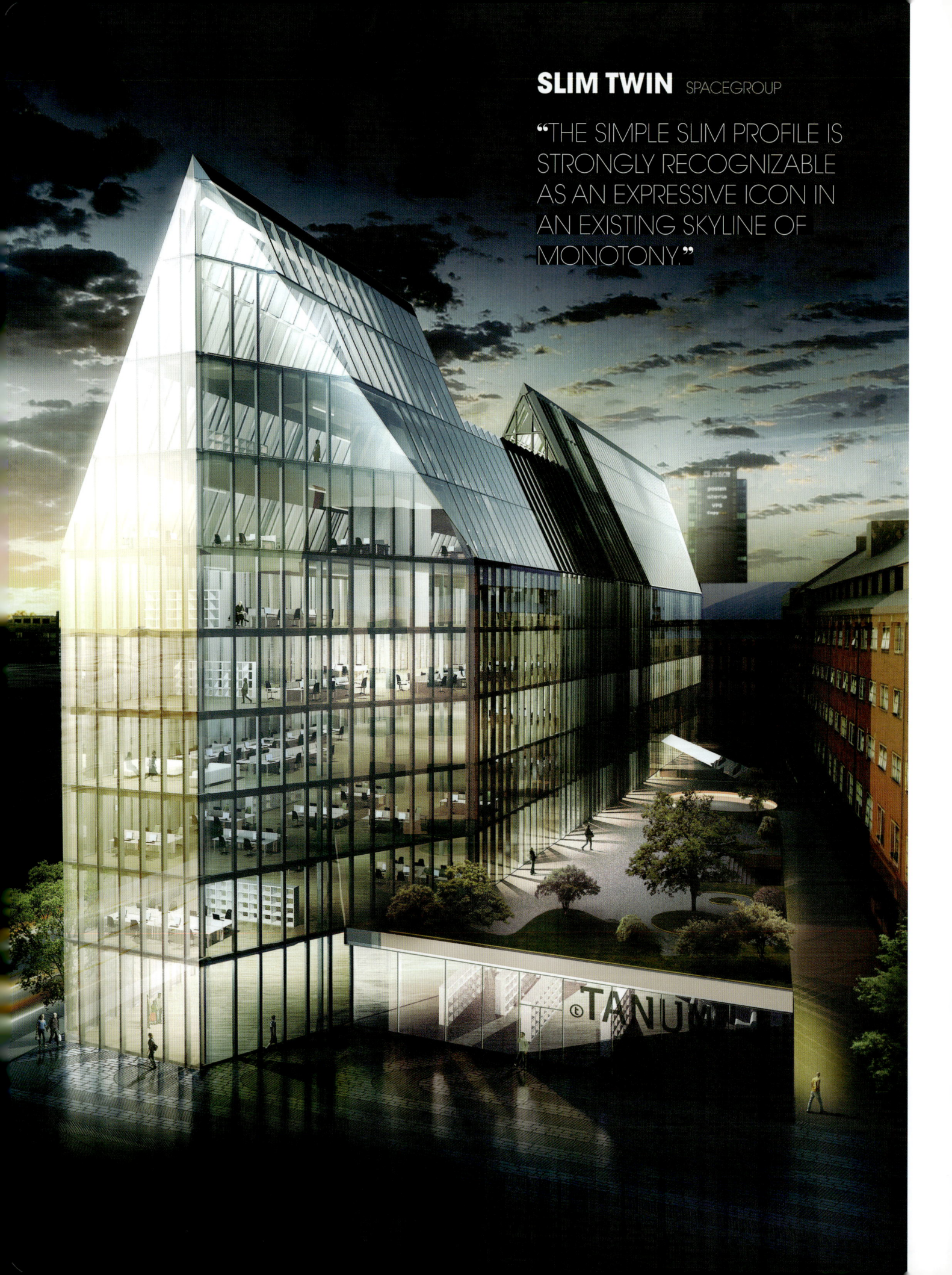

"THE SIMPLE SLIM PROFILE IS STRONGLY RECOGNIZABLE AS AN EXPRESSIVE ICON IN AN EXISTING SKYLINE OF MONOTONY."

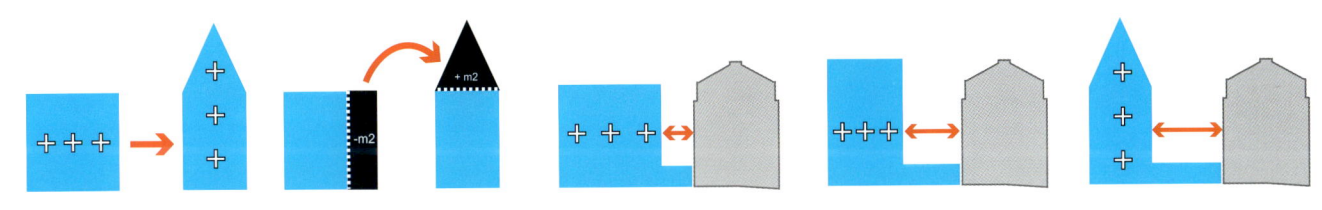

Façade generation

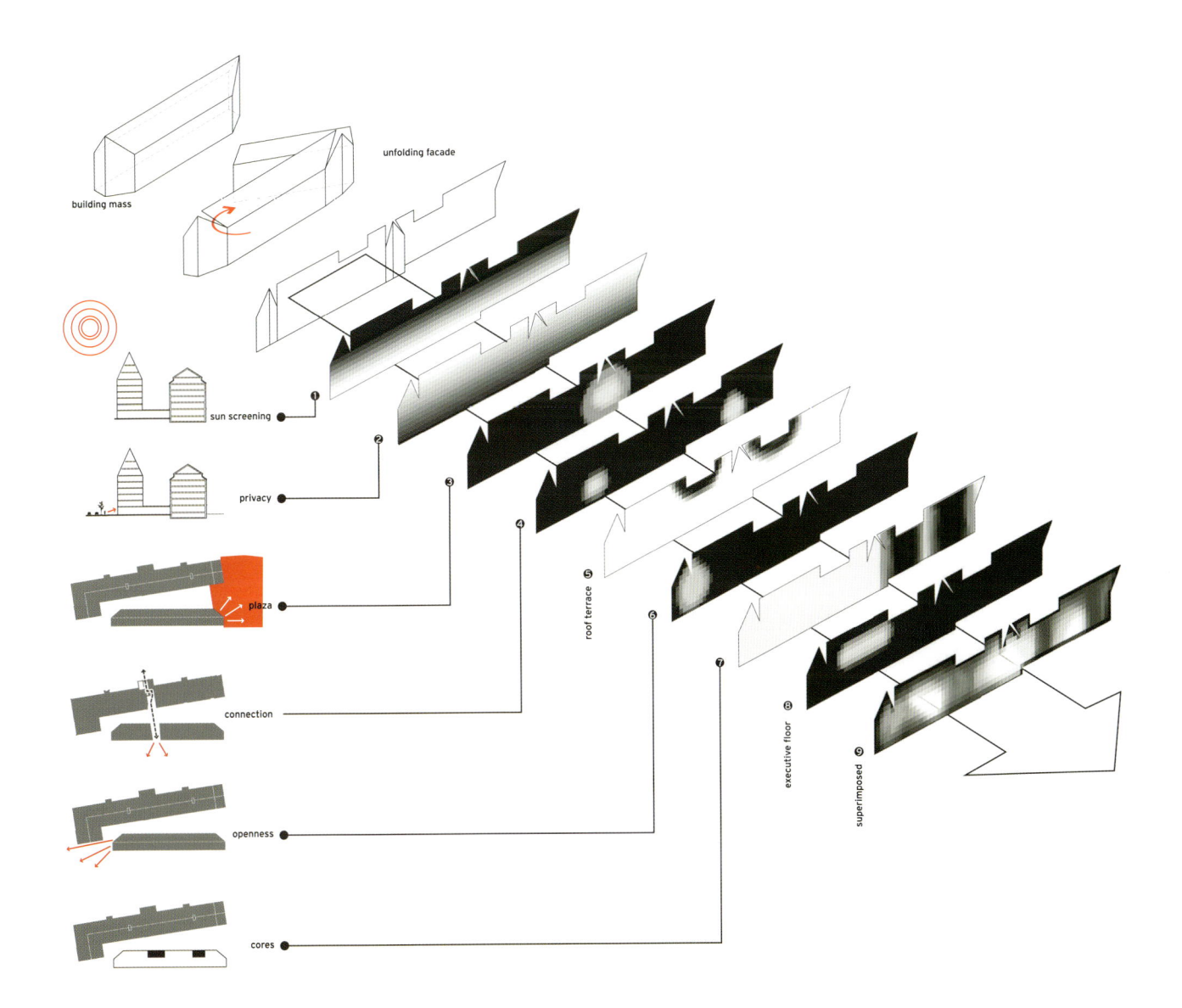

building mass
unfolding facade

sun screening
privacy
plaza
connection
openness
cores

roof terrace
executive floor
superimposed

ARCHITECTURAL DIAGRAMS 501

S_MAHAL Moonbalsso + DN

"THE WAVING OF THE SOFT WALLS ON A BREEZY DAY MADE IT CLEAR TO ME."

1. The UFO (unfriendly flying object) is sucking in the boiler building. Thank God! we have time to escape.
2. The UFO seems to be not so greedy. Anyhow my multi-legs have begun to grow, I might as well just start travelling.
3. I wonder which fellow will come with me.
4. How wonderful it is to be afloat and moving across the vast sea of gentle water.
5. The curtain has grown just right to give enough lift, and the legs are doing also very well in giving extra propulsion.
6. Without knowing, the S_Mahal is passing over the Taj Mahal.
7. Time have passed. we do not know how long it took us to be here. We somehow have arrived in the red stone district. The red and yellow suns are welcoming us.
8. Shall we go back?

ARCHITECTURAL DIAGRAMS

STAR HOTEL SPACEGROUP

"THE HOTEL REDEFINES THE CLASSICAL ATRIUM HOTEL TYPOLOGY TO A NEW AND STRONG IDENTITY."

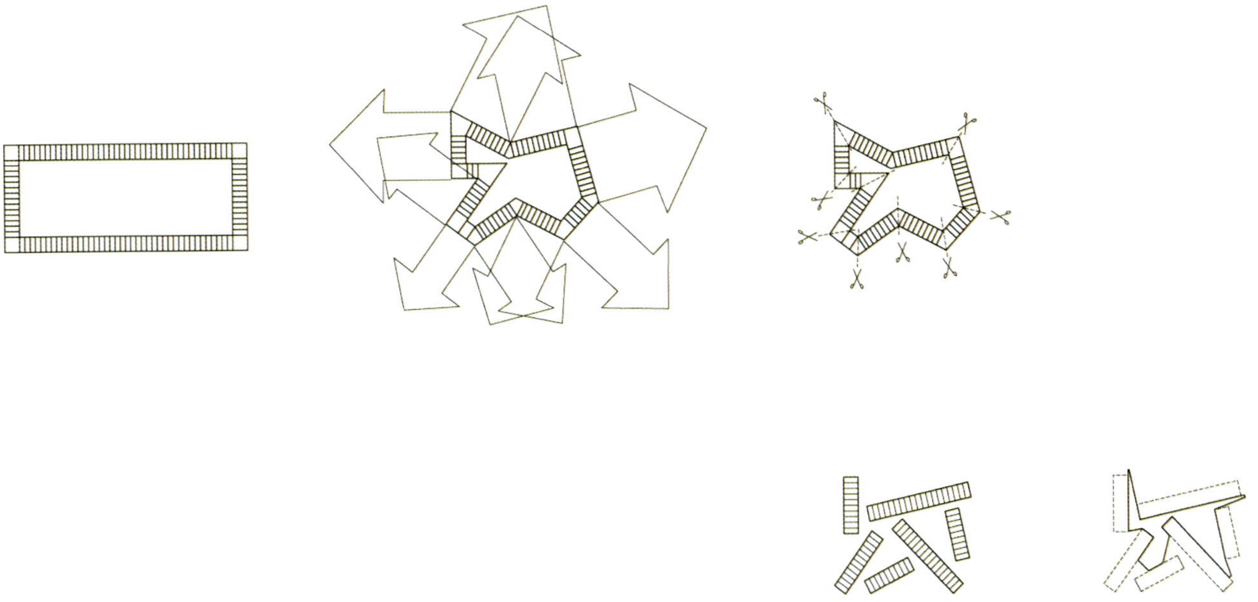

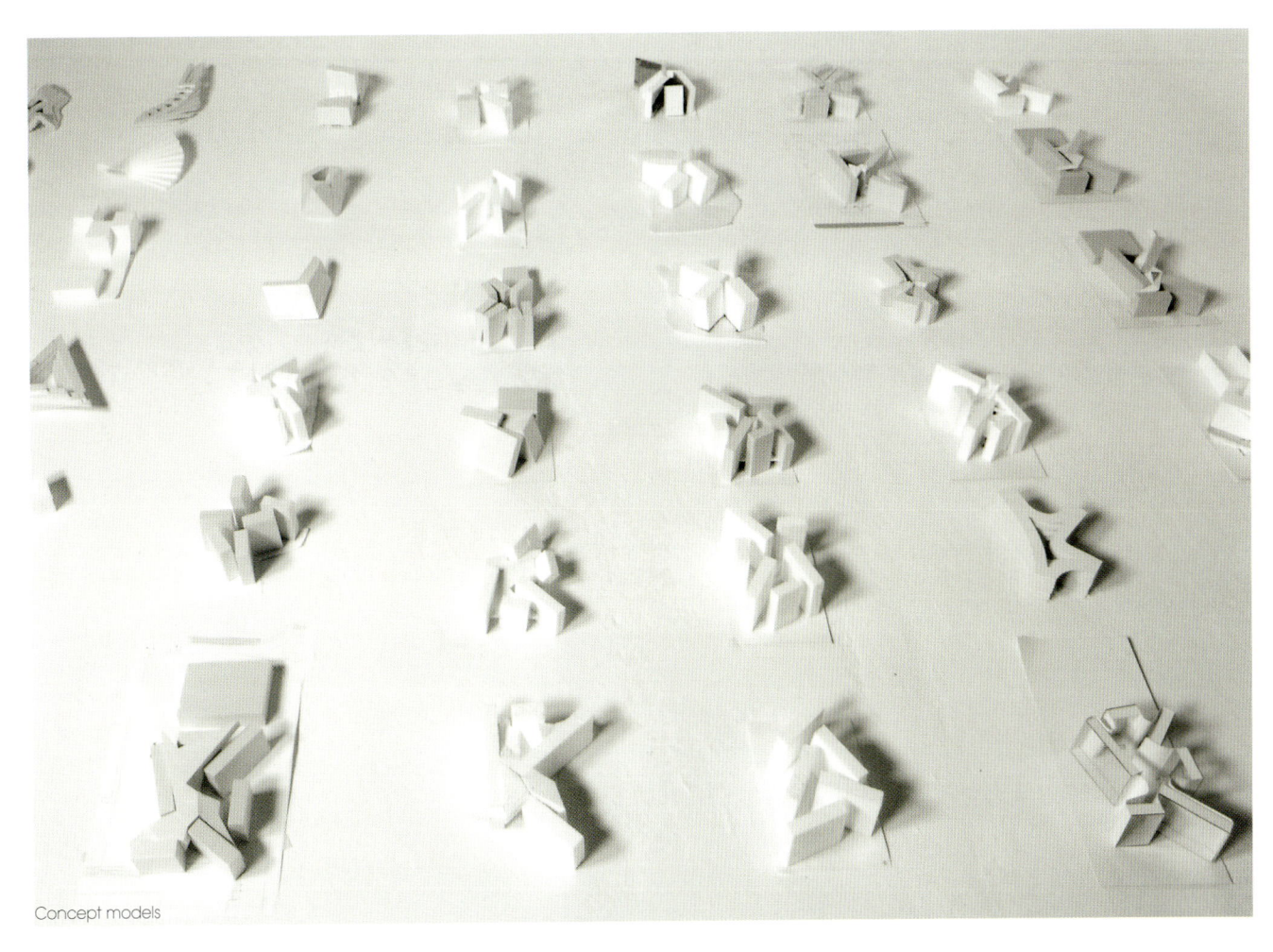

Concept models

ARCHITECTURAL DIAGRAMS 505

SUSTAINABLE OFFICE BUILDING VMX Architects

"OUR DESIGN COMBINES THE MOST NATURAL SUMMER AND WINTER SITUATION."

elevator
central staircase

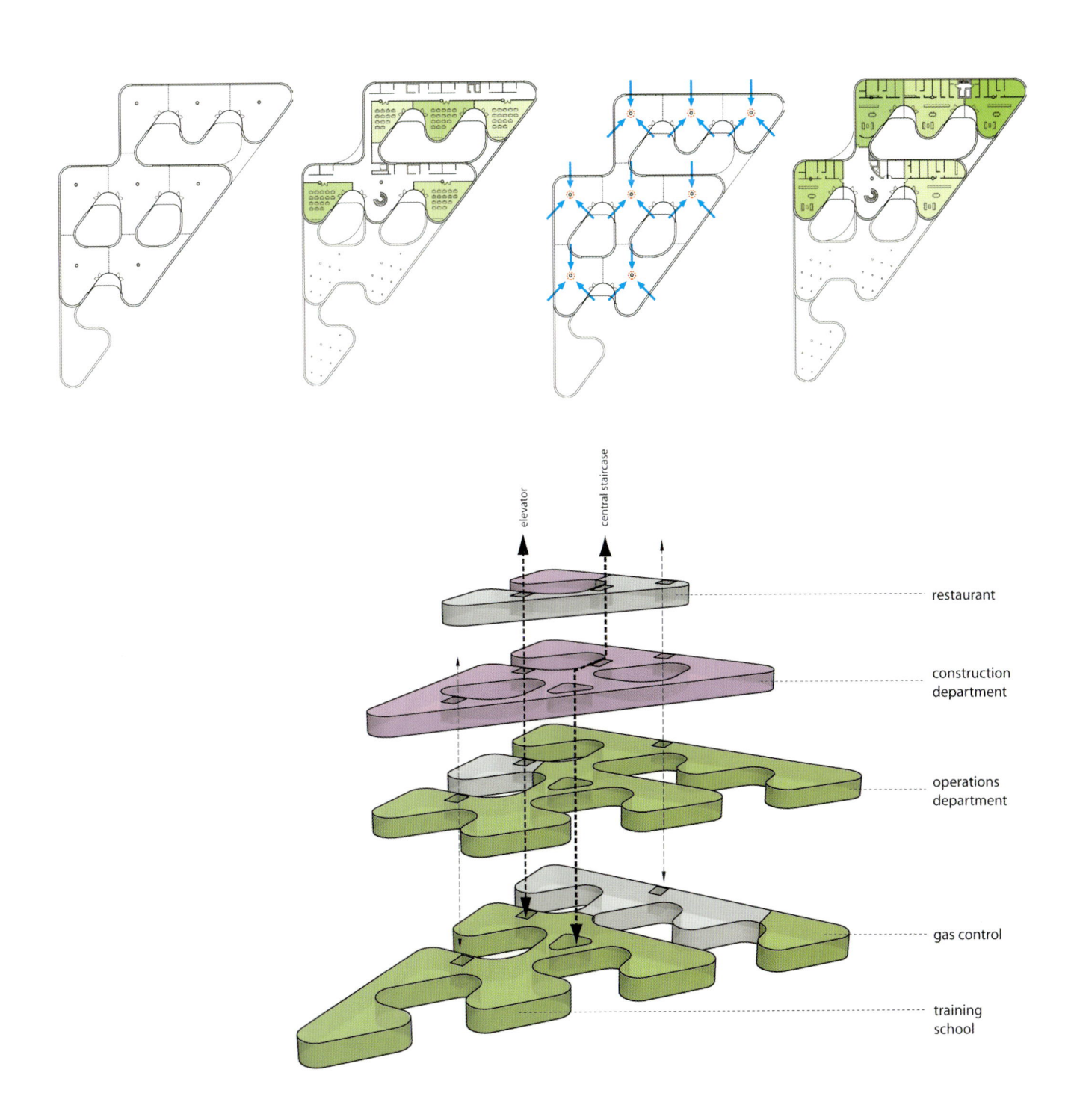

restaurant

construction department

operations department

gas control

training school

ARCHITECTURAL DIAGRAMS 507

SWITCH BUILDING
nARCHITECTS

"THE FRONT FACADE SWITCHES BACK AND FORTH, ALLOWING VIEWS UP AND DOWN NORFOLK STREET."

SOUTH VIEW

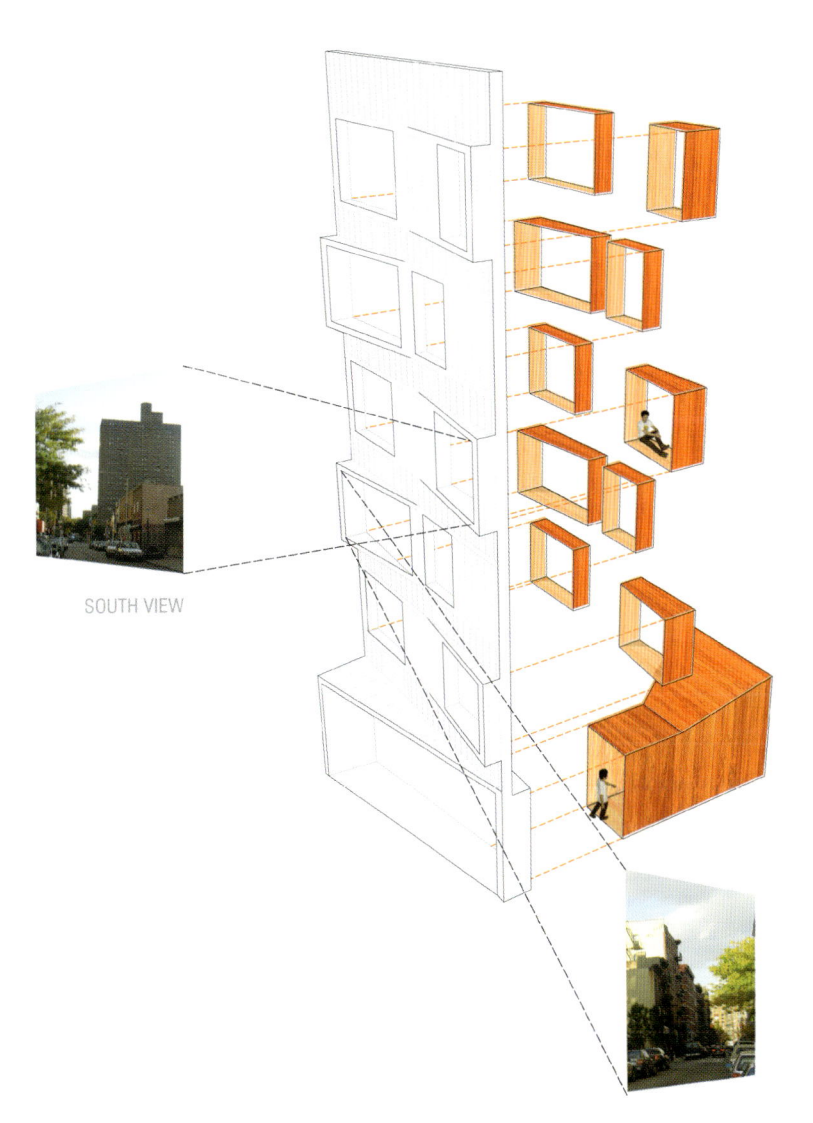

NORTH VIEW

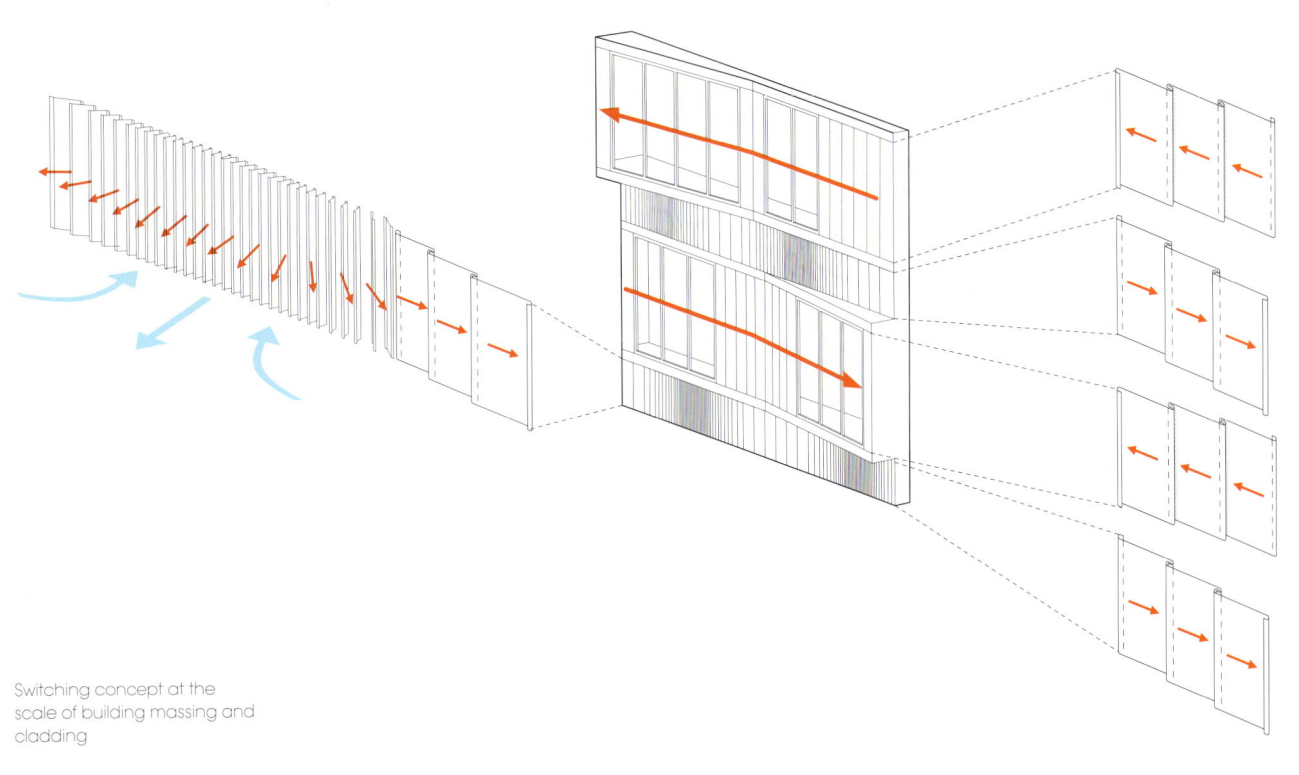

Switching concept at the scale of building massing and cladding

ARCHITECTURAL DIAGRAMS 509

THE MOUNTAIN JDS Architects

"WE DECIDED TO MERGE THE TWO FUNCTIONS INTO A SYMBIOTIC RELATIONSHIP."

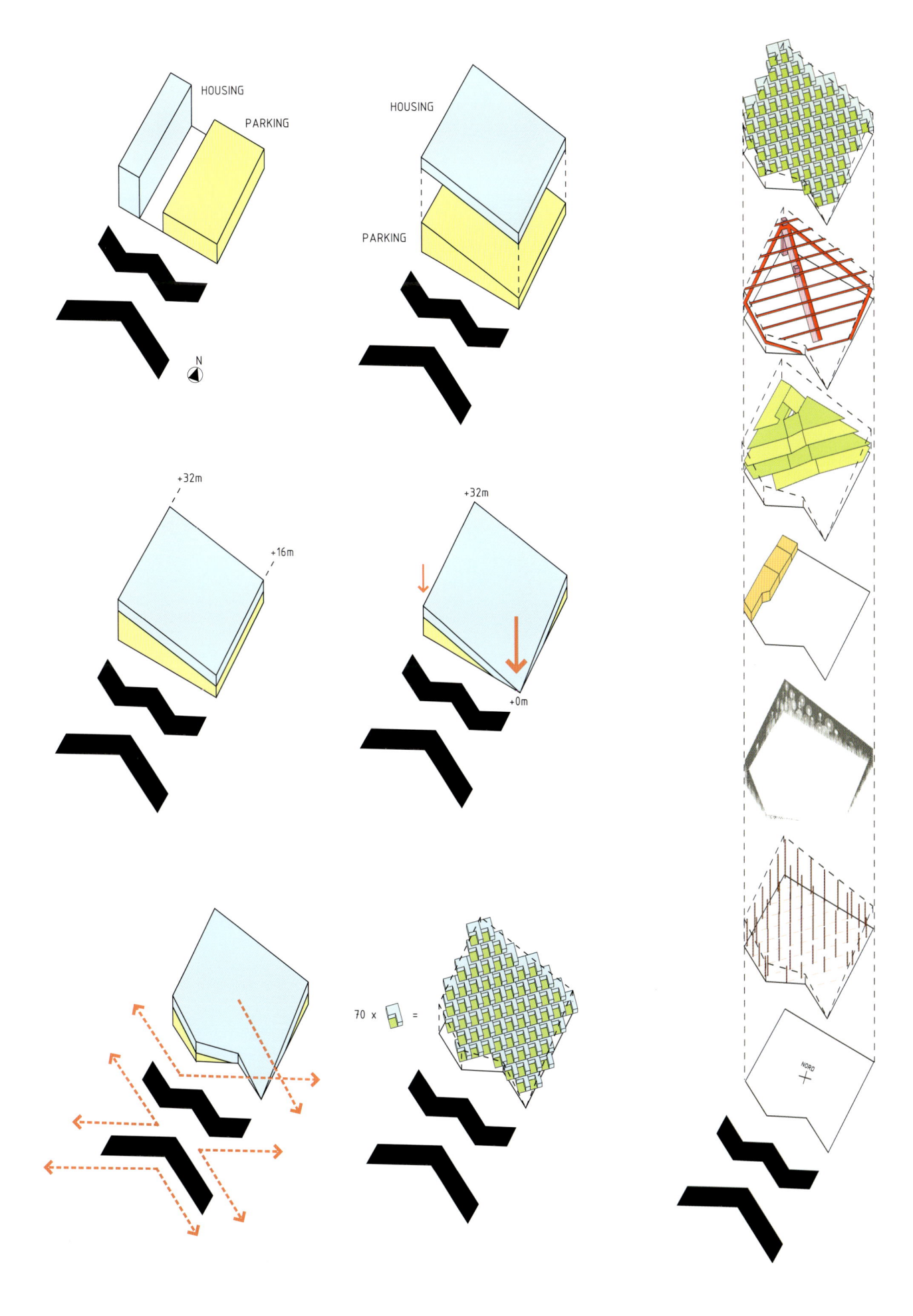

ARCHITECTURAL DIAGRAMS 511

THERMAL BRIDGE
nARCHITECTS

"THERMAL BRIDGE DEVELOPS A THERMAL LOGIC FOR THE ORGANIZATION OF HOUSING AND PUBLIC SPACE."

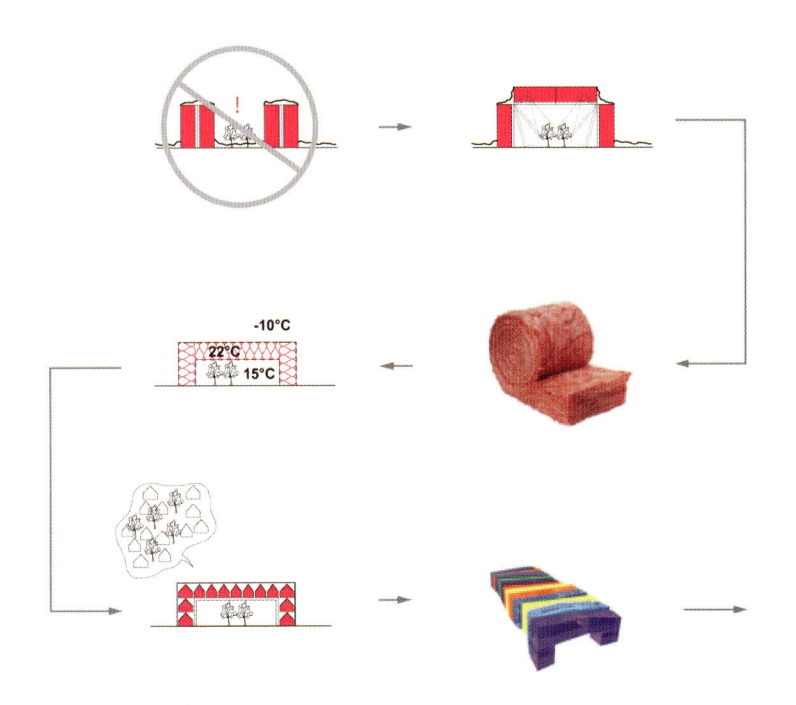

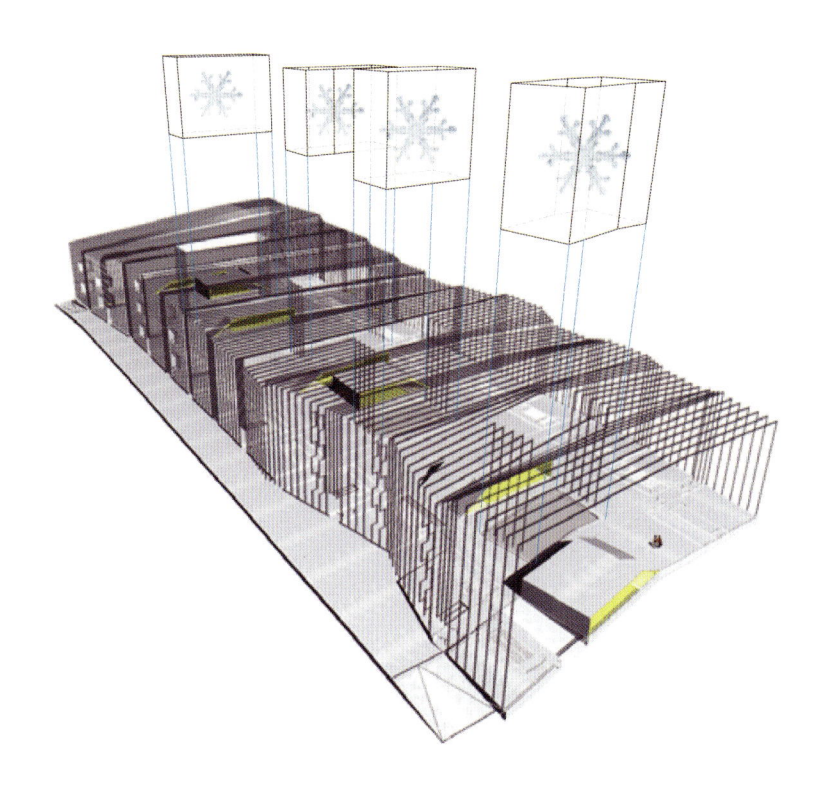

ARCHITECTURAL DIAGRAMS 513

TOWER COMPLEX AT THE SULEJMAN PASHA MONUMENT AREA
SADAR VUGA ARHITEKTI

"ALL THREE VERTICALS ALIGN VISUALLY AND THUS SYMBOLICALLY CONNECT RELIGIOUS, SECULAR AND URBAN."

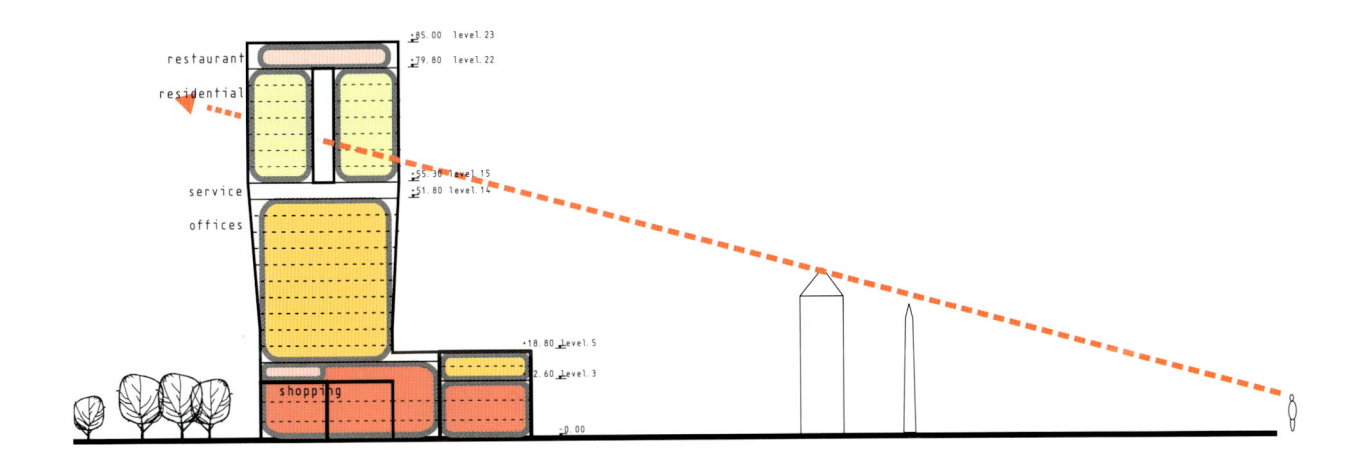

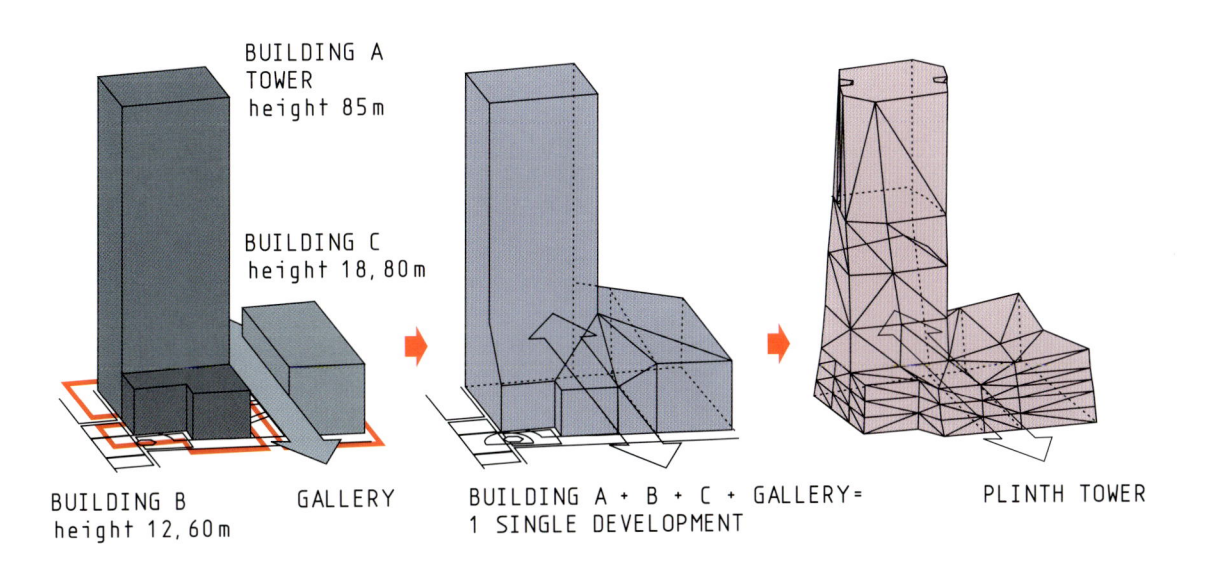

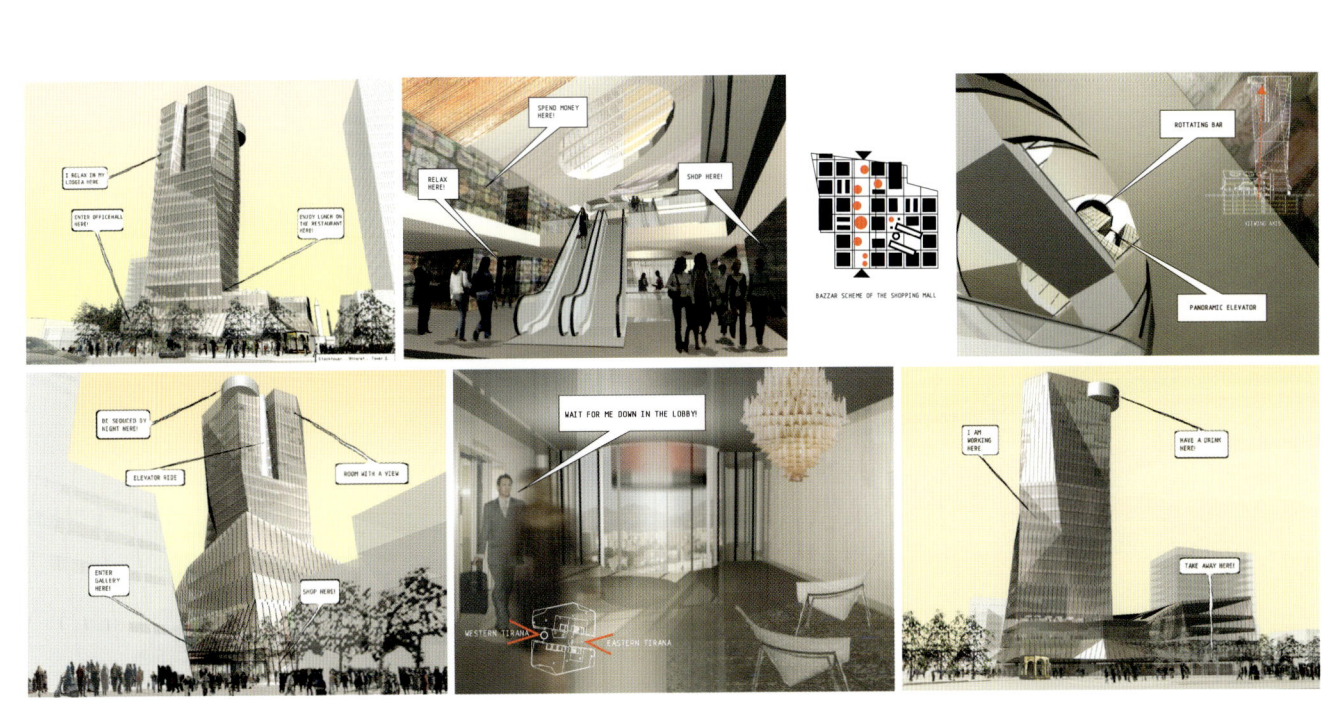

ARCHITECTURAL DIAGRAMS 515

TOWER COSTA RICA
Moho Architects

"THE CONCEPT IS DRIVEN BY A PROGRESSIVE ENVIRONMENTAL STRATEGY THAT IS EXPECTED TO ESTABLISH NEW BENCHMARKS FOR THE REGION."

Main access

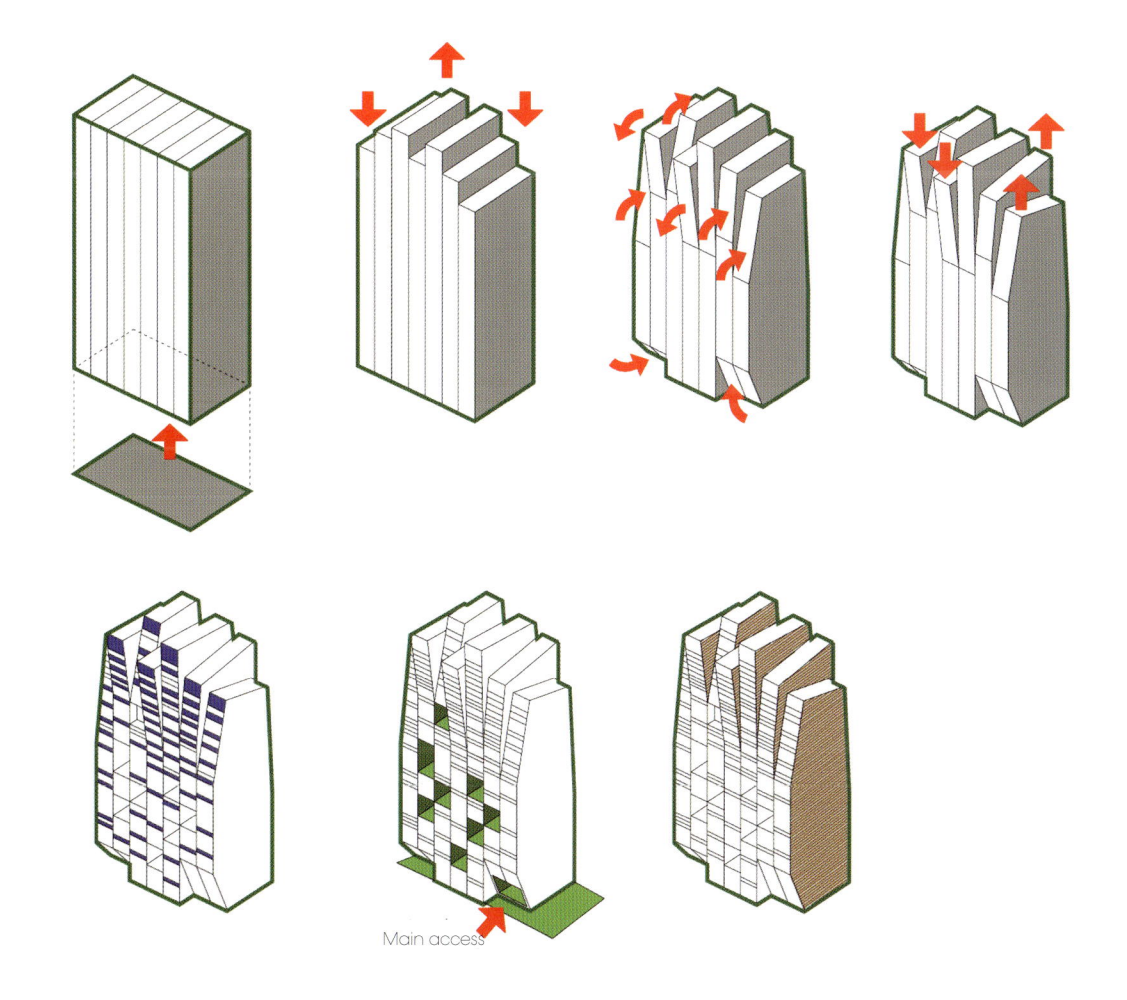

ARCHITECTURAL DIAGRAMS 517

TRP AMID [cero9]

"WE WOULD LIKE TO PROPOSE AN ARCHITECTURE THAT IS CHARACTERISED BY A CERTAIN INCORPOREAL."

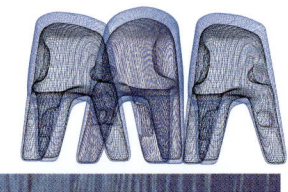

Collectors

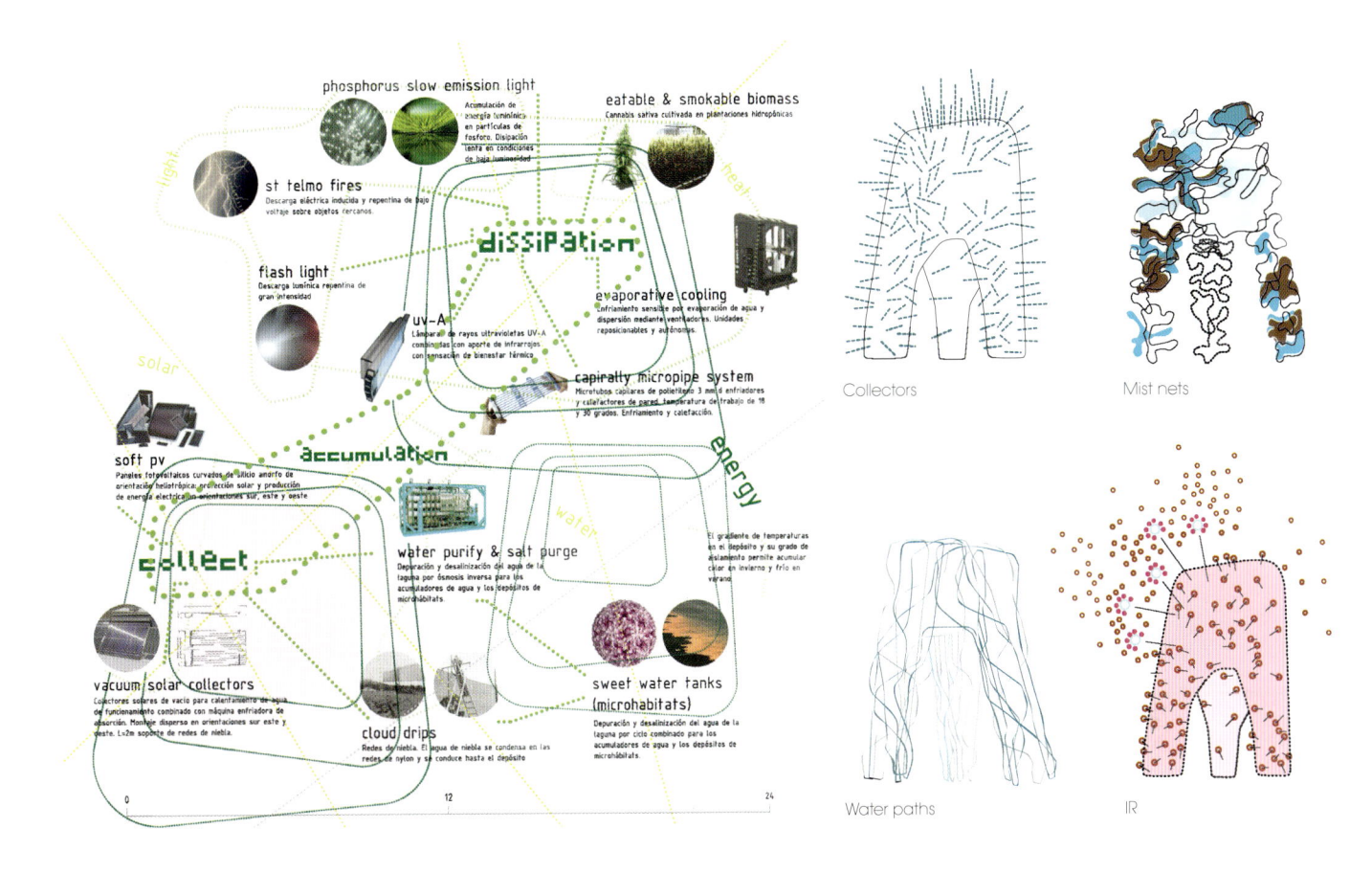

Mist nets

Water paths

IR

Marriage

Capillary microtubes

UV-a

Marijuana

Silicon pv

Sensors

Evaporative cooling

Differentiation autonomous systems

ARCHITECTURAL DIAGRAMS 519

UIB AMID [cero9]

"A LARGE, SPREADING, CONTINUOUS SPACE WITH ENORMOUS PILLARS AND CONTROLLED LUMINOSITY."

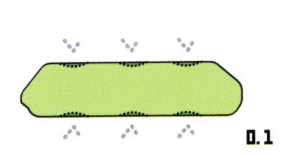

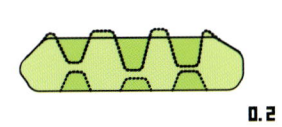

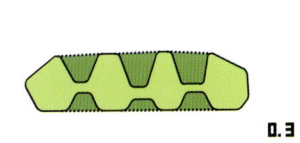

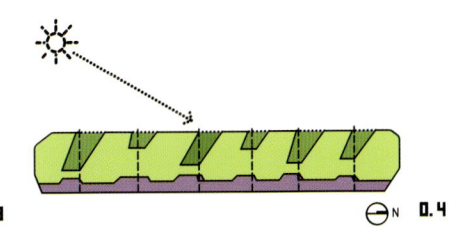

Pattern generation section

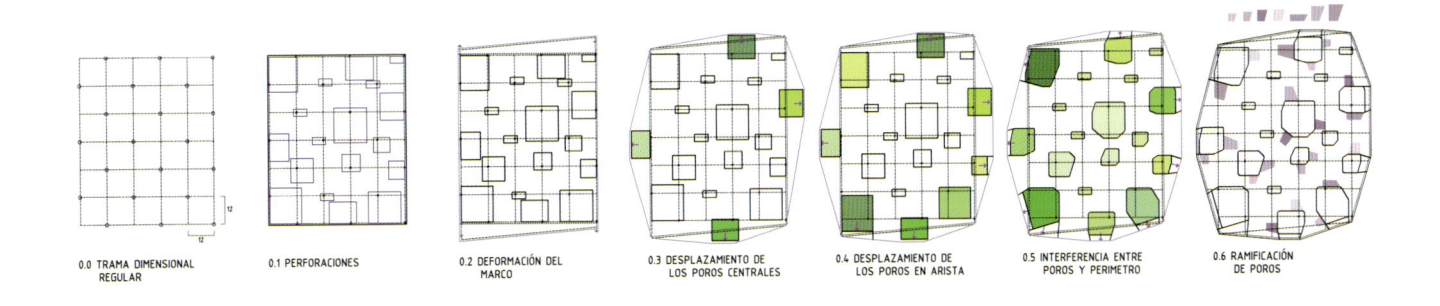

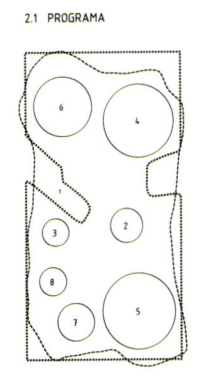

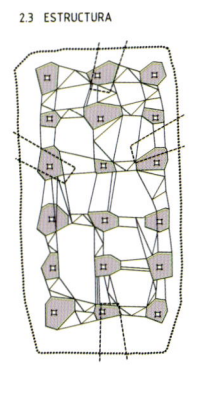

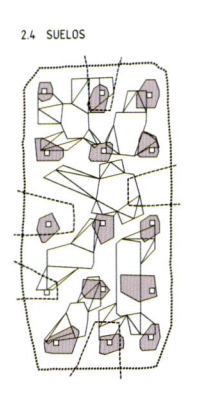

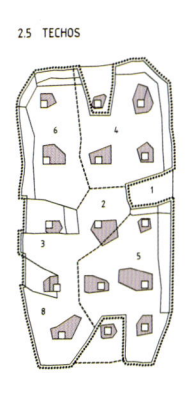

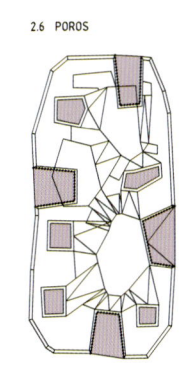

0.0 TRAMA DIMENSIONAL REGULAR
0.1 PERFORACIONES
0.2 DEFORMACIÓN DEL MARCO
0.3 DESPLAZAMIENTO DE LOS POROS CENTRALES
0.4 DESPLAZAMIENTO DE LOS POROS EN ARISTA
0.5 INTERFERENCIA ENTRE POROS Y PERIMETRO
0.6 RAMIFICACIÓN DE POROS

2.1 PROGRAMA
2.2 EJES
2.3 ESTRUCTURA
2.4 SUELOS
2.5 TECHOS
2.6 POROS

Pattern generation plan

ARCHITECTURAL DIAGRAMS 521

URBAN RESORT ST. PE-TERSBURG Willy Müller Architects

"THE RIBBONS, WILL BE TREATED LIKE A FAÇADE AND A ROOF AT THE SAME TIME."

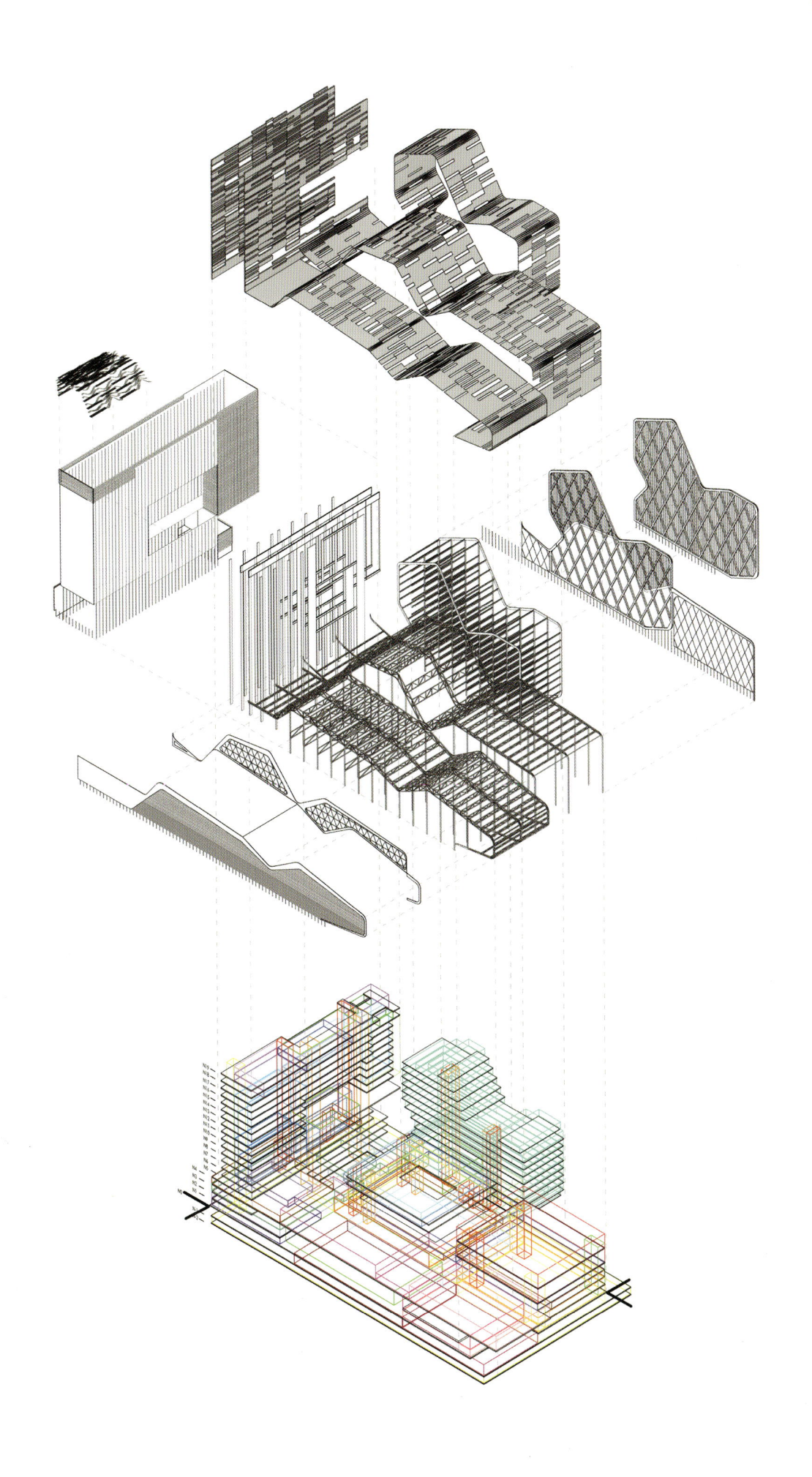

ARCHITECTURAL DIAGRAMS 523

VERTICAL TERRACED VILLAS nodo17 Architects

"GREAT FLORAL CURTAINS ENVELOP THE EXTERIOR OF THE BUILDING."

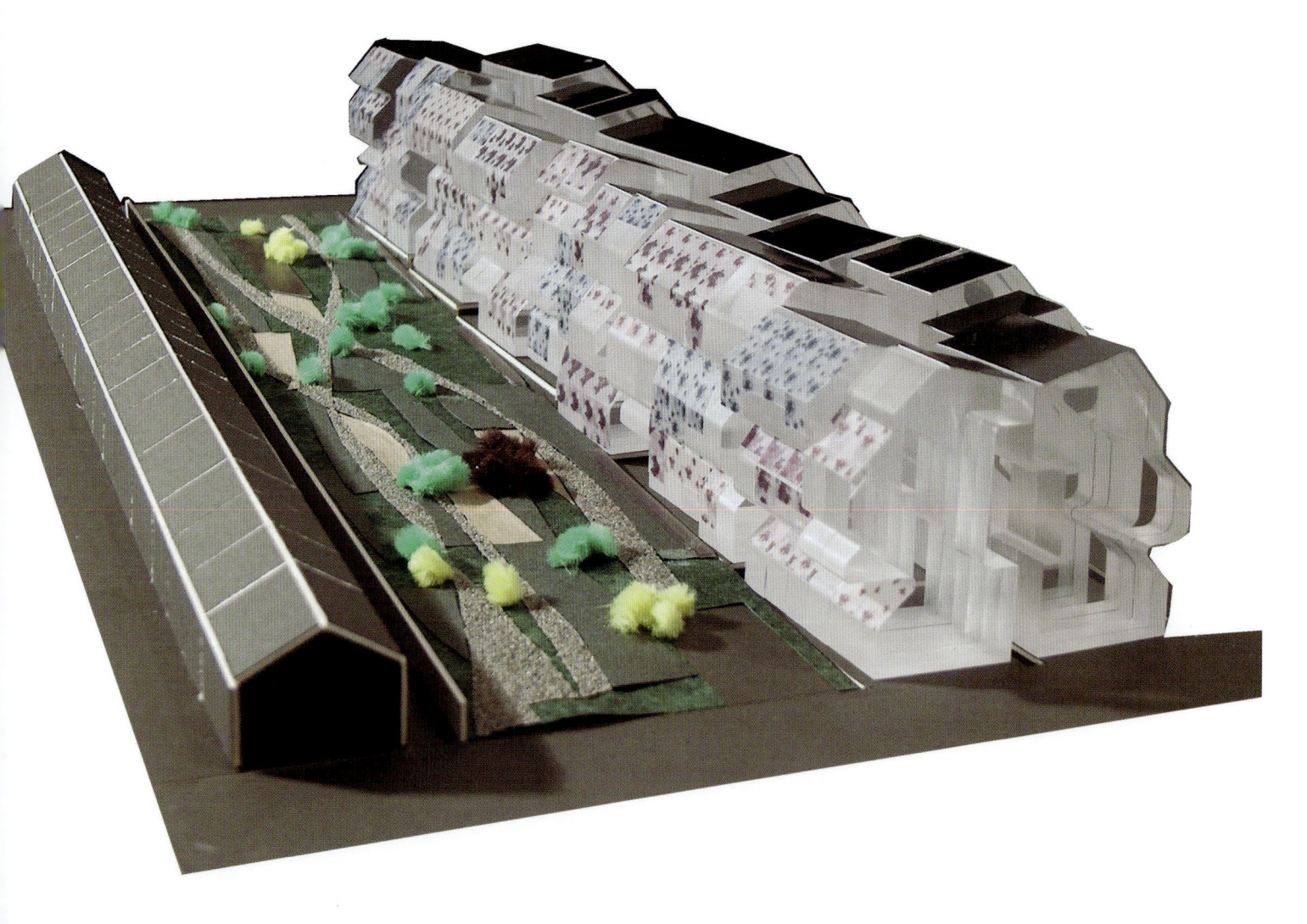

Extract

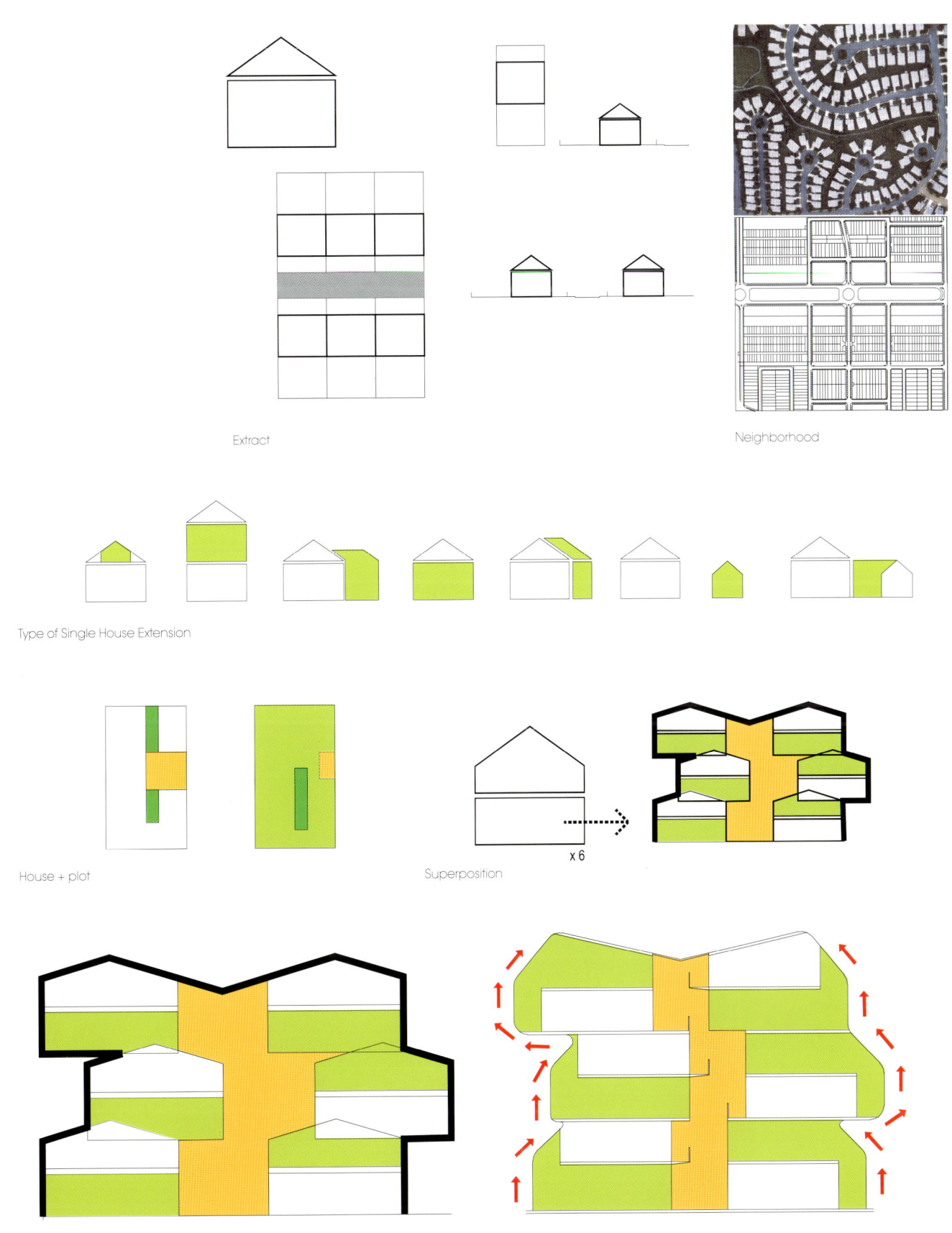

Neighborhood

Type of Single House Extension

House + plot

Superposition

Facade enrollable

ARCHITECTURAL DIAGRAMS 525

VESTBANEN SPACE GROUP

"OUR PROPOSAL ALSO REDEFINES CONTEXT BY DESIGNING SPECIFIC SITES WITHIN THE SITE."

Program interaction

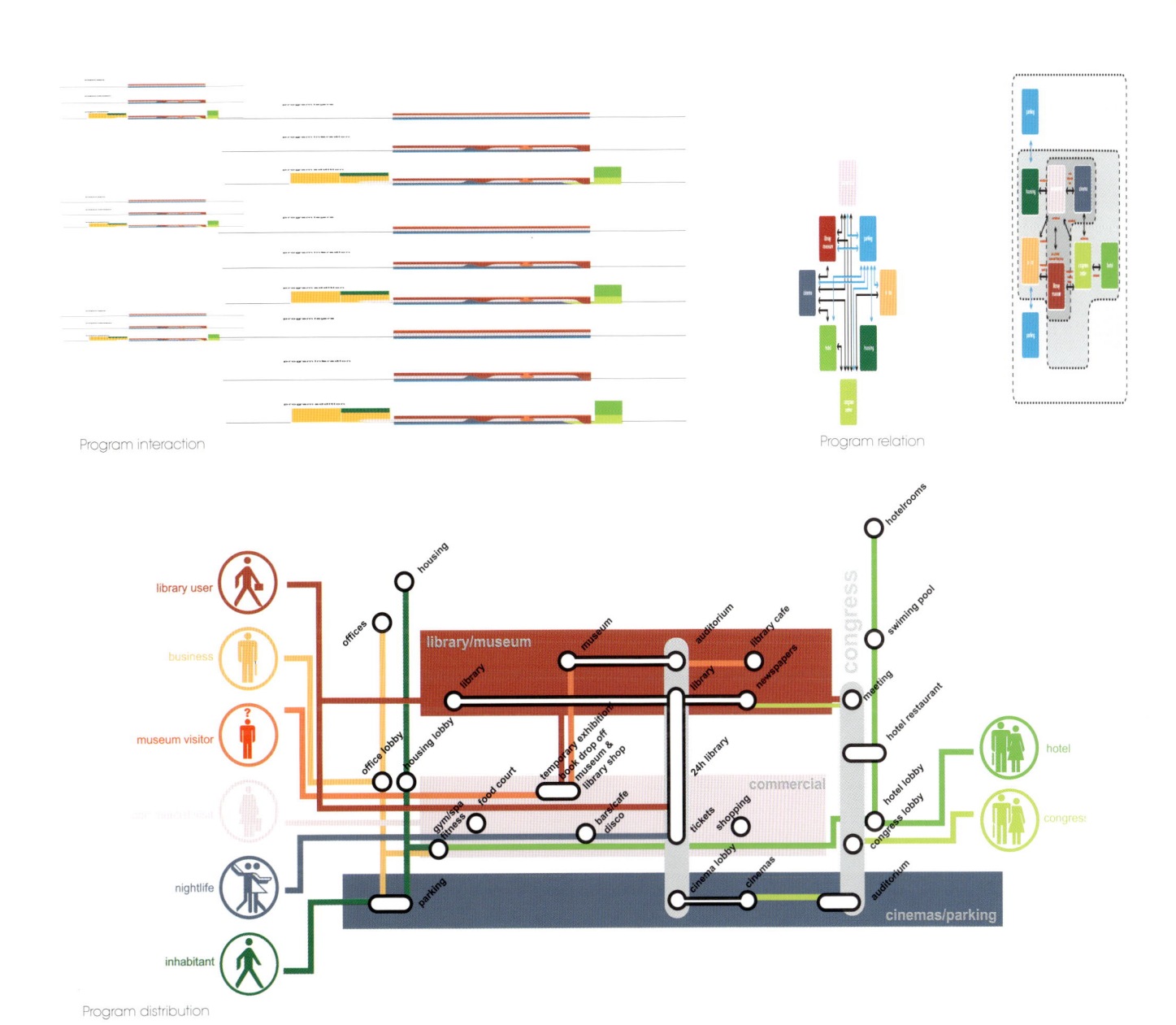

Program relation

Program distribution

Concept + Site circulation

ARCHITECTURAL DIAGRAMS 527

VILLA NM UNStudio

"THE MATERIALIZATION OF THE DESIGN IS A COMBINATION OF CONCRETE AND GLASS WITH A LIGHT METAL CONSTRUCTION."

Structure of volume

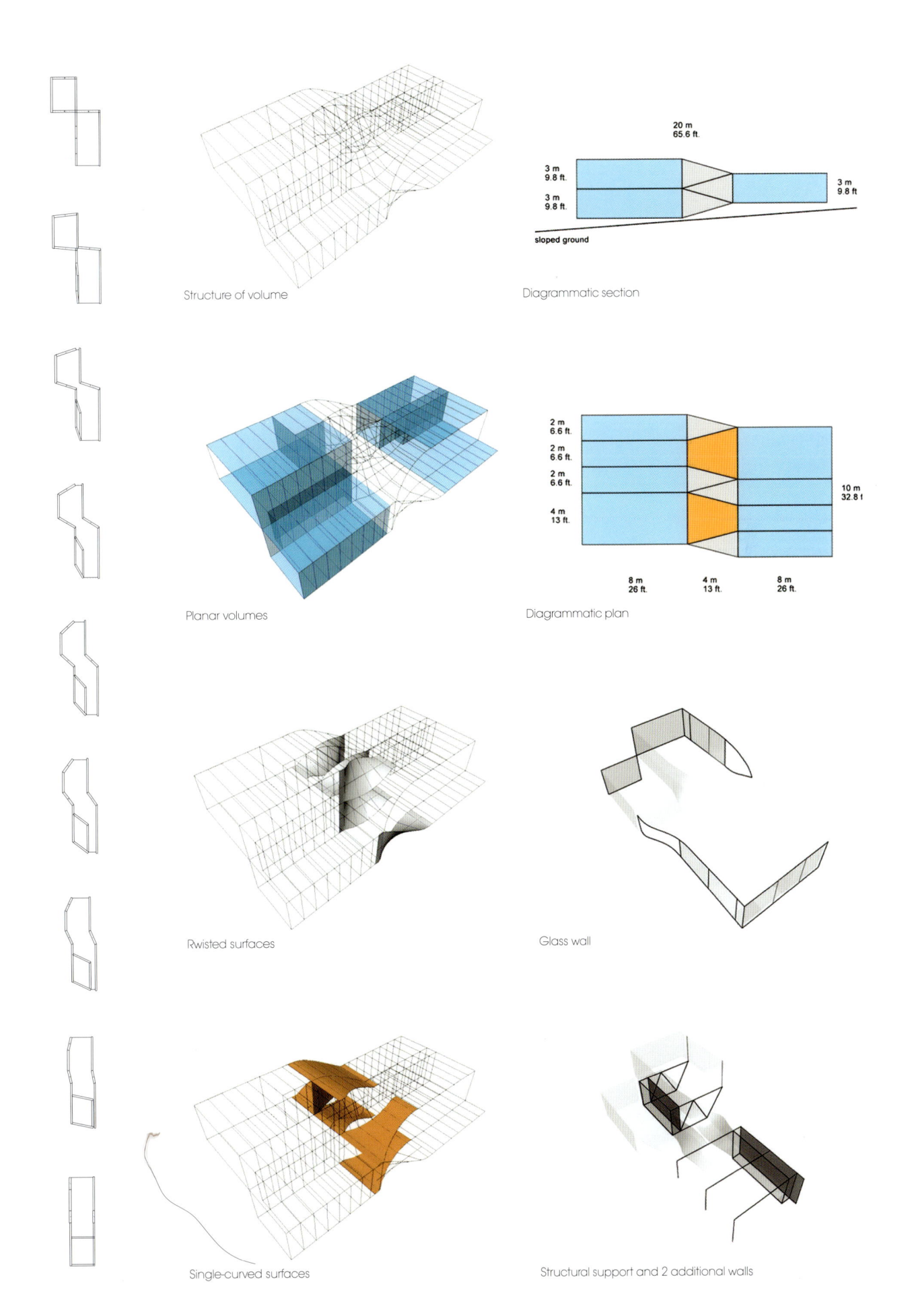

Diagrammatic section

Planar volumes

Diagrammatic plan

Rwisted surfaces

Glass wall

Single-curved surfaces

Structural support and 2 additional walls

ARCHITECTURAL DIAGRAMS 529

VILLA - VILLA nARCHITECTS

"CONCEIVED AS A HOUSE WITHIN A HOUSE, OUR VILLA COMBINES TWO DISTINCT SPATIAL AND THERMAL CONDITIONS."

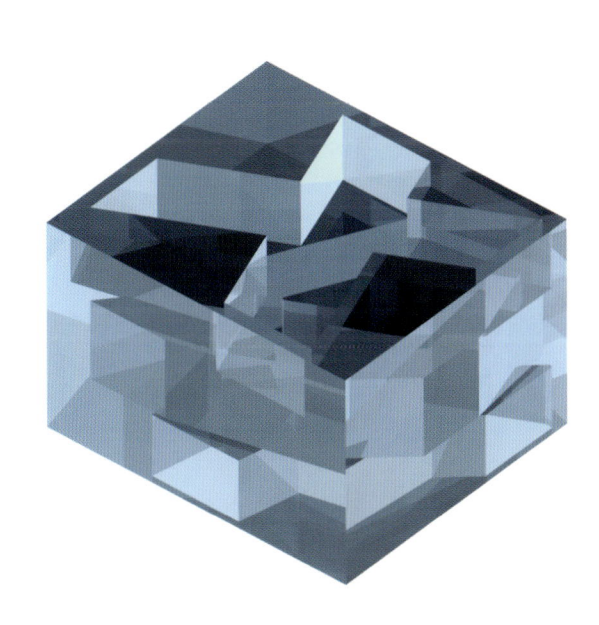

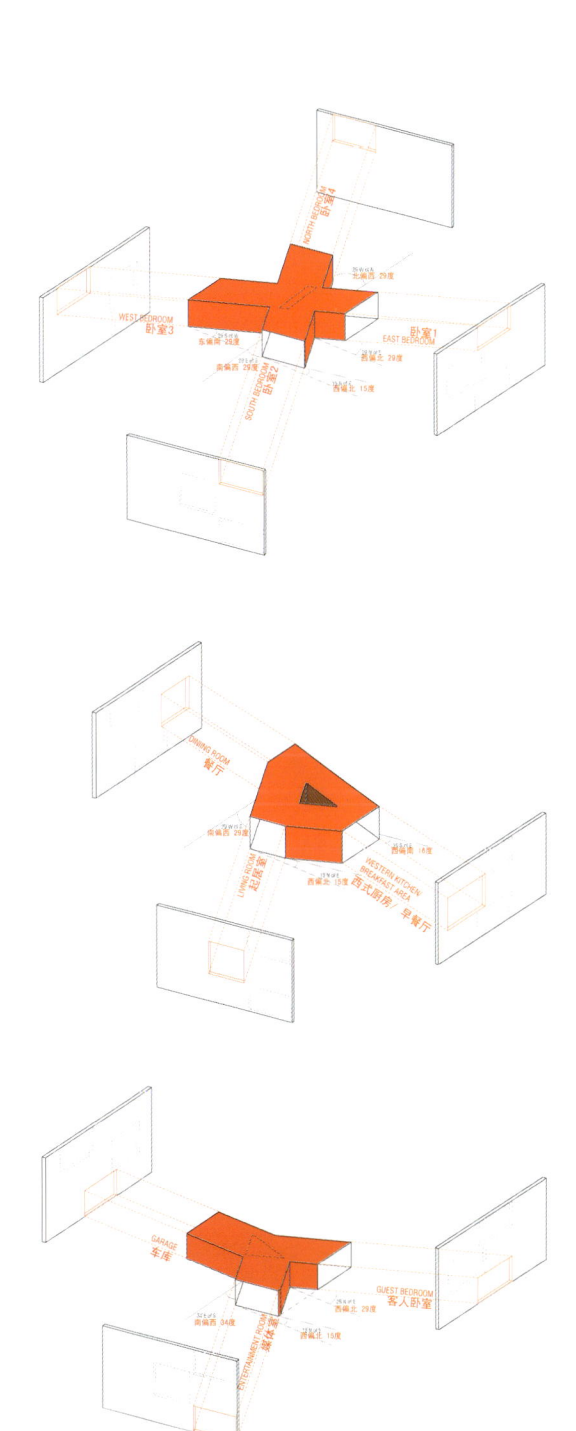

Three single-storey volumes stack on top of each other....

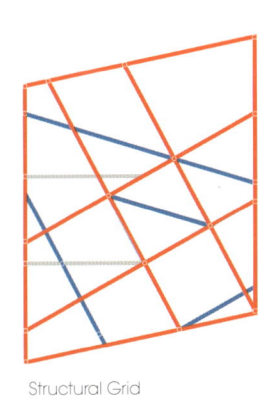

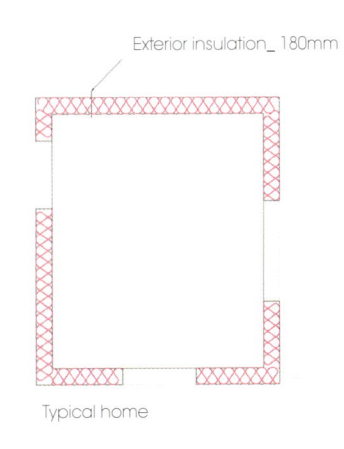

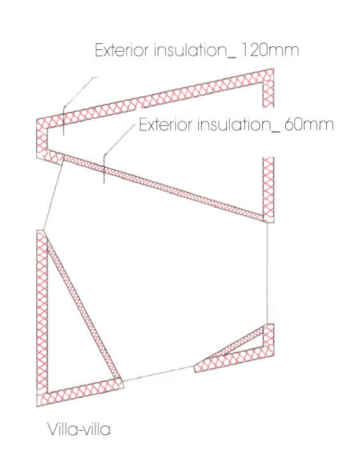

Exterior insulation_ 180mm
Exterior insulation_ 120mm
Exterior insulation_ 60mm

Structural Grid

Typical home

Villa-villa

ARCHITECTURAL DIAGRAMS 531

VILLA FAMILIE MAX MAIER J. MAYER H. ARCHITECTS

"THE RESULT ARE ASLOPE WARPED, SCULPTURAL OUTER WALLS IN THE MIDDLE FLOOR VISUALISING DYNAMICS AND FORCE PROGRESSION."

Visual Axes / Lines of sight

Movement and circulation

Core / Program / Skin
- Lobby
- Entrance Hall
- Living Space
- Parlor
- Dining / Kitchen

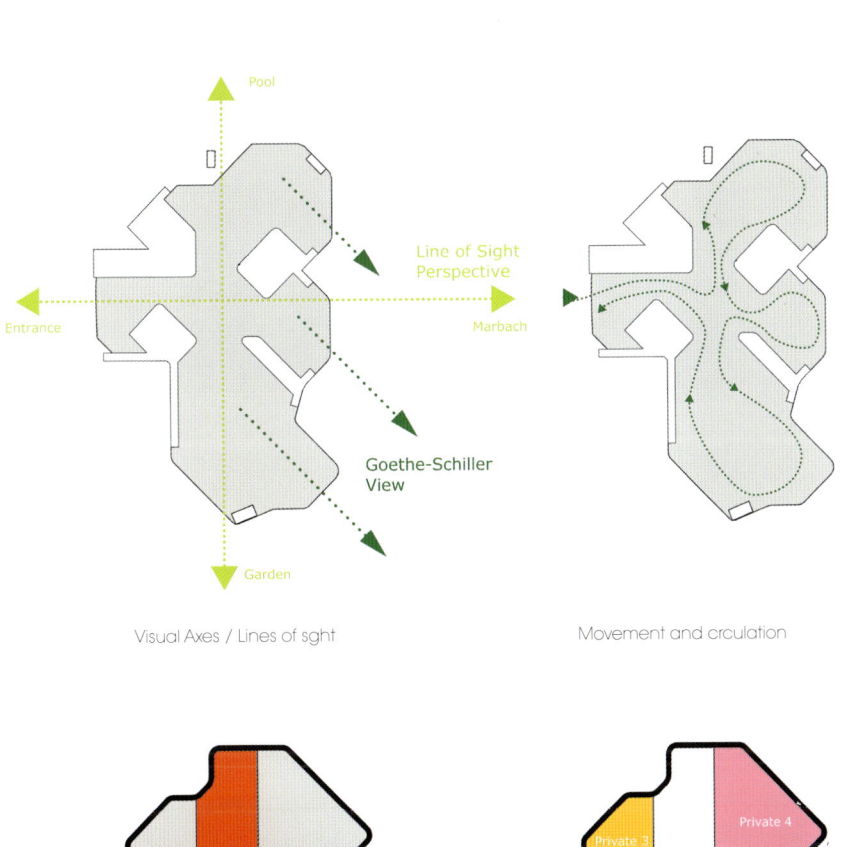

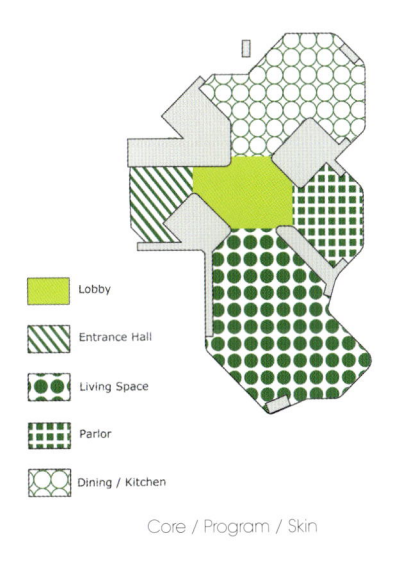

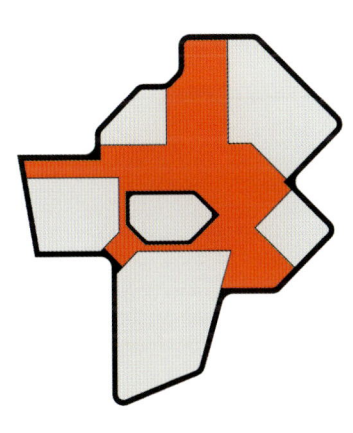

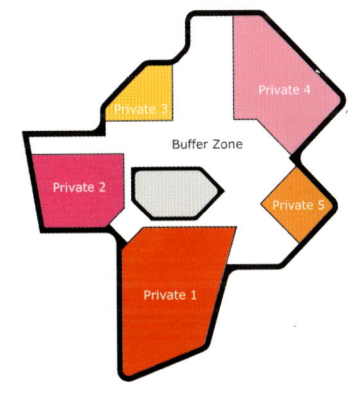

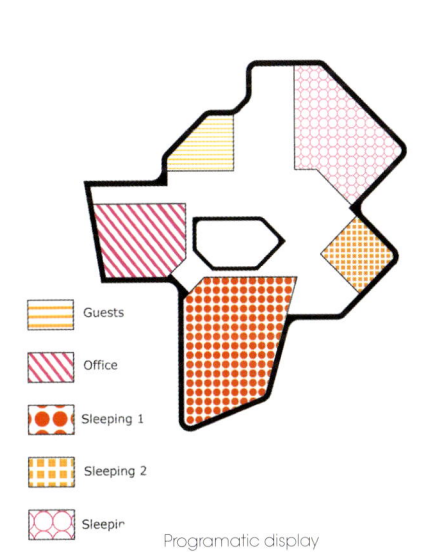

Spatial concept

Maximum of privacy

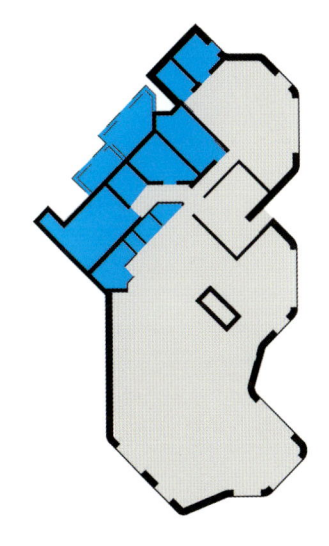

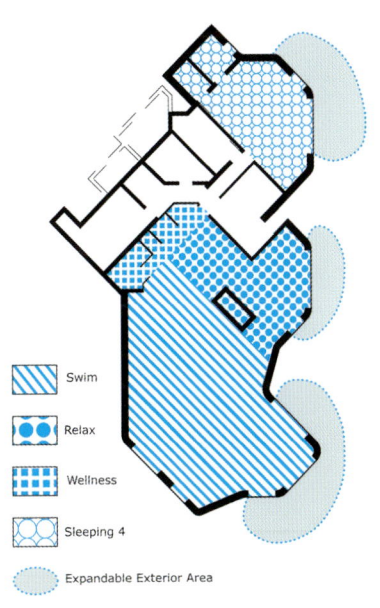

Programatic display
- Guests
- Office
- Sleeping 1
- Sleeping 2
- Sleeping 3

Spatial concept

Movement and circulation

Programmatic display
- Swim
- Relax
- Wellness
- Sleeping 4
- Expandable Exterior Area

ARCHITECTURAL DIAGRAMS 533

VM HOUSES JDS Architects

"IN THIS PROJECT THE TYPOLOGY OF THE UNITE D'HABITATION OF LE CORBUSIER IS REINTERPRETED AND IMPROVED."

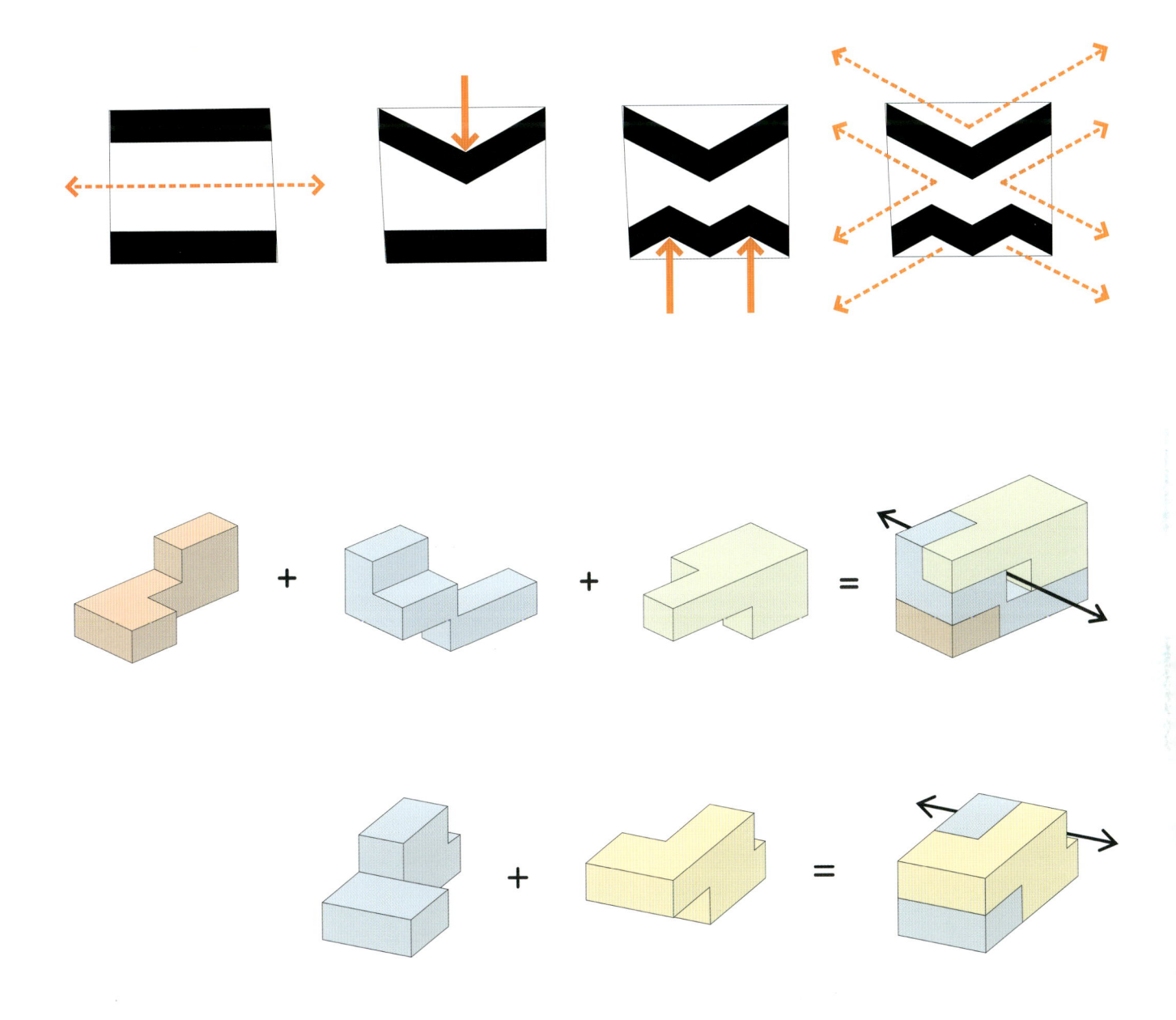

ARCHITECTURAL DIAGRAMS 535

WBW: WILLE URBANIE

Bernd Kniess Architects Urban Planners

"THE VILLE URBAINE HOUSE WITH COURTYARD FUSES URBAN DENSITY WITH THE DESIRE FOR EXTERNAL PRIVATE GREENERY."

Lageplan M. 1:500

Pocket gardens

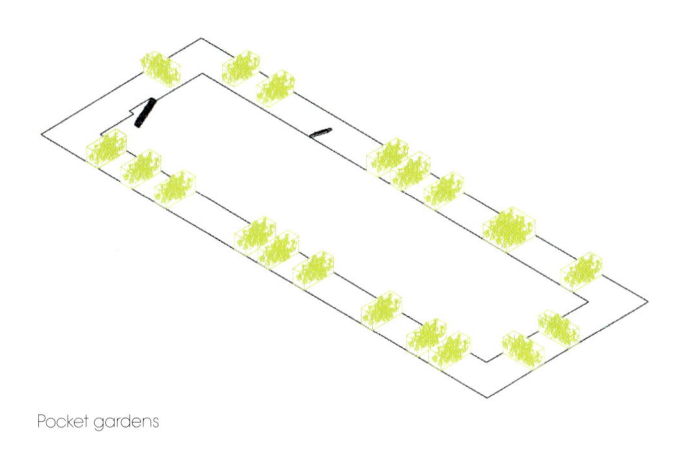

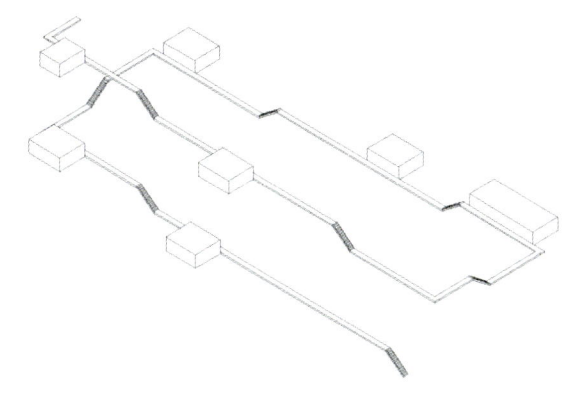

Spiral access balcony with shared plus-functions

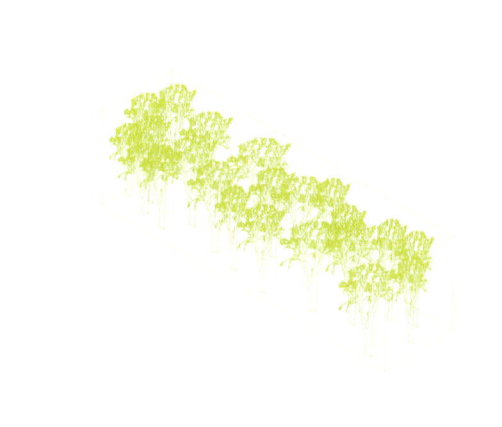

Shared garden

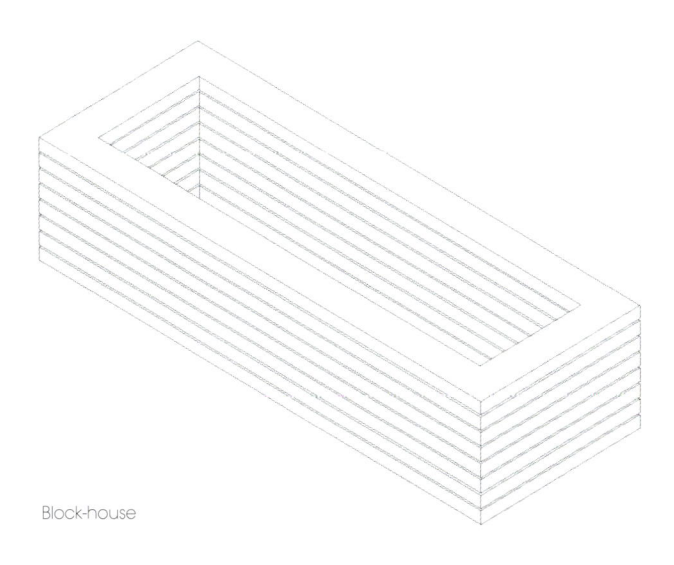

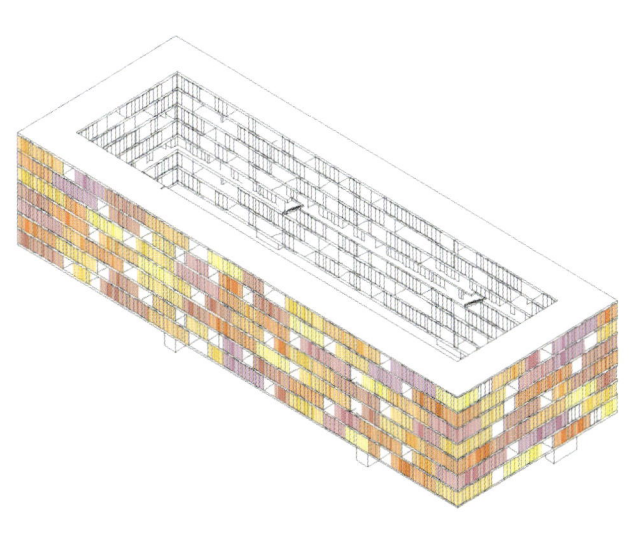

Block-house

Mixed use program

Mix of different dwellings

ARCHITECTURAL DIAGRAMS 537

ZAMBONINI HEAD-QUARTER IaN+

"ARCHITECTURE IS INTENDED BETWEEN AN IDEAL SPACE, THE LANDSCAPE, AND A REAL SPACE, SYMBOLIZED BY A TRADITIONAL COURTYARD BUILDING."

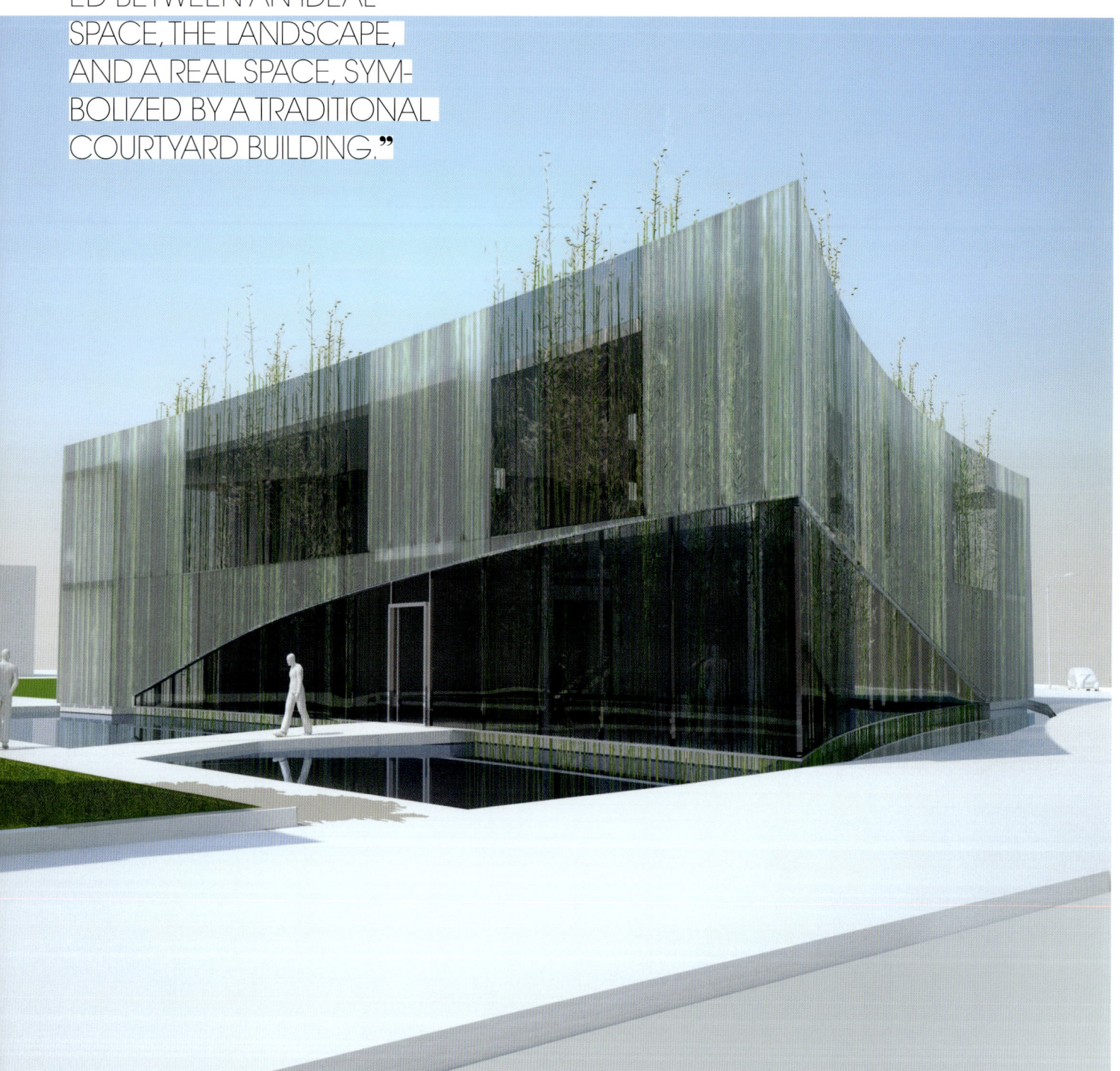

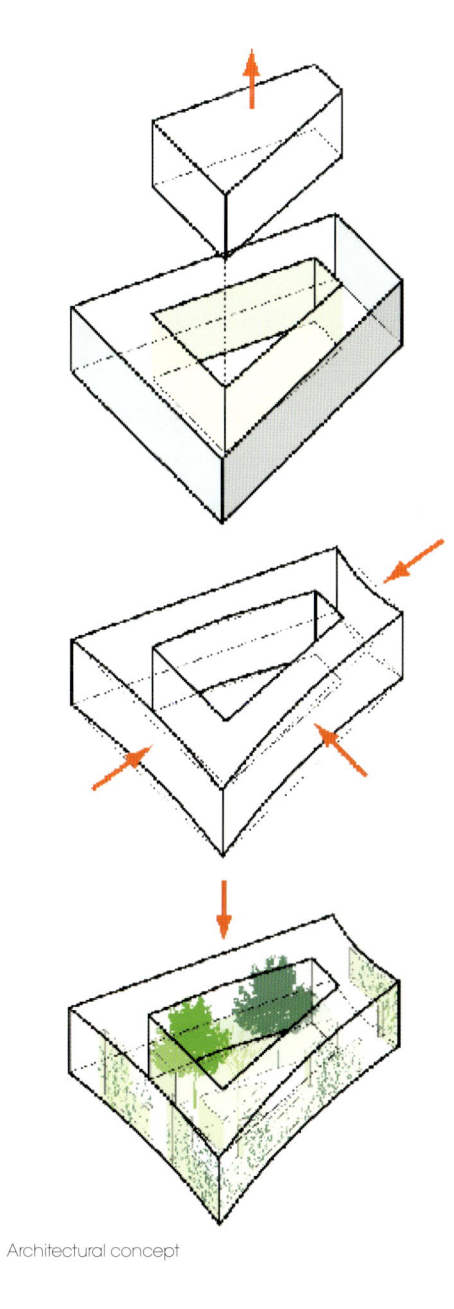

B
Services
Stairwells
Guest
Archive
Deposited

A
Hall
Representation
Offices
Meeting

1. main entrance
2. secondary input
3. pedestrian
4. distrivuzione internal
5. guest entry

A. offices
B. toilet building

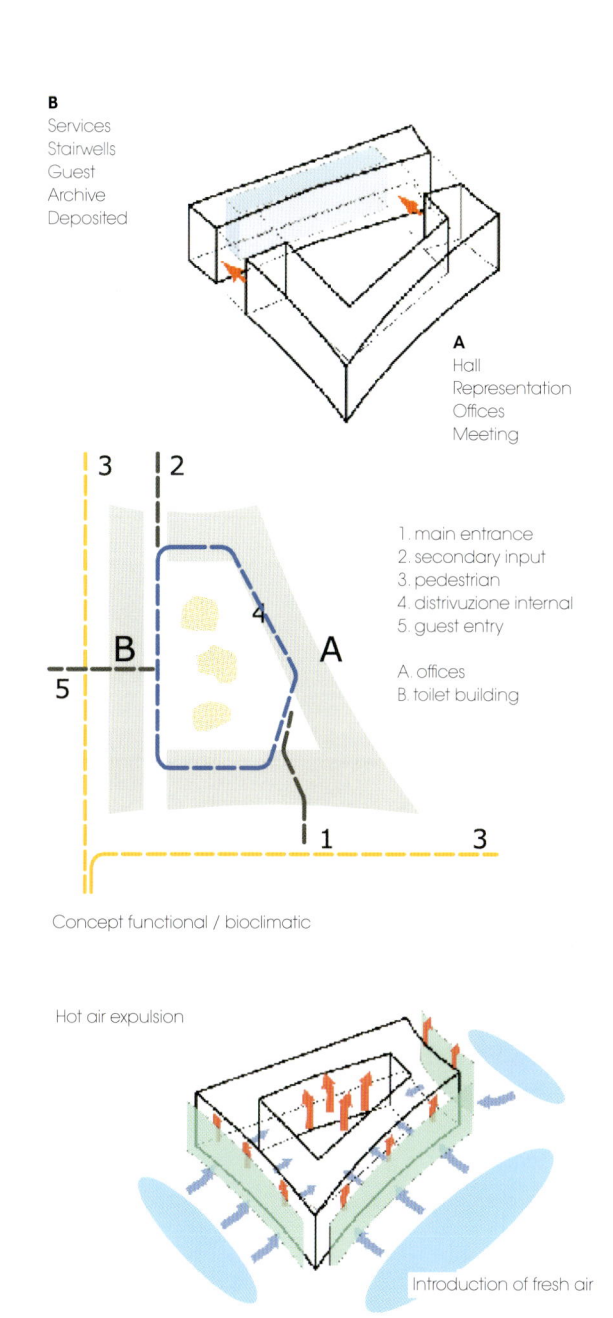

Concept functional / bioclimatic

Hot air expulsion

Introduction of fresh air

Architectural concept

ARCHITECTURAL DIAGRAMS 539

3 ACADEMIES LJUBLJANA
SADAR VUGA ARHITEKTI

"THE VERTICAL HALL IS THE POINT OF STIMULATED INTERACTION, GET-TOGETHER, AND MEETINGS BETWEEN STUDENTS, GUESTS AND VISITORS AT EVENTS."

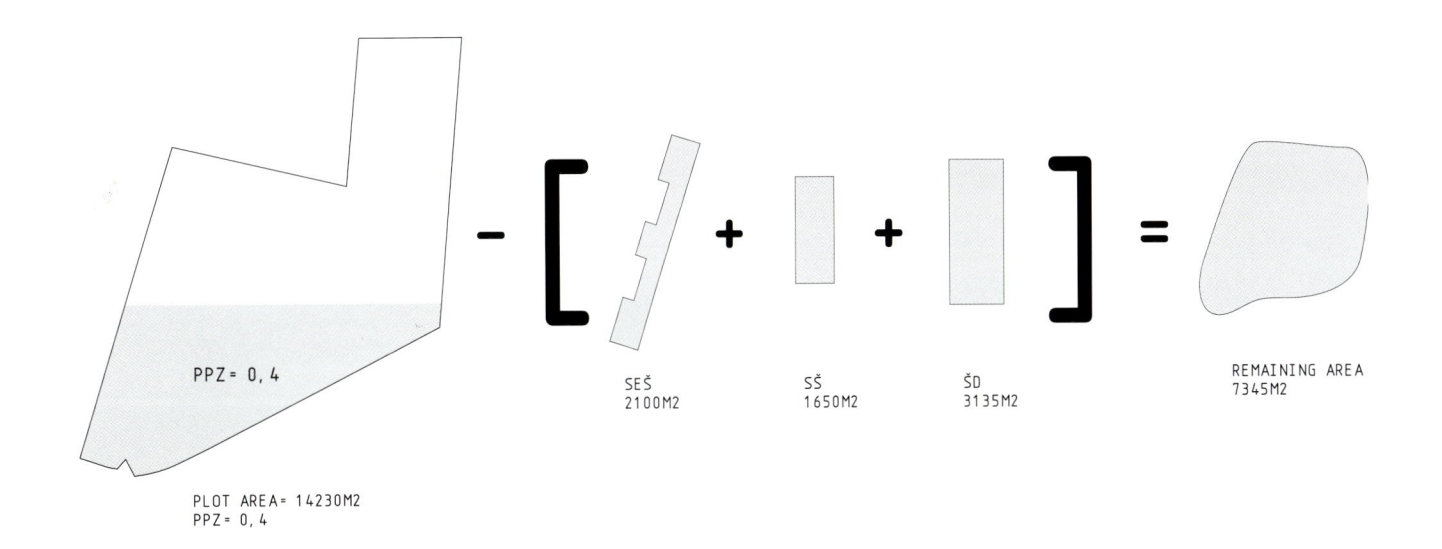

PLOT AREA= 14230M2
PPZ= 0,4

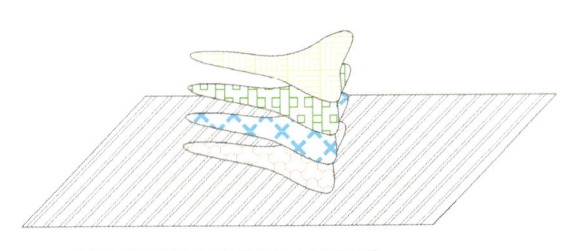

SEŠ
2100M2

SŠ
1650M2

ŠD
3135M2

REMAINING AREA
7345M2

5 horizontal slabs of same atmosphere on each level

Slab

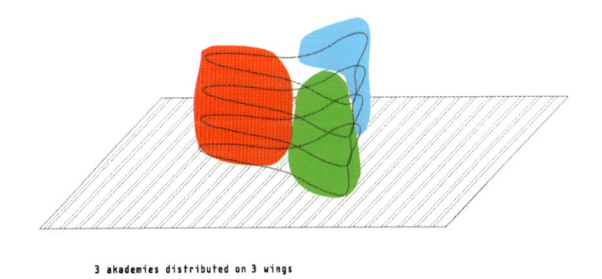

3 akademies distributed on 3 wings

Academies

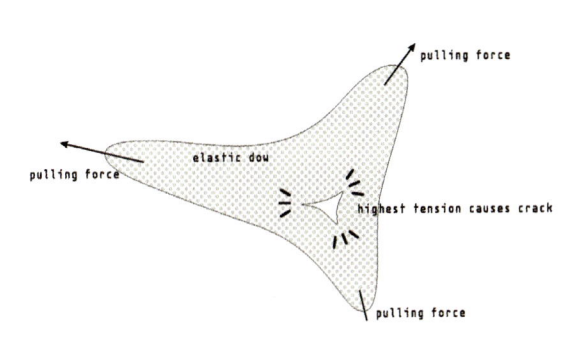

pulling force
elastic dou
pulling force
highest tension causes crack
pulling force

Forces

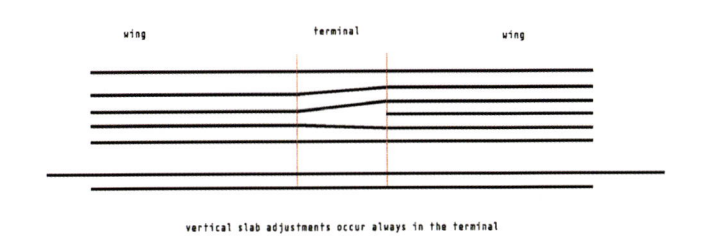

wing — terminal — wing

vertical slab adjustments occur always in the terminal

Adjustment

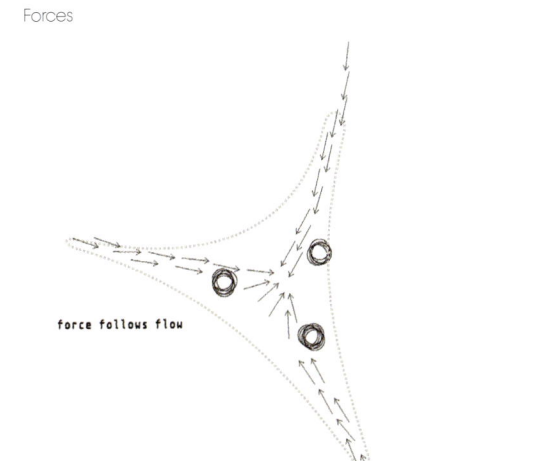

force follows flow

Flow

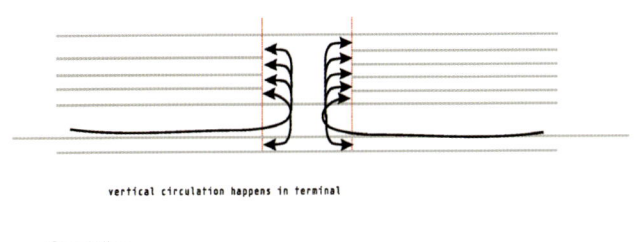

vertical circulation happens in terminal

Circulation

ARCHITECTURAL DIAGRAMS 541

3 EXTENDED HOUSES
nodo17 Architects

"HOW FAR CAN WE TRANS-FORM AN ICON WITHOUT IT LOSING ITS SHAPE."

■ Private
■ Communal

Planning

Maximum volume

Extension

Ground multiplication

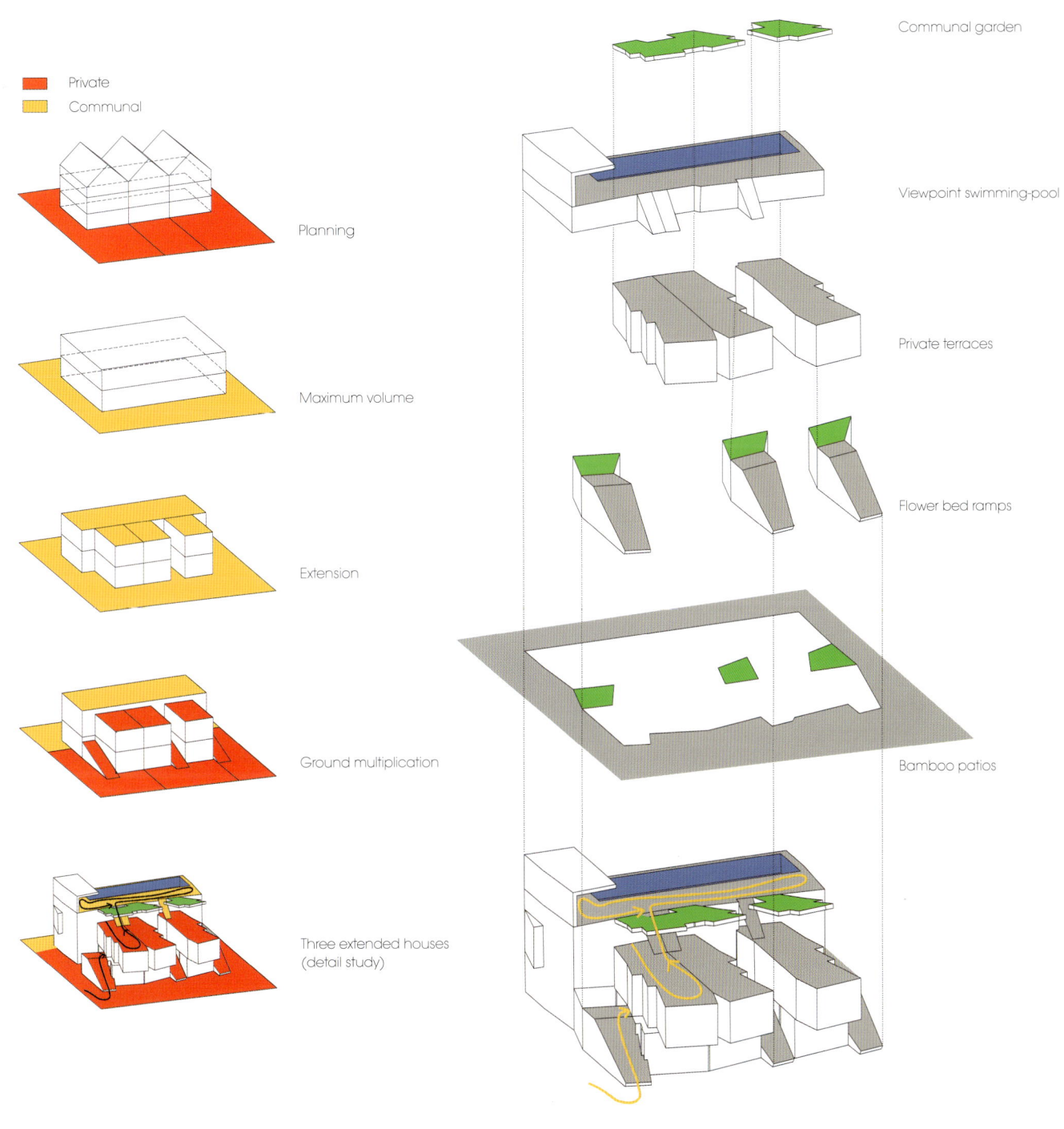

Three extended houses
(detail study)

Communal garden

Viewpoint swimming-pool

Private terraces

Flower bed ramps

Bamboo patios

Multiplication/ extension_ Ground plan

ARCHITECTURAL DIAGRAMS 543

360° HOTEL SPACEGROUP

"AIMS TO REPAIR RUPTURES, INITIATE/TRIGGER/ENCOURAGE NATURAL PROCESSES AND REVEAL REAL SITE QUALITIES."

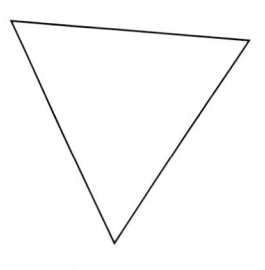

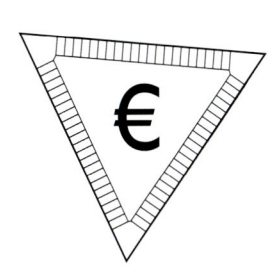

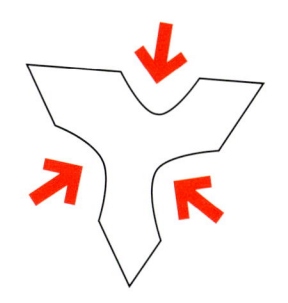

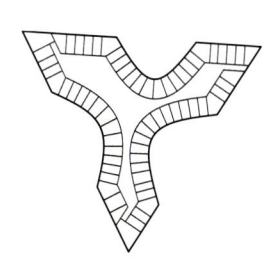

Hotel efficiency

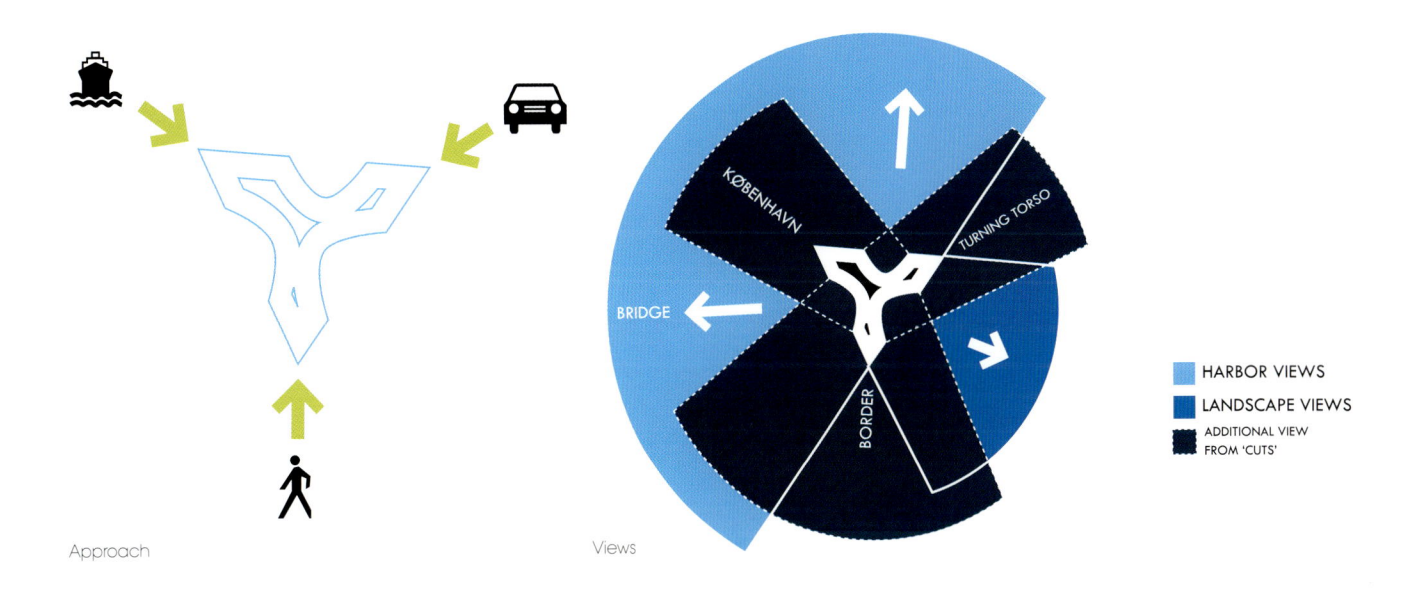

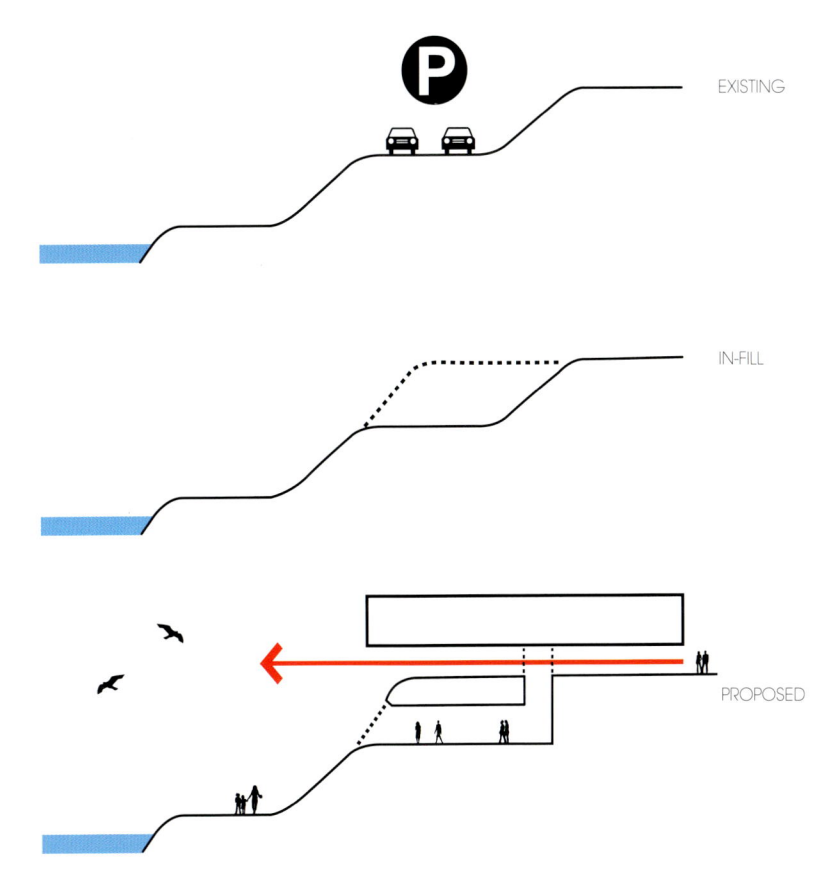

Approach

Views

HARBOR VIEWS
LANDSCAPE VIEWS
ADDITIONAL VIEW FROM 'CUTS'

KØBENHAVN
TURNING TORSO
BORDER
BRIDGE

EXISTING

IN-FILL

PROPOSED

ARCHITECTURAL DIAGRAMS 545

7-FINGERS Moonbalsso + DN

"THE WAVING AND LARGE CLOTH FLUTTERS ABOVE A MASS-PRODUCED HOUSING UNIT."

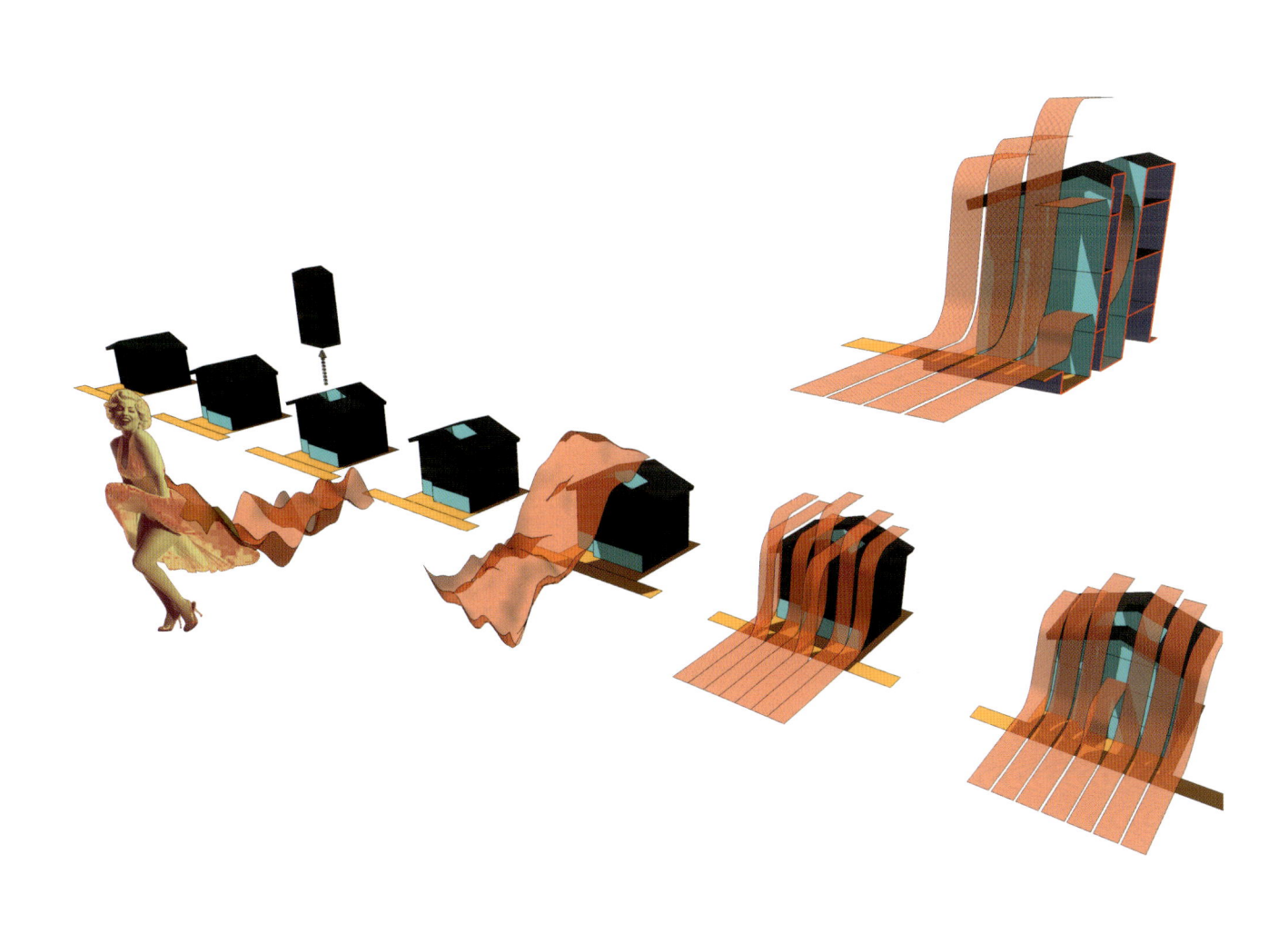

ARCHITECTURAL DIAGRAMS 547

INTERIOR DES|

ik weet niet precies hoe
mijn glansrijke toekomst
eruitziet ik weet eigenlijk
alleen maar dat hij gaat
kosten geld hebben om
de rekeningen te betalen
en de rekeningen
moeten door mij willen
worden voldaan verd
wil ik nu niet vergeet
maar ook niet niet
meeslepen te moei
aan te bagage ten
gaan de toek
glanst maar blijf b

panta rhei
alles stroomt
is steeds in
wording niets
staat vast

soms begrijp ik je niet
dan spreek je de taal
van de straat maar ik
hoor alleen maar weetje
weetje soms begrijp ik je
niet dan spreek je de taal
van de professor maar ik
hoor alleen ahum ahum
soms begrijp ik je niet dan
spreek je een taal die
niemand verstaat soms
begrijp ik je wel als kij in je ogen
kijk dan lees ik een boek

ALMIRA SADAR BOUTIQUE
SADAR VUGA ARHITEKTI

"IT IS DYNAMIC AND PRONOUNCEDLY PROTEAN."

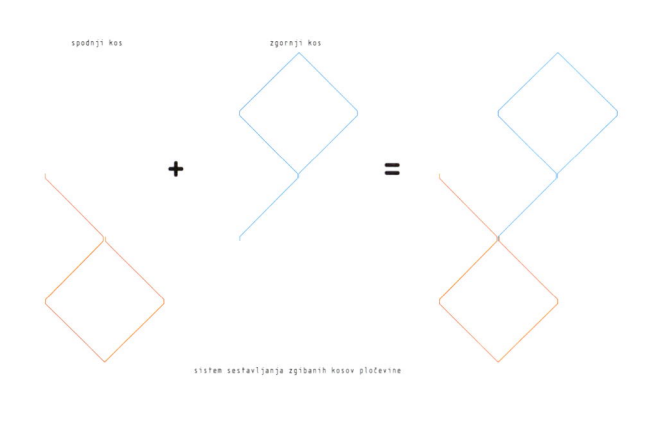

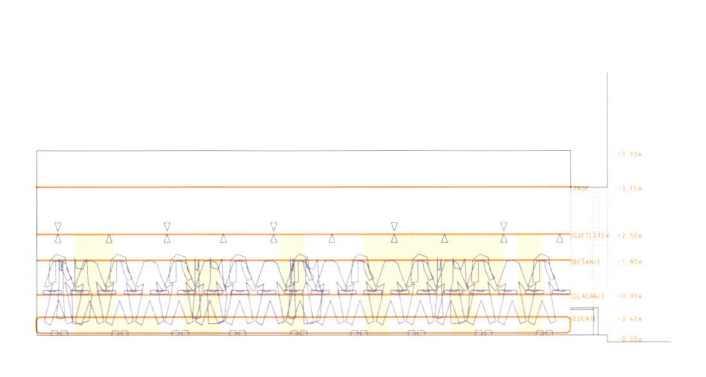

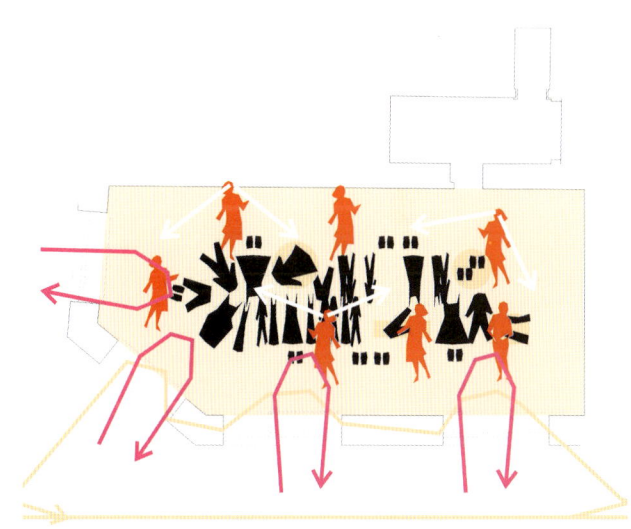

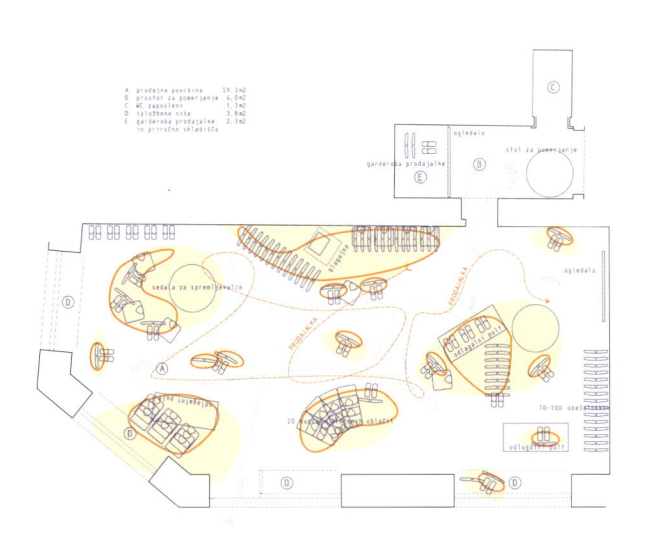

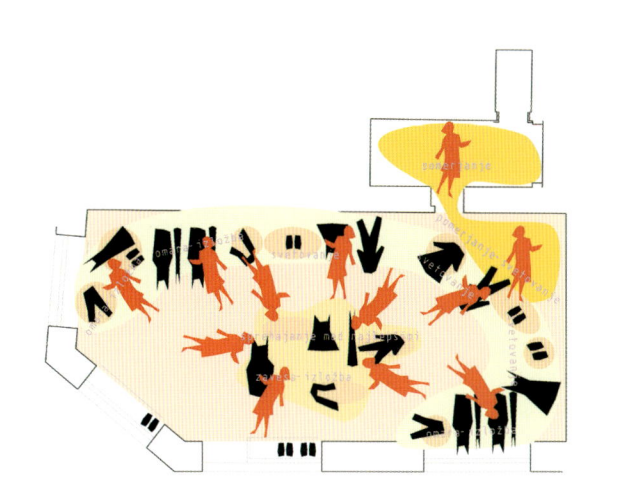

ARCHITECTURAL DIAGRAMS 551

AUTOMOTIVE SHOWROOM & LEISURE CENTRE
MANUELLE GAUTRAND ARCHITECTURE

"THE VOLUME IS CONCEIVED WITH THE CIRCLE AS A BEGIN, AND DEVELOPS ITSELF IN A VAST SCULPTURE OF CIRCLES AND SPHERES."

Module type

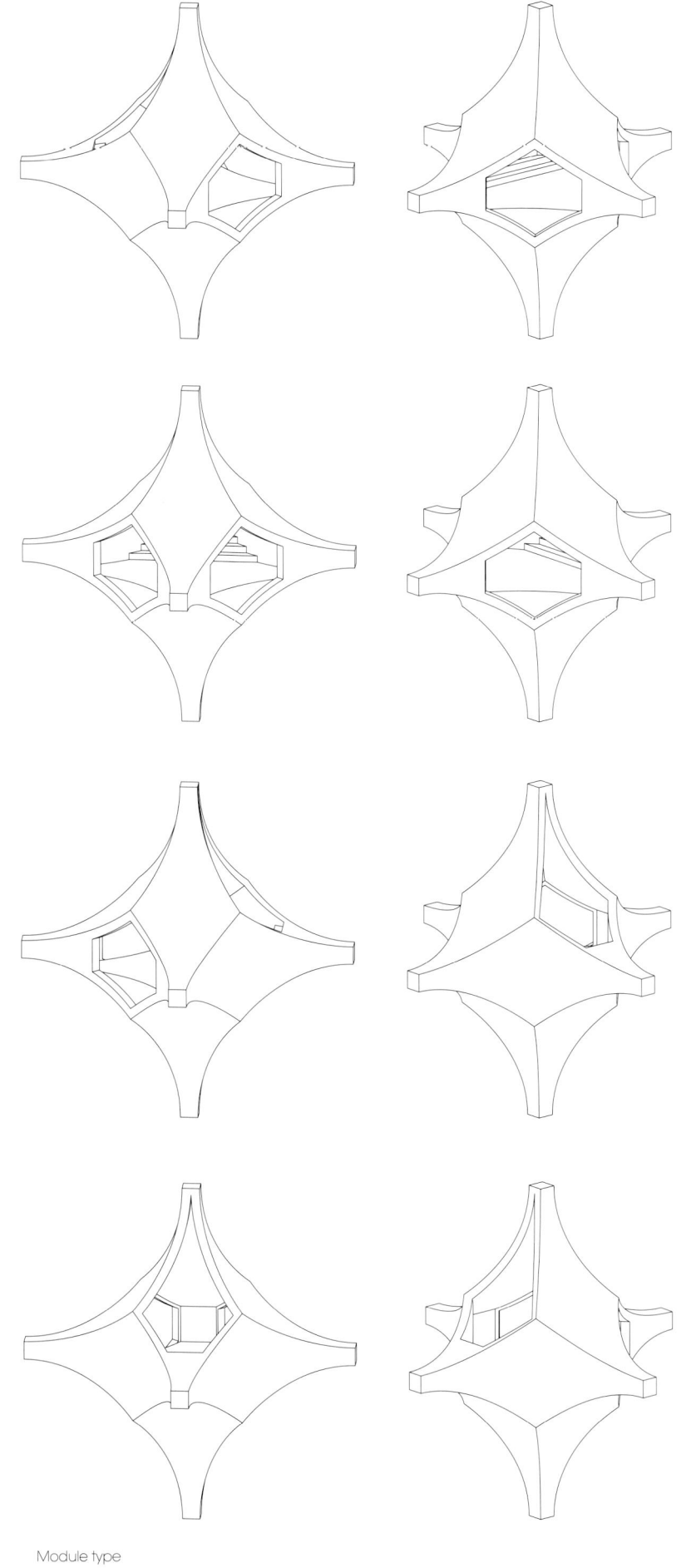

ARCHITECTURAL DIAGRAMS 553

BIG TEN BURRITO
PLY Architecture

"THE PATTERN AND SPACING FOR THE CEILING MAKE IT SIMULTANEOUSLY OPEN AND CLOSED DEPENDING ON THE PERSPECTIVE."

PACKED   INSTALLED

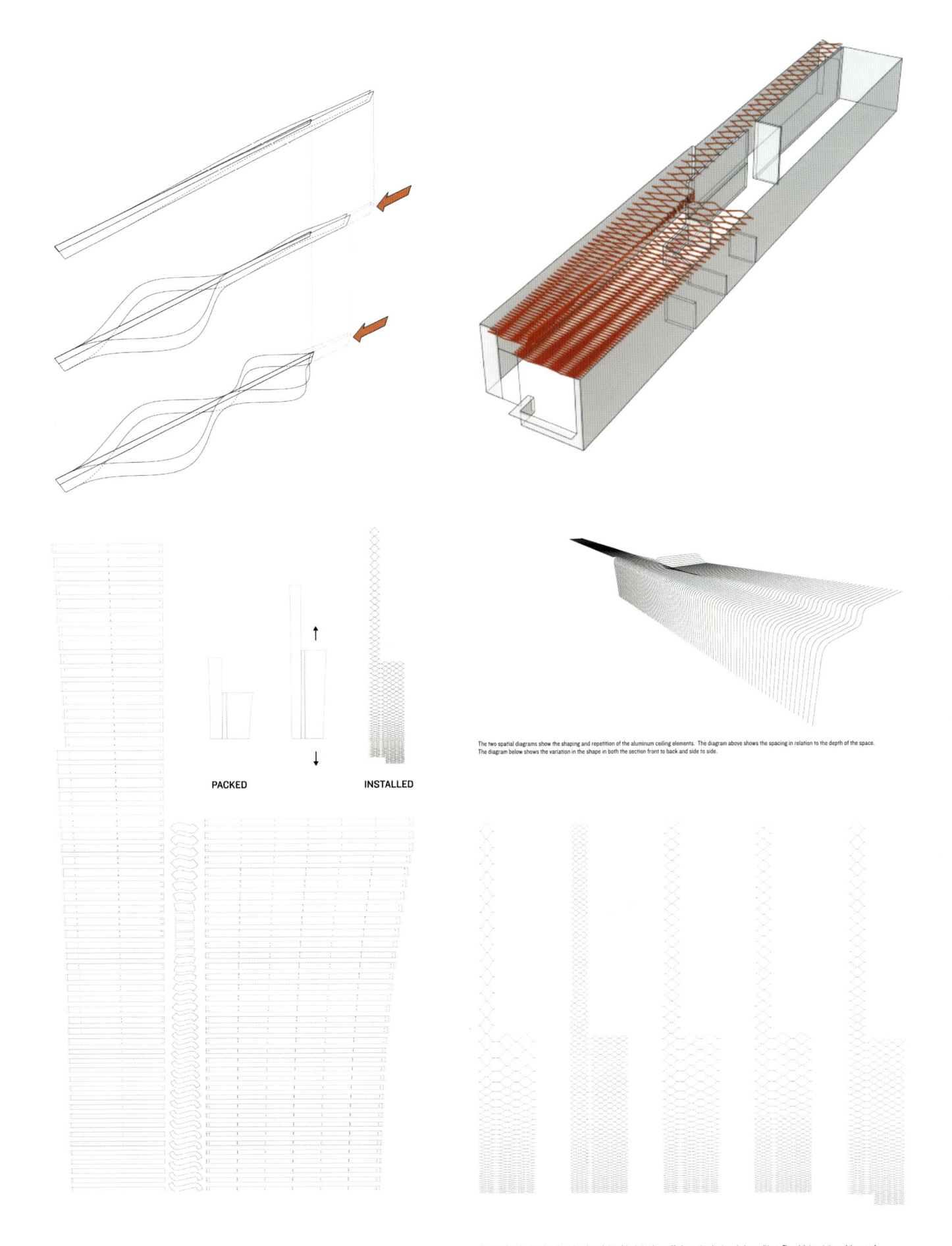

The two spatial diagrams show the shaping and repetition of the aluminum ceiling elements. The diagram above shows the spacing in relation to the depth of the space. The diagram below shows the variation in the shape in both the section front to back and side to side.

The five reflected ceiling plans above show the evolution of the design that modify the spacing, density and edge conditions. The subtly in variation and the ease of fabrication were critical issues for consideration during the design.

ARCHITECTURAL DIAGRAMS 555

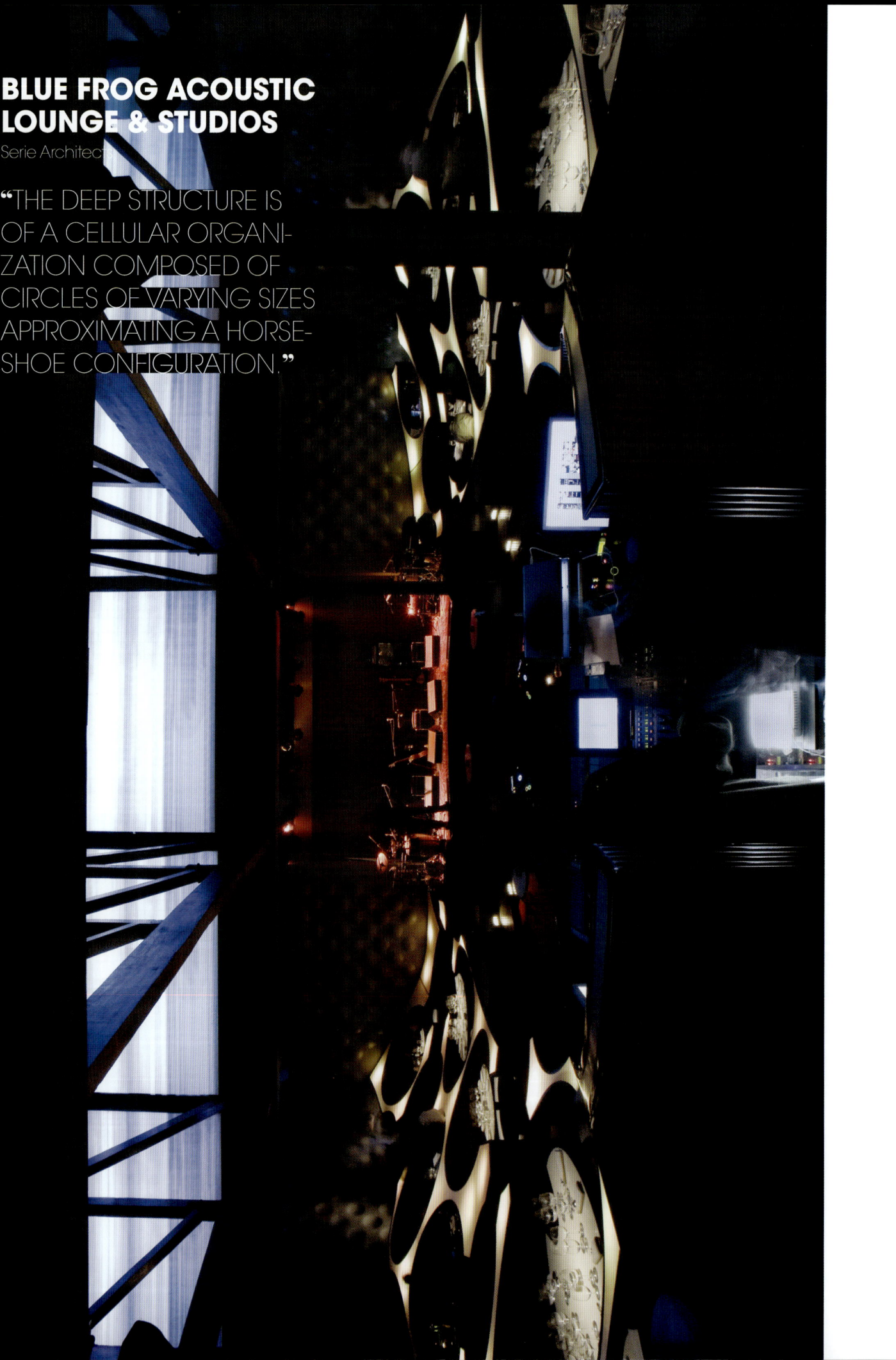

BLUE FROG ACOUSTIC LOUNGE & STUDIOS
Serie Architects

"THE DEEP STRUCTURE IS OF A CELLULAR ORGANIZATION COMPOSED OF CIRCLES OF VARYING SIZES APPROXIMATING A HORSESHOE CONFIGURATION."

Operahouse + Restaurant

Typological Change

Typological Transformation

Initial circular grid for modular seating

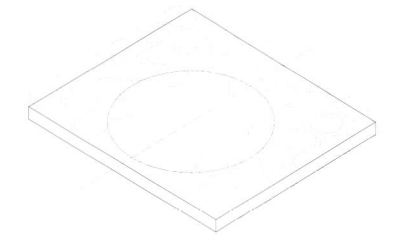

Insertion of epi-centre : dance area

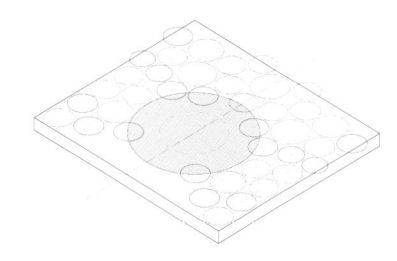

Modulation of circulr grid for optimal circulation

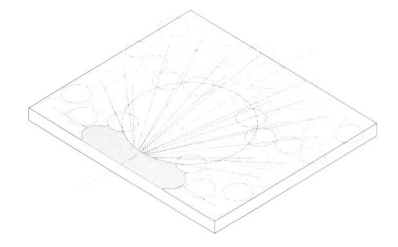

Imposition of sight lines from each pods towards the stage

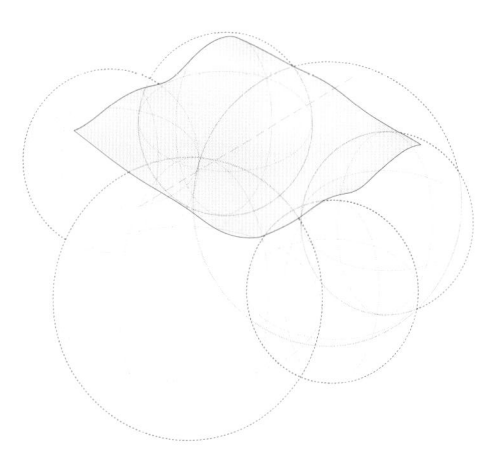

Optimization of sight lines by introducing a series of valleys and peaks

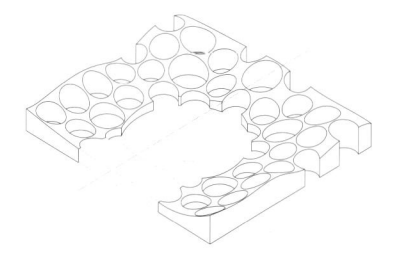

The final pod- seating adjusted to meet the valleys and peaks of the undulating surface

ARCHITECTURAL DIAGRAMS 557

BTB BURRITO PLY Architecture

"THE JOINT AND SURFACE ARE OF PARTICULAR INTEREST AS A MEANS OF SIMULTANEOUSLY ARTICULATING."

A
Typical pattern

B
Lights - compressed

C
Diffuser - stretched

Ceiling pattern strategy

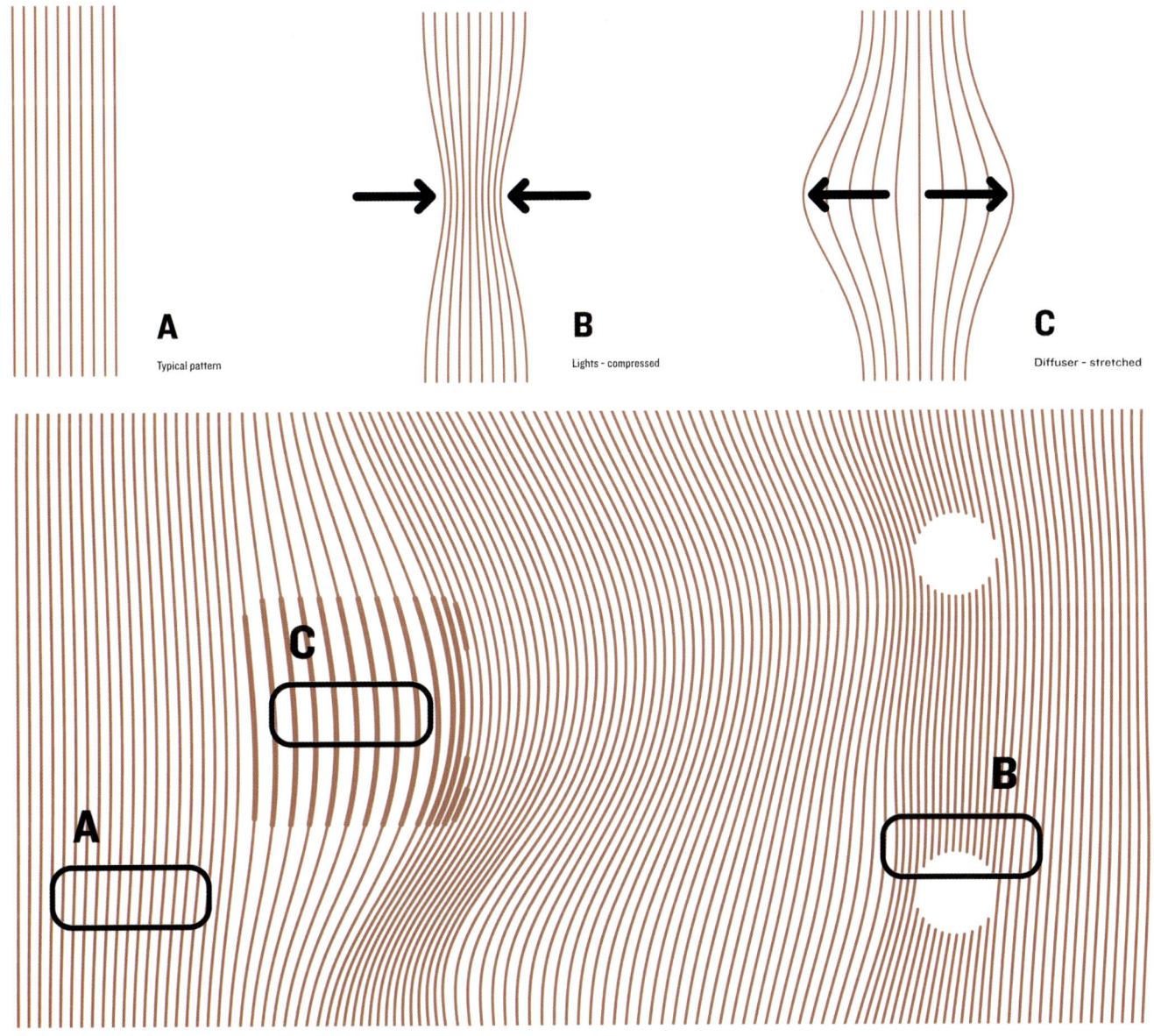

ARCHITECTURAL DIAGRAMS 559

CLINIC THE H jay is working.

"THE UNIQUE IDENTITY OF THE OUTCOME SEEMS TO LAST STRONGER THAN ANY OTHER WALL DISPLAYS."

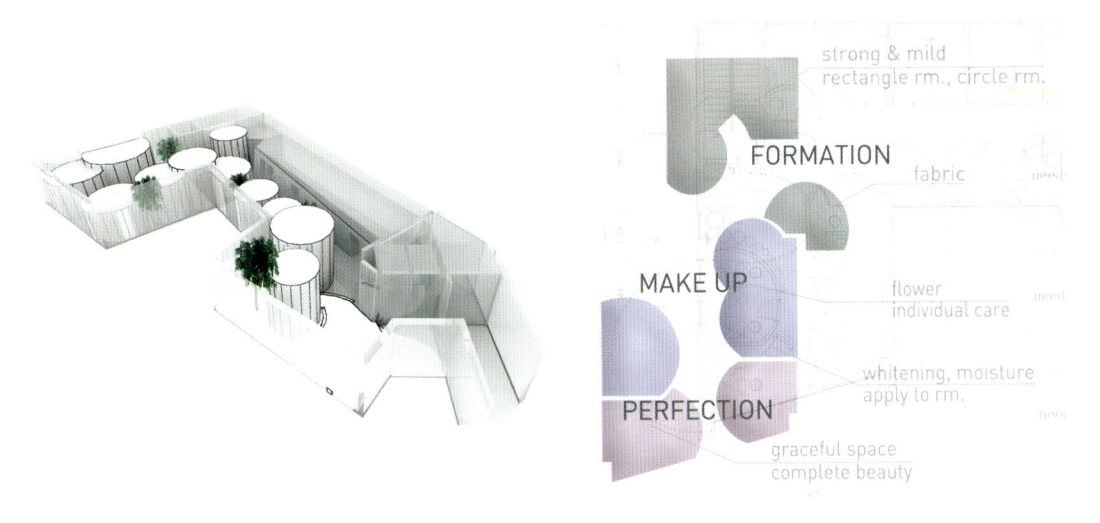

strong & mild
rectangle rm., circle rm.

FORMATION

fabric

MAKE UP

flower
individual care

whitening, moisture
apply to rm.

PERFECTION

graceful space
complete beauty

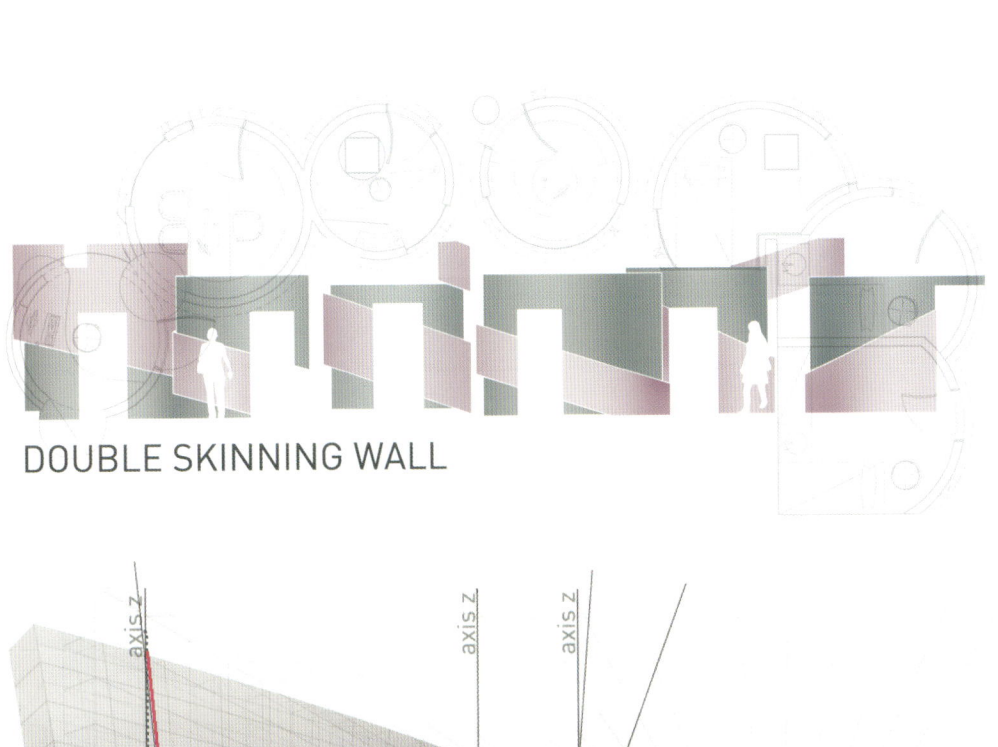

DOUBLE SKINNING WALL

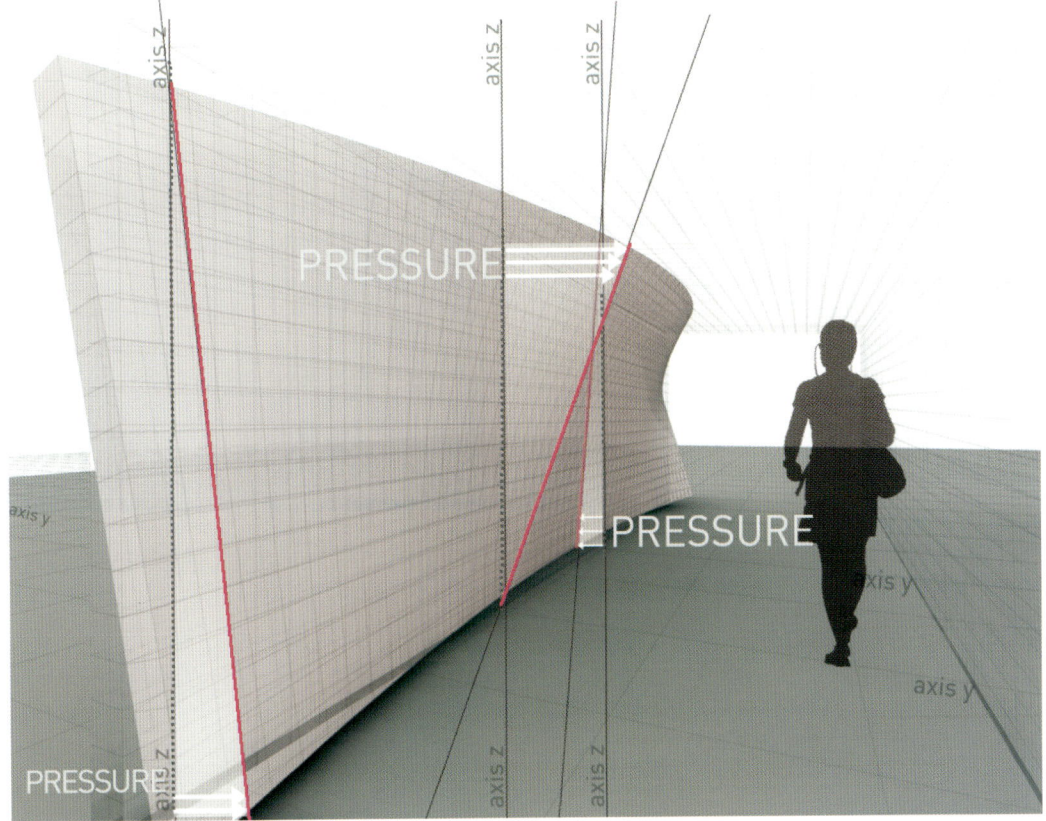

PRESSURE

PRESSURE

PRESSURE

ARCHITECTURAL DIAGRAMS 561

CLOUD BOX servo

"THE RELATIONSHIP IS BLURRED AND INTENSIFIED THROUGH THE GUISE OF DISPLAY SYSTEMS WHERE DIFFERENT DIAGONAL SYSTEMS ARE EMBEDDED WITHIN THE GRID GENERATING OBLIQUE PATTERNS."

Photograph of servo's solo exhibition at the Storefront for Art and Architecture in New York in 2000, featuring the projects Cloud Box, Nurbia, and Speetoy.

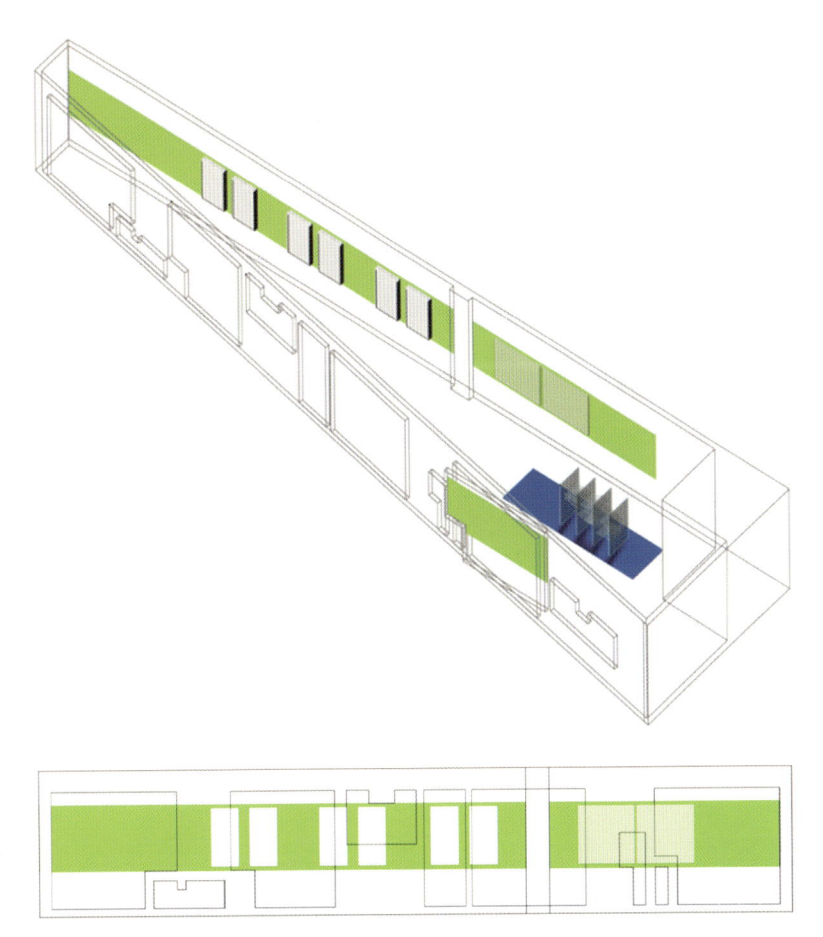

Installation design for servo's solo exhibition at the Storefront for Art and Architecture in New York in 2000, featuring the projects Cloud Box, Cloud Bar, Nurbia, and Speetoy.

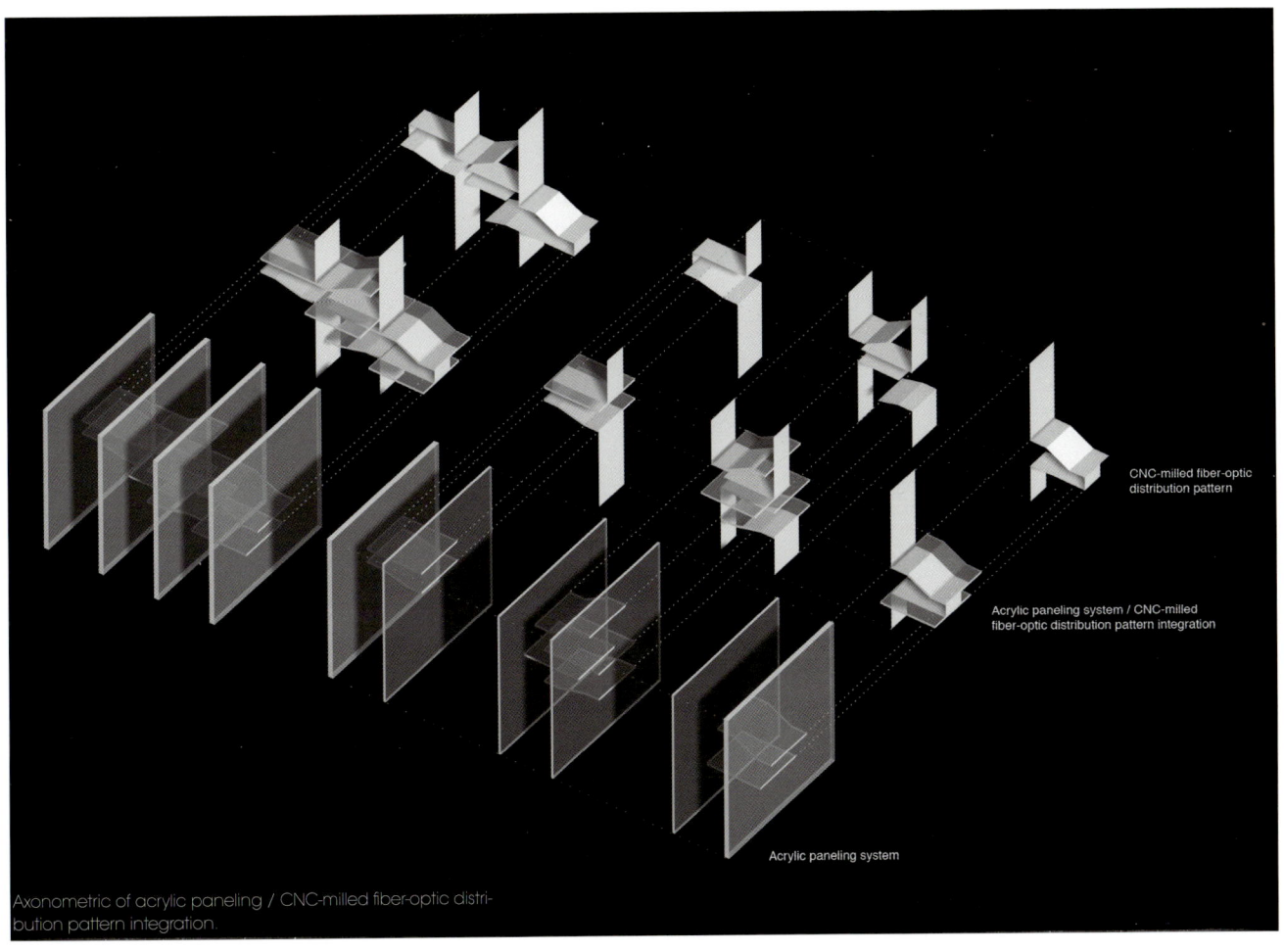

CNC-milled fiber-optic distribution pattern

Acrylic paneling system / CNC-milled fiber-optic distribution pattern integration

Acrylic paneling system

Axonometric of acrylic paneling / CNC-milled fiber-optic distribution pattern integration.

ARCHITECTURAL DIAGRAMS 563

CREATIVE HUB OF EURO RSCG

Atelier Philéas (member of PLAN01)

"IT LIVES IN SYMBIOSIS WITH THE TEAM WHO SPENDS A LOT OF TIME INSIDE, IN A FRAMEWORK ALWAYS IN MOVEMENT."

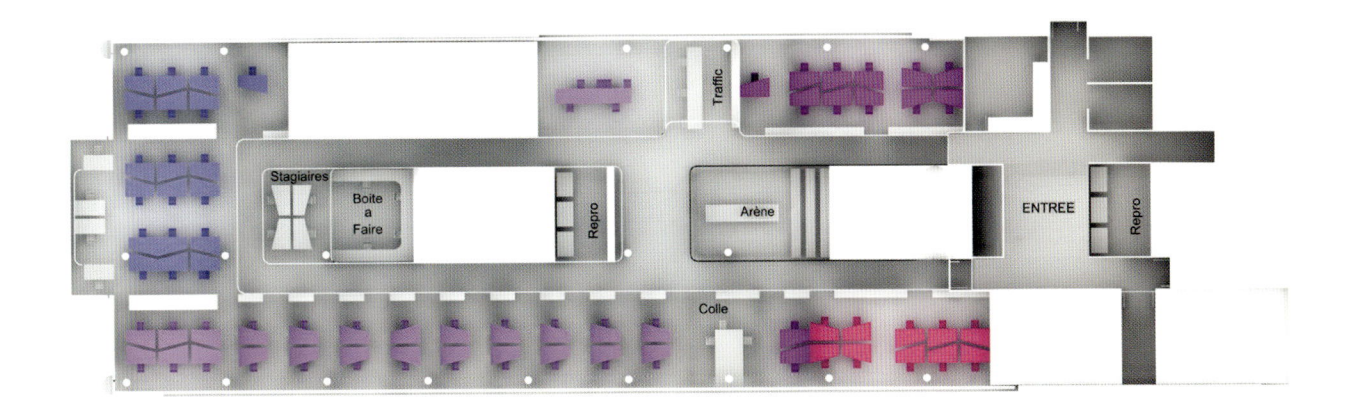

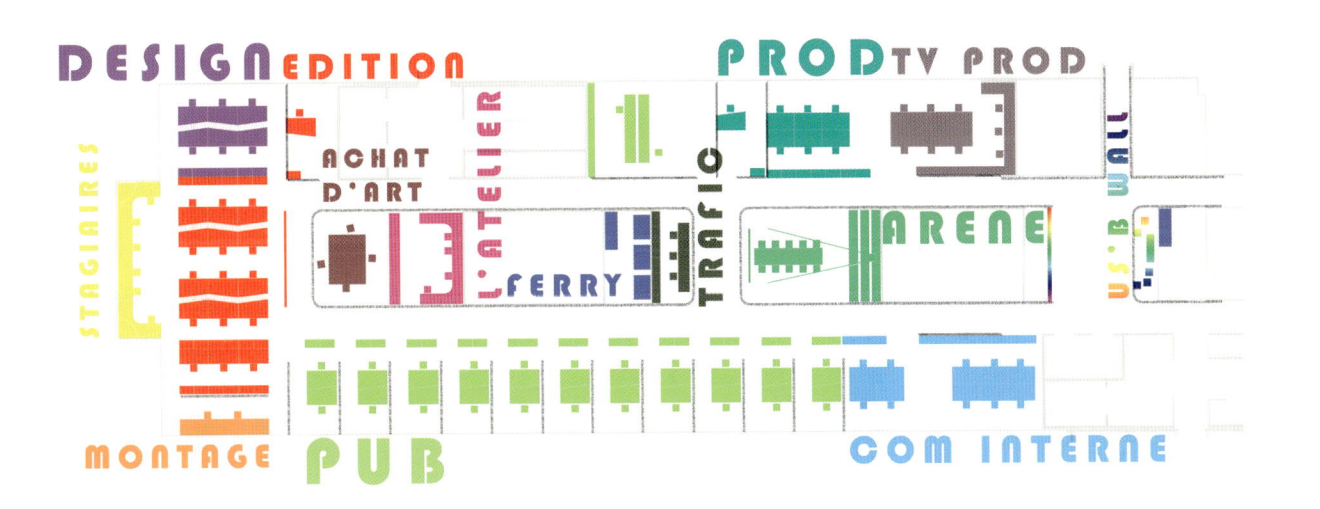

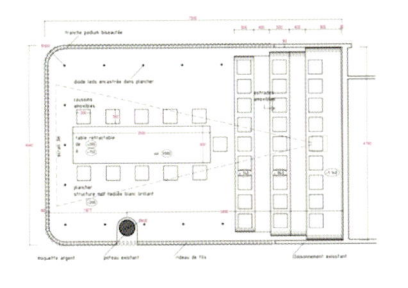

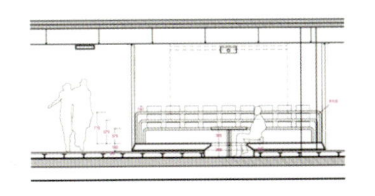

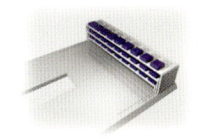

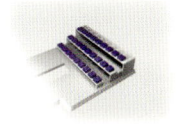

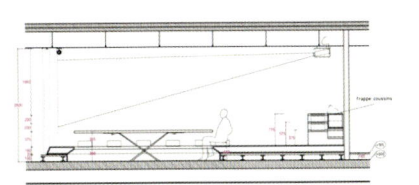

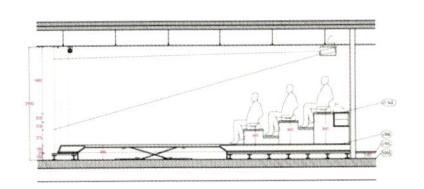

ARCHITECTURAL DIAGRAMS 565

DANBO FUN
MoHen Design International

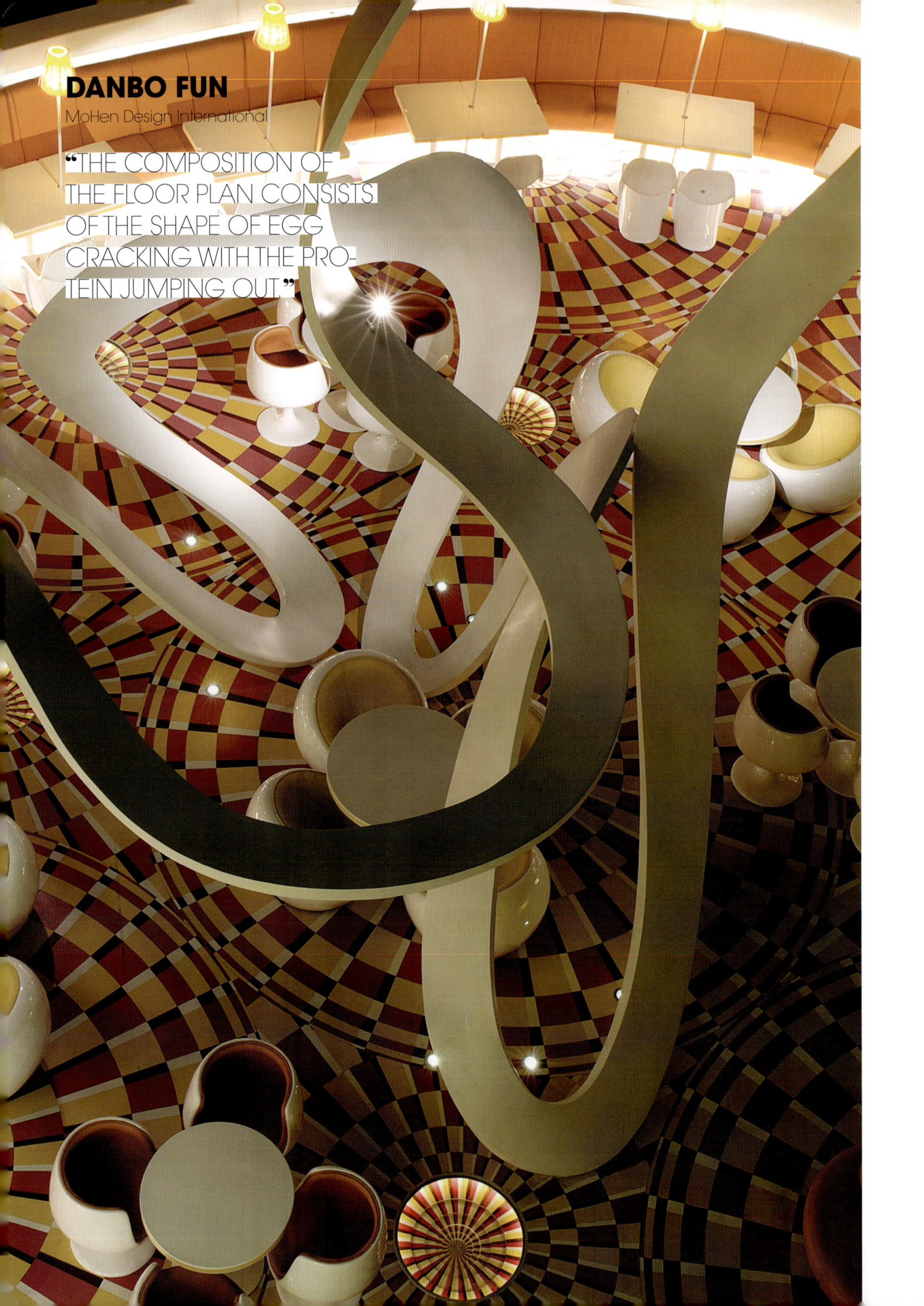

"THE COMPOSITION OF THE FLOOR PLAN CONSISTS OF THE SHAPE OF EGG CRACKING WITH THE PROTEIN JUMPING OUT."

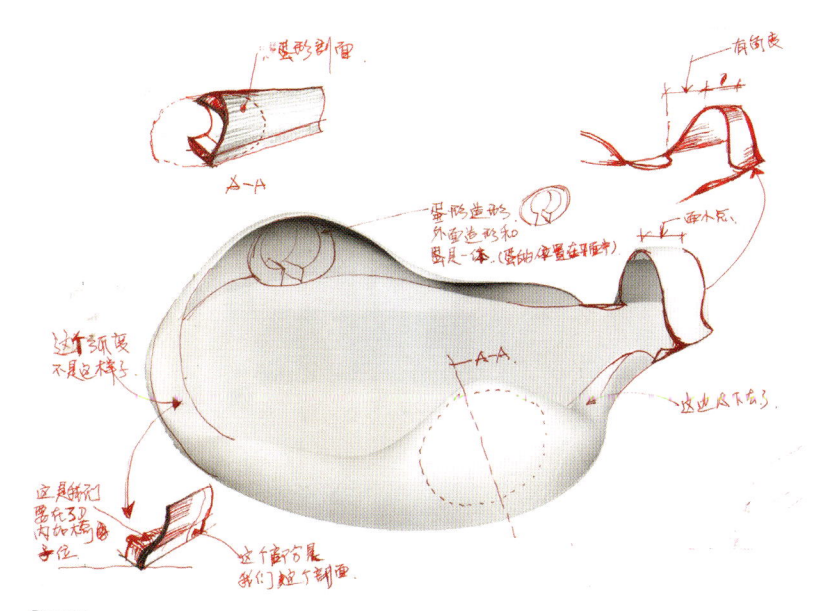

Process

Floor pattern

ARCHITECTURAL DIAGRAMS 567

DIGITAL ORIGAMI LAVA

"DIGITAL ORIGAMI USES RECYCLED AND RECYCLABLE CARDBOARD MOLECULES IN TWO DIFFERENT SHAPES."

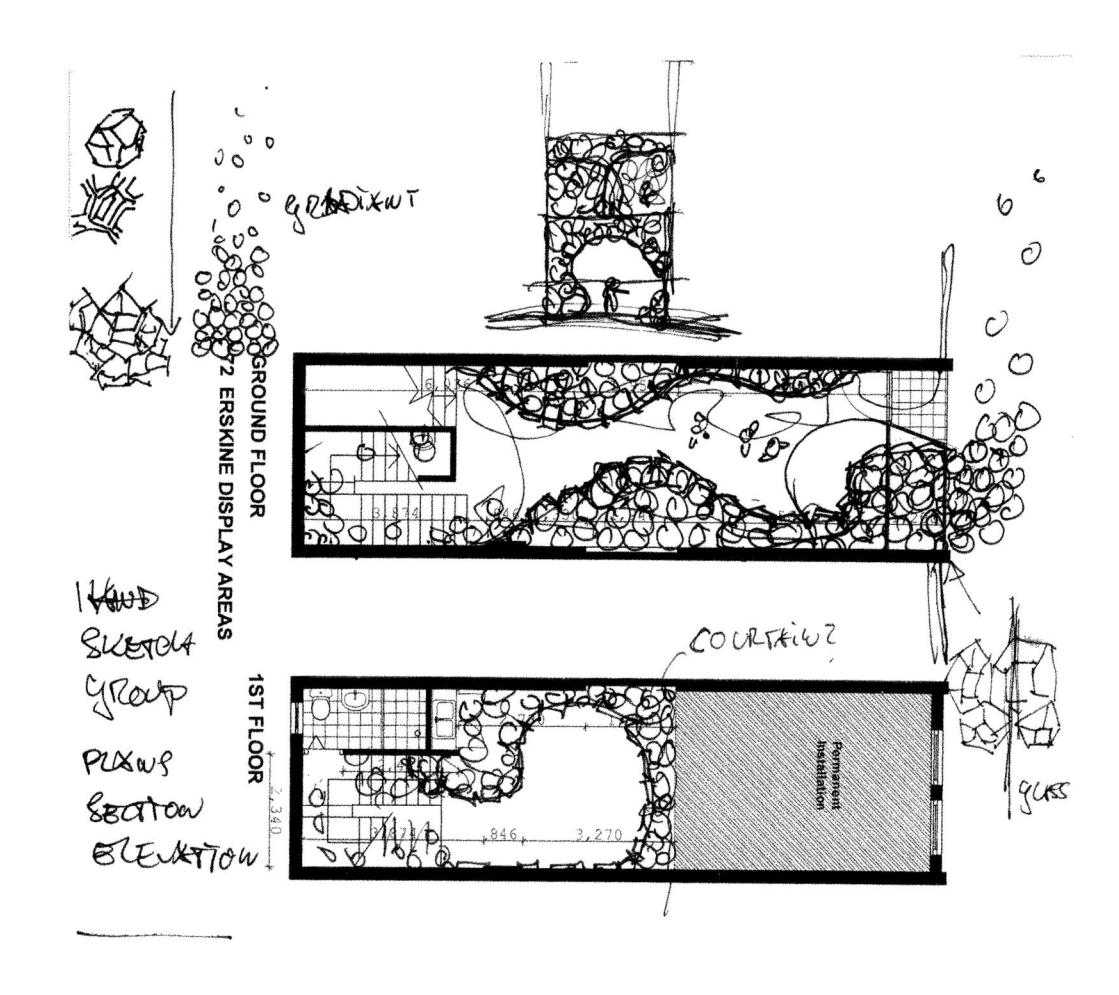

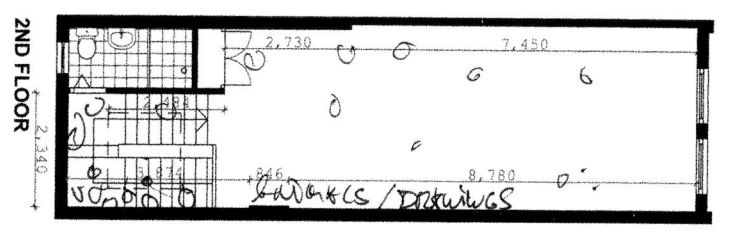

GROUND FLOOR
22 ERSKINE DISPLAY AREAS
1ST FLOOR
2ND FLOOR

GRADIENT

COURTAIN?

GLASS

HAND
SKETCH
GROUP

PLANS
SECTION
ELEVATION

Permanent installation

BOOKS/DRAWINGS

ARCHITECTURAL DIAGRAMS 569

DOUBLE JEOPARDY
PEG office of landscape + architecture

"THE CHALLENGE OF THE SURFACE DIAGRAM WAS TO ARRIVE AT A SYSTEM THAT COULD BE A DERIVATION OF THIS LANGUAGE."

20 LEVELS OF PATTERN OBJECTS TRANSITIONING FROM + to O

Rather than modulate light though depth (3-D subtractive) as the existing sunshades do, we chose to modulate the artificial light through shape (2-D). We devised a **non-uniform pattern** to regulate the geometry. The effect is an indeterminate pattern defined by the strict control between a point and a line. The plywood, mdf and linoleum is milled through and plugged with translucent, laser-cut acrylic, thus creating a flat surface. The pattern then continues as a 3-D additive where the acrylic takes the form of a button for tufting the felt cushions.

Green ceramic paint on mdf

Brown linoleum on mdf

Orange ceramic paint on mdf

Ebony stained birch plywood

Subtraction (existing) → Stitch (new)

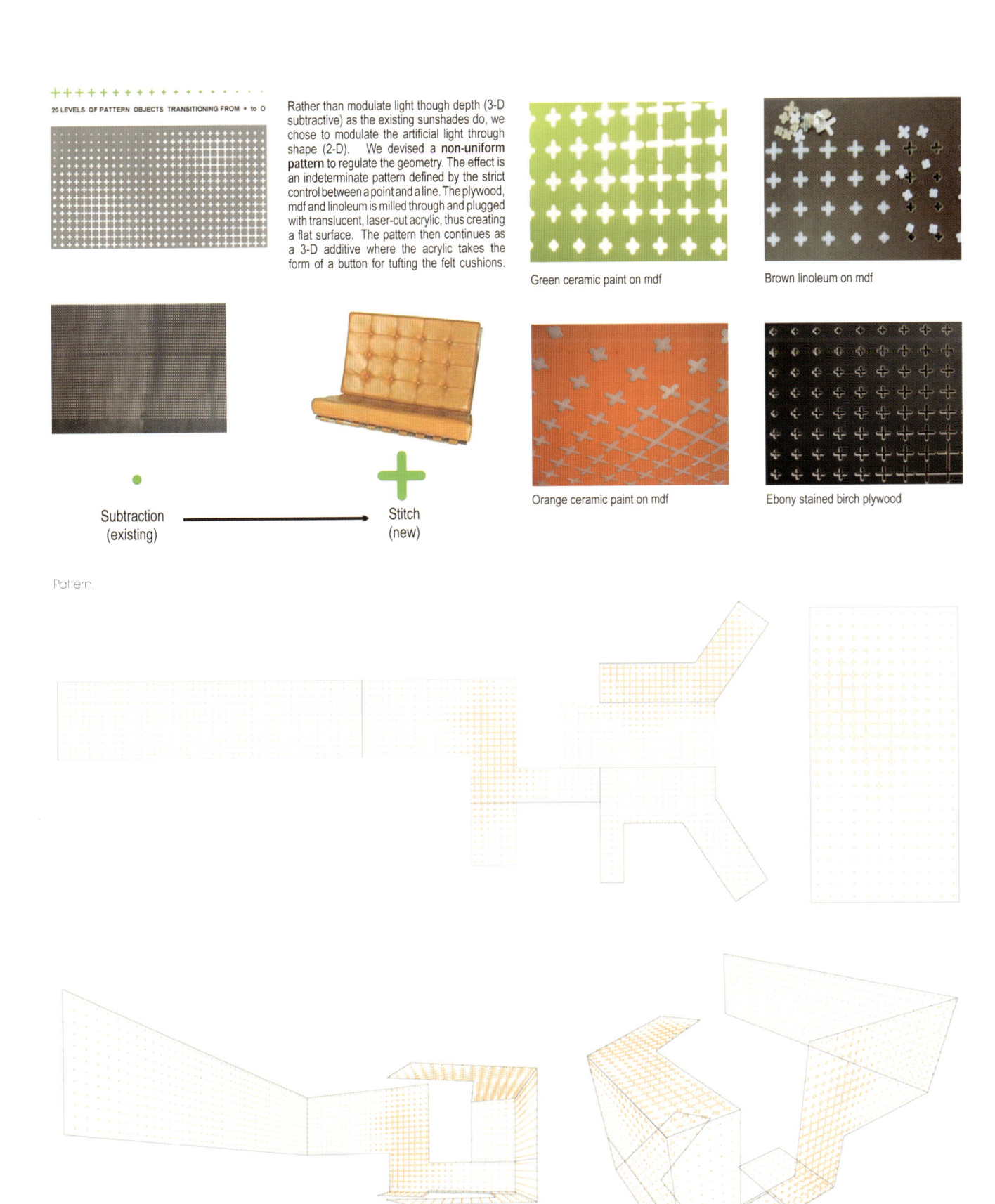

Pattern

Dynamic pattern diagram

ARCHITECTURAL DIAGRAMS 571

EXHIBITION DESIGN OF FISH STILL LIVES
Studio Ramin Visch

"THE SPACES AND WALLS FORMED EXCELLENT SUPPLEMENTARY FRAMES, IN A DYNAMIC BUT FLUID RELATION THAT ALLOWED THE PAINTINGS AND OBJECTS TO SPEAK FOR THEMSELVES."

KLEUREN

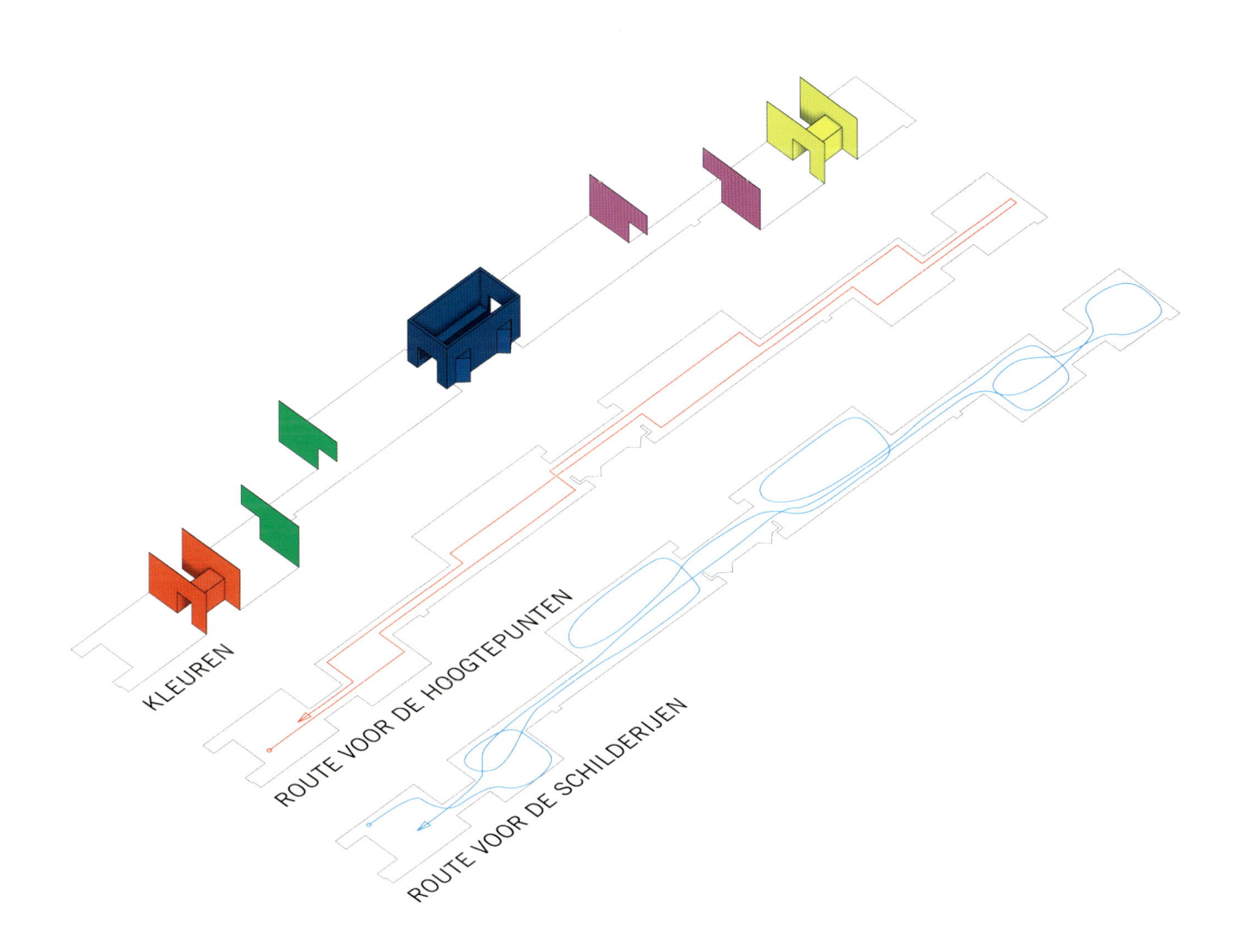

ROUTE VOOR DE HOOGTEPUNTEN

ROUTE VOOR DE SCHILDERIJEN

ARCHITECTURAL DIAGRAMS 573

EYE OF SQUARE
Kim Kai-chun

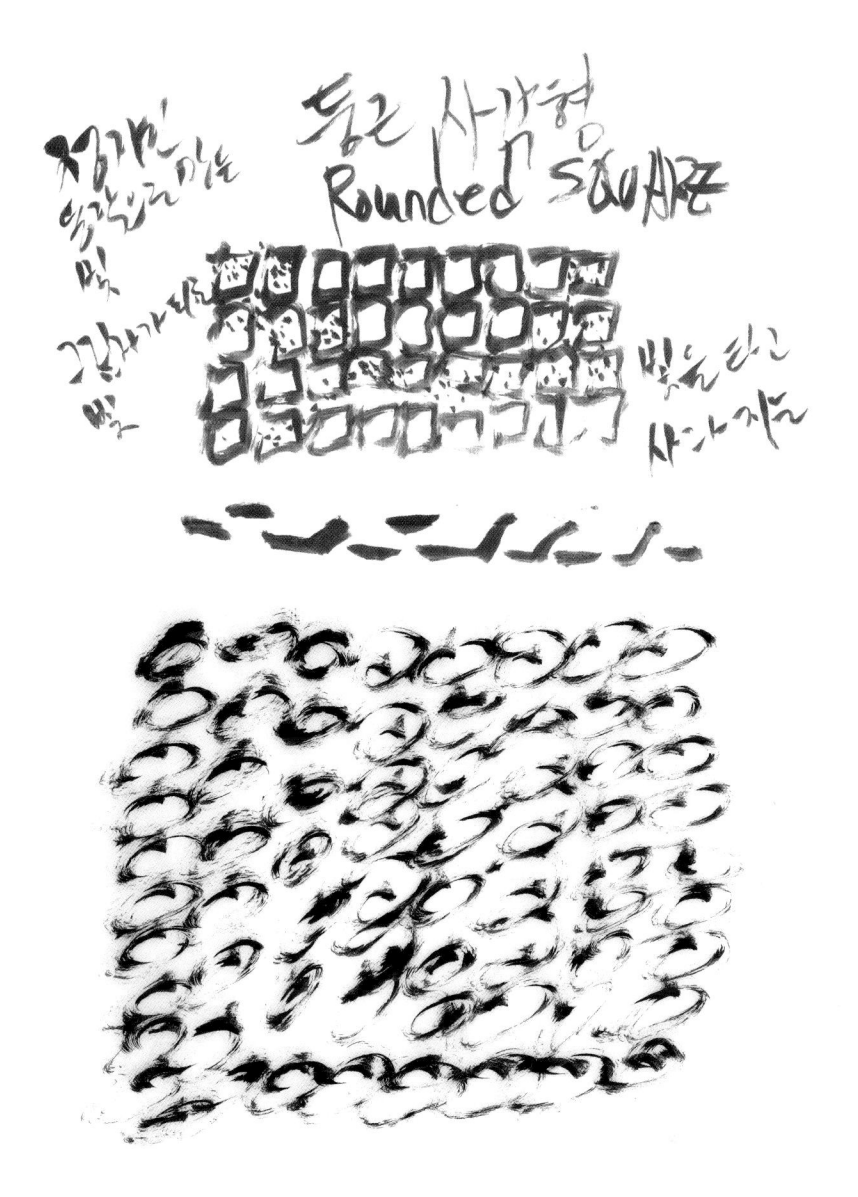

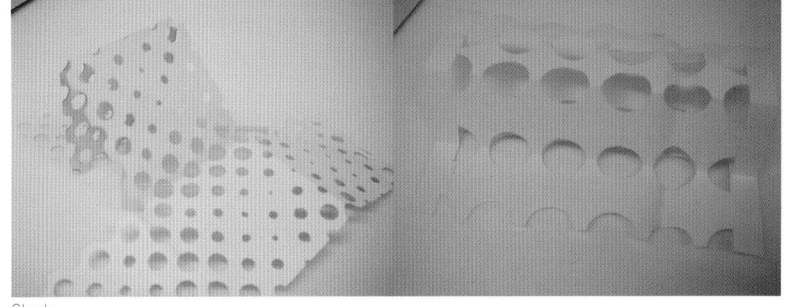

Study

HOTEL CASINO PARK
SADAR VUGA ARHITEKTI

"THE GUEST WILL PASS FROM THE NATURAL GARDENS OF SPACE AND THE ATMOSPHERE IN THE CASINO."

ARCHITECTURAL DIAGRAMS

HOUSEWARMING MY-HOME
J. MAYER H. ARCHITECTS

"BUILT IN HOT WIRES ARE PROGRAMMED TO TURN ON AND OFF, CREATING TEMPORARY ORNAMENTAL CLUSTERS OF PARALLEL WHITE LINES."

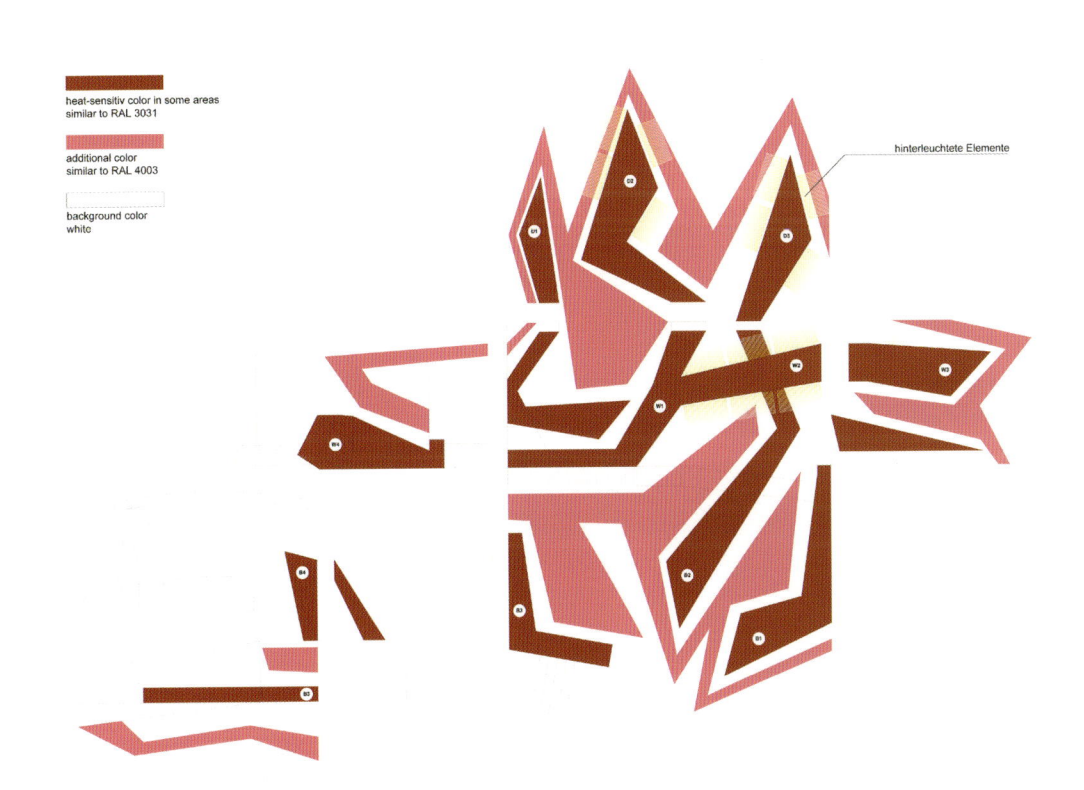

heat-sensitiv color in some areas
similar to RAL 3031

additional color
similar to RAL 4003

background color
white

hinterleuchtete Elemente

ARCHITECTURAL DIAGRAMS 579

INTERPOLIS NL Architects

"THE CENTRAL IDEA IS THAT EMPLOYEES NO LONGER NEED A FIXED WORK-SPACE."

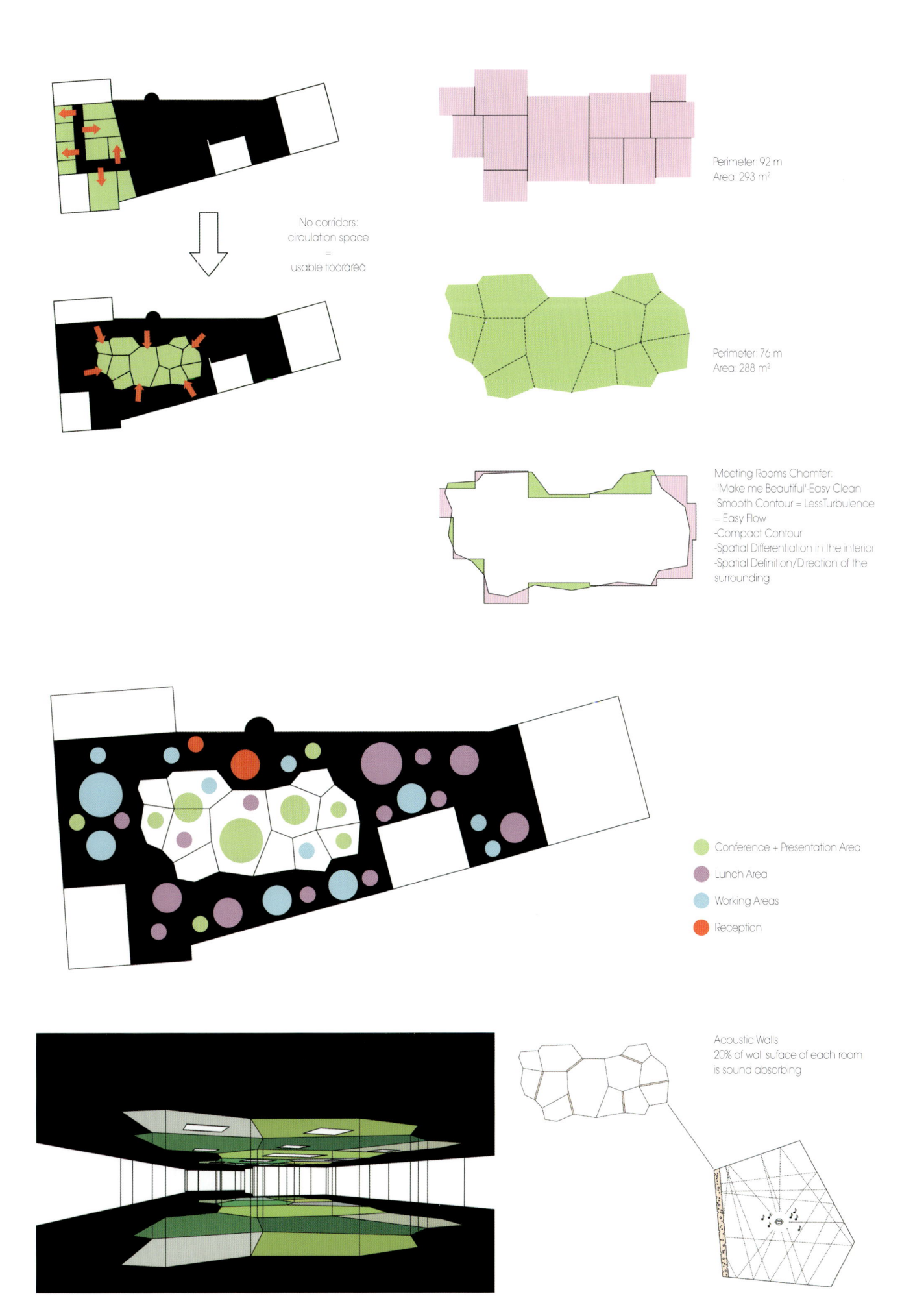

No corridors:
circulation space
=
usable floor area

Perimeter: 92 m
Area: 293 m²

Perimeter: 76 m
Area: 288 m²

Meeting Rooms Chamfer:
-'Make me Beautiful'-Easy Clean
-Smooth Contour = LessTurbulence
= Easy Flow
-Compact Contour
-Spatial Differentiation in the interior
-Spatial Definition/Direction of the surrounding

- Conference + Presentation Area
- Lunch Area
- Working Areas
- Reception

Acoustic Walls
20% of wall surface of each room is sound absorbing

ARCHITECTURAL DIAGRAMS 581

INTRA STUDIO
SADAR VUGA ARHITEKTI

"THE CASES ARE MOVABLE AND ADAPT TO THE ACTIVITIES AND OCCASIONAL EVENTS AT THE SALON."

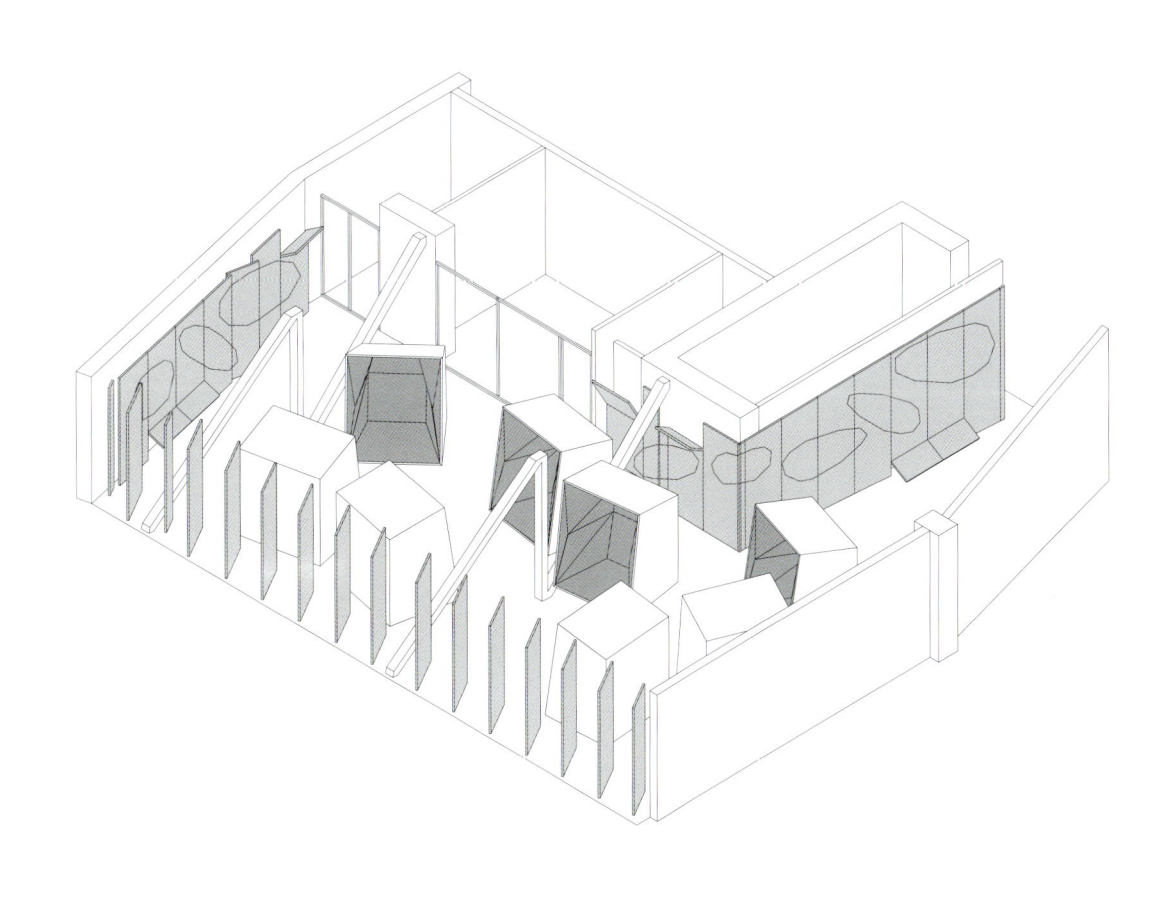

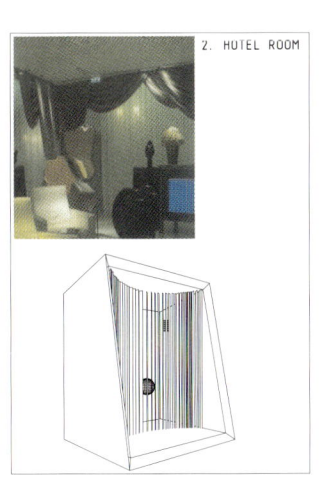

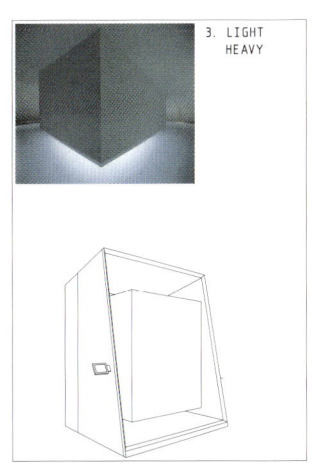

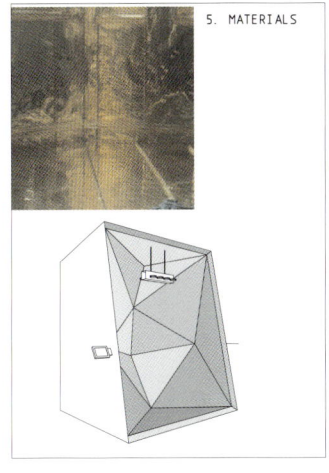

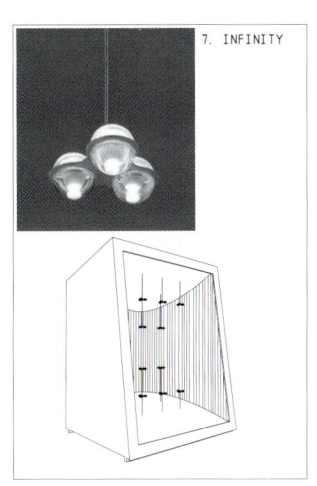

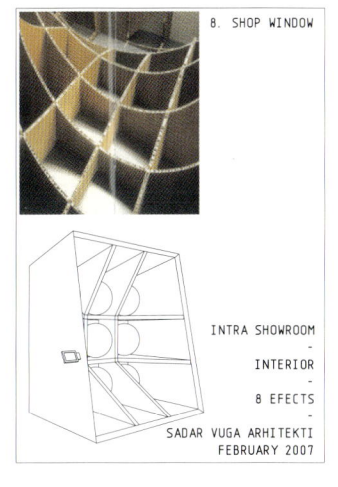

1. SHADOWS
2. HOTEL ROOM
3. LIGHT HEAVY
4. CURVE
5. MATERIALS
6. GRID
7. INFINITY
8. SHOP WINDOW

INTRA SHOWROOM
-
INTERIOR
-
8 EFECTS
-
SADAR VUGA ARHITEKTI
FEBRUARY 2007

ARCHITECTURAL DIAGRAMS 583

KANTOOR DUPON
Studio Ramin Visch

"BIG OPEN WORK SPACES WERE CREATED BY KNOCKING DOWN AS MUCH WALLS AS POSSIBLE."

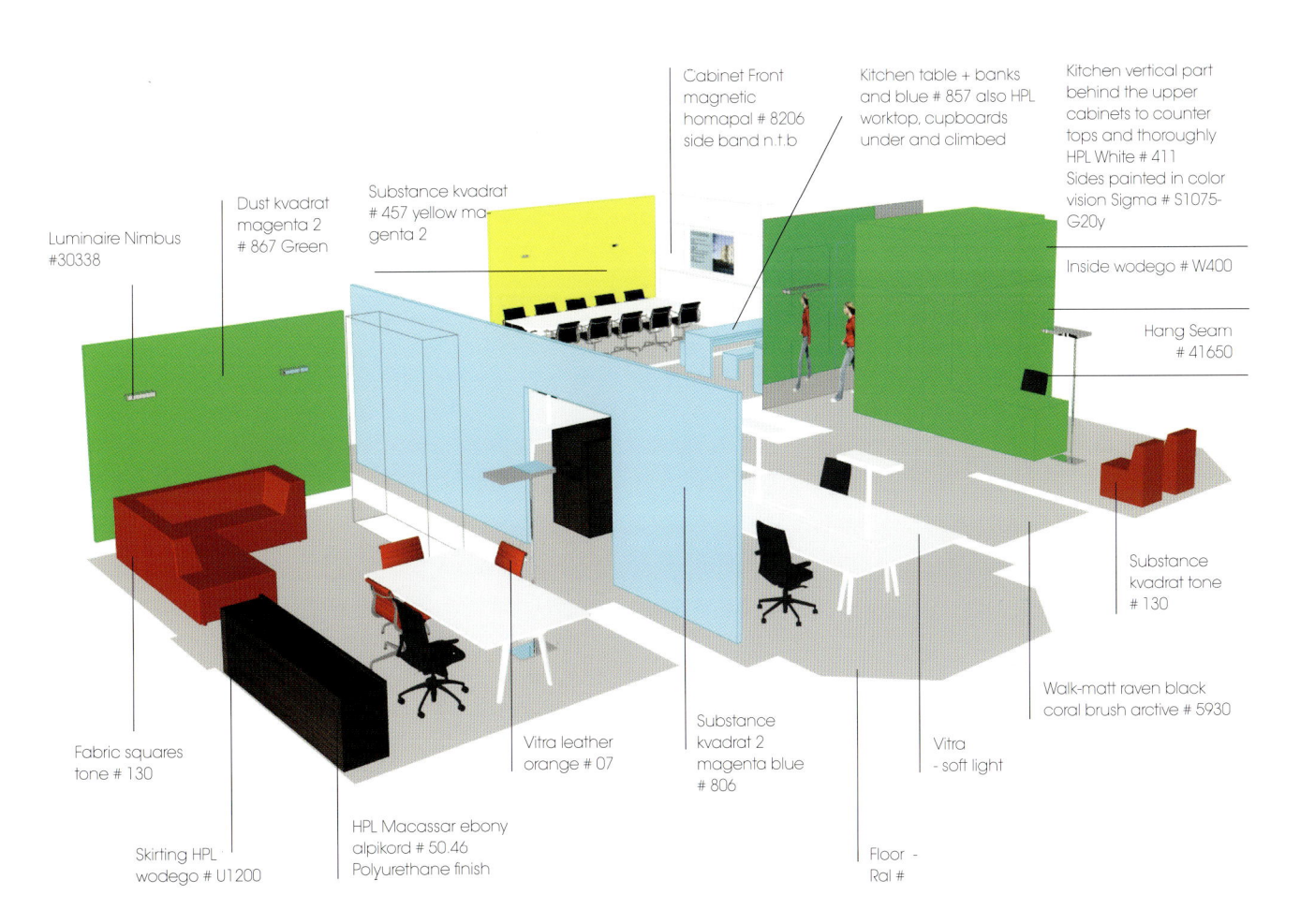

Luminaire Nimbus #30338	
Dust kvadrat magenta 2 # 867 Green	
Substance kvadrat # 457 yellow magenta 2	
Cabinet Front magnetic homapal # 8206 side band n.t.b	
Kitchen table + banks and blue # 857 also HPL worktop, cupboards under and climbed	
Kitchen vertical part behind the upper cabinets to counter tops and thoroughly HPL White # 411 Sides painted in color vision Sigma # S1075-G20y	
Inside wodego # W400	
Hang Seam # 41650	
Substance kvadrat tone # 130	
Walk-matt raven black coral brush arctive # 5930	
Fabric squares tone # 130	
Skirting HPL wodego # U1200	
HPL Macassar ebony alpikord # 50.46 Polyurethane finish	
Vitra leather orange # 07	
Substance kvadrat 2 magenta blue # 806	
Vitra - soft light	
Floor - Ral #	

Colors and materials schedule

KUNSTHAUS GRAZ
the next ENTERprise

"TO TRANSFORM THE ENVELOPE INTO A DISTANT HORIZON, MIRRORED PANELS WERE LEANED AGAINST THE CURVED PERIMETER WALLS."

Olafur Eliasson, Fivefold funnel, 2000 / Los Carpinteros, Frio Estudio Desastre, 2005

Section

Sectional sketch mirror flat Museum Graz

2.5m   5m

ARCHITECTURAL DIAGRAMS 587

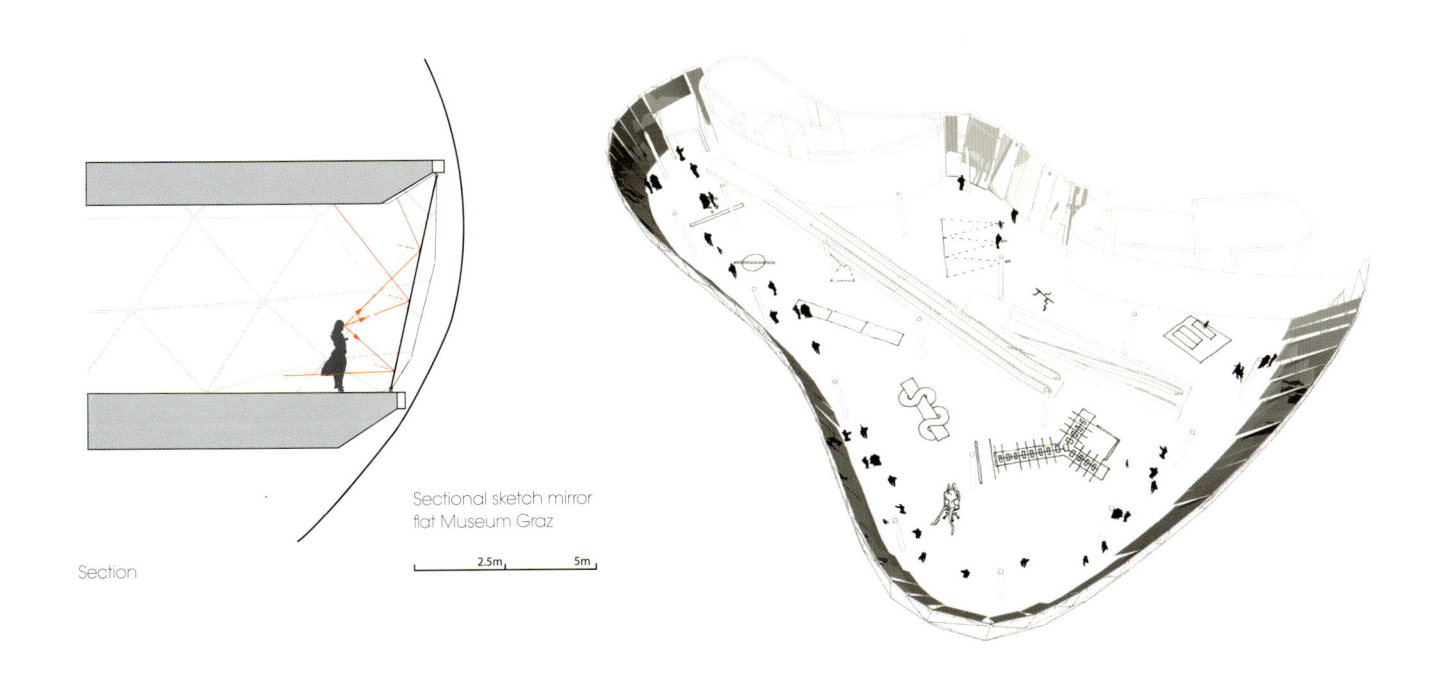

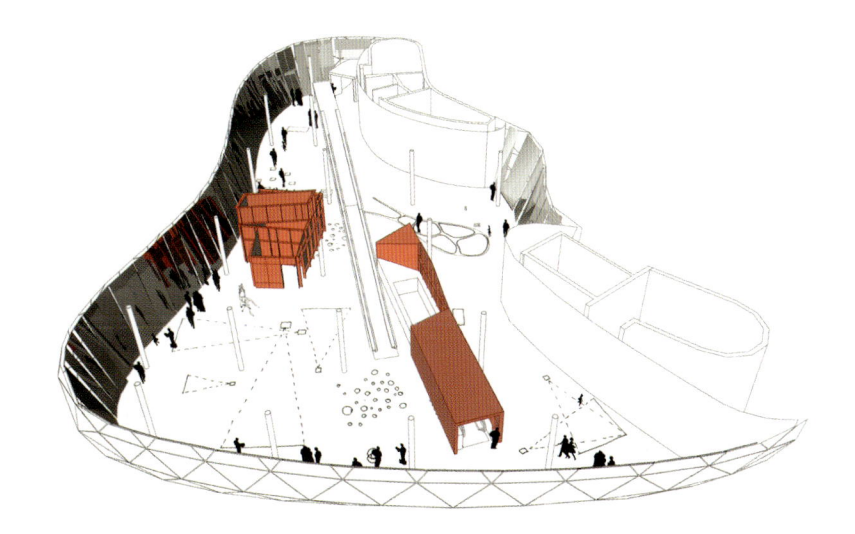

LA BELLE PAUSE
jay is working.

"JUST LIKE THE SCENES OF THE VILLAGE, EACH SIDE HAS A DIFFERENT SHAPE AND PRESENTS DIFFERENT LOOKS."

ELEVATION A

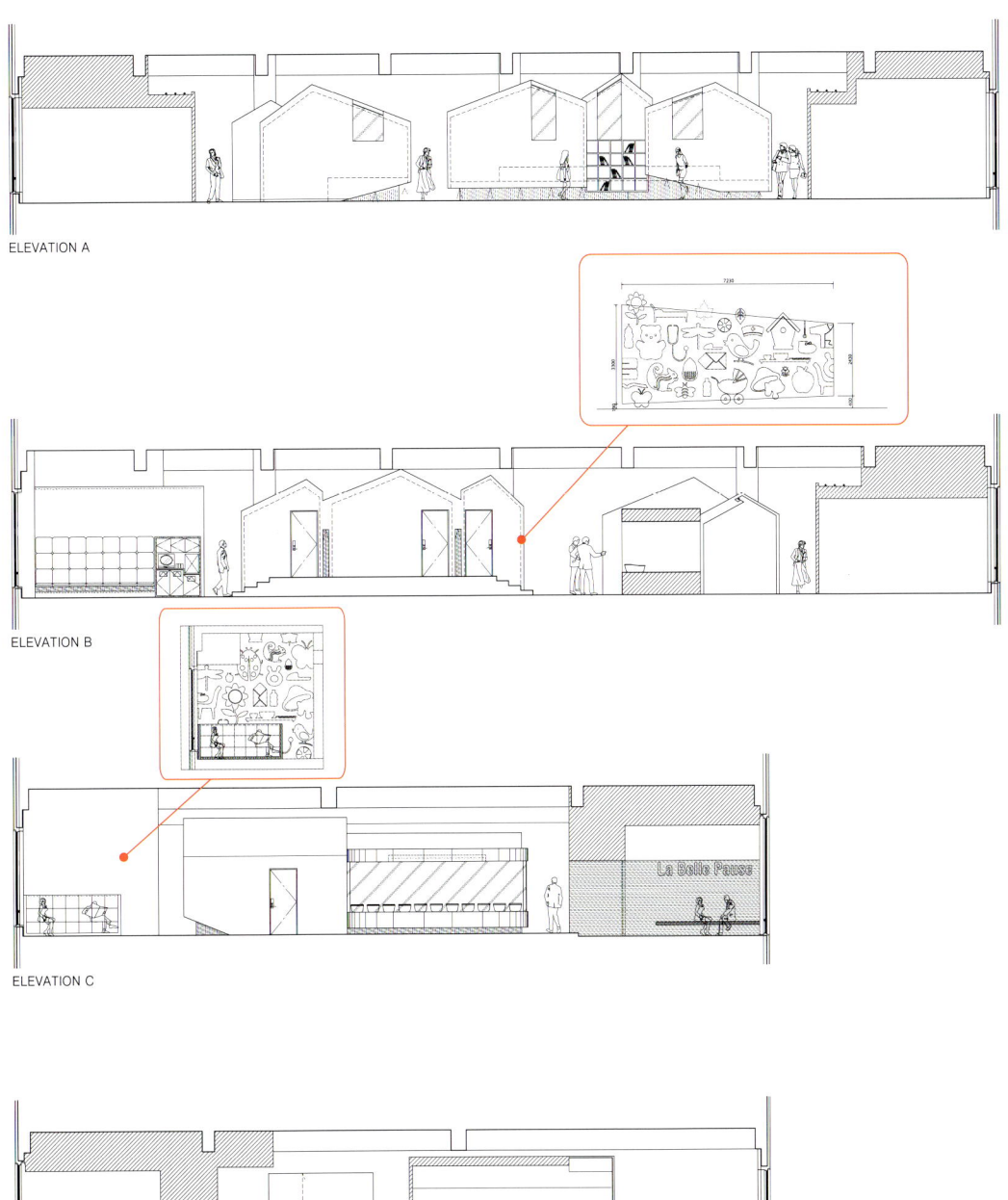

ELEVATION B

ELEVATION C

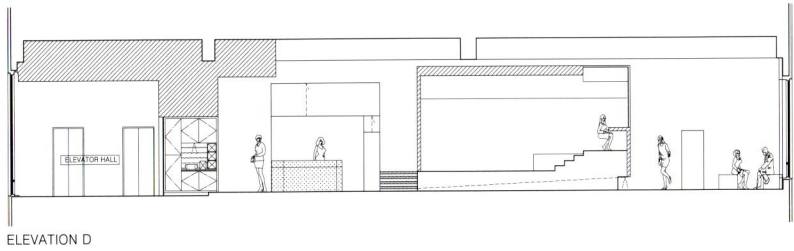

ELEVATION D

ARCHITECTURAL DIAGRAMS   589

LA GUARDIA SALON
Z-A studio and Cheng+Snyder

"THE WHITE SHEETROCK WALL WAS TREATED AS A PLIABLE MATERIAL AND THE RED FRAMES ARE CARVED INTO THE WALL."

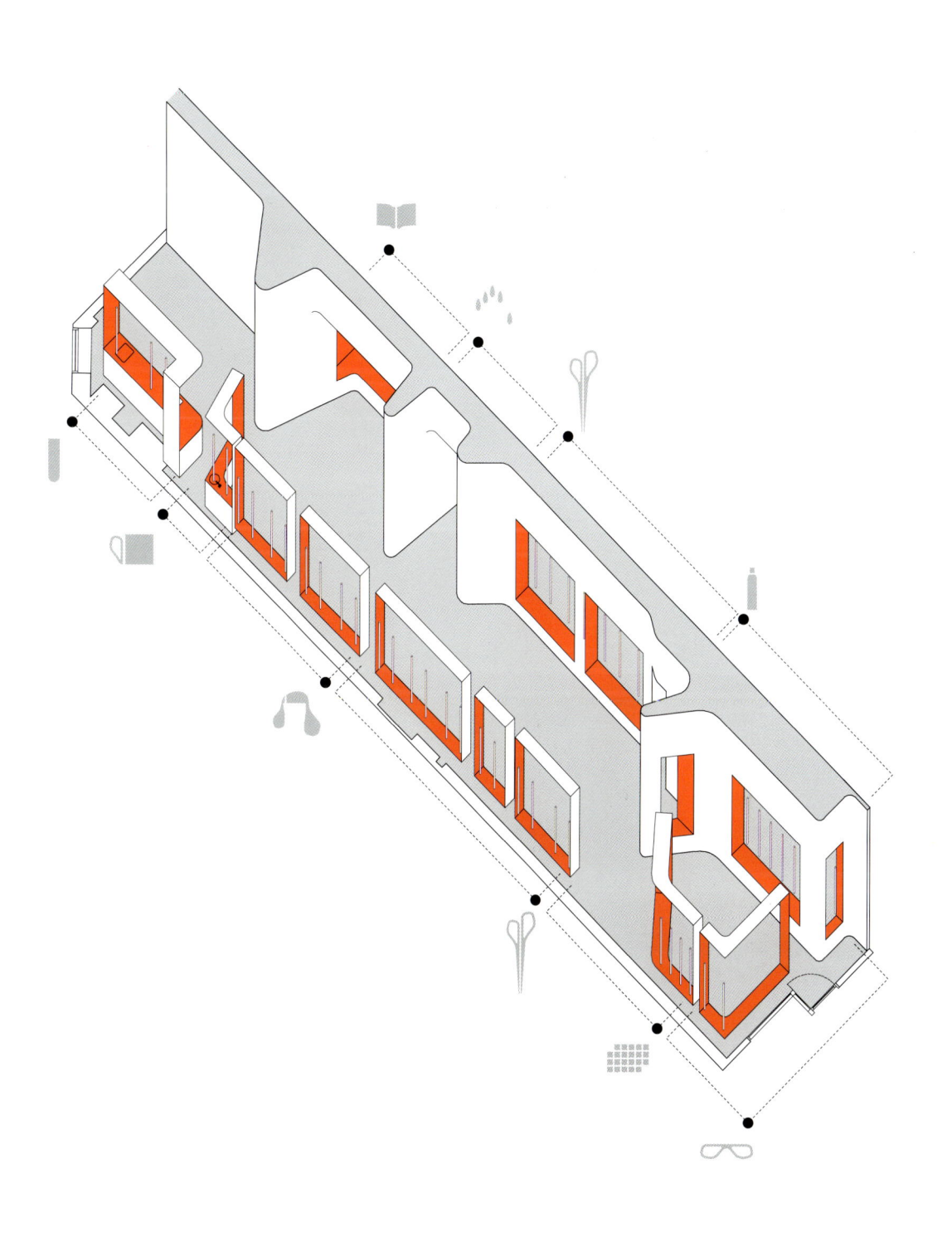

ARCHITECTURAL DIAGRAMS 591

MAISON DU DANE-MARQUE JDS Architects

"ONE UNDULATING SURFACE THAT WOULD REMIND US OF THE DANISH COUNTRYSIDE HILLS OF ABLE-TOFT."

Concept

How can we transform it existed something that radiates Denmark?

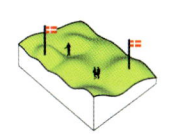

Ebeltoft hills, a beautiful landscape in Denmark

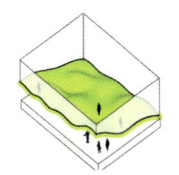

The landscape turned upside down

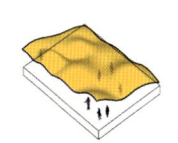

This results in a spatially interesting landscape

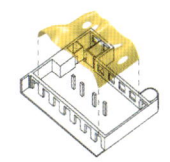

The landscape intention machined with specific programs and space

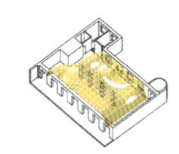

The Danish House in Paris!

Program

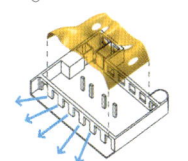

View from the balcony Champs-Elysees

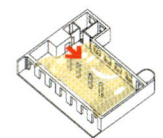

Main Entrance

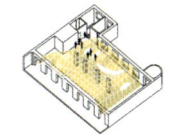

Desk and wardrobe

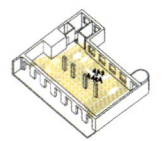

Meeting rooms in the cave ceiling landscape

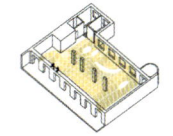

Bench overlooking the landscape

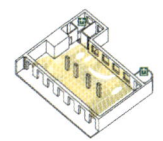

Exils

Scenarios of Use

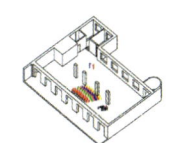

Conference

Exhibition furniture feast

Party

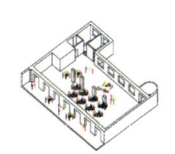

Evening of Danish food culture

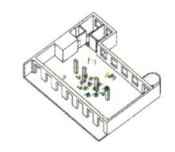

Project

Danish movie night

Construction

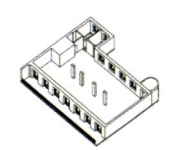

Existing situation

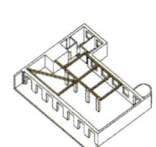

Beams

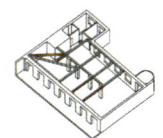

Secondary tree structure

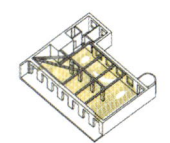

Beam layer connected to tree structure

Approach

Existing structure

New design

Habitable parts of the landscape

Secondary beams to / parts are not to be 'inhabited'

Tertiary tree structure

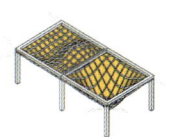

Shape held outside

ARCHITECTURAL DIAGRAMS 593

MASTERPLAN HALL 11
UNStudio

"AN 'URBAN MASTERPLAN', BASED ON THE HALL AS A CITYSCAPE WITH ITS OWN GRID OF ROADS."

Pattern_metro

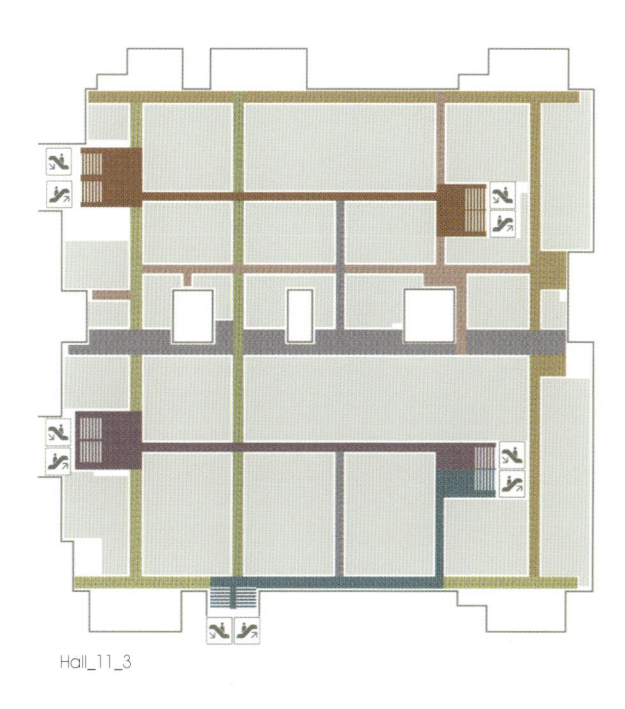

Hall_11_1

Hall_11_2

Hall_11_3

ARCHITECTURAL DIAGRAMS 595

MTV DESIGN STAGE
LAVA

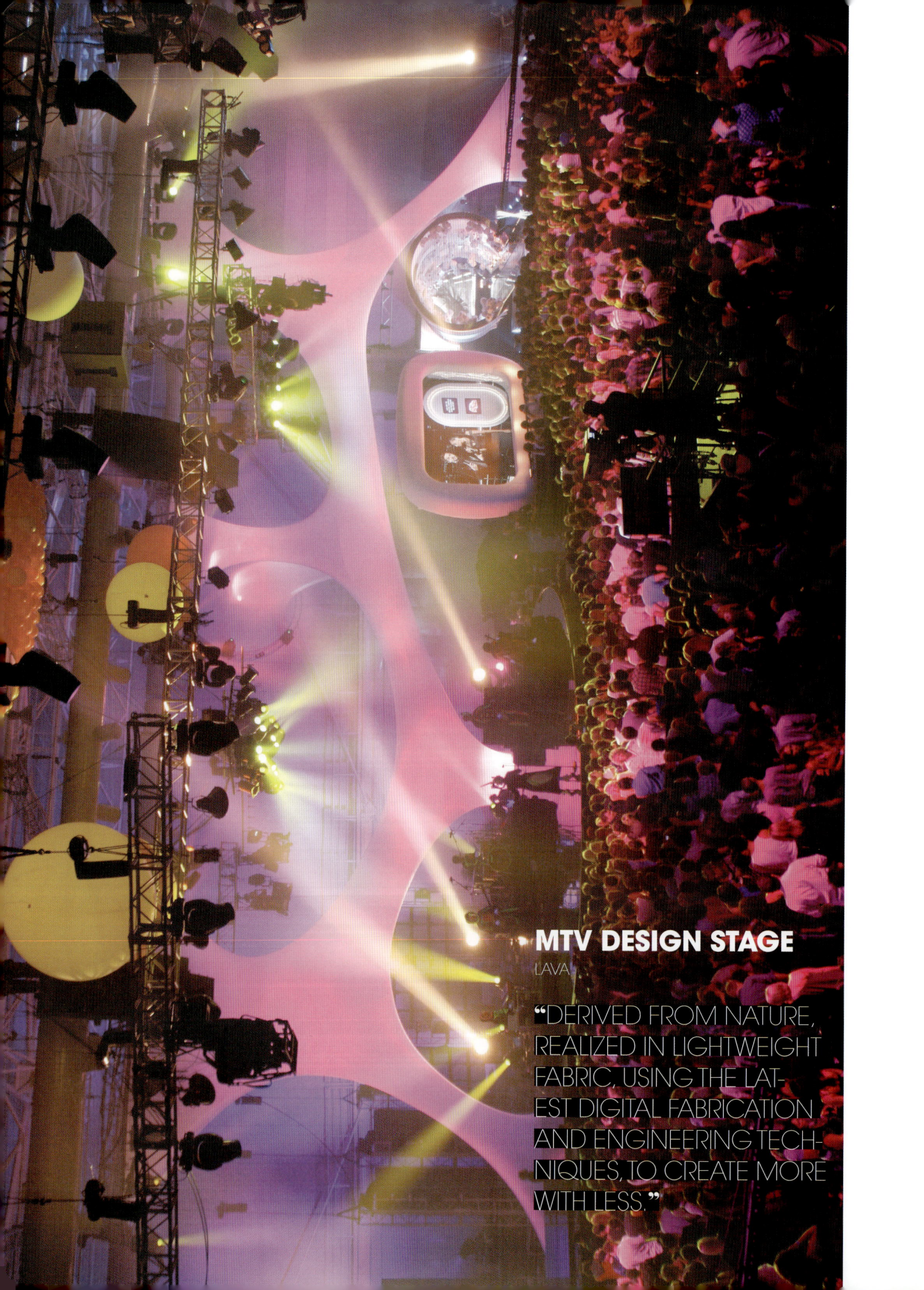

"DERIVED FROM NATURE, REALIZED IN LIGHTWEIGHT FABRIC, USING THE LATEST DIGITAL FABRICATION AND ENGINEERING TECHNIQUES, TO CREATE MORE WITH LESS."

ARCHITECTURAL DIAGRAMS 597

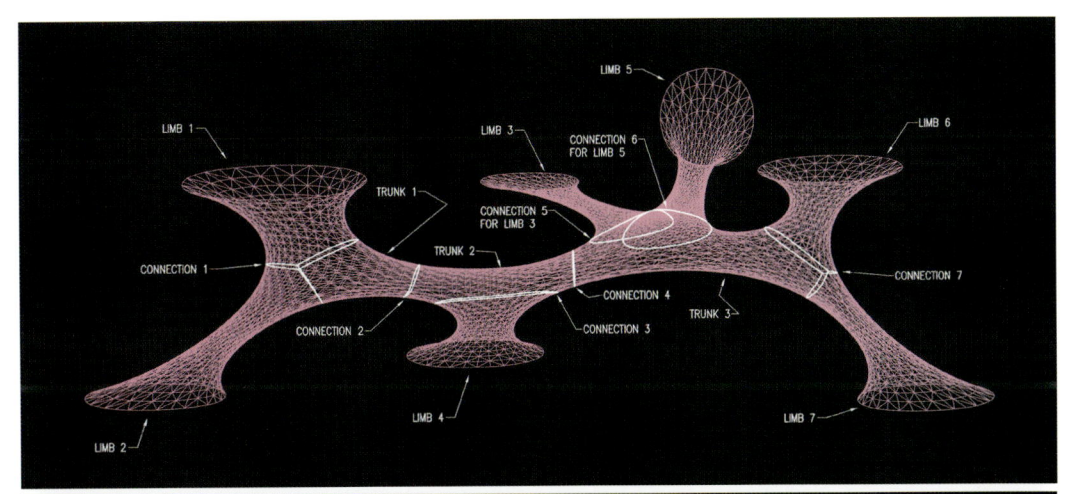

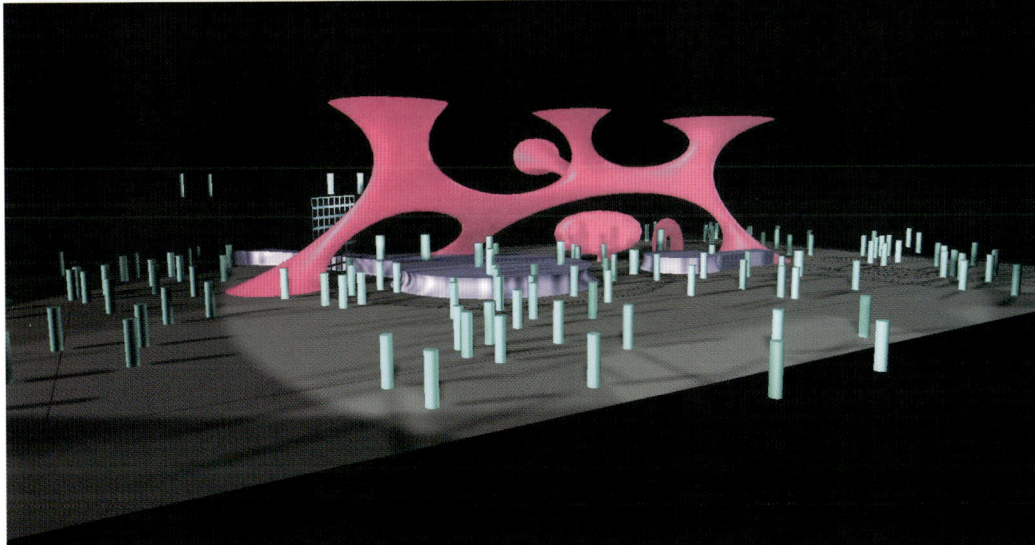

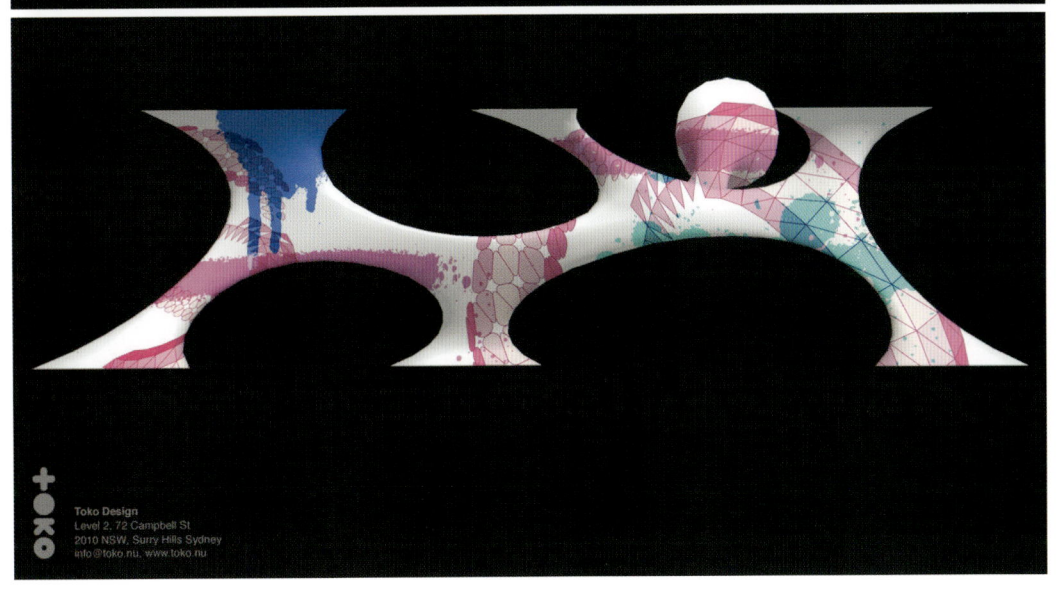

MUSIC THEATRE UNStudio

"THIS TWIST FORMS A 3D INTERPRETATION OF THE REPETITIVE PATTERN."

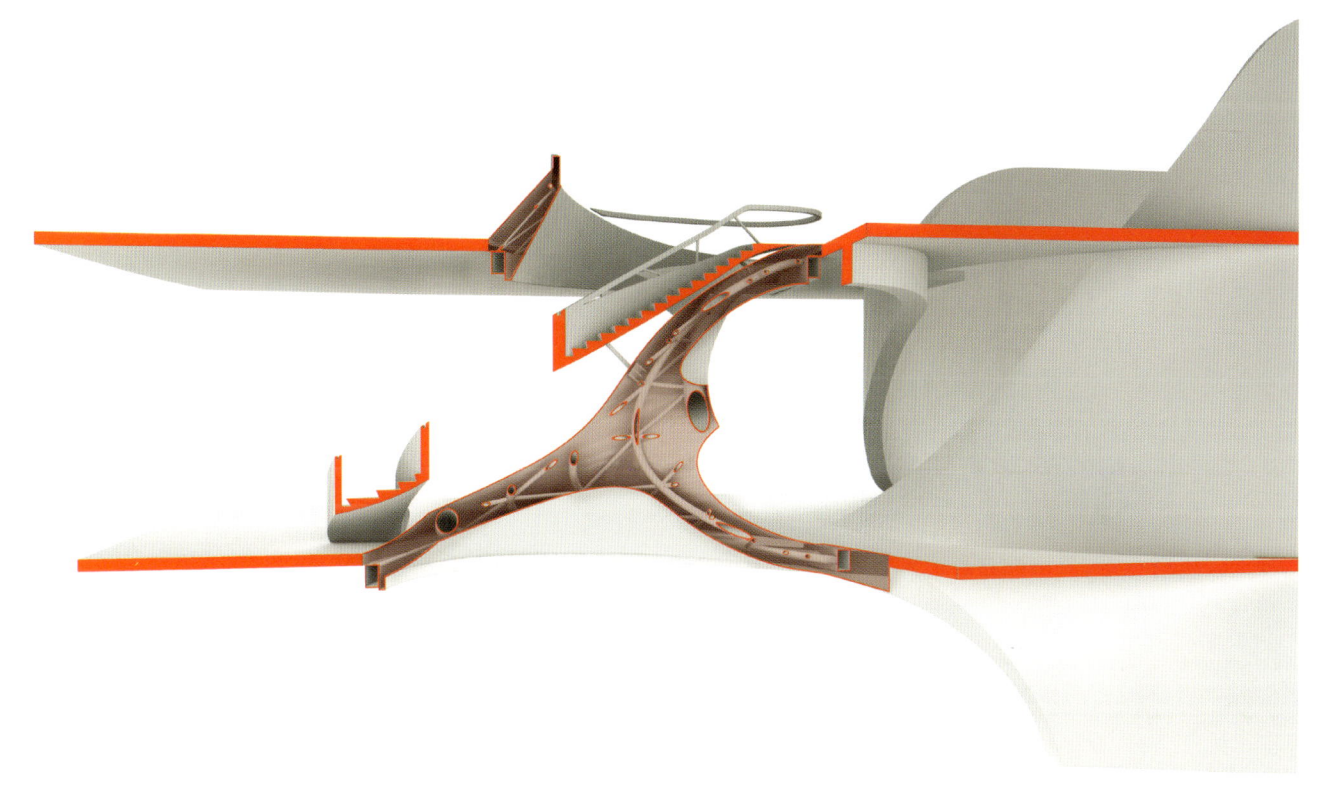

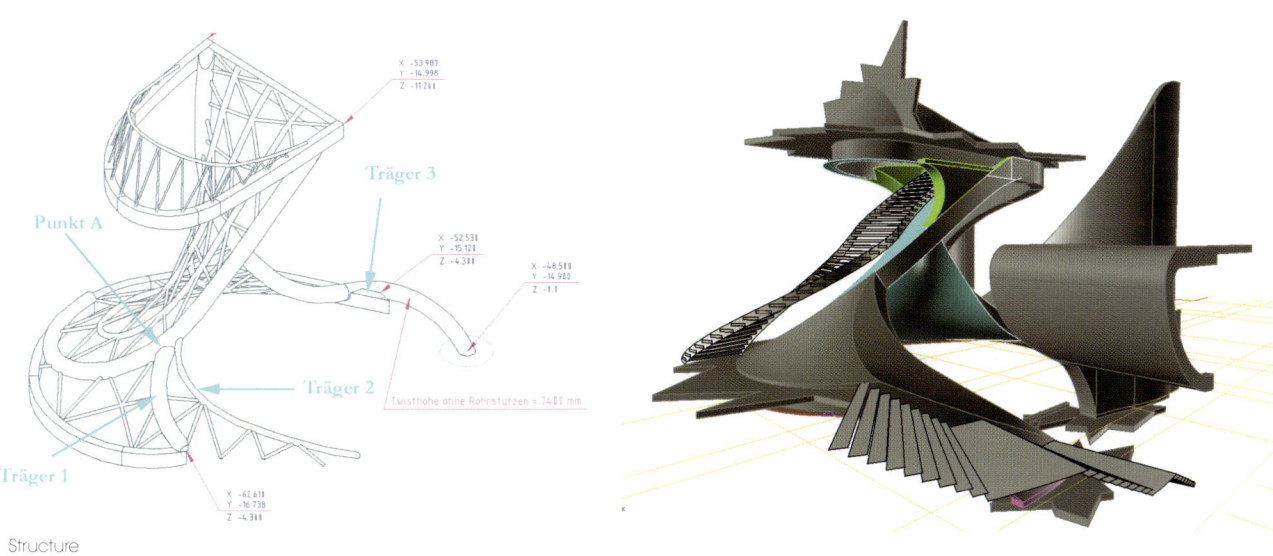

Structure

ARCHITECTURAL DIAGRAMS 599

ORIENTAL CLINIC
BOM_FLOW SPACE
jay is working.

"THE CURVED AXIS AND VISUALLY LAYERED DIAGONAL LINES ARE IMPORTANT ELEMENTS."

eyes to lotteworld

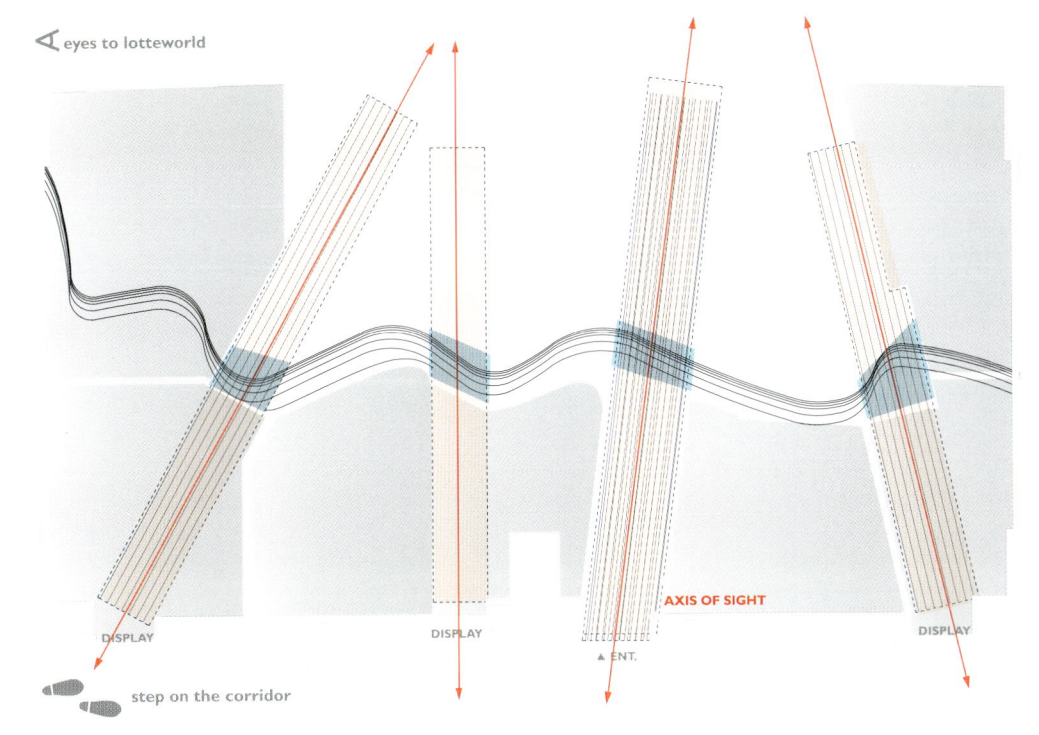

AXIS OF SIGHT

DISPLAY   DISPLAY   DISPLAY   DISPLAY

▲ ENT.

step on the corridor

Thouugh the volume shape - Extension of sight

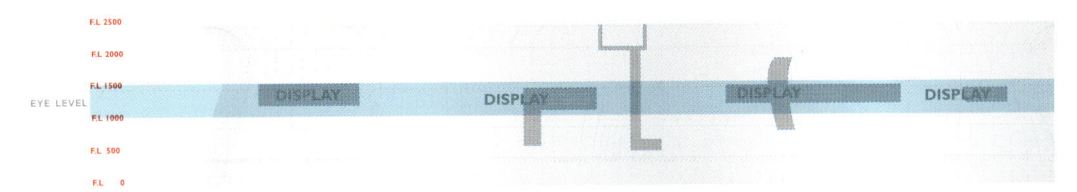

F.L 2500
F.L 2000
F.L 1500
EYE LEVEL
F.L 1000
F.L 500
F.L 0

DISPLAY   DISPLAY   DISPLAY   DISPLAY

Curved line + volume shape system

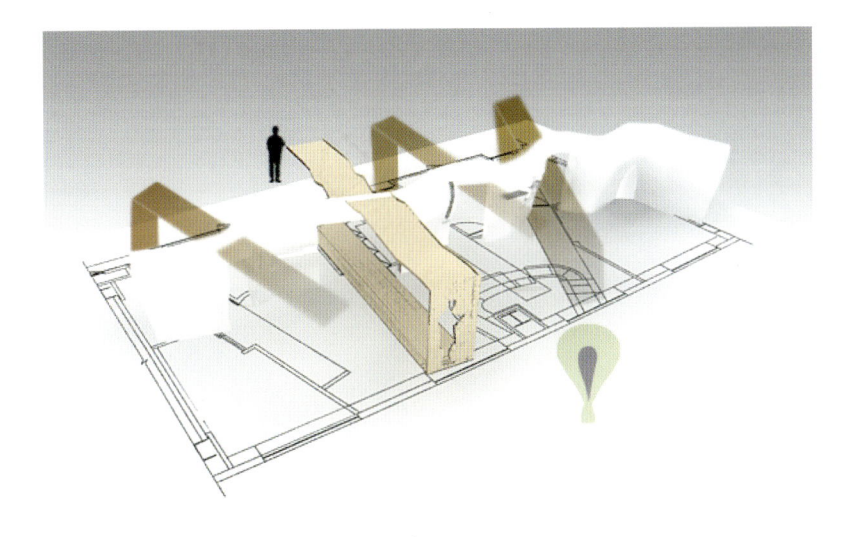

Spatial Ceiling

ARCHITECTURAL DIAGRAMS 601

PLY LOFT nARCHITECTS

"A SINUOUS SURFACE OF BENDABLE PLYWOOD SEPARATES PRIVATE AND STORAGE SPACES FROM THE LIVING AREA."

doors as light dimmers

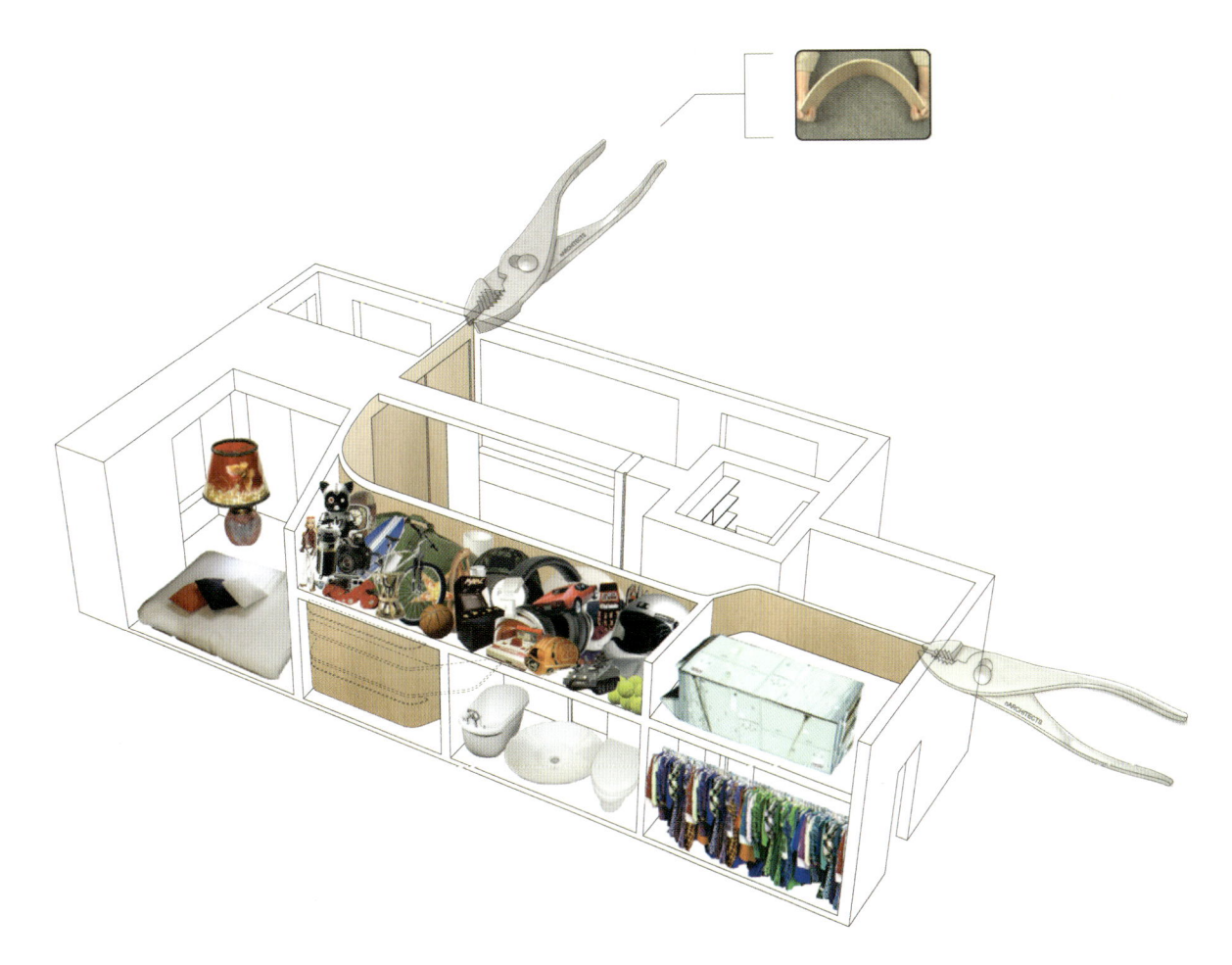

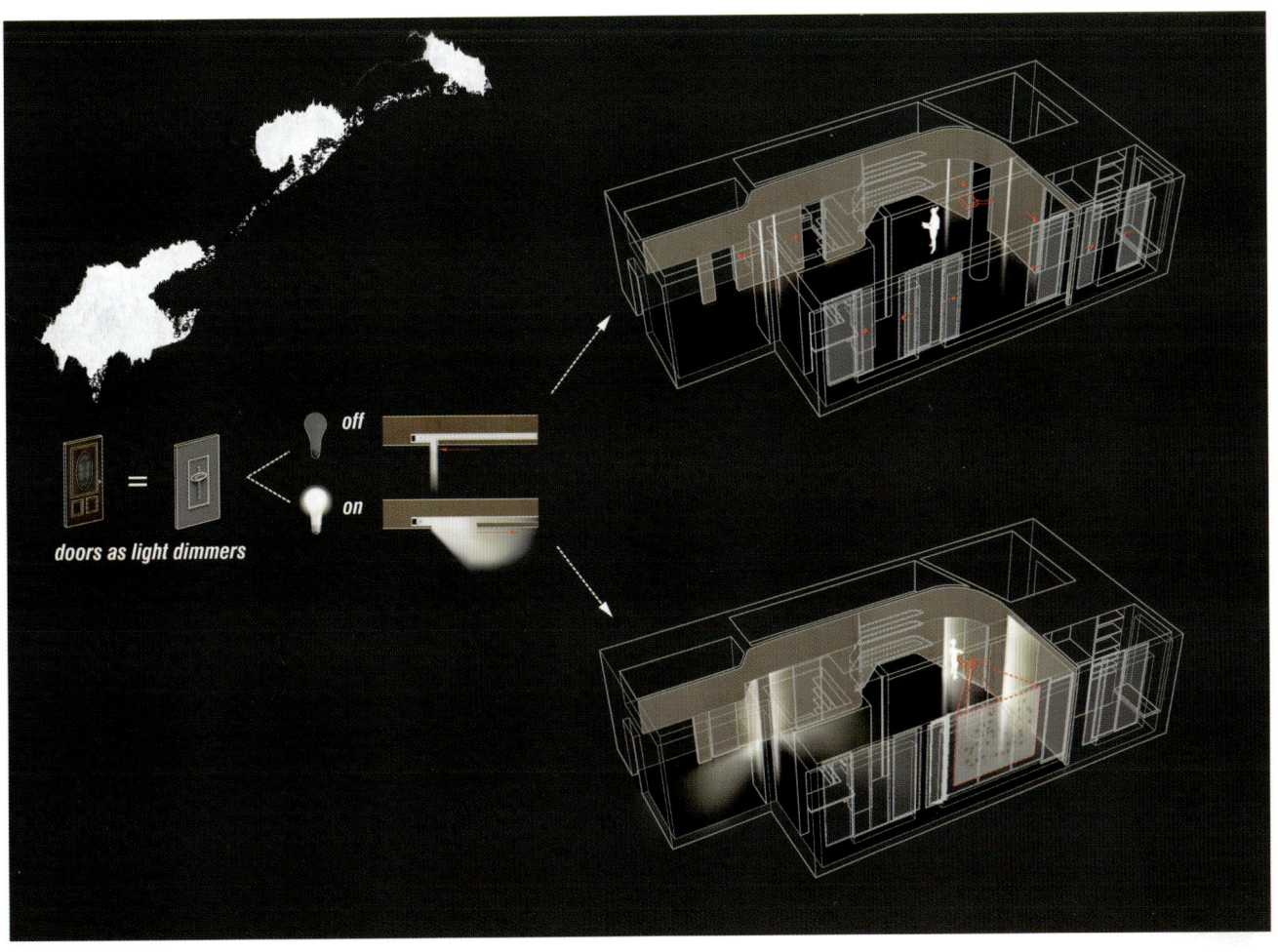

ARCHITECTURAL DIAGRAMS 603

ROBBINS ELEMENTARY SCHOOL
PLY Architecture

"THE NEW SCHOOL COMPLEX IS ORGANIZED AS THREE CONCENTRIC LAYERS THAT WRAP AN INTERNAL COURTYARD AND PLAZA."

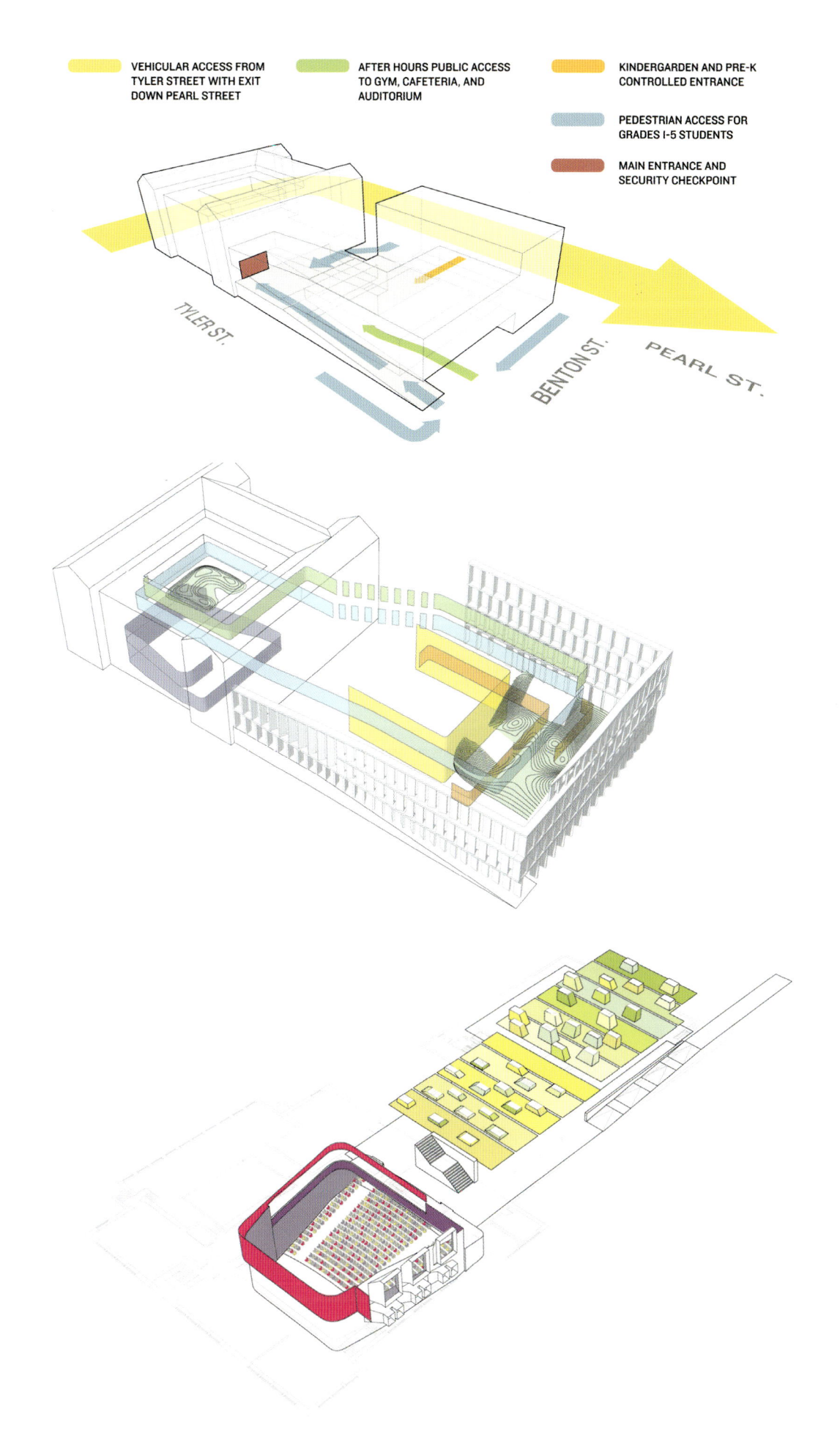

- VEHICULAR ACCESS FROM TYLER STREET WITH EXIT DOWN PEARL STREET
- AFTER HOURS PUBLIC ACCESS TO GYM, CAFETERIA, AND AUDITORIUM
- KINDERGARDEN AND PRE-K CONTROLLED ENTRANCE
- PEDESTRIAN ACCESS FOR GRADES 1-5 STUDENTS
- MAIN ENTRANCE AND SECURITY CHECKPOINT

TYLER ST.

BENTON ST.

PEARL ST.

ARCHITECTURAL DIAGRAMS 605

ROSSO RESTAURANT
sO Architecture

"THE FURROWED FIELDS, WHICH ARE FRAMED BY THE STRIP OF WINDOWS, FIND ITS CONTINUATION IN THE CEILING, AND EMBRACE THE DINER AS IF BY THE FOLIAGE OF TREES."

Concept ©Hayuta Dubnov

Ceiling elments

SCHOOL 03
129 interior architects

"THROUGHOUT THE ENTIRE SCHOOL POEMS HAVE BEEN APPLIED TO THE LINOLEUM FLOORS AND THE FURNITURE."

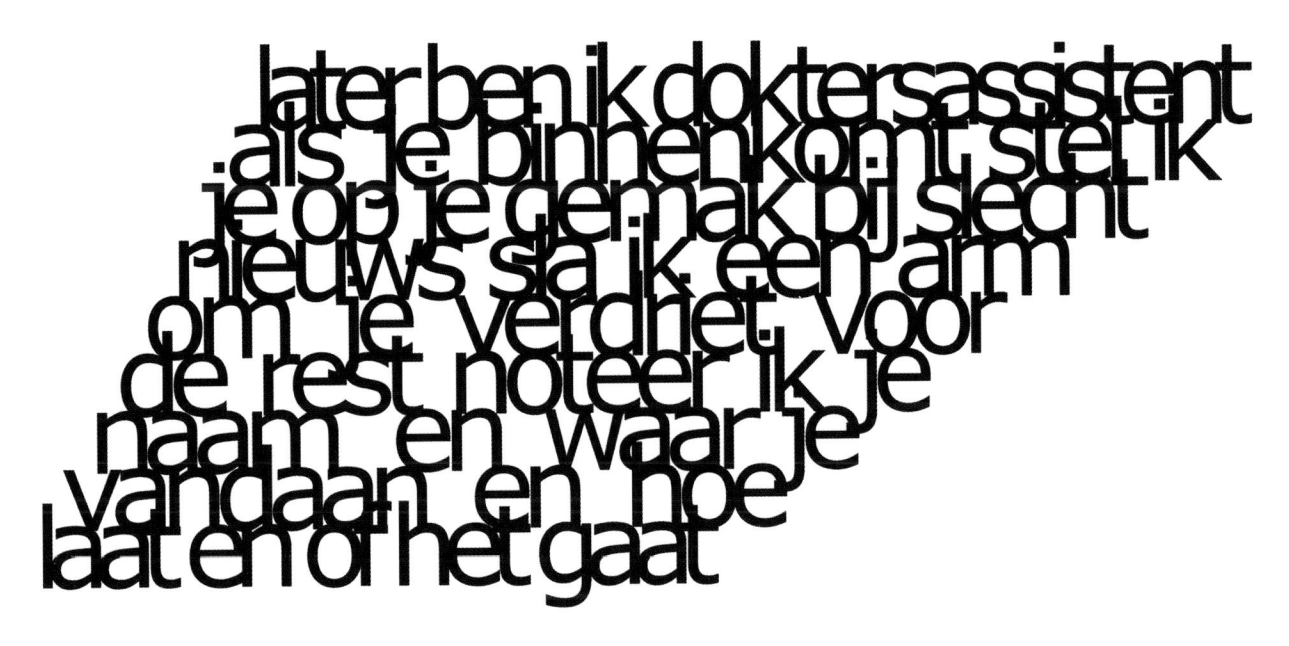

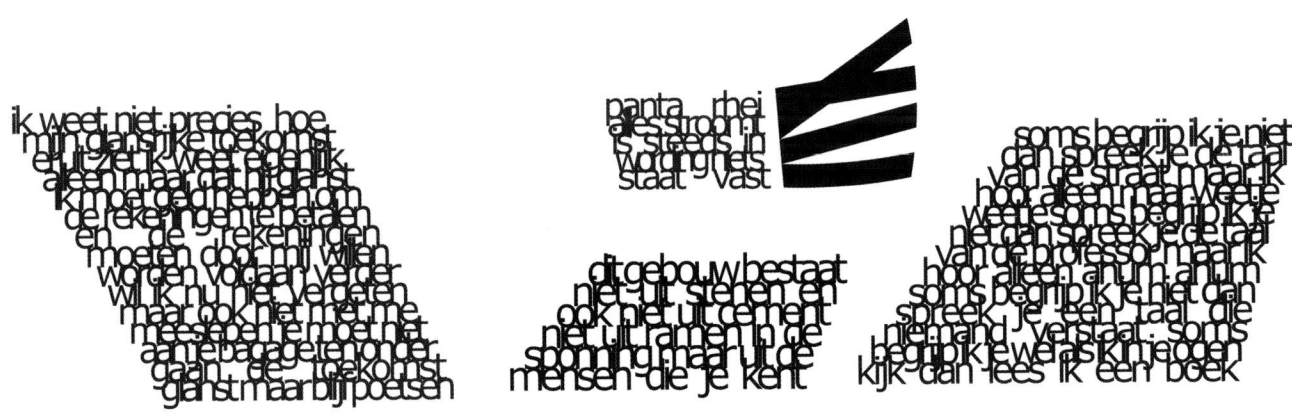

later ben ik doktersassistent
.als je binnenkomt stel ik
je op je gemak bij slecht
nieuws sla ik een arm
om je verdriet. voor
de rest noteer ik je
naam en waar je
vandaan en hoe
laat en of het gaat

ik weet niet precies hoe
mijn glansrijke toekomst
eruit ziet. ik weet alleen
alleen maar dat het zal
komen. die toekomst.
de rekening. de rekening
en de rekening. ook
moeten de dingen willen
worden voor dat verder
wil. ik. nu niet vergeten.
niets begeren. moet niet.
aan bagage. men niet.
gaan. de toekomst.
glans maar bij poetsen

panta rhei
alles stroomt
is steeds in
beweging niets
staat vast

dit gebouw bestaat
niet uit stenen en
ook niet uit cement
niet uit ramen in de
sponningen maar uit de
mensen die je kent

soms begrijp ik je niet
dan spreek je de taal
van de straat waar ik
nooit kom maar weet je
het eigenlijk iedereen kent
weet soms begrijp ik je
van de professor die ik
hoor alleen maar aan om
soms begrijp ik je niet dan
spreek je een taal
die niemand verstaat. soms
begrijp ik je wel als ik je ogen
kijk dan lees ik een boek

ARCHITECTURAL DIAGRAMS 609

SECRET STAGE Axi:Ome

"THE SPACE RELIED ON DARKNESS AND VOIDS FROM DIGITAL PROJECTIONS TO ELICIT THE NUMEROUS CROSSINGS OF CENSORED TEXT."

Shadow puppet diagram

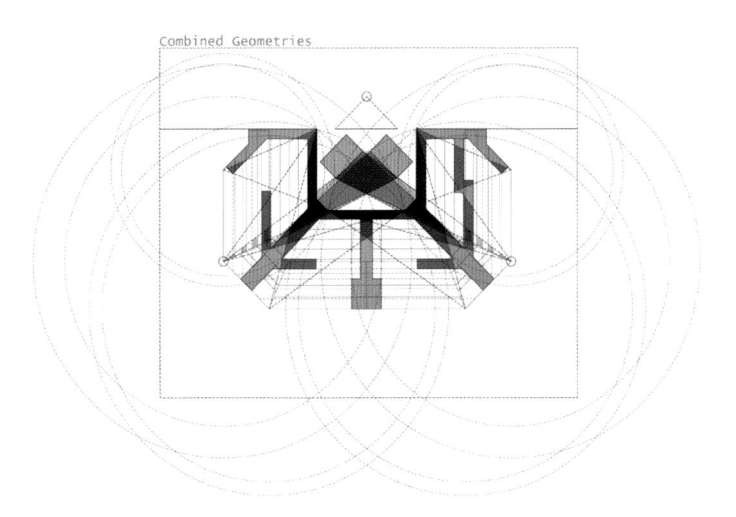

Projector Interaction Diagrams

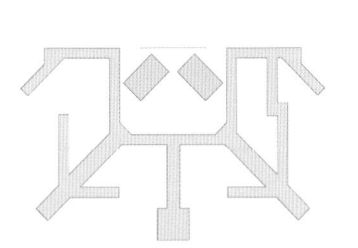

Given

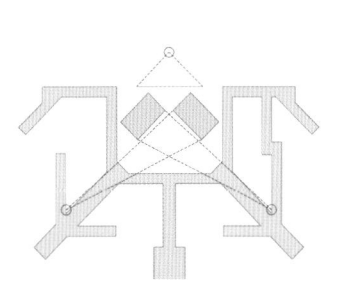

Inner projector

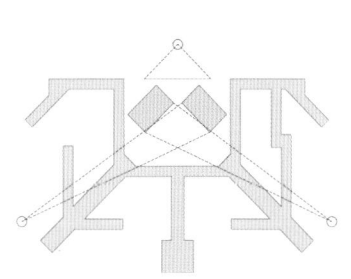

Outer projector

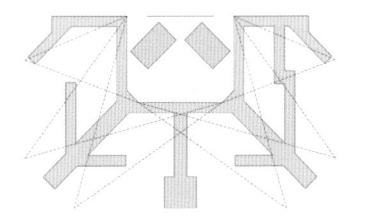

Sight extremes

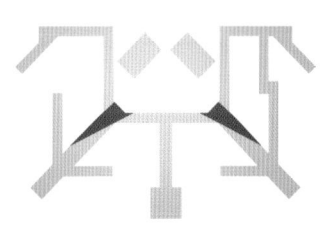

Inner projector / circulation

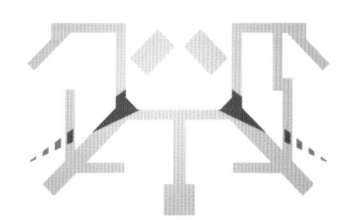

Outer projector / circulation

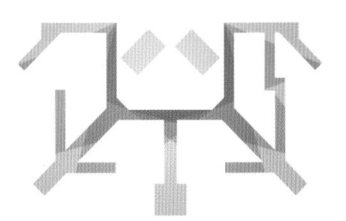

Sight extremes / circulation

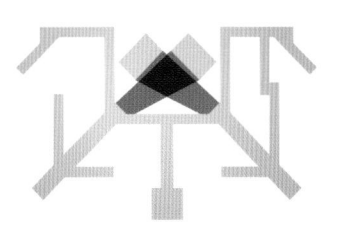

Inner projector / actors

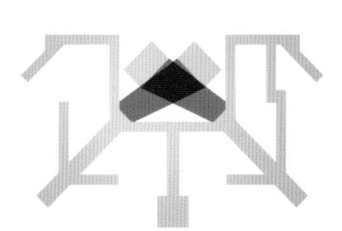

Outer projector / actors

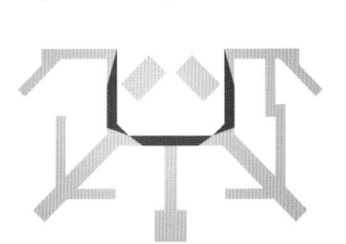

Sight overlaps / circulation

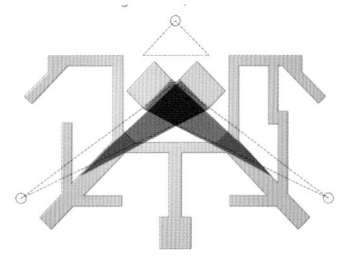

Circulation / stage combined

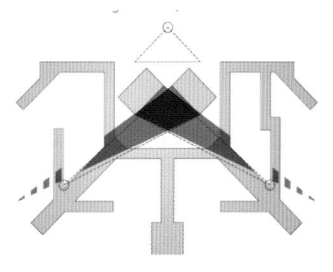

Circulation / stage combined

ARCHITECTURAL DIAGRAMS 611

SKY OFFICE OFF-SPRING PSA

"OUR PROPOSAL EXPLORES THE POTENTIAL OF NETWORKED LINEARITY."

FS3 – FBK3 – BS1
SEK2 – ES4 – EEK4
DS3 – CDK1 – DS2
AAK2 – AS3 – AFK3

FS3 – FBK3 – BS1
SEK2 – ES4 – EEK4
DS3 – CDK1 – DS2
AAK2 – AS3 – AFK3

FS3 – FBK3 – BS1
SEK2 – ES4 – EEK4
DS3 – CDK1 – DS2
AAK2 – AS3 – AFK3

AS1 – ABK1 – BS1
BFK3 – FS3 – FDK3
DS3 – DDK2 – DS2
DEK2 – ES2 – EAK1

BS3 – BBK3 – BS4
BEK2 – ES4 – EEK4
DS3 – CEK2 – ES2
EAK1 – FS3 – ADK3

FS3 – FBK3 – BS1
SEK2 – ES4 – EEK4
DS3 – CDK1 – DS2
AAK2 – AS3 – AFK3

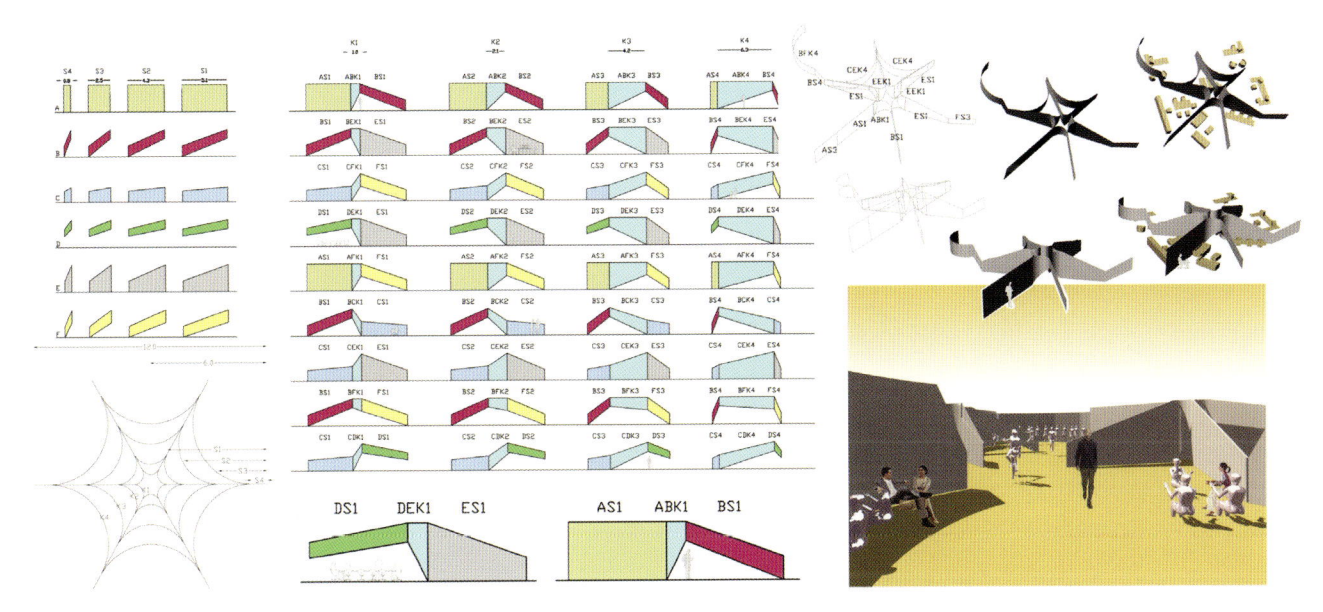

Case study

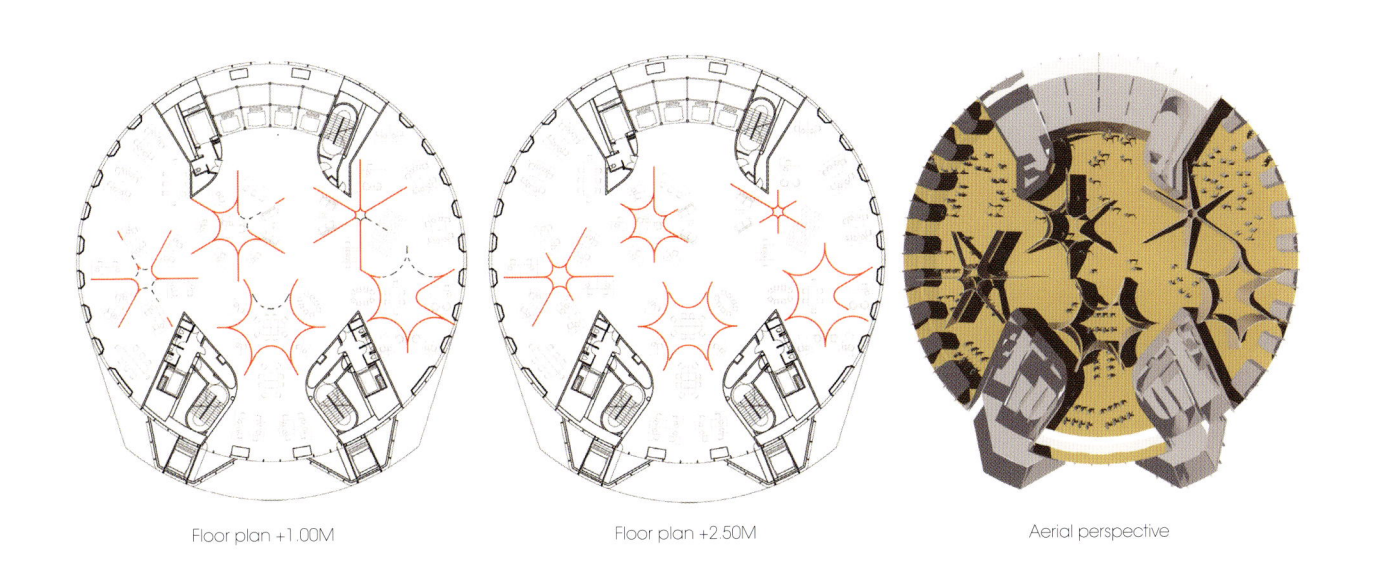

Floor plan +1.00M

Floor plan +2.50M

Aerial perspective

ARCHITECTURAL DIAGRAMS 613

STAND AND DELIVER
NL Architects

"BY LEAVING A VOID AT EYE LEVEL THE EMPHASIS IS ON THE PEOPLE, ON THE CORE BUSINESS, ON COMMUNICATION."

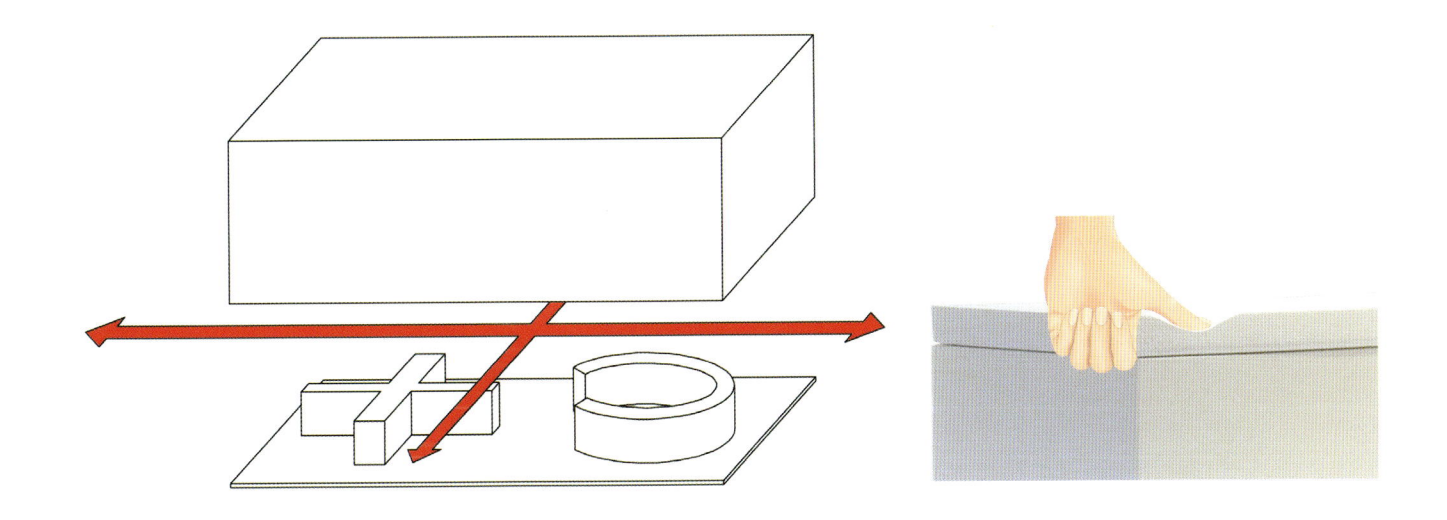

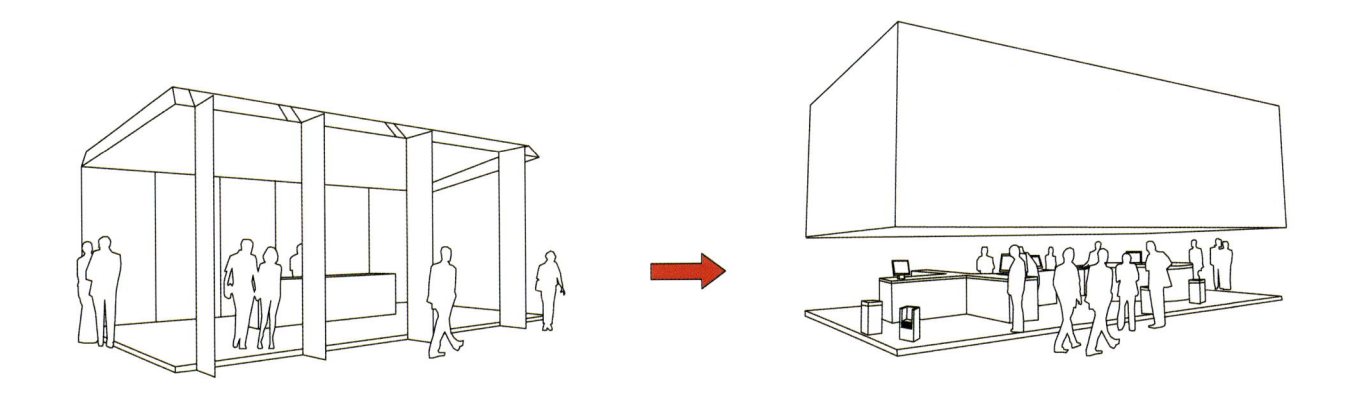

ARCHITECTURAL DIAGRAMS 615

STASH Maurice Mentjens Design

"THE IDEA WAS QUICKLY CONCEIVED TO WORK WITH MAGNETS, THE BAGS COULD BE 'STUCK' TO STEEL PLATES."

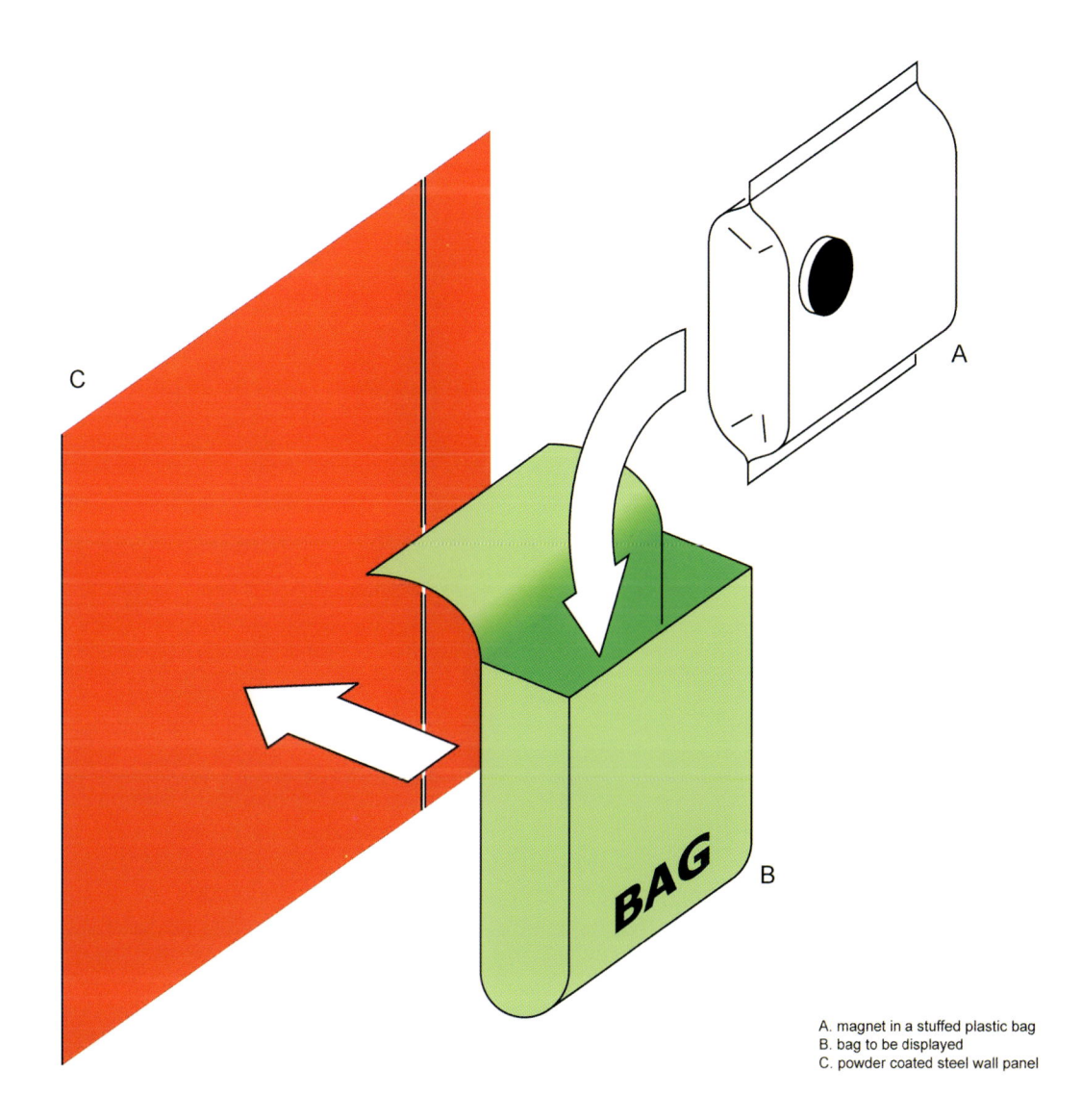

A. magnet in a stuffed plastic bag
B. bag to be displayed
C. powder coated steel wall panel

Magnet system

ARCHITECTURAL DIAGRAMS 617

TELEKOM STREAMS CEBIT kadawittfeldarchitektur

"WIDELY CURVED PERSPEX BANDS IN THE COMPANY COLORS, CONVINCINGLY SYMBOLIZING THE COMPANY'S MAIN FOCAL POINT."

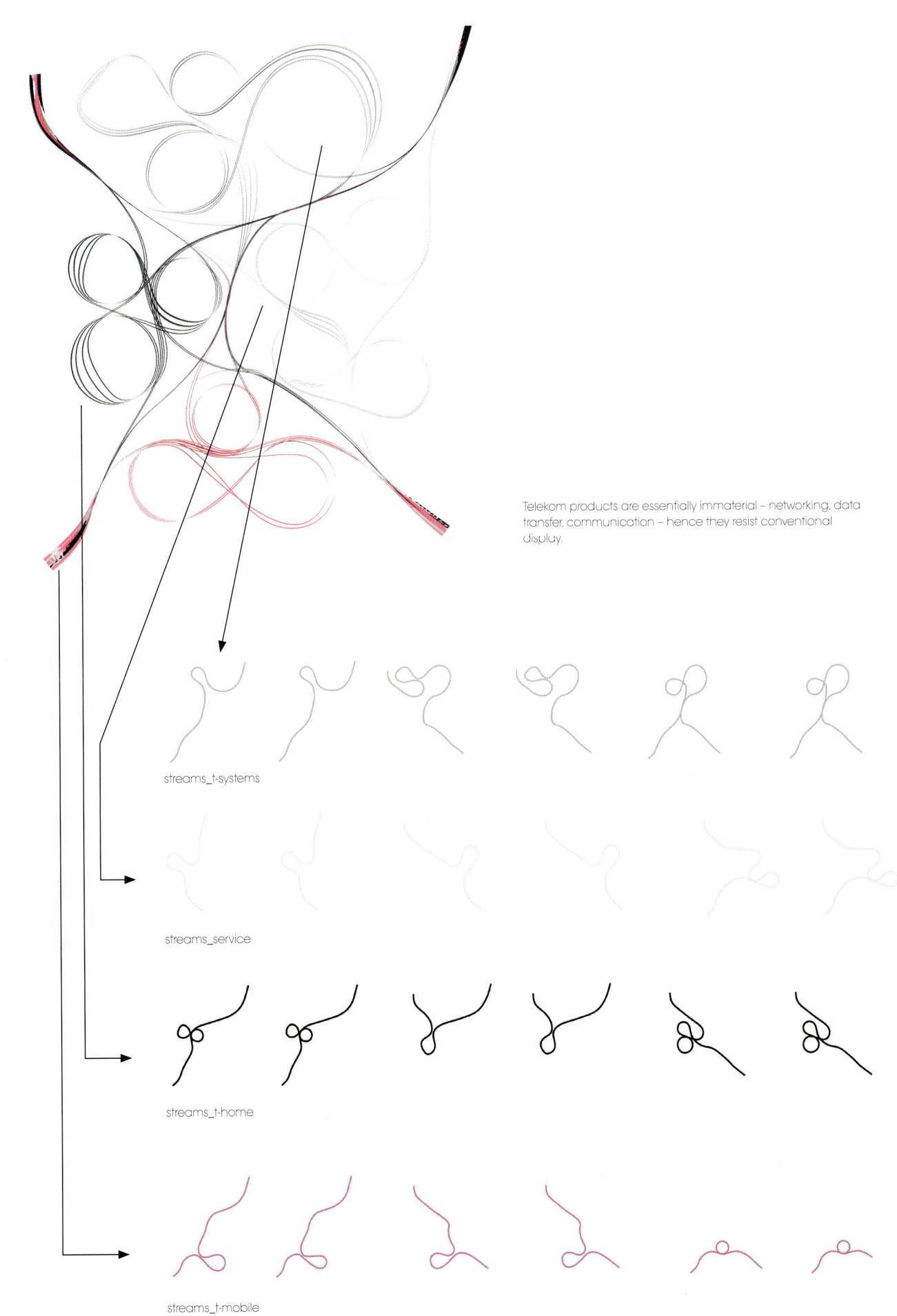

Telekom products are essentially immaterial – networking, data transfer, communication – hence they resist conventional display.

streams_t-systems

streams_service

streams_t-home

streams_t-mobile

ARCHITECTURAL DIAGRAMS 619

THEODORE – CAFÉ BISTRO SO Architecture

"THE GRAPHICAL LANGUAGE OF THE SITE IS REPEATED IN THE MENU THAT WAS DESIGNED AS A BOOK."

Cross section of secondary module

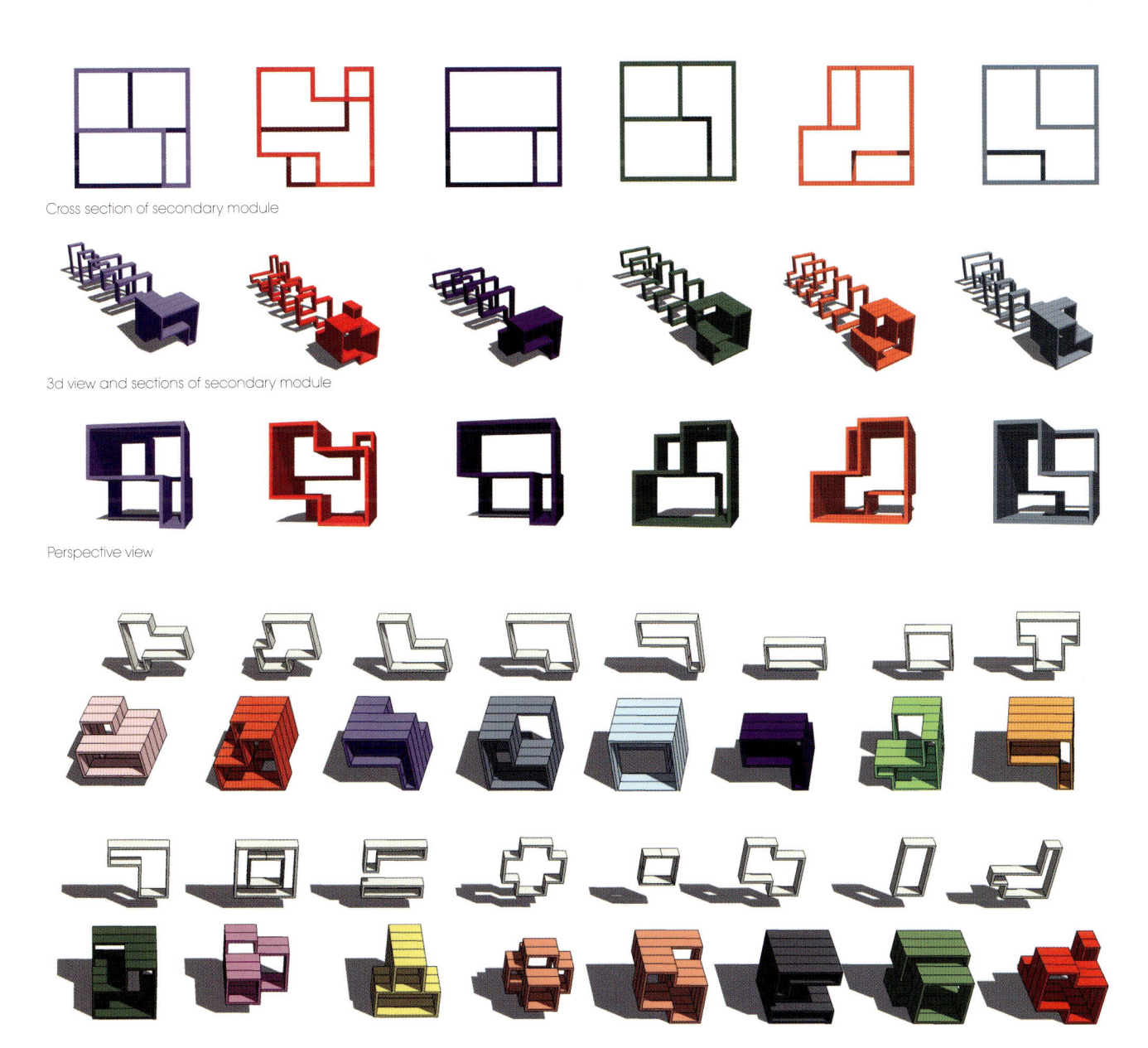

3d view and sections of secondary module

Perspective view

Combination proposal

ARCHITECTURAL DIAGRAMS 621

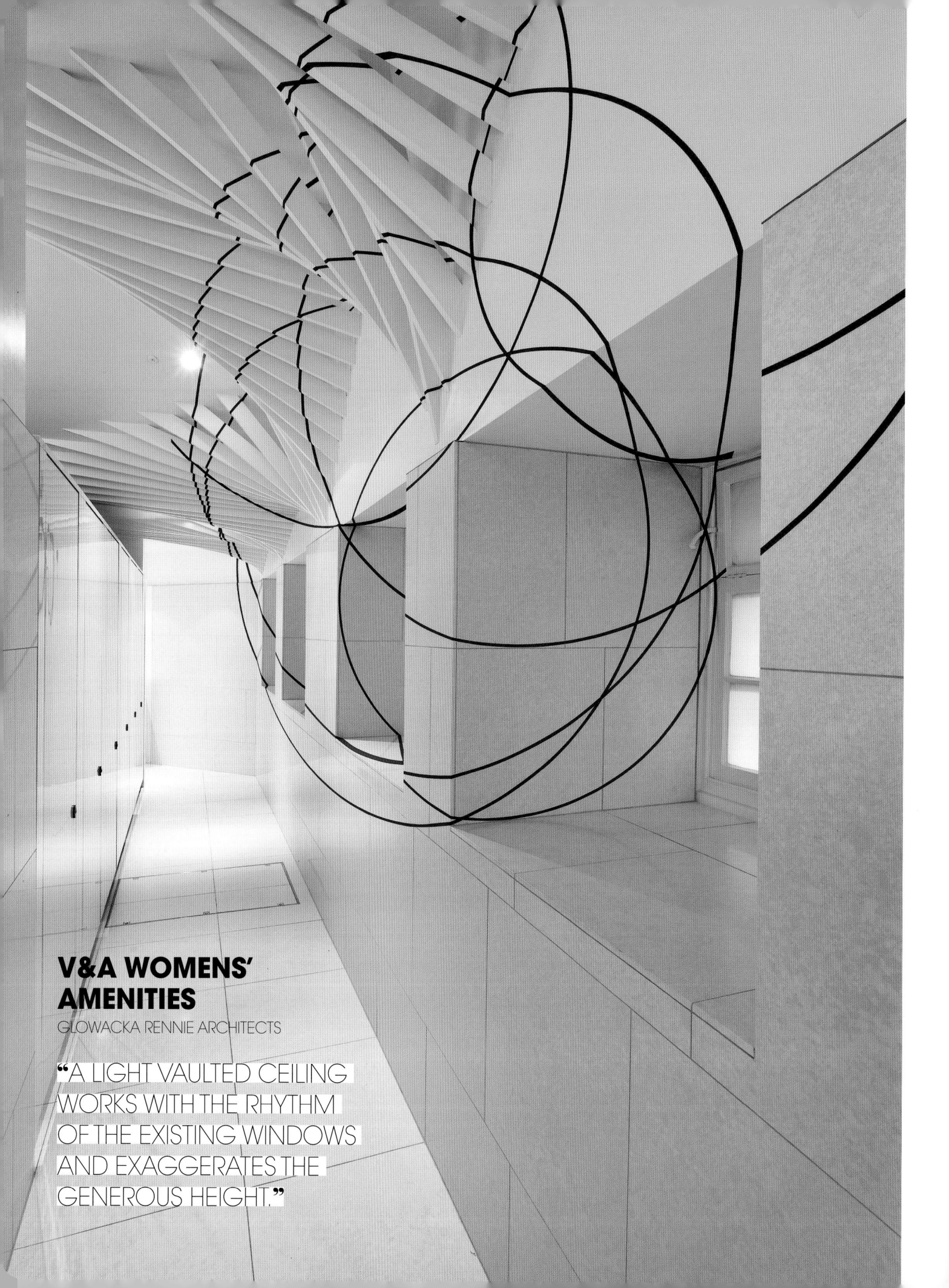

V&A WOMENS' AMENITIES
GLOWACKA RENNIE ARCHITECTS

"A LIGHT VAULTED CEILING WORKS WITH THE RHYTHM OF THE EXISTING WINDOWS AND EXAGGERATES THE GENEROUS HEIGHT."

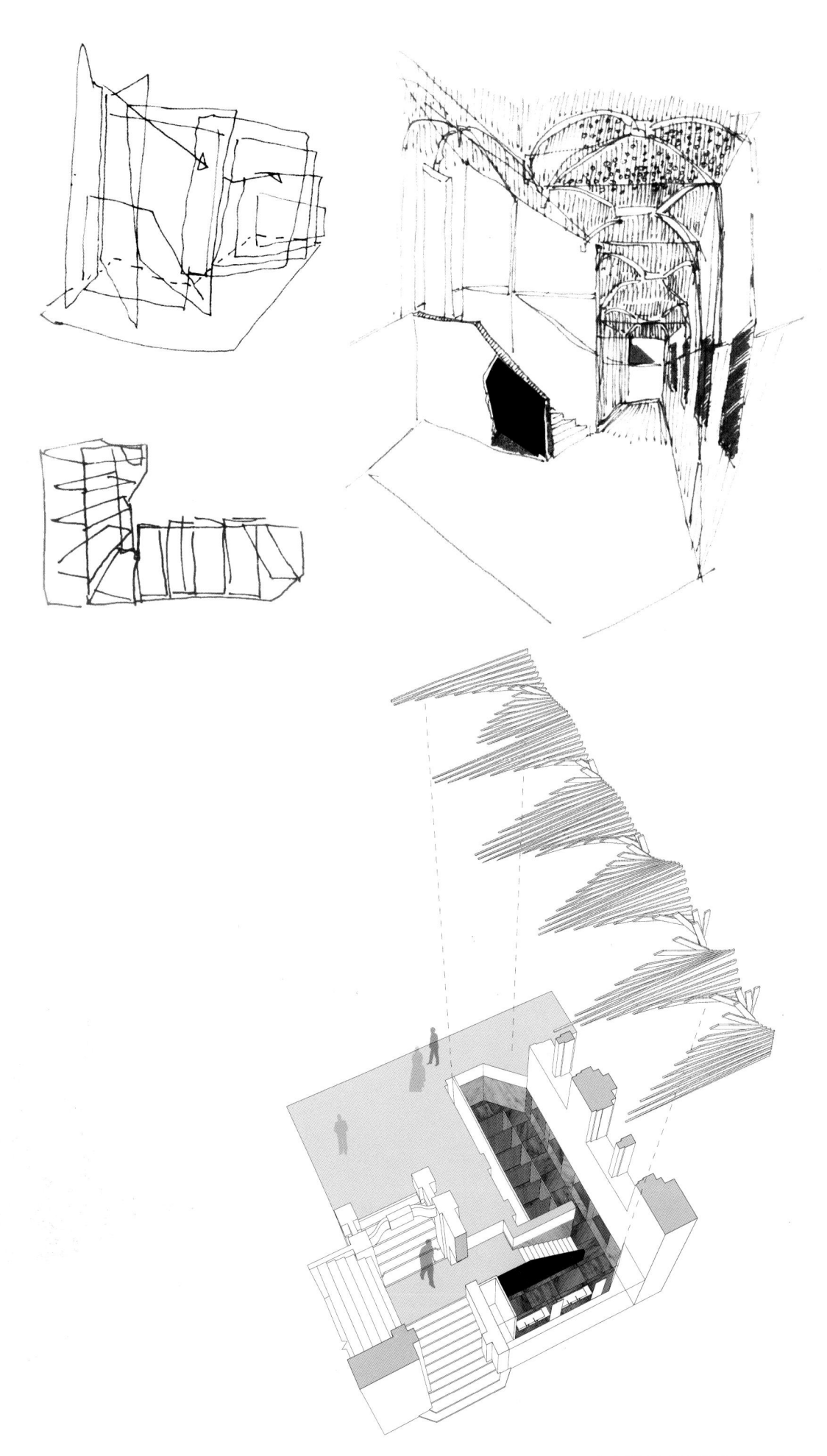

ARCHITECTURAL DIAGRAMS

VINEXPO 2009 ITALIAN STAND BORDEAUX

2TR ARCHITETTURA & Laura Federici

"THE IDEA IS TO HAVE A FLUID SPACE WHERE, LIKE BUBBLES IN THE WINE."

Concept

prospetto A

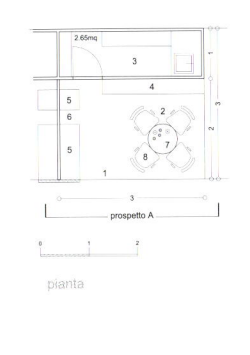

pianta

legenda
1. stand individuale
2. tavoli - degustazione - incontro
3. deposito
4. espositore vini cornice in multistrato betulla contenente illuminazione
5. vetrino d'esposizione
6. parete rivestita in D-BOND bianco con grafica applicata
7. tavolo in MDF laccato bianco h 70cm
8. Sedute KARTELL tipo MAUI bianco lucido

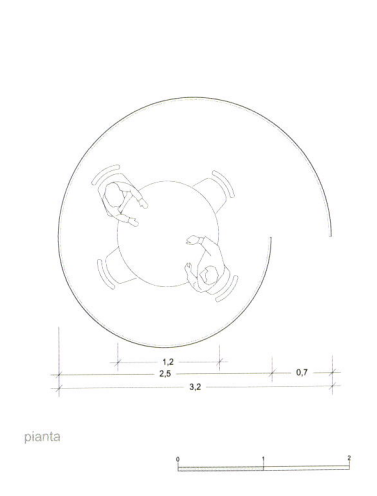

pianta

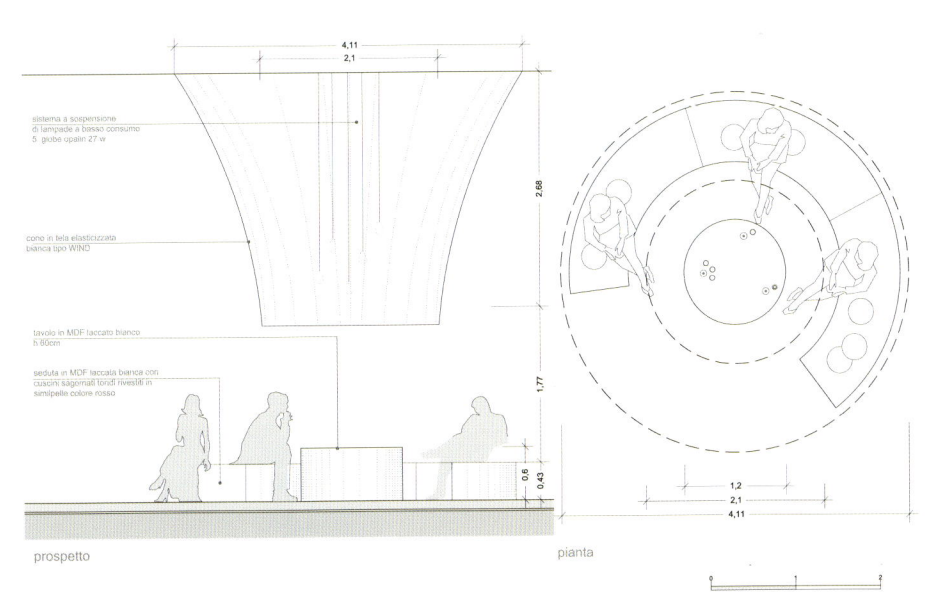

prospetto

pianta

ARCHITECTURAL DIAGRAMS 625

WOMEN'S SHELTER
Axi:Ome

"PROVIDING THEM SEMI-TEMPORARY LIVING ACCOMMODATIONS AS THEY SEEK MORE PERMANENT LINKS WITHIN ST. LOUIS."

Sunlight Density Maps

Top Third of Window Light

All of Window Light

Full Day, Four Months, ALL Year

Five Times a Day, Full Year

Combined

Light diagrams

Light field and program activation

ARCHITECTURAL DIAGRAMS 627

INSTALLATION

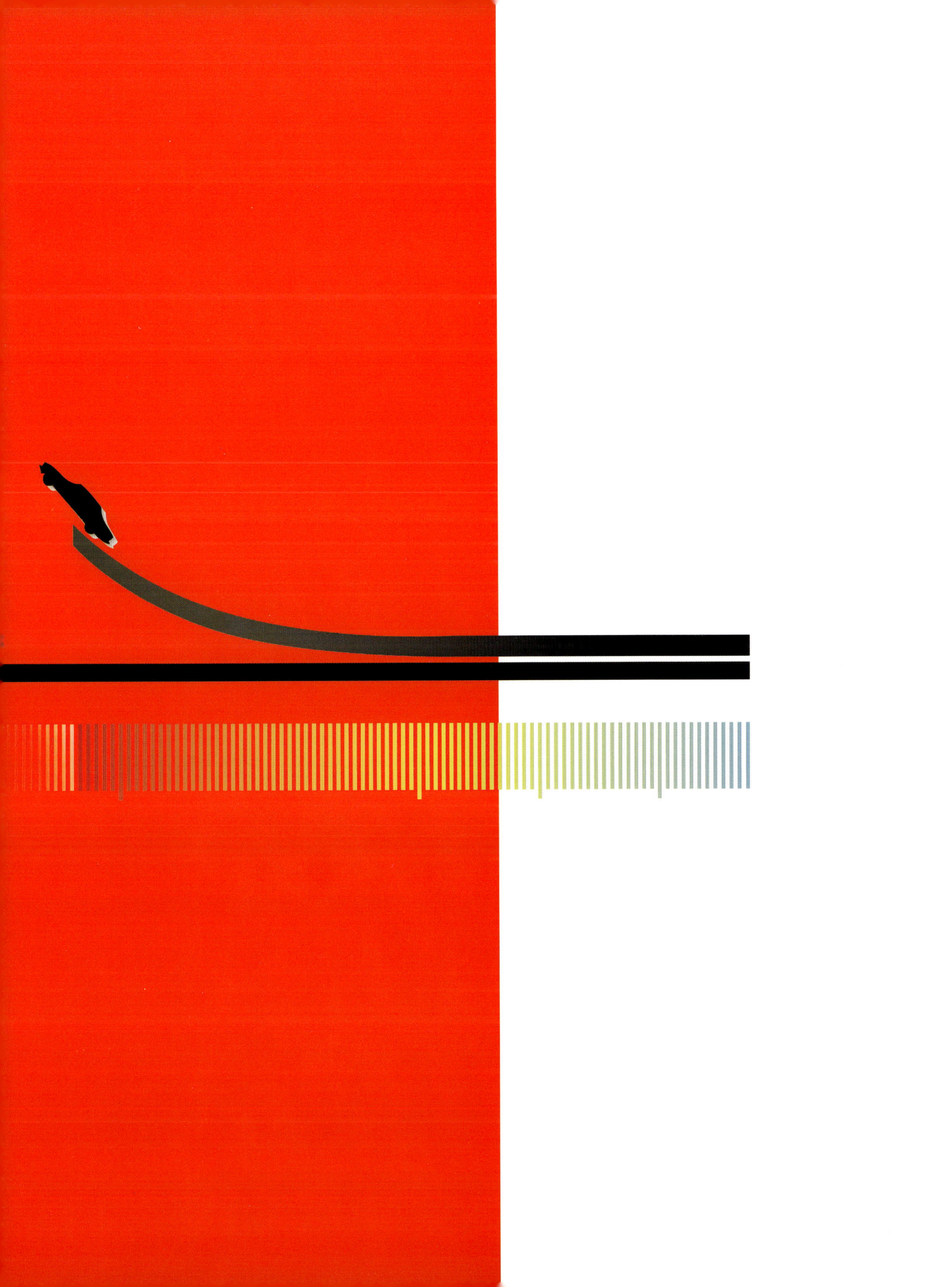

ALISHAN TOURIST ROUTES

Reiser+Umemoto RUR Architecture PC

"THE OPPOSITION OF NATURE AND CULTURE CAN NO LONGER BE CONCEIVED OF AS A SIMPLE DIALECTIC."

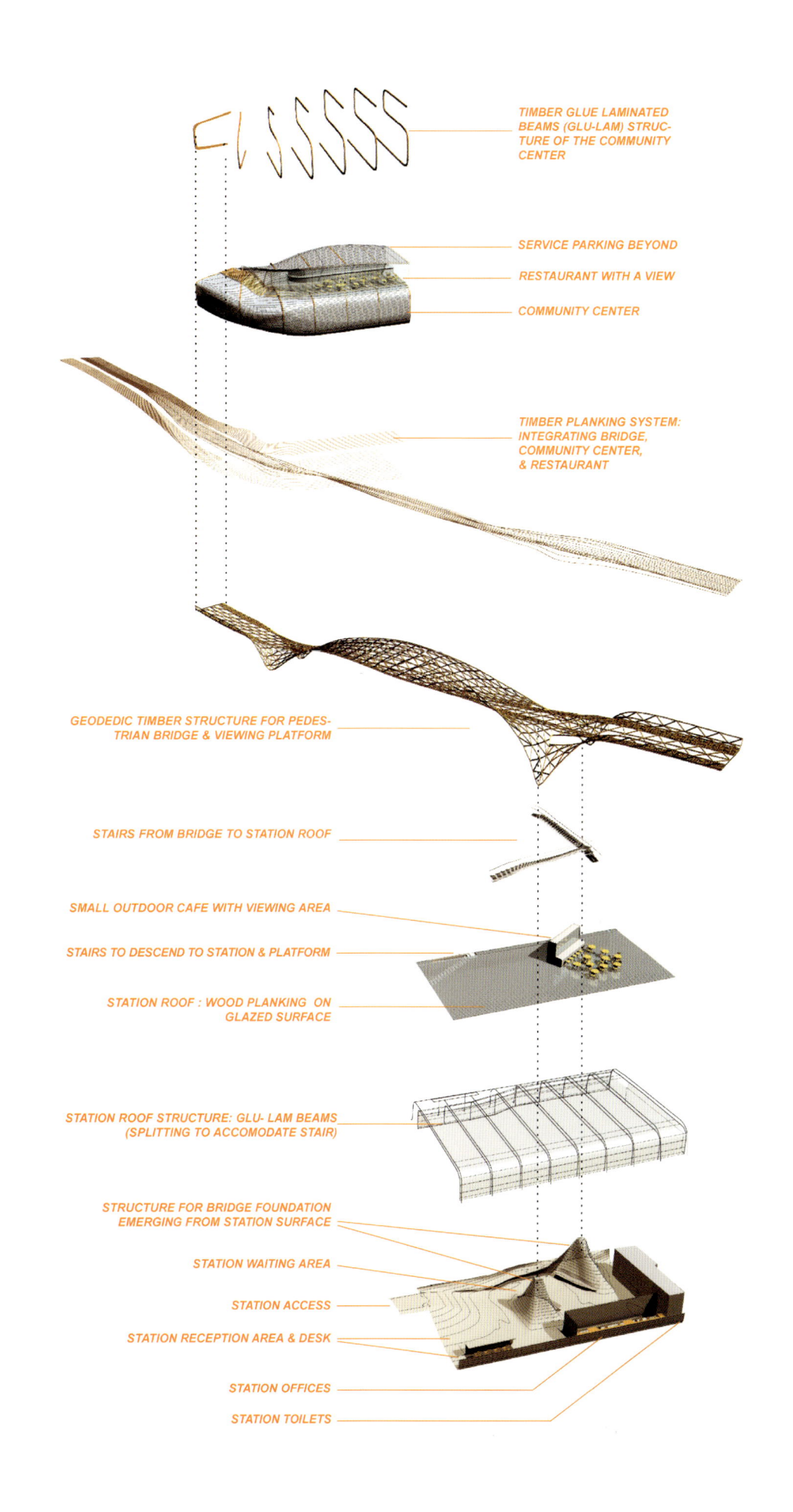

TIMBER GLUE LAMINATED BEAMS (GLU-LAM) STRUCTURE OF THE COMMUNITY CENTER

SERVICE PARKING BEYOND
RESTAURANT WITH A VIEW
COMMUNITY CENTER

TIMBER PLANKING SYSTEM: INTEGRATING BRIDGE, COMMUNITY CENTER, & RESTAURANT

GEODEDIC TIMBER STRUCTURE FOR PEDESTRIAN BRIDGE & VIEWING PLATFORM

STAIRS FROM BRIDGE TO STATION ROOF

SMALL OUTDOOR CAFE WITH VIEWING AREA
STAIRS TO DESCEND TO STATION & PLATFORM
STATION ROOF : WOOD PLANKING ON GLAZED SURFACE

STATION ROOF STRUCTURE: GLU- LAM BEAMS (SPLITTING TO ACCOMODATE STAIR)

STRUCTURE FOR BRIDGE FOUNDATION EMERGING FROM STATION SURFACE
STATION WAITING AREA
STATION ACCESS
STATION RECEPTION AREA & DESK
STATION OFFICES
STATION TOILETS

ARCHITECTURAL DIAGRAMS 631

ALTAMIRANO WALKWAY
EMILIO MARIN architect

"A SIMPLE PREFABRICATED HEXAGON-SHAPED CONCRETE SLAB BECAME THE CONSTRUCTIVE BASE FOR THE WITH VARIATIONS OF TEXTURE AND COMPOSITION."

MARCO

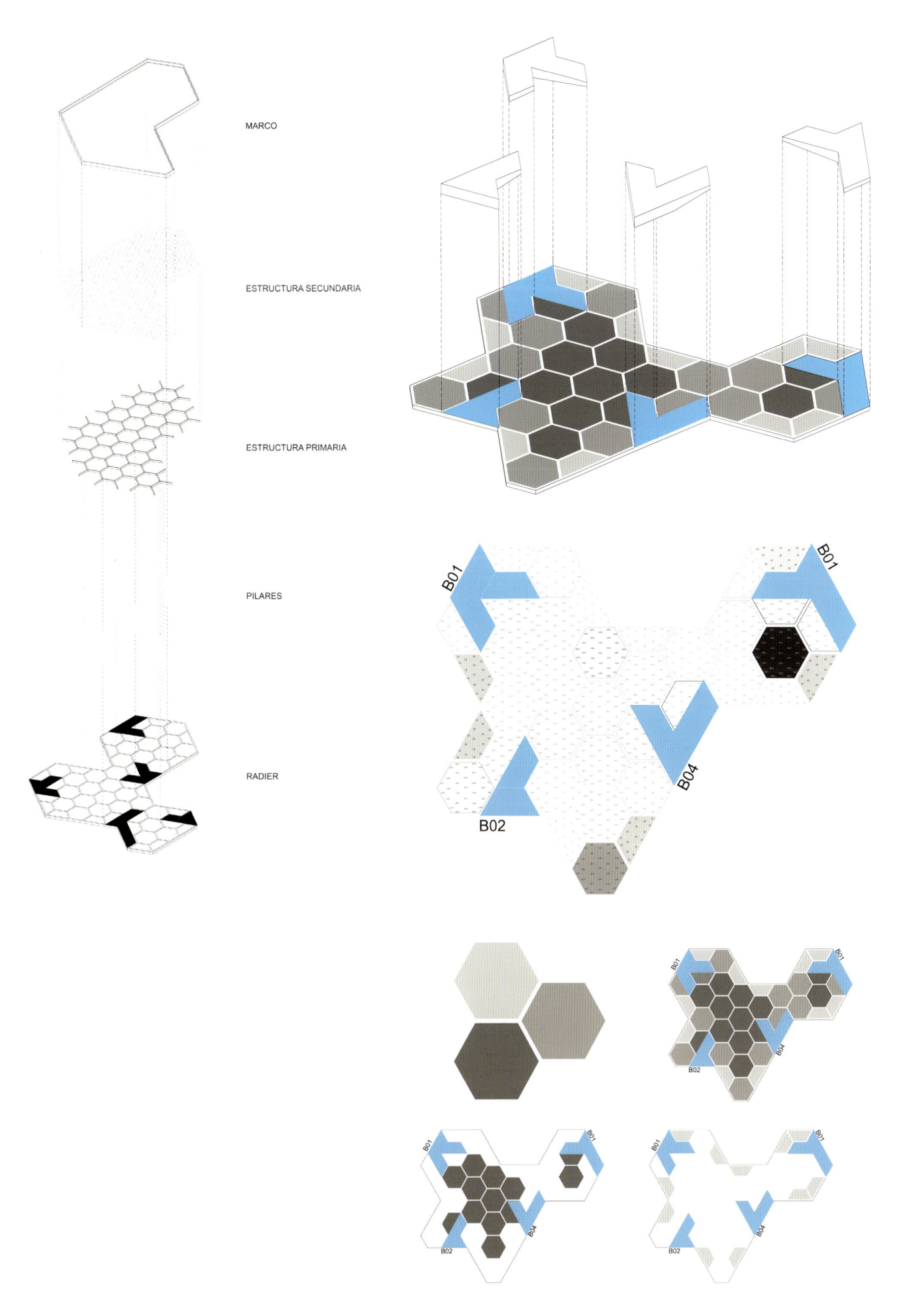

ESTRUCTURA SECUNDARIA

ESTRUCTURA PRIMARIA

PILARES

RADIER

B01

B01

B02

B04

ARCHITECTURAL DIAGRAMS 633

'AKTIPIS' FLOWERSHOP
Point Supreme Architects

"PLACING THE TABLES IN THE CENTRE OF THE SPACE FOCUSES THE CUSTOMERS' VIEW."

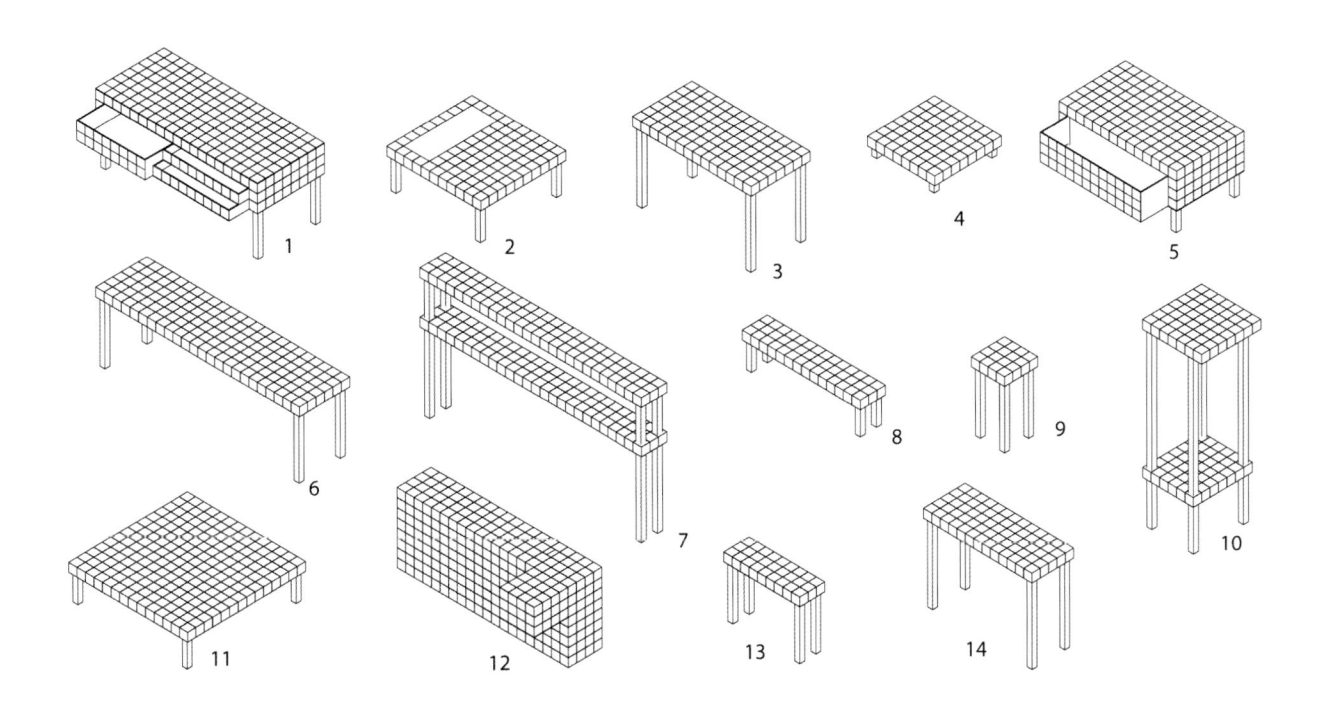

1. cashier/preparation table
2. low table/client seat
3. high table for low plants
4. very low table for heavy pots with big plants
5. table with big drawer for storing pots
6. high and long table for medium size plants
7. high, narrow and long table for small pots with flowers
8. vitrine table; fits in the 3dimensional facade void
9. table for special plant
10. table for plants with hanging branches
11. exhibition table
12. 'technical' table for computer, fax, phone
13. small table for special plants in the fridge
14. table in the fridge

Tables

BENCHES, BECOME A PART OF LANDSCAPE
Jungwoo Ji

"THE CONCEPT OF MOUNTAINS DEFINED AS ELEVATED LANDS SUCH AS MT. NAM OR MT. BUKHAN MOTIVATES THE SHAPE OF BENCHES."

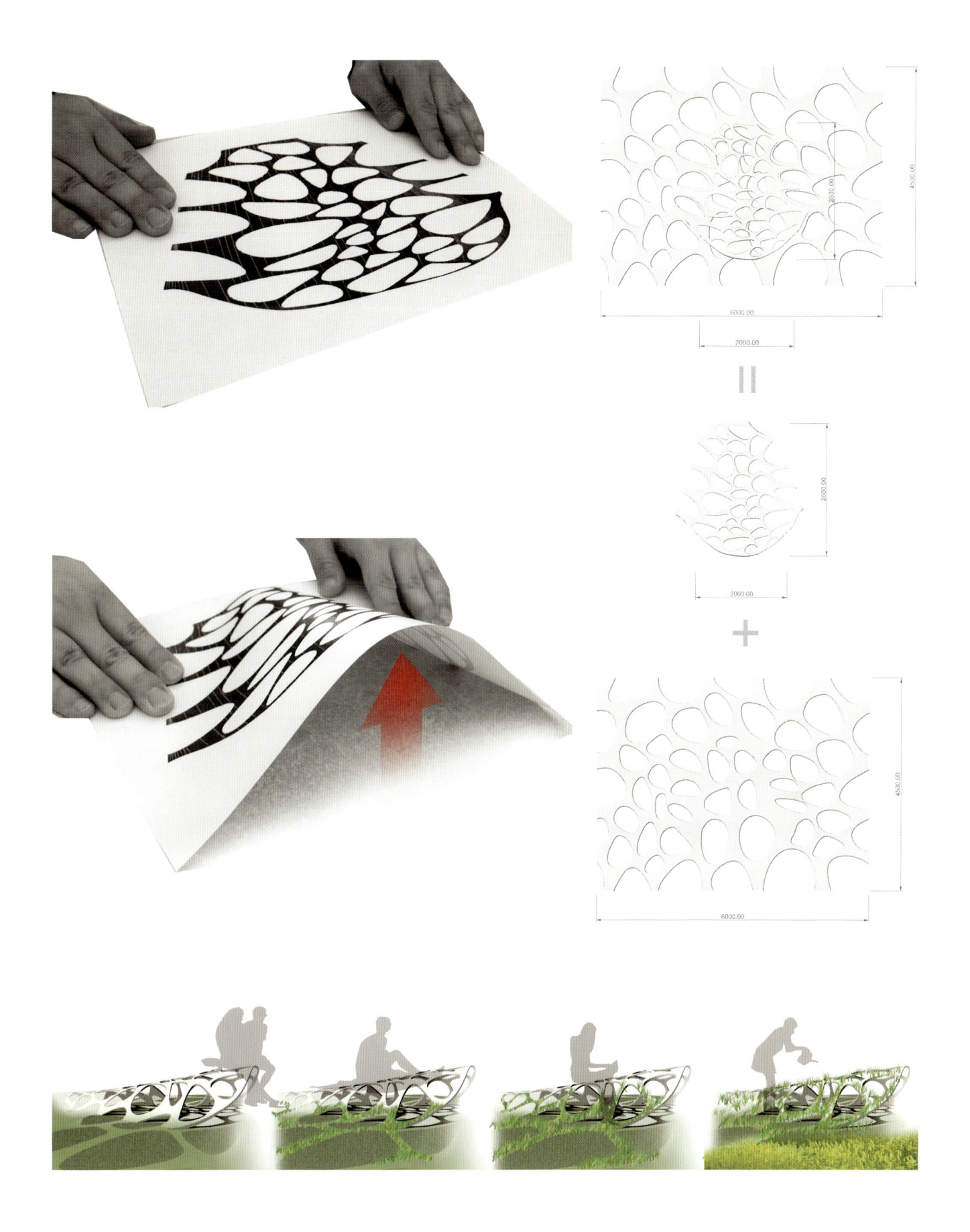

ARCHITECTURAL DIAGRAMS 637

BENCH DESIGN JDS Architects

"THIS BENCH IS A PALETTE OF ACTIVITIES INCLUDED IN A SINGULAR NECKLACE."

The heat is blocked.

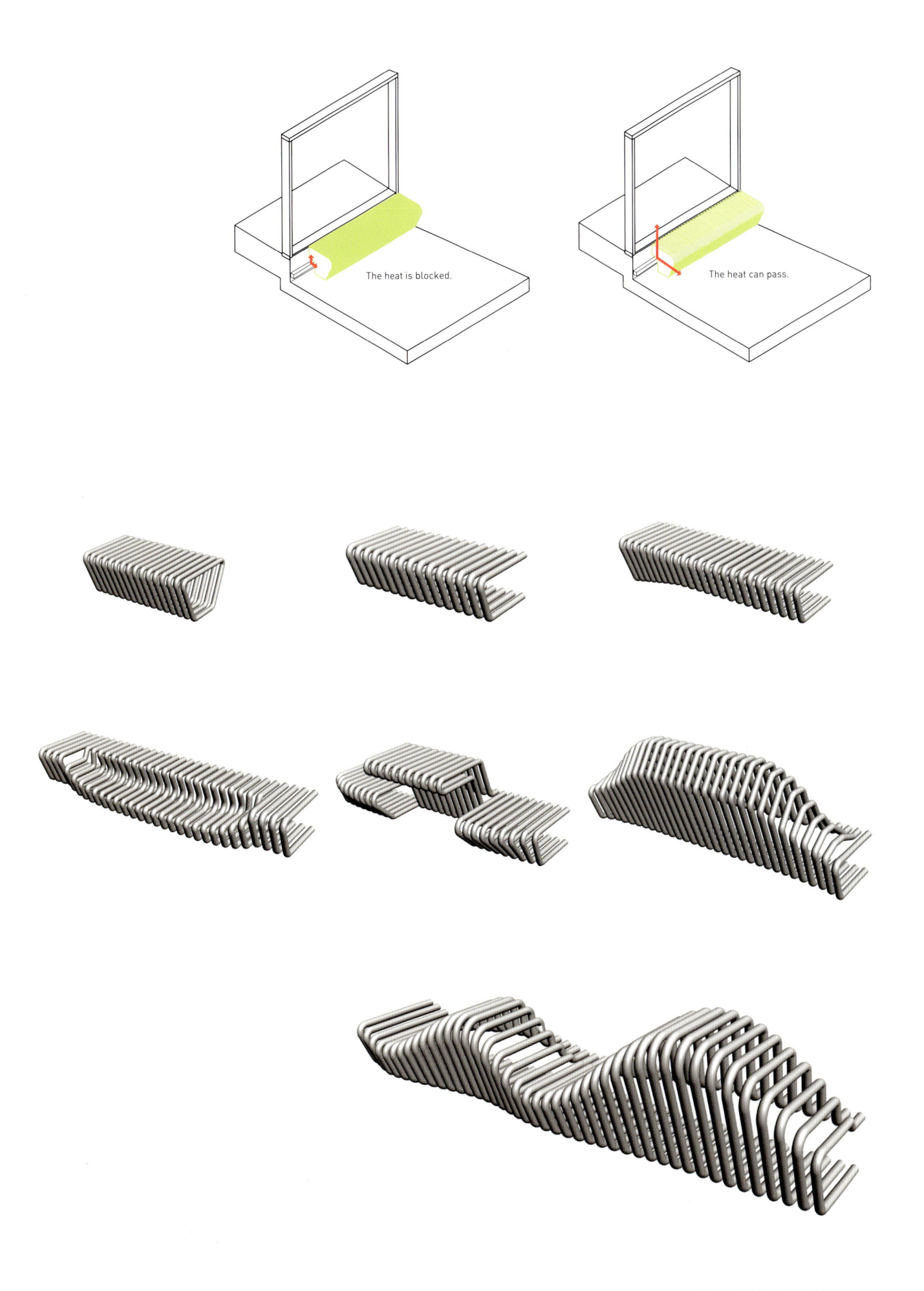

The heat can pass.

ARCHITECTURAL DIAGRAMS 639

BIOZONE servo

"CATALOG OF MATERIAL AND TECHNOLOGICAL PATCHES WHOSE DISTRIBUTION ALLOW FOR A WIDE RANGE OF RECREATIONAL, AGRICULTURAL, AND INFRASTRUCTURAL USES."

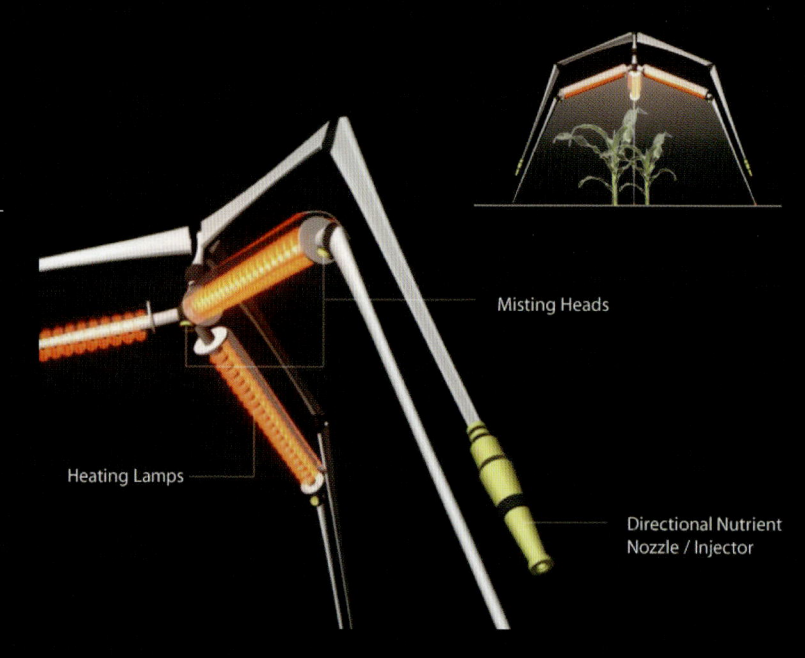

Misting Heads

Heating Lamps

Directional Nutrient Nozzle / Injector

640 INSTALLATION

	PIXELATION	PERIMETER	MATERIAL

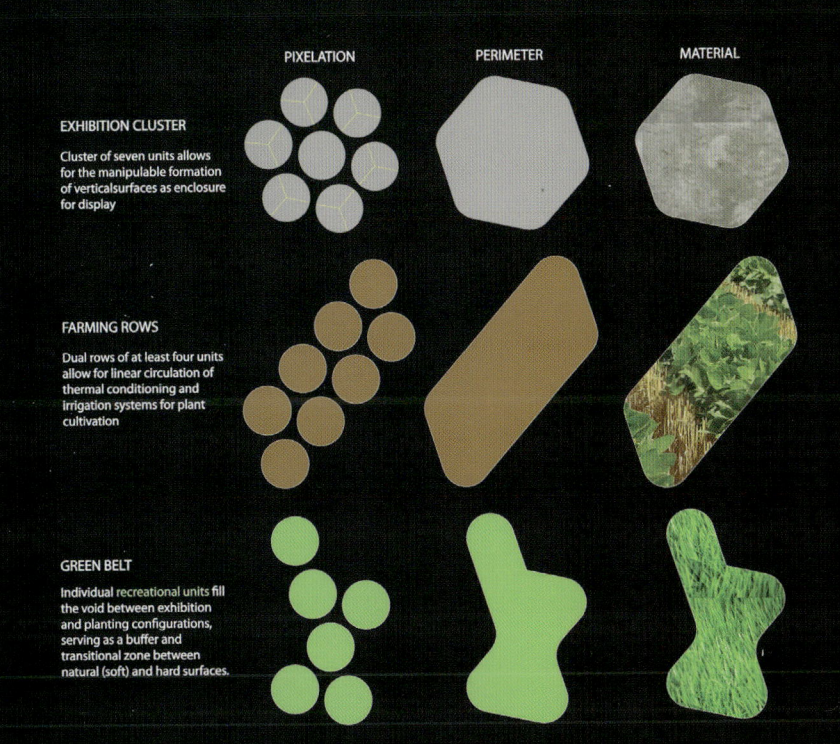

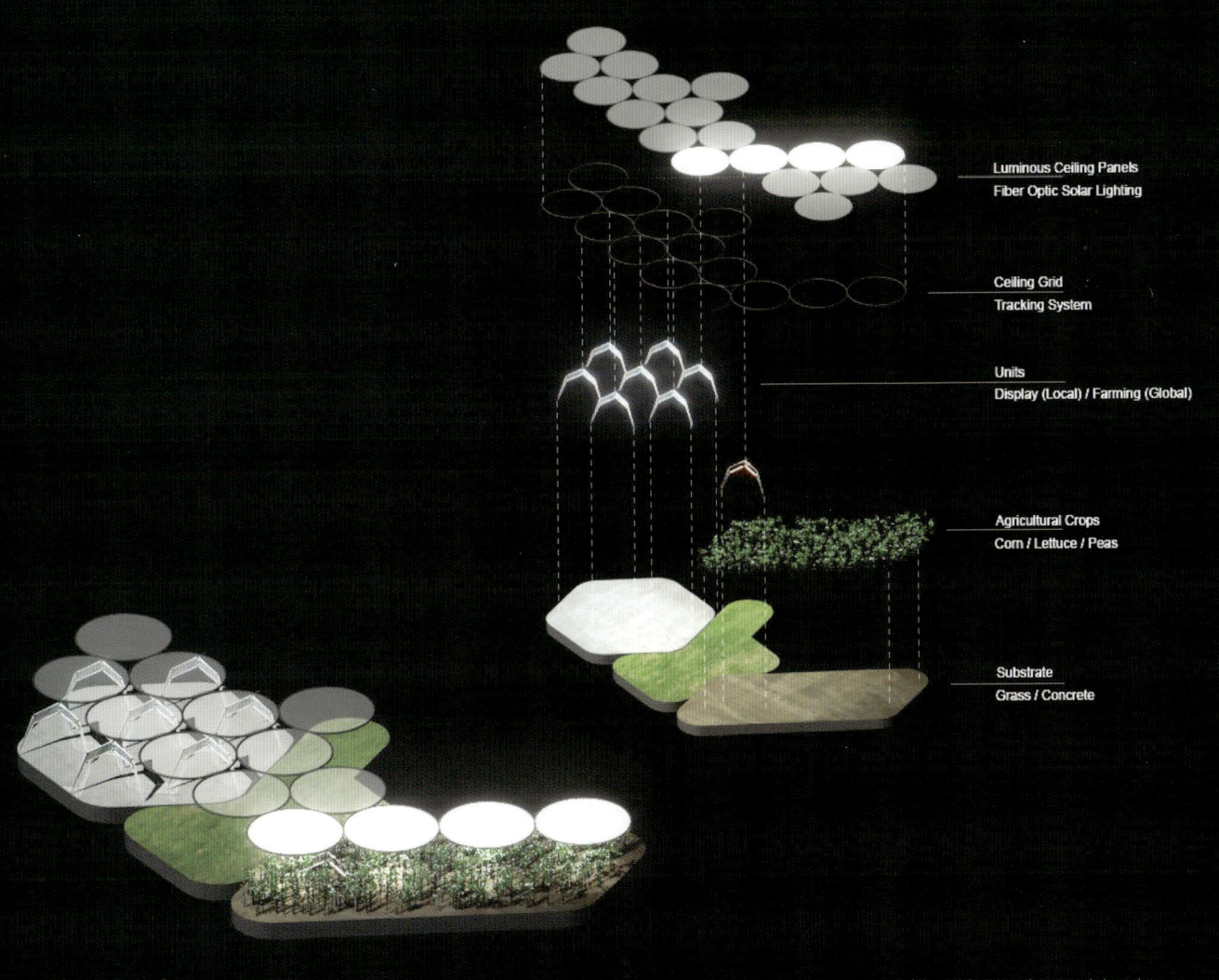

EXHIBITION CLUSTER
Cluster of seven units allows for the manipulable formation of vertical surfaces as enclosure for display

FARMING ROWS
Dual rows of at least four units allow for linear circulation of thermal conditioning and irrigation systems for plant cultivation

GREEN BELT
Individual recreational units fill the void between exhibition and planting configurations, serving as a buffer and transitional zone between natural (soft) and hard surfaces.

- Luminous Ceiling Panels / Fiber Optic Solar Lighting
- Ceiling Grid / Tracking System
- Units / Display (Local) / Farming (Global)
- Agricultural Crops / Corn / Lettuce / Peas
- Substrate / Grass / Concrete

Exploded axonometric of the various environmental and programmatic systems.

ARCHITECTURAL DIAGRAMS 641

BOOKS ON EARTH-QUAKE Smånsk Design Studio

"THE PLAYFUL DESIGN HAS BEEN DESCRIBED AS BOTH PRACTICAL AND FUNCTIONAL AND BARBIES HOUSE AFTER AN EARTHQUAKE."

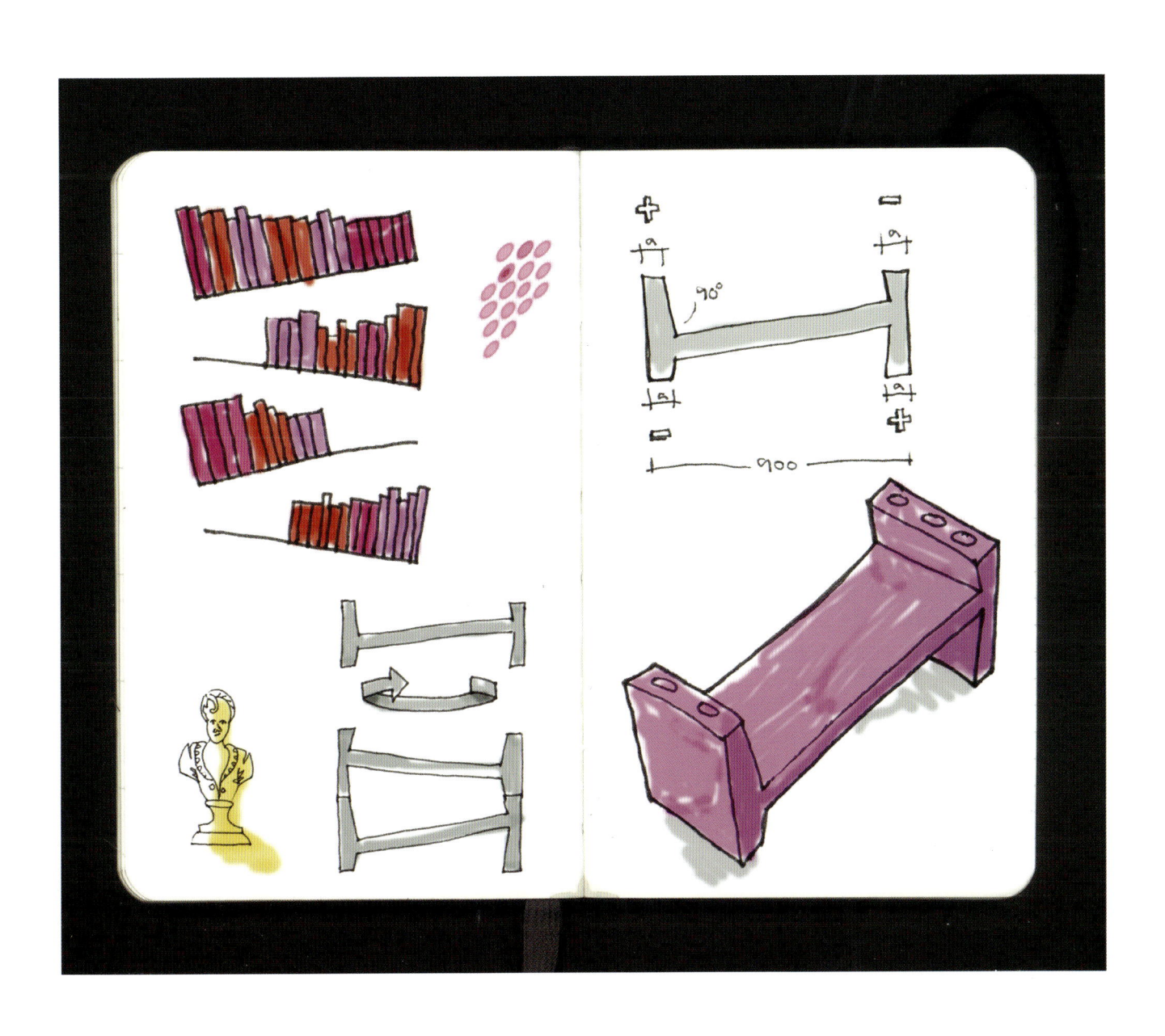

ARCHITECTURAL DIAGRAMS 643

CANOPY: MoMA / P.S.1
nARCHITECTS

"DIPS IN THE CANOPY PROVOKE DIFFERENT MODES OF LOUNGING IN FOUR DISTINCT ENVIRONMENTS."

	Landscape	Weather

Sand Hump	Pool Pad	Fog Pad	Rainforest
☀ 100 deg 💧 5% humidity	☀ 90 deg 💧 15% humidity	☀ 80 deg 💧 90% humidity	☀ 70 deg 💧 100% humidity

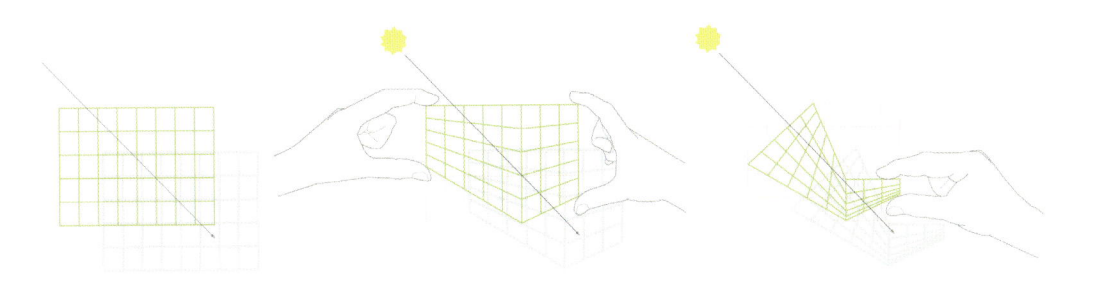

ARCHITECTURAL DIAGRAMS 645

CIRCLE UNStudio

"THE ARCHES CAN STAY LOOSE OR CAN BE ATTACHED IN DIFFERENT WAYS TO EACH OTHER."

ARCHITECTURAL DIAGRAMS

CROSS-WIND BRIDGE
Jorge Pereira

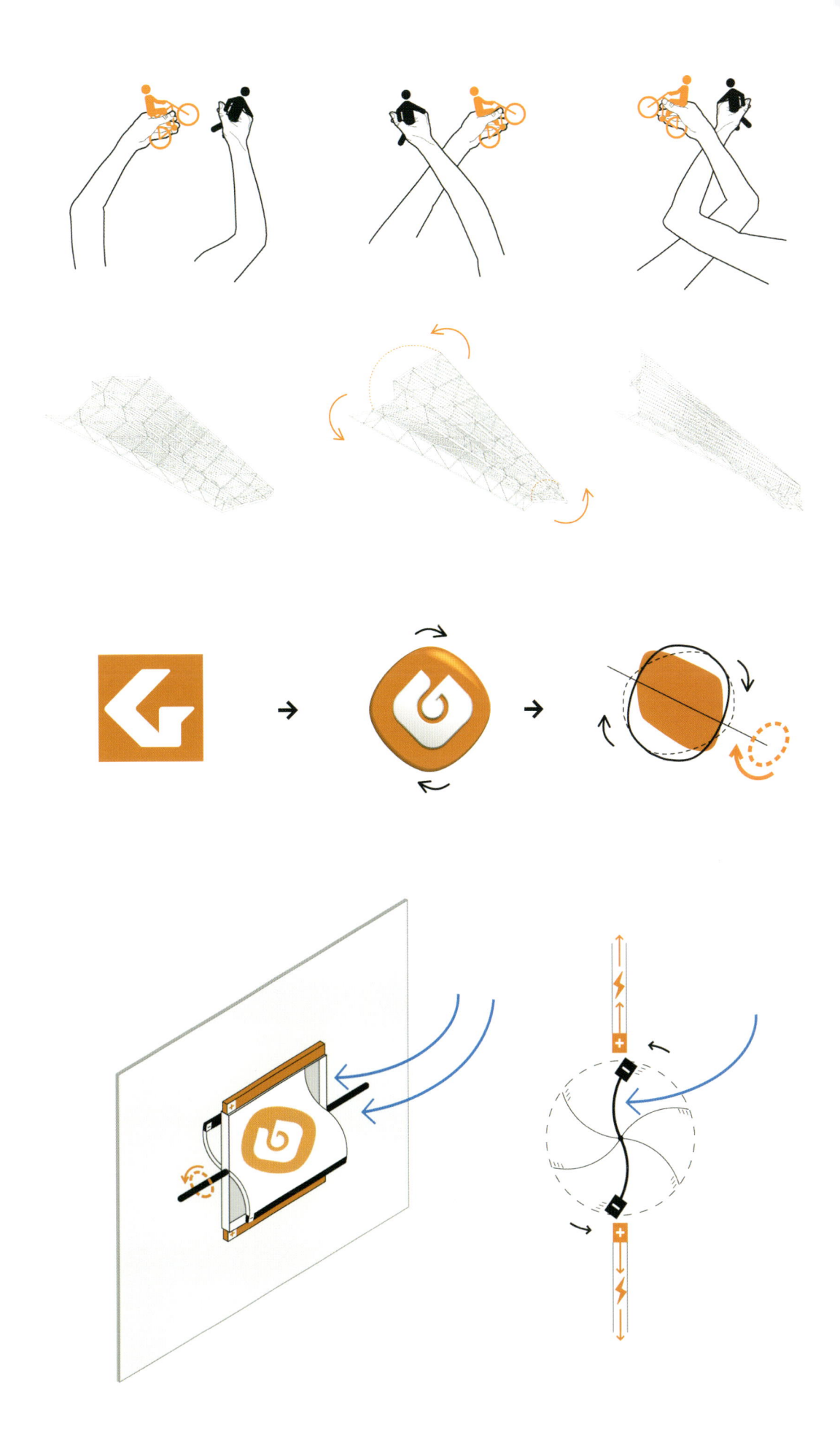

ARCHITECTURAL DIAGRAMS 649

CULTURAL GATE TO ALBORZ
Guallart Architects

"THE PROJECT WILL ACT AS A MONUMENTAL GATEWAY, CREATING A VIRTUAL BOUNDARY BETWEEN CITY AND NATURE."

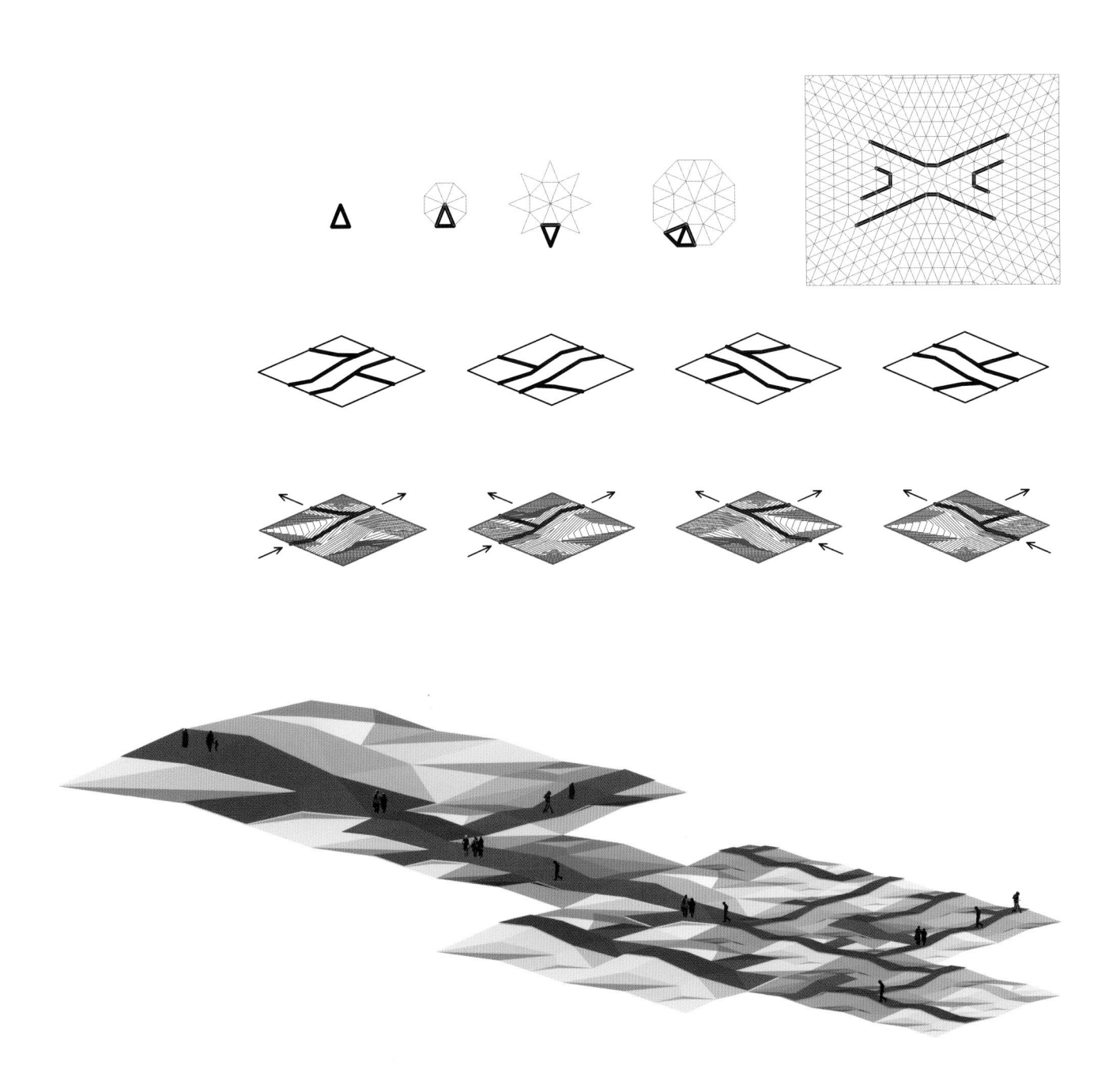

ARCHITECTURAL DIAGRAMS 651

DAS NETZ NL Architects

"IT HOPEFULLY INVITES THE PUBLIC TO USE IT IN MANY DIFFERENT WAYS."

Cinema

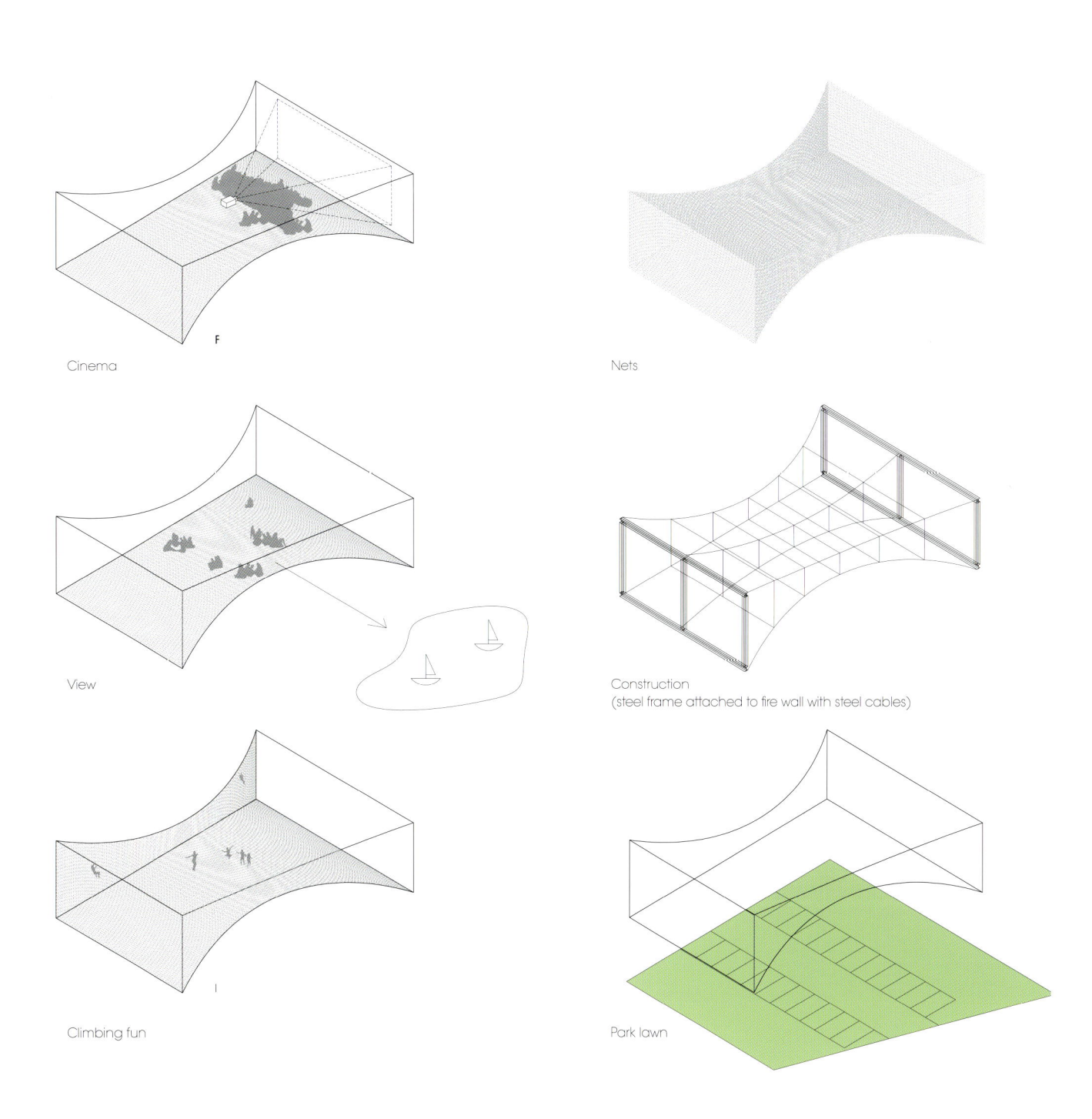

Nets

View

Construction
(steel frame attached to fire wall with steel cables)

Climbing fun

Park lawn

ARCHITECTURAL DIAGRAMS 653

DISPLAY ENVIRONMENT 1 servo

"THE STALACTITES PLUG INTO A SUSPENDED CEILING SYSTEM COMPRISED OF VACUUM-FORMED ACRYLIC CONDUITS."

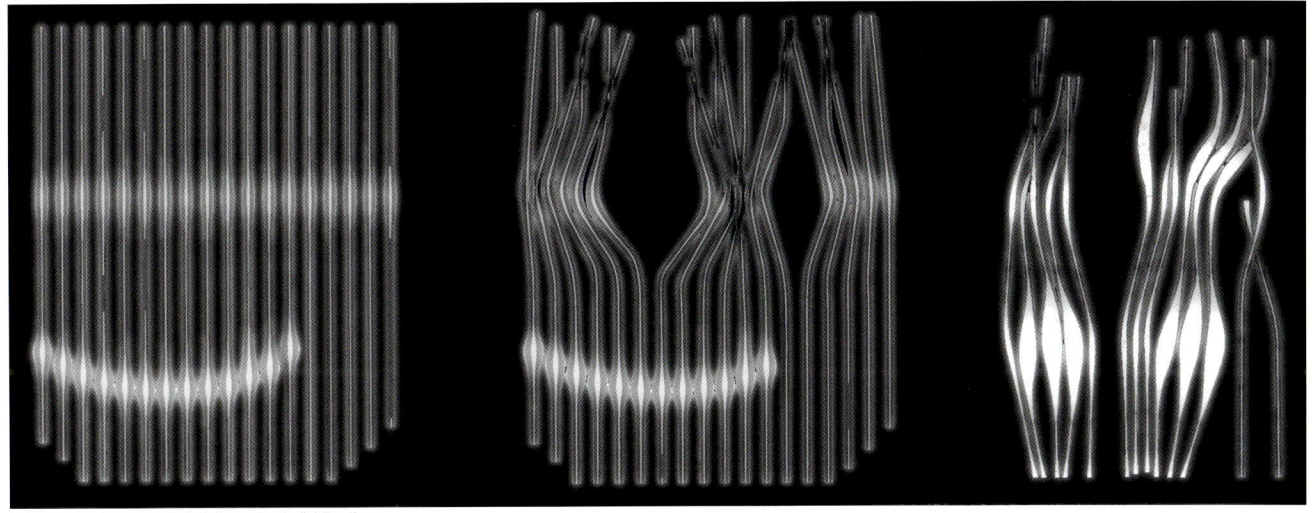

Diagram of fiber-optic lighting duct distribution.

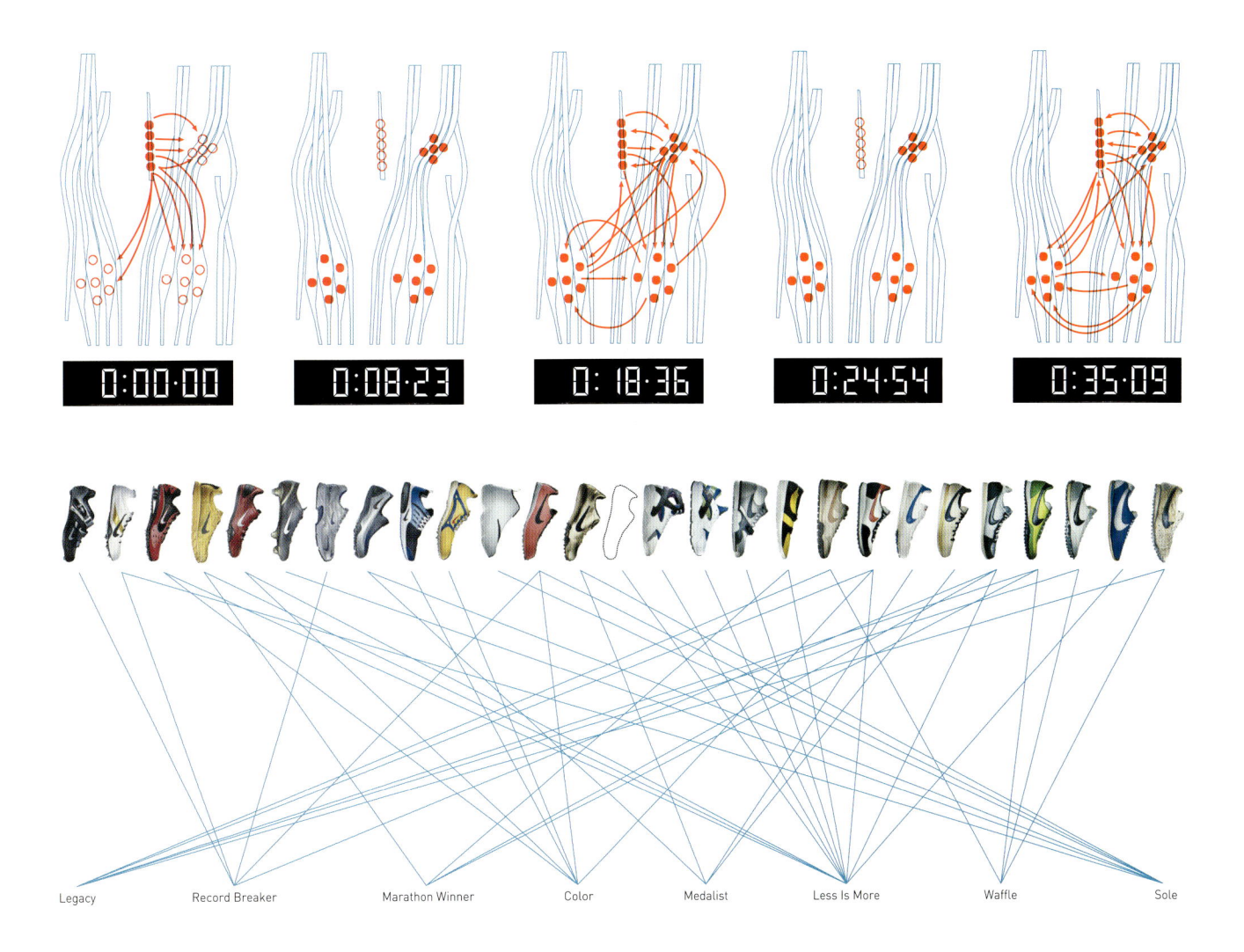

0:00:00   0:08:23   0:18:36   0:24:54   0:35:09

Legacy   Record Breaker   Marathon Winner   Color   Medalist   Less Is More   Waffle   Sole

Curatorial distribution system: Reconfigurable display canisters allow for shoes to continuously circulate based on variable thematic sequencing logics.

ARCHITECTURAL DIAGRAMS 655

DISPLAY ENVIRONMENT 2 servo

"THE PROJECTION SYSTEM PROVIDES FOR A PASSIVE ENGAGEMENT WITH THE DISPLAY MATERIAL, ALLOWING USERS TO VIEW ART IN A MORE INFORMAL WAY AS THEY MOVE THROUGH THE GALLERY."

Photograph of Dark Places exhibition infrastructure
Image Credit: Erdman Photography

Schematic diagram of the display infrastructure for the Dark Places project, integrating audio, visual, and interactive technologies in the formation of a responsive exhibition environment.

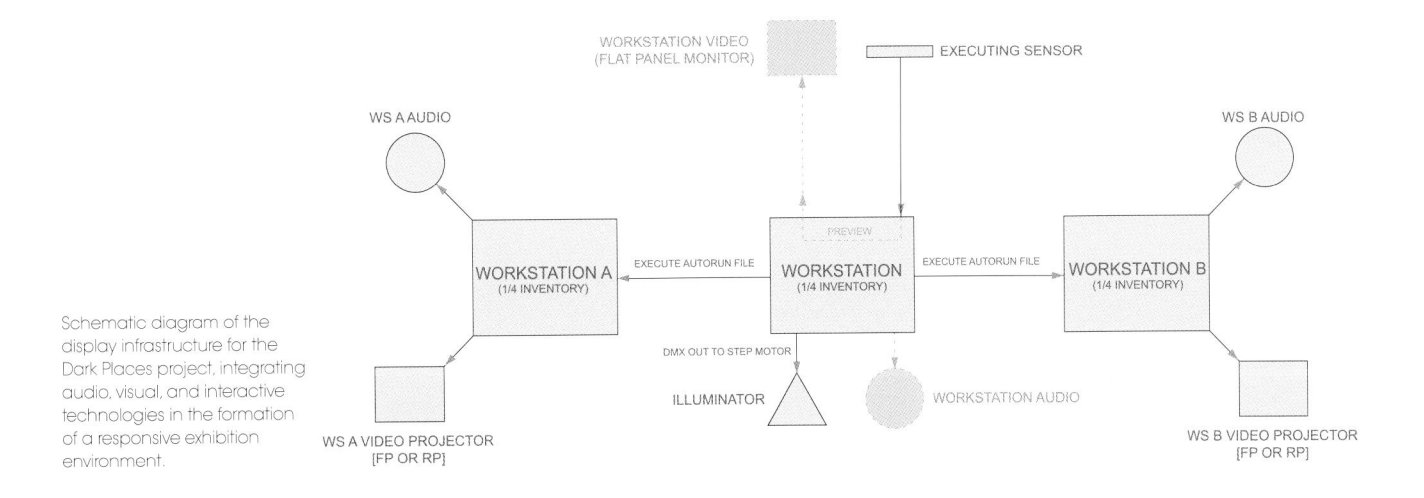

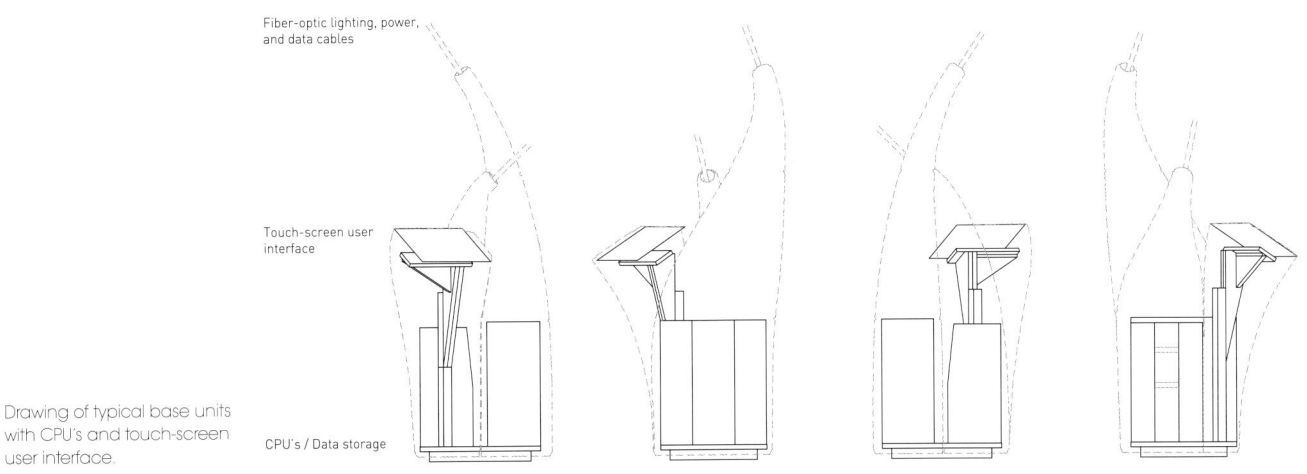

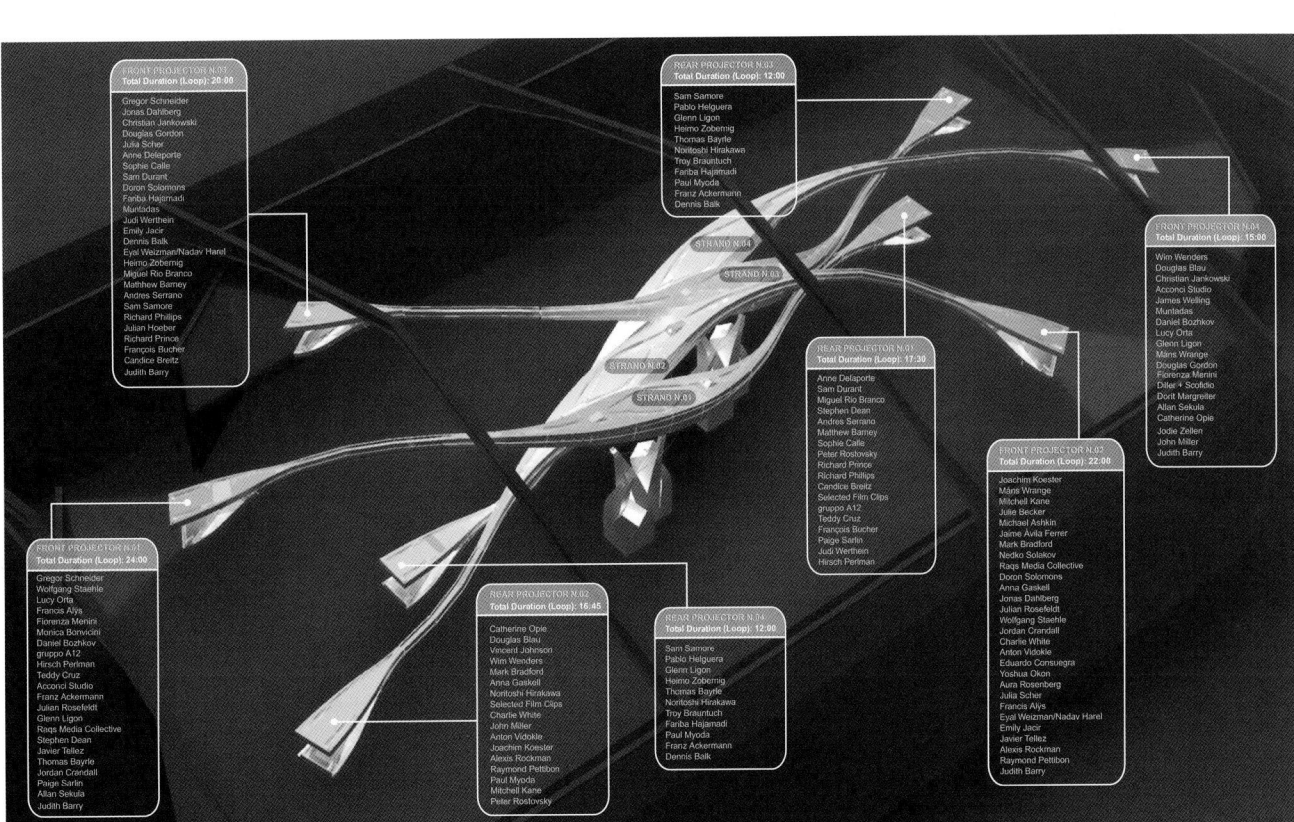

Drawing of typical base units with CPU's and touch-screen user interface.

ARCHITECTURAL DIAGRAMS 657

DUNE Moho Architects

"DUNE IS EASILY CONSTRUCTED WITH THIRTY SIX 100% RECYCLABLE TRIPLEX CARDBOARD RIBS, PERFORMING AN ECONOMIC, RESISTANT, SOFT STRUCTURE."

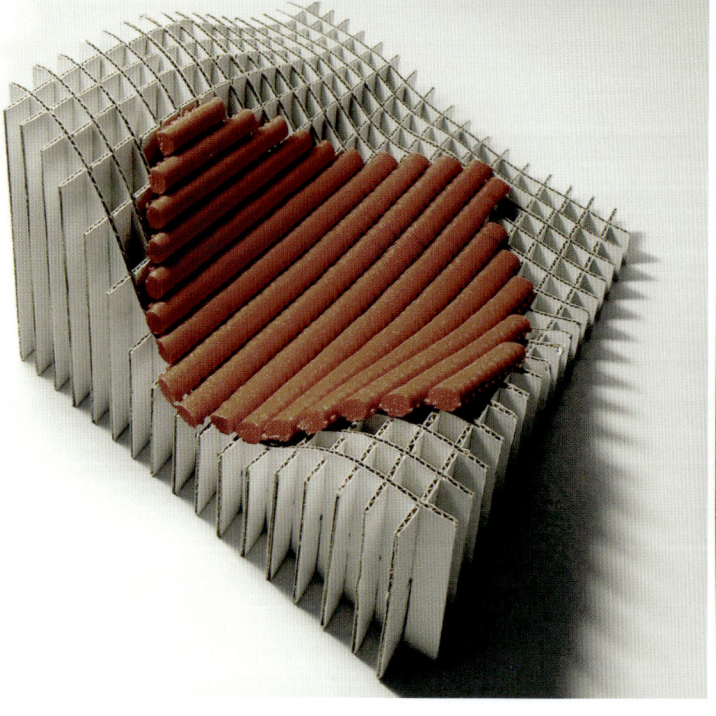

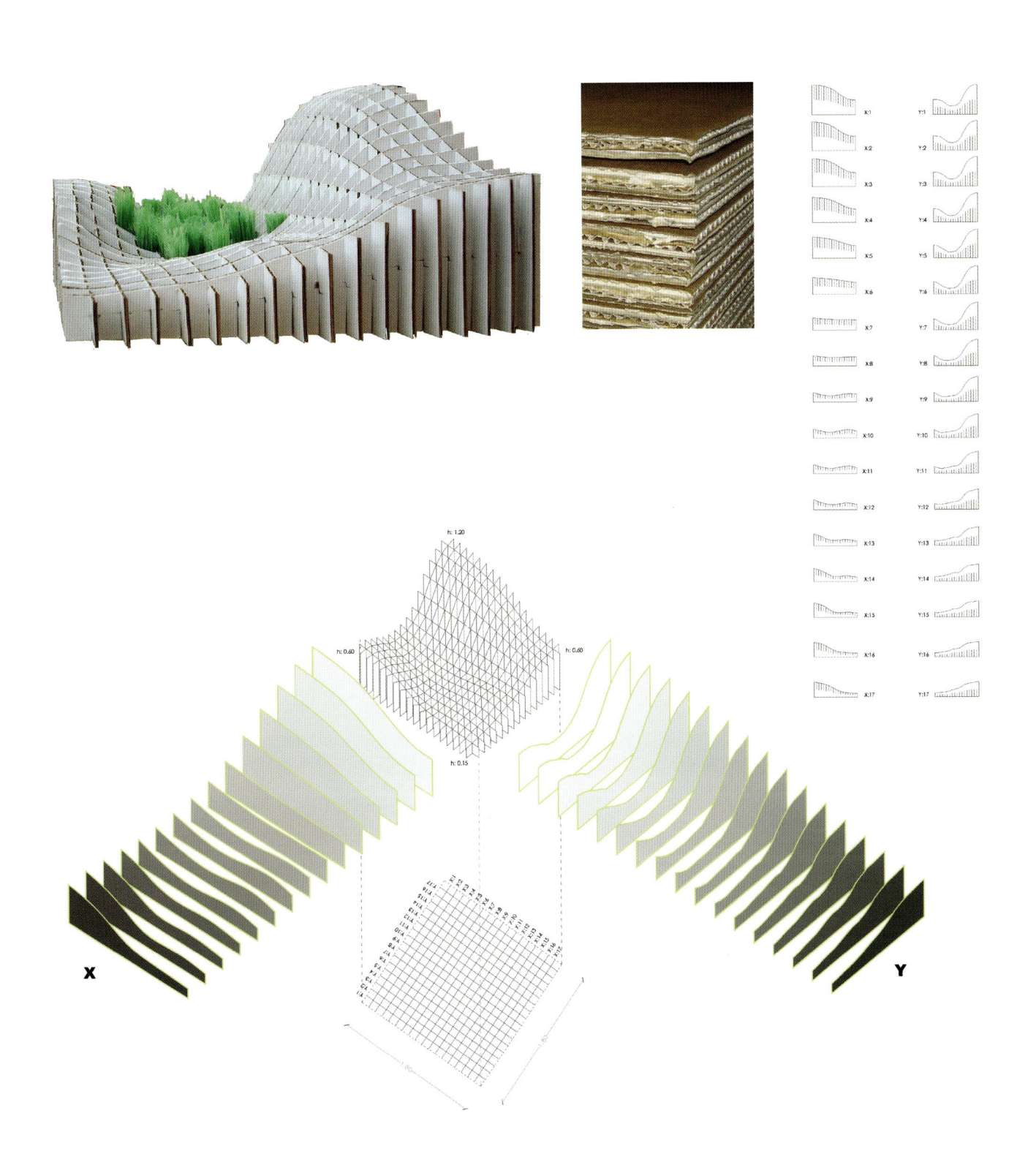

ARCHITECTURAL DIAGRAMS 659

DURCHBLICK
the next ENTERprise

"A PROMINENT ENTRANCE FROM BREITE GASSE INTO THE MUSEUMSQUARTIER, VIENNA'S NEW CULTURAL DISTRICT."

Deformed loop

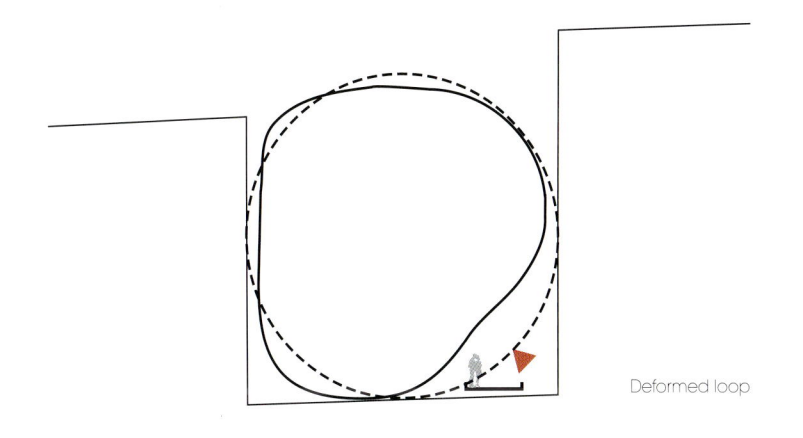

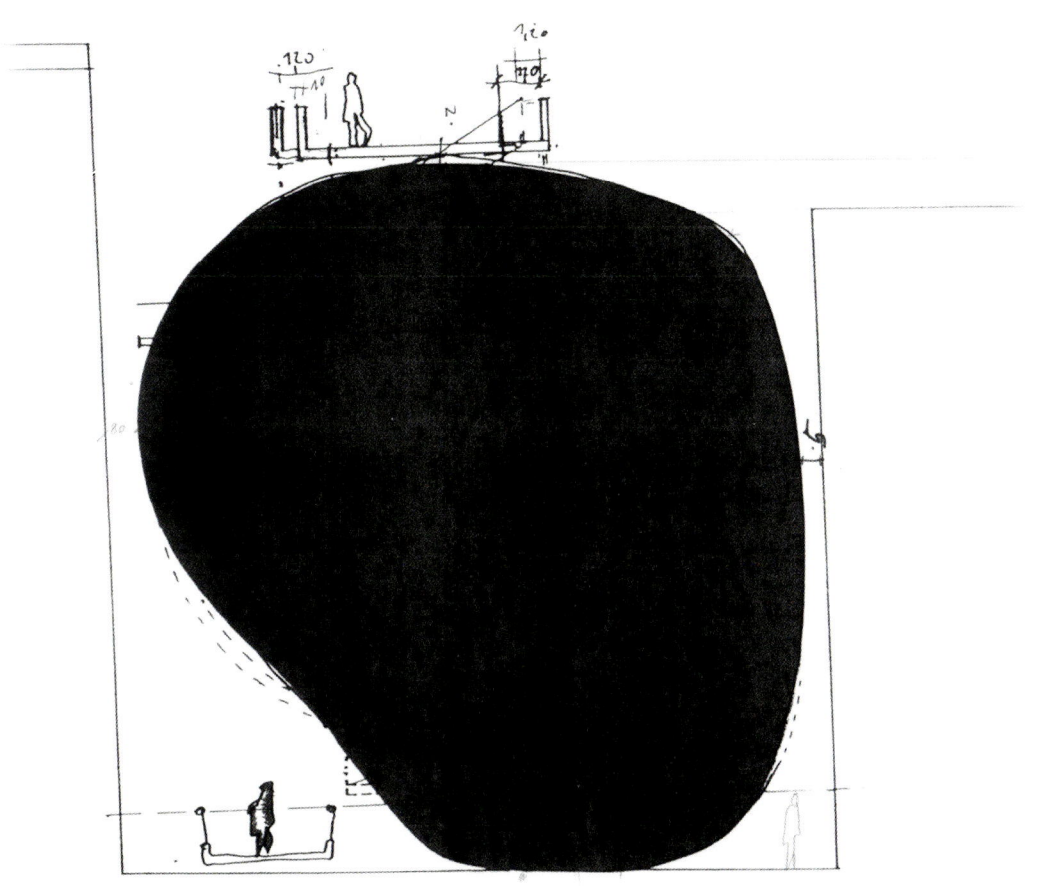

Sketch illustrating concept of site occupation.

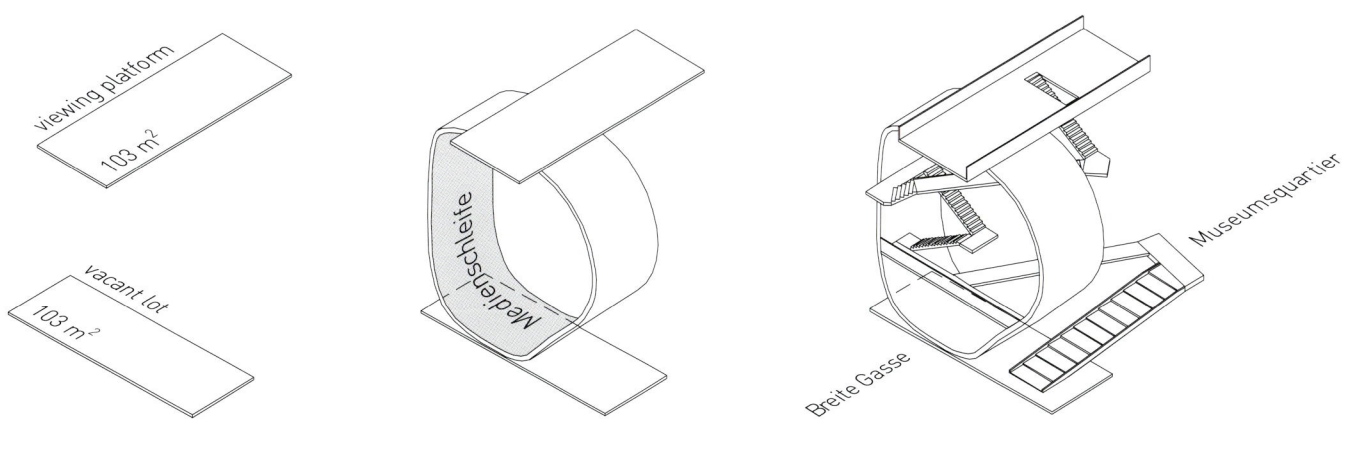

Lifted vacant lot — viewing platform 103 m², vacant lot 103 m²

Media loop

Circulation

ARCHITECTURAL DIAGRAMS 661

EARPHONE STAND PSA

"THE DESIGN OF THE PRODUCT EMERGED FROM THE CHOICE OF THE MATERIAL. THE WEIGHT (SELF-SUPPORTING) AND MALLEABILITY (ONE BENT PIECE) OF CORIAN."

ELEVATION 1

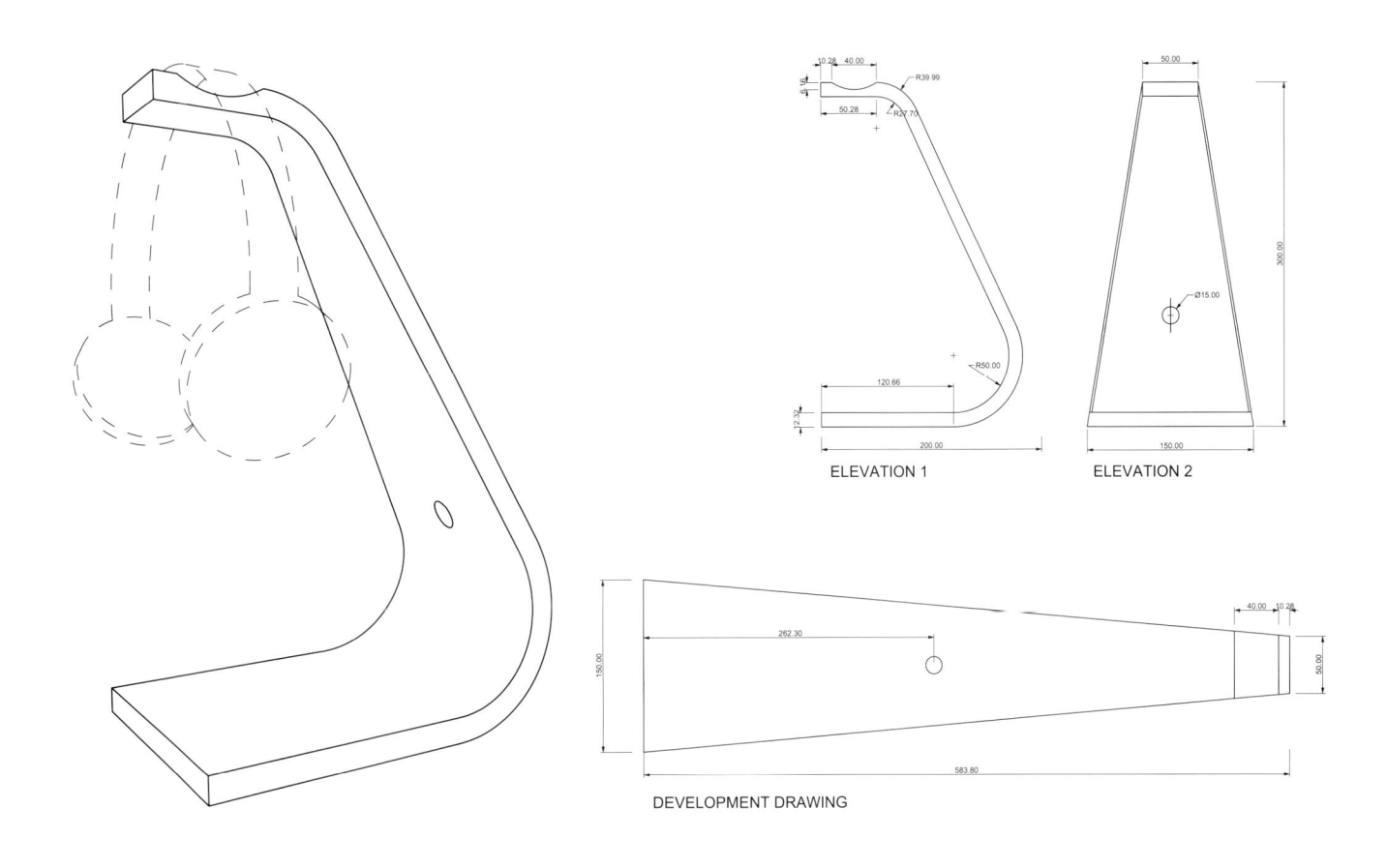

ELEVATION 2

DEVELOPMENT DRAWING

ARCHITECTURAL DIAGRAMS 663

ECO-BULEVARD, NEW SUBURBAN DEVELOPMENT OF VALLECAS

Ecosistema Urbano + TECTUM

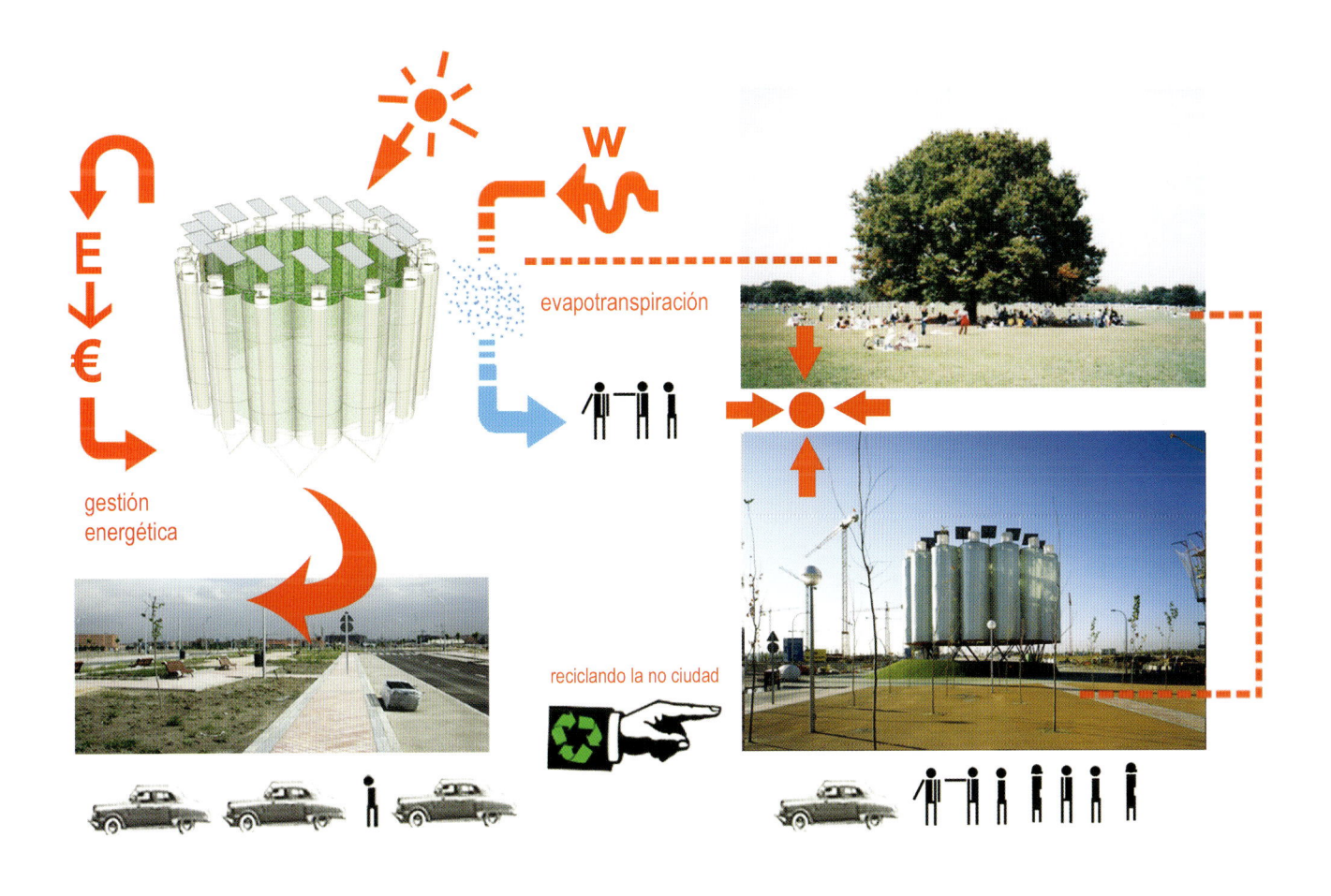

gestión energética

evapotranspiración

reciclando la no ciudad

year 0

year 20

ARCHITECTURAL DIAGRAMS 665

FLIP
marco hemmerling architecture design

"FLIP INTEGRATES FOUR DIFFERENT SEATING POSITIONS IN ONE CONTINUOUS SHAPE."

ARCHITECTURAL DIAGRAMS 667

HIGH-SPEED CAR
RAMP Tiago Barros + Jorge Pereira

A8 OESTE

Ramp Ahead
Please go Faster...

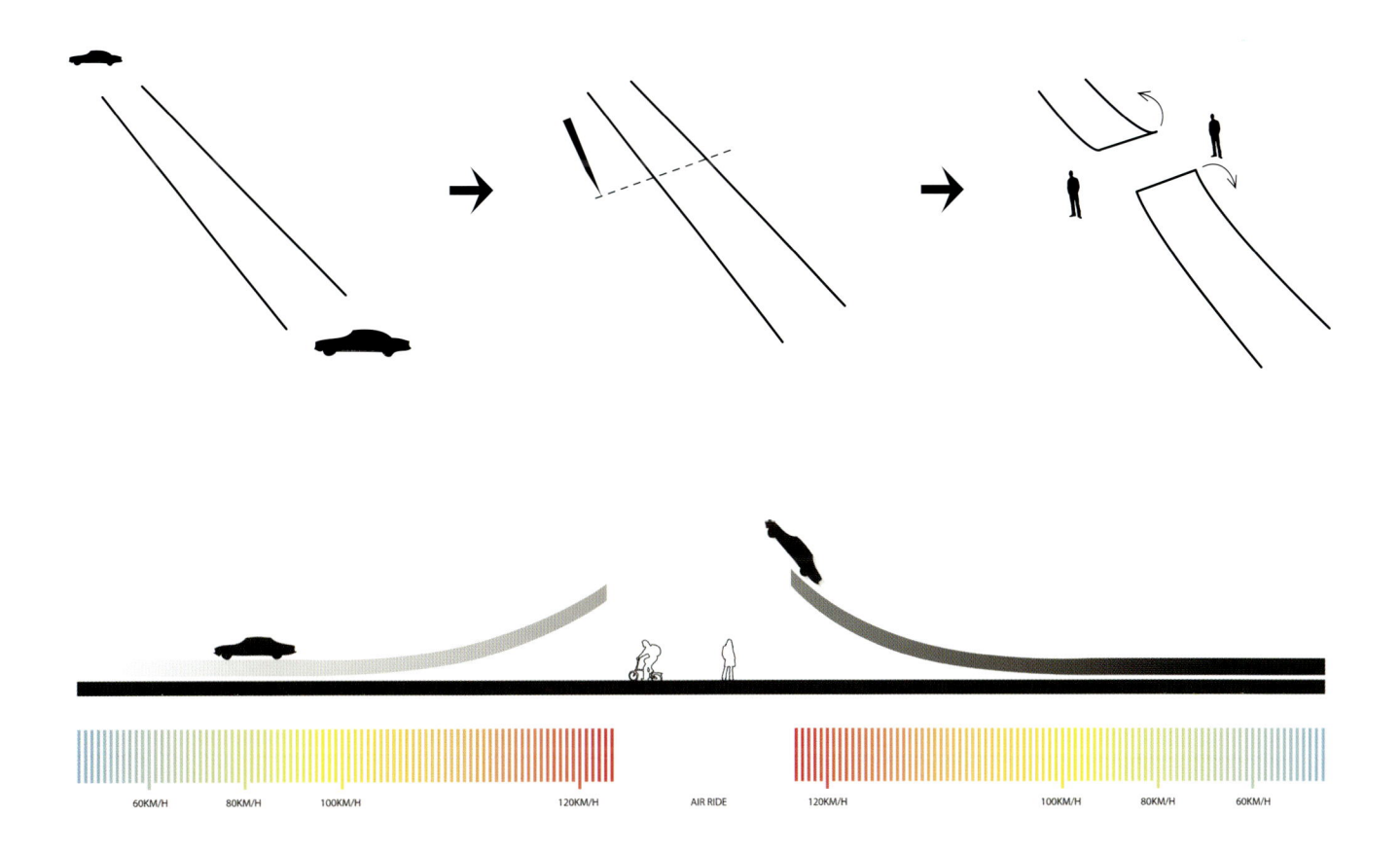

60KM/H 80KM/H 100KM/H 120KM/H   AIR RIDE   120KM/H 100KM/H 80KM/H 60KM/H

ARCHITECTURAL DIAGRAMS 669

HOME (FOR A HOMELESS KID) KOMATEIKA

Zizi&Yoyo

"...IS A MULTIFUNCTIONAL BACKPACK, MAKING THE CHILD FEEL AT HOME WHERE EVER HE OR SHE GOES."

Spiral inflatable structure

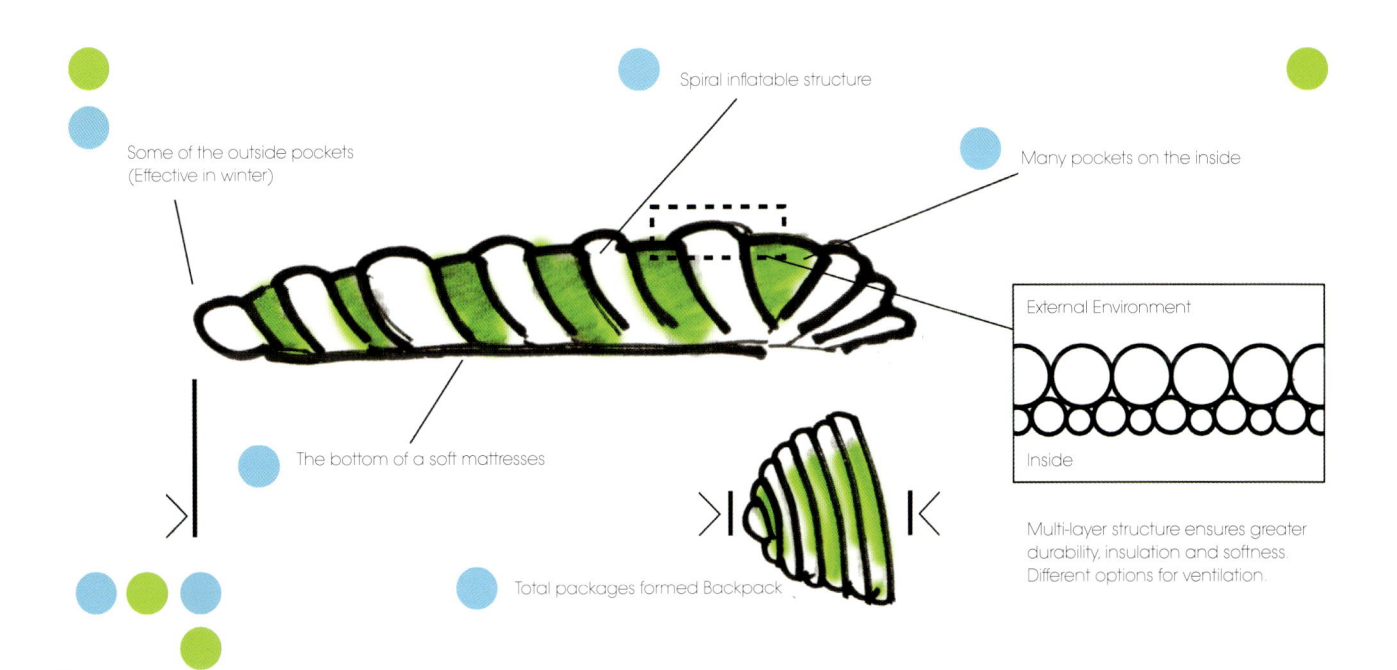

Some of the outside pockets
(Effective in winter)

Many pockets on the inside

The bottom of a soft mattresses

Total packages formed Backpack

External Environment

Inside

Multi-layer structure ensures greater durability, insulation and softness. Different options for ventilation.

ARCHITECTURAL DIAGRAMS 671

IN THE LATTICE servo

"A PROTOTYPE GEOMETRY INSCRIBING AN INTRICATE LATTICE PATTERN IS DEPLOYED AS A NAVIGATIONAL SYSTEM WITHIN A SERIES OF FOUR LIGHT TABLES."

Photograph of Lattice Archipelogics installation at UCLA's Department of Architecture

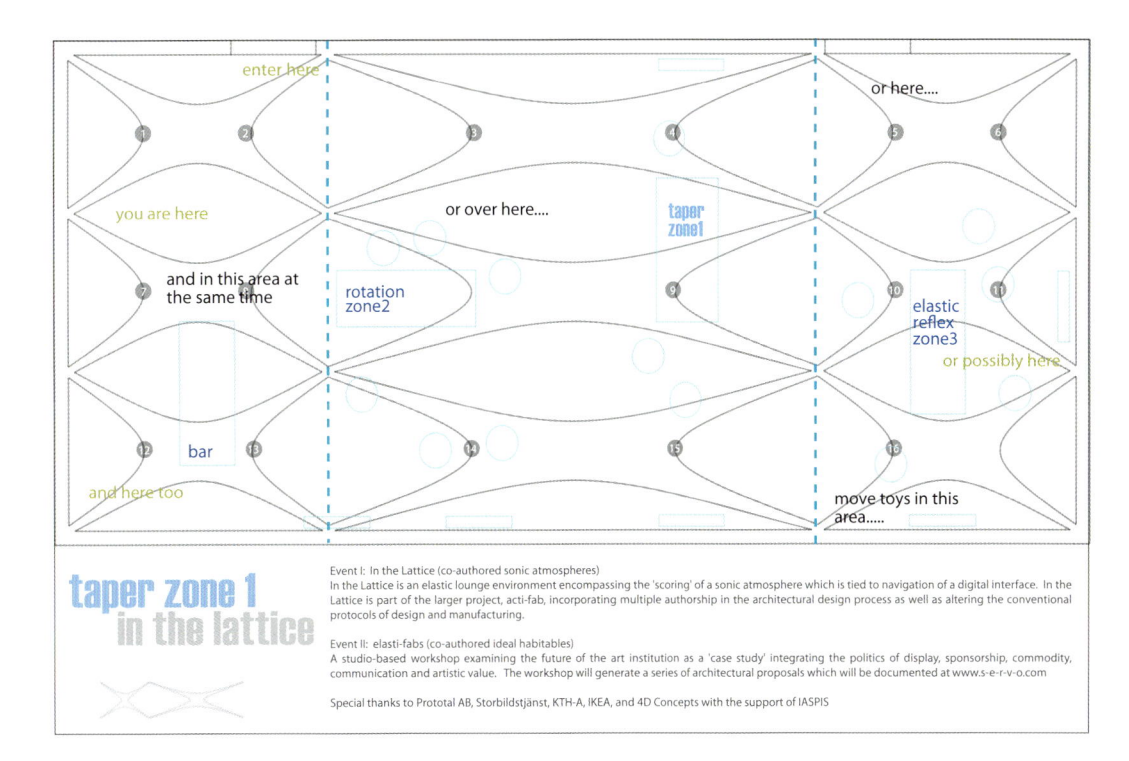

enter here
or here....
you are here
or over here....
taper zone1
and in this area at the same time
rotation zone2
elastic reflex zone3
or possibly here
bar
and here too
move toys in this area.....

taper zone 1
in the lattice

Event I: In the Lattice (co-authored sonic atmospheres)
In the Lattice is an elastic lounge environment encompassing the 'scoring' of a sonic atmosphere which is tied to navigation of a digital interface. In the Lattice is part of the larger project, acti-fab, incorporating multiple authorship in the architectural design process as well as altering the conventional protocols of design and manufacturing.

Event II: elasti-fabs (co-authored ideal habitables)
A studio-based workshop examining the future of the art institution as a 'case study' integrating the politics of display, sponsorship, commodity, communication and artistic value. The workshop will generate a series of architectural proposals which will be documented at www.s-e-r-v-o.com

Special thanks to Protatal AB, Storbildstjänst, KTH-A, IKEA, and 4D Concepts with the support of IASPIS

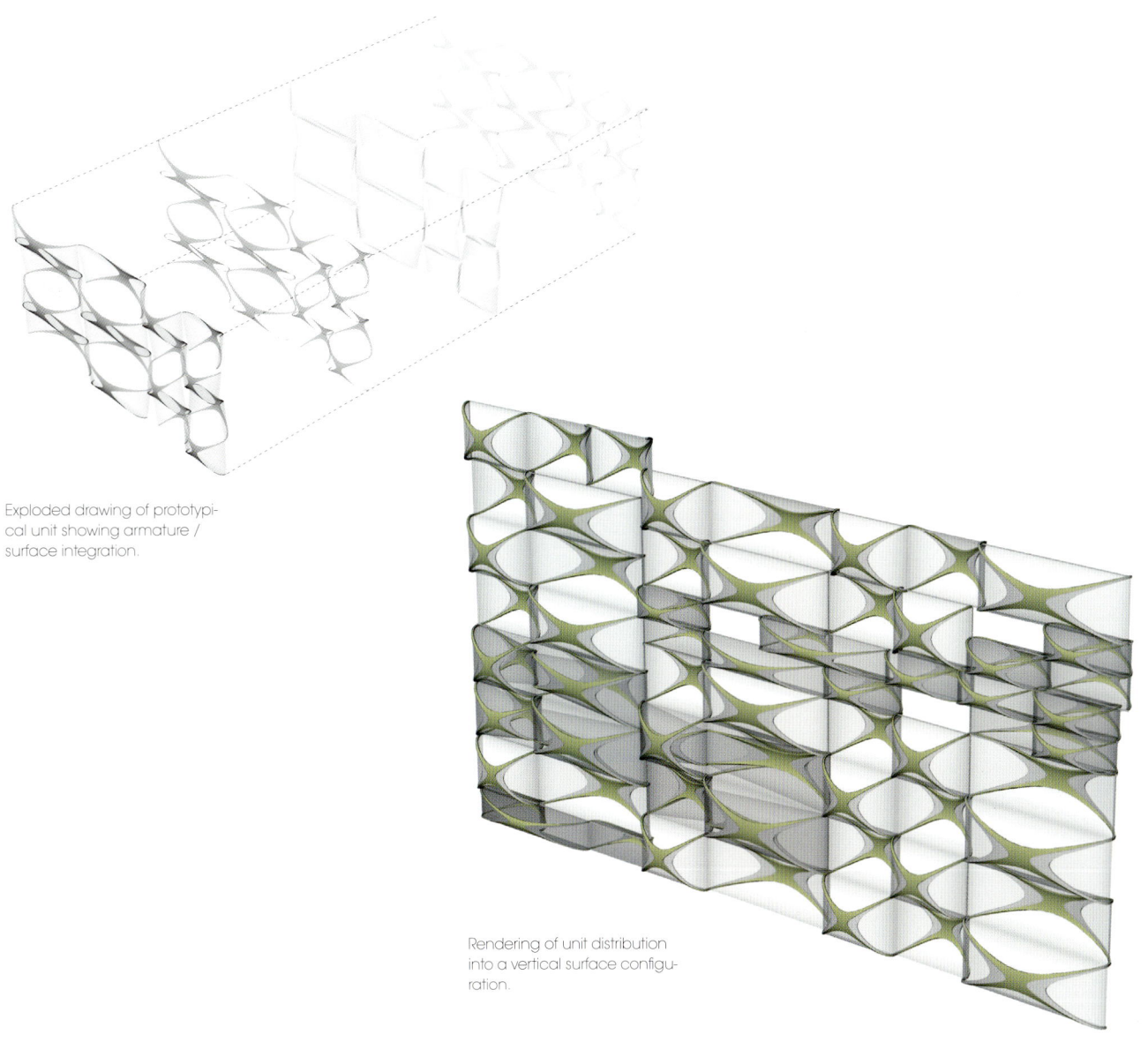

Exploded drawing of prototypical unit showing armature / surface integration.

Rendering of unit distribution into a vertical surface configuration.

ARCHITECTURAL DIAGRAMS 673

KERYKES J. MAYER H. ARCHITECTS

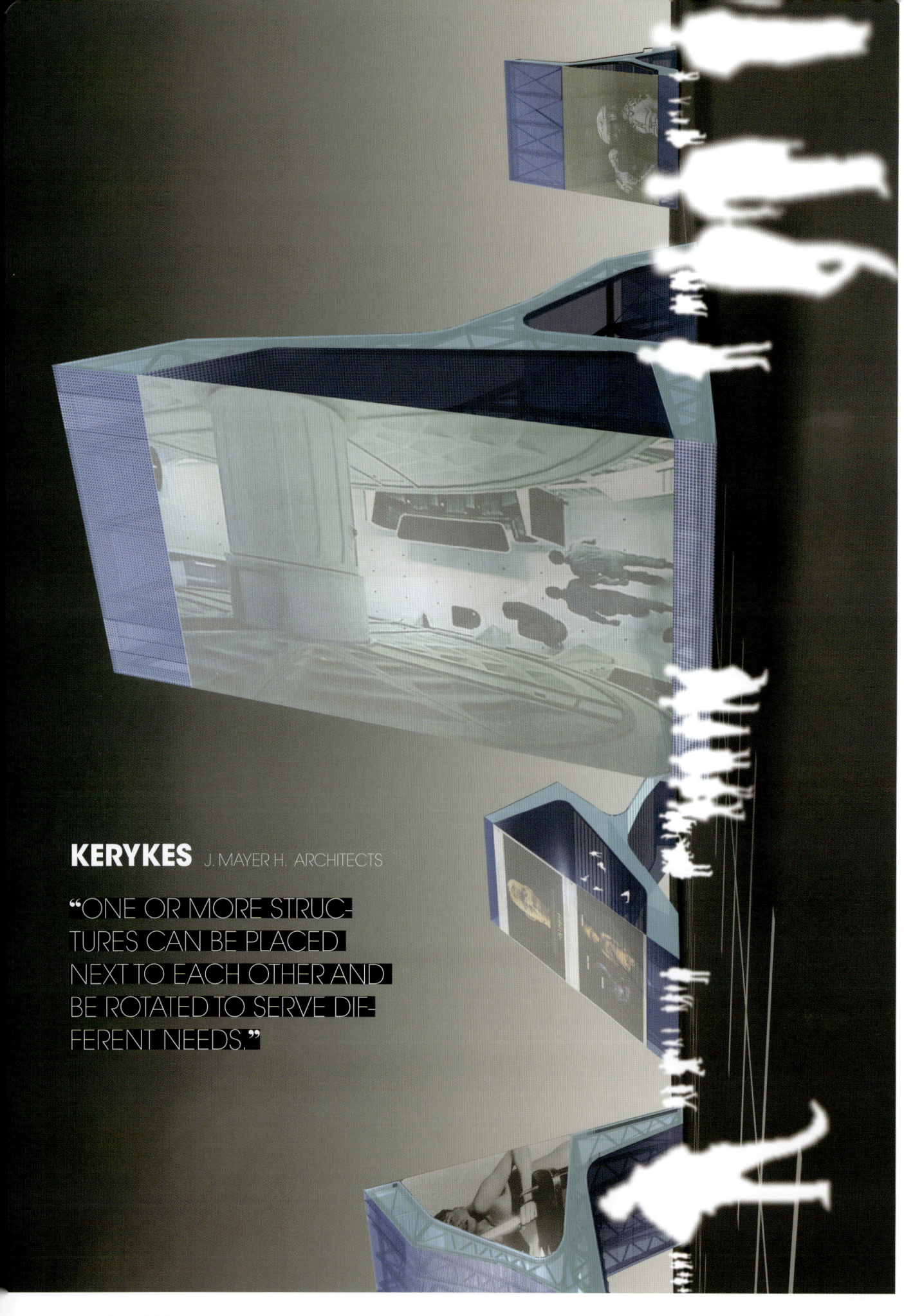

"ONE OR MORE STRUCTURES CAN BE PLACED NEXT TO EACH OTHER AND BE ROTATED TO SERVE DIFFERENT NEEDS."

674 INSTALLATION

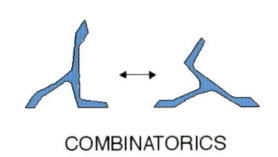

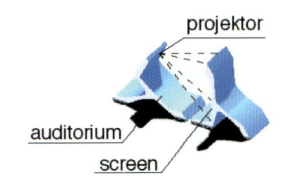

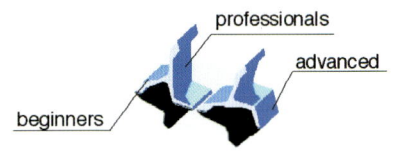

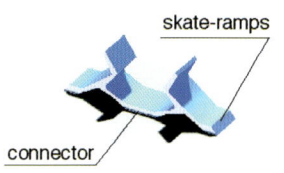

COMBINATORICS

projektor
auditorium
screen

professionals
advanced
beginners

skate-ramps
connector

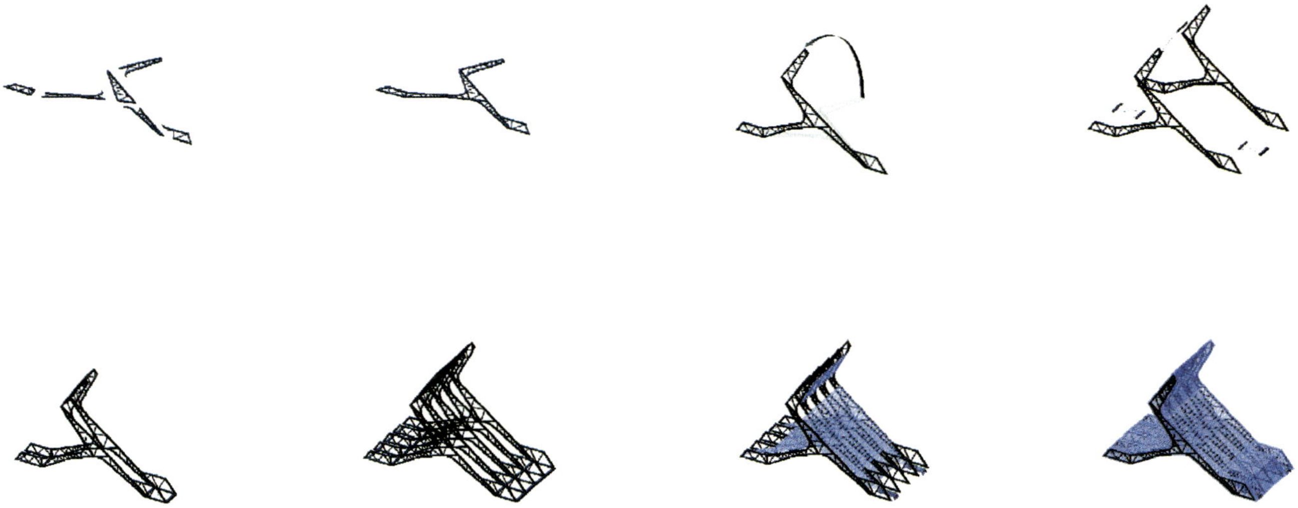

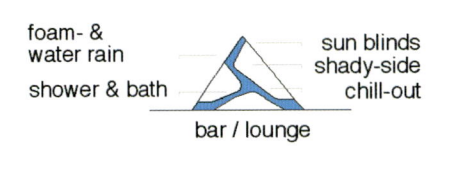

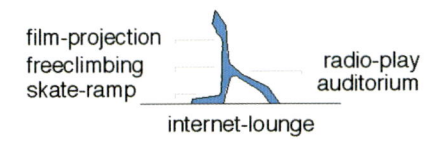

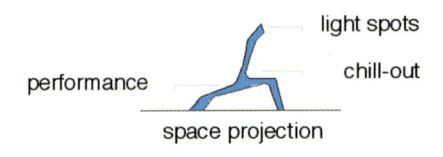

foam- & water rain
shower & bath
sun blinds
shady-side
chill-out
bar / lounge

film-projection
freeclimbing
skate-ramp
radio-play
auditorium
internet-lounge

performance
light spots
chill-out
space projection

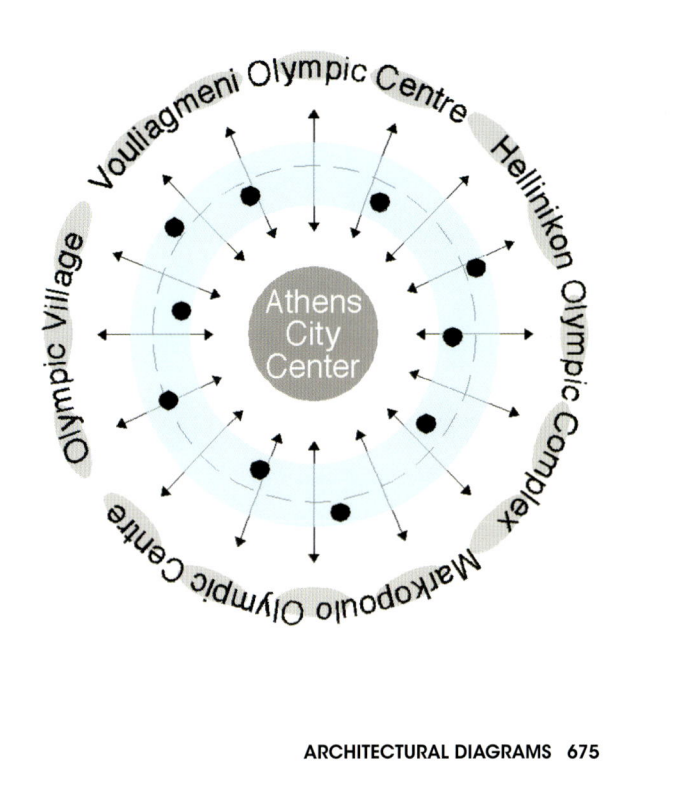

Vouliagmeni Olympic Centre
Hellinikon Olympic Complex
Markopoulo Olympic Centre
Olympic Village
Athens City Center

ARCHITECTURAL DIAGRAMS 675

LA BALLENA PEDESTRIAN BRIDGE UNStudio

"THE BRIDGE IS A HYBRID, COMBINING INFRASTRUCTURE AND BUILDING."

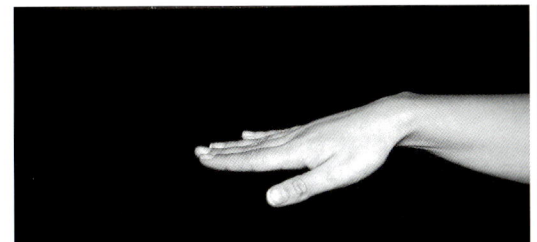

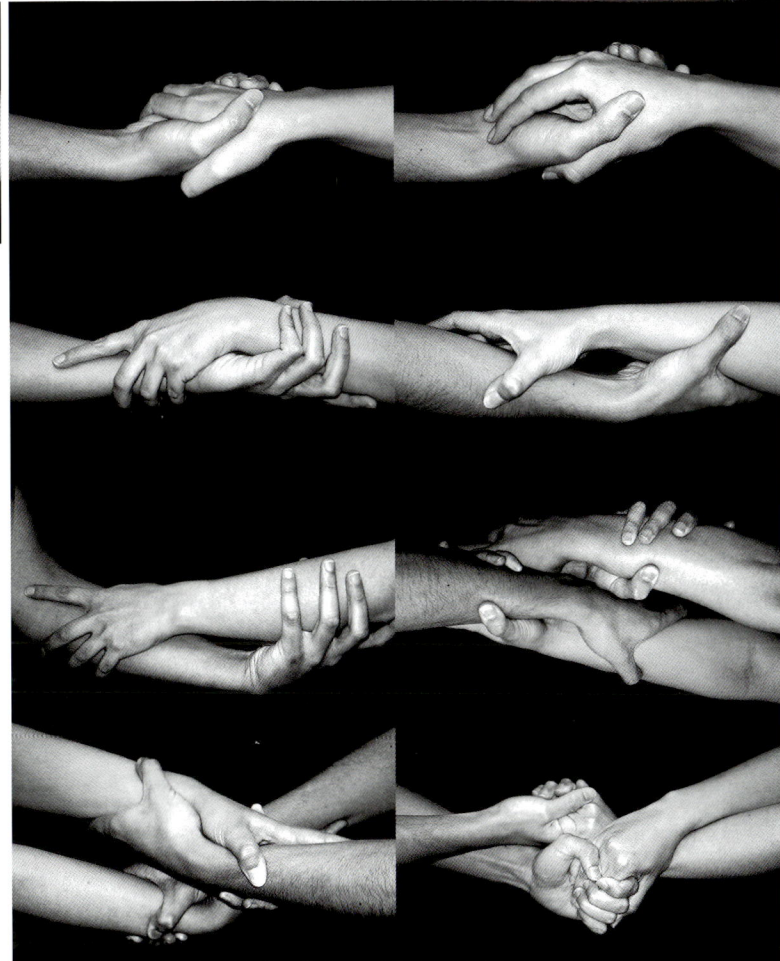

Concept bridge connection

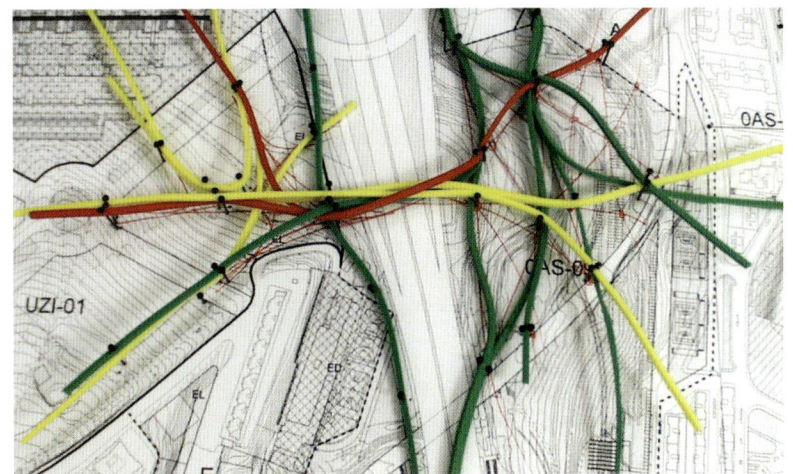

Flows of infrastructure

ARCHITECTURAL DIAGRAMS 677

LOBBI-PORTS servo

"ALLOWING IT TO REGISTER THE EFFECTS OF THAT ACTIVITY IN THE FORM OF LIGHTING PATTERNS ON THE BUILDING'S SKIN."

Rendering/montage of a hypothetical site for the distribution of Lobbi-Ports in an existing residential building on the west side of Manhattan.

678 INSTALLATION

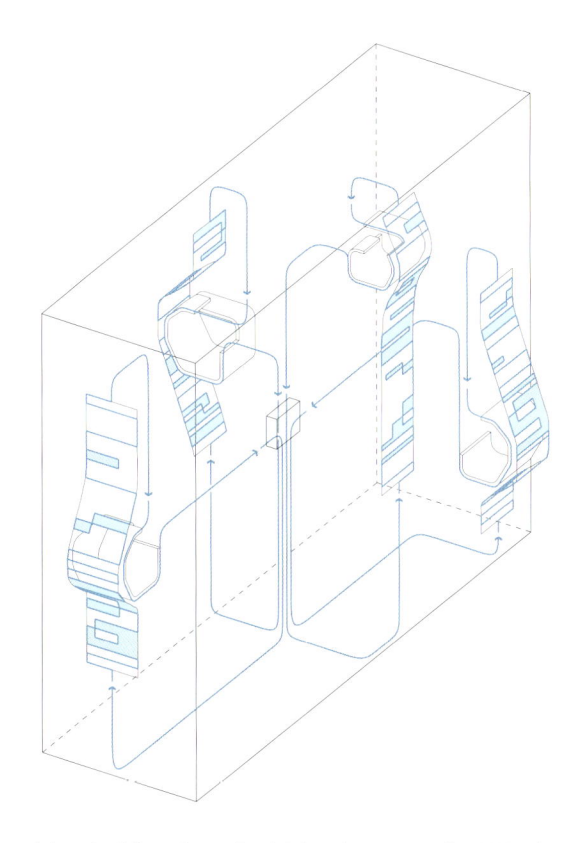

Interactive information network: Internal programmatic sensors / central data processing computer / external lighting infrastructure

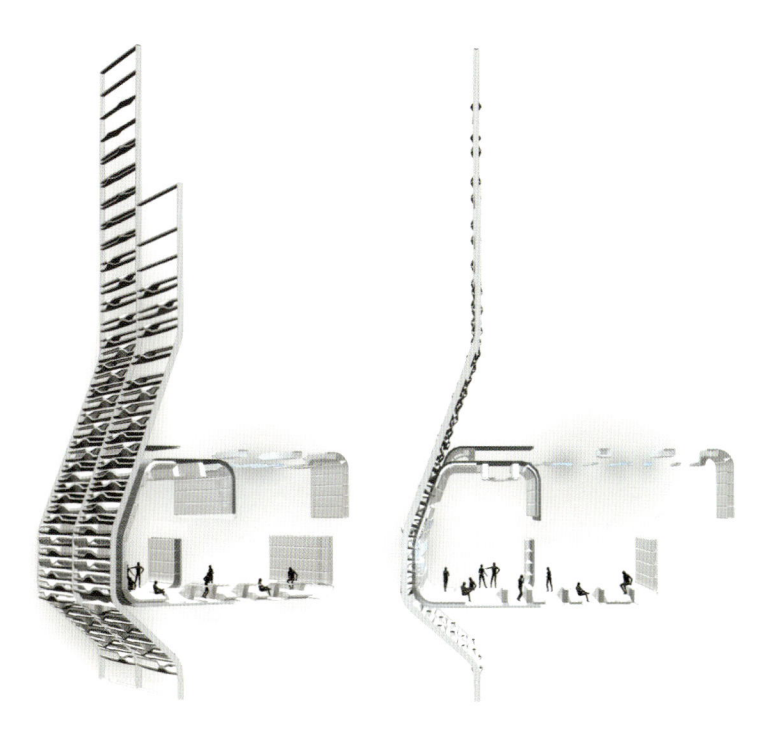

Renderings of Lobbi-Port building skin and programmatic implant system.

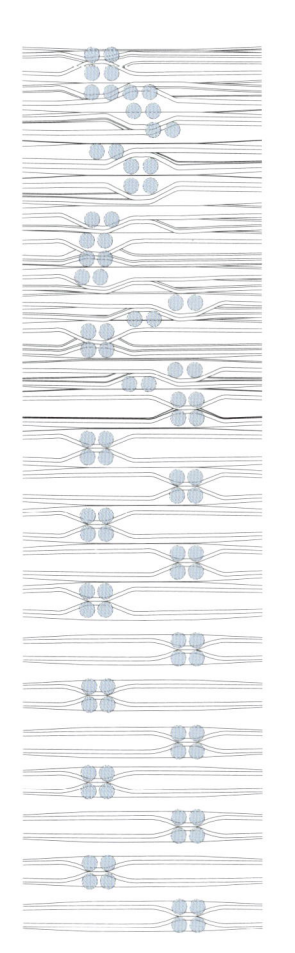

Distributional Regions

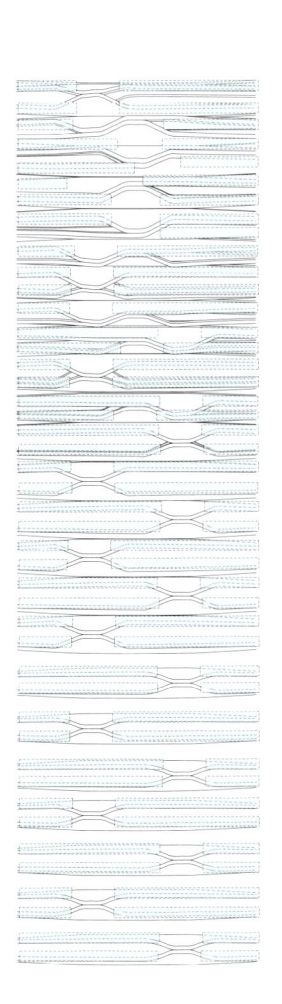

Luminous Skin Display Zones

Live Video Mapping
Key:

1. width — VIOLENCE
2. height — SEX
3. offset x — MUSEUMS
4. offset y — PARKS
5. width — TICKETS
6. height — GRAFFITI
7. offset x — DOGS
8. offset y — DANCING

ARCHITECTURAL DIAGRAMS 679

LOOP-THE-LOOP
NL Architects

"BY ONE RELATIVELY SIMPLE OPERATION -BISECTING, ROTATING AND REASSEMBLING- INTRIGUING NEW CONFIGURATIONS ARE POSSIBLE."

Container Diagram

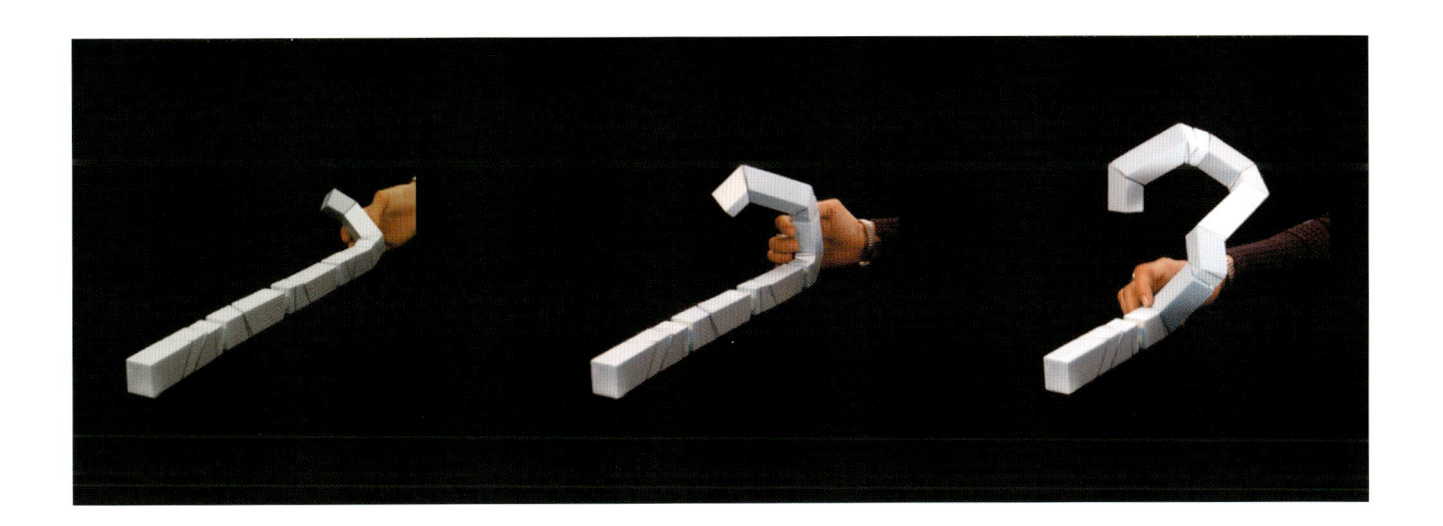

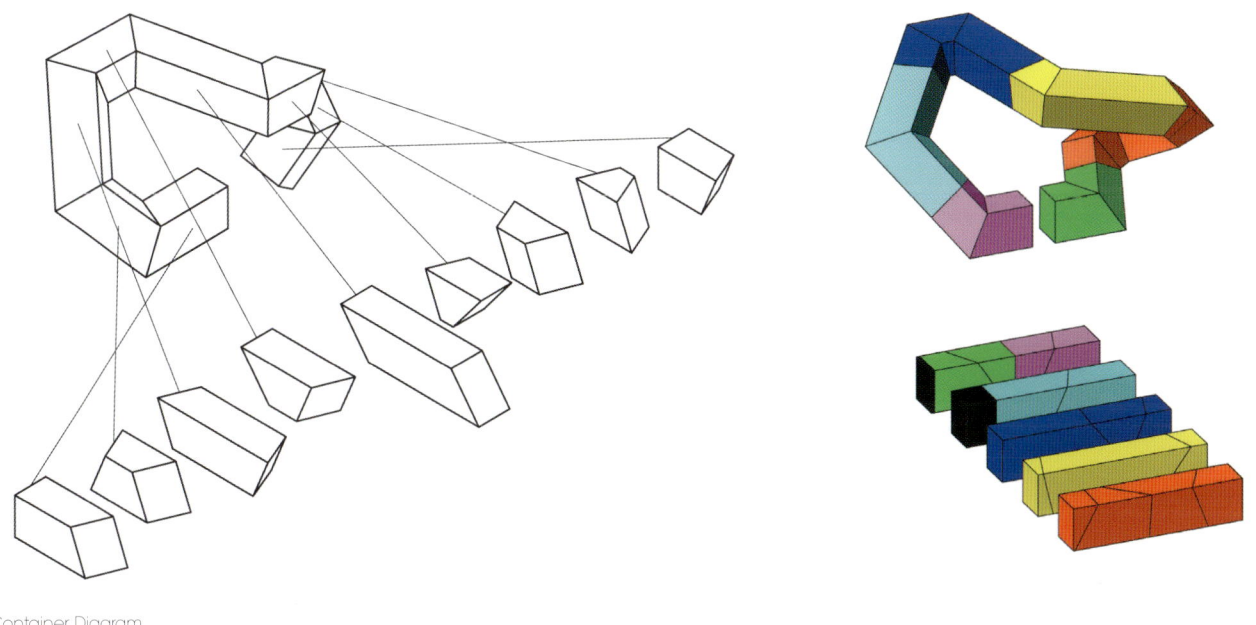

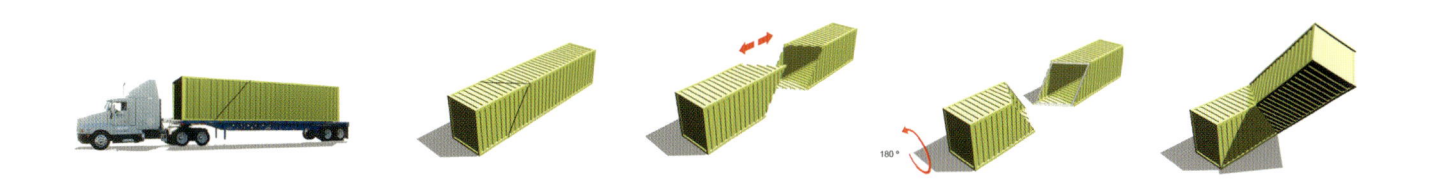

ARCHITECTURAL DIAGRAMS 681

MACHINE IN THE GARDEN
Responsive Systems Group

"A ROBOTIC LANDSCAPE ENVIRONMENT TO EXPLORE THE GENERAL INTERFACE BETWEEN ENVIRONMENTAL AND PROGRAMMATIC FORCES."

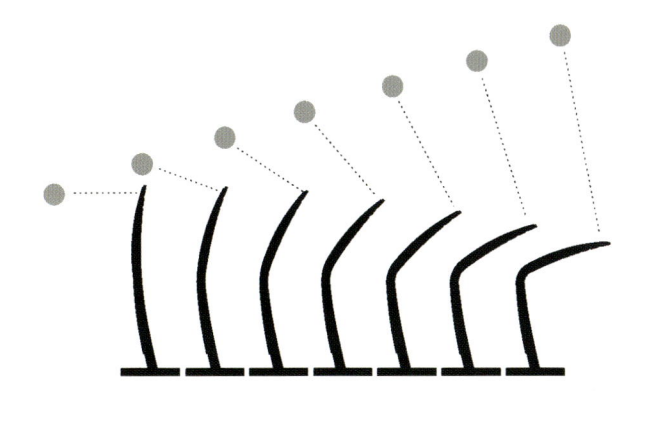

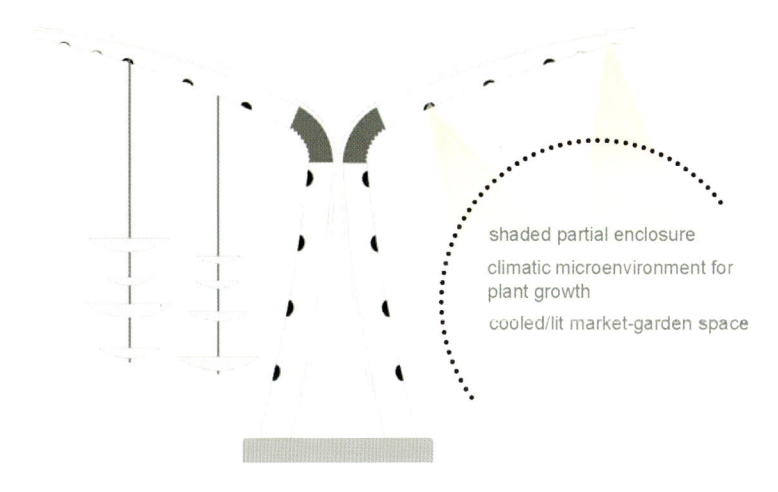

shaded partial enclosure
climatic microenvironment for plant growth
cooled/lit market-garden space

Diagrams indicating the range of movement within the robotic stalk system, which adjusts to both environmental and programmatic forces.
© Responsive Systems Group

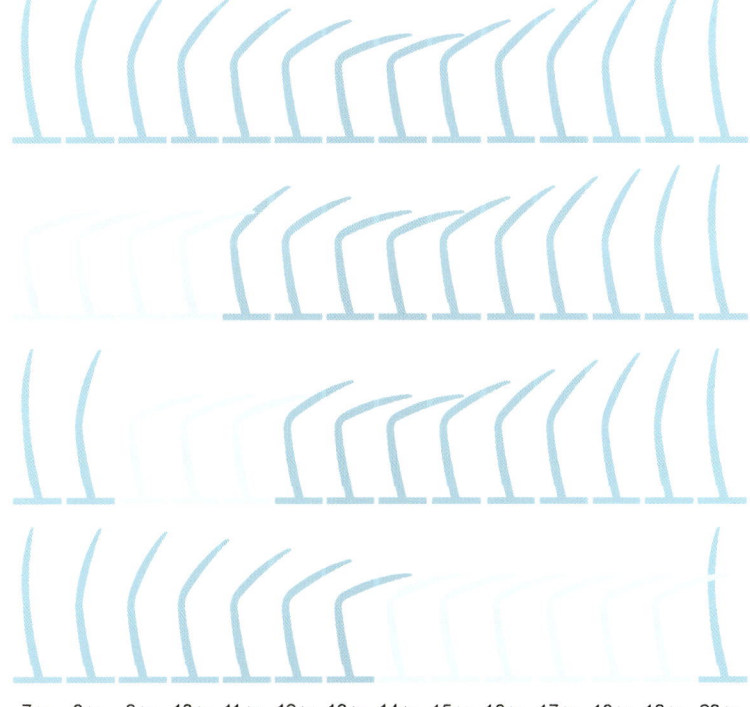

7 hr 8 hr 9 hr 10 hr 11 hr 12 hr 13 hr 14 hr 15 hr 16 hr 17 hr 18 hr 19 hr 20 hr

solar engagement/ sleep state

programmatic engagement
market, shading, lighting, misting

ARCHITECTURAL DIAGRAMS

OLZWEG R&Sie...architects

"THE ELEMENTS OF GLASS ARE FROM A CITIZEN GLASS RECYCLING PROCESS IN ORDER TO REDUCE THE RAW MATERIAL COSTS."

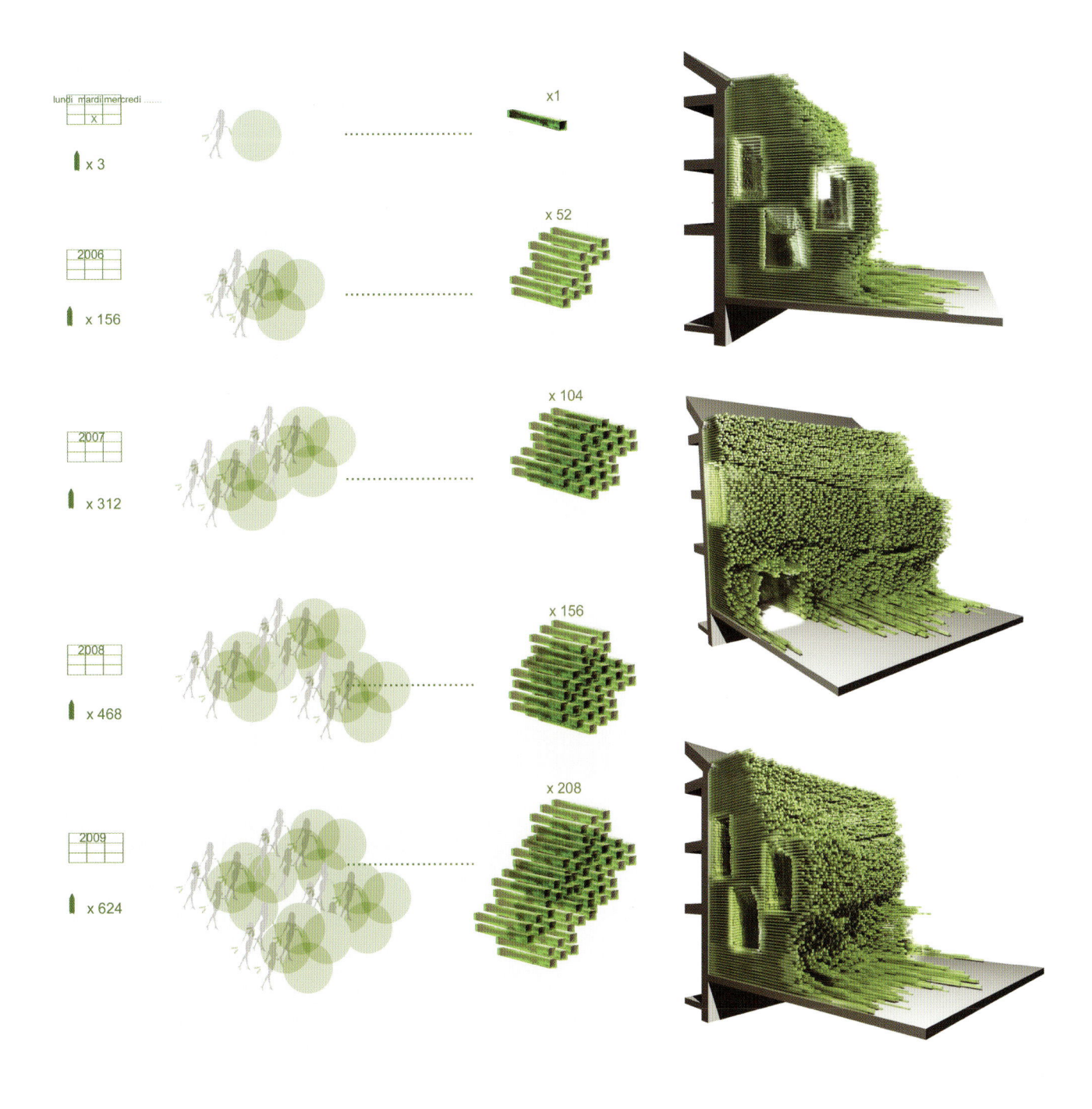

ARCHITECTURAL DIAGRAMS 685

OPEN SPACE AWARDS
TOKYO PSA

"SHE IS VIRTUALLY CONNECTED INTO THE NETWORK OF OTHER SHOPS IN REAL-TIME."

PROJECTIVE HISTORY OF RETAIL TYPOLOGIES

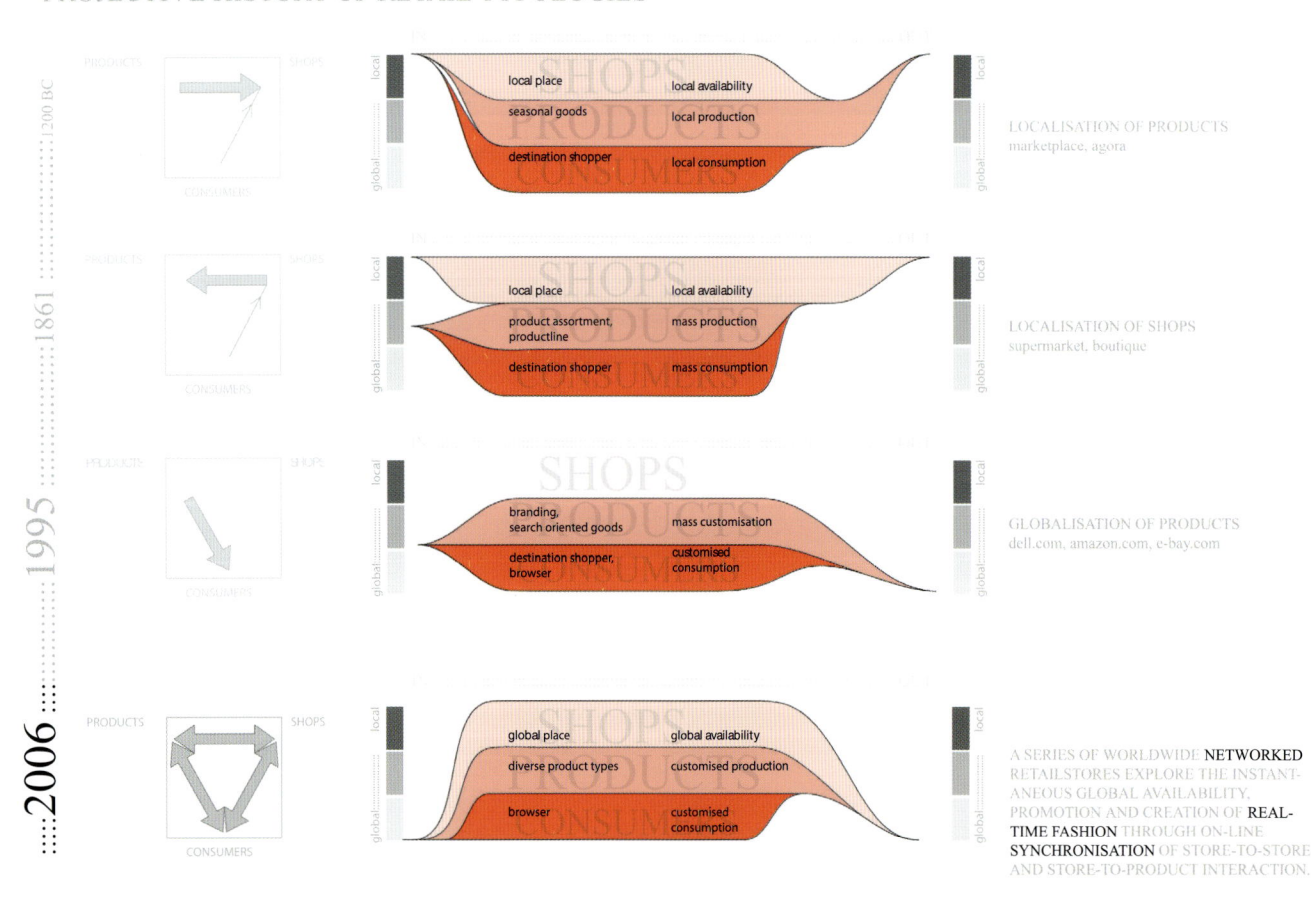

1200 BC

local place	local availability	
seasonal goods	local production	LOCALISATION OF PRODUCTS
destination shopper	local consumption	marketplace, agora

1861

local place	local availability	
product assortment, productline	mass production	LOCALISATION OF SHOPS
destination shopper	mass consumption	supermarket, boutique

1995

branding, search oriented goods	mass customisation	
destination shopper, browser	customised consumption	GLOBALISATION OF PRODUCTS dell.com, amazon.com, e-bay.com

2006

global place	global availability	
diverse product types	customised production	
browser	customised consumption	

A SERIES OF WORLDWIDE **NETWORKED** RETAILSTORES EXPLORE THE INSTANTANEOUS GLOBAL AVAILABILITY, PROMOTION AND CREATION OF **REAL-TIME FASHION** THROUGH ON-LINE **SYNCHRONISATION** OF STORE-TO-STORE AND STORE-TO-PRODUCT INTERACTION.

686 INSTALLATION

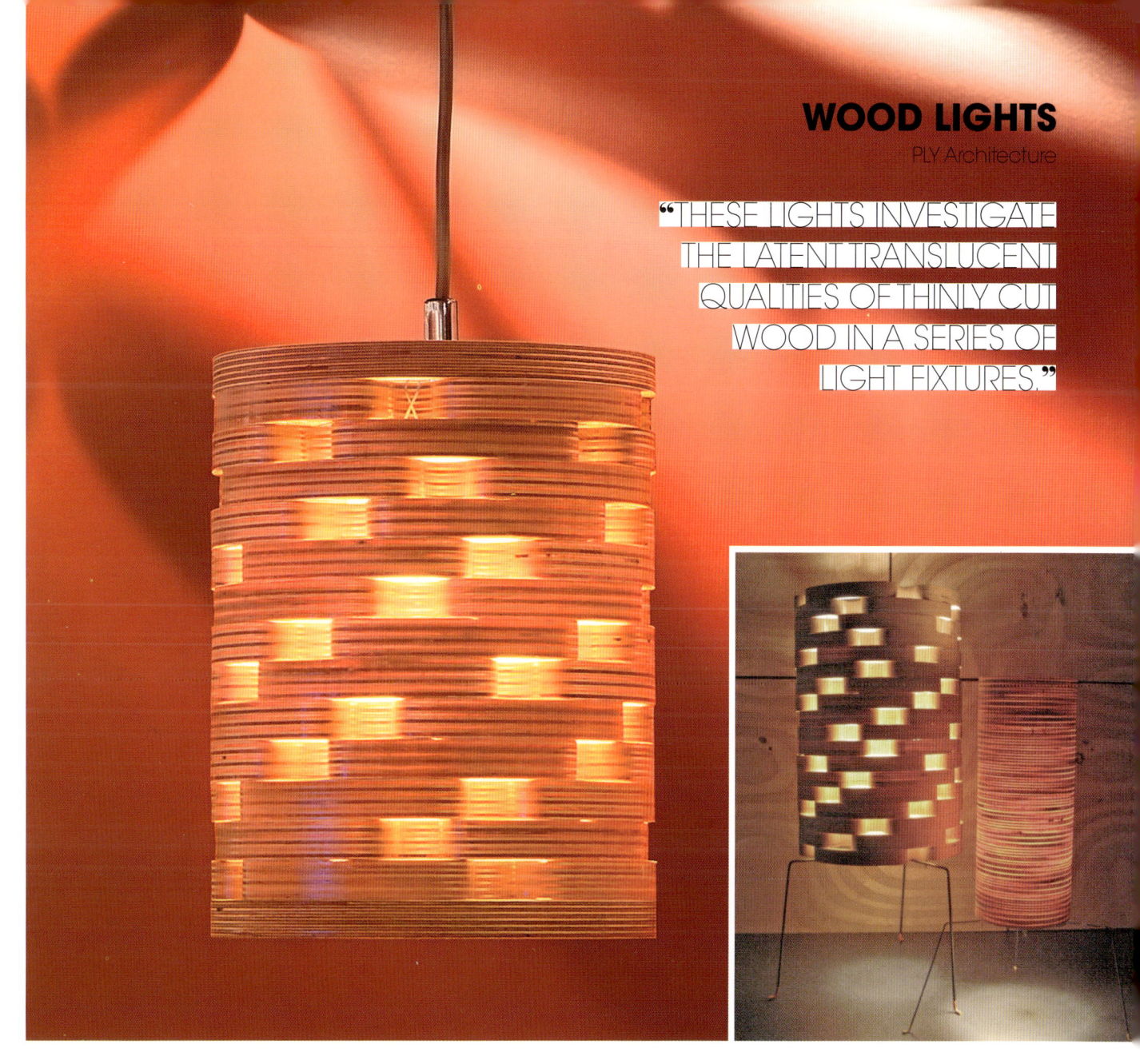

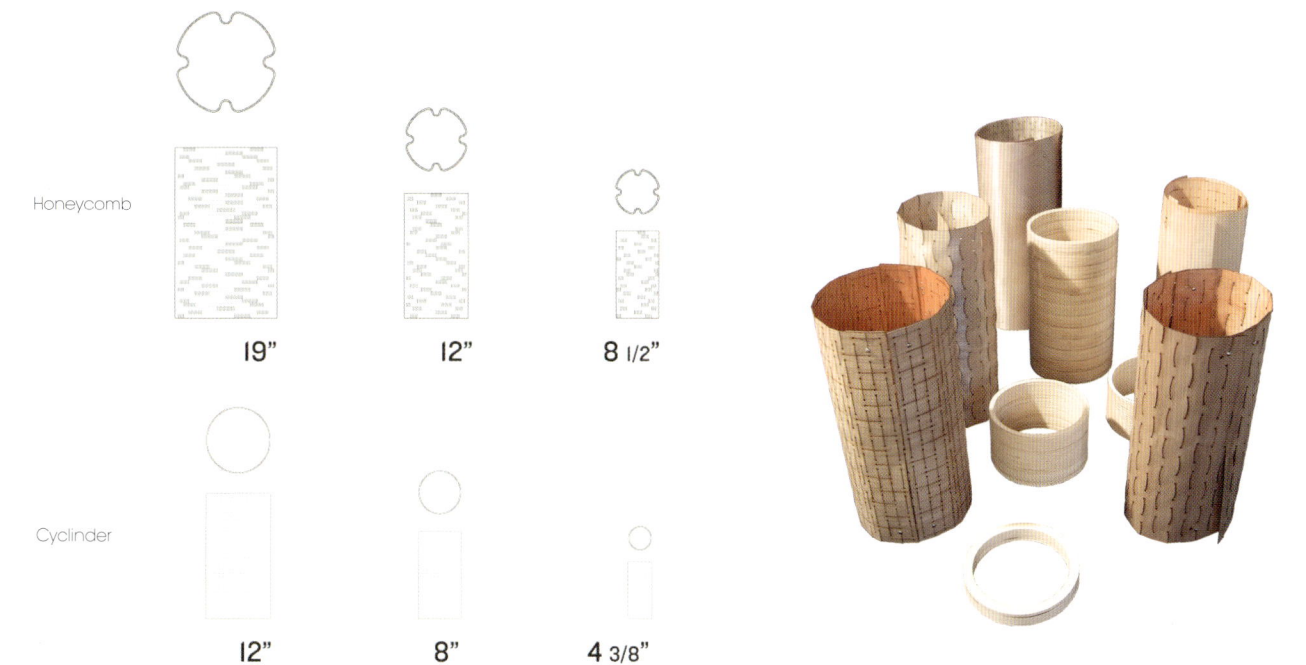

WOOD LIGHTS
PLY Architecture

> "THESE LIGHTS INVESTIGATE THE LATENT TRANSLUCENT QUALITIES OF THINLY CUT WOOD IN A SERIES OF LIGHT FIXTURES."

Honeycomb — 19" | 12" | 8 1/2"

Cyclinder — 12" | 8" | 4 3/8"

ARCHITECTURAL DIAGRAMS 687

PAPER LIGHTS
PLY Architecture

"THESE LUMINARIES INVESTIGATE THE TRANSLUCENT QUALITIES OF PAPER BY EXPLOITING ITS ABILITY TO TRANSMIT LIGHT AND CAST SHADOWS."

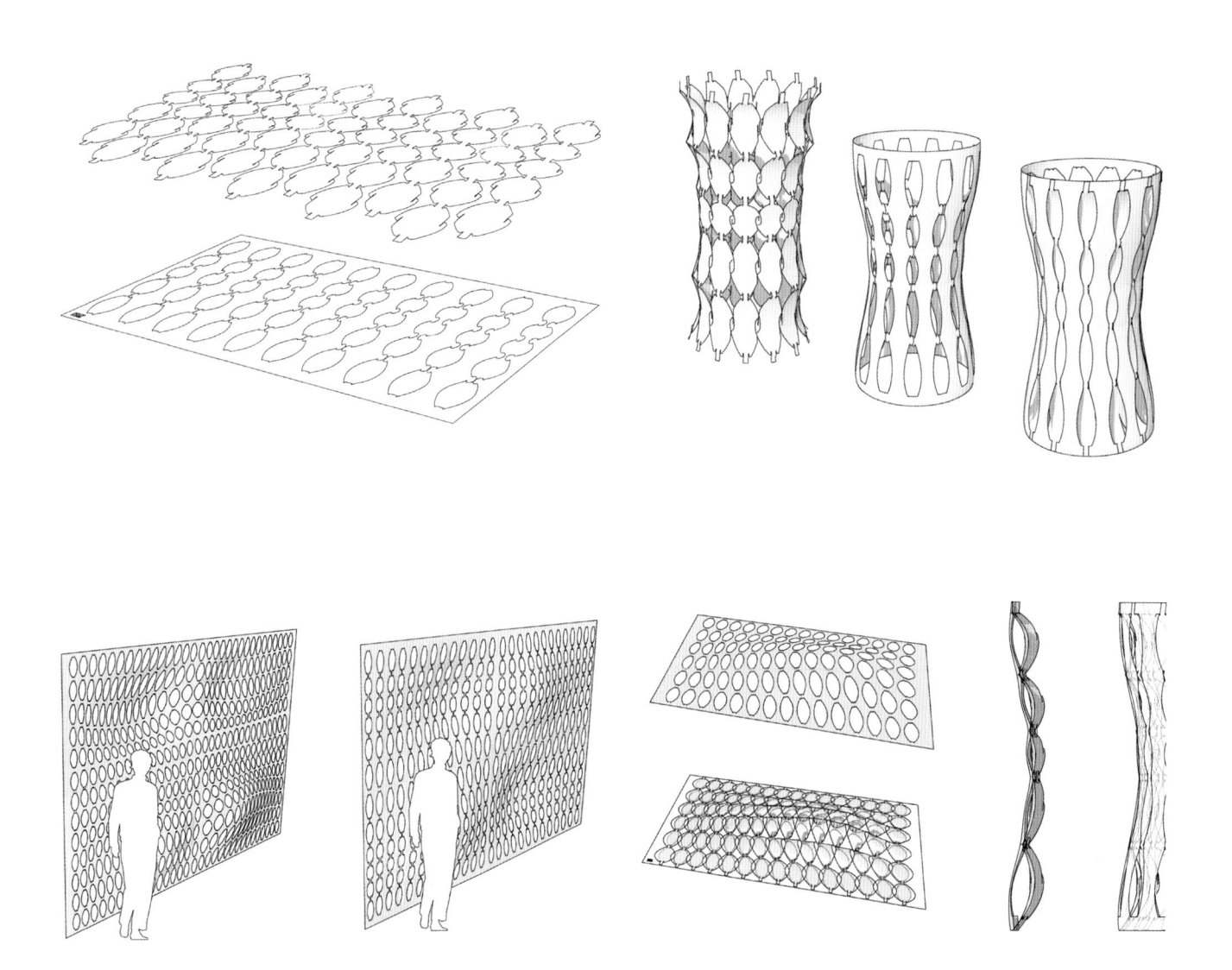

ARCHITECTURAL DIAGRAMS 689

PARK BENCH HOUSE
sga : sean godsell architects

"HOUSE IN ITS MOST FUNDAMENTAL TERM – 'SHELTER' AND ATTEMPTS TO EXPOSE A PRESSING SOCIAL NEED WITHIN WHICH ARCHITECTS CAN PROVIDE A VITAL ROLE."

Sketch

STEINER GARDEN
Zizi&Yoyo

"WIND-PUSHED WHITE REFLECTOR PLATES FLING CIRCLES OF LIGHT AROUND THE GARDEN, IN WINTER CALMED DOWN BY SNOW TOPS."

Paragraph | Surfaced recessed lighting | A seat pay 40 x 40cm | 150 cm diameter white metal arm bent metal reflector | Reflector

ARCHITECTURAL DIAGRAMS 691

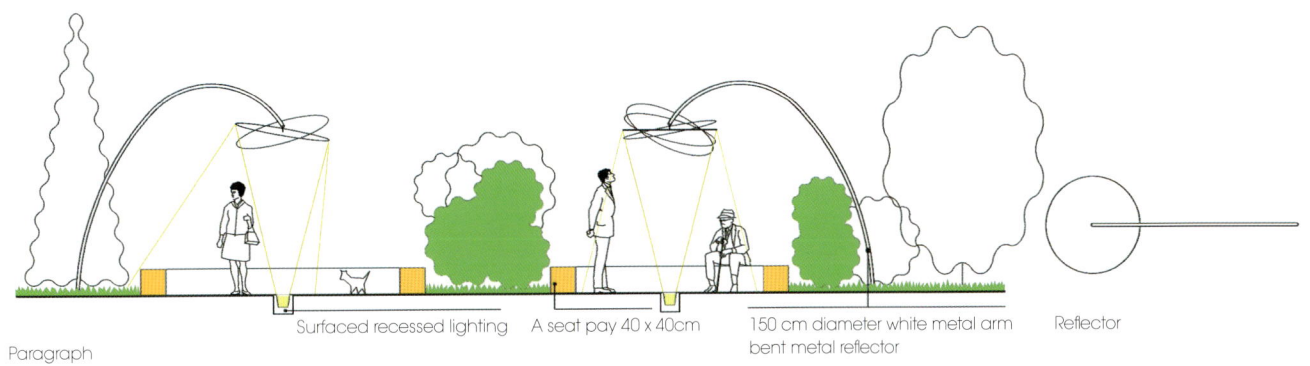

PARTY WALL nARCHITECTS

"AS ONE APPROACHES, EMBEDDED PROXIMITY SENSORS SIGNAL MICRO-PROCESSORS TO ACTIVATE TINY MOTORS..."

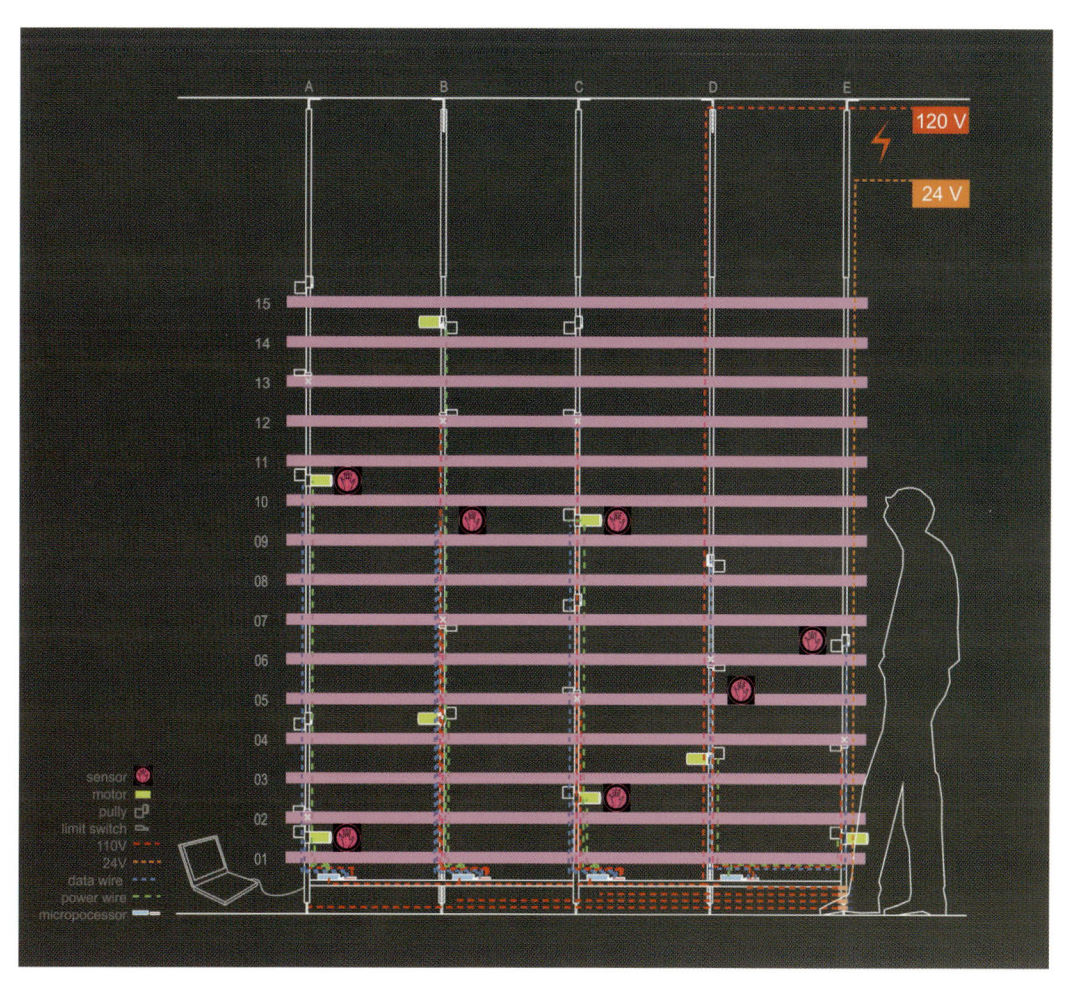

ARCHITECTURAL DIAGRAMS

PLAY GROUND
Andreas Angelidakis

"AS THE KIDS PLAY, THE OBJECTS GET MOVED AROUND, ANIMATING THEIR LANDSCAPE COLLABORATION WITH ELENI KOSTIKA."

ARCHITECTURAL DIAGRAMS 695

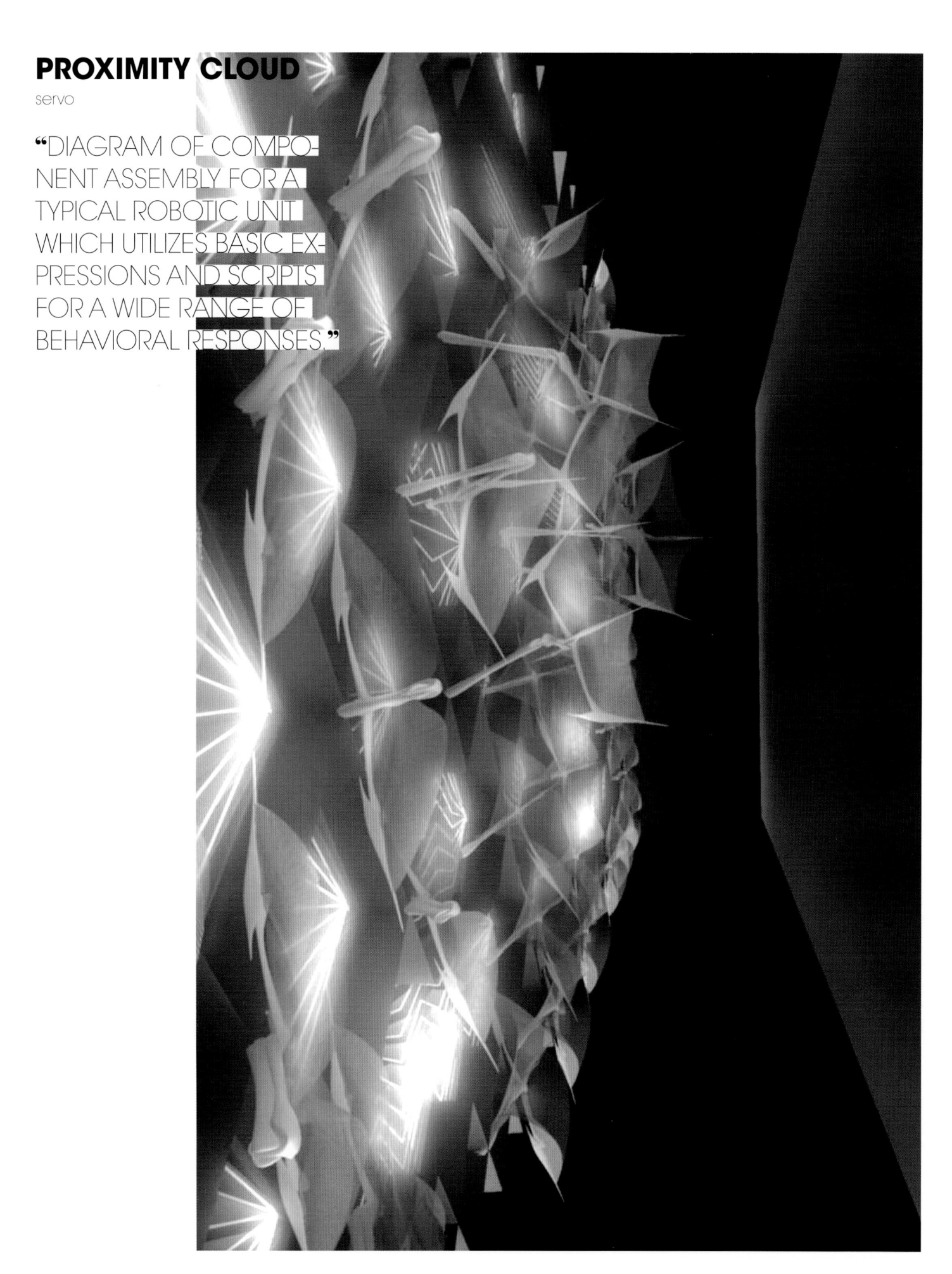

PROXIMITY CLOUD
servo

"DIAGRAM OF COMPONENT ASSEMBLY FOR A TYPICAL ROBOTIC UNIT WHICH UTILIZES BASIC EXPRESSIONS AND SCRIPTS FOR A WIDE RANGE OF BEHAVIORAL RESPONSES."

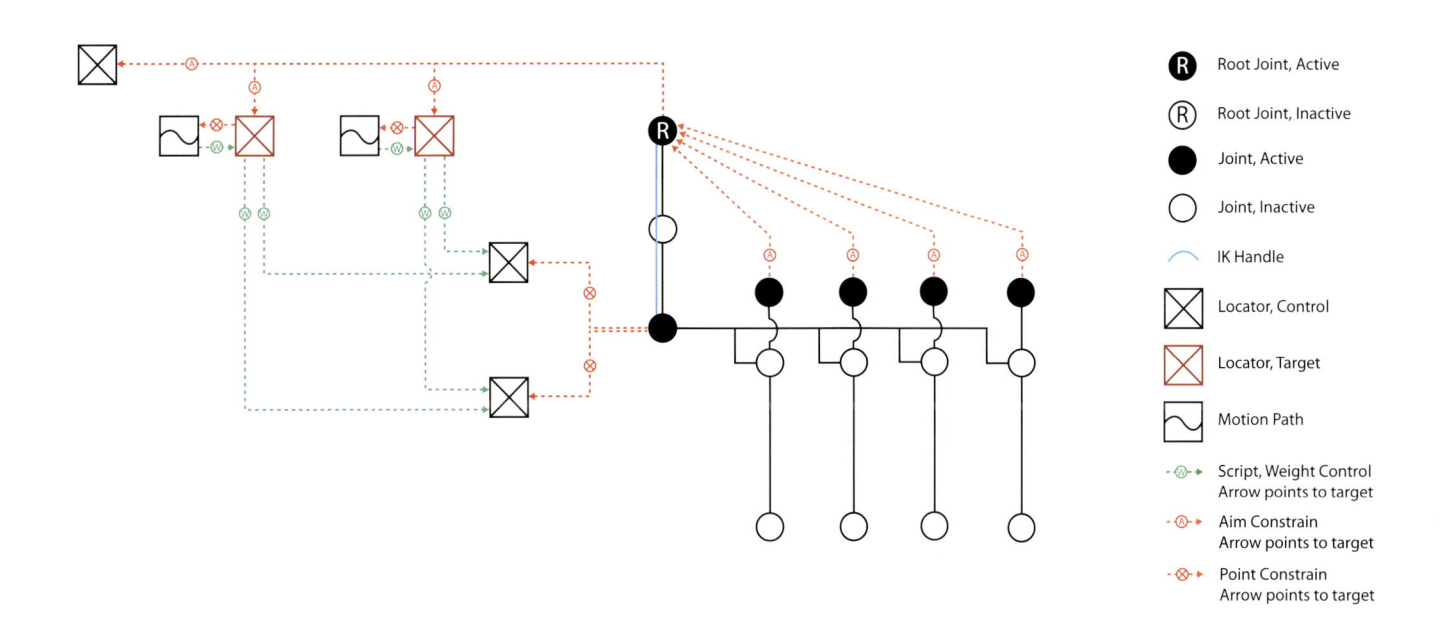

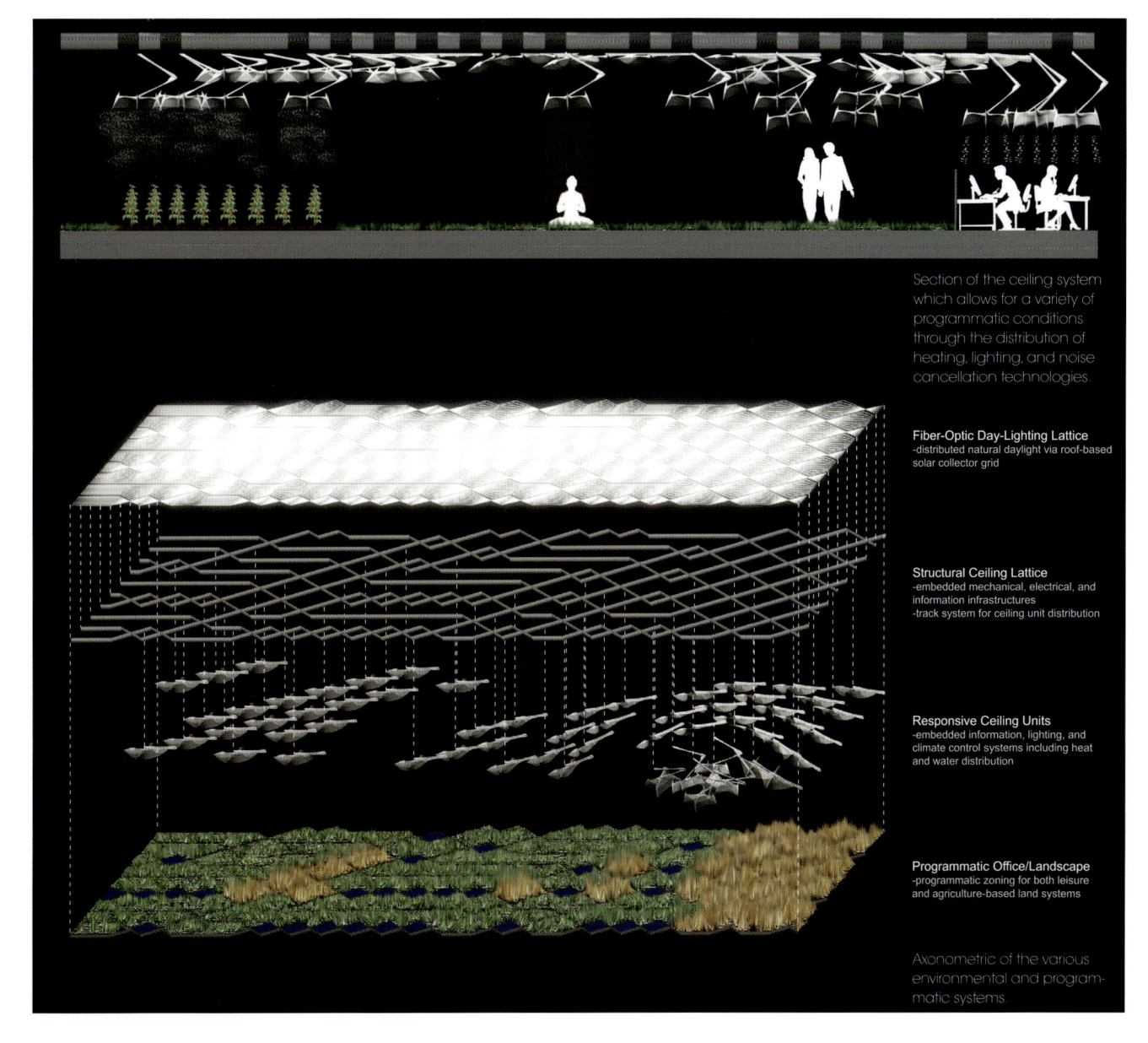

®	Root Joint, Active
Ⓡ	Root Joint, Inactive
●	Joint, Active
○	Joint, Inactive
⌒	IK Handle
⊠	Locator, Control
⊠ (red)	Locator, Target
∿	Motion Path
-⊚-▶	Script, Weight Control — Arrow points to target
-Ⓐ-▶	Aim Constrain — Arrow points to target
-⊗-▶	Point Constrain — Arrow points to target

Section of the ceiling system which allows for a variety of programmatic conditions through the distribution of heating, lighting, and noise cancellation technologies.

Fiber-Optic Day-Lighting Lattice
-distributed natural daylight via roof-based solar collector grid

Structural Ceiling Lattice
-embedded mechanical, electrical, and information infrastructures
-track system for ceiling unit distribution

Responsive Ceiling Units
-embedded information, lighting, and climate control systems including heat and water distribution

Programmatic Office/Landscape
-programmatic zoning for both leisure and agriculture-based land systems

Axonometric of the various environmental and programmatic systems.

ARCHITECTURAL DIAGRAMS 697

RED+HOUSING MANIFESTO OBRA ARCHITECTS

"THE FIRST-YEAR ANNIVERSARY OF THE SICHUAN EARTHQUAKE THROUGH PARTICIPATION IN CROSSING."

Roof

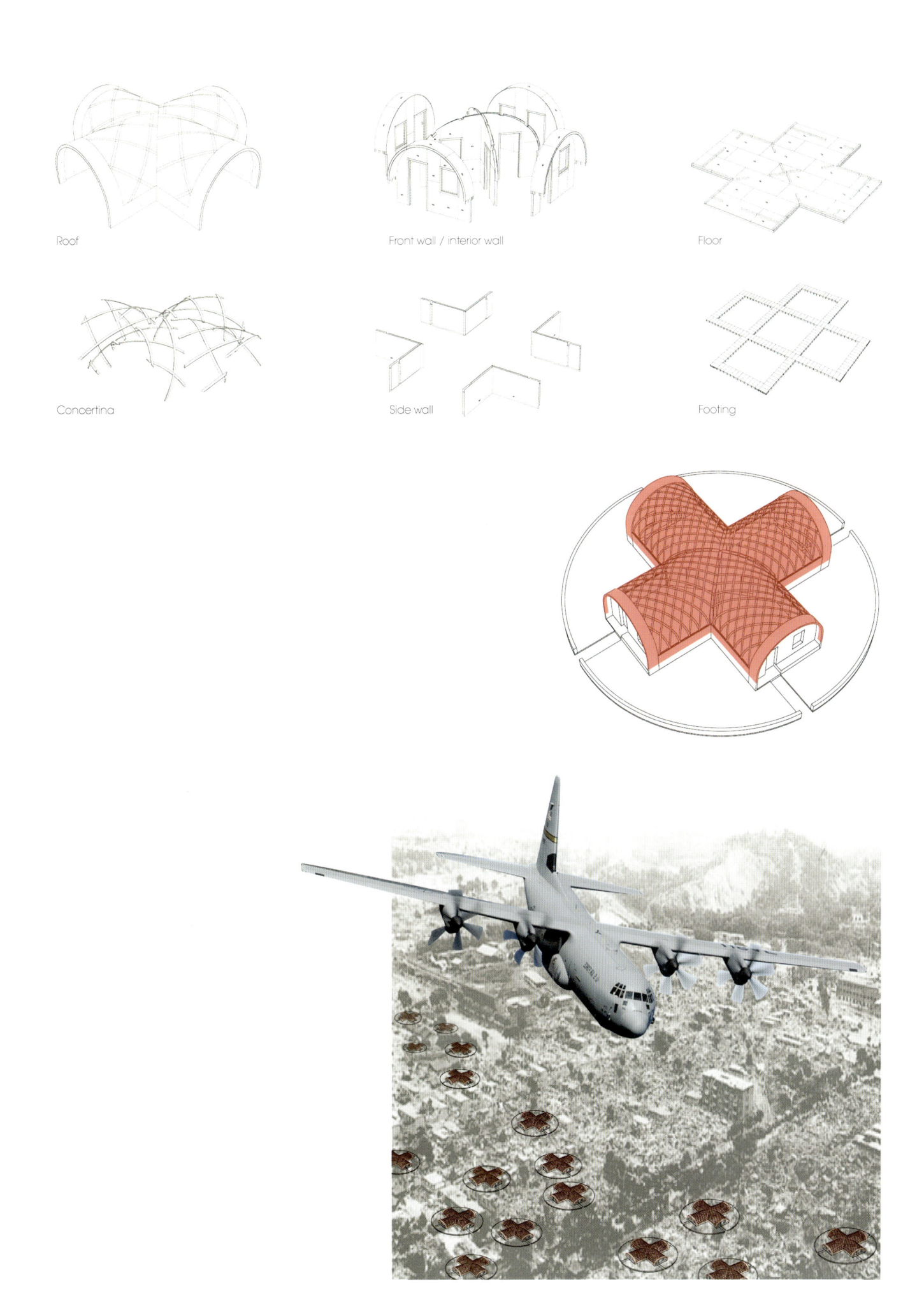

Front wall / interior wall

Floor

Concertina

Side wall

Footing

ARCHITECTURAL DIAGRAMS 699

SCREEN WALL PROTOTYPE PLY Architecture

"THE RESULTING PARTS VARY IN SIZE AND PROPORTION, DEPENDING ON ITS LOCATION IN THE WALL."

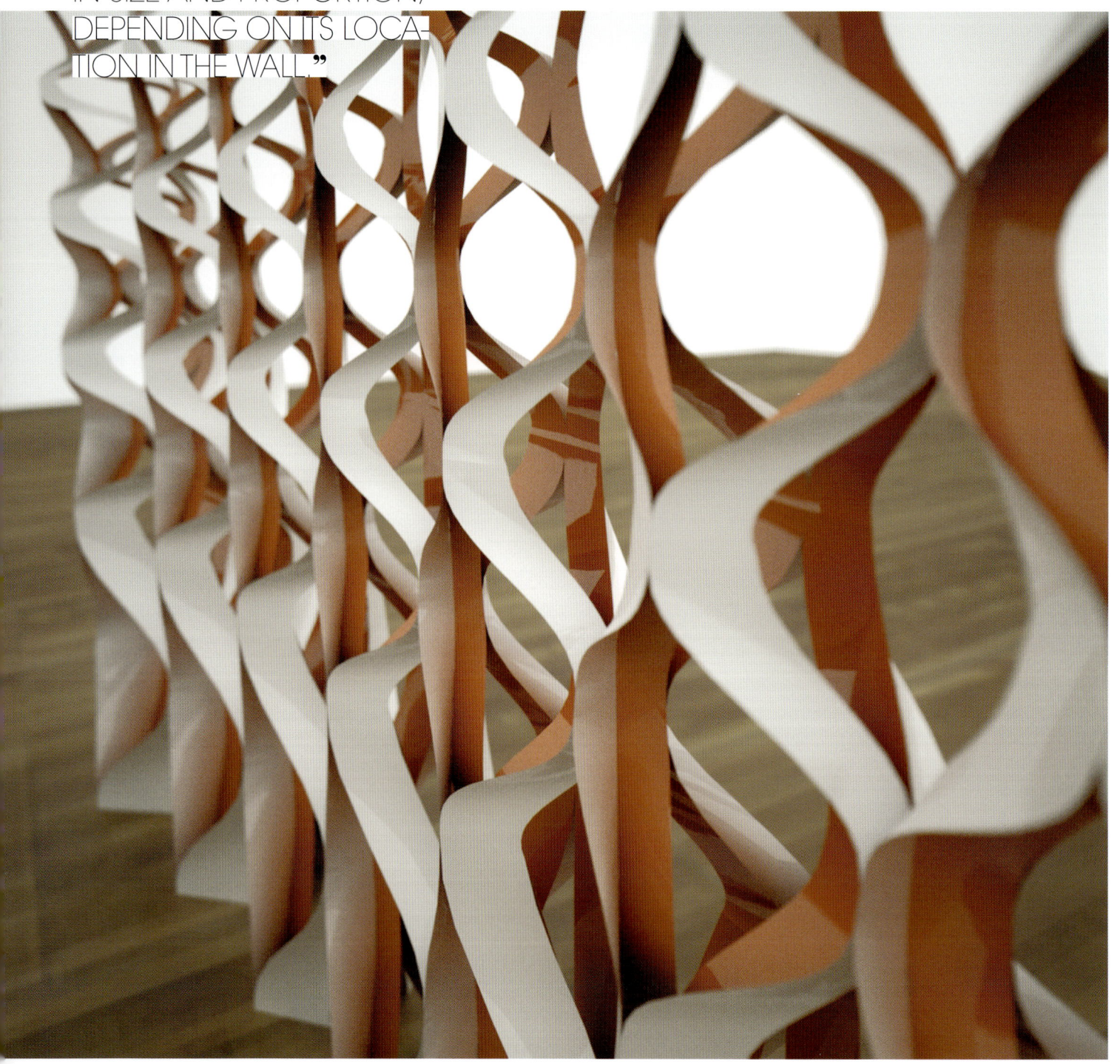

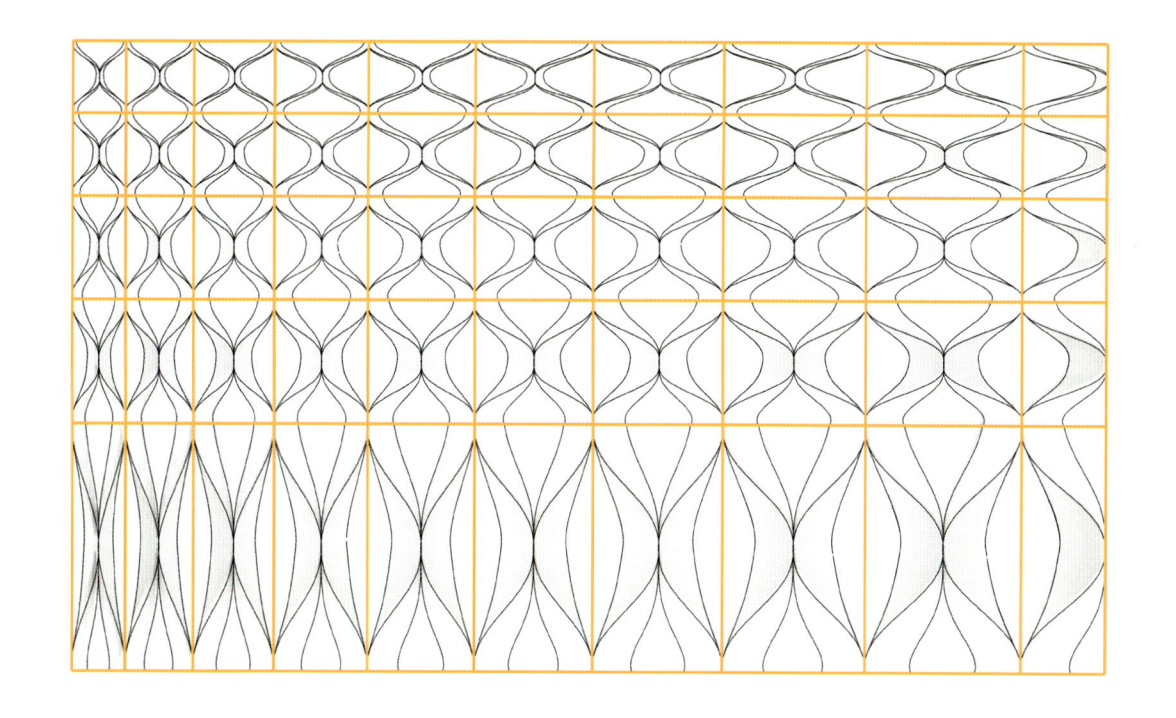

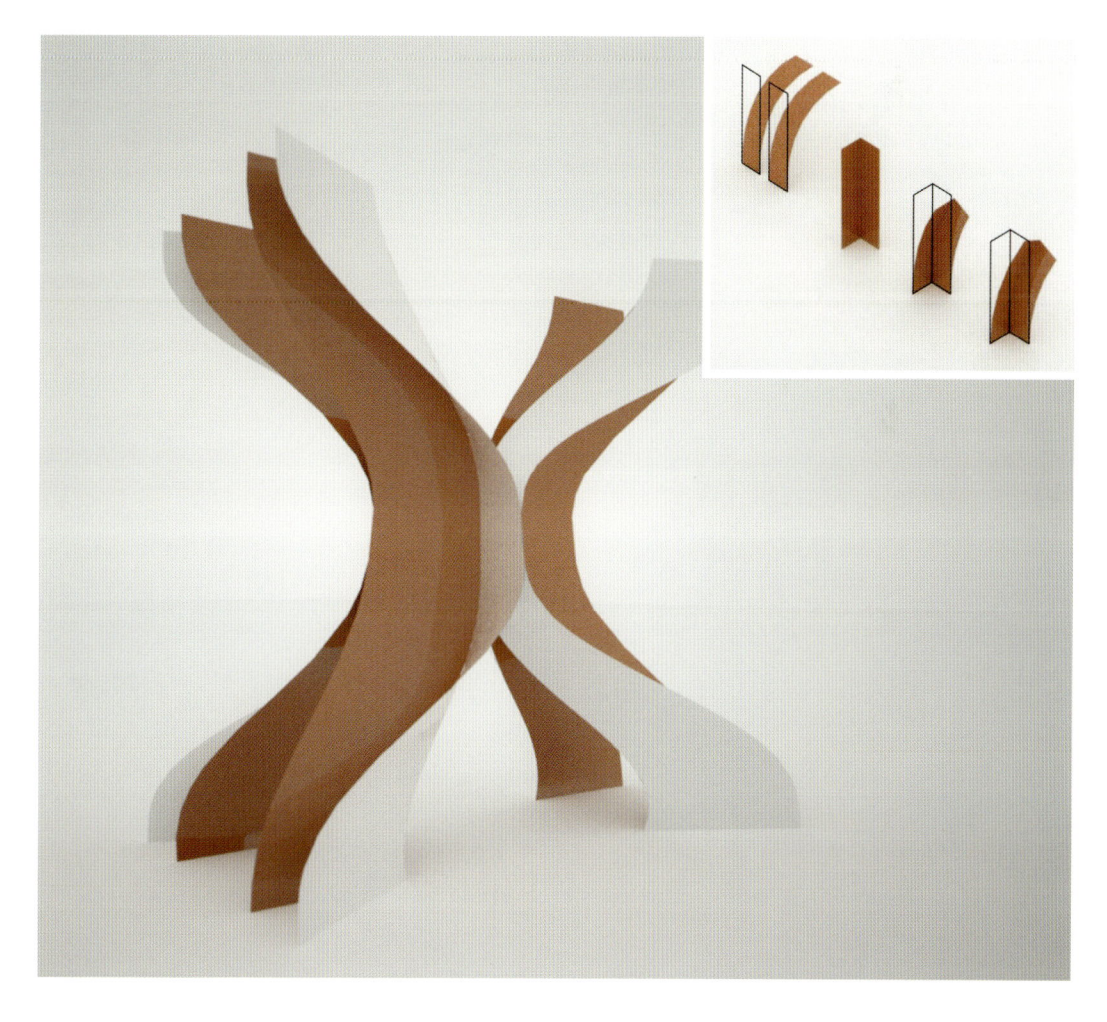

ARCHITECTURAL DIAGRAMS

SPLAT
Andreas Angelidakis

SUPERNEEN
ANGELIDAKIS
SPLAT CHAIR
BASE <A>

ARCHITECTURAL DIAGRAMS 703

STACKED
JDS Architects

"THE STACKED SHELVING SYSTEM PROVIDES A CONVENTIONAL STORING SYSTEM WITH AN UNCONVENTIONAL EFFECT."

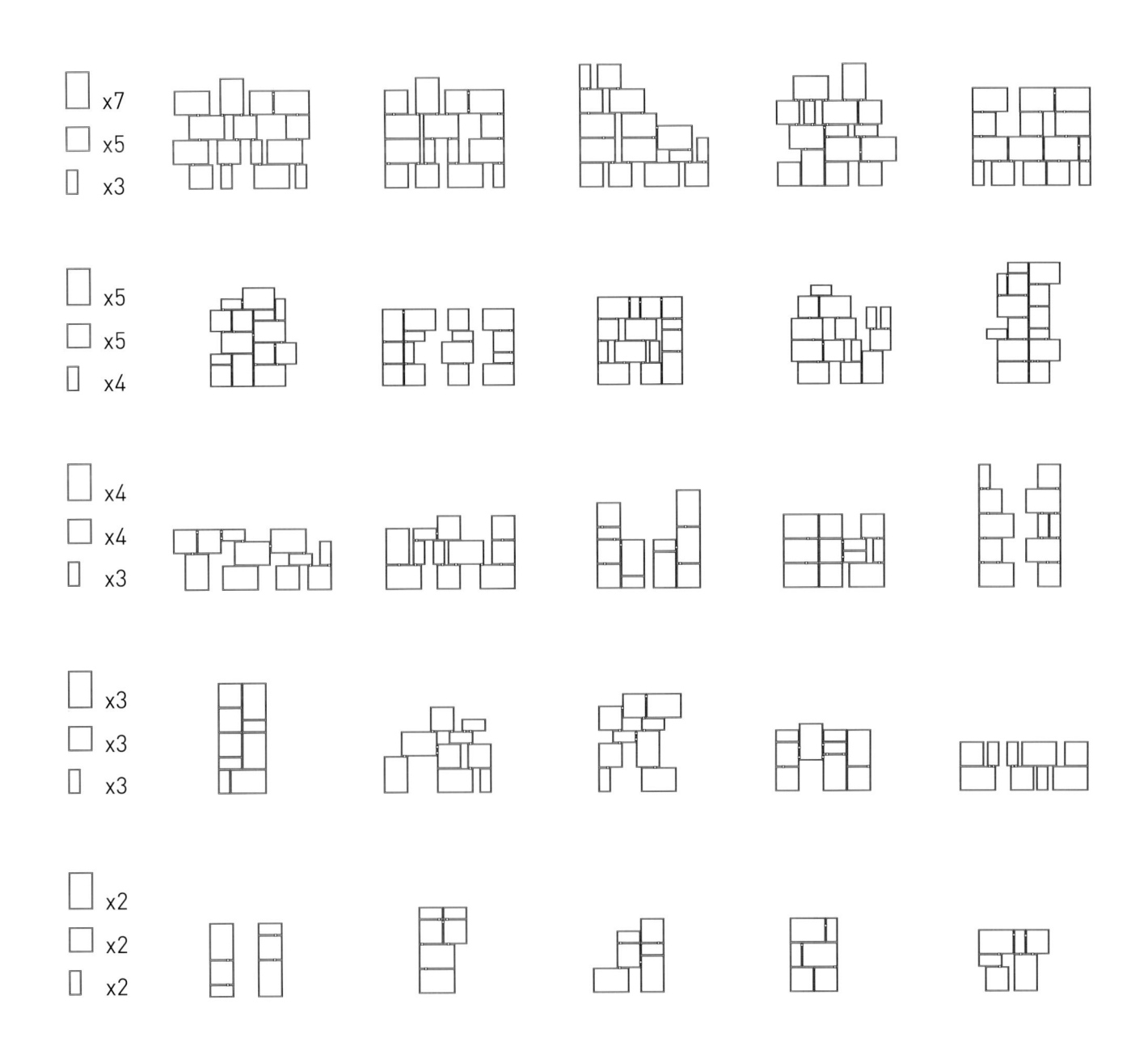

ARCHITECTURAL DIAGRAMS 705

SUM UNStudio

"THE THREE SEMI-CIRCULAR BLADES AT DIFFERENT ALTITUDES STIMULATE THE USER TO WORK IN DIFFERENT POSITION."

14:00 - 17:00
cooperating, meeting

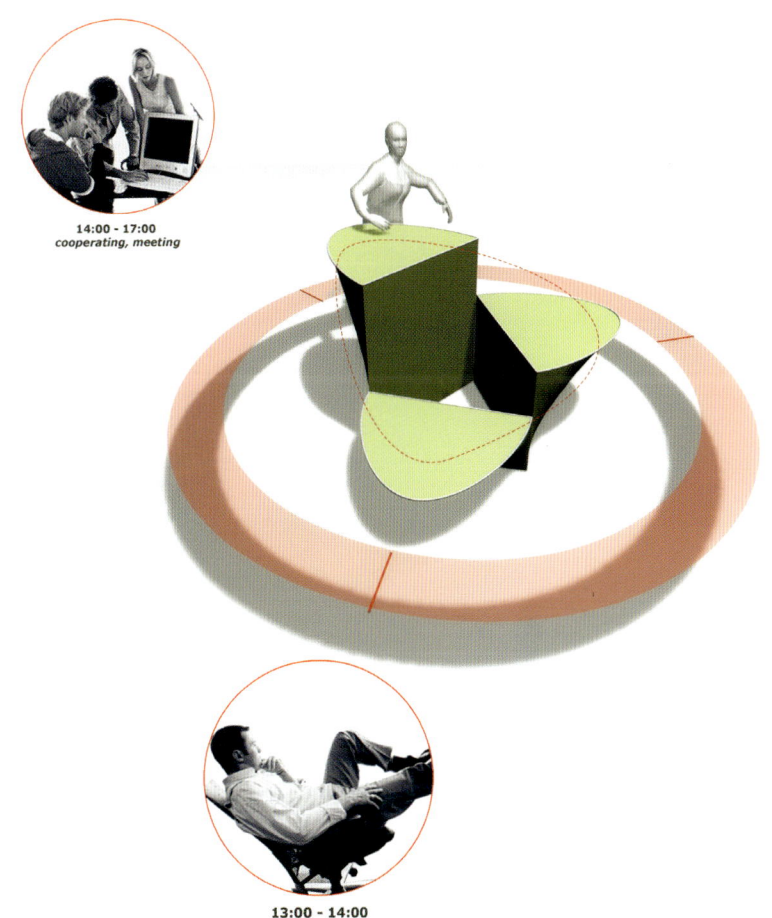

09:00 - 13:00
concentrated working

13:00 - 14:00
relaxing

Concept

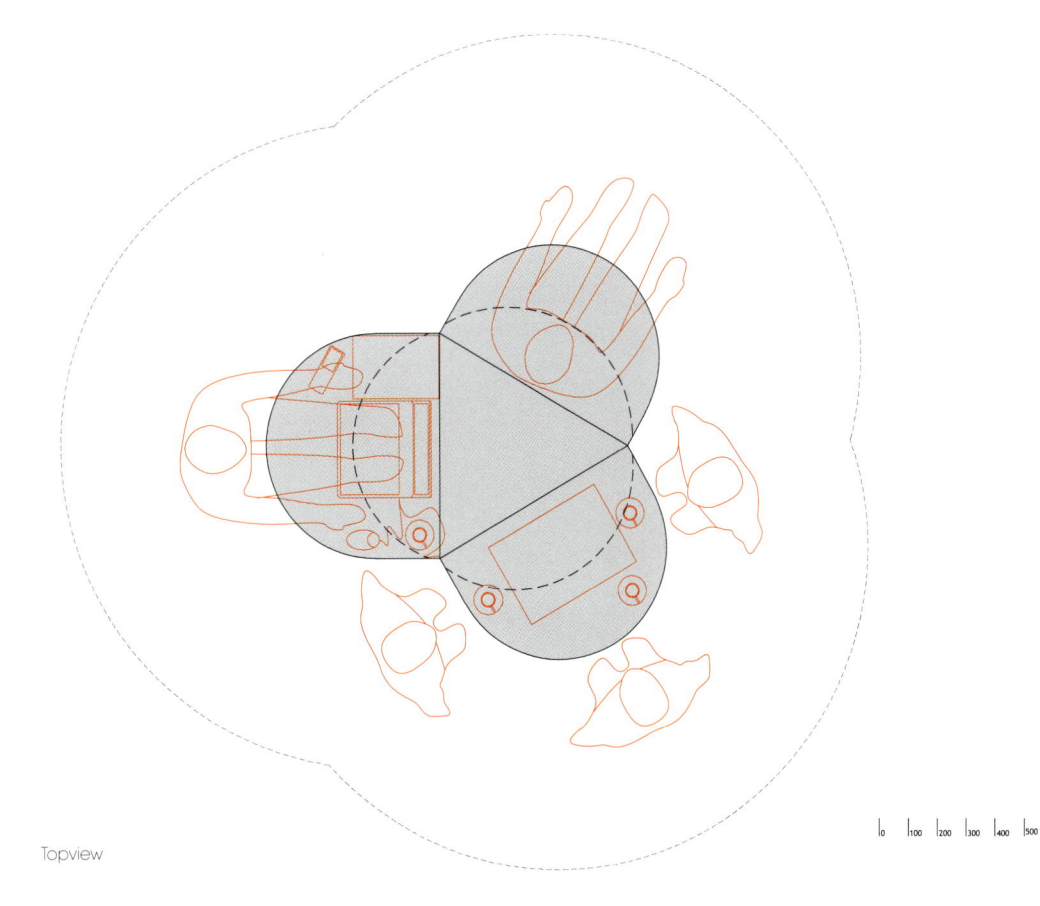

Topview

ARCHITECTURAL DIAGRAMS 707

SUN/S.E.T.
GEOTECTURA

"WE TRIED TO EMPHASIZE OUR CONTEMPORARY RESPONSIBILITIES AS DESIGNERS IN A SUSTAINABLE ERA: SOCIAL FLEXIBILITY OF INDIVIDUAL COMPOSITION."

sun\S.E.T. details

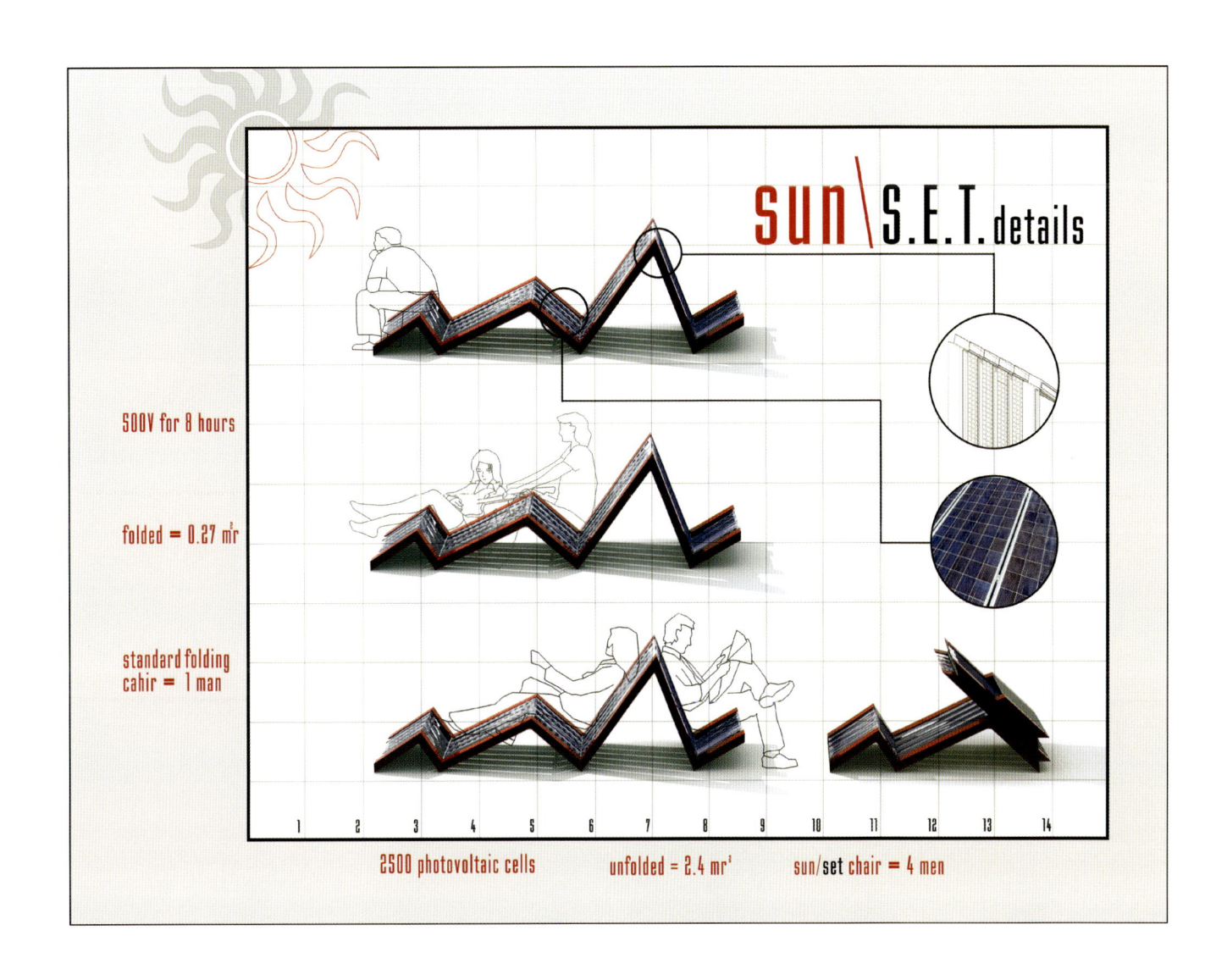

500V for 8 hours

folded = 0.27 m²

standard folding cahir = 1 man

2500 photovoltaic cells   unfolded = 2.4 m³   sun/set chair = 4 men

THE EXCHANGE
Z-A studio, Inbar Barak Studio & Claudia Herasme

"CREATING AN OPENING FOR A PASSERBY / TOURIST TO SEE INTO THE COMMUNITY."

AT PUBLIC INTERFACE

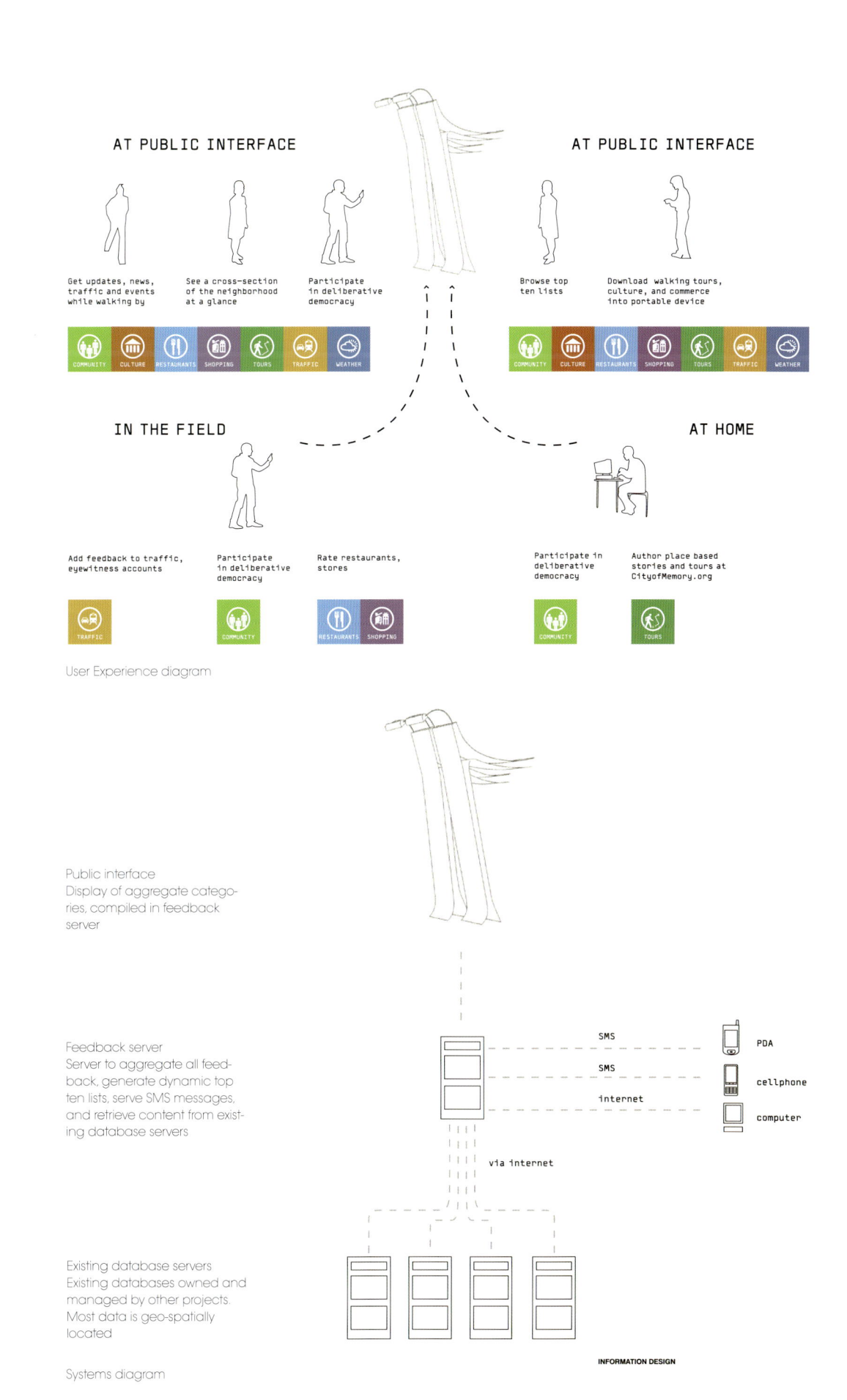

- Get updates, news, traffic and events while walking by
- See a cross-section of the neighborhood at a glance
- Participate in deliberative democracy

COMMUNITY | CULTURE | RESTAURANTS | SHOPPING | TOURS | TRAFFIC | WEATHER

AT PUBLIC INTERFACE

- Browse top ten lists
- Download walking tours, culture, and commerce into portable device

COMMUNITY | CULTURE | RESTAURANTS | SHOPPING | TOURS | TRAFFIC | WEATHER

IN THE FIELD

- Add feedback to traffic, eyewitness accounts
- Participate in deliberative democracy
- Rate restaurants, stores

TRAFFIC | COMMUNITY | RESTAURANTS SHOPPING

AT HOME

- Participate in deliberative democracy
- Author place based stories and tours at CityofMemory.org

COMMUNITY | TOURS

User Experience diagram

Public interface
Display of aggregate categories, compiled in feedback server

Feedback server
Server to aggregate all feedback, generate dynamic top ten lists, serve SMS messages, and retrieve content from existing database servers

SMS — PDA
SMS — cellphone
internet — computer

via internet

Existing database servers
Existing databases owned and managed by other projects. Most data is geo-spatially located

Systems diagram

INFORMATION DESIGN

ARCHITECTURAL DIAGRAMS 711

TOKYO DAY-TRIPPER
Studio Makkink & Bey bv

"DAY-TRIPPER IS BASED ON A STUDY OF THE DIFFERENT POSTURES PEOPLE ASSUME ON THE STREET DURING A DAY."

24 hours

500 years   7 days   1 year

ARCHITECTURAL DIAGRAMS 713

TOUCH SCREEN ma0

"A PLACE FOR RANDOM ENCOUNTERS, BRUSH UP AGAINST EACH OTHER, HIDE AND TOUCH EACH OTHER, UNDERNEATH THE SHEETS, SO TO SPEAK."

Enter   Sit back, look image   Be opening

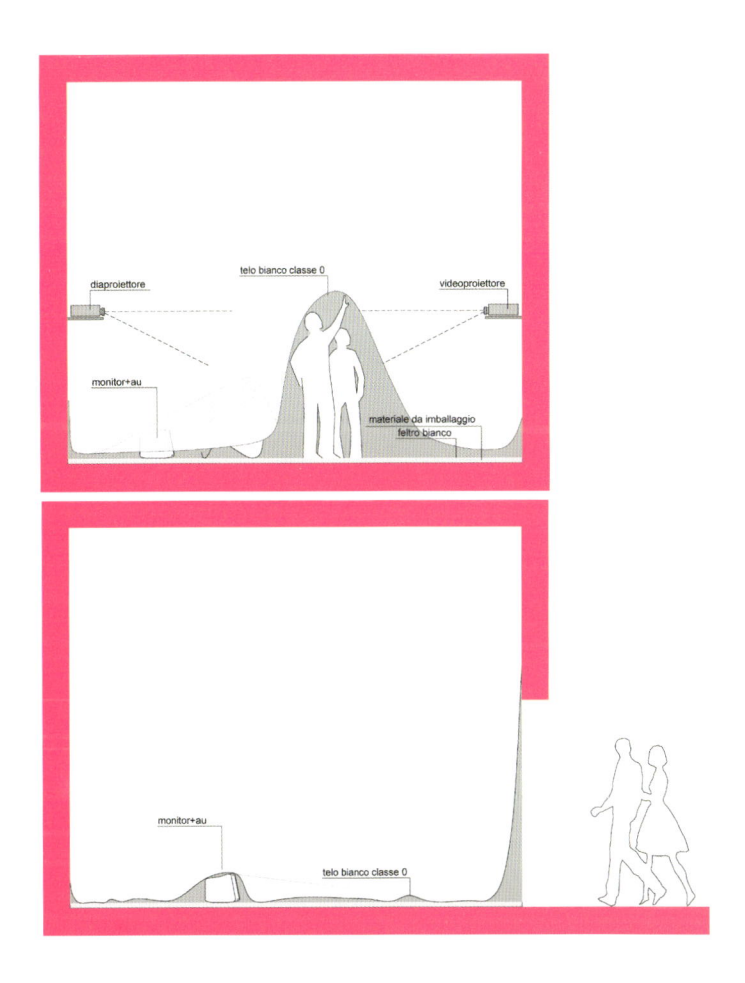

ARCHITECTURAL DIAGRAMS 715

TSUMARI ART TRIENNALE 2003
PERIPHERIQUES architectes

"PROJECT THAT PLAYS WITH THE LANDSCAPE, THE WINTER SNOW THE VISTAS, AND THE TREKKING THAT VISITORS DO."

Esquisse

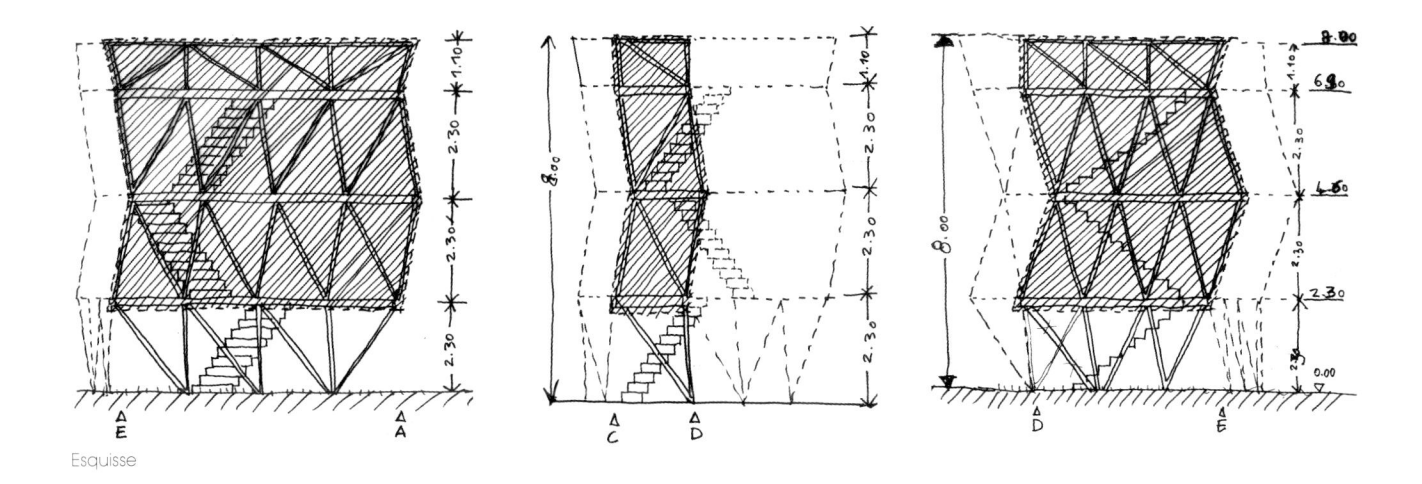

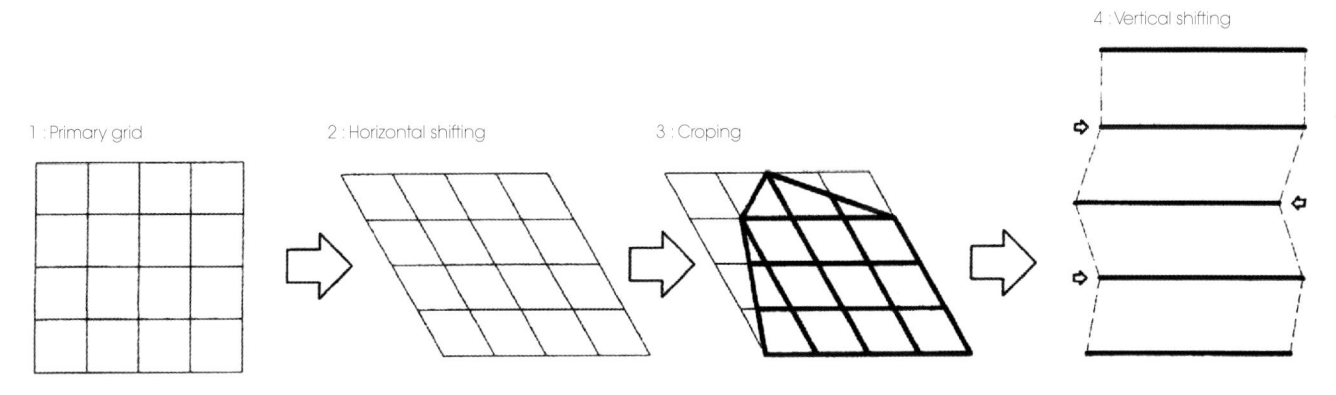

1 : Primary grid   2 : Horizontal shifting   3 : Croping   4 : Vertical shifting

Generating complexity

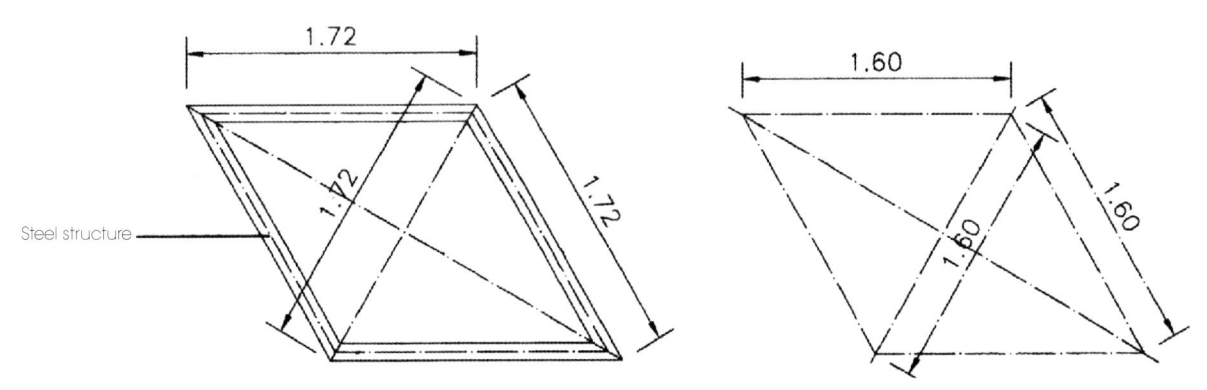

Steel structure

Basic Floor module

ARCHITECTURAL DIAGRAMS 717

VAGABOND TRAVEL BOOKSTORE
Smånsk Design Studio

"THE IDEA WAS TO BRING THE OUTSIDE WORLD INTO THE SHOP."

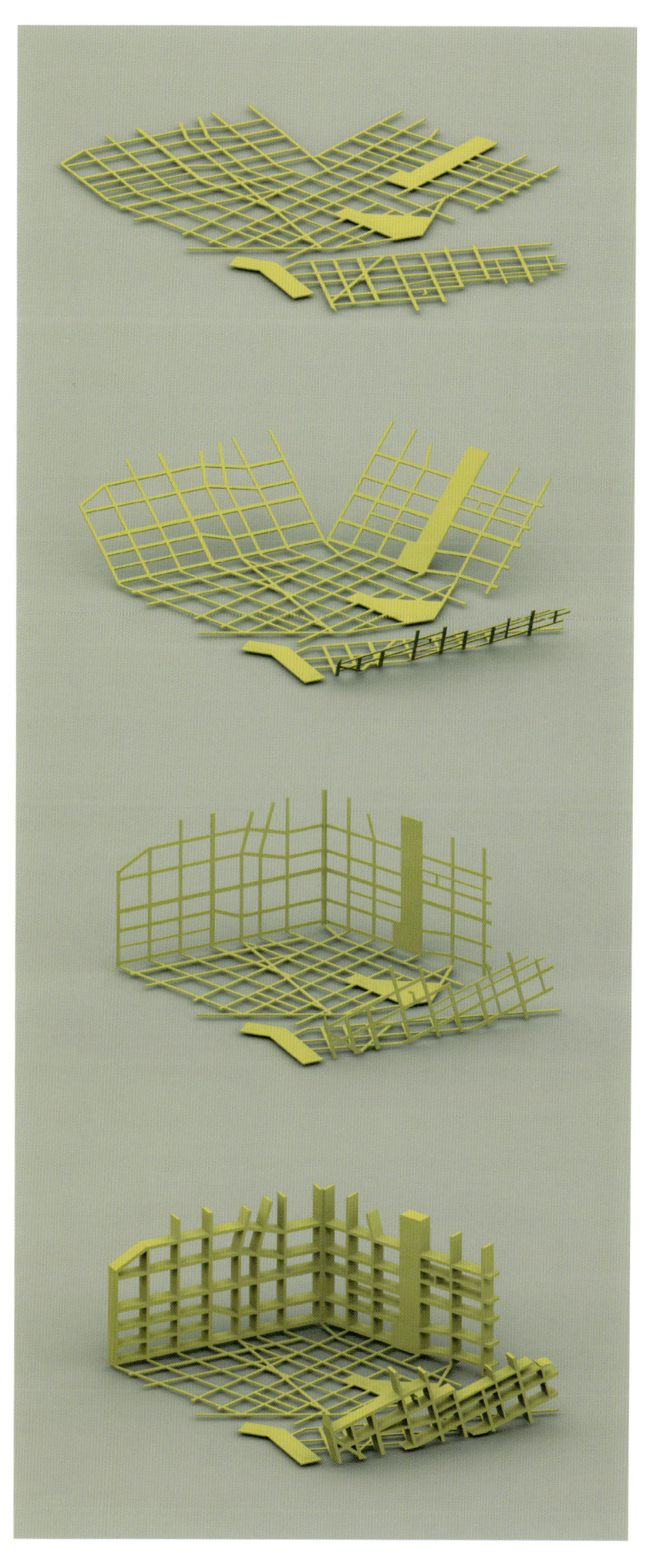

ARCHITECTURAL DIAGRAMS

WINDSHAPE nARCHITECTS

"FIFTY KILOMETERS OF WHITE POLYPROPYLENE STRING WERE THREADED THROUGH THE LATTICE TO CREATE SWAYING ENCLOSURES."

Wind passes through permeable structure

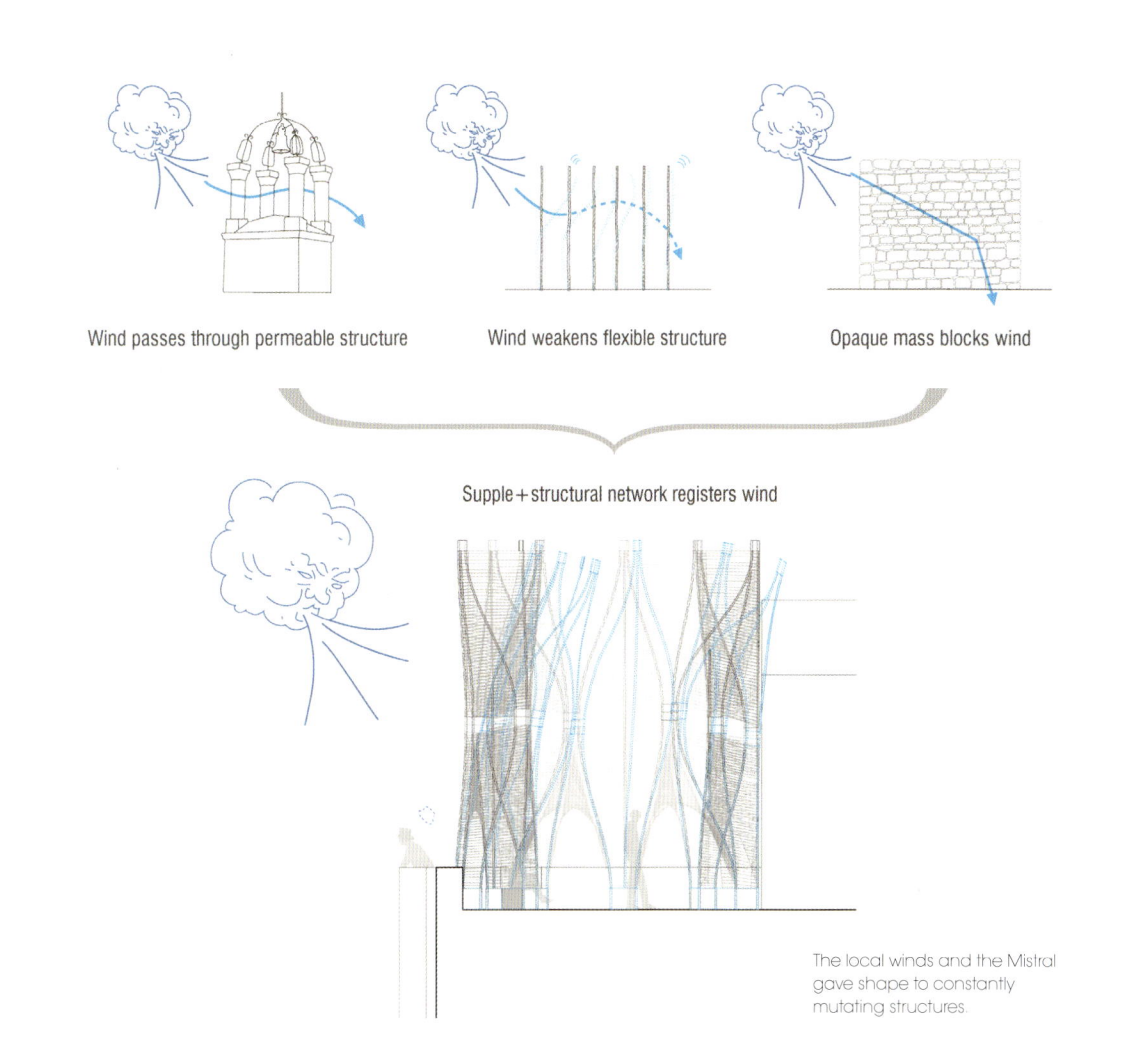

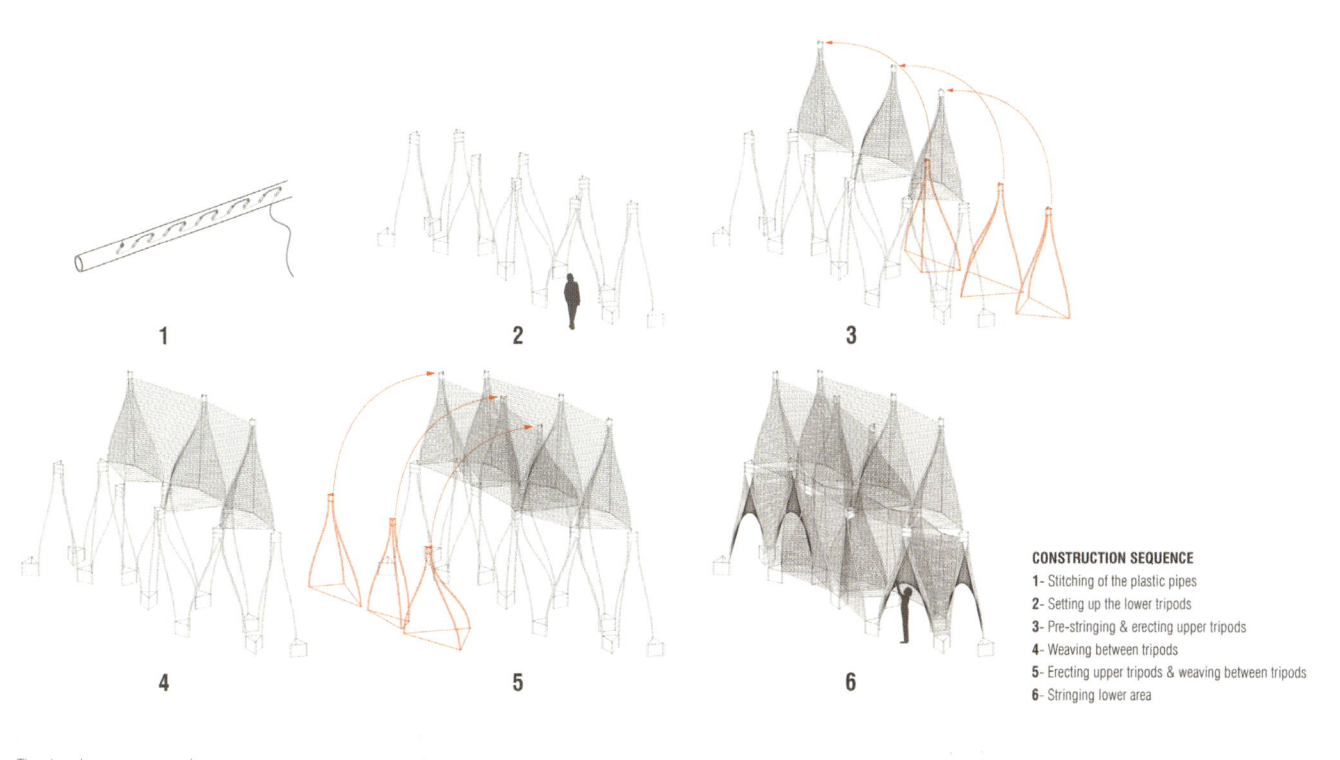

Wind weakens flexible structure

Opaque mass blocks wind

Supple + structural network registers wind

The local winds and the Mistral gave shape to constantly mutating structures.

CONSTRUCTION SEQUENCE
1 - Stitching of the plastic pipes
2 - Setting up the lower tripods
3 - Pre-stringing & erecting upper tripods
4 - Weaving between tripods
5 - Erecting upper tripods & weaving between tripods
6 - Stringing lower area

The basic components were digitally modeled and translated into a set of 2D drawings and data.

ARCHITECTURAL DIAGRAMS 721

60CH EMILIO MARIN architect

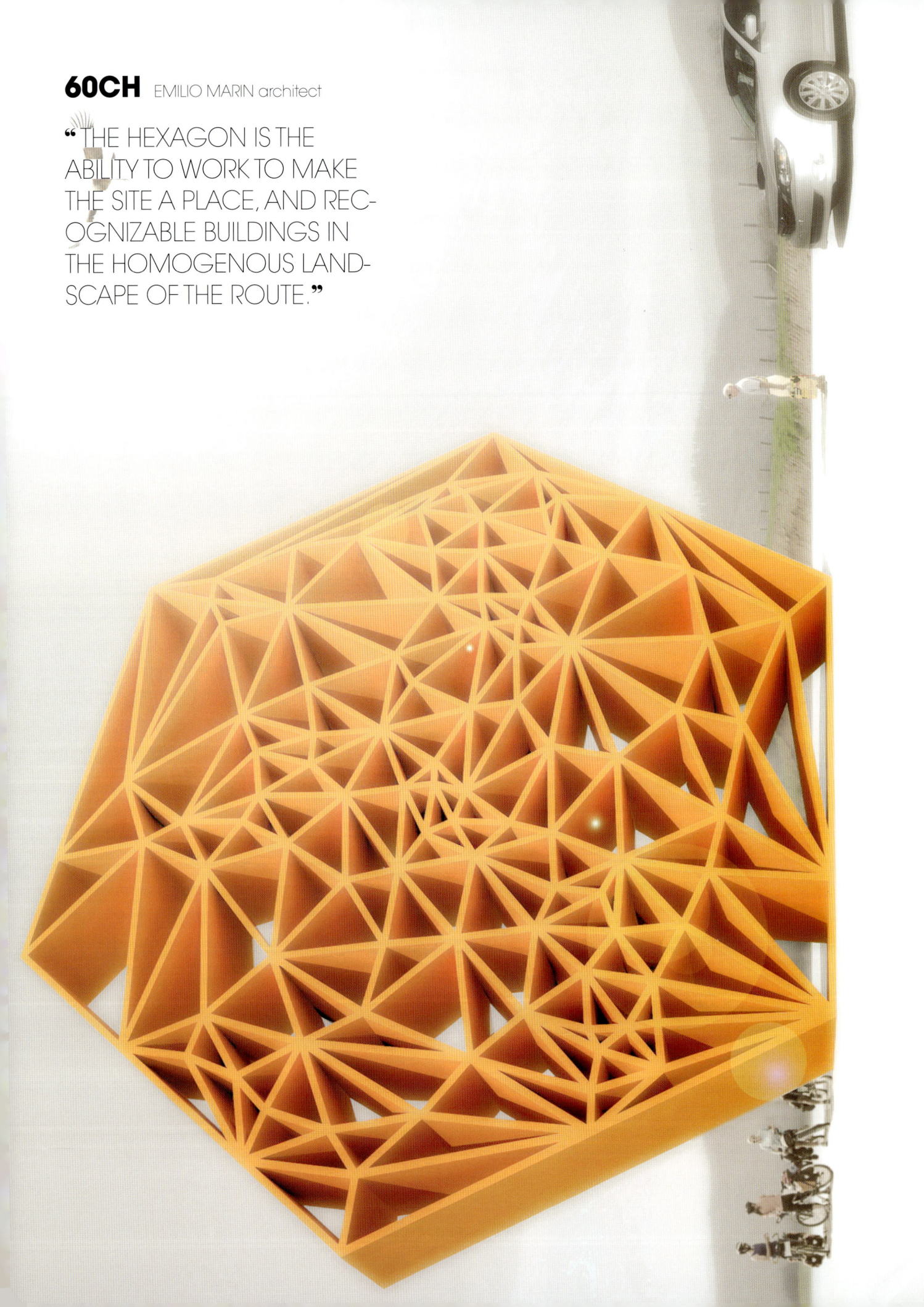

"THE HEXAGON IS THE ABILITY TO WORK TO MAKE THE SITE A PLACE, AND RECOGNIZABLE BUILDINGS IN THE HOMOGENOUS LANDSCAPE OF THE ROUTE."

- MOUNTAINS
- OCEAN
- ROAD
- VALLEY

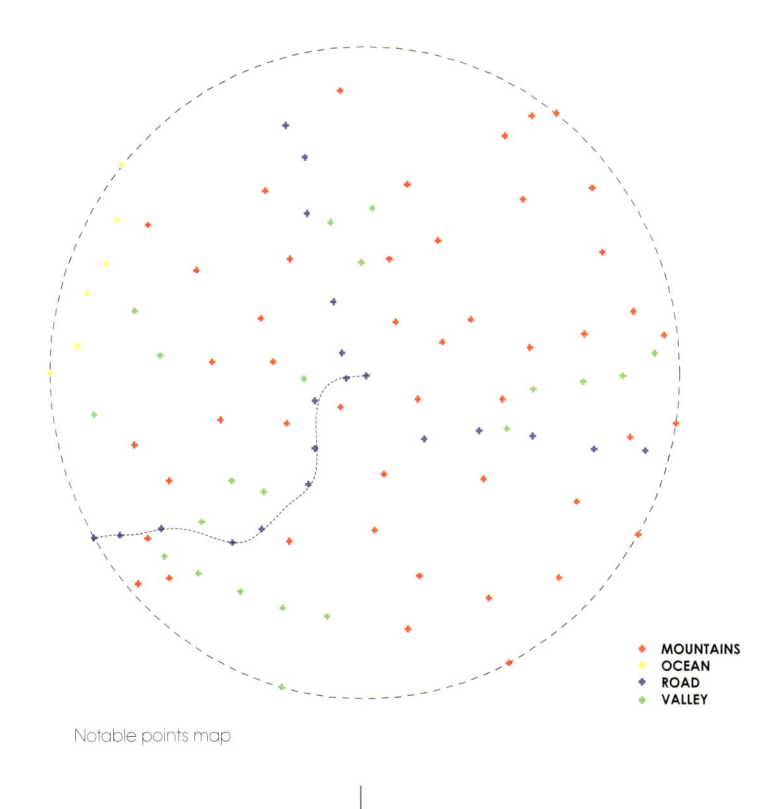

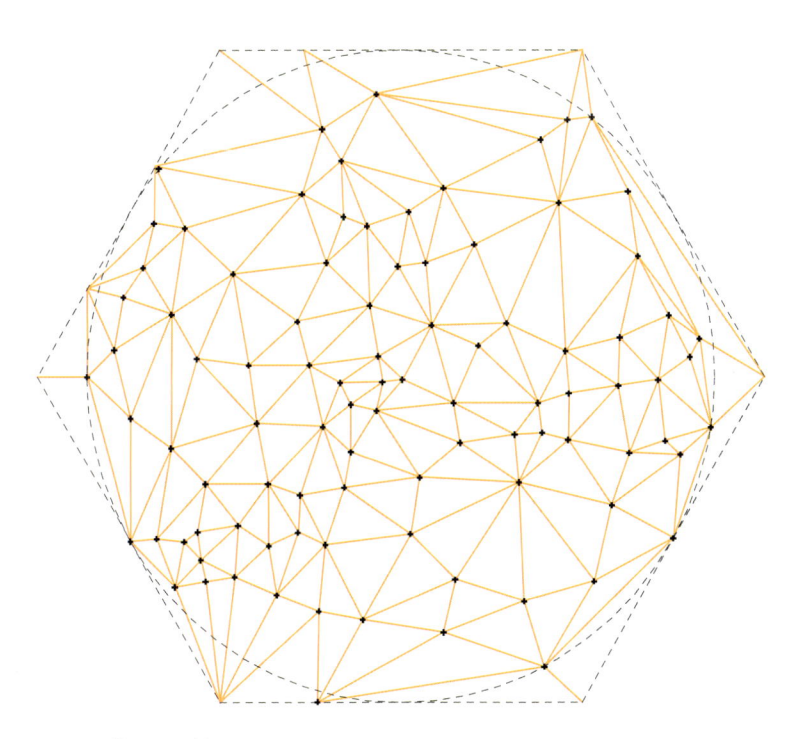

Notable points map

Diagrma delaunay

ARCHITECTURAL DIAGRAMS 723

...!!? BUREAU DES MÉSARCHITECTURES

"A HALF-EMERGED, OPAQUE MASS, ...!!? BORROWS ITS FORM FROM SUBMARINES AND ICEBERGS."

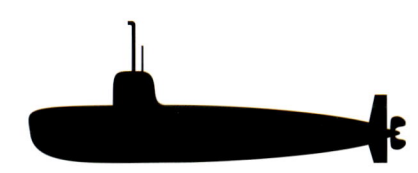

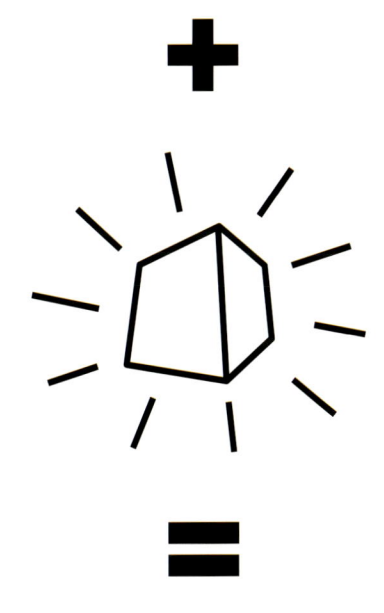

ARCHITECTURAL DIAGRAMS

PROFILE & IND[EX]

"2TR ARCHITETTURA / AA+U partnership for Ar[chitecture] / AMID [cero9] / Andreas Angelidakis / Atelie[r] Architeccts Urban Planners / beva / BIG / B[...] 8 Architects / DATA architects / EBPC / ECDM architect / Enrique Arenas Laorga & Luis Bas[...] zorek / GEOTECTURA / GLOWACKA RENNIE [...] pettersson / i29 interior architects / IaN+ / Io[...] jay is working. / JDS Architects / Jorge Pereira [...] chun / LAVA / LEON 11 ARCHITECTS / ma0 [...] hemmerling architecture design / Maurice [...] / Moho Architects / Moonbalsso / mxg arc[h...] TECTS / NL Architects / nodo17 Architects / [...]fice of landscape + architecture / PERIQHERI[C] / Point Supreme Architects / PSA / R&Sie… ar[...] / Re_Load / Responsive Systems Group / SA[...] neers / SeARCH / Serie Architects / servo / sg[...] dio / SMAQ / SO Architecture / SPACEGR[...] / Studio Ramin Visch / Tania Conko Architect[s...] lebaut Architectrue / VMX Architects / W[...]

...tecture, art and urbanism / Actar Arquitectura ...ileas / Axi:Ome / b4architects / Bernd Kniess ...AU DES MESARCHITECTURES / CJ Lim | Studio ...Ecosistema Urbano / EM2N / EMILIO MARIN ... Montalvo / Florian Krieger / Galvez + Wiec-...CHITECTS / Guallart Architects / gunnarsson ...Pavarani Architetti / J. MAYER H. ARCHITECTS / ...ungwoo Ji / kadawittfeldarchitektur / Kim Kai-...ANUELLE GAUTRAND ARCHITECTURE / marco ...ntjens Design / MoHen Design International ...ts / NABITO ARQUITECTURA S.C.P / nARCHI-...A ARCHITECTS / ONE ARCHITECTURE / PEG of-...S architects / platformbelin / PLY Architecture ...ects / Reiser + Umemoto RUR Architecture PC ...R VUGA ARHITEKTI / Samoo Architects & Engi-...sean godsell architects / Smansk Design Stu-... / studio asylum / Studio Makkink & Bey bv ...the next ENTERprise / UNStudio / Vincent Cal-...Müller Architects / Z-A Studio / Zizi&Yoyo"

2TR ARCHITETTURA

2TR ARCHITETTURA is a studio born in 2001 with two associates: Luca Montuori and Riccardo Petrachi. The studio works on a concept of un-volumetric architecture, the open/empty space is the primary element of every project: this means to work on public spaces and landscape from different approaches and ideas.
www.2tr.it

192
FREGENE SEASIDE
Project team: 2tr_Luca Montuori, Riccardo Petrachi with SMAA Architects.

278
CIPPS
Project team: 2tr with arch. Flora Ruchat Roncati
Model: M. Galofaro

624
VINEXPO 2009 ITALIAN STAND BORDEAUX
Project team: Laura Federici, 2T_R architettura (Luca Montuori e Riccardo Petrachi)
With: Alice Lentisco, Simone Stabile

AA + U partnership for Architecture, art and urbanism

AA + U, For Architecture, Art and Urbanism is an agent for interdisciplinary activities regarding the public domain. It was born out from collaborations of Socrates Stratis with architects and artists. It has a variable size depending on the projects undertaken. The main partner is Socrates Stratis, Dr. architect, urbanist with Riccardo Urbano, architect as the main associate and Maria Loizidou, as partner for visual arts. AA + U considers the projects at urban-architectural scale as an experimental device for creating knowledge which is constantly fed back to the making of projects. It has developed an integrating approach between architecture, art and urbanism in order to tackle issues about public space. The work of AA+U has been exhibited in both 9th and 10thVenice Biennales of Architecture. AA + U has participated in the design and implementation of projects such as residents, parks and public spaces and has won several prizes in local and European architectural competitions.

074
INCOGNITO
Study team : Socrates Stratis, Dr. architect, urbanist, Aggela Petrou, architect, Riccardo Urbano, architect
Assistants: Anastasia Aggelidou, Christos Pasadakis, architectural students

188
ELEFTHERIA SQUARE
Architect: Socrates Stratis, Dr. architect, planner, Christos Hadjichristos, Dr. architect (Lecturer of architecture, University of Cyprus)
Collaborating architects: Riccardo Urbano, Ercim Ulug

Actar Arquitectura

Manuel Gausa(1959), Oleguer Gelpi(1964), Ignasi Perez Arnal(1965), Florence Raveau(1965), Marc Aureli Santos(1960)
Founded in Barcelona Spain in 1994, Actar Architecture likes to think of itself as the place where multifaceted lines of activity come together and undergo radical exploration, producing, in no particular order, projects, buildings, books and exhibitions, all players on the architectural stage, are involved in a continuous and reciprocal relationship with these spheres of activity, and reject any form of division between theory and practice.
www.actar.es

270
BRUXELLES LANDSFLOW

AMID [cero9]

a! (Cristina Diaz Moreno +Efren Garcia Grida + Luis Cabrejas Guijarro + Hsiao Tien Hung)
a! Is a researching group of architects, designers and graphic producers able to develop any production related with new media and synthetic environments: movies, advertisements, graphic design, artificial landscapes, characters and, of course, imaginary architecture and artificial worlds.
www.a-synthetic.com

088
LK 0
Architects: Amid (Cristina Diaz Moreno + Efren Garcia Grinda)
ALIAS: LKm0
Project: Administrative building and Town Hall
Location: Lalin, Pontevedra with Galicia, (Spain)
Collavorators: Luis Cabrejas, Inigo Gonzalez-Haba, Jorge Martin Sainz de los Terreros, Hsiao-Tsien Hung, Javier Munoz Galan, David Marsinyach, Isabel Caballero and Javier Lopez Soldado
Structure: Schlaich Bergermann und Partner GBR
LANDSCAPE: Teresa Gali Izard

100
MM
Architects: Cristina Diaz Moreno + Efren Garcia Grinda
Project: The Magic Mountain. Ecosystem Mask For Ames Thermal Power Station
Collaborators: Dries Van De Velde, Luis Cabrejas Guijarro, Hsiao Tien Hung, Inigo Gonzalez-haba, Miguel Paredes

518
TRP
Architects: Cristina Diaz Moreno + Efren Garcia Grinda
Project: Forms of Energy. La Biennale di Venezia
Location: Venice Lagoon (Italy)
Collavrators: Luis Cabrejas, Inigo Gonzalez-Haba, Aritz Gonzalez

520
UIB
Architects: Cristina Diaz Moreno + Efren Garcia Grinda
Project: Central Library for UIB
Location: Palma de Mallorca (Spain)
Collaborators: Inigo Gonzalez-Haba, Gabriel Lassa, Luis Cabrejas Guijarro, Hsiao Tien Hung

Andereas Angelidakis

Andreas Angelidakis is an architect working at the intersection of digital culture and architectural production. In these parallel realities, Angelidakis treats the internet as a place where ideas are born and get tested, where new social behaviors define the way our society will develop in years to come. By assuming the role of architect inside online communities such as Second Life, and closely watching the development of technology's effect on our understanding of the world, he has developed an architecture that responds to the habits and particularities of the oncoming generation of citizens that grows up inside social networking sites like myspace and facebook.
In-between the internet and real life, Angelidakis has for a long time worked in the field of contemporary art, and it is this work which forms a bridge between different realities, between experimentation and implementation, between ideas and buildings.
These experiments always have a real life counterpart, as Angelidakis firmly keeps a base in both worlds, transferring the ideas from the internet to exhibition and installation design, furniture, urban planning, public space and more recently housing developments, always treating the client as a partner who is crucial to the projects' success.
www.angelidakis.com

694
PLAY GROUND

702
SPLAT

Atelier Philéas

Workshop Phileas is today composed of 10 persons: 7 architects, 1 interior designer, 1 draftsmen and 1 secretary. Our interest for architecture relies on pleasure that we have, to resolve complex equations. Taking into account the unique characteristics of a site context, added to our focus in respect of functional and economics data leads us, for each project and whatever its size, to find, with our own architectural touch, a unique project. The three partners provide together the design of the projects. It is a team work enriched by many discussions and by the experience of this common work. Then the project is supported by one of the three, from beginning to endwith the collaboration of the architects and draftsmen of the workshop (many of them have been part of the team for a long-time).
The clients are assured to have the same contact, including during the construction. The construction phase is a part of the work that we valued most and that enables us to maintain all the ideals developed till the end of the work.
Moreover, each partner has one or more speciality: Dominique is in charge of the communication with the constructors, Julien for the public relations and Anne-charlotte is responsible of the management. We pleasured to supervise the construction site; we often discuss and exchange our ideas and experiences weekly which allows us to have a perfect knowledge of the progress of all our projects.
www.atelier-phileas.co

564
CREATIVE HUB OF EURO RSCG
Client : Euros RSCG
Photos : Stephan Lucas

Axi:Ome

The Axi:Ome name derives from two Latin words axiom and forme. We engage architecture as research; a mode of practice directly interfaced in social, cultural, economic and environmental influences. Architects are on the edge of performance and material opportunities with the developing digital operations that allow for increased participation in the building process. We encourage technological conditions that enable freedom within our design choices, and we believe that original work in today's climate involves a spirit of collaboration.
In 2003 Heather Woofter and Sung Ho Kim re-structured Axi:Ome llc of St. Louis, MO. Heather and Sung Ho are involved in all phases of the practice in a desire for the projects to operate in a continuous dialogue at multiple scales, experimenting with shared ideas. Axi:Ome llc focuses on the concept that a building's spatial form and innovation are inextricably woven to one another and that architecture's progressive future lies in imagination, research and resolution of the intellectual and material development of design process.
www.axi-ome.net
www.axi-ome.blogspot.com

418
CARBON TOWER

610
SECRET STAGE

626
WOMEN'S SHELTER

728 PROFILE & INDEX

b4architects

The group was founded in Romein 2003, by Gianluca Evels, Francesco Fazzio, Lorenza Giavarini, Stefania Papitto, as a free association of architects that work in a synergic way, joining several knowledges. Measuring us from urban and landscape design until interior design and restoration, in a process that involve specific competences, always respecting the environmental characteristics. We are interested in producing works that contribute to the debate of the complexity of modern life. Our approach to any project is to involve all parties in a creative collaboration to define the objectives of the project with a balanced combination within critical readings of the local context and the "outsider" perspective of us. We also dedicate to further activities, like some different experiences at the university of Rome or taking part at some international workshops, with the aim to be active in the architectural debate about contemporary cities. From 2008 the active partners are Gianluca Evels and Stefania Papitto.
www.b4architects.com

350
TOUCHING WATER

Bernd Kniess Architects Urban Planners

Born 1961, was trained and worked as a landscape gardener before studying architecture and urban planning at the Technical University Darmstadt and the Academy of Arts, Berlin. Since 1995 he has works as both architect and urban planner. He was the co-founder and partner of b&k+ brandlhuber & kniess from 1996-2001. There after, he leads a research and design studio bernd kniess architects urban planners in Cologne. Since 1997 he has held several teaching positions, from 2003-2005, as visiting professorship for planning methodology and design (EPmLab) at the University of Wuppertal. He is one of the founders and a board member of "Loch e.V.", Cologne (a registered non-profit organization), which initiated the institution "European Kunsthalle" and a member of the advisory board of the International Design Forum (IFG) Ulm.
www.berndkniess.net

314
LJ:SONIC POLDER

316
MAPPING:PLAY

330
PANIC&PLANTING

364
WID

442
G55

472
NL-KB

474
NL-WI

536
WBW:WILLEURBANIE

beva

After earning their degrees from the Paris La villette School of Architecture in 2006, the two architects set up the beva practice the following year. With projects ranging in size from 6sqm to 60 hectares, they are just as happy giving free rein to their intuition and aspirations in ideas contests (such as Europan 9 – for which they received the first price –, such as the Paris Court of Justice contest – for which they received an honourable mention) as pursuing work in the field on much smaller sites (such as refurbishment of Parisian apartments). Each project they undertake seeks to make a statement and project an image in keeping with a story or plot line they wish to share. Their contemporary architectural thinking is therefore built both on due care for a given site and its cultural and other sensitive context, and on compliance with a programme and its contracting authority
www.beva.fr

226
ON CANAL STREET

252
URBAN STUDY

BIG

BIG is a Copenhagen based group of more than 50 architects, designers and thinkers operating within the fields of architecture, urbanism, research and development. BIG has created a reputation for completing buildings that are programmatically and technically innovative as they are cost and resource conscious. In our architectural production we demonstrate a high sensitivity to the particular demands of contexts and mixed use programs.

By practicing what Bjarke Ingels likes to describe as 'programmatic alchemy', BIG often mixes conventional ingredients such as living, leisure, working, parking and shopping into new forms of symbiotic architecture.
BIG recently opened their first Danish solo exhibition "YES IS MORE" at the Danish Architecture Center in Copenhagen and has also won the competition of representing Denmark at the World EXPO Exhibition in Shanghai, in 2010. These projects clearly represent BIG's ongoing effort to free architectural imagination from habitual thinking and standard typologies in order to deal with the constantly evolving challenges of contemporary life.
www.big.dk

154
TALLINN TOWN HALL

Project: The Public Village
Client: Union of Estonian Architects
Collaborators: Adams Kara Taylor, Grontmij – Carl Bro, Ramboll
Size: 28.000m²
Location: Tallinn, Est
Partner-In-Charge: Bjarke Ingels
Project Leader: Jakob Lange
Contributors: Daniel Sundlin, Hanna Johansson, Ondrej Janku, Ken Aoki, Benjamin Engelhardt, Maxime Enrico, Frederik Lyng, Joao Albuquerque, Aet Ader, Harry Wei, Alex Coma, Jin Kyung Park

304
KLM

Project: Kløverkarréen
Client: Kløvermarken Development Company
Partner-in-Charge: Bjarke Ingels
Project Leader: Andreas Pedersen
Contributors: Bo Benzon, David Zahle, Jakob Christensen, Julie Schmidt-Nielsen, Ole Schrøder, Stefan Mylleager Frederiksen
Collaborators: Jds Architects, The Municipality of Copenhagen
Size: 200.000m² / 2,000 Residences

368
WORLD VILLAGE OF WOMEN SPORTS

Client: H-Hagen Fastighets Ab
Collaborators: Akt, Tyréns, Transsolar
Size: 100.000m²
Location: Malmø, Sweden
Partner-in-Charge: Bjarke Ingels
Project Leader: Nanna Gyldholm Møller
Contributors: Gabrielle Nadeau, Daniel Sundlin, Jonas Barre, Nicklas Antoni Rasch, Jin Kyung Park, Fan Zhang, Steve Huang, Flavien Menu, Ken Aoki

374
ZIRA ISLAND MASTERPLAN

Size: 1,000,000m²
Client: Aurositi Holding
Collaborators: Ramboll
Project credits: Big + Ramboll + Pihl
Partner in charge: Bjarke Ingels
Project leader: Andreas Klok Pedersen
Team: Sylvia Feng, Kinga Rajczykowska, Pål Arnulf Trodahl, Pauline Lavie, Maxime Enrico, Oana Simionescu, Alex Cozma, Molly Price

BUREAU DES MESARCTECTURES

Didier Fiuza Faustino, born in 1968, has been carrying out between France and his country of origin, Portugal, installations, videos and projects for the public domain, while leading his career as an architect. Award winner at the New Albums of Young Architects exhibition in 2002 (with his "Bureau des Mésarchitectures", founded together with Pascal Mazoyer in 2001), and exhibited on several occasions at the Venice Architecture Biennale. His deliberately cross-disciplinary approach explores the chinks between public and private space, between political and architectural space.

724
...!!?

Specificity: Floating art center
Material: Wheel structure, steel panels, coated steel stairs and walkways, glass
Dimension: 15 x 24 x 10.5 m l 450m²

CJ Lim | Studio 8 Architects

CJ Lim is the founder of Studio 8 Architects, and the Professor of Architecture and Cultural Design at the Bartlett University College London.
His design focuses on innovative interpretations of cultural, social and environmental sustainability programmes. His recent award winning eco-cities are for the Chinese and Korean Governments. CJ is listed in Debrett's People of Today and the International Who's Who for his architecture and academic contributions. The Guardian and the Independent newspapers, and Iakov Chernikhov Foundation Moscow have included CJ in their talent listings. In 2006, the Royal Academy of Arts London awarded CJ the Grand Architecture Prize, the prestigious award with past winners including Lord Rogers and Lord Foster.
His most celebrated architecture, "Virtually Venice", investigated East-West cultures and identities – commissioned by the British Council UK for the Venice Architecture Biennale. Monographs publications include "441/10... we'll reconfigure your space when you're ready" (1996), "Sins + Other Spatial Relatives" (2001), "How Green is Your Garden?" (2003), "Museums [work in process]" (2004), "NeoArchitecture: Studio 8 Architects" (2005), "Virtually Venice" (2006), and "Smartcities + Eco-warriors" (2010).
www.cjlim-studio8.com

184
BONN SQUARE

Project: Bonn Square Oxford Redevelopment
Location: Oxford, UK
Client: Oxford City Council
Design team: CJ Lim with Jonathan Hagos
Consultant: Techniker (Structural Engineers)

200
GUANGMING SUSTAINABLE CENTRE PARK

Location: Shenzhen, China
Client: Shenzhen Municipal Planning Bureau
Design team: CJ Lim With Dimitris Argyros, Barry Cho, Kelly Chan
Consultants: Techniker (Structural Engineers), Fulcrum (Environmental + Sustainability Engineers)

224
NANYU SHOPPING PARK

Client: Shenzhen Municipal Planning Bureau, Jin Long Real Estate Co
Design team: CJ Lim with Yongzheng Li, Pascal Bronner, Sarah Mui, Tom Hillier, Maxwell Mutanda, Barry Cho, Jacqueline Chak, Martin Tang
Consultants: Techniker (structural engineers), Fulcrum (environmental + sustainability engineers)

342
STU CAMPUS

Client: Shenzhen Municipal Planning Bureau
Design team: CJ Lim with Pascal Bronner, Sarah Mui, Barry Cho, Tom Hillier, Maxwell Mutanda, Jacqueline Chak, Martin Tang, Loui Lim, Yongzheng Li
Consultants: Techniker (structural engineers), Fulcrum (environmental + sustainability engineers)

ARCHITECTURAL DIAGRAMS 729

DATA architects

Carolina Ruiz-Valdepeñas Guerrero and Daren Gavira Persad are graduated in architecture from E.S.A.Y.A. of the European University of Madrid, where they have been projects lecturers since 2004. In 2003 founded DATA, a space created with the purpose of creating the environmental conditions necessary to develop their work. Their projects are characterized by establishing continuous interference with other knowledge fields. This line of work allows them to coexist, in a natural way, with the error and uncertainty, with the ingenuity of those who wonder, why things are like that?

320
MAYDAY

EBPC

EBPC is an interdisciplinary studio based in Milan and was born out of the collaboration between Emanuela Bartolini and Paolo Cardin. EBPC goes through the research on the development of the contemporary city, exploring the importance of architecture in the city.
The rolling process of the space organization through the different scales, from the object to the city, is the theoretical structure of our method. The boundary between architecture and urbanism was never cosidered part of our work. Emanuela Bartolini studied at the Politecnicodi Milano and at the TU Delft. In 2005 she graduated in Milan, where she lives and works. She also collaborates with the Urban Design Department of the Politecnico di Milano. Paolo Cardin studied at the Politecnico di Milano and at the ETSA Barcelona. In 2005 he graduated in Milan, where he lives and works. He also collaborates with varied New Yorkfirms.
www.ebpc.it

280
CONTEMPORARY RAUMPLAN

292
FBM PERUGIA

Architect: Emanuela Bartolini Paolo Cardin

ECDM

Emmanuel Combarel and dominique Marrec Architects (ECDM) is an office for architecture based in Paris. ECDM's work focuses on transformational and flexible concepts as well as on issues of sustainable development. The open programming provides an overall conceptual platform to define specific scenarios for specific projects. The method may be characterized as an integrative approach. In close collaboration with the client, associated ingeniers, consultants and future occupants, our work consists of bringing forth fundamental concepts and guiding a design response, appropriate for a specific time, place and program. The pertinent solution is as much concerned with functional legibility and technical appropriateness, as with architecture's significant and poetic content.
www.ecdm.fr

326
NOUVEAU BASSIN

360
VORESBY CARLSBERG

Program: Urban planning of Carlsberg district
Client: Carlsberg
Images: Thomas Raynaud
Site Area: 330,000m²
Collect conditions of post-urbanity | Reuse the vintage fabric in a new ensemble | A collage of urban strategies.
Uses, programs and functions take place regardless of forms | Limits as interface.

398
A BIG HOUSE

426
CLAUDE BERNARD

Ecosistema Urbano

[ecosistema urbano] is an architecture and engineering team that focuses on the research and ecological design of new architecture projects that understand sustainable development as a resource for innovation and enthusiasm. Its principle members have backgrounds in architecture and civil engineering from Madrid Polytechnic University, the Bartlett School of Architecture at the University College London, Institut d'Architecture Victor Horta of Brussels as well as Cambridge University Engineering Department. They are design studio professors in the School of Architecture of Madrid, International University of Catalonia in Barcelona and visiting professors at several universities in Spain, South America, Asia and United States (Cornell, Yale, Cooper Union, California, Arizona, Shanghai, Mexico DF, Chile…).
They have received more than 30 awards since the year 2000 in national and international architecture design competitions. On the year 2005, they have received the European Acknowledgement Award from the Holcim Foundation for Sustainable Construction (Geneva, 2005) and the selection as one of the "Top ten spanish architects under 40" by the Antonio Camuñas Foundation. In 2006 they have received the Architectural Association and the Environments, Ecology and Sustainability Research Cluster Award (London, 2006). In 2007 they have been nominated for the European Union Prize for Contemporary Architecture Mies van der Rohe Award "Emerging European Architect" and they received the AR AWARD for emerging architecture in London, selected between more than 400 teams from all around the world. In 2008 they received the ARQUIA Award from the Caja de Arquitectos and the silver award for Europe from the Holcim Foundation for Sustainable Construction.
Exhibitions of their work have been shown in several national and international institutions. Their work has been covered by the national and international press, television programs, and specialized publications (Holland, Germany, France, Denmark, Sweden, Portugal, Italy, Austria, Czech Republic, Romania, Slovenia, Chile, Colombia, Cuba, Taiwan, Thailand, Russia, China, UAE, Canada and USA).
Recently a monograph of their projects, entitled Monoespacios 8, was published by the Association of Architects of Madrid. Presently their work is being shown in the collective exposition FRESHMADRID (www.freshmadrid.com), in Milan (Spazio gallery) and been invited to present their work in the latest edition of the Venice Architecture Biennale by the director of the biennial Aaron Betsky under the flag of Italy.
At present, outlined in the Louisiana Museum of Modern Art in Copenhagen a laboratory-installation within the exhibition "Green Architecture for the Future.
Currently the team is involved in research projects about future paths of city design called "eco-techno-logical cities", financed by the Spanish Ministry of Industry and in parallel develop outreach through new information technologies that has materialized with the launch of the Internet first participatory television on creative urban sustainability (www.ecosistemaurbano.tv).
As for their latest project construction, they have achieved the second phase of the EcoBoulevard project in Madrid (pilot project of bioclimatic revitalization of a public space) and the Meteorological Museum in the historical Buen Retiro Park in Madrid.
In 2010 they will inaugurate an interactive public space for the World Expo 2010 Shanghai representing the city of Madrid and the PLAZA ECOPOLIS project in Rivas Vaciamadrid.
ecosistemaurbano.com

260
WATER PARK

Concept: Water Park Universal Exhibition Zaragoz

354
URBAN VOIDS

664
ECO-BULEVARD, NEW SUBURBAN DEVELOPMENT OF VALLECAS

Architects: Belinda Tato, Jose Luis Vallejo, Diego Garcia-Setien
Project Team: Ideas Competition- Patricia Lucas, Asier Barredo, David Benito, Jaime Eizaguirre, Ignacio Prieto | Constructive Project- Ignacio Prieto, Maria Eugenia Lacarra, David Delgado, David Benito, Jaime Eizaguirre, Patricia Lucas, Ana Lopez, Laura Casas, Fabricio Pepe, Michael Moradiellos

EM2N

We aim to produce architecture that is powerful and personal, architecture with the capability of developing its own character. As a result our projects may polarize the public, which is fine with us. One may love or hate our architecture, but one should never be left indifferent. We are convinced that there never is just one solution. Our projects must cope with the unforeseen, even the accidental. Therefore, we tend to think in scenarios, we work with hypotheses and generate oppositional alternatives. Each one of these projections into the future originates from different assumptions and has its own history or story to tell. If we manage to develop projects that can stand for themselves in the urban fabric, we have achieved our goal.
www.em2n.ch

492
PUBLIC RECORDS OFFICE

EMILIO MARIN architect

Emilio Marín was born in the city of Concepcion, Chile, in 1972 and graduated as an Architect in 1998,from the Faculty of Architecture and Urbanism of the Universidad de Chile. In 1999 he founds "TIDY2MARIN architects" (T2M architects), an independent office of Architecture participating in diverse projects of Urbanism, Architecture, Inner Design and Industrial Design. During that period his work was recognized in several National and International Architecture Biennials, as well as in specialized publications. In the year 2005 he becomes independent to launch the oficinadearquitectura.clproject, this happens from a personal glance, acute and critical of the exercise of the profession. Thus becoming a new work place, OA tries to propose and to develop projects that can go somehow beyond "the traditional" exercise of the architect.
www.oficinadearquitectura.cl

632
ALTAMIRANO WALKWAY

Location: Walkway Altamirano, La Pólvora Road, Valparaíso, V Región Chile
Architects: Emilio Marín, Nicolas Norero (Competition Phase) / Special Credit: Diego Rossel (Development Phase)
Structural Engineer: Ingevsa S.A
Materials: Prefabricated Hexagon-Shaped Concrete Slab, Concrete , Steel
Photographer: Emilio Marin

722
60CH

Location: International road, Route 60ch, V region, Chile
Architects: Emilio Marín
Collaborator: Juan Carlos Lopez

Enrique Arenas Laorga & Luis Basabe Montalvo

Enrique Arenas Laorga (1974) graduated at ETSAM (Madrid, Spain). He has developed projects in very different areas: rehabilitations, housing, institutional, furniture, events architecture, etc. He has held lectures at several academic institutions, and is now researcher at ETSAM.
Luis Basabe Montalvo (1975) graduated at the TU Graz (Austria). Since 2003 he teaches design studio at ETSAM, where he is also working on his PhD. He was guest researcher and faculty at various Universities: RWTH Aachen (Germany), Cambridge (UK) and CEPT Ahmedabad (India).

336
SEEDS AND VECTOR

Colaborators: Alejandra climent & Luis Palacios

Florian Krieger

Born in Darmstadt, Germany 1968. Studied sociology in Bologna, Italy and architecture at the Technical University Darmstadt and the Technical University (ETSA) Madrid, Spain, Graduating 2000 in Darmstadt, worked in the Frankfurt based architectural office PAS-Jourdan&Müller, and Stadtbauplan, Darmstadt. 2003 founding Florian Krieger Architektur und Städtebau / office for architecture and urban design 2003-05 teaching at the Technical University Darmstadt. 2007 member of the german council for the culture of architecture (Bundesstiftung Baukultur) Potsdam. www.florian-krieger.de

340
STEPSCAPE - GREENSCAPE - WATERSCAPE

344
SUBURBAN FRAMES

346
SUN - FIELDS

366
WIESENFELD

378
3X2 - ELEMENTS FOR THE URBAN LANDSCAPE

Authors: Florian Krieger, Benjamin Künzel, Urs Löffelhardt, Ariana Sarabia
Urban design: masterplan, 16 hectares, by Florian Krieger and Urs Löffelhardt
Architecture: studies for housing types, by Florian Krieger and Urs Löffelhardt

Gálvez + Wieczorek

MªAuxiliadora Gálvez and Izabela Wieczorek collaborate since 2003, working either autonomously or in association. They work on an active sensorial architecture, linked to nature, developing housing and facilities projects. Both share those interests with research and teaching. Their work has been awarded in several national and international competitions, as Europan, and shown in different institutions like I.F.A París or monographic publications like "Excepto 21. Galvez+Wieczorek. Active Cartographies".
www.galvez-wieczorek.com

130
SAMI CULTURAL CENTRE

Developer : State provincial Office of Lapland/ European Regional Development Fund.
Architects : Mª Auxiliadora Gálvez Pérez+Izabela Wieczorek
Collaborators : Juan Lobato, Jean-Baptiste Joye, Carla de Prada, Plácido González, Lara Freire, Hector Torres y Jaime Traspaderne
Built area : 5,000sqm

218
LINEAR PARK

Location: Canal del Guadalmellato, Córdoba, Spain
Developer: C.O.A.Co/ UIA/ Confederación Hidrográfica del Guadalquivir
Architects: Mª Auxiliadora Gálvez Pérez+Izabela Wieczorek
Collaborators: Mª Luisa Reques
Consultants: Carlos Rodríguez (Ingeniero de Montes)
Area: Central stretch: 594 Ha

GEOTECTURA

GEOTECTURA means merging land and architecture together with ecological values, cost effective technologies, psychological considerations and social responsibility.
GEOTECTURA is an award winning architectural studio founded by architect Dr. Joseph (Yossi) Cory. Our work was published and exhibited worldwide. We use in the office green design techniques combined with social awareness and creativity.
Specializing in innovative design GEOTECTURA is committed to explore new sustainable horizons by preserving and restoring the balance between natural and built environment. Our projects are based on multi-disciplinary research and the office uses an open source design approach to optimize the best result for each challenge through the collaboration with designers from various fields such as science, architecture, art, landscape architecture, sociology and psychology.
www.geotectura.com

708
SUN/S.E.T

Architecture team: Dr. Joseph Cory (Geotectura Studio), Oded Rozenkier

GLOWACKA RENNIE ARCHITECTS

Agnieszka Glowacka and Eleanor Rennie set Glowacka Rennie in 2004 after winning an international design competition for a Landmark in the East of England. They have recently successfully completed a Feasibility Study for their Landmark idea for the East of England Development Agency, for which they were appointed lead consultants to a team of renowned sub-consultants including Arup, Expedition Engineering and Quantity surveyors Savant International.
Agnieszka Glowacka and Eleanor Rennie's design skills were recognized whist at University. They studied at the Bartlett School of Architecture in London and were both awarded Distinctions for their architectural Diplomas and also the Sir Bannister Fletcher Medal for the highest marks for architecture in their respective Diploma years. They were both nominated for the RIBA Presidents Silver Medal, Eleanor was awarded the RIBA Serjeant Award for drawing in 2000. Her diploma project was published in Young Blood - Architectural Digest.
Glowacka Rennie's approach to design is not stylistically driven, but a response to a project's specific context and Client brief. In our eyes each design solution and client is unique, no two projects or solutions are the same. We use physical clues such as the orientation, weather and topography of a site as well as its historical context and planned future and as starting points. We always understand who will be occupying the building and tailor our responses to their needs.
glowacka-rennie.com

622
V&A WOMENS' AMENITIES

Location : London, UK
Client : Victoria and Albert Museum
Architect and Lead Designer : Glowacka Rennie
Artist : Felice Varini
Project Manager : Thinc Projects
Structural Engineer : Price and Myears
Services Engineer : Consultant Design Engoineers
Contractor : Longcross
Photo : Glowacka Rennie, Archimage
Budget : £130,000

Guallart Architects

Vicente Guallart (Valencia 1963) is one of the most relevant emerging architects in Spain. He opened his studio in Barcelona in 1992. He works in the confluence of architecture, nature and new technologies. He spends part of his time with research and educational projects as director of the new Institute for Advanced Architecture of Catalonia (Iaac), in Barcelona, that hold a international postgraduate program on architecture and urbanism working in many scales "from Bits to geography". In 2000 he co-directed with MIT's Media Lab and other research Center, the Media House Project, the prototype of an informational house, based, as first time, in distributed computation.
www.guallart.com

166
WROCLAW 2012

Client : Wroclaw City Council
Main architects : Vicente Guallart, María Díaz
Collaborators : Enrico Crobu, Asaduzzaman Rassel, Marian Albarrán, Fernando Meneses, Daniela Frogheri, Andrea Imaz, Rainer Goldstein, Ana Cabellos
3D images : Lucas Cappelli, Gaëtan Kohler, Néstor David Palma
Work models : Christine Bleicher, Laure-Hélène Pélissot, Filipa Barraquero / Methacrylate model : Fabián Asunción, Diego Gutiérrez, Ángel Gaspar, Juan Robledo, Rafael DeMontard
Lights : Toño Saeinz
Photography of model: Nuria Díaz (construction), Adrià Goula (final images)

178
BATOUTZ PORT AND OCEAN PLAZA

Main architects: Vicente Guallart, María Díaz
Local Architects: J.M. Lin The Oberver Design Group
Images: Laura Cantarella, Sabine Mayer
3D: Lucas Cappelli + Uoku.com.net artchitects; Lucas Jagodnik, Julieta Serena,Mariano Castro, Horacio Suaya / 3D images: YLAB Tobias Laarmann / 3D images Ocean Plaza: Néstor David Palma
Models: Fabián Asunción, Soledad Revuelto, Ángel Luis Gaspar, María JoséBizama, Ruth Martín Ocean Plaza Model: Theodora Christoforidou, Fotis Vasilakis, Andrea Imaz, Daniela Frogheri, Fernando Meneses
Collaborators: Christine Bleicher, Ester Rovira, Maria Osa, Kika Estarella, Ekhiñe Nieto, Michael Strauss, Rodrigo Landáburu, Melissa Magallanes, Carlos Valdés, Ricardo Guerreiro
Parametric Rocks Video: Oriol Ferrer
Advisors: Tourism_ José Miguel Iribas, Sustainability_ Rafael Serra Florensa. UPC, Solar Energy _ Oscar Acebes. TFM, Structure_ Willy Muller, WMA, Port Engeneering_ Vicente Cerdà, UPV, Crystallographic advisor_ Albert Soler, Photography of rocks_ Universitat de Barcelona, Chinese translation_ Lin Yi, Chinese culture_ Li-An Tsien

196
FUGEE PORT

Client: Taipei County Government
Architecture: Guallart Architects & J.M. Lin, The Observer Design Group
Main architects: Vicente Guallart, María Díaz
v.1_ Collaborators: Christine Bleicher, Ester Rovira, Maria Osa, Kika Estarella, Francisco Nieto, Michael Strauss, Rodrigo Landáburu, Melissa Magallanes, Carlos Valdés, Andreas Allen
3D: Lucas Cappelli + Uoku.com-net architects; Lucas Jagodnik, Julieta Serena,Mariano Castro, Horacio Suaya
3D images: YLAB Tobias Laarmann
Images: Laura Cantarella, Sabine Mayerv. 2_Collaborators: Christine Bleicher, Amaya Coello, Ignacio Toribio, Francesco Moncada, Massimo Tepedino, Rainer Goldstein, Gawel Tyrala, Wobciech Szubinski, Torsten Altmeyer, Francis Holding, Inti Vélez, Mariano Arias, Katharina Schendl , Moritz Treese, Csíkva˝ri Gergely
v. 3_Collaborators: Rainer Goldstein, Fernando Meneses, Daniela Frogheri, Marian Albarrán, Ana Cabellos, Marta Vélez, Andrea Imaz, Enrico Crobu
Models: Fabián Asunción, Soledad Revuelto, Ángel Luis Gaspar, María José Bizama, Ruth Martín, Christine Bleicher, Ricardo Guerreiro
3D images: Néstor David Palma
Advisors: Sociologist_ José Miguel Iribas, Sustainability_ Rafael Serra Florensa. UPC, Solar energy_ Oscar Acebes. TFM, Crystallographic_ Albert Soler, Chinese translation: Lin Yi, Taiwanese traditions: Li-An Tsien

214
KEELUNG

Main Architects: Vicente Guallart, Maria Díaz
Local Partner for development: J.M. Lin The Oberver Design Group
Collaborators: Dirk Barchstaedt, Christine Bleicher, Magnus Lundstrom, Rodrigo Landáburu, Melissa Magallanes, Ester Rovira, Manuel Shvartzberg Michael Strauss, Ricardo Guerreiro
Models: Christine Bleicher
Final model: Fabián Asunción, Soledad Revuelto, Ángel Luis Gaspar, María José Bizama, Ruth Martín
Images: Laura Cantarella, Sabine Mayer
3D images: Néstor David Palma, Lucas Cappelli + UokU.com net-architects. Lucas Jagodnik, Julieta Serena, Mariano Castro, Horacio Suaya, Martin Eschoyez, Franco Cappelli
Advisors_ Tourism: Jose Miguel Iribas, Sustainability: Rafael Serra Florensa. PC, Solar energy: Oscar Acebes. TFM., Structure: Willy Muller, WMA, Port Engeneering: Vicente Cerdà, UPV, Crystallography: Albert Soler, Rock images: Universitat de Barcelona, Chinese translation: Lin Yi, Chinese culture: Li-An Tsien

254
VINAROS PROJECT

Client : Ayuntamiento de Vinarós, Generalitat Valenciana and Tourism Ministry
Site : Costa Sur, Vinarós.
Main architects : Vicente Guallart, María Díaz
Geometry : Marta Malé Alemany
Collaborators : Rainer Goldstein, Christine Bleicher, Wobciech Szubinski, Csikvari Gergely, Marta Vieira Baptista, Julia Futó, Moritz Treese, Massimo Tepedino, Amaya Coello, Ignacio Toribio, Francesco Moncada, Gawel Tyrala, Diego Martin
Photography : Laura Cantarella, Nuria Díaz
Models : Christine Bleicher, Theodora Christoforidou, Fotis Vasilakis, Gabriella Castellanos, Daniela Frogheri, Fernando Meneses, Andrea Imaz, Marta Velez, Laure-Hélène Pelissot, Filipa Barraquero, Asaduzzaman Rassel
Construction : Binaria
Wooden platforms : Gestalt

650
CULTURAL GATE TO ALBORZ

Client: Development of Cultural Environment Co.
Local partner: Bonsar Architecture Studio
Main architects: Vicente Guallart, María Díaz
Collaborators: Fernando Meneses, Daniela Frogheri, Luis Fraguada, Marcin Siekaniec, Katarzyna Zabczyk, Iwona Tajer, Pilar Díaz Rodríguez, Karen Kemp, Shahrzad Rahmani, Guillermo I. López Domínguez
Images: Soléne Couet, Romain Lelièvre, Cyril Breton

ARCHITECTURAL DIAGRAMS 731

gunnarssonpettersson

In our projects we try to find the accurate scale and work with the building volumes in relation to the context and surrounding landscape. We want to explore new ways of interpretingthe landscape and traditional structures. In this process we use environmental and social parameters to find new solutions.
Peter Morander studied architecture at Chalmers, Gothenburg and at ETSAM, Madrid. He is now working in Stockholm, partly with his own practice.
Liisa Gunnarsson studied architecture at KTH, Stockholm, and is now at ETH in Zürich, Switzerland.
Maria Pettersson studied architecture at KTH, Stockholm and at EPFL in Lausanne, Switzerland. She has now a practice of her own.

246
THE NEW ENTRANCE TO TJORN

i29 interior architects

We are Jaspar Jansen (1970) and Jeroen Dellensen (1972). In 2001 we joined forces and a year later office at i29 was born, creative and versatile design studio. Our aim is to create intelligent designs and striking images. Space is the leitmotiv, the result always clear, with a keen eye for detail.Our approach is practical yet based on strong ideas articulated in clear concepts. We try to get to the core of things but keep it looking simple. Our clients are open minded and involved. It is most important to us to enjoy the process together and to get everything out of it.
We are not alone in our voyage. In a short period of time many projects have been realized for a wide variety of clients, both private and business. We have been nominated for several prizes, and won the Dutch design Prize for best interior design.
www.i29.nl

608
SCHOOL 03
Client : Panta Rhei, Amstelveen
Floor area : 4000m²
Photography : Jeroen Musch
Poems : ErikJan Harmens
Architect : Snelder Architects
Constructor : Wouters Bouw
Interior builder : Zwartwoud

IaN+

IaN+ was set up in 1997 and materializes around the core of its three members with different professional formation and experience. Carmelo Baglivo and Luca Galofaro, design project and theory, Stefania Manna engineering consultant. IaN+ multy-disciplinary agency aims at being a place where theory and practice of architecture overlap and meet, in order to redefine the concept of territory as a relational space between the landscape and its human user. They have been participating to many national and international architectural competitions, gaining prizes and mentions. In 2006, with the "Tor Vergata" University scientific research building, they obtained the Italian Architecture Gold Medal for the first realized work at the Triennale in Milan, they participated at the London Biennale of Architecture and to the exhibition Talking Cities in Germany.
www.ianplus.it

098
METRO D
Project team: Andrea Leonardi, sara Bernardi, Marco Colaiacomo, Fabrizio Micocci

106
MY SCHOOL IS A FLOWER
Project team: Serena Mignatti, Andrea Leonardi, Federico Giacomarra, Nadav Engel, sara Bernardi

110
NEW TERAMO THEATRE COMPLEX
Project team: Serena Mignatti, Andrea Leonardi, Nadav Engel, Paolo Fusco, Nina Artioli
Area : 10,000 sqm

160
TITTOT GLASS MUSEUM

206
INDRE SOGN ARTS CENTRE

328
OSAKA CENTRAL STATION AREA

436
ESO HEADQUATERS
Project team: Giuseppe Vultaggio, Felix Silbermayr, Andrea Leonardi, Eloisa Susanna

450
HOUSING ALMERE

538
ZAMBONINI HEADQUARTER

Iotti + Pavarani Architetti

The Architectural practice "iotti + pavarani architetti" was set up in 2001, arising from the professional partnership of Paolo Iotti and Marco Pavarani. The practice is involved in work over a wide range of architectural scales (from desin to landscaping) for both the public and private sectors. Current design and construction projects are spread over a number of different sectors: museum, teaching, sporting, commercial, residential and landscaping. The Practice is particularly involved in building rehab, urban renewal and landscaping, taking part in numerous competitions and workshops. The design work which typifies the projects undertaken by our practice is aimed at the understanding and interpretation of the relations existing between building and landscape, a commitment which remains a constant, irrespective of the scale of the intervention or indeed, the subject matter of the individual project.
iotti-pavarani.com

290
ECO VILLAGE RIGA
Site: Kizesers Lake, Riga, Latvia
Area: 24 ha
Team: Paolo Iotti, Marco Pavarani
Collaborator: Valentina Adami, Anita Cova, Matteo Francesconi (render), Fabrizio Gruppini, Cristina Haumann, Carlotta Meneguzzo , Federica Pennacchini, Perla Rebecchi, Giulia Sacchetta, Simone Tortini

338
SLOW TOWN VEMA
Team : Paolo Iotti, Marco Pavarani
Artists invited : Botto & Bruno
Collaborator : Valentina Adami, Anita Cova, Matteo Francesconi (render), Fabrizio Gruppini, Cristina Haumann, Carlotta Meneguzzo , Federica Pennacchini, Perla Rebecchi, Giulia Sacchetta, Simone Tortini

352
URBAN LIVING ROOMS
Site: Jugla Lake, Riga - Latvia
Area: 27 ha
Team: Paolo Iotti, Marco Pavarani
Collaborators: Michele D'Ariano, Matteo Ferrari, Anna Malaguti, Federica Pennacchini, Stefano Spada, Giulia Tardini, Francesco Tosi, Dario Varotti, Alberto Verde

J. MAYER H. ARCHITECTS

Founded in 1996 in Berlin, Germany, J. MAYER H. studio, focuses on works at the intersection of architecture, communication and new technology. Recent projects include the Town Hall in Ostfildern, Germany, Potsdam Docklands Masterplan 2002, a student center at Karlsruhe University and the redevelopment of the Plaza de la Encarnacion in Sevilla, Spain. From urban planning schemes and buildings to installation work and objects with new materials, the relationship between the human body, technology and nature form the background for a new production of space. Juergen Mayer H. is the founder and principal of this cross-disciplinairy studio. He studied at Stuttgart University, The Cooper Union and Princeton Universty. His work has been published and exhibited worldwide and is part of numerous collections including MoMA New York and SF MoMA. He has taught at Princeton University, University of the Arts Berlin, Harvard University, Kunsthochschule Berlin, Architectural Association in London and is currently teaching at Columbia University, New York.
www.jmayerh.de

060
GUBEN GUBIN
Client: IBA Fuerst-Puecklerland
Architect: J. MAYER H., Team: Juergen Mayer H., Wilko Hoffmann, Marc Kushner, Dominik Schwarzer, Maczek Woroniecki In collaboration with Landscape Architects: Coqui-Malachowska-Coqui

096
MENSA KARLSRUHE
Client: Vermoegen und Bau, Baden-Wuerttemberg, Amt Karlsruhe
Architect: J. MAYER H.,
Team Realization: Juergen Mayer H , Project Architect: Sebastian Finckh, Julia Neitzel, Andre Santer, Team: Marcus Blum, Wilko Hoffmann, Jan-Christoph Stockebrand
Team Competition: Juergen Mayer H , Sebastian Finckh, Wilko Hoffmann, Dominik Schwarzer, Ingmar Schmidt, Daria Trovato
Architect on Site: Ulrich Wiesler
Multidisciplinary Engineers: ARUP GmbH
Kitchen Engineers: Martin Scherer, Darmstadt
Building Physics: Dr. Schaecke und Bayer
Landscape Architect: Karl Bauer, Karlsruhe

232
PLAYA LAVA
Competition team: Juergen Mayer H., Paul Angelier, Christoph Emenlauer, Alessandra Raponi, Steve Malloy, Jan-Christoph Stockebrand, Ana I. Alonso de la Varga
Client: City of El Hierro
Structural engineers: Juan Rey Rey, Luis Cea Gomez, Luis Diaz Diaz, Mecanismo, Madrid

532
VILLA FAMILIE MAX MAIER

578
HOUSEWARMING MYHOME
Location : Vitra Design Museum, Weil am Rhein, Germany
Project team : Juergen Mayer H., Jonathan Busse, Marcus Blum
Photographer : Thomas Dix for Vitra and J. MAYER H.

674
KERYKES
Client: Cultural Olympiad Athens
Team: Juergen Mayer H., Sascha NikolauschkeDominik Schwarzer,
Structural Engineer: Lydia Thiesemann

jay is working.

Jay is working began its operation in year 2000 as a design company providing an overall design solution for space and visual information. Under the firm belief that the most powerful marketing strategy is creating good designs, Jay is working integrated architectural and interior design, communication and visual media design into a three-dimensional space. As the result, it is recognized as an authentic image-creating group. Works of Jay is working were presented in residential and commercial spaces and cultural projects. The company has established the foundation of complete multi-dimensional identity by unifying individual design fields under single coherent concept. JIW has expanded its creativeness into building shop design manual of the companies for its power brands. Work Area_ Architectural Design, Interior Design, Space Identity, Sign Design, Display / Branding, C.I., B.I., Promotion Design, Exhibition Design, Motion Graphics.
www.jiw.com

490
PRUGIO VALLEY - UNIT & FACADE DESIGN
Location : Seoul, Korea
Designer : Jang Soon Gak
Team : Choi hae jin, Kang moon kuan, Bae se yeon / jay is working.
Execution drawing : Kwon tae hyun, Park yeo jin / jay is working.
Constructor : Daehye interior & architecture
Floor area : 2,577m2
Site area : 6,225m2
Floor : 4th floor
Finish : Facade_ app Paint Finish with gravels, Punching Metal, Unit_秀&流 / Floor_ crystal stone, wood flooring / Wall_ birch plywood, 3form, lacquer, wall paper, fabric / Ceiling_ lacquer

560
CLINIC THE H

Location : Seoul, Korea
Designer : Jang Soon Gak
Execution drawing : jay is working. / Kang moon kwan, Bbae se yeon
Constructor : jay is working. / Park sang bum
Sign design : jay is working. / Song jong hyun, Ko kyung il
Area : 314m²
Finishing : floor_ crystal stone, wood flooring, polishing tile, marmoleum, carpet tile, Bolon / Wall_ wood blind, white cushion mat, lacquer, textile wall paper, silk wall paper, import wall paper, fabric panel, glass wall, acryl tube / Ceiling_ VP painting, silk wall paper, import Wall paper
Design : interior design, furniture&lighting design, sign design
Photos : Jeong tae ho

588
LA BELLE PAUSE

Location : Seongnam-si, Korea
Designer : Jang Soon Gak
Local designer : jay is working. / Lee se young, Bae se yoen
Constructor : jay is working.
C.I. & sign design : jay is working. / Song jong hyun, Yoo hye jin
Area : 714.43m²
Finish : Floor_ wood flooring, epoxy on concrete finish, crystal stone, tile / Wall_ lacquer, oregon pine louver, wood louver , wall paper, fabric panel, mosaic tile, color tile / Ceiling_ VP painting, birch plywood, oregon pine louver
Photos : Jeong tae ho

600
OPIENTAL CLINIC BOM_FLOW SPACE

Location : Seoul, Korea
Designer : Jang Soon Gak
Local designer : jay is working. / Lee se young, Kang moon kwan
Constructor : jay is working
C.I. & Sign design : jay is working. / Song jong hyun, Lee hyun jin
Area : 123.48m²
Finish : Floor_ imitation stone, epoxy on birch plywood, wood flooring, tile / Wall_ lacquer, wall paper / Ceiling_ VP painting, urethane on birch plywood
Photos : Park Wan soon

JDS Architects

Julien De Smedt is the founder and director of JDS Architects based in Copenhagen, with offices in Brussels and Oslo. A designer and architect whose work is known in Europe and abroad, Julien"s commitment to the exploration of new architectural models and programs has helped to re-energize the discussion of architecture in Denmark with projects such as the VM Housing Complex, Maritime Youth House and Stavanger Concert Hall. Born in Brussels to French art enthusiast Jacques Léobold and Belgian artist Claude De Smedt, Julien attended schools in Brussels, Paris, and Los Angeles before receiving his diploma from the Bartlett School of Architecture. Before founding JDS Architects, Julien worked with OMA, Rotterdam and co-founded in well known architecture firm PLOT in Copenhagen.
www.jdsarchitects.com

018
AALBORG HARBOUR BATH

Location: Aalborg, Denmark
Size: 1,000m²
Client: Aalborg City Counsil
Collaborators: Sigurd ostergaard-andersen, Leif ansen group I-68 radgiven ingenior A/S
Project team: Julien De Sment, Kamilla heskje, Mads knak-nielsen, Michaela weisskirchner, Felix luong

022
ALTIENS BATHHOUSE

Location: Alta, Norway
Size: 2,800m²
Client: Alta Kommune, Nordlysbadet Aps
Collaborators: Carlsbro Enginneers
Project team: Julien De Smedt, Michaela Weisskirchner, Barbara Costa, Jussi Vuori, Tove Entin

026
BARCELONA ENCANTS

Location: Catalonia in Barcelona, Spain
Size: 34,000m²
Client: Bimsa
Collaborators: Ayesa
Budget: € 2.503.544,73
Project Team: Julien de Smedt, Francisco Villeda Arreola, Felix Luong, Javier Sancho Andrés, Jordi López Aguiló, Kristoffer Harling, Liz Kelsey

028
BELGIAN PAVILION SHANGHAI

Project: Shanghai Expo Pavilion
Size: 5,000m2
Budget: 4,000,000 Eur
Client: Commissioner General of Belgium For The World Fair Shanghai 2010
Collaborators: Auditoire, Greisch, Kahle Accoustics, D.T.S & Co., Nanton Sijan Construction Group
Location: Shanghai, China
Project Team: Julien De Smedt, Barbara Wolff, Andrew Griffin, Francisco Villeda, Drew Parli, Edna Lueddecke, Elina Manninen, Felix Luong, Heechan Park, Jouri Kanters, Lieven Schulz, Michaela Weisskirchner, Philipp Ohnesorge, Robert Huebser, Sandra Fleischmann, Sofie Degroote, Tabea Trier, Virgini Ryckeboer, Wouter Dons

038
DUBLIN DOCKLANDS OPEN AIR BATH

Location: Dublin, Ireland
Size: 5,300m²
Site: The Grand Canal
Client: Dublin Docklands Development Authority
Collaborators: Arup
Project Team: Julien De Smedt, Kamilla Heskje, Andrew Griffin, Andy Vann, Itzel Vargas, Katerina Lampri, Max Muller, Nicolas Kisic

054
GRAND EGYPTIAN MUSEUM

Location: Cairo, Egypt
Size: 86,000m²
Client: Egyptian Government, UN
Collavorators: Plot, Big
Project team: Julien De Sment, Bjarke Ingels, Barbara Wolff, Dorte Boresen, Henning Stuben, Henrik Juul Nielsen

066
HELSINGØR PSYCHIATRIC HOSPITAL

Location: Helsingor, Denmark
Size: 6,000m²
Client: Federiksborg County, Helsingor Hospital
Collavorators: Plot, Big
Project team: Julien De Sment, Bjarke Ingels, Leif Andersen, Ask Hvas, Christian finderup, David Zahle, finn Norkjaer, Hanne halvorsen, Jakob Eggen, Jakob Moller, Jamie Meunier, Jennifer dahm Petersen, Jesper wichmann, Jesper Bo Jensen, Jorn Jensen, Kasper Larsen, Lene Norgaard, Louise Steffensen, Nnna Gydholm Moller, Simon Irgens-moller, Xavier Pavia Pages.
Engineers: Moe Og Brodsgaard A/S
Programming: David Mollerup, Nurse
Consultants: Lise Weile, Nurse

068
HIGH SQUARE

Location: Copenhagen, Denmark
Size: 3,000m²
Client: Magasin Du Nord, Realdania foundation
Collavorators: Plot, big
Project team: Julien De Smedt, Bjarke Ingels, finn Norkjaer, Henrik Juul Nielsen, Jesper Wichmann, Thomas christoffersen, Xavier Pavia Pages
Consultants: Birch & Krogboe A/S
Photography: Jakob Galtt, Simon Ladeeoged

072
HUA_CULTURAL & SHOPPING CENTER

084
LINDESNES CULTURE SQUARE

Location: Lindesnes,Norway
Size: 1,500m²
Client: Lindesnes region
Project team: Julien De smedt, Nikoline Dyrup carlsen, Erica Osterlund, felix Luong, Jussi Vuorl

090
LOW ENERGY HOUSING

092
MARITIME YOUTH HOUSE

Locaton: Copenhagen, Denmark
Size: 2,000m²
Client: Lokale Og Anlaegsfonden, The urvan development Foundation

Collavorators: Plop Big
Project team: Julien De Sment, Bjarke Ingels, Alistair Williams, Anders Drescher, David Zahle Jakob Lange, Karsten Hammers, Anders Drescher, David Zahle, Jakob Lange, Karsten Hammer Hansen Marcjay, sandra Knobl, sune Nordby, Thomas chris Toffersen
consultants: Moe Og brodsgaard A/S, Jordan Acoustics, freddy Madsen, Klaus Wolter, Royal danish Theater, Shiptech, Benot Sangberg

126
ROLLING AQUA CENTER

Location: Aalborg, @counterstike, fanders, Hillerod, Ballerup, Valby, frederikssund, Odense
Size: 5,000m²
Client: Gigantium, Aarlborg City council, The Space And facility foundation, Odense City Counsil
Collavorators: Plot, Big
Project teamL Julien De Sment, Bjarke Ingels, Anette Jensen, Casper Larsen, Christian Gutter, Cristina Garcia Gomez, Xva Hvid, finn Nokjaer,Gudjon Kjartansson, Hanne Halvorsen, Helena Kristina Nygolm, Jamie Meunier, Jennifer Dahm Petersen, Jorn Jensen, Lene Norgaard, Oliver Grundahl, snorre Nash, Thomas Christoffersen, Thomas Tulinius

138
SJAKKET

Location: Copenhagen, Denmark
Size: 2,000m²
Client: Sjakket, Realdania foundaton
Collavorators: Plot, Big, Birch Og Kroboe
Project team: Julien De Sment, Bjarke Ingels, Sophus sobye, Anders Drescher, Bobenzon, Christian Dam, David Zahle, Julie Schmidt-nielsen, Kathrin Gimmel, Louise Steffesen, Nanna Gyldholm Moller, Narisara Ladawal, Nina ter-borch, Ole Nannberg, Olmo Ahlmann, soren Lambersen

140
SPINDERIHALLERNE

Location: Vejle, Denmark
Size: 20,000 m²
Client: Sjakket, Realdania Foundation
Collavorators: Nr2154, Jacob Wildschiodtz & Troels faber
Project team: Julien De Sment, Benny Jepsen, Brian friel, Jim Loewenstein, Jussi vuori Karin Bjorsmo, Karsten Hammer Hansen, Maythinie Eludut, Sabrina Engels, Stefan Filz

144
STAVANGER CONCERT HALL

Location: Stavanger, Norway
Size: 22,000m²
Type: Competition, Honourable Mention
Status: golden Lion at The venice Bienale
Client: Stavanger City Council, Stavanger Orchestra
Collavorators: Plot, Big
Project team: Julien De Sment, Bjarke Ingels, Alistair Williams, Anders Drescher, David Zahle Jakob Lange, Karsten Hammers, Anders Drescher, David Zahle, Jakob Lange, Karsten Hammer Hansen Marcjay, sandra Knobl, sune Nordby, Thomas chris Toffersen
consultants: Moe Og brodsgaard A/S, Jordan Acoustics, freddy Madsen, Klaus Wolter, Royal danish Theater, Shiptech, Benot Sangberg

146
STOCKHOLM'S GARDEN LIBRARY

Location: Stokholm, Sweden
Size: 33,000 m²
Client: City of Stockholm
Project team: Julien de Smedt, Michaela Weisskirchner, Alex Smith, felix Luong, Mikael Ling, Stefan Fofer

248
TRONDHEIM FJORDPARK

Project: Harbourfront, Park
Project team: JDS Team_ Partner in Charge | Julien De Smedt, Project Leader | Francisco Villeda, Project Team |
Andrew Parli, Felix Luong, Philipp Ohnesorge, Sofie Degroote, Virgini Ryckeboer, Wouter Dons
KLAR Team_ Partner in Charge | Henning Stüben, Project Team | Dorte Børresen, Morten Jeppesen, Ditte Bjerregaard, Sara Winther Andersen, Helena Ahlblom
Type: Invited Competition, 2009
Size: 2.3 Hectares
Budget: 40 000 000 Nok (4 500 000 Eur)
Client: Statens Vegvesen
Collaborators: Klar, Tyrens Ab, Åf Hansen og Henneberg
Location: Brattøra, Trondheim, Norway
Status: Settled
Services Provide: Lead Consultant, Complete Architectural Design

268
BRUSSELS ADMINISTRATIVE CITY

Location: Brussels, Belgium
Size: 200,000m²
Client: Breevast
Collavorators: ARUP, PLOT, BIG
Project team: Julien De Smedt Bjarke Ingels, David Zahle Jakob Lange, Karsten Hammers, Anders Drescher, David Zahle, Jakob Lange, Thomas Garvin, Yoonju No

454
IMEC TOWER

Project: Offices, Laboratories And Public Function
Location: Leuven, Brussels
Size: 12,000m²
Client: Imec Represented By Mr. Walter Fluit
Collaborators: Bopro, Boydens, Daidalos, Ney, Topotek
Budget: 16m Euro
Team: Julien De Smedt, Barbara Wolff, Lucy Jones, Cruz Garcia, Federico Pedrini, Felix Luong, Johan Tristan Kinnucan, Liz Kelsey, Nathalie Frankowski, Peter-Andreas Simonsen, Peter Vande Maele, Razvan Armeanu, Ryan Roettker, Victor Garcia, Wouter Dons

470
MERMAID ISLAND

Project : Mermaid Wellness Center
Size : 50,000m²
Client : Tække r
Collaborators : Tækker Rådgivende Ingeniører A/s, Plot, Big
Project Team : Julien De Smedt, Bjarke Ingels, David Benitez, Leon Rost, Karla Spennrath, Karsten Hammer Hansen, Kathrin Gimmel, João Vieira Costa, Julie Schmidt-nielsen, Simon Herup, Yooju No

498
SILO

Project: 900 apartments, museum and public
Type: 100,000 m²
Tors: Arup, moe og brødsgaard
Project team: Julien de Smedt, Charlotte Truwant, Andy Vann, Aitkaterini Lampri, Aleksander Torkaz, Barbara Costa, Aries Rodet, Emil Bäckström, Federico Pedrini, Mads Knack-Nielsen, Maria Konstantinopoulou, Nicolas Kisic, Therése Wallström,
Imaging: Auracab / P.M. De Vallon

510
THE MOUNTAIN

Code: MTN
Project: MOUNTAIN DWELLINGS
Location: ØRESTAD, DENMARK
Size: 33,000 M²
Type: COMMISION
Status: COMPLETION 2008
Client: HØPFNER A/S, DANSK OLIE KOMPAGNI A/S
Collaborators: PLOT, BIG, MOE & BRØDSGAARD
Project team: JULIEN DE SMEDT, BJARKE INGELS, ANNETTE JENSEN, DENNIS RASMUSSEN, EVA HVIID FINN NØRKJÆR, HENRIK POULSEN, AKOB LANGE JAN BOGSTRØM, JOÃO VIERA COSTA, JØRN JENSEN, KARSTEN HAMMER HANSEN, KARSTEN V. VESTERGAARD, LEON ROST, LOUISE STEFFENSEN, MALTE ROSENQUIST, MIA FREDERIKSEN, OLE ELKJÆR-LARSEN, OLE NANNBERG, SOPHUS SØBYE, WATARU TANAKA
Engineers: MOE OG BRØDSGAARD

534
VM HOUSE

Location: Ørestad, Denmark
Size: 25,000M²
Client: Høpfner A/S, Dansk Olie Kompagni A/S
Collaborators: Plot, Big
Project Team: Julien De Smedt, Bjarke Ingels, Alistair Williams, Annette Jensen, Bent Poulsen, Christian Finderup, Claus Tversted, Danid Zahle, Dorte Borresen, Finn Norkjaer, Henning Stuben, Henrick Poulsen, Ingrid Serritslev, Jakob Christensen, Jakob Lange, Jakob Moller, Jakob Wodschou, Jorn Jensen, Karsten Hammer Hansen, Mads H Sund, Marc Jay, Maria Tedby Ljungberg, Nadja Cederberg, Nadja Cederberg, Narisara Ladawal, Oliver Grundahl, Simon Irgens-Møller, Sophus Søbye, Søren Stærmos, Thomas Christoffersen, Xavier Pavia Pages
Engineers: Moe Og Brødsgaard

592
MAISON DU DANEMARQUE

Location : Paris, France
Size : 200m²
Client : Maison du Danemarque

638
BENCH DESIGN

Location: Helsingor, denmark
Client: Helsingor Psychiatric Hospital
Collavorators:Rolf Hay
Project team: ulien De smedt, Maria Ljungsten, candice Enderle

704
STACKED

Location : World Wide Distribution
Size : 380 X 380 X 380 Mm And Derivates
Client : Muuto / www.Muuto.Com
Project Team : Julien De Smedt, Wouter Dons, Lena Billmeier

Jorge Pereira

648
CROSS-WIND BRIDGE

668
HIGH-SPEED CAR RAMP

Team: Ines Valente, Natalie Brazile, Yoon-Young Hur, Joao Paulo Fernandes
Promoters: Fundacao Galp Energia and Experimenta Design

Jungwoo Ji

Jungwoo Ji is focusing on not only professional design practice of public space but also planning for public discourse with diverse experience from urban design to interior design. He has been practicing at EE&K Architects, New York as an associate architect and working on one of the future waterfront complex 'Huishan North Bund' in Shanghai, China as a project architect from landscape to office buildings. He established 'studio eu concept'with his wife for participating competitions and doing personal practice. He taught undergraduate students at SNU Frontline Workshop in 2008.
He graduated bachelor and master course of architecture at Korea University and had worked for JAD design research center. At Cornell University, he studied and researched his master thesis work with the issue of 'Seoul City Hall plaza'. Main conference hall of Seoul City Hall (Taepyung Hall) had been renovated by his competition winning scheme in 1999 and he attended Seoul Bench Competition ceremony at there in 2008. Now the Taepyung Hall has been destroyed for new city hall. He was the fellow of TSK Young Architects fellowship in 2000 and from 1998, has been an active columnist for several architecture and commercial magazines.'Another Scale of Architecture – new generation of Korean Architects' which was published at 'Architecture and Culture' magazine for two years since 2006 was his major article and it is going to be published as an indepentdent volume.
http://kr.blog.yahoo.com/jungwooji

236
PUBLIC GRADATION ON GREEN ARMED PLAZA

Team: Jungwoo Ji(Team Leader), Kyuseon Hong

322
NETWORKING FOR THE MULTI-FUNCTIONAL ADMINISTRATIVE CITY

Team: Hyungpyo Kwan, Joori Suh, Soonjoo Kim, Sung Goo Yang, Hyoungdu Bae, Kyoung Hun Jo, Teu Kim

636
BENCHES, BECOME A PART OF LANDSCAPE

kadawittfeldarchitektur

kadawittfeldarchitektur is a European architectural office, operating out of Aachen, Germany, with its founding office in Graz, Austria.
In the meanwhile, 50 full-time graduate employees are working at the office in Aachen.
The wide range of specialists among us include economic geographers and city planners, with most employees being architects, right up to the interior and product designers.
The projects of kadawittfeldarchitektur move in scale between architecture, city building, interiors, and urban studies to create meaning within a context of public buildings. Since 1996, the office has produced a number of internationally renown buildings. Among those are the Mercedes Benz's headquarters in Salzburg, the technical University of Salzburg, the adidas LACES administration building in Herzogenaurach and the AachenMünchener Insurance headquarters in Aachen. Parallel, kadawittfeldarchitektur has won numerous independent inter/ national competitions such as central station in Salzburg and the auditorium in Padova.
kadawittfeldarchitektur is a spatial strategy translated into built form. The building itself is understood as a functional object, designed to serve the user and spectator alike, from inside and out. The office tests reality: building and translating the meaning of tradition into appropriate contemporary spatial structures. kadawittfeldarchitektur provides a unique, innovative answer to each task, providing customized spaces rather than prefabricated solutions.
www.kwa.ac

114
PADUA AUDITORIUM

Typology: Concert hall
Construction volume: gfa 16.000m² / cubature 181.800m³
Client Comune di Padova
Competition 1st prize 2007

128
SALZBURG CENTTAL STATION

Typology: Railway station
Construction volume: ea 13.000m² / cubature 140.000m³
Client: OBB infrastruktur bau AG
Realization: 2008-2013
Project manager: Aldrik Lichtwark

174
A 10 HOGHWAY

Typology: Highway
Construction volume: Length 80 km
Client: Highway company ASFINAG

396
AACHENMUNCHENER HEADQUA

Typology: Office building
Construction volume: gfa 34.500 m² / cubature 121.000 m³
Client: AachenMünchener Versicherung AG
Representation: AMB Generali
Realization: 2007-2009
Project manager: Stefan Haass

400
ADIDAS LACES

Typology: Office building
Construction volume: gfa 60.000m² / cubature 356.000m³
Client: adidas ag
Project manager: Dirk Zweering

420
CENTER FOR EUROPEAN CULTURE

Typology: Cultural building
Construction volume: gfa 7.400m² / cubature 30.350m³
Client: City of Aachen

618
TELEKOM STREAMS CEBIT

Typology: Trade fair
Construction volume: gfa 2290m²
Client: Deutsche Telekom AG
Partners: Büro Uebele Visuelle Kommunikation

Kim Kai-chun

Professor of Interior design Dept. at the kookmin University in Seoul Korea, and majored in Zen philosophy at the Dongkuk University. He have been represented as a president and the 'invited designer' of KOSID. He write and design on relations between Zen philosophy and oriental esthetics in this century.
He is the author of several articles on esthetics of ancient Oriental Architecture. Most recently he has written widely in the Beauty of world Architecture.

574
EYE OF SQUARE

LAVA

At the vanguard of a nonconformist and inventive new generation in architecture, LAVA bridges the gap between the dream and the real world.
Essentially a network practice, directed by Chris Bosse and Tobias Wallisser who have worked on international icons such as the Beijing Watercube (PTW) and the Mercedes-Benz Museum in Stuttgart (UNStudio), the epicentres in Sydney and Stuttgart have become hotspots and breeding grounds for a new wave of architectural talent. Together with PNYG:Company we are working on a couple of ground-breaking large-scale projects in Abu Dhabi that will redefine the relationship between architecture and branding.
l-a-v-a.net

220
MASDAR PLAZA, OASIS OF THE FUTURE

Location: Masdar, UAE
Client: Masdar Future Energy Company
Status: competition win. Construction 2009-2013
Team: LAVA(Laboratory for Visionary Architecture)_ Chris Bosse, Tobias Wallisser, Alexander Rieck
In Cooperation with: Bob Nation/Kann Finch Group, Arup Sydney, SL Rasch, Transsolar, EDAW

412
BIONIC TOWER

Location : Abu Dhabi, UAE

430
CORNICHE TOWER

Location : Abu Dhabi, UAE
Area : 32.000 sqm
General Planing : Wenzel+Wenzel, Stuttgart, GER
Consultants : Kling Consult, Krumbach, GER

444
HEADLANDS HOTEL

Architects : Chris Bosse, Tobias Wallisser, Alexander Rieck
Team members: Chris Bosse, Jarrod Lamshed, Anh-Dao Trinh, Jonas Epper, Niklas Muehlich, Andrea Dorici, Alessio Coghene
Client: George Dimitrovski
Location: Austinmer, NSW
Cost: AUS$84 million
Status: design development
Size: 10.000m²

568
DIGITAL ORIGAMI

Building Materials : Cardboard
Size : 120 sqm
Photo credit : Ian Barnes/ERCO

596
MTV DESIGN STAGE

Client : MTV Austrlia
Location : Sydney, Australia
Size: 24x35x10m
Material : Digitally patterned nylon fabric
Photo : Chris Bosse, Peter Murphy

LEON11 ARCHITECTS

The team is part of a multidisciplinary group that 5 years ago formed a studio, Leon 11, which is developing projects in architecture, design, web page creation, animated films, among many others. This team has grown and now consists of 11 architects and two graphic designers. This group seeks to provide answers from a contemporary system of work and organization that allows being in contact with other people or teams in the same line of common interests, so it is constantly evolving design, cultural, and their own work tools.
www.leon11.com

094
MARKET IN SANCHINARRO

Project team: Lgnacio Alvarez-Monteserin, Manuel Alvarez-Monteserin, David Cardenas, Alicia Domingo, Elisa Fernandez Ramos, Javier Gutierrez, Jorge Lopez, Joann Ludorikow, Maria Mallo And Lys Villalba

244
SQUARE IN COPENHAGEN

266
BADAJOZ CH 852

274
CARLSBERG VORES BY

ma0

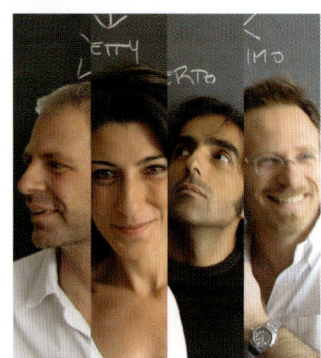

734 PROFILE & INDEX

Founded in 1996, ma0 has been active in a field that has expanded during these years due to the notion that architecture is an interdisciplinary medium, linked to territory. Literally acting as this medium, the studio works in both physical and immaterial fields. From wall to video interface, the studio's architectural vision is defined as a system of spatial rules –a playground – able to modify the relationships between space and its inhabitants, between public and private, interior and exterior, artificial and natural, real and virtual...

The firm's experience manifests the skills necessary to work within this broader conception of architecture, managing the design process with the appropriate technologies, from construction drawings to graphic design and interactive communication tools.

Constantly drawing upon the feedback between theory and practice through participation in commissions, competitions, lectures, and workshops, each project becomes an opportunity to explore the relationship between the form and the social role of architecture, which is, by choice, an open, interactive and process-based device. Therefore, architecture becomes adaptable to the phenomena of appropriation, transformation and progressive developments initiated by its inhabitants.

The aim of this research and practical experimentation is to give back to the inhabitant/user the power to shape the space, from the installations to the concrete mass of architecture, and to give back to the contemporary city an intensity of uses, multiplicity of relationships, sedimentation of identities, in other words that richness typical to the historical city.
www.ma0.it

080
LIBRARY

Design team: ma0
Collaborators: Pierluigi Ventura, Federica Greco, Lorraine Perrot
Client: Comune di Bari

132
SCHOOL IN ROME

Design team: ma0
Collaborators: Federico Dal Brun, Angelo Grasso, Veronica Erspamer
Client: City of Rome

198
GARDEN IN BARI

Design team: ma0 + Ing. Maurizio Franco
Client: City of Bari

238
ROZZOL MELARA

Design team: ma0
Collaborators: Alexander Valentino promoted by Ater Trieste, Department of Architecture of the University of Trieste, City and Province of Trieste, Ordine degli Architetti of Trieste, DARC

264
ALMERE HOUT

Design team: ma0 + with Angelo Grasso
Landscape consultant: Anne Caspari
Collaborators: Federico Dal Brun, Rosa Maria D'Antoni, Roberta Gallucci, Eliana Mangione

358
VEMAE

Design team: ma0
Collaborators: Enrica D'Aula, Diane Jaeger, Lisa Pavanello, Giacomo Pietrapiana, Carlo Tancredi, Piero Ventura

714
TOUCH SCREEN

Design team: ma0+Tecnovisioni/Formazero

MANUELLE GAUTRAND ARCHITECTURE

Born in 1961 and qualified as an architect in 1985. She set up her office in 1991, in Paris, where she lives and works. She has handled all kinds of projects, whether built or in study phase, ranging from housing and offices to cultural buildings, business premises and leisure facilities. Her clients are public contracting authorities as well as private firms, in France and abroad. The "C42" Citroën flagship showroom building, at the Champs-Elysée Avenue in Paris, has contributed to make a name for herself with the large public and the International. 2008 has seen the start-up of the Gaîté-Lyrique work-site, converting a theatre to contemporary music and digital arts, as well as the planning permission"s deposit for the AVA tower, office building, at La Défense.
www.manuelle-gautrand.com

044
ENTERTAINMENT COMPLEX

Location: Place Andre Thome, Rambouillet - France
Client: Ville de Rambouillet
Client project manager: Jean-Pascal Reux
Client consultants: Cafe Programmation (programmer)
Architect: Manuelle Gautrand
Architect project manager: Philippe Solignac
Architect project team: Alexandre Dumoulin, Irina Bruscky, Yves Tougard, Marie Duval, Julien Roge
Scenography: Jean-Paul Chaert
Engineers O.T.H. Tisseyre (acoustic)
Models: New Tone, Gautrand Office
Numeric Images   Platform, Gautrand Office
Dimensions: 4.200m², 11 millions US$ incl taxes

046
EXTENSION OF THE LILLE MODERNE ART MUSEUM

Location: Allee du Musee, Villeneuve d'Ascq - France
Client: Lille Metropole
Client project manager: Francois Rohart
Client consultants: Joelle Pijaudier, museum director
Architect: Manuelle Gautrand
Architect project manager: Yves Tougard
Architect project team: Shirin Raissi, Miguel Conde Silveira, Julie Nabucet, Julien Roge
Museography: Renaud Pierard
Engineers: Khephren (structure), Alto (fluid), Lucigny-Talhouet (economist), Labeyrie (multimedia), Casso (security)
Models: New Tone, Gautrand Office
Numeric Images   Platform, Gautrand Office
Autors: Raymond Balau
Dimensions: 9.000m², 9 millions US$ incl taxes

116
PINAULT FOUNDATION FOR CONTEMPORARY ART

Location: Seguin Island, Boulogne - France
Client: Artemis - Francois Pinault
Client consultants: Francois Barre
Architect: Manuelle Gautrand
Architect project team: Hermann Kollhoffel, Eric Pannetier, Jean-Francois Py, Sophie Delhay, Hiroo Nishiyama, Chizuko Kawarada
Museography: Renaud Pierard
Engineers: R.F.R. (structure), Alto (fluid), Lucigny-Talhouet (economist), Casso (security)
Consultants: Paul Ardenne, Alice Laguarda, Christophe LeGac
Models: New Tone, Gautrand Office, Patricia Lefranc
Numeric Images   Platform, Jalil Amor
Photograph: Philippe Ruault
Dimensions: 34.000m², 150 millions US$ incl taxes

416
BUSINESS CENTRE

Client: COGEDIM RIC & P NALLET IMMOBILIER
Location: Château Creux District, Saint-Etienne, France
Program: Office
Area: 27,000 sqm
Construction cost: 30m2 vat excl
Consultants: KHEPHREN (structure), ARCORA (envelop)
Project manager: Thomas Daragon

424
CITROEN EXHIBITION CENTER

Location: 42, avenue des Champs-Elysees - Paris, France
Client: Automobiles Citroen
Client project manager: Yves Boutin
Client consultants: Amadeus, Maps
Architect: Manuelle Gautrand
Architect project manager: Anne Feldmann
Architect project team: Philippe Solignac, Hiroo Nishiyama, Yves Tougard, Alexandre Dumoulin ,Nicolas Vrignault, Cedric Housset, Shirin Raissi, Miguel Silveira, Julien Roge
Engineers: Arnaud de Bussiere (envelope), Spectat (mobil equipement), Khephren (structure), Alto (fluid), Lucigny-Talhouet (economist), Lamoureux (acoustic), Labeyrie (multimedia), Eciac (scheduling), Casso (security)
Constructors: Gartner (envelope)
Models: New Tone, Gautrand Office
Numeric Images   Platform, Gautrand Office
Autors: Anna Mc Queen
Dimensions: 1.200m², 11 millions US$ incl taxes

448
HOUSING

Location: Rue des Longs Pres, Rennes - France
Client: Espacil
Architect: Manuelle Gautrand
Architect project manager: Philippe Solignac
Architect project team: Benoit Imbert, Nicola Marchi, Sophie Delhay, Sonja Kiehlneker, Amandine Batsele
Engineers: I.2 C
Consultants: Tribu (green building)
Models: Gautrand Office
Numeric Images   Platform
Dimensions: 100 flats, 9.000m², 10 millions US$ incl taxes

460
LIFE IN TOWN

Client: UNIBAIL-RODAMCO
Location: France (confidential)
Program: shopping mall, retail, markot, housing, offices.
Area: 75,000 sqm.
Project manager: Bertrand Colson

552
AUTOMOTIVE SHOWROOM & LEISURE CENTRE

Client: GB AUTO
Surface: 12.000 m²
Location: Cairo, Egypt
Exterior elevations: Manuelle Gautrand Architecture
Interior showroom vues: Arthur Couprie

marco hemmerling architecture design

Marco Hemmerling, born 1970, studied Architecture and Interior Design at the Bauhaus-University in Weimar and at the Politecnico di Milano. From 2000 –2005 he was project architect at UN Studio van Berkel & Bos in Amsterdam and Stuttgart where he was jointly responsible for - among other projects - the design and realisation of the Mercedes-Benz Museum in Stuttgart. In 2005 he established his own office for architecture and design in Cologne and completed in 2006 his postgraduate Master of Arts in Architecture and Media Management at the University of Applied Sciences in Bochum. Since 2007, he has been teaching and researching as Professor for Computer Aided Design at the Detmold School of Architecture and Interior Design, University of Applied Sciences Ostwestfalen-Lippe.
Marco Hemmerling has lectured at various universities and conferences across Europe and in South America and has published extensively on Digital Design.
marcohemmerling.com

666
FLIP

Maurice Mentjens Design

MauriceMentjensDesign's aim is to realize high-quality designs with a small, but dynamic team of enthusiastic and talented staff members.
Interesting small-scale projects, which have quality and creativity as main purpose, are preferred to shopping malls and other large-scale projects.
Quality has top priority in all aspects of the design process and the execution.
mauricementjens.com

616
STASH

Location: Maastricht, the Netherlands
Client's name: Yves Vola & Joelle Bastin
Lighting: UTI-licht, Sittard
Graphics (logo): Rico Bastin, Maastricht
Engineers: Maurice Mentjens Design
Manufacturers: WS-Interieurs, Maastricht
Floor: Atelier Winterink, Brunssum
Capacity: 74m2 (presentation surface)
Total floor area: 34 m2
Photographer: Arjen Schmitz

MoHen Design International

MOHEN DESIGN INTERNATIONAL is an award-winning company creating schemes for residential, contract, office and hospitality design in Shanghai, Tokyo and Taiwan. The practice was initially set up by Mr. Hank M. Chao as a platform for cross-disciplinary collaborations. Today the German, Spanish, American, Japanese, Australian, Taiwanese and Chinese press has reviewed the practice's work.
MOHEN DESIGN INTERNATIONAL projects range from public buildings to individual interiors for private clients. The practice has particular experience in the leisure and hospitality industry, developers, focusing on the design of contemporary bars, clubs and restaurants, hotels and private villas. Using a unique language of color, light and geometry, our interiors are sensuous and eventful. Space is carefully choreographed into stylish environments.
mohen-design.com

566
DANBO FUN

ARCHITECTURAL DIAGRAMS 735

Moho Architects

Joy is the engine of growth and the inspiration of our work. Laugh is as a measure of how comfortably we are express ourselves. We like to think about our projects as beautiful experiments, iterations, attempts, trials, and errors. Little jumps over irrational tradition and disciplinary fences.
www.mohoweb.com

516
TOWER COSTA RICA
Location: Bulevar Las Americas, Sabana Norte, San Jose, Costa Rica.
Built Surface: 28.000 sqm

658
DUNE

Moonbalsso

Born in Korea, 1968. Attended Taroona High in Hobart, Tasmania, Australia. After graduating from Inha University in Korea, received M.Arch from MIT, USA. Served in the ROK army as an engineer, and draftsman for 2 years. Few years of internship in Korea and USA, before starting up practice in Seoul in 2001. Sangsang Museum was awarded Korean Institute of Architects prize for year 2005. Other Recently completed works include S-Mahal, Neurosurgery21, Junju Zoo, Hyundai High school, Pochon House, and Mookdong Multi-housing. Held many group and single exhibitions with Architecture and Drawings. Participated as an Art director for an Urban magazine called Citymongkey, and also directed and produced few short films on Architecture and Drawings.
www.moonhoon.com

502
S_MAHAL

546
7-FINGERS

mxg architects

Above all mg is the meeting and the friendship of 2 people: maxime le trionnaire and gwénaël le chapelain.
This encounter occurred in 1997 in the School of Architecture of Nantes.
During their studies, they create a deep bond and polish their architect's visions.
Graduated in 2004, they work in many architecture agencies with good reputation like Architecture Studio, Block, Duncan Lewis, Stéphane Maupin, X'tu, ...
In parallel, they carry through several design competitions and a cycle of installations about sport and architecture.
Bolstered up by this experience, they decide in 2006 to set up their own business and they constitute "mg architectes".
Their first orders came from the west of France.
For this reason and by love of this region, they begin a contemporary regional reasoning.
This thinking could be defined as the pursuit of an original style very attached to a region, to a place. A style that could tell and perpetuate the local history. An architecture disconnected from its past but without any contempt of it.
With this style and with their different project, they try to go against a sort of "new international style" that is spread by different media flooding books, magazines and internet of images and forms.
They do not want to adopt the same style in Brittany as an architect working in Patagonia.
On the contrary, they gladly chose the local instead of the global and the specific instead of the generic.
This approach was rewarded by the publication of their first execution (twin houses in Rennes (France)) in the book entitled Architecture Contemporaine en Bretagne.
Moreover, this project was nominated to the "Prix d'Architecture du Moniteur 2009 : la Première Oeuvre".
This local and contextual approach, coming from the west of France, was recently extended to Ardennes, Franche-Comté and to Paris thanks to the increasing interest of state project sponsor.
In conclusion, their objective is to execute a simple and understandable architecture, an architecture close to its surroundings.
www.mgarchitectes.com

112
NURSERY SCHOOL
Place: Prato, Italy
Client: City of Prato
Area: 1,254 m²
Cost: 1,695,340.00 €
Project Architect: mxg (le trionnaire maxime + le chapelain gwénaël)
Project Team: Ingrid vindis + virginie prié + manuella vibi

284
CRYSTAL PALACE
Place: Bodo, Norway
Client: City of Bodo
Area: 26,000m²
Project Architect: mxg (le trionnaire maxime + le chapelain gwénaël)
Project team: manuella vibi

380
16 DWELLINGS CHERLEVILLE-MÉZIÈRES
Team : [mxg] (le trionnaire m. x le chapelain g.) + zebra 3 ing.
Location : ZAC Alphonse Guérin _Rennes_France
Client : OPAC des ARDENNES
Area : 1110m²
Program : 16 individual dwellings

382
288 DWELLINGS
Team: [mxg] (le trionnaire m. x le chapelain g.) + klnb architectes
Place: L'isle d'abeau, France
Client: L'isle d'abeau, France
Program: 288 dwellings + commercial area + parking

404
AQUATIC CENTER
Location: Saint-Brice-en-Cogles, FRANCE
Client: COGLAIS COMMUNAUTE
Cost: 3 300 000 €
Area : 1400 m²
Project Architect: Representative_ a/LTA jean-luc le trionnaire - alain tassot j Associates_ [mxg] maxime le trionnaire x gwénaël le chapelain
Project Team : mathias robert (a/LTA architectes), cécile combelle ([mxg] architectes), jean-françois leblanc (Ouest-structures), rémy kervadec (ETHIS MEP), yves hernot (HERNOT acoustics)

414
BUREAUX BESANÇON
Team : [mxg] (le trionnaire m. x le chapelain g.) + ALDO architectes
Location : Besançon, France
Client: SAIEMB.
Area : 3 500m²
Program : Health and social center + offices + commercial area

NABITO ARQUITECTURA S.C.P

NAbito (Alessandra Faticanti 1975, Roberto Ferlito 1973) is a multidisciplinary team based in Barcelona and active on the mediteranean territories like Italy Spain and France looking for similarities and differences. His attempt is to redefine a different process of elaboration for a new contemporary culture, from the social and economic point of view. The goal of nabito arquitectura is to develop a cultural mix related and in communication with parallels realities. Nabito Won the important european award "Nouveaux albums des jeunes architectes Paris 2006", given by the ministry of culture. They won several competitions in Europe starting to build his first buildings.
www.nabit.it

242
SENSATIONAL PARK
Partners: Luca Faticanti , Damiano BaucoV

250
UPGRADE PILONI

nARCHITECTS

nARCHITECTS_2000-2008 charts the first 8 years of the New York - based practice founded in 1999 by Eric Bunge and Mimi Hoang.

040
DUNE TERRACE
Status: Grand Egyptian Museum Competition
Program: Archeological Museum, Conference Center
Location: Giza, Egypt
Dimension: 860,000 sf / 86.000m²
Client: Grand Egyptian Museum
Materials: Perforated concrete, glass, stone, steel.
Consultant: Ove Arup & Partners, NY

234
P.O.R.T
Status: Competition, official runner-up (2nd Prize)
Program: Toronto Central Waterfront
Location: Toronto, Canada
Client: TWRC / City of Toronto
Consortium: In collaboration with Balmori, H3, Snohetta and Weisz + Yoes, also with Joe Lobko, Halcrow Yolles, Sasaki

446
HOTEL PRO FORMA
Program: Theater / Hotel
Location: Ørestad, Denmark
Area: 42,000 sf / 4.200m²
Client: Hotel Pro Forma Performance Group
Consultants: Ove Arup & Partners, Arkitektgruppen, Bigert & Bergstrom

466
LIVING STEEL
Status: Living Steel International Competition Finalist
Program: Residential Apartments
Location: Wuhan, China
Area: 90,000 sf

508
SWITCH BUILDING
Program: Residential Apartments & Art Gallery
Location: Lower East Side, Manhattan, New York
Area: 14.000 sf
Client: 109 Norfolk LLC
Materials: Galvalume cladding, wood window liners, glass, ceramic
Consultants: Sharon Engineering

512
THERMAL MRIDGE
Status: Aomori Northern Housing Competition
Program: 200 Housing Units, Shared public programs
Location: Aomori, Japan
Dimension: 400,000 sf / 40.000m²
Client: City of Aomori
Consultant: Ove Arup & Partners, NY

530
VILLA - VILLA
Status: Ongoing, Ordos 100 Project
Program: Villa
Location: Ordos, Inner Mongolia, China
1000m²
Client: Jiang Yuan Water Engineering Ltd
Curator: Ai Wei Wei, FAKE Design
Materials: Local Brick, Concrete, Wood, Glass

602
PLY LOFT
Program: Artists' Live / Work Space
Location: New York
Area: 1,000 sf
Client: Lee Day & Ursula Endlicher
Materials: Bendable plywood

644
CANOPY: MOMA / P.S.1
Status: 1st Prize, National Competition
Program: Ephemeral public area / outdoor lounge
Location: P.S.1 Contemporary Art Center, New York
Area: 30,000 sf
Client: MoMA / P.S.1
Materials: Green bamboo, steel, EPS foam, cedar
Fabrication: nARCHITECTS; steel components by Amuneal
Consultants: Dave Flanagan, President, Northeast Chapter, American Bamboo Society, Boston; Markus Schulte, Ove Arup & Partners, NY; Garden: Marie Viljoen, NY

692
PARTY WALL
Program: Interactive installation; design and fabrication of wall prototype, part of Artists Space's Architecture & Design Project Series
Location: Soho, New York
Dimention: 10'x 12'x 1'-4"
Client: Artists Space Gallery
Materials: Filter foam, steel, motors, pulleys, cables, sensors, brainstems, motor controllers
Fabrication: Interactive design: Parul Vora, Jeff Weber
Funding: Artists Space, Elise Jaffe & Jeffrey Brown

720
WINDSHAPE
Program: Ephemeral pavilions
Location: Lacoste, France
Client: Savannah College of Art and Design
Materials: 50km 2.5mm polypropylene string, plastic pipes, aluminum collars, concrete

NL Architects

Kamiel Mark
Walter Pieter

736 PROFILE & INDEX

Pieter Bannenberg (1959), TU Delft 1995
Walter van Dijk (1962), TU Delft 1991
Kamiel Klaasse (1967), TU Delft 1995
Mark Linnemann (1962), TU Delft 1991 (Left the office in 2003)

NL Architects is an Amsterdam based office. The four principals, Pieter Bannenberg, Walter van Dijk, Kamiel Klaasse and Mark Linnemann, officially opened practice in January 1997, but have shared workspace already since the early nineties. All were educated at Delft University while living in Amsterdam. NL's 'commuting' office started while carpooling between these cities (in that sense the principals like to think of themselves as autodidactic; the recurrent fascination with mobility and tarmac perhaps could be traced back to being 'educated' on the highway). Often projects focus on ordinary aspects of everyday life, including the unappreciated or negative, that are enhanced or twisted in order to bring to the fore the unexpected potential of the things that surround us. NL Architects currently employs an international staff of five to ten people. Mark Linnemann recently left the office.
www.nlarchitects.nl

036
CWBG

048
FILMMUSEUM

Client : Rijksgebouwendienst, Atelier Rijksbouwmeester: ir. M. Crouwel and Filmmuseum Amsterdam
Architect : NL Architects, Pieter Bannenberg, Walter van Dijk, Kamiel Klaasse
Team : Sören Grünert and Kirsten HüsigWith : Michael SchonerAnd : Corine Dikkers, HS Kim, Katharina Meier, Rachel Herbst, Andreas Krompass, Victoria Sjöstedt
Structural engineers : Arup Amsterdam, ir. Arjan Habrakon and David Gilpin
Model 1:500 : Made By Mistake

056
GRONINGER FORUM

Design : NL Architects_Pieter Bannenberg, Walter van Dijk, Kamiel Klaasse / Team_Thijs van Bijsterveldt, Sören Grünert / Collaborators : Britta Harnacke, Jana Heidacker, Sybren Hoek, Ana Lagoa Pereira Gomes, Florent Le Corre, Thomas Scherzer, Michael Schoner, Vittoria Volpi
Bureau Bouwkunde : Jan Calkoen, Peter Houtman
Advisors : Construction_ABT / Walter Spangenberg / Climate - Fire regulation_Peutz BV - Peter Wapenaar / Automatic Parking system_VDL Technics - Leon Hamelink / Model_Made by Mistake

058
GROUNDNOISE SCHIPHOL

Team: Thijs van Bijsterveldt, Chris Collaris, Florent Le Corre, Michael Schoner
With: Nora Aursand Iversen, Kim Guldmand Ewers, Jorge Redondo, Philip Schläger, Troels Steenholdt Heiredal
Consultants: Arno Eisses / TNO (Acoustics), Henk Krüs / Cyclone (Aerodynamics), Jeannet van Antwerpen, Edo Muller / INBO

076
LAVA LAND

Team: Rachel Herbst, Kirsten Huesig, Victoria Sjostedt, Sebastian Janusz,
Client: Municipality of Amsterdam, Stadsdeel Osdorp, Sociale vernieuwing Osdorp

104
MUZIEKPALEIS

Architect/Urbanist : Architectuurstudio HH Architects and Urban designers
Co-Architects : Architectuurstudio HH (Supervision and Chamber Music, Vredenburg), Jo Coenen & Co Architekten (Pop, Tivoli),
Architectuurcentrale Thijs Asselbergs (Jazzzaal, SJU), NL Architects (Crossover Zaal)
Architect Crossover Zaal : NL Architects, Amsterdam
Collaborators : Kirsten Husig, Soren Grunert, Thomas Scherzer, Michael Schoner, Wim Sjerps, Gerbrand van Oostveen,
Marc Dahmen, Martijn StoffelsClient : Muziekcentrum Vredenburg_Tivoli and SJU, Ontwikkelingsbedrijf Gemeente Utrecht OGU
Structural engineers : Ingenieursbureau Zonneveld
Mechanical engineers : Ingenieursburo Linssen
Building Physics and Acoustics : DHV Bouw en Industrie
Project Management : Samenwerkingspartners SMP, OGU/VGM Ontwikkelingsbedrijf en Vastgoedmanagement Utrecht
Costs Management : BBN
Lighting and Audio Design : Team Projects
Contractor : Heijmans

148
STRIJP S

Client: Stichting Trudo
Program: Parking, Foodcourt, Skateаrea, BMW Showroom, Supermarket
Size: 36,600m²
Team: Thijs van Bijsterveldt, Chris Collaris, Florent Le Corre, Kirsten Hüsig, Gen Yamamoto With: Nora Aursand Iversen, Kim Guldmand Ewers, Philip Schäger, Janine Tüschen
Consultant Construction: Arjan Habraken, Arup Amsterdam

150
TAIPEI PERFORMING ARTS CENTER

168
X SITE

NL Architects: Pieter Bannenberg, Walter van Dijk, Kamiel Klaasse
Team: Kirsten Huesig, Barbara Luns, Jungwha Cho

170
ZWALUWEN UTRECHT 1911

Client: Gemeente Utrecht, DMO
Architects: NL Architects, Pieter Bannenberg, Walter van Dijk, Kamiel Klaasse
Team: Sybren Hoek, Lukas Haller, Rachel Herbst, Erik Moederscheim
Contractor: Ton Versteeg
Structural engineer: Pieters Bouwtechniek Amsterdam BV
Installations: Ingenieursburo Linssen BV
Floor area: 1,265m²
Building costs: approx. 1,100,000 Euro

176
A8ERNA

Client: Gemeente Zaanstad
Architect: NL Architects, Pieter Bannenberg, Walter van Dijk, Kamiel Klaasse
Project leader: Sören Grünert
Team: Erik Moederscheim, Sarah Möller, Annarita Papeschi, Michael Schoner, Wim Sjerps, Crystal Tang
Artists: Arie van den Berg, Horst Rickels, Marc Ruygrok
Skatepark design: Carve, Amsterdam
Program: Public space - Church Square, covered square, marina, park, kid zone, Shopping - supermarket (facade), fish/flower shop
Size: Public space 22,500m², Shopping 1,500m²
Budget: 2,100,000 €

208
ISOLE D'ACQUA

Competition (by invitation): Santa Cesarea Therme, Italy
Client: Brioschi Finanziaria spa
Program: Holiday Village, 8000 housing Units + Additional Program
Size: 1.3Km²
Architect: NL Architects, Pieter Bannenberg, Walter van Dijk, Kamiel Klaasse
With: Sören Grünert, Daan Roggeveen and Britta Harnacke, Ana Lagoa, Florent Le Corre, Michael Schoner, Vittoria Volpi Gen Yamamoto
Landschapsarchitect: Bureau B+B, Martiene van Vliet
With: Anne Fleur Aronstein, Michiel Akkerman, Ulrike Centmayer, Adelaida Larrain

410
BEND UP/ BEND OVER

Collaborators: Caro Baumann, Jennifer Petersen, Misa Shibukawa
Client: CV Park Brederode (Thunnissen Ontwikkeling bv / TRS ontwikkelings groep/ BPMT), represented by BVR

422
CHO RESIDENCE

Location: Heiry Art Valley, Korea
Client: Young-Wook, Cho
NL Architects: Pieter Bannenberg, Walter van Dijk, Kamiel Klaasse
Collaborator: Kirsten Huesig Initiator
Consultant and Architect on Site, our friend and 'man on the inside': Young Joon Kim, YO2
Additional Consultant: Seung Soo Shin
Structural Engineer: Arup Amsterdam, Pieter Moerland

486
ORDOS 100

Client : Jiang Yuan Water Engineering Ltd.
Curator : AI WEI WEI / FAKE DESIGN
Project Leader : Michael Schoner
Team : Jung-Hwa Cho, Gen Yamamoto, Florent Le Corre, Wei-Nien Chen, Amadeo Linke
Structural Engineer : ABT - Walter Spangenberg
Facade pattern : LANDLAB - Arnhem and, OSLO - Berlicum
Climate : DGMR - Paul van Bergen
Air Installation : Huisman & Van Muijen - Will van der Weijden

488
PRISMA

Client : Stichting De Huismeesters (housing corporation), Ed Moonen
Architect : NL Architects, Pieter Bannenberg, Walter van Dijk, Kamiel Klaasse
Project leader : Sören Grünert
Team: Rachel Herbst, Sebastian Janusz, Erik Moederscheim, Wim Sjerps (competition)
Lukas Haller, Gerbrand van Oostveen, Michael Schoner, Wim Sjerps (approval planning), David de Bruin, Arjen Fruitema, Britta Harnacke (contract documents)
Cost Consultant : ABT Delft, Charles Boks
Structural Engineer : ABT Velp, Rob Nijsse, Erwin ten Brincke
Building services Engineer : Van der Weele Groningen, Frits Weijers, Radek Nosek
Fire Consultancy : DGMR Arnhem
Contractor : Ballast Nedam Regio Noord
Program : Housing (52 rental apartments), nursery with consultation office
Size : Plot size_2600m², Footprint_1600m², Gross floor area_8650m² (nursery 1000m², housing 7650m²), Height_49,5m (16 floors), Floor area ratio_3.3
Budget : 9.000.000m2

580
INTERPOLIS

Address: Dr. Hub van Doorneweg 195 NL-5026 RE Tilburg
Client: N.V. Interpolis Tivoli: Hans Koense
Architects of the 'High Rises': Architectenbureau Storimans
Supervisor interior design: Kho Liang Ie, Nel Verschuuren
General office concept: Veldhoen & Company, Pierre Buijs
Architects of the 'Base': Pieter Bannenberg / Walter van Dijk / Kamiel Klaasse
Collaborators: Kirsten Husig, Sarah Moller
Structural engineering: Adviesburo Tielemans: R. van Helvoirt
Acoustics consultant: Adviesbureau Peutz: K. Hoogendoorn
Mechanical engineers: Technisch adviesburo Becks: M. Walraven
Light consultant: Centrum voor Lichtarchitectuur: Egbert Keen
Audiovisual consultant: MK2
Artist: Franc Bragigand
Contractors: Bouwcombinatie BBF-Heijmans Bouw: R.van de Ven
Interior/furniture manufacturers: Brouwers Interieurs / DF Industrials/ De Jager / Walter van Lier / G&S Project

614
STAND AND DELIVER

Stand and Deliver: a stand for TPG Post at DIMA 2002, Dusseldorf and Frankfurt
Architect: NL Architects, Amsterdam
Collaborators: Kirsten Husig, Sarah Moller
Client: TPG Post

652
DAS NETS

Client: Stadtkunstprojekte e.V / Kunst und Architektur in Alt Köpenick (KAIAK)
Curator: Heike Catherina Mertens
NL Architects: Pieter Bannenberg, Walter van Dijk, Kamiel Klaasse
Team: Sören Grünert and Sarah Möller
Structural engineers: Happold Ingenieursbüro
Contractor: COROCORD RAUMNETZ GmbH
Building Costs: 190,000 Euro

680
LOOP-THE-LOOP

Client: Stichting 'Leve de Bouwput'
Team: Wim Sjerps, Christoph Wassmann, Annarita Papeschi, Sören Grünert, Beatriz Ruiz, Sarah Möler

nodo17 Architects

Manuel Pérez Romero.
Santa Cruz de Tenerife, Canary Islands. (1972)
E.T.S.A. de Las Palmas de Gran Canaria, 1998.
From 2001- Associate lecturer at the Architecture Dept. at the E.T.S.A.G. in Alcalá de Henares. Madrid. Spain.
2000-2001- Assistant lecturer at the Design Dept. at the E.T.S.A. Polytechnic in Madrid. Spain.
www.nodo17.com

032
BULLFIGHTER'S COSTUME

Competition: First Prize
Site: Blanca, Murcia. Spain
Architects: nodo17 (Manuel Pérez Romero)
Design Team: Aitor Casero, Mercedes Peña, Felix Toledo, Birga Wingenfeld, Alegría Zorrilla
Structure: Joaquín Antuña. Installations: ACH + Euring
Graffiti: Boamistura
Textile cover: Batspain
Vet consultants: Jimesa
Foreman builder: Pilar Perez
Infography: Jaime López
Model: Gilberto Ruiz Lopes

142
SPORT PARK

Site: Salamanca_ Spain
Architects: nodo17 (Manuel Pérez Romero)
Design Team: Mercedes Peña, Birga Wingenfeld, Alegría Zorrilla, Félix Toledo Lerín

158
THUNNUS THYNNUS

Site: Sanchinarro. Madrid. Spain
Architects: nodo17 (Manuel Pérez Romero)
Design Team: Aitor Casero, Félix Toledo Lerín, Birga Wingenfeld, Alegria Zorilla
Infography: Jaime López

194
FROM FLOWER TO FLOWER

Site: Getafe. Madrid. Spain
Architects: nodo17 (Manuel Pérez Romero) + BOAMISTURA
Desing Team: Birga Wingenfeld, Alegría Zorrilla, Mercedes Peña

310
LACTARIUS

Site: Guadalajara. Spain
Architects: nodo17 (Manuel Pérez Romero)
Design Team: Mercedes Peña, Birga Wingenfeld, Alegría Zorrilla

432
DASYPUS

Competition: Honorable Mention
Site: Alfafar. Valencia_ Spain
Architects: nodo17 (Manuel Pérez Romero)
Design Team: Birga Wingenfeld, Michael Moradiellos, Félix Toledo Lerín

524
VERTICAL TERRACED VILLAS

Site: Guadalajara. Spain
Architects: nodo17 (Manuel Pérez Romero)
Design Team: Birga Wingenfeld, Mercedes Peña, Michael Moradiellos, Javier Serrano and Dimitris Tsimopoulos

542
3 EXTENDED HOUSES

OBRA Architects

OBRA Architects was founded by Pablo Castro and Jennifer Lee in the year 2000 in New York City. The projects undertaken by OBRA Architects span a wide rangeof programs and sizes yet consistently seek to evoke invention and interest through explorations of material, structure, site and experience. Their practice and their work seek to challenge and expand the range of metaphors in which architecture finds itsmeaning. OBRA considers each and every project to be intimately bound to its surroundings, extending afield into site and landscape the conceptual understanding of the architectural work. As a result many proposals and built works include outdoor components and integration into the natural or urban landscape.
www.obraarchitects.com

698
RED+HOUSING MANIFESTO

Location: National Art Museum of China, Beijing, PR China
Credits: OBRA Architects / Pablo Castro and Jennifer Lee
OBRA Architects Project Team: Shin Kook Kang / Project Architect, Atsushi Koizumi, Sihyung Lee, Sara Kim, Orla Higgins, Michel Dinis
Special thanks to: National Art Museum of China, United Nations Development Programme China, China Central Academy of Fine Arts
Photo credits: OBRA Architects
Program: Emergency housing prototype commissioned as part of the exhibit
Crossing: Emergency Dialogues for Architecture to acknowledge the anniversary of the Sichuan earthquake area: 40m²

ONE ARCHITECTURE

Since its foundation, nearly a decade ago, One Architecture has engaged in a wide variety of projects, ranging from designs for luxury villas to the organization of the Atelier Delta Metropolis for the Dutch Ministry of Spatial Planning.
In the early days, the office explored the boundaries of architecture through conceptual projects, and published numerous articles on architecture and architectural theory, such as 'The Virtuous Horse, or Empiricism in Urbanism' and 'Disneyland with Euthanasia: The Vicissitudes of the Welfare State.'
In this period, One Architecture embarked on its first 'foreign adventures,' winning competitions with its exciting urban plans for Salzburg and former industrial areas of Germany.
After the original founders Matthijs Bouw and Joost Meuwissen parted ways in 2001, Bouw embedded, initially with Donald van Dansik, One Architecture's work more in professional practice, by integrating design and process and focusing on what we call 'conversational practice'. Through an understanding and engagement of the deep structure of planning (stakeholder agendas, organizational aspects, technology and programme), combined with design intelligence, a diverse range of projects was tackled. One Architecture expanded its working range throughout Europe with projects in Denmark (Hotel Pro Forma, Copenhagen), Italy (Genoa Harbour), and France (three urban plans, in Paris and Lille); it even made the crossover to North Africa with a thrilling design for a lively waterfront area in Nador (Morocco).
www.one-architecture.nl

240
SCHOOLS

256
VOSSELVELD
Team: Matthijs Bouw, Jan Willem Petersen, Carola Böker Client: ICS Adviseurs, on behalf of Universitair Medisch Centrum Utrecht

288
DUTCH MOUNTAINS

298
GPRU PORTE DE MONTREUIL

312
LES HALLES

376
ZOETERMEER AFRIKAWEG

464
LINZ LANDESFRAUEN KLINIK

PEG office of landscape + architecture

PEG office of landscape + architecture is an award-winning design and research office based in Philadelphia, PA. We engage a wide range of projects in terms of content, scale, and medium. Whether through competitions, writing or client-sponsored work, we explore the overlapping terrain between the disciplines of architecture and landscape architecture. Utilizing the techniques or conventions inherent in one discipline enables us to scrutinize the conventions of the other in order to imagine new formal and material arrangements. This does not, however, lead to the uniform application of technique. If we believed in manifestos, ours would be that scale matters.
www.peg-ola.com

180
BAYWATCH
Size: 26 acres
Location: Buzzard's Bay, MA
Project team: Karen M'Closkey, Keith VanDerSys, Jason O'Meara, Patricia Gruitts

210
JOIE DE VIE(W)
Size: 1,000 sf
Project team: Karen M'Closkey, Keith VanDerSys, Lizzie Rothwell

222
MIES VAN DER ROHE PLAZA
Size: 4,000 sf
Location: Detroit, MI
Project team: PEG and PLY Architecture KPF

258
WATERCOURSE
Size: 48 hectares
Location: Sacca San Mattia, Italy
Project team: Karen M'Closkey, Keith VanDerSys, Kristen Dean, Matt Ducharme-Smith, Jamie Witherspoon

570
DOUBLE JEOPARDY
Client : University of Michigan
Principal Designers : Karen M'Closkey + Keith VanDerSys (PEG office of landscape + architecture)
Project Team : Mark Davis, Neil Thelen, Matt Saurman; Leigh Stewart
Photographer : Beth Singer

PERIPHERIQUES architects

For 10 years, PERIPHERIQUES has been a structure in constant evolution exploring production and diffusion of architecture while proposing the negociation and sharing of ideas between several partners as a platform for creation. Currently animated by the 2 agencies of each one ten people, Emmanuelle MARIN + David TROTTIN architects on the one hand and twin Anne-Françoise JUMEAU, architect on the other hand. PERIPHERIQUES proposes a creation with several, based on the negotiation and the division of the ideas like on the multidisciplinarity of the activities.
PERIPHERIQUES: these are two agencies which having to confront their ideas validate them in manner self-criticism at the time of workshop, before presenting them at the building owner.
Our agencies have a great practice to work together. We study and carry out a number of joint projects, always attaching a great importance to the precision and the rigour of the studies, to the respect of the programs and the follow-up of the budgets.
PERIPHERIQUES carries on mainly its activities in the fields of architecture and town planning, while intervening regularly in the related fields of scenography, the design, the graphics and the production of installations.
www.peripheriques-architectes.com

078
LES HALLES

308
LA PIROTTERIE
Project team: L. Paillard, S. Razafindralambo, G. Mangeot, D. Graignic Ramiro, P.E. Loiret with S. Truchot, R. Picaper, F. Rognone, G. Bousquet
Program Urban planning : a residential area in Rezé
Site Rezé, France
Client Rezé City, Terre Océane
Floor area 18 ha
Budget 2.5 M€ excluding VAT
Schedule Completion 2005

452
ILE DE NANTES

716
TSUMARI ART TRIENNALE 2003
Project team L. Paillard, H. Kangas, S. Razafindralambo, M. Hamada
Program View-point and camping place
Site Tsumari, Japan
Client Art Front Gallery, Tokyo
Floor area 200 m²
Schedule Completion 2003

plattformberlin

Born in Karlsruhe, 1967. Architectural and urban studies in Darmstadt, Paris and Berlin, 1986~1994. Diploma (Dipl.-Ing. Architekt) TH Darmstadt, 1994. Jens Metz architecte founded of the planning network plattformberlin in Berlin 2002, and in Paris 2001. ENSAS Strasbourg, visiting professor for urban planning, master course, 2006~2007. BTU Cottbus, assistant professor for building construction and architectural design, 2000~2003. Europan Vice-president of the German Europan committee, member of the Europan Europe technical committee. Contributions to the programs and catalogues Europan 8 and 9. Workshops Lectures, workshops and diploma juries in various architecture schools, a. o. TU Berlin, Masterclass. Doordrecht, HCU Hamburg, LU Hannover, EAML Marseille, HS Müunster, EAPVS Paris, ENSAS.
www.plattformberlin.com

190
ESA STAHLHOF
Client: agora SA (Luxembourg)
Program: Design of a public square
Status: Competition 01 / 2005
Partners: Atelier Tangente, landscape architects
Surface: approx. 1.1 ha

202
HAG ST. JOSEPH
Client: City of Haguenau (France)
Program: Regeneration of a nineteen-sixties settlement
Status: Study 07 / 2007, in process
Partners: Atelier Tangente, landscape architects, OTE, engineers
Surface: approx. 2.7 ha

216
LA JOLIETTE

230
PLANKEN MANNHEIM
Client: City of Mannheim (Germany)
Program: Urban masterplan, public spaces
Partners: Atelier Tangente, landscape architects
Surface: approx. 12 ha

276
CBO COTTBUS
Client: City of Cottbus (Germany)
Program: Urban development scheme
Partners: E. Weber, University of Cottbus, biologist
Surface: approx. 24 km²

PLY Architecture

PLY Architecture is Craig Borum and Karl Daubmann. Both Borum and Daubmann are registered architects and both are tenured professors at the University of Michigan.
PLY(verb) means to practice or perform diligently, 'to ply a trade'.
PLY operates between academia and the profession, two worlds that seem to not always understand one another. Academia critiques the profession for being too passive, simply providing a service, while the profession argues that academia is in the clouds, not able to understand the issues on the ground. PLY leverages the best of each against the other, taking on client-generated commissions and attempting to unpack inherent potentials, reformulating them through questions of the discipline, and responding with innovative solutions.
PLY is recognized as a design research practice. A research agenda pervades the design process, exploring material and the logic of construction. Since 1999 our portfolio has grown to include more than 50 projects, 38 that are built. The work ranges from designs for public schools to gallery installations, from client commissioned projects to open design competitions.
www.plyarch.com

554
BIG TEN BURRITO
Location : East Lansing, USA
Square Footage : 1700 sf, seating for 30
Design + Construction : Craig Borum + Karl Daubmann (Principals), Jeana D'Agostino, Jen Maigret, Michael Powers, Liz Kuwada

558
BTB BURRITO
Location : Ann Arbor, USA
Design + Construction : Karl Daubmann, Craig Borum (principals); Carl Lorenz, Pete Stavenger, Maria Walker
Square Footage : 150 sf.

604
ROBBINS ELEMENTARY SCHOOL
Teams: Craig Borum, Karl Daubmann (Principals)/ Jen Maigret, Michael Powers, Sam Barclay, Jeana D'Agostino, Josh Bard, Lizzie Rothwell, Kasey Vilet, Na Young Shim, Ka Young Shim, Nick Quiring

687
WOOD LIGHTS
Design + Construction : Craig Borum + Karl Daubmann (Principals), Jeana D'Agostino, Kristen Little, Jen Maigret, Michael Powers, Maria Walker

688
PAPER LIGHTS
Design + construction : Craig Borum + Karl Daubmann (Principals), Jeana D'Agostino, Kristen Little, Jen Maigret, Michael Powers, Maria Walker

700
SCREEN WALL PROTOTYPE
Materials Include : water-jet cut aluminum sheet
Design : Karl Daubmann (Principal)

Point Supreme Architects

Point Supreme Architects was founded in Rotterdam in 2007 and is now based in Athens. The office is led by four collaborators of diverse background; Konstantinos Pantazis, Marianna Rentzou, Beth Hughes and Yiorgos Pantazis. Prior to forming Point Supreme they worked for a variety of international firms including OMA –Rem Koolhaas and MVRDV in the Netherlands, Jun Aoki in Tokyo and 51N4E in Brussels. Their work integrates architecture, urbanism, landscape and graphic design thinking in order to reach the 'point supreme'.
www.pointsupreme.com

634
'AKTIPIS' FLOWERSHOP
Location : Patras, Greece
Graphics : Point Supreme Architects
Light consultant : Athina Papanikou
Photos : Yiannis Drakoulidis
Area : 40m2
Budget : 20.000 euros

PSA

PSA (Pschill Seghatoleslami Architektur) was founded 2004 by Lilli Pschill (MSc) and Ali Seghatoleslami (MSc) in Vienna. PSA defines itself as an architectural studio where project-specific solutions with a strong emphasis on technological and design innovation are sought after.
Lilli Pschill (born 73 in Wien) und Ali Seghatoleslami (born 75 in Teheran) graduated from the Technical University in Vienna and the Architectural Association in London.
www.p-s-a.org

228
OPATIJA NEW SQUARE

612
SKY OFFICE OFFSPRING

662
EARPHONE STAND
Client: McShark Apple Premium Reseller

686
OPEN SPACE AWARDS TOKYO

R&Sie...architects

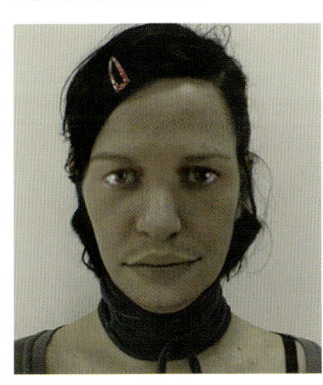

R&Sie(n) is an architectural office sey up in 1989 and lead by Francois Roche (1961, France), Stphanie Lavaux (1966, France), based in Paris. The organic, oppositional architectural projects of their practice is concerned with the bond between building, context and human relations. Roche explains his concept of spoiled climate chameleon architecture, which links and hybrids the human body to the body of architecture by a re-scenarization on the rules of all the natures, even artificial. They use speculations and fictions as process to dis-alienate the post-capitalism subjectivities, in the pursuit of Toni Negri. R&Sie(n) consider architectural identity as an unstable concept, defined through temporary forms in which the vegetal and biological become a dynamic element. R&Sie(n) are currently undertaking a critical experiment with new warping technologies to prompt architectural "scenarios" of cartographic distortion, substitution, and genetic territorial mutations to create protocols in apparatuses that merge fiction, subjectivation and processes of transformation with "bachelors and desirable" machines, simultaneously re-scenarizing the aesthetic relationship with nature(s) - artificial, paranoiac and/or real.
www.new-territories.com

042
DUSTY RELIEF / B-MU
Creative team: Francois Roche, Stephanie Lavaux, Jean Navarro, Pascal Bertholio
Local architect: A49 / Bangkok
Landscape architect: Michel Boulcourt, Paris
Furniture designer: Mathieu Lehanneur, Paris
Structural steel engineer: Nicolas Green, Paris, London
Light engineer: ACT / B. Lalloz
Client: Petch Osathanugrah, Bangkok
Key dimensions: 5,000m²

684
OLZWEG
Creative team: Francois Roche, Stephanie Lavaux, Jean Navarro, Pascal Bertholio
Local architect: A49 / Bangkok
Landscape architect: Michel Boulcourt, Paris
Furniture designer: Mathieu Lehanneur, Paris
Structural steel engineer: Nicolas Green, Paris, London
Light engineer: ACT / B. Lalloz
Client: Petch Osathanugrah, Bangkok
Key dimensions: 5,000m²

Reiser + Umemoto RUR Architecture PC

Jesse Reiser and Nanako Umemoto have practiced in New York City as Reiser + Umemoto RUR Architecture P.C. since 1986. Jesse Reiser is currently an Associate Professor of Architecture at Princeton University.
Reiser + Umemoto, RUR Architecture P.C. an internationally recognized architectural firm has built projects at a wide range of scales: from furniture design, to residential and commercial structures, up to the scale of landscape design and infrastructure. The firm approaches each project as the continuation of an ongoing inquiry, delving into relationships among architecture, territory and systems of distribution. By working on projects of varying scales, from the architectural to the regional, the firm has developed flexible strategies and techniques that seek open structures that are now ossified and to integrate domains that historically have been kept apart.
www.reiser-umemoto.com

136
SHENZHEN INTERNATIONAL AIRPORT - TERMINAL 3
Location: Shenzhen, China
Principals: Jesse Reiser + Nanako Umemoto
Design Team: Mitsuhisa Matsunaga (Lead), Kutan Ayata, Michael Overby, Roland Snooks
Assistants and Interns: Steven Lauritano, Juan De Marco, Neil Cook, Michael Loverich, Lindsey Cohen, Luis Costa, Yan Wai Chu, Roselyn Shieh, Max Kuo, Robin Liu, Devin Jernigan, Robert Soendergaard, Victor Chei, Penelope
Structural Engineering: Dan Brodkin, Matthew Clark, Ove Arup and Partners, New York
MEP / Acoustics / Sustainability / Lighting Consultant: Ashok Raiji, Ove Arup and Partners, New York
Animation Assistance: Sean Daly, Windtunnel Visualization, New York

296
FOSHAN SANSUI URBAN PLAN

362
WEST SIDE CONVERGENCE
Principals: Jesse Reiser + Nanako Umemoto
Design Team: Jason Payne, Yama Karim, Nona Yehia, David Ruy
Assistants and Interns: Wolfgang Gollwitzer, Astrid Piber, Matthias Blass, Keisuke Kitagawa, Ade Herkarisma, Joseph Chang
Consulting Engineers: YSRAEL A. SEINUK P.C.
Planning and Transportation Consultants: BUCKHURST FISH & JACQUEMART

478
O-14
Location: Dubai, UAE
Principals: Jesse Reiser + Nanako Umemoto
Design Team: Mitsuhisa Matsunaga, Kutan Ayata, Jason Scroggin, Cooper Mack, Michael Overby, Roland Snooks, Michael Young
Assistants and Interns: Tina Tung, Raha Talebi, Yan Wai Chu
Structural Engineer: Ysrael A. Seinuk, PC, New York, NY
Architect of Record: Erga Progress, Dubai, UAE
Window Wall Consultant: R.A.Heintges & Associates
Client: Creekside Development Corporation
General Contractor: Dubai Contracting Company
Size: 31,400 sq. m
Structure: Perforated Concrete Exoskeleton

630
ALISHAN TOURIST ROUTES
Size: 3600 sq. m.
Type: Tourist, infrastructure
Structure: Multiple

Principals Architects: Jesse Reiser + Nanako Umemoto
Design Team: Eva Perez de Vega Steele, Jason Scroggin, Jonathan D. Solomon
Interns and Assistants: Joe Kobayashi, Yuya Suzuki, Keisuke Kitagawa, Alver Mensana, Akari Takebayashi, Akira Nakamura, Aki Eto, Arthur Chu, David Nam, Ian Gordon
Structural Engineer: Cecil Baimond, Charles Walker, Ove Arup & Partners, London
Architectural Consultant: Philip Fei, Fei and Cheng, Taipei

Re_Load

Marco Plazzogna (1981) and Silvia Bertolone (1982) bore in Treviso, Italy. They studied at the University of Architecture IUAV in Venice where graduated in 2006 with full marks. Especially interested in the new architectural tendencies developing in Spain, in 2007 decided to undertake there an experience of study and work.
They worked with 'Estudio Entresitio' and DL+A (Madrid, Spain) and CZA, Cino Zucchi architetti (Milano, Italy). They are also attending the doctorate of planning at the ETSAM University in Madrid.
Their approach with architecture is based on the geometric relationship between interior and exterior spaces, the vibrating border that clearly divides what it's motionless and unchangeable (architecture) from what it's changeable (nature). Their architectural research is addressed to buildings developing from a geometrical idea and creating multidirectional points of view in a still and immutable space.
www.bertoloneplazzogna.eu

082
LIGHT HOUSE

162
TREVISO CULTURAL CENTRE

212
KALEIDOSCOPE STREET

334
REFILLING GREEN

Responsive Systems Group

Founded and directed by Chris Perry, the Responsive Systems Group operates as a peripheral design research practice within servo's general collaborative network. The group was originally formed in 2006 at Cornell University as a means of exploring the potential of responsive design through an integrated curriculum of advanced design studios, research seminars, and technology courses, and has since conducted visiting studios and seminarsat a number of other architectural institutions including Rice University, the University of Toronto, and Pratt Institute.

682
MACHINE IN THE GRADEN
A design research subsidiary of servo
@ Rice School of Architecture
Design studio directed by Chris Perry
Design proposal by Sarah Simpson

SADAR VUGA ARHITEKTI

Sadar Vuga Arhitekti (SVA) was founded by Jurij Sadar and Bostjan Vuga in Ljubljana in 1996. Over the past twelve years it has focused on open, innovative and integral architectural design and urban planning.
The office has been driven by a quest for quality, with a strong belief that forward-leaping architectural production contributes to our well-being, and generates a sensitive and responsive development of the physical context we live in, broadening our imagination and stimulating our senses.
The growing portfolio of built work ranges from innovative town planning to public space sculpture, from interactive new public buildings to interventions within older existing structures. SVA designs extended living areas in residential buildings, guided by the culture and climate of place. SVA shapes interior environments that respond to very personal tastes and desires.
The client base reflects the diversity of built and project experience. Ranging from municipal councils and Central Government, encompassing national and private arts bodies and multi nationals to the best developers in Slovenia.
www.sadarvuga.com

034
BUTCHER'S BRIDGE
Client: City Council Ljubljana
Site: The Ljublijanica river and embankments in the centre of Ljubljana, Slovenia
Site area: 5,722sqm
Building area: 722sqm
Total floor area: 7,166sqm
Storeys: ground floor + 2 storeys
Programme: market opening, public event space, bridge
Structure: cast-on-site reinforced concrete, prefab reinforced concrete
Architect: Jurij Sadar, Boštjan Vuga, Nataša Mrkonjic, Bor Pungercic, Margarida Dias, Adrian Petrucelli
Structural engineer: Atelier One, London/Manchester
Service engineers & Lighting: N/A

086
LJUBLJANA PASSENGER STATION
Client: Emonika
Site: Ljubljana City Centre
Site area: 26,118sqm
Total floor area: 25,152sqm
Storeys: ground floor + 2 storeys
Programme: train and bus station + retail
Structure: bridge steel truss
Cladding: glazed facade
Architect: Jurij Sadar, Boštjan Vuga, Miha Cebulj, Bor Pungercic, Risto Avramovski, Bruno Henriques
Structural Engineer: Elea IC - Miha Žibert

102
MUSEUM NEUGAUS LIAUNIG COLLECTION
Client: private client
Site: Neuhaus, Carinthia, Austria
Building Area: 36.565m²
Total Floor Area: 4.585m²
Collection Area: 2.365m²
Storeys: sculpture field under main floor + main floor
Parking: 50 cars + 4 buses
Program: art exhibition (permanent and temporal), performance / events for 150 visitors, cafeteria, storage
Structure: concrete platform, brick vaults, lightweight space frame
Architect: Sadar Vuga Arhitekti (Jurij Sadar, Bostjan

ARCHITECTURAL DIAGRAMS 739

Vuga, Or Ettlinger, Tina Hocevar, Tomaz Kristof, Lucijan Sifrer, Luka Jancic - model, Matjaz Kofol - graphics)
Structural Scheme: Arup, London (Charles Walker, Project Director - Structural Engineering and Advanced Geometry, Martin Self, Project Engineer - Structural Engineering and Advanced Geometry)
Environmental Scheme: Arup,London (Paul Lander, Project Services Director - Mechanical Engineering Duncan Campbell, Project Engineer - Mechanical Engineering and Microclimate Design)
Lighting Scheme: Atelje Japelj

402
APARTMENT HOUSE GRADASKA

Client: Lesnina Inzeniring d.d.
Site: Gradaska Street 20, Ljubljana
Site Area: 1.545m²
Building Site Area: 795m²
Total Floor Area: 3.800m² / 12 apartments, biggest 350m², smallest 90m²
Parking: 39 | Total Volume: 14.850m³
Storeys: UF + GF + 3 storeys
Program: housing appartament
Structure: reinforced concrete, steel
Cladding: structered stone panels, glass, reflecting glass
Architect: Sadar Vuga Arhitekti (Jurij Sadar, Bostjan Vuga, Beno Masten, Goran Golubic, Tadej Zaucer, Tomaz Celigoj, Lucijan Sifrer, Ana Struna)
Structural Engineer: Elea IC | Mechanical Services: Klimaterm | Electrical Services: Norma | Site Engineering: Kono
Photo: Ziga Koritnik, SVA Archive

428
CONDOMINIUM TRNOVSKI PRISTAN

Client: Begrad, Novo Mesto
Address / Site: Trnovski Pristan, Ljubljana, Slovenia
Site Area: 4640m²
Building Area: 1365m²
Total Floor Area: 4010m²
Storeys: basement + GF + 2 storeys
Program: residential building
Cladding: ventilated facade, ceramic tiles on alu plates, alu double glazing
Architect: Sadar Vuga Arhitekti (Jurij Sadar, Bostjan Vuga, Tina Hocevar, Miha Pesec, Tadej Zaucer, Mojca Kocbek)
Structural Engineers: Elea | Service Engineers: TE Biro (Mechanical & Electrical)
Landscape Design: Andrej Strgar
Traffic / Site Engineer: Gasper Blejec
Photo: Hisao Suzuki, SVA Archive

514
TOWER COMPLEX AT THE SULEJMAN PASHA MOUMENT AREA

Tendency: Matrix Volume
Site: Skenderbej Plaza zone, Tirana, Albania
Building Area: 4.815m²
Total Floor Area: 22.825m² plus 1.100m² shopping on -1
Storeys: 4B + GF + 23
Program: shopping / retail (7.400m² + 1.100 m² On -1), office (9.460m²), residential (4.755m²), top floor restaurant / bar (770m²), technical rooms (440m²)
Parking: 390 Cars
Architecture: Sadar Vuga Arhitekti (Jurij Sadar, Bostjan Vuga, Lucijan Sifrer, John Paul Americo, Ines Schmid)
Structural Scheme: Atelier One, London (Aran Chadwick, Neil Thomas)
Cladding Consultant: Aks, Ljubljana (Stephan Lungmuss)

540
3 ACADEMIES LJUBLJANA

Source: open competition
Client: Ministry of Education of the Republic of Slovenia, University of Ljubljana
Site: Ljubljana, Slovenia
Site Area: 35.530m²
Building Area: 5.465m²
Total Floor Area: 27.770m²
Storeys: 2 basements + ground Floor + 4 storeys
Program: Academy for Music, Academy for Performative Arts, Academy for Visual Arts
Structure: precast concrete slabs, concrete pillars
Cladding: insulated glass panels, alu frames
Architect: Sadar Vuga Arhitekti (Jurij Sadar, Bostjan Vuga, Tina Hocevar, Adrian Petrucelli, David Ruic, Goran Golubic, Ines Schmid)
Structural Engineer: Andrey Mladenov
Environmental Engineer: Miha Praznik
Service Engineers: Biro ES
Theatre Project Consultant: TPC (David T. Staples)

550
ALMIRA SADAR BOUTIQUE

Site Area: Ground floor of historicaly preserved secession building
Total Floor Area: 75m²
Program: Women fashion store
Structure: Steel structure, hanging element
Ceiling: permeable metal mash suspended element
Architect: Sadar Vuga Arhitekti (Jurij Sadar, Bostjan Vuga, Tinka Prekovic)
Service Engineers: Biro ES
Lighting: Marko Japelj
Photo: Hisao Suzuki

576
HOTEL CASINO PARK

Client: HIT, hoteli igralnice turizem
Site: Nova Gorica, Slovenia
Net Area: 3.750m² gaming and entertainment area
Storeys: basement + GF + 1 storey
Parking Spaces: 37 for automobiles, 2 for taxis, 1 for bus
Purpose: hotel and casino center
Structure: existing

Materials: light threads made of semi-elastic and heat resistant plastic, lowered ceiling made of perforated metal, semi-reflecting wall cladding, printed glass
Architect: Sadar Vuga Arhitekti (Jurij Sadar, Bostjan Vuga, Tinka Prekovic, Lucijan Sifrer, Uros Strel)
Lighting Concept: Atelje Japelj
Traffic / Site Planning: Gasper Blejec
Structural Engineering: Spit, Nova Gorica
Construction Cost: EUR 3.5 Million

582
INTRA STUDIO

Location : Diamant building, BTC City, Ljubljana, Slovenia
Client : Intra lighting
Total floor area : 260m²
Material : laminated wooden plates, lighting
Architect : SVA (Jurij Sadar, Boštjan Vuga, Tina Hocevar, Adrian Petrucelli)
Lighting : Matej B. Kobav
Graphics : Gigo Design
Photos : Aljosa Rebolj & SUA

Samoo Architects & Engineers

Established in 1976, Samoo Architects & Engineers looks back on 30 years of history. From the beginning, Samoo has maintained its status as Korea's number 1 architectural design firm with the goal of becoming one of the world's leading companies in this field. In 2008, Samoo ranked 11th among architectural firms on the renowned journal ENR's list of top global architectural design firms. Through creativity and excellent overseas marketing, Samoo continue to expand internationally by promoting projects in Algeria, Vietnam, Cambodia, Kazakhstan, Abu Dhabi, Saudi Arabia, China, Japan and U.S.A. etc. Samoo currently have three branch offices in Dubai, Shanghai and New York. Kim Kwan Joong is executive director of Architectural Studio 1 in Samoo Architects & Engineers. He graduated in architectural engineering department from Yonsei university. His major projects include (Yongsan International Business District), (Korea Cultural Center in Japan), (DMC Landmark Tower), (Bundang NHN Venture Tower)
www.samoo.co.kr

204
HEART OF MAGOK IS NATURE OF LIVING WATER

Client: Seoul City, SH
Location: Magokdong, Gangseogu, Seoul, Korea
Area: 1,170,780M2
Design Team: Samoo Architects & Engineers_ Kim Kwan Joong, Kwon Soon Woo, Kim Ki Yeon, Choi Chang Soon, Nam Kung In, Yang Sung Min, Sun Shuli, Han Mi Ok, Kim Sung Joon, Bang Seung Hwan, Baek Ho Jjung, Wm. Jack T. Phillips, Silas Jeffrey, Harry H. Park, Wei Chuang, Min Joon Ki, Jung Sang Moon / Thomas Balsley / Seoyeong Engineering_ Yoo Duk Hee, Rim Hae Wook / PMD Landscape Architecture_ Lee Sang Jong

SeARCH

Architect-directors: Bjarne Mastenbroek and Uda Visser. Consisting of 40 international architects, designers and staff members, SeARCH develops architectural and urban projects and does research on architecture, landscaping, urbanism and new building products and materials. SeARCH collaborates with different disciplines to experiment and test the results of collective design sessions in order to give an opportunity to innovative, original and unexpected proposals.
www.search.nl

164
WELZIJNSCLUSTER ZOETERMEER

Location : Diamant building, BTC City, Ljubljana, Slovenia
Client : Intra lighting
Total floor area : 260m2
Material : laminated wooden plates, lighting
Architect : SVA (Jurij Sadar, Boštjan Vuga, Tina Hocevar, Adrian Petrucelli)
Lighting : Matej B. Kobav
Graphics : Gigo Design
Photos : Aljosa Rebolj & SUA

Serie Architects

Founding Principals : Christopher CM Lee is an architect, teacher, and the Principal of Serie Architects London. He graduated with the AA Diploma [Honours] in 1998 from Architectural Association School of Architecture London and awarded the RIBA President's Medal Commendation Award. Christopher Lee lectures widely and has delivered guest-lectures in Tsinghua University China, Central Academy of Fine Arts China, Beijing Institute of Architectural Design China, UIA Conference in Kuala Lumpur, Barbican London, Chinese University Hong Kong.
Kapil Gupta is the principal of Serie Architects India and a director at the Urban Design Research Institute, Mumbai. He graduated with honours from Sir J J College of Architecture, Mumbai followed by post-graduate studies at the Architectural Association, London. Kapil has delivered guest lectures at UIA Conference in Kuala Lumpur, Urban Design Research Institute, Mumbai, the Annual IALD Awards, Hyderabad, and at various architecture schools in Mumbai some at which he is a regular Visiting Critic.
www.serie.co.uk

062
GUIYANG HUAXI URBAN CENTRE

Building Type : Commercial, Live/ Work, Public Space
Total Area : 16,000 sqm
Client : Homnicen Group China
Credits : Serie Architects London / Serie Architects India
Design Team: Chris Lee, Bolam Lee, Udayan Mazumdar, Kevin Hung

064
HEALTH SCIENCES CAMPUS

152
TAIPEI PERFORMING ATS CENTRE

556
BLUE FROG ACOUSTIC LOUNGE & STUDIOS

Client : Blue Frog Media Pvt. Ltd
Area : 1000 sqm
Design : Chris Lee / Kapil Gupta
Project Team : Tomas Ruis Osborne, Santosh Thorat, Purva Jamdade, Suril Patel, Dharmesh Thakker, Niti Goursaria, Vrinda Seksaria and Udayan Mazumdar
Acoustic Design : Munroe Acoustics (UK)
Lighting Design : Abhay Wadhwa Associates
Project Management : Masters Management Consultants
General Contractor : Zigma Enterprises
Photographer : Fram Petit

servo

An architectural design collaborative with partners in Europe and the U.S., servo adopts the organizing principles of a network, integrating geographically discrete nodes of operation through various forms of telecommunication. The group's work focuses on the development of architectural environments, active design systems comprised of temporal conditions, shifting material states, the proliferation of electronic and digital equipment and interfaces, and in general the ebb and flow of information in real-time. Recent projects include a full-scale interactive installation for the International Biennial of Contemporary Art in Seville and a digital media exhibition design for at the Santa Monica Museum of Art.
servo's work has been exhibited at a wide variety of prominent galleries and museums including the Venice Architecture Biennale, the Centre Pompidou, SF-MoMA, the Cooper-Hewitt National Design Museum, the Wexner Center for the Arts, MoMA/QNS, Artists Space, and the Storefront for Art and Architecture in New York.
www.s-e-r-v-o.com

124
REEFMOD

Project Credits: servo
David Erdman, Marcelyn Gow, Ulrika Karlsson, Chris Perry
Design Team: Erik Hökby, Ebba Hallin

182
BIOBOX

562
CLOUD BOX

Project Credits: servo
David Erdman, Marcelyn Gow, Ulrika Karlsson, Chris Perry
Design Team: Emily Grandstaff, Jung Ho, Don Schneider

640
BIOZONE

654
DISPLAY ENVIRONMENT 1

Project Credits: servo in collaboration with Stephen Kinder Design Partnership and Karen Kimmel

656
DISPLAY ENVIRONMENT 2

Project Credits: servo

672
IN THE LATTICE

Project Credits: servo
David Erdman, Marcelyn Gow, Ulrika Karlsson, Chris Perry
Design Team: Daniel Norell, Thomas Broome, Olaf Bendt, Fredrik Petersson

678
LOBBI-PORTS

Project Credits: servo in collaboration with Perry Hall (2002) and Small Design Firm (2004)

696
PROXIMITY CLOUD

740 PROFILE & INDEX

sga : sean gosell architects

Sean Godsell was born in Melbourne in 1960. He graduated with First Class Honours from The University of Melbourne in 1984. He spent much of 1985 traveling in Japan and Europe and worked in Londonfrom 1986 to 1988 for Sir Denys Lasdun. In 1989 he returned to Melbourne and worked for The Hassell Group. In 1994 he formed Godsell Associates Pty Ltd Architects.
In July 2003 he received a Citation from the President of the AIA (American Institute of Architects) for his work for the homeless. His Future Shack prototype was exhibited from May to October 2004 at the Smithsonian Institute's Cooper Hewitt Design Museum in New York, in the USA, China and Australia.
www.seangodsell.com

690
PARK BENCH HOUSE

Architect: Sean Godsell
Construction: Steel frame, Woven stainless steel 'bed', Aluminium Roof / Seat, Photovoltaic cell
Photographer: Hayley Franklin

Smånsk Design Studio

Smånsk is a young Swedish design group formed in 2007 in connection with the Salone Satellite in Milan. Simon Jarl and Martin Pålsson met at Konstfack University College of Arts, Craft and Design in Stockholm and soon they decided to launch their best ideas under a common name.
Smånsk we gain space to develop the creative process. We realised that we had a similar approach to design where we analyse the upstart of ideas itself in different ways and try to control that process, says Martin Pålsson.
we work with interiors we refer to it as 'brand architecture'. We try to find the core of the clients work and express this through the interior. This concept is applicable for both retail and workplaces. What if a workplace could express, to clients andto the people working there, what you want and what you represent?
www.smansk.com

642
BOOKS ON EARTHQUAKE

718
VAGBOND TRAVEL BOOKSTORE

All photos : Carl Kleiner

SMAQ

SMAQ is a collaborative studio that operates in the field of architecture, urbanism and research. SMAQ was founded by the architects Sabine Müller and Andreas Quednau in Rotterdam and is now based in Berlin. Sabine Müller holds a position as assistant professor for architecture and urbanism at the Karlsruhe University of Technology and Andreas Quednau at the Berlin University of Technology. Both partners hold a Master's Degree from Columbia University, New York. SMAQ has conducted to a number of urban research projects in Germany, Latin America and Africa dealing with everyday urbanisms and infrastructure and co-published the book "BRAKIN – Visualizing the Visual".
www.smaq.net

070
HIGHWAY...ING

Client : Loetje bv, Amsterdam
Location : Noord Holland, the Netherlands
Project team : Rob Wagemans, Erik van Dillen, Jari van Lieshout, Jeroen Vester
Manufacturers : Interior_ V.o.f. van der Schaaf, Fitted furniture_ Roord Binnenbouw, Lighting_ Moooi, Piet Hein Eek, various suppliers, Installations_ Miwo, luchtbehandelingstechniek
Photography : Ewout Huibers
Total area : 270m2

134
SCOOP

Client : City of Hammerfest, Hammerfest Naeringsinvest AS and Hammerfest Harbour Authority
Design : SMAQ – Sabine Müller and Andreas Quednau
Collaborator : Caroline O' Donnell
Bioclimatic Consultant : Caroline O' Donnell
Use : Arctic Culture Centreincl. a music school for rehearsal, performance, cinema and exhibitions
Size : 4,100sqm

282
CUMULUS

Project Team: Sabine Müller, Andreas Quednau, Felipe Flores, Silvia Izquierdo, Martino Sacchi
Client: City of Oslo
Program: 195 apartments, 14,370 m2 retail and public program, 10,450 m2 offices, 8,500 m2 cultural and social facilities, 19,200 m2 underground parking
Site Area: 5.5 ha
Study Area: 15 ha
Building Area: 9,995 m2 (building foot print only - with parking garage: 19,200 m2)
Gross Floor Area: 49,950 m2
Building Scale (no. of floors): 5 - 11 floors

286
DOTSANDLOOPS

Master Plan Team : Sabine Mueller, Andreas Quednau, Marta Male Alemany
Landscape Design Team : Sabine Mueller, Andreas Quednau
Site Area : 3.75 ha
Program : 245 apartments, 1,500sqm retail, 750 parking places, sports facilities
Status : in development
Client : Aragon Izquierdo, S. L. Burgos
Collaborator : Marta Male Alemany

306
L.A.R.S

370
XERITOWN

Urban Design: SMAQ – architecture urbanism research (Berlin)_ Sabine Müller and Andreas Quednau with Joachim Schultz, Team_ Therese Granberg, Ludovica Rogers, Felipe Flores, Kathrin Löer, Valle Medina
Local architect/ coordination: X-Architects (Dubai)_ Ahmed Al-Ali, Farid Esmaeil, Mathan Ramaiah, Kamal M. Musallam, Bashar Suliman
Landscape Design: Johannes Grothaus + Partners Landscape Architects (Potsdam/Dubai)_ Johannes Grothaus, Joachim Genest, Dörthe Ritter, Juliane Lehmphul, Jörn Mikoleit, Danuta Dias
Renderings: LeBalto, Marc Pouzol
Lighting Design: Reflexion (Zurich):Thomas Mika, Oliver Königs
Infrastructure: Buro Happold (London/Dubai):
Bill Addis, Ed Bartz, Bernardo Vazquez, Bill Coupe, Gerry Prodohl
Commissioner/Developer: Dubai Properties (Dubai)

SO Architecture

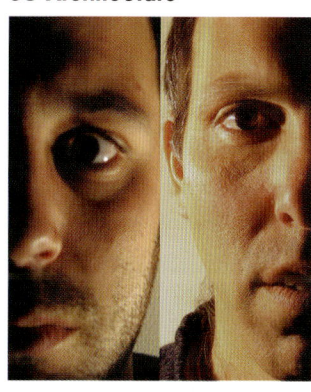

So Architecture office was created in 2007 by architect shacar Lulav and Oded Rozenkier. Lulav and Rozenkier were both born in Kibbutzim in the North of Israel and raised in these Socialist agricultural villages. Shachar Lulavwas born in 1970 in Israel. He had studied Interior design in Holon Design Academy and then architecture in Vizo art Academy and is graduated with honorable excellence. Oded Rozenkier was born in 1978 in Israel. He studied architecture at the Technion –Israel Institute of Technology and Ecole National SUperioeur d'Architecture Paris La-Villette and graduated with honorable excellence. Rozekier had worked as a stager-architect in Jean Nouvel's office in Paris.
www.soarch.co.il

606
ROSSO RESTAURANT

Team : Shachar Lulav, Oded Rozenkier
Location : Ramat Ishay, Israel
Floor area : 60 m²

620
TEODORE - CAFE BISTRO

Team : Oded Rozenkier, Shachar lulav, Alejandro Feinerman
Graphic design : Maya Eyal Rozenkier
Photograph : Asaf Oren

SPACEGROUP

SPACEGROUP is directed by Gary Bates (USA), Gro Bonesmo (NO), and Adam Kurdahl (DK).
SpaceGroup (est. 1999) is an architecture and design office based in Oslo, Norway.
A land of protected differences and hyper-similarity, Norway provides the backdrop and need for investigation and innovation – a laboratory of curiosity open for failure and radical success.
The profession of architecture has exploded into infinitesimal parts and processes.
Our work provides SPACE for the staging of uncertainty – CONDITIONS for friction and coincidence – FORMULATIONS on the built environment, through a meshwork of people, materials, information/knowledge, and ideas.
Through design research, we actively engage the performance of architecture, autonomously and in the city – what it does, and where it does it. Politics, economics, aesthetics, and culture form our communication platform.
Space Group is a network-based practice – a diverse international base with a compact core that attacks both small and large projects with similar ambition – strategic and inventive, flexible and specific. The office nurtures intense collaborative processes, guiding clients and teams to find new logics and strategies. Consistency in approach coupled with the specificity and challenges of each task generates diversity in the work, providing unique results.
We operate in the business of intelligence gathering, combining and disseminating intelligence.
We buy intelligence, trade it, add value to it, deconstruct it, filter it, transform it, and make it operational through a generative process of design: We are agents of intelligence.
www.spacegroup.no

120
PROSTNESET TERMINAL

Location: Prostneset, Tromsø Norway
Site: Centrally located Habor Front in the center of Tromsø
Area: 28,000 m2
Program: Terminal for Hurtigruta, bus terminal, speed boat terminal, offices, conference center and spa. Redesign of Roald Amundsens Plaza, Urban seafront promenade, fish market, reorganization of traffic patterns (land and water).
Client: Tromsø Harbor, Nordic Management
Status: Competition 2003 (First Price), Completion 2010
Budget: 70mill €
Design: Space Group
Team: Gary Bates, Gro Bonesmo, Adam Kurdahl, Grant Cooper, Håvard Fagernes, Thomas Fagernes, Daniel Fordman, Franco Ghilardi, Tai Grung, Karoliina Hartiala, Ellen Hellsten, Thor Arne Kleppan, Margrethe Lund, Matteo Poli, Minna Riska.
Structure: Arup w/ Barlindhaug, ARUP & Partners Rory McGowan, Carolina Bartram, David Johnston, Jo Marples and Francesca Galeazzi)
Mechanical: Arup w/ Erichsen & Horgen
Electric: Arup w/ Erichsen & Horgen
Traffic: Arup
Civil: Arup w/ Noteby
Maritime: Arup w/ Barlindhaug
Facades: Van Santen / Metallplan: Franco Blöchlinger (Hotel)
Fire: Reinertsen
Cost: Bygganalyse
Adm.: Byggpro
Landscape: West 8, Netherlands (Adriaan Geuze and Jerry van Eyck with Anders Melsom)
PGL: Space Group
Photography: Ivan Brodey
Vizualizations: MIR as
Model: Vincent de Rijk

294
FILIPSTAD

Location: Filipstad, Oslo, Norway
Site: Former harbor area on reclaimed land.
Area: 450-600,000 m2
Program: Urban redevelopment of former container harbor and train depo. 30HA site including new ferry terminal, hotel, super gym, head quarter, offices, housing, new urban beach, park. Reorganization of traffic patterns existing highway and train.
Client: Oslo Harbor, ROM Eiendom
Status: First Prize Competition 2005-06
Budget: NA
Design: Space Group
Team: Gary Bates, Gro Bonesmo, Adam Kurdahl, Fredrik Krogeide, Mirza Mujezinovic, Tim Prins, Jeremy Richey, Lotte Sponberg
Engineering: Arup
Landscape: West 8
Visualizationi: MIR as

356
VELIKA PLAZA

Client: Ministry of Economic and Spatial Development, Montenegro
Program: 30 000 hotels beds and support programs including urban design for local population. 6 villages. Nature reserves, marina, environmental strategy and preservation, parks
Site: Velika Plaza in Montenegro
Design: Space Group Architects in collaboration with Julien de Smedt Architects
Team: SPACE GROUP ARCHITECTS AS_ Adam Kurdahl, Gro Bonesmo and Gary Bates with Fredrik Kjelman, Naofumi Namba, Wenche Andreassen, Kasia Heijerman, Jose Hernandez, Fredrik Krogeide and Mark Bol / JDS_ Julien de Smedt and Andrew Griffin with Francisco Villeda, Aleksandra Kiszkielis, Josephine Giller, Roberto Aparici, Philipp Ohnesorge, Elena Prendergast, Antonio Tan
Strategic consultant : Donald van Dansik
Engineering : ARUP London_ Carolina Bartram, Ian Carradice, David Johnston, David Dack, Stuart Jordan and Peter Bryant

372
ZAKUSALA RIGA

Location: Riga, Latvia
Site: 14 ha site on natural island just outside the Unesco protected Riga city centre in the river Daugava
Area: 290,000m2
Program: Culture and leisure resort: Hotels, casinos, spa, live venue, logistics center, offices, condos, marina, beaches, plaza and park.
Client: Withheld
Status: Commission 2005, Construction 2009
Budget: NA
Design: Space Group
Team: Gary Bates, Gro Bonesmo, Adam Kurdahl, Wenche Andreassen, Gerald Bliem, Grant Cooper,

ARCHITECTURAL DIAGRAMS 741

Fredrik Krogeide, Naofumi Namba, Tim Prins, Jeremy Richey, Minna Riska, Lotte Sponberg. Sketch phase (2007) in collaboration with Julian De Smedt Architects   Engineers: Arups & Partners AS
Structure: Florian Koch
Visualizations: MIR as

458
LERVIG BRYGGE

Client : Withheld
Location : Lervig Brygge, Stavanger, Norway
Site : Reclaimed land
Program : 4 apartment towers, 19.000sqm, 232 apartments
Team : Space Group_Gary Bates, Gro Bonesmo and Adam Kurdahl with Jens Noach, Kasia Heijerman, Karsten Huitfeldt, Naofumi Namba
Environment : Norconsult, Pal Eian Kjetil
Model : SuperModell

482
OKERN CENTER

Location: Oslo, Norway
Site: Økern Senter
Area: 160.000 m2
Program: Urban regeneration and retail development, including retail, water world, entertainment, cinema, housing and offices.
Client: Økern Sentrum ANS
Status: First prize, Competition 2007
Budget: NA
Design: Space Group in collaboration with Ghilardi & Hellsten
Team: Space Group: Gary Bates, Gro Bonesmo, Adam Kurdahl, Wenche Andreassen, Kasia Heijerman, José Hernández, Fredrik Kjelman, Yik-To Ko, Naofumi Namba, Tim Prins, / Ghilardi + Hellsten Arkitekter AS: - Franco Ghilardi, Ellen Hellsten, Morten Adamsen,
Ida Winge Andersen, Pau Canals, Espen Krogstad, Llatzer Planas, Erik Stenman, Johanne Borthne
Engineering: Arup & Partners London
Landscape: Arquitectura Agronomia
Visualizations: MIR AS

500
SLIM TWIN

Location: Oslo, Norway
Site: Narrow plot sandwiched between historical building and existing train station.
Area: 12.000m2
Program: office and commercial building, urban square with pedestrian connection to the Oslo Central station thoroughfare and the new Bjørvika plan.
Client: Entra Eiendom
Status: Invited competition 2006
Budget: NA
Design: Space Group
Team: Gary Bates, Gro Bonesmo, Adam Kurdahl, Grant Cooper, Tim Prins, Nathan Smith
Engineering: Norconsult
Visualizations: MIR as

504
STAR HOTEL

Location: Brattøra, Trondheim Norway
Site: Disused industrial Waterfront
Area: 35.000m2
Program: Hotel with conference facilities and an adjoining aquarium.
Client: Realinvest, Choice
Status: First prize, Competition 2006-2007
Budget: 100 MILL Euro, NA
Design: Space Group
Team: Gary Bates, Gro Bonesmo, Adam Kurdahl, Wenche Andreassen, Fredrik Krogeide, Gerald Bliem, Grant Cooper, Karoliina Hartiala, Karsten Huitfeldt, Naofumi Namba, Tim Prins, Minna Riska, Lotte Sponberg.
Engineering: Arup & Partners London
Hotel Room Interiors: Quinze & Milan
Fire: Reinertsen Engineering
Visualizations: MIR AS
Photography: Ivan Brodey

526
VESTBANEN

Location: Oslo Norway
Site: Former station area on the waterfront in the center of Oslo by the Town Hall plaza and new Nobel Peace Prize institute.
Area: 125.000 m2
Program: Cultural functions including Deichmanske Library, Stenersen and Munch museum, cinema, conference centre plus retail, hotel, offices and housing
Client: Statsbygg, City of Oslo
Status: Competition 2002, completion 2010
Budget: NA
Design: OMA in collaboration with Space Group. Second phase (2007)   REX in collaboration with Space Group.
Structure: Arup & Partners London
Mechanical: Arup & Partners London

544
360° HOTEL

Location: Lernacken, Malmö, Sweden.
Site: Pristine waterfront site in close vicinity to the Øresund Bridge.
Area: 32 000 m2
Program: Hotel with Conference and Spa Centre in Malmö. In addition to the Hotel's 250 rooms, there exists a conference facility with a 900 seat congress Hall and a Spa Centre of more than 2000 m2

Client: Home Properties, Choice
Status: First prize, Competition 2007-2008
Budget: NA
Design: Space Group
Team: Gary Bates, Gro Bonesmo, Adam Kurdahl, Wenche Andreassen, Grant Cooper, Fredrik Krogeide, Kasia Heijerman, Karsten Huitfeldt, Naofumi Namba and Tim Prins.
Consultants: Atkins Global Malmö

studio asylum

Founded by Kim Hun. He graduated Architectural Engineering, Hanyang University and University of Michigan Graduate School. Currently teaching at Kyunghee University
Current, Seoul National University, Kunkuk University, Kyonggi University architecture school (GSAK). Institute of Architects Award 2004 and 2007, Korea Pavilion Venice Biennale International Architecture Exhibition 2006 and 2008, Japan Institute of Architects (JIA), Osaka Branch invited exhibition and lecture. Salobrena Spain in 2007 invited international design.
www.studio-asylum.com

476
NUMEN

Architect : Kim Hun
Location : Publishing Intelligence Industrial Complex, Paju, Korea
Area and district : Semi Industrial Area, Industrial Establishment Area
Site area : 1,696.80sqm
Floor area : 429.99sqm
Total floor area : 977.62sqm
Building scope : 4 floors
Structure : Reinforced concrete/ steel
Photographer : Park Wan-soon

Studio Makkink & Bey bv

Born in 1965, Jurgen Bey graduated from Design Academy Eindhoven in 1989. He ran a design office for eight years together with Jan Konings, and after that set up his own business. Best known product: Light Shade Shade, a one-way mirror that reflects its environment and conceals/reveals the chandelier within. Studio Makkink & Bey designs for public spaces, interiors and applied art. Analyzing the contents, searching for the relation of the things and its users, design supporting a story and the things having an interaction with its users are starting points for the projects.
www.jurgenbey.nl

712
TOKYO DAY - TRIPPER

Studio Makkink & Bey for Droogdesign assisted by Silvijn v/d Velden, Christiaan Oppewal

Studio Ramin Visch

Studio Ramin Visch was established in 1998. A professional team up to five employees with an office in Amsterdam.
Our projects are best described as large scale interior projects. Projects vary from a cinema to an espressobar, apartments, furniture, offices and exhibitions. Large part of our projects is realized in industrial heritage or industrial monuments.
The old and new are clearly kept separate, both in materialization and volume. This clear distinction between new and old, enhances both. Although the function of the building changes, it's spaceousness and character are preserved and remain omnipresent throughout the building. Together with a team of architects, constructors, acoustics- and light experts we are involved during all phases of the process, from design until delivery.
www.raminvisch.nl

572
EXHIBITION DESIGN OF FISH STILL LIVES

Client: Centraal Museum Utrecht
Brief: Exhibition of fish still lives, fish on strong water, fish skeletons and antiquarian books
Project team: Ramin Visch, Rick Abbenbroek, Petra Dekker
Area : 1.100m²

584
KANTOOR DUPON

Client : Dupon Real Estate Development bv
Brief : Office in a former Mayor Villa in Hoofddorp
Project team : Ramin Visch, Femke Poppinga, Peter van der Geer(acoustic)
Photos : Jeroen Musch
Area : 280 m²

Tania Concko Architects

Born in Paris, grew up in Pointe-Noire and now lives in the Netherlands. Having graduated as a qualified architect and as Urban Planner, she opens an architecture and urban design office in Amsterdam in 1997, based on her personal experience through international competitions and urban planning research. Her approach is based on a critical understanding of the urban reality: "the nature of the cities", their evolution over time, their connection within architecture, art and landscape... architecture as a tool for urban strategy. Today the company is comprised of an international team of proffesionals currently working on major masterplans among many other residential projects.

272
CAMPUS BORDEAUX

the next ENTERprise

Ernst J. Fuchs and Marie Therese Harnoncourt founded the next ENTERprise – architects in 2000 in Vienna. They have cooporated   with other partners –since the early 1990s. From the beginning the next ENTERprise has operated in a field that ranges from experimental installations (Blindgänger 2000; Audiolounge 2002; Trinkbrunnen 2003) to architectural practice (Zirl House 1997; Underground swimming pool, Vienna 2001; Lakeside bath, Caldaro / Kaltern, 2006) treating both approaches as equal and mutually influential. The two latest projects are the Open-Air Pavilion for Grafenegg Castle Park, opened in 2007and the new Thermal Bath in Villach Warmbad currently at the planning stage. tnE has held teaching engagements in Vienna, Innsbruck, Linz, Bratislava and Paris. Work by the studio has been widely exhibited and published (Venice Biennale 2006 and 2004; 5th Biennale for Architecture, São Paulo / Brazil, 2003; Archilab 5, Orléans 2003; Latent Utopias, Graz 2002;).
www.thenextenterprise.at

586
KUNSTHAUS GRAZ

Location : Graz, Austria
Curator : Adam Budak (Kunsthaus Graz), Daniela Zyman (Thyssen-Bornemisza Art Contemporary)
Exhibition Design : the nextENTERprise - architects
Photo : Niki Lackner, Landesmuseum Joanneum

UNStudio

Ben van Berkel - Principal Architect/ Director UN Studio - studied architecture at the Rietveld Academy in Amsterdam and the Architectural Association in London, receiving the AA Diploma with Honours in 1987.
In 1988 he and Caroline Bos set up architectural practice in Amsterdam. The Van Berkel & Bos Architectuurbureau has realized among other projects the Karbouw office building, the Erasmus bridge in Rotterdam, museum Het Valkhof in Nijmegen, the Moebius house and the NMR facilities for the University of Utrecht. In 1998 Ben van Berkel and Caroline Bos established a new firm: UN Studio(United Net). UN Studio presents itself as a network of specialists in architecture, urban development and infrastructure. Current projects are the restructuring of the station area of Arnhem, a new Mercedes Benz Museum in Stuttgart(Germany), a music theatre for Graz(Austria) and the design and restructuring of the Harbor Ponte

742 PROFILE & INDEX

Parodi in Genoa(Italy)
www.unstudio.com

024
ARNHEM CENTRAL

118
PONTE PARODI

Client: Porto Antico
Design team: Ben van Berkel, Caroline Bos with Astrid Piber, Nuno Almeida, Cristina Bolis, Peter Trummer, Tobias Wallisser, Ergian Alberg, Stefan Miller
Advisors: Arup & Partners, Arup Projectmanagement, Grootint bv.
All images and photographs are copyrights by UNStudio

156
THEATRE AGORA

Program: Regional theatre
Building surface: 5890m2 bvo
Seats: large theatre hall 725
Small theatre hall: 200
Volume: 30.000m³
Building site: 2925 m² and expedition area
All images and photographs are copyrights by UNStudio

302
IFCCA 42ND-23RD STREET

Location: Manhatten NY, USA
Program: Proposal for the implementation of a new urban package for the area between the 42nd and 23rd Street of New York to function as a lobby for Manhattan
Credits: Ben van Berkel, Caroline Bos, Tobias Wallisser, with Olaf Gipser, Hans Sterck, Jasper Jaegers, Philip Koehler, Stephanie Kulmann, Bas Kwaaitaal, Alexander Jung, Ludo Grooteman, Remco Bruggink, Andreas Bogenschutz

Urban Filter.com (Vienna): Armin Hess, Susanne Boyer
Ove Arup (London): Cecil Balmond, David Johnston, Paul Whitehouse, Juan Alavo
Office 21 Fraunhofer (IAO (Stuttgart): Alexander Rieck, Stephan Zinser

408
BATTERSEA WEAVE OFFICE BUILDING

Client: Parkview international LTD, London and ARUP - AGU, London
Program: building with showcase spaces and office spaces
Gross floor surface: 51,000m²
Design: UN Studio_ Ben van Berkel, Caroline Bos with Gerard Loozekoot, Astrid Piber and Ger Gijzen, Holger Hoffmann, Colette Parras, Albert Gnodde, Christian Veddeler, Hape Nuenning, Markus Berger, Markus Hudert, Matthew Johnston, Michaela Tomaselli, Elke Uitz, Jeroen Tacx, Louis Gadd, Eric Coppoolse, Jan Schellhoff, Katrin Härtel, Maria Eugenia Diaz, Marie Morin
Advisors: Masterplan_ Arup AGU
Engineering: Arup, London
Building Services: Arup, London
Landscape: West 8, Rotterdam
Lighting: ArupLighting
All images and photographs are copyrights by UNStudio

438
FIVE FRANKLIN PLACE

Location: Five Franklin Place, New York, USA
Developer/Sponsor: Sleepy Hudson LLC, New York, NY
Design Architect: UNStudio_Ben van Berkel, Caroline Bos, Gerard Loozekoot with Wouter de Jonge and Holger Hoffmann, Kristin Sandner, Jack Chen, Miklos Deri, Christian Hoeller, Nanang Santoso, Derrick Diporedjo, Erwin Horstmanshof, Colette Parras, Stefan Nors Jensen, Jesca de Vries
Local Executive Architect: Montroy Anderson DeMarco LLP, New York, NY
Construction Management: Leeds United
Structural Engineer & Facade Consultant: Gilsanz Murray Steficek LLP, M.E.P. Engineer: MGJ Associates, Inc., Lighting Designer_ UNStudio, Soils Consultant_ Geo Tech and Surveyor, Langan Engineering and Environmental Services, Waterproofing Consultant_ River Consultants, Cold Spring, Code Consultant_ William Vitacco Associates, Ltd.; Appliance Contractor_ B&B Italia

468
MERCEDES-BENZ MUSEUM

Architect: UN Studio van Berkel & Bos
Museum design: Prof. H.G. Merz, Stuttgart
Builder/owner
DaimlerChrysler: Immobilien (DCI) GmbH
Height of the building: 47.5 meters
Total area: Approx. 53,000 sq. meters
Floor space: 4,800 sq. meters
Exhibition space: 16,500 sq. meters
Interior space: 210,000 cubic meters Levels 9
Number of vehicles: exhibited 175
Contracts with companies and engineering firms: 246
Plans: 35,000
Cables in concrete: 630,000 meters
Concrete: 120,000 tons

Building foundations: 850 reinforced concrete piles
Polyethylene pipes: 100 kilometers
Lights: 12,000
Glass frontage: 14,000 sq. meters
Site factors
Geographic position: Latitude 48.76° north
Longitude: 9.18° east
Elevation above sea level: 359 meters
Local temperature conditions: Min. temperature – 15.4 °C, Max. temperature 33.2 °C
All images and photographs are copyrights UNStudio & Photographer

484
OMOTESANDO

Client: Tokyu Land Corporation
Location: Meiji dori, Tokyo, Japan
Building surface: 12,000 m²
Building volume: 60,000 m3
Building site: 1,750 m²
Program: Commercial (flagship stores, shops, restaurants)
Status: Competition entry
Design: UNStudio_Ben van Berkel, Caroline Bos, Astrid Piber with Florian Heinzelmann, Rudi Nieveen, Patrick Noorne and Marina Bozukova
Advisors: Local architect_Kanji Matsushita
All images and photographs are copyrights by UNStudio

494
RESEARCH LABORATORY

Project team: UN Studio _ Ben van Berkel with René Wysk, Ton van den Berg, Boudewijn Rosman and Eric den Eerzamen, Erwin Horstmanshof, Jacques van Wijk, Thomas de Vries, Nanang Santoso, Michaela Tomaselli, Andreas Bogenschuetz, Pablo Rica, Wouter de Jonge, Jeroen Tacx, Gerard Loozekoot, Eugenia Zimmermann, Stephan Albrecht, Anika Voigt
All images and photographs are copyrights by UNStudio

528
VILLA NM

Location: Upstate New York, Catskills, USA
Client: Anonymous
Building surface: 230m2
Function: Residence
Credits: Ben van Berkel with Olaf Gipser and Andrew Benn, Colette Parras, Jacco van Wengerden, Jan Debelius, Olga Vazquez-Ruano, Martin Kuitert
Local consultant: Roemer Pierik
Photographer: Chr. Richters

594
MASTERPLAN HALL 11

Design team: Ben van Berkel, Caroline Bos with René Wysk, Cristina Bolis and Daniela Hake, Jürgen Heinzel, Cynthia Markhoff, Isak Birgersson, Florian Zschüttig, Adriana Schein
Longest street: 120m
Total length of all streets: 4300m
Total surface of the floor coverings: 17000m2
Total covering of walls and staircases: 3000m2

598
MUSIC THEATRE

Location: Graz, Austria
Client: Building_ BIG, Bundesimmobiliengesellschaft m.b.H., Interior_ KUG, University for music and dramatic arts
Program: University faculty building
Gross floor surface: 6.200 m²
Volume: 31.600 m³
Site: 2.800 m²
Credits: UNStudio_ Ben van Berkel, Caroline Bos, Hannes Pfau and Miklos Deri, Kirsten Hollmann, Markus Berger, Florian Pischetsrieder, Uli Horner, Albert Gnodde, Peter Trummer, Maarten van Tuijl, Matthew Johnston, Mike Green, Monica Pacheco, Ger Gijzen, Wouter de Jonge
Engineering: Arup London _ Cecil Balmond, Volker Schmid, Charles Walker, Francis Archer
Engineering execution: Peter Mandl and PartnersSpecifications: Housinc Bauconsult, Vienna Accoustics and building physics: ZT Gerhard Tomberger, Graz, Pro Acoustics Engineering
Stage technique: e.f.f.e.c.t.s. technisches Büro GmbH, Klosterneuburg
Photos: Iwan Baan

646
CIRCLE

Design: UNStudio_ Ben van Berkel and Caroline Bos with Khoi Tran, Thomas de Vries, Job Mouwen

676
LA BALLENA PEDESTRIAN BRIDGE, LAS PALMAS

Location: Las Palmas de Gran Canaria, Spain
Program: Infrastructure, park
Bridge span: 93m
Site area: 2500m² in a four-path crossing
Credits: Ben van Berkel with Caroline Bos, Alicia Velazquez, Daniel Borruey, Olga Vazquez, Astrid Piber, Igor Kebel, Cynthia Markhoff, Andrew Benn, Colette Parras, Santiago H. Matos, Fabian Hernandez, Tiago Nunes, Cristina Bolis, Khoi Tran, Ger Gijzen, Tobias Wallisser, Harm Wassink

706
SUM

Client: Gispen International
Design: Ben van Berkel and Caroline Bos with Khoi Tran and Thomas de Vries

Vincent Callebaut Architectrues

Born in 1977, Belgium, Diploma in 2000 awarded with René Serrure First Prize at ISAIVH, Brussels, Belgium. Since then, in the framework of his Parisian agency and great collaborations (Jakob+MacFarlane, Claude Vasconi, Jacques Rougerie), he militates continuously for the sustainable development of the new Ecopolis via «parasitical»strategies for an investigation architecture mixing biology to information and communication technologies. From New York to Hong Kong crossing Brussels and Paris, Vincent Callebaut proposes with determination and conviction prospective and ecological projects by insufflating locally dialogs and meetings that try to raise our questionings on the society in which we live as citizen of a global world!
www.callebaut.org

050
FLOATING ISLANDS

Program: Arctic Culture Centre and Hotel/Congress Centre
Location: The Findus Site of Hammerfest, Multi-Energy Town
Surface area: 3,600m² for ACC + 6,000m² for HCC
Client: Municipality of Hammerfest
Cost: 9† Millions NOK for ACC
Perspectives of the Artic Culture Centre: Benoît Patterlini

108
NEURONAL ALIEN

Program: Prospective Master Plan for Vatnsmyri Airfield of Reykjavik
Location: Airfield of Reykjavik
Surface area: 150ha
Proponent: The Planning and Building Department of the City of Reykjavik on behalf of the City Council

122
RED BAOBAB

332
PERFUMED JUNGLE

Program: Master Plan Eco-designing the Central Waterfront of the Business District
Surface area: 2.7 linear km
Competition promotor: City of Hong Kong
Team: Vincent Callebaut + Arnaud Martinez + Maguy Delrieu

348
THE URVAN CORSET,
A HYBRID INTERMEDIARY

Program: Contemporary Art Centre
Location: Porte de Namur of Brussels
Surface area: 28.000 m²
Client: Presented at the Paul Bonduelle's Prize, Royal Academy of Sciences, Letters and Arts of Belgium
Photographer: Daniel Callebaut

434
ECOCOON FOR RECYCLING

440
FRACTURED MONOLITH

456
LANDSCRIPT

Surface area: 4,500,000m² in a mixing program for 100,000 new inhabitants and 40,000 new housings

462
LILYPADS

VMX Architects

The office was established after winning Europan 3, Den Bosch, 1994. Various projects have been worked on since that time. These projects vary from the design of a table to the design of a temporary bicycle storage, and from the complete modification of an existing house to the design of large, complex public buildings, hospitals, offices and schools. VMX Architects consists of two partners: Don Murphy and Leon Teunissen. Don Murphy was one of the first graduates of the Berlage Institute. He is responsible for the architectural position of the office. Leon Teunissen graduated at TU Delft in both Architecture and Building Management. He is responsible for the management of projects and the office as a whole.
www.vmxarchitects.nl

030
BICYCLE STORAGE

Client: Municipality of Amsterdam
Location: Central Station, Amsterdam
Size: 3,000m2
Costs: 1 million Euro

052
GENERAL AVIATION TERMINAL

Client: Schiphol Real Estate
Location: Amsterdam Airport Schiphol (NL)
Size: 6,600m2

406
AZIEWEG

496
S-HOUSE

Client: Family Van der Steen
Location: IJburg, Amsterdam (NL)
Size: 225m2
Costs: 260.000 Euro

506
SUSTAINABLE OFFICE BUILDING

ARCHITECTURAL DIAGRAMS 743

Willy Müller Architects

Willy Müller_ Argentina, 1961. 1984_Architect. 1985_Settles down in Barcelona. 1986/88_Doctorate studies at the ETSAB, UPC school of architecture. Preparation of doctoral thesis. 1996_Opens his own office in Barcelona: WMA. Willy Müller Architects. In 1998 he founded and directed the Metápolis group together with M. Gausa and V. Guallart. Became Development Manager at IAAC, the Institute of Advanced Architecture of Catalonia, directed Agenda 21 for the Construction Industry, and Lab. Lab, Latinoamerica Laboratory. He is now director of the Master of Advanced Architecture in the IaaC. The office is currently developing projects in Spain, Russia, Dominican Republic, Brazil and Mexico.

Frédéric Guillaud(Associated Architect)_ France, 1973. 1992_Architect. Studied at EAG (Grenoble, France) and UQAM (Montreal, Canada). 2000 Licensed architect DPLG. 2000 Settles down in Barcelona. 2001 Studied in the Metapolis Master of Advanced Architecture: The Media House Project. 2005 Invited with WMA to the International week in the Ecole Nationale Supérieur of Nancy, France. 2008 Associated Professor in the ENSAG, France. Associated architect in WMA office since 2000.
www.willy-muller.com

300
HICAT: NEW PORT, NEW CITY

Site: Industrial harbour of Barcelona
Collaborators: Sergio Pinto, Joana Lages., Anne-irene Valais, Juan pablo Porta
Model maker: Juan carter
3D models: Gabriel Serrano, Rupert Maurus
3D rapid prototype modeling: Esarq
Photos: , Laura Cantarella, WMA

318
MARITIME FRONT OF ALMERIA

Site: Port of Almeria
Area port extencion: 120 000m2
Area urbanization: 170 000m2
Constructed area: 64 000m2
Cost: 162 000 000 euros
Collaborators: Andre Mota, Isabella Pintani, Kelly Hendriks, Ben Olszyna-Marzys, Luuk van der Broek, Sofie Kvist
WMA+Nodotec (Jose a. Ferrer, Fernando Mateos)
Photos: Laura cCantarella, WMA

324
NEW TAINAN TAIWAN BY DESIGN

Site: Tainan, Taiwan
Collaborators: Sergio Pinto, Justin Piercy, Christine Spetzler, Andre Mota, Isabella Pintani
Model's photos: WMA

480
O.I.C HEADQUARTERS BUILDING

Authors : WMA, Willy Müller Architects, Barcelona, Spain
Main architect : Guillermo Müller Zappettini (Willy Müller)
Associated architect : Fréderic Guillaud
Team Architects : Francisco Villeda, Isabella Pintani
3d modeling : Simona Assiero Brá, Mariano Arias-Diez
Rendering : Lucas Capelli, Julia Morgado, Daniel Corsi
Collaborators : Iris Cantante, Bruno Louzada, Edgardo Arroyo, Claudia Barata, Bart Hooijen, Katrine Kunstz
Model: ARRK,s.l., Fabio Castelblanco, Fabian Asunción

522
URBAN RESORT ST. PETERSBUG

Area : 135,000m2
Budget : 300,000,000 Euros
Client : GC Development Group
Design : WMA - Willy Müller Architects (in collaboration with: BPG Arquitectes and THB Consulting)
Principal architect : Willy Müller
Associate architect : Fred Guillaud
Architects : Mario Perez Botero, Sabine Bruinink, Bruno Louzada, Christian Kreifelts, Fransisco Villeda, Augusto Alvarenga, Samuel Martin Guerra, Sergio Pruccoli
Collaborators: Elke Gall, Sergio Ramos, Gijs Verhoofstad

Z-A Studio

Z-A is dedicated to exposing the unexpected in the mundane. Z-A explores extreme material implications of the most ordinary constraints. Structural efficiency, budget limitations or camouflaged identity generate the selection of adequate material or material quality in response. Z-A uses these "found" materials in conjunction with one mode of operation to create a specific material organization.

Guy Zuckeris the principle and founder of Z-A. In addition to running his practice he currently teaches Graduate Architecture Studio at the University of Pennsylvania and has previously taught at the Columbia Graduate School of Architecture and at Parsons Graduate School of Design. Mr. Zucker holds a Master of Science in Advanced Architectural Design from Columbia University, and a Bachelor of Architecture from the Technion Institute of Technology.
www.guyzucker.com

020
A BUILDING FOR BOOKS

Location : Paris, France
Architect: R&Sie(n) ... Paris
Creative team: François Roche, Stéphanie Lavaux, Jean Navarro
Hydroponic system from R&Sie(n)
Key dimensions: 130 m2
Situation: Confidential

590
LA GUARDIA SALON

710
THE EXCHANGE

Design Team : J Mayer H, Andre Santer, Alex Arnold, Steve Molloy

Zizi & Yoyo

Architecture+production+design company manifests its partners' profiles, approaching spatial issues from two different angles. Veronika Valk, as the architect of the office, has constructed both public and private buildings, designed interiors and landscapes, won some 30 prizes at various competitons as well as published a number of critical essays on urban issues. Helene Vetik as a graphic designer has made several logotypes, webpages, prints, moving pictures, ideas' solutions. Zizi&Yoyo supports Tallinn Festival of Light, life long learning at University of Third Age in Tallinn and creative industries incubator Kultuurikatel.
www.ziziyoyo.com

186
COMPOSER TUBIN MONUMENT

Project team: Veronika Valk (architect), Aili Vahtrapuu (sculptor), Louis Dandrel (sound).
Images: Zizi&Yoyo

670
HOME (FOR A HOMELESS KID) KOMATEIKA

Authors : Veronika Valk_ architect, Liisi Eesmaa_ fashion designer, Martin Voltri_ graphic design

691
STEINER GARDEN

Architects: Veronika Valk & Villem Tomiste
Images: Zizi&Yoyo.